Male, Female

Male, Female

The Evolution of Human Sex Differences, *Second Edition*

David C. Geary

American Psychological Association • Washington, DC

Second Printing, March 2010.

Published by
American Psychological Association
750 First Street, NE
Washington, DC 20002
www.apa.org

To order
APA Order Department
P.O. Box 92984
Washington, DC 20090-2984
Tel: (800) 374-2721; Direct: (202) 336-5510
Fax: (202) 336-5502; TDD/TTY: (202) 336-6123
Online: www.apa.org/books/
E-mail: order@apa.org

In the U.K., Europe, Africa, and the Middle East, copies may be ordered from
American Psychological Association
3 Henrietta Street
Covent Garden, London
WC2E 8LU England

Typeset in Goudy by Circle Graphics, Inc., Columbia, MD

Printer: Edward Brothers, Inc., Ann Arbor, MI
Cover Designer: Naylor Design, Washington, DC

The opinions and statements published are the responsibility of the authors, and such opinions and statements do not necessarily represent the policies of the American Psychological Association.

Library of Congress Cataloging-in-Publication Data

Geary, David C.
  Male, female : the evolution of human sex differences / David C. Geary. — 2nd ed.
    p. cm.
  Includes bibliographical references and index.
  ISBN-13: 978-1-4338-0682-7
  ISBN-10: 1-4338-0682-7
  1. Sex differences. 2. Human evolution. I. Title.
  QP81.5.G43 2010
  612.6—dc22
                                        2009025924

British Library Cataloguing-in-Publication Data

A CIP record is available from the British Library.

Printed in the United States of America
Second Edition

To Corie and Nicholas

CONTENTS

LIST OF EXHIBITS, TABLES, AND FIGURES

EXHIBIT

TABLES

FIGURES

PREFACE

Darwin's (1871) discovery with Alfred Wallace of the principles of natural selection has long been hailed as one of the greatest achievements in the history of science. Yet at the same time, his discovery of the principles of sexual selection—the evolutionary sources (e.g., male–male competition for mates) of most sex differences—was largely ignored by biological scientists for nearly 100 years (Cronin, 1991). In recent decades, however, sexual selection has emerged as a vibrant area of research in evolutionary biology, one that explains a myriad of sex differences across invertebrate and vertebrate species (Andersson, 1994). In the 1970s and 1980s, evolutionary anthropologists and psychologists, including David Buss, Martin Daly, Margo Wilson, and Donald Symons, began to apply the principles of sexual selection to human sex differences, primarily to sex differences in aggression, parenting, and mating strategies. Their work resulted in significant and groundbreaking achievements but did not provide an integration of human sex differences across the many domains in which these differences are found (e.g., in brain architecture and play patterns); this is, in part, because much of what researchers now know about sex differences was unknown even a few years ago.

My primary goal in writing the first edition of *Male, Female: The Evolution of Human Sex Differences* was to attempt to provide this integration and in doing so to provide the proof that Darwin's (1871) big picture of sex differences and their evolution (he got a few of the details wrong) provides the only theory that allows us to pull together human sex differences across a wide range of traits, from mating to play to brain and cognition. I was not fully successful in the first attempt but have come closer in this one.

The most difficult aspect of writing the first edition of *Male, Female* was to develop a model that tied together research on sex differences that are clearly related to sexual selection, including aggression, parenting, and mating strategies, with decades of research on sex differences that are not obviously related, including play, social development, and cognitive development. This model—the motivation to control—was developed over the course of about a year (the first sketch was published in a special issue of *Human Biology*; Geary, 1998a) and was presented as chapter 6 in *Male, Female*. I elaborated this in the context of brain and cognitive evolution in a subsequent book, *The Origin of Mind: Evolution of Brain, Cognition, and General Intelligence* (Geary, 2005b). Here, in the second edition of *Male, Female: The Evolution of Human Sex Differences*, I use the same general theoretical framework—including a taxonomy of evolved folk domains of mind—in combination with sexual selection to provide a means to understand the evolution as well as the here-and-now proximate expression of sex differences in many traits, from physical to behavioral to cognitive to neural.

In effect, when writing the first edition of *Male, Female*, I was convinced that Darwin (1871) was correct and that Buss, Daly, Wilson, Symons, and others were on the right track in using sexual selection as the theoretical frame for understanding human sex differences. I also knew that the vast majority of social scientists were unaware of the principles of sexual selection and the supporting research in nonhuman species. Even if they were aware of this work, most social scientists preferred to believe that humans were different, specifically, that human sex differences were due largely to socialization. In the decade or so since the first edition was published, the situation has improved, but there is a long way to go: Many social scientists and even some biological scientists still do not appreciate the power of sexual selection for understanding and organizing our knowledge about the many sex differences found in our species. L. Ellis et al. (2008) provided an extensive atheoretical cataloging of 100 years of empirical studies of human and nonhuman sex differences.

To counter this trend, in the first edition I provided a review of sex differences in nonhuman species as related to sexual selection. Even though these species are wide ranging and differ in many ways from humans, they all illustrate the take-home message: The same evolutionary (e.g., intrasexual competition) and proximate (e.g., testosterone) mechanisms are operating in all of these species, including our own. Since the publication of the first edition, the literature on human sex differences and on related topics, such as the evolution of sexual reproduction, has increased substantially. This required a thorough rewriting of all of the chapters, including breaking topics that were covered in a single chapter in the first edition into two chapters in this one, as well as adding new chapters. With the expanded coverage and more thorough organization and integration across chapters there was no room (in terms of page limitations) to include a chapter on implications for modern societies. However, I do cover the gist of these topics—sex differences in academic competence (e.g., reading, mathematics), behavioral (e.g., accidents) and psychological disorders (e.g., depression), and occupational outcomes (e.g., achievement level)—in the afterword.

I note that my referencing is extensive and perhaps excessive at times. I did this to provide a list of sources for the interested reader to pursue as well as to provide the documentation for my claims in light of the highly contentious nature of evolutionary accounts of human sex differences. I also tried to make the writing style more reader friendly (less academic) than in the first edition but no less scientifically documented. I believe the result is a book that is more accessible and useful for a wider audience, from the educated lay reader to the working scientist.

As when I wrote the first edition of this book, I contacted experts in a number of fields when writing this edition to ensure that I had not missed an important study, to ask questions, or to ask them to review one or several chapters. I would like to thank all of these individuals for responding to my queries and for their comments on one or more chapters: Rosalind Arden, Drew Bailey, Jay Belsky, Jennifer Byrd-Craven, Lee Ellis, Mark Flinn, Carl Gerhardt, Mary Heard, Lara Nugent, Viola Mecke, Amanda Rose, Meli Sheldon, Jonathan Thacker, Leah Thomas, Erin Twellman, Alex Wilkerson, and Jonathan Oxford. I thank Patricia Hoard for her work on many of the illustrations throughout the book. I am, of course, responsible for all statements herein.

Male, Female

1

BEGINNINGS

It is widely acknowledged that Darwin's (1859) *On the Origin of Species by Means of Natural Selection* is one of the most important works in the history of science. The principles of natural selection provide the key for understanding how new species emerge across evolutionary time, the relations among species, and many other facets of the biological world. One of Darwin's other pivotal contributions was the discovery of the principles of sexual selection, which were detailed in his 1871 book, *The Descent of Man, and Selection in Relation to Sex*. These principles (described in the paragraphs that follow) were debated, refuted, and largely ignored for 100 years (Cronin, 1991) but in recent decades have been confirmed as the key to our understanding of the evolution and here-and-now proximate expression of sex differences across a vast array of species, ranging from insects to plants to fish to mammals (Andersson, 1994). The one species in which the application of these principles is resisted is our own. The reasons for this resistance are multifaceted and might well deserve book length treatment in and of themselves, but this is neither my goal nor my interest.

My goals are in some ways more straightforward: to analyze, synthesize, and integrate our vast knowledge of human sex differences in terms of the principles of sexual selection and to integrate this knowledge with several

1982). Variation in these male traits is partly heritable and thus passed on to the offspring who in turn are healthier than offspring sired by less attractive males. Females may also choose mates on the basis of mating displays, physical stamina, or other traits that are not easily faked by less fit males (Zahavi, 1975). In some species, these males also provision (i.e., provide food to) the females and their offspring, in addition to providing good genes, and in other species, the males provide only genes. Sometimes female choice is not based on male looks or behavioral vigor but occurs through sperm competition. In these species, females mate with several males. Choice emerges through a combination of mechanisms in the female reproductive track that can bias fertilization toward one male or another (e.g., Andersson & Simmons, 2006) and through the characteristics of each male's sperm (Cornwallis & Birkhead, 2007).

More typically, though, males compete directly for access to mates or, as I stated, for control of the resources females need to raise their offspring. I review the many different ways in which males compete—physically, behaviorally, and cognitively—and the evolutionary result: The traits that aid in male–male competition will become exaggerated over evolutionary time (Andersson, 1994). The exaggeration of these traits and the traits females use in their choice of mates creates corresponding sex differences. Although female–female competition is less common than male–male competition, it does occur, especially for species in which males parent. When males invest in parenting or females differ in the quantity or quality of the offspring they will produce, males become choosey. Chapter 3 closes with examples of both male choice and female–female competition.

Chapter 4: Sexual Selection and Life History

Some people wonder why evolution has not resulted in our living forever or at least for a few hundred years. This is the wrong question. The real question is why humans live as long as we do, given that the life span of most species on this planet is a year or less (R. D. Alexander, 1987). Life history scientists study how evolution has shaped the length and pattern of the life span and how these patterns unfold in the environments in which individuals are situated (e.g., Stearns, 1992). These scientists study how evolution influences how quickly or slowly individuals grow up, their activities (e.g., play) while they are growing up, and the relation between these activities and later reproduction as well as why species differ in how they reproduce. Some species have a few high-quality offspring over the course of a long lifetime, whereas other species have many low-quality offspring over a short lifetime.

I cover all of these issues, with a particular focus on sex differences in developmental patterns (e.g., age of maturation), play, parenting, and the influence of sex hormones on the expression of these behaviors and those described in chapter 3. Within the context of life history evolution, chapter 4 provides readers the background needed to fully appreciate and understand human fatherhood (see chap. 6) as well as sex differences in human physical development, play patterns, and social behavior (see chaps. 10 and 11). More generally, the life history approach allows scientists to see how the results of evolution unfold during development as a dynamic interaction between genes and environment.

Chapter 5: Sexual Selection in Primates and During Human Evolution

In chapter 5, I bring readers one step closer to our own species, with a focus on living primates and the implications of the fossil record for understanding our ancestors. I begin with male–male competition and female choice in our primate cousins. The section on male–male competition illustrates the relation between the achievement of social dominance and reproductive dynamics among males. The dynamics largely manifest as one-on-one physical threats and fights for access to receptive females. As the reader will see, DNA fingerprinting to determine offspring paternity confirms that dominant males sire more offspring than do other males but not always as many as their social dominance would suggest (e.g., Muehlenbein & Bribiescas, 2005; Setchell & Dixson, 2001; Setchell & Wickings, 2005). Male chimpanzees (*Pan troglodytes*) also engage in between-groups coalitional competition (Goodall, 1986). They band together, enter the territory of neighboring groups, and search for males. If they isolate one of them, they will attack and kill him. If they manage to eliminate all of the males in the rival group, they expand into their territory, to their reproductive benefit and that of the females in their group. It is not all about male–male competition, however, because females can influence reproductive dynamics in many ways, although typically in more subtle ways. I review some of these aspects of female choice and then touch on some aspects of female–female competition and male choice; for instance, I discuss why male chimpanzees prefer older to younger females as mates.

The next step closer to our species is found with our early ancestors. I take us back about 4 million years to the australopithecine (i.e., early bipedal primates) fossil record and then to *Homo*. By contrasting the fossils that likely came from males to those of females and comparing these patterns with those found in living primates, scientists can learn a surprising amount about our ancestors. In living primates, physical male–male competition, for instance, is associated with polygyny and larger males than females. Our male ancestors of about 4 million years ago were much larger than our female ancestors, but this has changed considerably since that time (Plavcan, 2001); differences exist today, of course, but they are not as dramatic as they once were. I take these sex differences and others and combine them with patterns found in living primates to make inferences about the social and reproductive dynamics of our ancestors. Following Geary and Flinn (2001), I propose that our australopithecine ancestors were more like modern day gorillas (Gorilla gorilla)—for instance, in terms of male responsiveness to offspring—than our closer relatives, the chimpanzee or bonobo (Pan paniscus). This has profound implications for understanding the evolutionary history of long-term reproductive relationships between women and men, including men's parenting.

Chapter 6: Evolution of Fatherhood

In chapter 6, I deal with one of the puzzles of human evolution, specifically, why many men invest in the well-being of their children. Many readers will likely see this as an expectation and not a puzzle, but a puzzle it is. This is because male parenting is found in less than 5% of mammal species and not at all in our two closest relatives (Clutton-Brock, 1989), the chimpanzee and the bonobo. If our ancestors were more like gorillas than chimpanzees or bonobos, then men's parenting would be less of a puzzle. In any case, I organize the discussion of this parenting in terms of the cost and benefit trade-offs described in chapter 4 for male parenting in other species—offspring well-being, lost mating opportunities, and risk of cuckoldry (i.e., investing in another male's offspring). I then turn to a cross-cultural review of sex differences in investment in parenting. Although men parent more than most other male mammals, throughout the world they invest less than women do, as predicted from the principles outlined in chapter 3. I close chapter 6 with a discussion of the here-and-now factors that influence whether and how much men invest in parenting. These factors range from genetics to hormones to the quality of the spousal relationship and to wider cultural mores and marriage laws.

Chapter 7: Choosing Mates

Choosing a mate or mates is one of the most important decisions that one will make in one's lifetime and one of Darwin's (1871) core components of sexual selection. When viewed in terms of any resulting children and grandchildren, these are choices that will echo through subsequent generations. Given this, it is not surprising that in most hunter-gatherer societies these choices are not left to the whims of young adults or older adolescents (Apostolou, 2007). Of course, these young women and men may have a say in whom they marry, but the ultimate choice is typically made by their parents. In many cases, the parental choices and the preferences of their children converge. I consider both the actual choices that women, men, and their par-

ents make across many cultural contexts and the preferred choices of women and men that emerge in psychological studies (D. M. Buss, 1989b; Lippa, 2007). The psychological studies are important because they provide a window into evolved motivations that are not constrained by the competing interests of others or by wider social mores; these preferences also engage the conscious psychological control systems I describe in chapter 9.

When it comes to long-term marriage partners, men's and women's preferences are more similar than different, but there are sex differences in the traits that are prioritized by one sex or the other and differences in the trade-offs (e.g., physical appearance vs. income) women and men are willing to make in these choices. I cover these preferences and trade-offs in terms of personal and behavioral characteristics (e.g., cultural success, emotional intimacy), and physical and genetic traits. The latter tie human mate choices back to those described in chapter 3 and even tie choices to the factors that may have resulted in the evolution of sexual reproduction in the first place (see chap. 2). Along the way, I review women's and men's alternative—to long-term monogamy—mating strategies, changes in women's mate preferences across the ovulatory cycle, and men's sexual fantasies, among other topics.

Chapter 8: Competing for Mates

In chapter 8, I focus on the other core component of Darwin's (1871) sexual selection, that is, competition for mates. Darwin focused on male–male competition in large part because it is much more common than competition among females. In many species, in fact, females do not have to compete at all for mates because the males do not provide any parental investment, only a little mating time (G. C. Williams, 1966). The situation is different with our species because men do invest in their children. The more men have to offer, the more valuable they become to women as a reproductive resource.

I begin with men's competition for mates and review the different forms of this competition across traditional and modern societies. The concept that ties these forms of competition together is Irons's (1979) *cultural success*. Men in all cultures are highly motivated to attain social status and control of culturally significant resources. The resources are those needed to support survival and to attract a mate or mates and can vary from land to herds of cows to a large paycheck. Whatever the form of resource, the outcome is the same. Women prefer culturally successful men as mates, and thus these men have more reproductive options. It is not only about making themselves attractive to women, however; men sometimes compete in lethal ways to achieve control of social dynamics, independent of female choice (Betzig, 1986). I consider all of these different forms of competition and link them to those found in other species (see chaps. 3 and 4, this volume), to patterns that were likely

during our evolutionary history (see chap. 5, this volume), and to research on sex hormones, risk taking, and population genetics.

As with men, women compete in terms of mate-choice preferences of the opposite sex. They "dress to kill" in modern societies and adorn themselves in ways that enhance the traits men find attractive (e.g., use of makeup to enhance appearance of their eyes). They also derogate these same traits in potential competitors (D. M. Buss, 1988) and manipulate social information and relationships in other ways to drive competitors away from potential romantic partners and to disrupt their friendships with other women; women's same-sex friendships are social resources as well. Women do not resort to violence as often as men do, but they can in some circumstances (A. Campbell, 1995). In some polygynous societies in which land is inherited by sons, women will sometimes poison the sons of their cowives (Strassmann, 1997). In this way, the perpetrator's sons inherit more land than they would otherwise. In societies in which monogamy is socially imposed (i.e., polygynous marriages are illegal), women compete for cultural success just as men do but not as intensely; men's mate choices are influenced by women's income in these societies.

Chapter 9: Evolution and Development of the Human Mind

My goal for chapter 9 is to provide a bridge between the human sex differences described in the three preceding chapters to sex differences in affect (e.g., emotional expressions), fantasy, development, and brain and cognition described in chapter 9 and succeeding chapters. I provide overviews of my motivation-to-control theory and evolved domains of the human mind (i.e., folk psychology, folk biology, and folk physics), and a description of how developmental activities relate to the expression of these evolved biases; a full account is provided in Geary (2005b). This is the theoretical framework that allows us to more fully integrate the vast number of human sex differences in ways that make sense from an evolutionary perspective and at the same time allows for cultural variation in the expression of these differences.

I cover sex differences in how the motivation to control is expressed socially, in sexual fantasy and in affect. The former reflects the ways in which men and women would prefer to organize their social worlds and the strategies they use to achieve this goal. These motives are easily tied back to the sex differences in parental investment and to the costs and benefits of intrasexual competition. These sex differences are reflected, as one example, in the social and political biases of women and men. When it comes to politics, women are more inclined to advocate policies that result in a more equitable distribution of social resources and a greater investment in children (e.g., public day care), whereas men are more inclined to advocate policies associated

with group dominance (e.g., military spending; Pratto, 1996). These sex differences follow directly from the respective differences in investment in parenting (see chap. 6, this volume) and in the forms and intensity of intrasexual competition (see chap. 8, this volume). The reader will not be surprised to learn that young men fantasize about more sexual partners than do young women (B. J. Ellis & Symons, 1990); I describe these and how such fantasies aid in forming social strategies. The term *affect* covers observable emotional expressions (e.g., facial expressions) and unobservable feelings (Damasio, 2003). There are, of course, sex differences in both components of affect as well as some surprising similarities.

Chapter 10: Sex Differences in Infancy and at Play

In chapters 10 and 11, I cover a wide range of sex differences in children and integrate these with the principles of life history evolution (see chap. 4) and with sex differences in mate choice and competition for mates described in chapters 7 and 8, respectively. I begin with sex differences in physical development because these are readily linked to corresponding sex differences in other primates and to reproductive dynamics (Leigh, 1996). In addition to the pattern of physical development, boys and girls differ in the physical competencies that emerge during development. Many of these sex differences can be understood in terms of physical male–male competition and the use of projectile weapons, which is common in traditional cultures and, I argue, during human evolution.

One of Darwin's (1871) many insights was that nonhuman sex differences tend to be small early in life and become more pronounced as individuals approach reproductive maturity. On the basis of these patterns, scientists would not expect substantial differences between girls and boys during infancy, but there are differences nonetheless. I move from infancy to the different forms of play introduced for nonhuman species in chapter 4, specifically, social, locomotor, and object-oriented play. The reader will learn about sex differences in play fighting, parenting, exploration of the environment, and play with objects as related to tool use and in game play. These differences in turn provide children with the experiences needed to prepare them for the survival and reproductive demands of our adult ancestors, in keeping with the relation between developmental activities and the experiential adaptation of evolved cognitive competencies to local conditions described in chapter 9.

Chapter 11: Sex Differences in Social Development

In chapter 11, I continue the exploration of the lives of girls and boys but change the focus to their social development. Beginning by 3 years of age

and continuing throughout development, boys and girls segregate into distinct peer cultures. I provide a framework for placing these cultures and the associated social activities into a wider evolutionary picture, and through this framework I offer a means to link these early sex differences to differences in the forms of reproductive competition and other social relationships described in earlier chapters. Among other issues, I place the different ways in which girls and boys form social networks and maintain friendships into the broader context of male–male coalitional competition and in terms of the different types of same-sex relationships I propose were common during our evolutionary history (see chap. 5). Chapter 11 closes with reviews of parental treatment of girls and boys in Western culture, imitation of parents as a potential source of developmental sex differences, and how parental socialization of girls and boys varies from one culture to the next, as related to sex differences in adult reproductive competition in the society.

Chapter 12: Sex Differences in Folk Psychology

The two final chapters are devoted to sex differences in brain and cognition. The corresponding reviews are theoretically organized in terms of the taxonomy of evolved cognitive domains introduced in chapter 9, specifically, folk psychology, folk biology, and folk physics. For both chapters, I searched for sex differences in these domains as they relate to sex differences in reproductive and other social activities described in the chapters on mate choice (see chap. 7) and competition for mates (see chap. 8). Before presenting the analysis of sex differences in folk psychological domains in chapter 12, I provide an introduction to sex differences in brain size and organization (e.g., L. Cahill, 2006), including hormonal influences on the expression of these differences and sex differences in the expression of genes in the brain (Neufang et al. 2009; Reinius et al., 2008). My goal with the first section is not to provide an evolutionary analysis but rather to document the existence of extensive neural sex differences that beg explanation. I argue the explanation can be found in our evolutionary past and outline how and why with respect to sex differences in folk psychology, biology, and physics.

Folk psychology encompasses our ability to process social information (e.g., facial expressions) and our implicit understanding of other people. To the extent that our female and male ancestors' social relationships differed (e.g., in terms of intrasexual competition), sex differences in current folk psychological competencies will be found. As an example, when girls and women compete with same-sex rivals, the competition is much more likely to be relational—based on gossip, derogation of competitors, and so forth—than physical. The corresponding prediction is that the brain and cognitive systems that support relational aggression, such as language, will be more

highly elaborated in women than in men, just as physical male–male competition has resulted in the evolution of larger men with more lean muscle mass. I provide similar analyses for domains ranging from self-awareness to theory of mind to cognitions about in-group and out-group dynamics.

Chapter 13: Sex Differences in Folk Biology and Folk Physics

Folk biology refers to people's intuitive understanding of plants and animals in their local ecology and is quite extensive for people living in traditional societies (Atran, 1998). The evolutionary analysis of sex differences in folk biological knowledge is largely based on research by ethnobiologists who study the knowledge of people living in traditional cultures and on the division of labor in these societies, that is, women's foraging and men's hunting (Silverman & Eals, 1992). The number of studies available on sex differences in folk biology is small in comparison with those available for folk psychology and folk physics. The available research, nonetheless, reveals that women tend to know more about local flora than men, whereas men tend to know more about local fauna (Boster, 1985). Whether these differences result from sex differences in an evolved bias to learn about these different features of the biological world or from engagement in traditional activities remains to be determined.

Folk physics refers to the brain and cognitive systems that allow people to detect and respond to the physical world, to navigate in this world, to mentally represent physical space, and to learn to use objects as tools. As readers will learn, there are sex differences in all of these areas, some favoring boys and men and others, girls and women. I consider these cognitive sex differences in terms of the potential influence of prenatal and circulating hormones and in terms of the brain systems that support these cognitive competencies; I do this for the folk biological literature as well, but much less is known here and thus the hormone and brain sections are limited.

To illustrate, I ask the reader to consider that men's use of projectile weapons during between-groups raids in traditional societies (see chap. 8) is predicted to result in sex differences favoring men in skill at detecting subtle movement in complex visual arrays, estimating the velocity of moving objects, hitting targets with thrown projectiles, and dodging and blocking projectiles thrown at them. As predicted, men and sometimes boys have advantages in all of these areas (Peters, 1997; Schiff & Oldak, 1990; N. V. Watson & Kimura, 1991). Many of these competencies might also result from an evolutionary history of men's hunting. However, their skill at dodging and blocking projectiles is only consistent with male–male competition, given that humans are the only hunted species that fights back with weapons. Other sex differences covered in chapter 13 include women's advantage in remembering the location of objects—hypothesized by Silverman and Eals (1992) to be related to an evolutionary history of women's foraging—and boy's advantage in using objects as tools. I also review evidence that sex differences in these areas are influenced by prenatal exposure to male hormones and are associated with sex differences in the architecture of the corresponding brain regions (Amunts et al., 2007; Hines et al., 2003).

CONCLUSION

With this volume, I hope to convince the reader that Darwin's (1871) principles of sexual selection, and more recent discoveries about the evolution of sexuality and parenting, provide the only truly integrative scientific theory for the origins of sex differences, including those found in our own species. Humans are of course a species that creates culture and rules for social behavior; however, these constructions are not the origins of sex differences, but rather they add flavor to the way evolved biases are expressed. I walk the reader through many of these cultural nuances and explain how underneath the nuances are patterns that are found in all human cultures and can be tied in principled ways to the sex differences found in other species.

2

NATURAL SELECTION
AND THE EVOLUTION OF SEX

The discovery of the principles of natural selection is one of the pivotal events in the history of science. Natural selection is the net that captures all of the disparate findings in the biological and life sciences and pulls them together into a coherent whole. It is not surprising that much of the general public does not understand natural selection; it is, however, very surprising that many nonbiological scientists do not fully appreciate the eloquence and power of these mechanisms for understanding the natural world, including our own species. I therefore begin this chapter with a primer on Darwin's (1859) principles of natural selection and how these basic mechanisms profoundly influence the natural world. From there, my discussion turns to the evolution of sexual reproduction; it is helpful to begin here because an understanding of the factors that led to the evolution of sexuality and the distinct sexes sheds light on the persistence of variability across individuals, in general, and the dynamics of sexual reproduction, in particular. The unfolding of these sex differences is described in chapters 3 and 4 of this volume.

Across these chapters and in succeeding ones, I discuss a variety of species, ranging from bacteria (*Escherichia*) to guppies (*Poecilia*) to finches (*Geospiza*) to mandrills (*Mandrillus*) and more. The reader may wonder how discussion of these species informs our understanding of human evolution and human sex differences. These are good questions. On the surface, bacteria seem entirely irrelevant to human evolution, but the study of these species informs us about the evolution of sexual reproduction and the mechanisms (e.g., parasite resistance) that maintain sexual reproduction. By better understanding these issues, we can better frame our study of human mate choices and the processes that can influence these choices, as I cover in chapter 7. My discussion of a wide range of species also illustrates the power of the mechanisms of natural selection and sexual selection for understanding evolution in general and sex differences in particular. Even if the details differ from one species to the next, the basic mechanisms are the same. Sexual selection might result in bright male plumages in one species, elaborate mating displays in another, and large aggressive males in still another, but the basic mechanisms of competition, mate choice, and differential reproduction are the same. Humans, of course, have the added influence of cultural history and rules (e.g., whether men can marry polygynously), but this just adds a twist to how reproductive dynamics are expressed and does not change the basic mechanisms, as I discuss in forthcoming chapters.

NATURAL SELECTION

I begin with an overview of the basic mechanisms of natural selection. I then walk the reader through the major class of pressures that drive natural selection.

How It Works

Darwin and Wallace's (1858) and Darwin's (1859) fundamental observations and insights that led to the discovery of natural selection are shown in Table 2.1. One important facet of nature is that population size in most species remains stable, even though these populations should increase rapidly in size because each set of parents has more than two offspring in their lifetime. Both Darwin and Wallace concluded that it must be the case that more individuals are born than survive to reproduce themselves. This conclusion was fused with a keen awareness of individual variation within each species and with the recognition that some of this variation was passed from parent to offspring. The mechanisms of genetic inheritance were not understood at that time, but the results of selective breeding in domestic species showed Darwin that some of the variation across individuals in one generation was inherited from parents of the previous generation. The critical insight is that variation in key traits across individuals within a population and individual variation in the chances of survival are linked together or covary. Wallace

TABLE 2.1
Darwin's and Wallace's Observations and Inferences

Observation	Inference
All species have such high potential fertility that populations should increase exponentially. Except for minor annual and rare major fluctuations, population size is typically stable. Natural resources are limited, and in a stable environment they remain constant.	More individuals are born than can be supported by available resources, resulting in competition for those resources.
No two individuals are exactly the same. Much of this variability is heritable.	Survival is not random and covaries with heritable characteristics of individuals. The resulting differential survival is natural selection. Over generations, natural selection leads to change in the population (microevolution) and production of new species (macroevolution) or speciation.

Note. Observations and inferences are based on Darwin and Wallace (1858), Darwin (1859), and Mayr (1982). Darwin knew that selective breeding (artificial selection) influenced domestic species. This gave him the insight that traits, or characters, were passed on from parent to offspring. The science of genetics began in earnest after Darwin's death.

described this insight in a letter written in 1887 and reprinted in Darwin's autobiography (F. Darwin, 1887/2000):

> it suddenly flashed upon me that all animals are necessarily thus kept down—"the struggle for existence"—while *variations*, on which I was always thinking, must necessarily often be *beneficial*, and would then cause those varieties to increase while the injurious variations diminished. (pp. 200–201)

Although most people think of evolution in terms of cross-generational change in the mean or average of a trait or phenotype, such as height or coloration (Shtulman, 2006), variation is equally important, as noted by Wallace (in F. Darwin, 1887/2000). Indeed, there is considerable variation among individuals on most traits, and as noted, natural selection is driven by the relation between this variation—the result of mutations (Crow, 1997) and sexual reproduction (W. D. Hamilton & Zuk, 1982; G. C. Williams, 1975)—and the chances of surviving to adulthood and successfully reproducing (Price, 1970). A trait is *evolvable* when variation around the mean of the trait is due in part to genes (Houle, 1992); evolvable variation is not the same as heritability (h^2; for a critique, see Pigliucci, 2006). *Heritability* refers to the degree of genetic influence on the differences between individuals for any given trait, but it is also necessary to consider the distribution of a trait within a population. Most complex traits, such as size, are distributed close to a normal bell-shaped curve, with most individuals being average and some being larger or smaller. If being larger confers a survival advantage and if size is heritable, then the trait size is evolvable. In other words, when there are many individuals above (e.g., larger) or below (e.g., maturing at a younger age) average on a particular trait, and a significant proportion of these differences are heritable, there is potential for the mean of the trait to increase or decrease across generations. This potential is realized only if being above or below average confers survival or reproductive advantage.

The key components of heritable variation and the relation between this variation and individual differences in survival or reproductive outcomes are illustrated in Figure 2.1. For each generation, the strength of evolutionary selection is the product of these two components. If h^2 is 0.30, then 30% of the individual differences in trait variation is due to variation in the associated genes, and if the strength of the relation between these individual differences and survival or reproductive outcomes (in terms of standard deviation units) is 0.30, then the strength of evolutionary selection is 0.09 (.30 × .30).

It used to be theorized that a trait would evolve until it was highly suited to the conditions that promote survival and reproduction and at this point genetic variation in the trait would be eliminated (R. A. Fisher, 1930). But the puzzle remained that many apparently advantageous traits remain heritable; why do all beneficial traits not evolve to their optimal value? There are at least four mechanisms that help to explain this puzzle. First, the elimination of genetic variance requires cross-generational stability in the ecological and social conditions that drove the evolution of the trait. Although this sta-

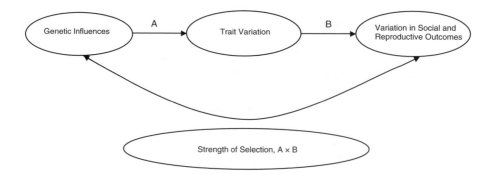

Figure 2.1. Strength of evolutionary selection. Evolution of a trait occurs when two conditions are present. First, individual differences must be heritable, represented by Line A. Second, individual differences in the trait must covary with individual differences in survival or reproductive outcomes, represented by Line B. The strength of evolutionary selection is the product (A × B) of these two components.

bility may be achieved for some traits and can result in a substantive reduction in the genetic influences on individual differences in the trait (e.g., Gustafsson, 1986), the required level of cross-generational stability is not always achievable. Second, genetic variability may also be maintained when the gene or genes that underlie trait expression have multiple effects in terms of cost–benefit trade-offs (G. C. Williams, 1957); this is called *pleiotropy*. The benefits of high levels of testosterone in terms of physical development and behavioral vigor and the corresponding benefits in the competition for mates in young adulthood may compromise immune functions (Folstad & Karter, 1992) or increase risk of disease and premature death later in adulthood (Adams et al., 1999). In this case, reproductive advantage at a younger age may lead to disadvantage at a later age and vice versa such that neither earlier nor later reproduction is better over the life span. With these trade-offs, genetic influences on both earlier and later reproduction will be maintained in the population.

A third contributor to the maintenance of genetic variation is called *frequency-dependent selection*. That is, the survival or reproductive advantage of one heritable version of a trait or another is dependent on how common each version is in the local population (e.g., M. R. Gross, 1985; Olendorf et al., 2006). The concept is illustrated in Figure 2.2. On the basis of Olendorf et al.'s findings for guppies (*Poecilia reticulata*), males with the more novel or less common coloration pattern are at an advantage because they are less likely to be eaten by predators and because females prefer them as mating partners. For the top leftmost group, the lighter males are at an advantage, and therefore their frequency increases and in this example peaks after three generations (bottom rightmost group). For this generation, the darker males are now at an advantage, and the cycle begins to reverse. The cycle need not continue, as the frequencies may eventually stabilize, but in either case the genetic variation underlying the differences in coloration is maintained. A fourth mechanism might be *sexually antagonistic genes*, that is, genes that promote the reproductive fitness of fathers can reduce the reproductive fitness of their daughters (Foerster et al., 2007). These cross-generational trade-offs will prevent such genes from becoming dominant in the population.

For these reasons, individual differences in many of the traits that covary with survival or reproductive outcomes show small to moderate genetic influences and are therefore continually subject to evolutionary change (Roff, 1992). Mousseau and Roff's (1987) comprehensive review of the genetic (h^2 in this case) variability of life history (e.g., age of maturation) and physiological (e.g., cardiovascular capacity), behavioral (e.g., mating displays), and morphological (e.g., body size) traits across 75 species provided an assessment of the first component shown in Figure 2.1 (i.e., Line A). Their analysis indicated that "significant genetic variance is maintained within

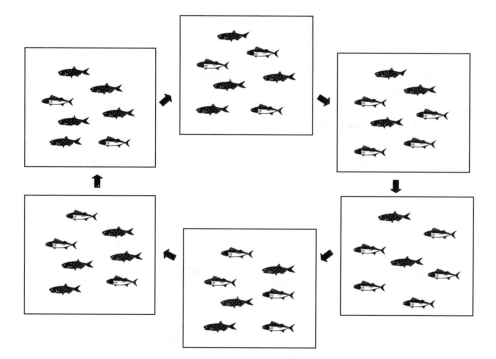

Figure 2.2. Frequency-dependent selection. With frequency-dependent selection, survival or reproductive advantage is dependent on the relative frequency of different traits in the local population. In this example, males with the less common color pattern suffer less predation and are preferred as mating partners. As a result, their frequency increases across generations. This results in their color pattern becoming common. Whichever variant has the rarer pattern has a survival edge over the other.

most natural populations, even for traits closely affiliated with fitness" (Mousseau & Roff, 1987, p. 188), as predicted by R. A. Fisher (1930), but researchers have shown that this is not always the case (e.g., M. R. Gross, 1985). A further twist is that the relative importance of heritable and environment influences on many phenotypes can change across the developmental period and from one context to the next and that many heritable influences emerge through epigenetic, gene–environment interactions (e.g., West-Eberhard, 2003; A. J. Wilson & Réale, 2006). The complexity of these interactions is not well understood and beyond the scope of this work, but the importance of developmental experience is highlighted in this volume in chapter 4 for nonhumans and in chapters 10 and 11 for humans.

In any case, an analysis of the second component shown in Figure 2.1 (i.e., Line B) was provided by Kingsolver et al.'s (2001) review of field studies of variation in survival and reproductive outcomes in wild populations. Across species and traits, the median effect size—the correlation between individual differences in the trait and individual differences in the survival or reproductive outcome—indicated that being 1 standard deviation above (e.g., later maturation) or below (e.g., earlier maturation) the mean was associated with a 16% increase in survival (e.g., probability of surviving to the next breeding season) or reproductive fitness (e.g., number of offspring). If the heritability of any such trait was only 0.25, "then selection of this magnitude would cause the trait to change by 1 standard deviation in only 25 generations" (Conner, 2001, p. 216) or in 12 to 13 generations with a heritability of 0.50.

These patterns suggest that evolutionary change can occur much more rapidly than Darwin (1859) originally assumed. Rapid changes have indeed been empirically documented for a variety of traits (e.g., beak shape, scale coloration) and species (e.g., Barluenga, Stölting, Salzburger, Muschick, & Meyer, 2006; P. R. Grant & Grant, 2002; Pergams, Barnes, & Nyberg, 2003; Reznick, Shaw, Rodd, & Shaw, 1997). However, as suggested by Darwin, studies of evolutionary change across a large array of species and time scales, including the fossil record, indicate that rapid change is not the norm (Estes & Arnold, 2007). Rather, rapid changes occur when there is dramatic change in climate, food availability, or social conditions. Natural selection then results in rapid adaptation to these new conditions such that a species reaches stability or a stasis point; for discussion of intermediate steps in the evolutionary process, see Poelwijk, Kiviet, Weinreich, and Tans (2007). This is not actually a stasis point per se, but rather a small plateau on which the means of the evolved traits shift around from one generation to the next. The trait means will not stray far from the center of the plateau unless there are dramatic changes in ecological or social conditions.

Ecological Selection Pressures

The second component shown in Figure 2.1 (i.e., Line B) represents the link between trait variation and variation in survival and reproductive outcomes. Peter and Rosemary Grant provide one of the best empirical documentations of such a linkage (B. R. Grant & Grant, 1993; P. R. Grant, 1999; P. R. Grant & Grant, 2002). For the past several decades, the Grants and their colleagues have been studying multiple species of Darwin's finches on the Galápagos islands. They have clearly documented that cross-generational change in the physical traits of these finches is linked to variation in survival and reproductive outcomes that follow dramatic changes in food availability and climate. Their research also provides a useful illustration of two important concepts, natural selection acting on variability to create change within a species (*microevolution*) and to create new species, that is, speciation or adaptive radiation (*macroevolution*; Reznick & Ricklefs, 2009).

Studies of the medium ground finch (*Geospiza fortis*) have illustrated how individual differences in a trait can covary with individual differences in survival and reproductive outcomes and thus evolve; at the top right of Figure 2.3 is an illustration of this species (Darwin, 1845). The trait of interest is beak size and its variation across individuals. These differences are moderately to highly heritable for beak length ($h^2 = 0.65$), depth ($h^2 = 0.79$), and width ($h^2 = 0.90$; Boag, 1983; Boag & P. R Grant, 1978), and are highly evolvable in terms of heritable variance around the mean (Boag, 1983). As might be expected, beak size covaries with body size.

When food is plentiful and varied, there is little relation between beak size and survival prospects. Under these conditions, the value of the second component in Figure 2.1 (i.e., Line B) is close to 0.0, and thus natural selec-

1. Geospiza magnirostris. **2.** Geospiza fortis.
3. Geospizaparvula. 4 Certhidea olivacea.

Figure 2.3. Four species of finch from the Galápagos islands. 1. large ground finch (*Geospiza magnirostris*), 2. medium ground finch (*G. fortis*), 3. small tree finch (*Camarhynchus parvulus*), 4. warble finch (*Certhidea olivacea*). From *Journal of Researches Into the Natural History and Geology of the Countries Visited During the Voyage of H.M.S. Beagle Round the World, Under the Command of Capt. Fitz Roy, R.N.* (2nd ed., p. 379), by C. R. Darwin, 1845, London: John Murray. In the public domain.

tion does not operate on beak size. When food is scarce, the value of this component becomes larger than 0.0 because the size and shape of an individual's beak determine which foods can be eaten and which foods cannot (B. R. Grant & Grant, 1993). Individual birds whose beak size and shape allow them to specialize in abundant food sources survive in greater numbers than do individuals whose beak size and shape force them to specialize in a scarce food source.

As an example, in 1973 a drought resulted in an 84% decline in the quantity of foods available to Darwin's finches and a sharp increase in mortality. One of the plentiful foods was the seeds of the caltrop plant (*Tribulus cistoides*), which are encased in hard and spiked shells called *mericarps*. Some medium ground finches or *fortis* were able to exploit this food source, whereas others were not. As described by Weiner (1995),

> *fortis* with bigger beaks can crack the mericarp and gouge out the seeds faster than those with smaller beaks. Tiny variations are everything. A *fortis* with a beak 11 millimeters long can crack caltrop; a *fortis* with a beak only 10.5 millimeters long will not even try. "The smallest grain in the balance" can decide who shall live and who shall die. Between a beak big enough to crack caltrop and a beak that can't, the difference is only half a millimeter. (p. 64)

For the medium ground finch and their cousins, life or death depended greatly on beak size. Even when small-beaked males survived, they were at a mating disadvantage. These males were poorly nourished and thus weaker than their better fed large-beaked peers, resulting in a difference in the vigor of their courtship displays. Females of this species choose mates on the basis of vigor of these displays and thus preferred large-beaked males. The combination of differential survival rates and female choice (see chap. 3) resulted in a shift in the next generation's average beak size; individual differences in beak size were still evident, but the average beak size increased, and there were fewer individuals with extremely small beaks and more individuals with extremely large ones. However, having a larger than average beak is beneficial only during droughts. In 1982–1983, an especially strong El Niño event resulted in a 14-fold increase in rainfall (B. R. Grant & Grant, 1993), a significant decrease in the number of caltrop plants and their mericarps, and a significant increase in the number of plants that produce smaller seeds. Small-beaked individuals are able to handle small seeds more deftly than their large-beaked peers. The results were that small-beaked individuals survived in greater numbers than did large-beaked individuals, and females preferred small-beaked males as mating partners. After several generations of differential survival and mating success, the average beak size of medium ground finches was now smaller than it was just after the drought.

In this seminal study, cross-generational changes in average beak size and shape were found to be linked to cross-generational changes in the distribution of available foods and with mating dynamics. Over the course of 30 years and seven generations, the overall evolutionary effects were significant reductions in beak and body size of medium ground finches and a significant change in beak shape, from somewhat blunted to moderately pointed (P. R. Grant & Grant, 2002). These adaptations resulted in microevolutionary changes in the medium ground finch such that the average individual in the population looked somewhat different from the average individual just seven generations earlier.

Macroevolution

When the microevolutionary changes illustrated in the preceding paragraph are sustained and directional (i.e., having the same effect) across many generations but differ for different populations within the species, selection can result in a single species diverging into two or more separate but related species. Although Darwin did not introduce natural selection until 1858 (Darwin & Wallace, 1858), he provided hints in earlier work. With respect to the Galápagos species shown in Figure 2.3 and their cousins, Darwin noted the following in 1845: "Seeing this gradation and diversity of structure in one small, intimately related group of birds, one might really fancy that from an original paucity of birds in this archipelago, one species had been taken and modified for different ends" (p. 380).

DNA studies have confirmed Darwin's keen insight, finding that all 14 species of Galápagos finch arose during the past 3 million years from a single ancestral species that originated from the South American mainland (P. R. Grant, 1999; Petren, Grant, & Grant, 1999; Sato et al., 1999). To illustrate one route by which multiple species can evolve from a single species, I consider again the medium ground finch (for a review, see Schluter, 2001). What appears to have happened is that several populations of these birds were separated from the original population and on different islands. If mericarps were more abundant on one island and smaller seeds more abundant on the other, then the microevolutionary changes described previously would result in the average beak and body sizes of the two populations moving away from each other and from the original population with each successive generation. After many generations the evolutionary emergence of distinct species is possible.

In fact, such a process readily explains the three species of ground finch that currently reside on the Galápagos islands, that is, small (G. *fuliginosa*), medium, and large (G. *magnirostris*) ground finches (Petren et al., 1999). These species specialize in different sources of food and, in addition to body size, differ primarily in beak size and shape, the morphological specializations that allow them to exploit one type of food source or another. Although there is no overlap in the distribution of beak sizes of small and large ground finches, there is some overlap between the beak size distributions of medium and large, and medium and small ground finches. The beak sizes of the largest medium ground finches, for instance, overlap those of the smallest large ground finches. These overlapping distributions are exactly what would be expected for species with a very recent common ancestor. In other words, the distributions of beak size in the three species of ground finch are understandable in terms of a common ancestor that was likely similar in size to the medium ground finch, with the large and small ground finches evolving from the tails, so to speak, of the distribution of medium ground finches.

Social Selection Pressures

In the same way that ecological changes in food availability influenced the evolution of body size and beak morphology in Darwin's finches, competition among members of the same species (i.e., conspecifics) can result in selection acting on traits that facilitate this competition to the extent these traits are evolvable and covary with survival or reproductive outcomes (Mayr, 1974). The coalitional behavior of females of many species of Old World (Africa and Asia) monkeys provides one example of how social competition can influence evolutionary outcomes (Wrangham, 1980).

Coalitional behavior is most common in species in which high-quality food sources, such as fruit trees, are clustered in one or a few locations (Sterck, Watts, & van Schaik, 1997). In these species, related females cooperate with one another to compete with other female kin groups for control of these high-quality foods, and the larger matrilineal coalitions typically succeed. The combination of social dominance—associated with the ability to influence the behavior of conspecifics—and better nutrition results in increased survival rates for individuals of successful coalitions and significant changes in reproductive patterns. In comparison with females in less successful coalitions, females in dominant coalitions mature earlier and have shorter interbirth intervals, and their offspring have higher survival rates (Silk, 1993). The result is a significantly higher lifetime reproductive success for dominant as opposed to subordinate females. Silk, Alberts, and Altmann (2003) demonstrated that even within matrilineal coalitions, the infants of female baboons (*Papio cynocephalus*) with larger social networks have higher survival rates than the infants of more socially isolated mothers.

Given the strong link between coalitional dominance and size of within-coalition social networks and the wide array of survival and reproductive outcomes, selection will necessarily favor individuals with the social and cognitive competencies needed to develop, maintain, and use social relationships (e.g., Bergman, Beehner, Cheney, & Seyfarth, 2003). In other words, the survival and reproductive advantages associated with between- and within-coalitional behavior create a social ecology that influences the evolution of behavioral and presumably cognitive social competencies (Dunbar, 1993; Dunbar & Bever, 1998), just as the nonsocial ecology (i.e., available foods) influences the evolution of beak morphology in Darwin's finches.

WHY REPRODUCE SEXUALLY?

The principal advantage of asexual reproduction is that one does not have to mix one's genes with another individual to produce offspring; barring mutations, offspring are genetically identical to the parent. With sexual reproduction, in contrast, there is only a 50% overlap, on average, between the genes of offspring and those of each parent (Bulmer, 1994; Ridley, 1993; G. C. Williams, 1975; G. C. Williams & Mitton, 1973). Because of this substantial genetic cost and other costs (e.g., finding a mate), sexual reproduction will not evolve to be a viable alternative to asexual reproduction unless the benefits of the former are more than double the benefits of the latter (G. C. Williams, 1975). Indeed, there are potential long-term costs to asexual reproduction and long-term benefits to sexual reproduction that can result in important evolutionary advantages to reproducing sexually. Although many nuances remain to be settled (de Visser & Elena, 2007; Rice, 2002), theoretical models and experimental studies of the advantages and disadvantages of sexual and asexual reproduction have focused on the deleterious effects of accumulating mutations, the creation of variability, the accompanying ability of offspring to adapt to their ecology, and resistance to parasites. These models are briefly discussed in the sections that follow. These are not exclusive mechanisms; they may interact, or the importance of one or the other might differ across species (Cooper, Lenski, & Elena, 2005; de Visser & Elena, 2007).

Accumulating Mutations

Genetic mutations can arise in several ways, such as mistakes in DNA replication during cell divisions (Crow, 1997). Although the frequency with which these mutations occur is currently debated and may vary across species—being higher for species with longer developmental periods and thus more cell divisions before reproduction (Keightley & Eyre-Walker, 2000)—it is clear that a small number of mutations, and sometimes a single mutation, can affect the individual's behavior, physiology, development, and other phenotypes (Ajie, Estes, Lynch, & Phillips, 2005; Kondrashov, 1988). The majority of mutations that affect the individual are harmful, although each typically results in only small reductions in life span and in the number of offspring contributed to the next generation (Crow, 1997). In most cases, the accumulation of mildly harmful mutations gradually reduces the ability of affected individuals to reproduce and through this eliminates them from the population (e.g., Poon & Chao, 2004).

Asexual reproduction results in a faster accumulation of harmful mutations over generations than does sexual reproduction (Kondrashov & Crow, 1991; H. J. Muller, 1964). With sexual reproduction, some individuals in the population have only a few mutations, whereas other individuals have many mutations. Those individuals with many mutations are less likely to survive and reproduce than are their cohorts with fewer mutations (Ajie et al., 2005; Cooper et al., 2005; Crow, 1997). The net result is that relatively harmful mutations are eliminated from sexually reproducing populations without endangering an entire population. With asexual reproduction, all harmful mutations that arise in one generation will necessarily be passed on to all members of the next generation, which, in turn, will eventually result in the accumulation of a large number of harmful mutations over successive generations. H. J. Muller (1964) explained the process in terms of a ratchet—Muller's ratchet—whereby the number of mutations from one generation to the next necessarily ratchets up, or increases. Ridley (1993) likened the process to photocopying:

> Muller's ratchet applies if you use a photocopier to make a copy of a copy of a copy of a document. With each successive copy the quality deteriorates. . . . Once the original is lost [through mutations], the best copy you can make is less good than it was before. (p. 48)

In addition to providing a mechanism that can eliminate harmful mutations without affecting the entire population, sexual reproduction appears to afford a number of other advantages over asexual reproduction (Crow, 1997; Kondrashov, 1988). With the genetic recombination associated with sexual reproduction, many offspring will have fewer potentially harmful mutations than their parents; others will, of course, have more. Sexual reproduction also creates the opportunity for beneficial mutations that have arisen in each parent to be combined in their offspring. Empirical comparisons of asexual and related sexual species are difficult to conduct but generally suggest that the accumulation of harmful mutations places asexual species at an evolutionary disadvantage (Ajie et al., 2005; Poon & Chao, 2004). The more rapid accumulation of mutations in asexual species might not be sufficient to maintain sexual reproduction but likely contributed to its original evolution (Cooper et al., 2005; de Visser & Elena, 2007).

Speed of Adaptation and Advantages of Variation

Compared with asexual reproduction, sexual reproduction results in greater genetic and phenotypic variation within a population (Bell & Maynard Smith, 1987; B. Charlesworth, 1993; G. C. Williams, 1975; G. C. Williams &

Mitton, 1973). Large populations are necessarily at greater risk of both harmful and beneficial chance mutations (Colegrave, 2002). Greater variability within a population allows more rapid adaptation to conditions that change from one generation to the next (Darwin, 1859; Reznick et al., 1997; G. C. Williams & Mitton, 1973). This suggests that asexual reproduction will be most successful when the ecology of the parent and the offspring are the same. The parent is adapted to this ecology, and the genetically highly similar offspring will also suit the conditions. But what happens when the ecology changes? In that case the characteristics that enabled the reproduction and survival of the parent may not be well suited to the new ecological conditions. Sexual reproduction ensures variability in offspring, which increases the chances that some of the offspring will survive and reproduce under the new ecological conditions.

G. C. Williams (1975) used a lottery analogy to explain these reproductive strategies. The ecological conditions that support survival and reproduction represent the winning number. Asexual reproduction is like having 100 lottery tickets, all with the same number. With sexual reproduction, you get fewer tickets—50 in this case—but they all have different numbers. If you do not know the winning number in advance, that is, if the conditions that support survival and reproduction frequently change or are very harsh, then sexual reproduction, although more costly (you cannot buy as many tickets), is more likely to result in a winning number. Experimental studies have confirmed that sexual reproduction results in the more rapid creation and combination of potentially beneficial mutations and that under harsh conditions these mutations result in phenotypes that survive and reproduce in greater numbers than do asexual members of the same species (Rice, 2002).

The elbow-room model represents another potential advantage to offspring variability (Bulmer, 1994). The basic premise is that offspring that differ to some extent, genetically and phenotypically, do not compete for identical environmental resources. In other words, offspring that differ from one another—those resulting from sexual reproduction—are better able to seek different niches within the same environment and thus reduce the intensity of competition among them (Dawkins & Krebs, 1979). With asexual reproduction, the primary competitors for survival are often one's identical siblings. Even in relatively stable environments, this competition can be severe if resources are limited (G. C. Williams & Mitton, 1973). Thus, intense competition favors niche seeking (Dawkins & Krebs, 1979), which, in turn, is made possible through the phenotypic variability that results from sexual reproduction.

Parasite Resistance

W. D. Hamilton's (1980, 1990; W. D. Hamilton, Axelrod, & Tanese, 1990) and Jaenike's (1978) hypothesis that the need to adapt to parasites drove the evolution of sexual reproduction has been the focus of intense study and discussion (Baer & Schmid-Hempel, 1999; Cooper et al., 2005; W. D. Hamilton & Zuk, 1982; A. D. Morgan, Gandon, & Buckling, 2005; Sorci, Morand, & Hugot, 1997). Parasites such as viruses, bacteria, and worms are ubiquitous and typically negatively affect the fitness of the host. One review found that species ranging from mollusks to mammals were infected, on average, by 16 parasitic species (Torchin, Lafferty, Dobson, McKenzie, & Kuris, 2003). The presence of these parasites creates strong selection pressures for the evolution of antiparasite adaptations such as immune responses to viruses or bacteria. However, because parasites generally have shorter life spans than their hosts, the parasites are often able to evolve away from the host's antiparasite adaptations. The result is that the host's defenses against these parasites are weaker, at least in the short term. With asexual reproduction, the antiparasite defenses of the parent and the offspring are nearly identical, differing only as the result of mutations. Any such mutations are unlikely to result in an effective long-term defense against the more rapidly evolving adaptations of the parasites (W. D. Hamilton et al., 1990). Thus, once adapted to the defenses of the parent, the parasites are equally well adapted to the defenses of the offspring. In such situations, harmful parasites will quickly reduce the viability of, or even eliminate, the lineage (W. D. Hamilton, 1980).

In this view, the principal function of sexual reproduction is to create highly variable antiparasite defense systems that can respond to a variety of different parasites and can be reshuffled, to some extent, from one generation to the next. If the parasites have adapted to the specific defenses of the parent, then a reshuffling of these defenses will typically benefit their offspring (Penn & Potts, 1999). The parasites will then make adaptations to these new defenses (Neu, 1992), which, in turn, will be reconfigured in the next generation of the host. The process of successive adaptations creates a coevolutionary cycle between parasites and the host's defenses (Dawkins & Krebs, 1979). The coevolution of hosts and parasites is reciprocal, however. It does not lead to any particular end point, such as permanent immunity, but rather to a potentially never ending pattern of resistance and susceptibility to parasites (Ridley, 1993). Van Valen (1973) illustrated this concept by means of Lewis Carroll's (1871) Red Queen.

> The Red Queen is a formidable woman who runs like the wind but never seems to get anywhere: . . . [She states to Alice], you see, it takes all the running you can do to keep in the same place. (Ridley, 1993, p. 64)

Stated otherwise, the coevolution of hosts and parasites ensures constant change and individual variability for the characteristics, such as the immune system, that are the focus of this coevolution, but the mean viability of the host does not necessarily change (e.g., Decaestecker et al., 2007).

The immune system provides an excellent illustration of the evolution of a system of defenses against parasites; another is the chemical defenses of many plant species. The genes that code for aspects of immune responses—major histocompatibility complex (MHC)—are the most variable family of genes ever identified (Nei & Hughes, 1991), supporting the prediction that variation is the key to keeping ahead of parasites. There are specific MHC mechanisms that trigger immunological responses to specific parasites. Thus, natural selection should favor individuals with a varied MHC because almost all organisms are threatened by many such parasites (Torchin et al., 2003). The specific evolutionary mechanisms maintaining MHC variation are not fully understood, however (Apanius, Penn, Slev, Ruff, & Potts, 1997; Gould, Hildreth, & Booth, 2004; Penn & Potts, 1999).

One possibility for how this came about is that natural selection would result in an increase or decrease in the variants (alleles) of the genes that code for specific immune responses across generations, depending on the parasites in the particular region (A. V. S. Hill et al. 1991). The advantage of these variants would begin to decline as parasites adapted to the accompanying immune responses, thereby making less common variants more reactive to these parasites. Another possibility is that MHC responses have actually evolved to detect nonself material, such as mucus or sperm, from conspecifics (Gould et al., 2004); living in large communities thus favors variation in these genes. Detection of this material triggers an adaptive immune response because many viruses hitchhike on it.

Results from field and experimental studies have not yet settled the matter but are consistent with the importance of variation in MHC genes and the relation of this variation to the evolution of the immune system (Milinski, 2006; Wegner, Reusch, & Kalbe, 2003). Although mutations contribute to variation in these genes, overall variation may be maintained primarily through sexual reproduction, specifically, disassortative mating—the mating of individuals with differences in their MHC (MHC differences appear to be detected by olfactory cues, or odor). In one related study, Potts Manning, and Wakeland (1991) examined the relation between mating patterns in mice (*Mus musculus domesticus*) and MHC disparity between mating partners. Females largely control choice of mating partners in this species and consistently chose males with an MHC different from their own. Moreover, Potts et al. found that "females seek extraterritorial matings with males that are relatively more MHC disparate than their own territorial mate" (p. 620). For other species, the results from mate-choice studies sometimes support these findings (Garver-Apgar, Gangestad, Thornhill, Miller, & Olp, 2006; J. I. Hoffman, Forcada, Trathan, & Amos, 2007; Wedekind, Seebeck, Bettens, & Paepke, 1995), and sometimes do not (Paterson & Pemberton, 1997; Penn, 2002; Penn & Potts, 1999).

Inconsistencies across studies may be due to the potential cost of an extremely variable MHC system, that is, increased risk of autoimmune disorders (Milinski, 2006). The best outcome would thus be a mate that would result in an intermediate level of MHC variation in offspring (Wegner et al., 2003), which, in turn, would make mates with highly dissimilar MHC genes less preferable. The combination makes the study of MHC-based mate choices more complicated than simply choosing an MHC-dissimilar mate. Whether or not MHC variability is maintained primarily by disassortative mating, the results of the Potts et al. (1991) study and many other studies (e.g., Møller, 1990b; W. D. Hamilton et al., 1990; Wedekind et al., 1995) are consistent with the hypothesis that the evolution of sexuality was driven, at least in part, by the benefits associated with maintaining a diverse and ever changing system of defense against parasites.

The model of host–parasite coevolution does not preclude the earlier described influence of mutations or facility of adaptation to changing ecologies on the evolution of sexuality (Kondrashov, 1988; W. D. Hamilton et al., 1990). In fact, all of the models make many of the same predictions: The central feature of both the speed of adaptation and host–parasite coevolution models is that the principal function of sexual reproduction is to maintain genetic and phenotypic variability (i.e., individual differences). Moreover, there is some evidence that multiple mechanisms may be involved in the evolution and maintenance of sexual reproduction (de Visser & Elena, 2007). In an experimental study, Cooper et al. (2005) manipulated the number of mutations and parasite exposure (exposed or not exposed) for the bacteria *Escherichia coli*. The ability of these bacteria to reproduce decreased as the number of mutations increased, consistent with Muller's ratchet, and decreased with exposure to the parasite, consistent with the Red Queen model. The bacteria strain with the lowest reproductive success had the combination of parasite exposure and a high number of mutations. Sexual reproduction in these bacteria would reduce mutation load, thereby reducing susceptibility to the parasite, in keeping with multiple benefits to sexual reproduction.

CONCLUSION

The discovery of the principles of natural selection was pivotal in the development and unification of the biological sciences. These principles provide a meta-theoretical organization to these sciences and explain three important phenomena: the diversity of life in the natural world, the mechanisms by which this within- and between-species diversity arose, and how and why species will continue to change. This is not to say that all aspects of natural selection have been fully resolved. There are multiple ways in which ecological and social selection pressures can influence the dynamics that result in speciation (e.g., Schluter, 2001), but these involve nuances in the process of natural selection and not evidence that refutes these principles. Ecological, social, and genetic studies continue to provide support for the theory of evolution and supply an ever finer grained understanding of how these principles work at multiple levels, from genes to behavior (Baglione, Canestrari, Marcos, & Ekman, 2003; McKinnon et al., 2004) and across a few generations to thousands of generations (Estes & Arnold, 2007; Kinnison & Hendry, 2001).

An intriguing area of evolutionary research concerns the evolution of sex and sexual reproduction. The considerable genetic cost to sexual reproduction—one has to give up 50% of one's genes to reproduce—raises the intriguing question of how this form of reproduction evolved. Although nuances remain to be resolved, there is consensus that one of the principal benefits of sexual reproduction is the generation of variability or individual differences (Kondrashov, 1988). Variation is, of course, the grist on which evolution works and provides several benefits in contrast with asexual reproduction. These benefits include the cross-generational elimination of deleterious mutations, the ability to adapt to changing ecologies, niche seeking in socially competitive environments, and an ever changing system of defense against rapidly evolving parasites (Apanius et al., 1997; Dawkins & Krebs, 1979; W. D. Hamilton & Zuk, 1982). These benefits affect the overall survival of the species but do not mean that evolution is for the good of the species (Dawkins, 1989; W. D. Hamilton, 1964). Rather, individual variation largely determines which individuals within the species or sex survive and reproduce and which do not. With the evolution of sexual reproduction came the evolution of sex differences, which is the subject of the next chapter.

3

SEXUAL SELECTION

With the publication of *On the Origin of Species* in 1859, Darwin laid out the argument for natural selection and largely proved the power of these mechanisms for creating evolutionary change. In this treatise, he also introduced another class of evolutionary mechanism, sexual selection, but only devoted about three pages to the topic. Twelve years later, Darwin greatly elaborated on these mechanisms in *The Descent of Man, and Selection in Relation to Sex.* In Darwin's words, sexual selection

> depends on the advantage which certain individuals have over other individuals of the same sex and species, in exclusive relation to reproduction. When the two sexes differ in structure in relation to different habits of life . . . they have no doubt been modified through natural selection. (1871, Vol. 1, p. 256)

Thus, for Darwin, natural selection was the principle evolutionary force that shaped the behavior and physiology of the species, including many sex differences (Ghiselin, 1974). Sexual selection was largely restricted to the physical and behavioral traits and accompanying social dynamics that were directly related to and influenced mate choice and competition for mates. Despite a compelling argument for distinguishing sexual from natural selection, Darwin's theory of sexual selection languished for about 100 years before being considered seriously as an evolutionary pressure (Cronin, 1991).

The principle components of sexual selection—*intersexual choice* (Which mate do I want?) and *intrasexual competition* (How can I get the mate I want?)—have now been studied and firmly established as potent evolutionary forces (Andersson, 1994; Andersson & Simmons, 2006). These processes are also core influences on the social dynamics of many species (West-Eberhard, 1983). They contribute to the maintenance of sexual reproduction (Agrawal, 2001) and may influence the emergence of new species (Gavrilets, 2000; Seddon, Merrill, & Tobias, 2008). In this chapter, I introduce and illustrate the dynamics of intersexual choice and intrasexual competition, and focus on the most common forms—female choice and male–male competition. These were Darwin's (1871) original foci, but scientists now know that the processes of competition and choice operate in both sexes, as I discuss (see also Clutton-Brock, 2007). Before moving to consideration of these components of sexual selection, it is important to step back and consider another key aspect of reproduction—parenting. The evolution of parenting, and sex differences in the amount of effort devoted to parenting, sets the stage for the evolution of sex differences in intersexual choice and intrasexual competition.

PARENTAL CARE

Although Darwin (1871) identified and defined the basic principles of sexual selection, he did not elaborate on their evolutionary origin. G. C. Williams (1966, 1975) and Trivers (1972) proposed that the evolution of intersexual choice and intrasexual competition is associated with the degree to which each sex invests in parental care, specifically, sex differences in the relative costs and benefits of producing and investing in offspring. For example, a female bird that needs a male to feed her while she is nesting must choose a mate that seems capable of provisioning; the cost of making the wrong choice could be fatal to her and to her offspring. Scientists now understand that the relation between parenting and sexual selection works both ways (Andersson, 2004). For instance, females may invest more in the offspring of healthy than unhealthy males (Burley, 1986; B. C. Sheldon, 2000). Nonetheless, the basic insight remains valid. As G. C. Williams (1966) noted,

> It is commonly observed that males show a greater readiness for reproduction than females. This is understandable as a consequence of the greater physiological sacrifice made by females for the production of each surviving offspring. A male mammal's essential role may end with copulation, which involves a negligible expenditure of energy and materials

on his part, and only a momentary lapse of attention from matters of direct concern to his safety and well-being. The situation is markedly different for the female, for which copulation may mean a commitment to a prolonged burden, in both the mechanical and physiological sense, and its many attendant stresses and dangers. (pp. 182–183)

Trivers (1972) formalized these observations and proposed that each individual's overall reproductive effort is a combination of mating effort (e.g., time spent searching for mates, the energy spent in vigorous mating displays), parental investment (e.g., the effort spent on finding food for offspring and defending them from predators), and in some cases nepotism (i.e., aiding the survival or reproductive prospects of relatives), as shown in Figure 3.1. *Parental investment* includes any cost (e.g., time, energy) associated with raising offspring that reduces the parent's ability to produce or invest in other offspring (see also Trivers, 1974). Both parents must invest something if they are to have any reproductive success, even if it is only the energy to produce gametes (e.g., sperm). But the proportion of effort that is typical in each sex varies substantially among species. In Trivers's (1972) words,

> the sex whose typical parental investment is greater than that of the opposite sex will become a limiting resource for that sex. Individuals of the sex investing less will compete among themselves to breed with members of the sex investing more. (p. 140)

The reproductive success of members of the lower investing sex is more strongly influenced by the number of mates that can be found than by investment in the well-being of individual offspring, whereas the reproductive success of members of the higher investing sex is more strongly influenced, in most cases, by investment in offspring than in competing for mates. The dynamics of sexual selection are influenced by the ways in which members of each sex distribute their reproductive efforts across mating and parenting

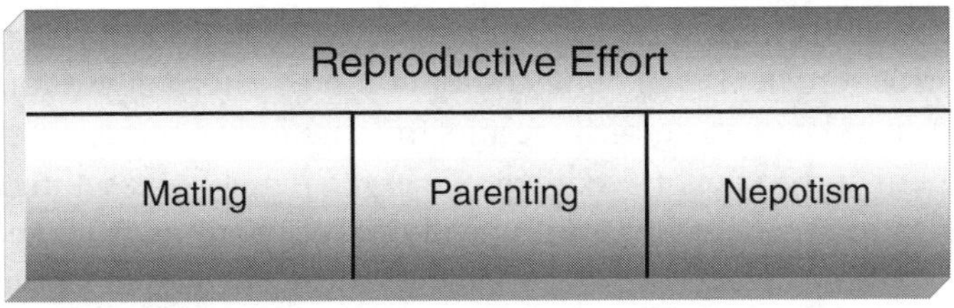

Reproductive Effort		
Mating	Parenting	Nepotism

Figure 3.1. Components of reproductive effort. Reproductive effort is distributed among mating effort (e.g., competing for mate); parental investment (e.g., provisioning and protecting offspring); and, in some species, nepotism (i.e., behaviors that aid survival or reproductive prospects of more distant relatives).

(Clutton-Brock, 1991), and those reproductive efforts in turn are influenced by a variety of factors, including the potential reproductive rates of males and females, the operational sex ratio (OSR), and the mating system of the species. All of these factors are interrelated (Kvarnemo & Ahnesjö, 1996) but are discussed separately in the sections that follow.

Reproductive Rate

The potential rate of reproduction is the biological limit on how quickly an individual can produce offspring, that is, the time between producing one offspring or a clutch of offspring and readiness to produce the next (Clutton-Brock & Vincent, 1991). The limit is determined by the amount of time needed to produce sperm, ova, clutch of eggs, gestation time, and so forth. A male elephant can sire many offspring in a single day, but it takes a female elephant 22 months to produce a single offspring. Across species, sex differences in the potential rate of reproduction are systematically related to sex differences in the relative mix of effort devoted to mating or parenting (Clutton-Brock & Vincent, 1991; Lorch, 2002). The sex with the higher potential rate of reproduction typically invests relatively more in mating than in parenting, whereas the sex with the lower rate of reproduction invests relatively more in parenting than in mating. Once they have mated, members of the sex with the higher potential rate of reproduction can rejoin the mating pool more quickly than can members of the opposite sex. It is often in their reproductive best interest to do so, particularly when biparental care is not necessary for the viability of offspring (Clutton-Brock, 1991; Maynard Smith, 1977). In most species, males have a higher potential rate of reproduction than do females as a result of sex differences in the time and cost associated with the production of sperm and eggs and any cost associated with gestation and postnatal care (Bateman, 1948; G. A. Parker & Simmons, 1996).

For species with internal female gestation and obligatory postnatal female care, as with suckling in mammals, the rate with which females can produce offspring is considerably lower than the potential reproductive rate of conspecific males (Clutton-Brock, 1991). The combination of internal gestation and the need for postnatal care necessarily results in more initial maternal than paternal investment and creates a sex difference in the benefits of seeking additional mates. Males in most species can reproductively benefit from seeking and obtaining additional mates, whereas females cannot (Maynard Smith, 1977). Thus, the sex difference in reproductive rate, combined with offspring that can be effectively raised by the female, creates the potential for large sex differences in the mix of effort devoted to mating and parenting, and this potential is often realized in nature if other conditions are also met (see the discussion that follows). In more than 95% of mammalian species, females can effectively provide all of the parental care and in fact do so; notable exceptions are the carnivore and primate families in which some level of paternal care is evident in 30% to 40% of genera (i.e., groups of highly related species), as described in the section of chapter 4 titled Paternal Investment. Female care of offspring frees males to invest in mating effort: In most mammalian species the reproductive effort of males is almost exclusively focused on competing with one another for access to mates (Clutton-Brock, 1989).

Support for reproductive rate as a key mechanism in the evolution of sex differences in the bias toward mating effort or parental effort is found for species in which females can potentially reproduce faster than males (Clutton-Brock & Vincent, 1991). In many of these *sex-role-reversed* species, males incubate, or internally gestate, the fertilized egg (Andersson, 2004; Berglund, Rosenqvist, & Bernet, 1997; Eens & Pinxten, 2000). The latter is common in species of pipefish and seahorse in which females transfer fertilized eggs into a front pouch on the male; an example of such a pouch is shown for the big-belly seahorse (*Hippocampus abdominalis*) in Figure 3.2. In many of these species, females compete intensely for reproductive access to parental males (A. B. Wilson, Ahnesjö, Vincent, & Meyer, 2003).

Intense female–female competition is also found in the mating system of the red-necked phalarope (*Phalaropus lobatus*), a polyandrous shorebird (J. D. Reynolds, 1987). In this species, males provide most or all of the parental care: They build the nest and incubate the eggs. The fledglings are precocial, that is, they fend for themselves once hatched. The high level of obligatory paternal care makes it possible for the female to pursue other mates, and she typically does. The crucial feature of this mating system is that females are ready to produce another clutch about 1 week after laying their first clutch, whereas the incubation time for males is close to 3 weeks. The result is that the effective rate of reproduction is potentially higher in females than in males. Females can produce about two clutches of eggs for every single clutch of eggs that can be incubated by a male. The limiting factor in the number of offspring that can be produced by females is thus the number of unmatched males. Female red-necked phalaropes show many of the characteristics that are typically associated with males in other species. They are slightly larger than males, have brighter plumage, fight with other females for access to males, and once paired, guard their mates against competitors (J. D. Reynolds, 1987). Male red-necked phalaropes, in contrast, rarely threaten or attack one another, although they will guard their mate until the eggs are laid. Mate guarding by males is very common; it ensures that any offspring are indeed his, that is, it ensures *paternity certainty* (see the section titled Male Parenting in chap. 4, this volume).

Figure 3.2. The male big-belly seahorse (*Hippocampus abdominalis*). This seahorse incubates eggs and provides protection for his offspring in a ventral (front) pouch. Illustration by Anthony Campolo. Printed with permission.

There is another important consequence of the sex-role reversal in the red-necked phalarope. The reproductive success of females is more variable than the reproductive success of males; for every female that produces two clutches in a breeding season, one female goes unmated and thus fails to reproduce. Unmated males, in comparison, are rare. Females that capitalize on the high level of paternal care will produce more offspring than females who assist the male in clutch incubation. As long as the male can effectively incubate the eggs himself, evolution—through differential reproduction— will favor females who are successful in gaining additional mates, that is, females who invest more in mating effort than in parental effort. Of course, the converse is also true: In species in which females invest more in parenting, males compete for sexual access and maternal investment, and a few males sire many offspring and many males sire no offspring.

Operational Sex Ratio

OSR is the ratio of sexually active males to sexually active females in any given breeding area at a given time. Because the OSR is related to the rate of reproduction (Emlen & Oring, 1977; Kvarnemo & Ahnesjö, 1996), it is a useful way to quantify the outcomes of some different behavioral strategies. In a population in which there are as many sexually mature females as there are sexually mature males—an actual sex ratio of 1:1—any sex difference in the rate of reproduction will result in an unbalanced OSR. Among the red-necked phalarope, the OSR is unbalanced because there are more unmated females than males in the breeding population at most points in the breeding season (J. D. Reynolds, 1987). The result is there are fewer unmatched males than there are females searching for mates (see also Oring, Lank, & Maxson, 1983; Owens, Burke, & Thompson, 1994). The higher demand for males results in an unbalanced OSR and the previously described female–female competition. The OSR is influenced by other factors as well, including sex differences in the time of arrival at breeding sites, the degree of synchrony in female sexual receptivity, and the spatial distribution of resources and mates (Emlen & Oring, 1977; Shuster & Wade, 2003). These differences can result in changes in mating dynamics within the species and at different points in the same breeding season (J. W. A. Grant & Foam, 2002; Kvarnemo & Ahnesjö, 1996).

An example of the importance of the time of arrival at the breeding site is provided by the spotted sandpiper (*Actitis macularia*), another polyandrous shorebird in which males provide most of the parental care (Oring et al., 1983). One way in which females of this species compete with one another is to arrive at the breeding site before the males, resulting in more females than males at the beginning of the mating season. As individual males arrive, females fight among themselves, sometimes to the point of injury, for access to these males. As with the red-necked phalarope, there are considerable reproductive benefits to successful females despite the cost of competition (i.e., risk of injury). This is because early breeders are more likely to produce additional clutches than are later breeders.

For species in which males compete for access to females, the degree to which female sexual receptivity is synchronized has an important influence on the OSR, as can the ecological distribution of potential mates. If all females are sexually receptive at the same time, then males are severely limited in the number of females with whom they can mate (Emlen & Oring, 1977). Under these conditions, the OSR will mirror the actual sex ratio, and if this ratio is close to 1:1, little male–male competition is likely. Asynchronous or prolonged female receptivity, in contrast, creates the potential for polygyny and results in a shift in the OSR such that there are more unmated males than females in the mating pool. Males then compete for access to sexually receptive females.

Takahashi's (2004) studies of the Japanese macaque (*Macaca fuscata fuscata*) provide a striking example of how the timing of sexual receptivity affects mating behaviors. The social groups of this species include several adult males and a larger number of adult females and their offspring. The females do not go into estrous every mating season, and thus there can be considerable variation across seasons in the number of reproductive females. Across four mating seasons, the ratio of reproductive females to males ranged from 1:5 to 3:1. When there were more males than estrous females, dominant males monopolized mating access to these females. During these seasons, low-ranking macaque males mated with estrous females less than 20% of the time. In seasons in which there were more estrous females than males, dominant males could not control mating dynamics. In these seasons, low-ranking males mated almost 50% of the time.

Dramatic changes in the OSR can even occur within a single breeding season, as documented for the two-spotted goby (*Gobiusculus flavescens*), a species of fish (Forsgren, Amundsen, Borg, & Bjelvenmark, 2004). At the beginning of the breeding season the OSR is unbalanced with more reproductive males than females. At this time, males compete intensely for nesting sites, court females, and then fan and protect eggs. These activities are very costly for the male and result in high male mortality; by the middle of the breeding season, there are many more females than males. When the OSR reaches about a 4:1 ratio of females to males, females start adopting male-typical behaviors. They begin to court males—"individual males were often surrounded by up to 20 round females courting them at close range" (Forsgren et al., 2004, p. 553)—and they chase other females away from the males to get access to mating opportunities with them.

Ecology of the Mating System

Any sex difference in the rate of reproduction or OSR means that one male may monopolize the reproduction of many females or one female may monopolize many males. Sex differences in the rate of reproduction or OSR are not enough, however, to result in polygamy, that is, either polygyny or polyandry. Polygamy arises when "multiple mates, or resources critical to gaining multiple mates, are economically defendable" (Emlen & Oring, 1977, p. 215). The sexual division of labor, particularly parental care, is also crucial for polygamous species, that is, one sex has to provide most or all of this care. For polygamy to be realized, the resources that support the species need to be clustered in space, and in most cases, members of the higher investing sex need to be sexually receptive at different times and clustered together. If resources or potential mates are sparsely distributed or sexual receptivity is limited to a very short period, then there is little opportunity for members of one sex to monopolize the reproductive efforts of members of the opposite sex. In these situations, social monogamy and high levels of biparental care may evolve, as is found in many species of bird (J. M. Black, 1996). In many of these species, resources are sparsely distributed, and as a result, biparental care is often needed to successfully raise nestlings (Clutton-Brock, 1991). If the spatial distribution of resources and the temporal distribution of potential mates coalesce, then there is a potential for polygamy, several different forms of which are described in Table 3.1 (see also Shuster & Wade, 2003).

Males of many species compete for control of the highest quality territory, that is, one that offers the most food and the best nesting sites and is defensible (Andersson 1994). Males controlling these territories are often able to attract more than one mate; this is called *resource defense polygyny*. Where females aggregate to lessen the risk of predation or because there are limited birthing sites *female defense polygyny* may arise (Andersson, 1994; Clutton-Brock & McComb, 1993). In this case, a very small number of males control large numbers of females. The northern elephant seal (*Mirounga angustirostris*) is an example: A few males dominate the many females who cluster on relatively confined beaches during the breeding season (Le Boeuf, 1974; Le Boeuf & Peterson,

TABLE 3.1
The Ecology of Mating Systems

Mating system	Variation within mating system
Monogamy	Neither sex has the opportunity to monopolize additional members of the opposite sex. Fitness is often maximized through shared parental care.
Polygyny	Individual males frequently control or gain access to multiple females.
	1. Resource defense polygyny. Males control access to females *indirectly,* by monopolizing critical resources.
	2. Female (or harem) defense polygyny. Males control access to females *directly,* usually by virtue of female gregariousness.
	3. Male dominance polygyny. Mates or critical resources are not economically monopolizable. Males aggregate during the breeding season, and females select mates from these aggregations.
Polyandry	Individual females frequently control or gain access to multiple males.
	1. Resource defense polyandry: Females control access to males *indirectly,* by monopolizing critical resources.
	2. Female access polyandry. Females do not defend resources essential to males but, through interactions among themselves, may limit access to males.

Note. From "Ecology, Sexual Selection, and the Evolution of Mating Systems," by S. T. Emlen and L. W. Oring, 1977, *Science, 197,* p. 217. Copyright 1977 by the American Association for the Advancement of Science. Reprinted with permission.

1969). This behavior is common in many ungulates (i.e., hoofed mammals) and pinnipeds (e.g., seals, sea lions). The elephant seal also provides an excellent example of *male dominance polygyny* and is discussed in greater detail in the section titled Male–Male Competition later in this chapter.

In another pattern of sexual behavior males aggregate in one place, called the *lek*, and compete with one another for the best spot. Competition can be direct, as in fighting or energetic displays, or indirect, as in ornamentation (e.g., bright plumage; Andersson, 1994). In some lekking species such as peacocks (*Pavo cristatus*), physical male–male competition is minimal; female choice largely determines which males reproduce and which do not (Höglund & Alatalo, 1995; Petrie, 1994; Petrie, Halliday, & Sanders, 1991). Peacocks develop large tail trains with varying numbers and sizes of eyespots. Males display their tails to females, and females choose mates on the basis of the length of the train and the number of eyespots (Petrie et al., 1991). Following copulation, females leave the lek to nest while the male remains to court other females. In lekking species, the combination of male–male competition and female choice of mates results in a small number of males fathering most of the offspring.

In lekking species in which the male provides most or all of the parental care, as with the Eurasian dotterel (*Charadrius morinellus*), females compete for access to males. Once a dotterel female has chosen a potential mate, she courts the male and attempts to isolate him from the lek. At this point, other females typically interrupt the courtship, and fighting then ensues between the two females, with additional females often joining the fray (Owens et al., 1994). This form of female–female competition provides a good illustration of *female access polyandry*, whereas the spotted sandpiper is an example of *resource defense polyandry*. As noted earlier, female spotted sandpipers arrive at the breeding site before the males arrive and compete for control of nesting territories. Successful females are able to attract one or more males to these territories and unsuccessful females remain unmated.

In addition to influencing the potential for polygamy, the ecology in which the species is situated can also influence sex differences in other ways. This can occur if males and females occupy different feeding niches that in turn require different physical adaptations, such as long legs for terrestrial foraging versus short legs for arboreal (in trees) foraging; examples are provided across species of *Anolis* lizard in the Caribbean (M. A. Butler, Sawyer, & Losos, 2007).

FEMALE CHOICE

Early naturalists found it impossible to deny male–male competition because it was so visible, whether or not it was important from an evolutionary perspective. Darwin's (1871) other proposal—that female choice was also a potent evolutionary force—was met with much more skepticism (Cronin, 1991). Today scientists know that females do choose mates; the research questions now center on finding the proximate (cues) and ultimate (functions) bases of their choices (Andersson, 1994). Female choice can operate at many points. There is precopulatory behavioral choice of a mating partner or partners and postcopulatory choice cryptically through choice of sperm from one male or another or through promotion of sperm competition (Birkhead & Møller, 1996; Griffith & Pryke, 2006; Neff & Pitcher, 2005; Ziegler, Kentenich, & Uchanska-Ziegler, 2005). I discuss core features of these two forms of choice in the following sections. In the final section, I provide a brief review of research on social learning and female choice.

Behavioral Precopulatory Choice

Aspects of early debates between Darwin and Wallace are a central issue today: Do females choose mating partners for reasons of aesthetics (Darwin's position) or does choice focus on more practical features, those that aid or predict offspring survival (Wallace's position, e.g., Wallace, 1892, although his view vacillated)? These two views are often described as the "good taste" and "good genes" versions of female choice. The predicted evolutionary outcomes of good taste and good genes mate choices, such as bright and colorful males, are often the same, and thus the relative contributions of these mechanisms are sometimes difficult to detect (Endler & Basolo, 1998) and in fact may lie more on a continuum rather than being distinct mechanisms (Kokko, Brooks, McNamara, & Houston, 2002). Nonetheless, separate discussions are warranted and are followed by discussion of trade-offs in female mate choices.

Good Taste

One of Darwin's (1871) most important insights presented in *The Descent of Man, and Selection in Relation to Sex* was that many physical differences or dimorphisms between males and females of the same species cannot be attributed to natural selection. In fact, the bright and oftentimes rather large plumage of the males of many species of bird—as illustrated in Figures 3.3 and 3.4—likely increase risk of predation. As a result, these sex differences not only cannot be explained in terms of natural selection but might in fact be eliminated by natural selection if some other process were not operating. Darwin argued that this other process is sexual selection, in particular female choice of aesthetically pleasing males. For Darwin (1871) and later R. A. Fisher (1930), the evolution of good-looking males could occur if females simply preferred more colorful or more elaborate males to their less flamboyant

Figure 3.3. Female and male humming birds (*Spathura underwoodi*). The large tail feathers of the male is a sexually selected trait and likely to be an honest indicator of the male's health. From *The Descent of Man, and Selection in Relation to Sex* (Vol. 2, p. 77), by C. R. Darwin, 1871, London: John Murray. In the public domain.

peers. Any such preference might initially result from a female sensory bias for certain color patterns or the brightness of certain colors that "may serve as a charm for the female" (Darwin, 1871, Vol. 2, p. 92) but that evolved for other reasons, such as detection of fruit (Ryan & Keddy-Hector, 1992) or ease of detecting males in different background environments (e.g., varying water depth; Seehausen et al., 2008).

Female choice of males that look attractive for reasons other than male quality will lead to the exaggeration of the trait in males, but unlike the good

Figure 3.4. The male resplendent quetzal (*Pharomachrus mocinno costaricensis*). From the Costa Rican Montane Oak Forest. Photo by Beth Kingsley Hawkins. Printed with permission.

genes models this male trait does not predict any particular benefit for females or their offspring (e.g., C. A. Marler & Ryan, 1997). In theory, it is possible for traits that are completely arbitrary—or arbitrarily complex (Gerhardt, Humfeld, & Marshall, 2007)—with respect to natural selection or male quality to become exaggerated through *runaway selection*. This can occur if the male feature and the female preference for that feature become genetically linked (R. A. Fisher, 1930). Such a link can evolve if daughters inherit a preference for the sexually selected features of their father and if sons inherit these same features. Any such "sexy son" will, especially in polygynous species, enjoy greater reproductive success than the sons of less elaborated males as long as the female preference does not change (Andersson, 1994) and as long as this trait does not become so exaggerated that it reduces the viability of the males (R. A. Fisher, 1930). In this way, a relatively arbitrary female preference could, in theory, result in the evolution of many of the secondary sex differences described by Darwin (1871), such as the elaborate plumage of the males of many species of bird. In practice, however, it is often difficult to determine exactly what is driving female choice of mating partners, and thus it is difficult to conduct rigorous tests of the predictions of runaway sexy son models (L. S. Johnson, Kermott, & Lein, 1994; Kirkpatrick & Ryan, 1991; Sargent, Rush, Wisenden, & Yan, 1998).

An exception is found in a large-scale study that extended 24 years and included more than 8,500 collard flycatchers (*Ficedula albicollis*), a species of bird (Qvarnström, Brommer, & Gustafsson, 2006). Qvarnström et al. were able to assess heritable variation in the primary male ornament in this species, that is, size of the forehead patch, and heritable variation in female preference for males with a large forehead patch. Both the size of the patch and the female preference for large patches showed heritable variation, but the heritable variation in female preference for this trait was independent of heritable variation in patch size. The failure to find a genetic link between females' preference for male patches and patch size is inconsistent with predictions of the sexy son model. Moreover, because of low levels of paternal provisioning and thus poorer health when they fledged (Gustafsson & Qvarnström, 2006), the sons of sexy fathers did not have a large, sexy forehead patch. Although it is possible that runaway selection occurs in some species (Dale, 2006), for the collard flycatcher and many other species it is more likely that females choose sexy fathers because these males and their sexy sons are healthier, more resistant to parasites, and generally more vigorous than their duller cohorts (Griffith & Pryke, 2006). Female choice of aesthetically pleasing males just makes good sense.

Good Genes

Good genes models of sexual selection typically focus on the genetic benefits provided by males to offspring (Borgia, 2006; Møller & Alatalo, 1999). However, good genes that promote male health may also be associated with males' ability to feed females or their offspring. In some species, including many species of bird, healthy males provide good genes and good food to offspring. It is hard to tease apart the relative contributions of these different kinds of benefits because in effect *good genes* often refers to higher quality males that are better able than other males to provide both genetic and material resources. Good genes lead to better offspring health—not simply more attractive sons—and to higher reproductive success of these offspring (e.g., B. C. Sheldon, Merilä, Qvarnström, Gustafsson, & Ellegren, 1997) and sometimes their grandoffspring (J. M. Reid et al. 2005). For these reasons, I discuss models of both indirect and direct investment by males.

The common prediction of these models of female choice is that the associated traits are reliable indicators of the likelihood the male will in fact provide these benefits (W. D. Hamilton & Zuk, 1982; Zahavi, 1975). Aspects of the male phenotype such as the degree of coloration, vigor of courtship displays, and quality of male song are sensitive to genetic and environment conditions. This provides essential information to the female about suitor quality (Andersson, 1994). Zahavi argued further that many sexually selected characteristics are a *handicap*, in the sense that the development and maintenance of such characteristics incurs some cost to the male. Selection favors the evolution of such handicaps because only superior males can bear the costs. For instance, inferior males would not be capable of deceiving potential mates by faking good health (Folstad & Karter, 1992). Handicaps are thus honest signals of the male's condition. The phenotypic quality of these male characteristics is *condition dependent*, that is, the attractiveness of these traits varies directly with the condition (including genetic condition) of the male. Females are predicted to use these characteristics in their evaluation of potential mates.

Although there are some questions that remain to be answered (e.g., Qvarnström, Pärt, & Sheldon, 2000), field and experimental studies support the prediction that the quality of sexually selected traits is particularly sensitive to individual differences in male health. There is evidence, too, that females benefit from mate choices that are based on the condition of these traits (G. E. Hill, 1991; Jennions, Møller, & Petrie, 2001; B. C. Sheldon et al., 1997; Siefferman & G. E. Hill, 2005; von Schantz, Wittzell, Göransson, Grahn, & Persson, 1996; Zuk, Thornhill, & Ligon, 1990). W. D. Hamilton and Zuk (1982) hypothesized that the condition of many sexually selected traits is specifically dependent on parasite load; I discuss potential mechanisms in chapter 4 (in the section titled Sex Hormones, Parasites, and Male Quality). If one of the selection pressures for the evolution and maintenance of sexual reproduction is resistance to parasites, as described in chapter 2 (in the section titled Parasite Resistance), then indicators of parasite resistance would be a good target for female choice. W. D. Hamilton and Zuk argued that the bright plumage of the males of many bird species varies directly with degree of parasite infestation; infected males sport duller displays than their healthier counterparts (Delhey, Peters, & Kempenaers, 2007).

In an early experimental test of this hypothesis, Zuk et al. (1990) infected a group of male red jungle fowl chicks (*Gallus gallus*)—a wild relation to the domestic chicken—with a parasitic worm (*Ascaridia galli*). Zuk compared the chicks' growth and their later success in adulthood in attracting mates to a group of uninfected males. Infected males grew more slowly than their healthy peers; in adulthood their sexually selected characteristics were more impaired than were other physical characteristics. For instance, the comb of affected males was smaller and duller than that of unaffected males, but many other physical traits did not differ across these groups. A mate-choice experiment demonstrated two points. First, uninfected males were preferred 2 to 1 to their parasitized peers. Second, female choice was related to sexually selected traits, such as comb length, but not to other physical traits (B. C. Sheldon et al., 1997; Zuk et al., 1990). Follow-up studies have confirmed that dominant males, those preferred by females as mates, have a healthier immune system and more elaborate sexually selected traits than subordinate males (Zuk & Johnsen, 1998).

In another test of the model, von Schantz et al. (1996) examined the relations between a sexually selected male characteristic, spur length (a projection on the wing of the male), male viability, and major histocompatibility complex (MHC) genotype in the ring-necked pheasant (*Phasianus colhicus*). Spur length varied with MHC genotype and both were significantly related to the likelihood of survival to 2 years of age. Longer spur lengths were associated with a higher likelihood of survival. Equally important, males with longer spurs are preferred as mating partners by females and father offspring with higher survival rates than their cohorts with shorter spurs (von Schantz et al., 1989). These and some, but certainly not all (Schall & Staats, 1997), other studies that have tested W. D. Hamilton and Zuk's (1982) hypothesis indicate that the quality of many of the secondary sexual characteristics of males often varies with degree of parasite infestation (Faivre, Grégoire, Préault, Cézilly, & Sorci, 2003; Milinski, 2006; Møller, 1994a; Penn & Potts, 1999; von Schantz, Bensch, Grahn, Hasselquist, & Wittzell, 1999).

In these situations, the sexually selected traits are good indicators of male quality, and thus it is not surprising that female choice targets these traits. Female choice is complicated by another dimension—her own MHC genes that are associated with immunocompetence. To enhance variation and immunity in their offspring, females must choose not only the healthiest male they can find but also a male with MHC genes that are moderately different from their own (Neff & Pitcher, 2005). So the male with the most elaborate secondary sexual characteristic might not be the best choice for every female in the population, especially for females with MHC genes that are similar to those of this male. Rather, females may choose mates from among the group of most elaborate males such that their offspring have a moderately different MHC set of genes than either parent. As I described in chapter 2 (in the section titled Parasite Resistance), moderate MHC differences between parents might provide the best immune-system outcome for offspring.

Male quality and female choice are not just a matter of parasite resistance. Female choice can be related also to direct benefits provided by males, such as their ability to forage. This may be influenced by parasite load, but it may not be (Borgia, 2006; Hadfield et al., 1991; Petrie, 1994; Petrie et al., 1991). Examples of the direct benefits signaled by sexually selected traits are provided by the socially monogamous house finch (*Carpodacus mexicanus*) and eastern bluebird (*Sialia sialis*). In these species, females prefer brightly colored males because degree of coloration is a good predictor of the male's later level of provisioning (G. E. Hill, 1991; Siefferman & G. E. Hill, 2005). Brighter males provide more food to their mate during clutch incubation and more food to the nestlings than do duller males. An example of female choice that is unrelated to parasites or provisioning is provided by Borgia's (1986) study of the satin bowerbird (*Ptilonorhynchus violaceus*), a species in which males provide no parental care. Males that are infected with a parasite are less likely to hold a courtship arena, that is, a bower, than are unaffected males. In this study, there was very little infestation among bower-holding males, but females still strongly discriminated among them, indicating that parasite load might influence the ability to acquire or keep a bower, but other factors also influenced female choice.

Males' ability to develop a bright plumage or other sexually selected traits is influenced by a combination of parental investment (especially their own earlier feeding), current conditions, and genetics (Møller, 1990b; Petrie, 1994). The contributions of genes and environments to the expression of these traits can vary considerably across species and across breeding seasons of the same species (Hadfield et al., 2006; P. M. Nolan, Hill, & Stoehr, 1998). As a result, a genetically healthy male may at times sport a dull plumage owing to a food shortage early in life, and a relatively unhealthy male may sport a brighter plumage during a food glut.

Mate Choice Trade-Offs

Even good mate choices may come at a cost. In many cases, there is a trade-off between the indirect (such as genetic quality) and direct (such as food) benefits provided by the male. Sometimes as one goes up, the other goes down. These trade-offs are most apparent in species in which males provide extensive parental care, as is nicely illustrated in a series of field and experimental studies of the socially monogamous barn swallow (*Hirundo rustica*).

Female barn swallows choose mates on the basis of the length and symmetry of the male's tail feathers, as shown in Figure 3.5 (Møller, 1988); length and complexity of male song is also important (Garamszegi, Heylen, Møller, Eens, & de Lope, 2005). Males with relatively long and symmetrical tail feathers obtain mates more quickly, are more likely to sire a second brood during any given breeding season, and obtain more extrapair copulations than their peers with shorter or asymmetric tail feathers (Møller & Tegelström, 1997; Saino, Primmer, Ellegren, & Møller, 1997). These longer tailed males also mate with higher quality females—indexed by the quantity of food provided by the females to their offspring (Møller, 1994b)—that in turn contributes to the greater reproductive success of longer tailed males. But it

Figure 3.5. Two pairs of male and female barn swallows (*Hirundo rustica*). The males have the longer tails. From *Sexual Selection and the Barn Swallow* (p. 159), by A. P. Møller, 1994, New York: Oxford University Press. Copyright 1994 by Oxord University Press. Reprinted with permission of Oxford University Press and Anders P. Møller.

is difficult to forage with long tail feathers, so long feathers are a cost to both the male and the female with whom he mates. Unlike among the house finch and the bluebird, this sexually selected trait is not a good indicator of later paternal investment in offspring; in fact, it indicates lower than average investment. Despite this cost, females obtain benefits from mating with males with longer tail feathers. Tail feather length appears to be a good indicator of parasite resistance and general physical viability (Møller, 1990a; Saino, Bolzern, & Møller, 1997). The direct benefit is reduced risk of parasite infestation during mating (an analog of a sexually transmitted disease).

The parasite resistance and general physical vigor indicated by the length of tail feathers is heritable and thus conveys indirect benefits in terms of more viable offspring. In one cross-fostering (i.e., "adoption") study, nestlings with shorter and longer tail feathers were switched such that one half of the nestlings were raised by their biological parents and one half by foster parents and one half of all nest sites were infected with a common parasite (Møller, 1990a). In infected nests, parasite resistance was strongly correlated with the length of the biological fathers' tail feathers, whether the nestling was raised by biological or foster parents. In contrast, the rearing fathers' tail feather length was not related to the parasite resistance of their foster nestlings. Field studies also indicate that the length of a male's tail feathers is a heritable indicator of the likelihood of his survival from one year to the next (Møller, 1994a).

The expression of these heritable characteristics is, however, condition dependent; that is, the phenotype of long tail feathers needs both the genes and good environmental conditions, such as availability of food, for it to be expressed (Møller, 1994a). One outcome of condition-dependent selection is that lower genetic quality males are more strongly affected by stressful conditions than are other males (Saino, Primmer, et al., 1997). This pattern was demonstrated for barn swallows by artificially making tail feathers longer (by gluing on an additional section) and thereby making foraging more difficult. The result was much larger costs—in terms of foraging ability and survivability—for naturally shorter than longer tailed males. Long tail ornaments can only be maintained by the most vigorous males and are indeed a handicap (Zahavi, 1975). Another outcome is greater variability among males than females on these traits (Pomiankowski & Møller, 1995). For the barn swallow, there are greater differences among males than females for length of tail features.

Females also have to balance the benefits of finding high-quality mates against the time and risks (e.g., of predation) associated with searching for better and better males. Gerhardt, Tanner, Corrigan, and Walton (2000) demonstrated this trade-off with the preference functions—"How much is enough?"—of female grey tree frogs (*Hyla versicolor*). In this species, females choose mates on the basis of the duration of the males' courtship call. Females prefer males with longer calls, and the offspring of these males are healthier than the offspring of males with shorter calls (Welch, Semlitsch, & Gerhardt, 1998); males do not provide any direct investment in the female or the offspring, and thus this is a heritable good genes effect. Gerhardt et al. presented females with pairs of shorter and longer courtship calls. When the duration of both calls was below average, females almost always preferred the longer call. When the duration of both calls was above average, the female preference for the longer call was much weaker. In other words, females consistently reject males with below average courtship calls, but once they find an above average male they are less likely to reject this male for a marginally better one.

Cryptic Postcopulatory Choice and Sperm Competition

There are now many examples across a wide variety of species of cryptic female choice and male–male sperm competition within the female reproductive tract (Andersson & Simmons, 2006; Bernasconi et al., 2004; Birkhead &

Møller, 1998; Bjork & Pitnick, 2006; J. P. Evans, Zane, Francescato, & Pilastro, 2003; Gil, Graves, Hazon, & Wells, 1999). *Cryptic choice* refers to mate choice hidden from view because it happens within the body of the animal. The term refers to mechanisms that increase chances of fertilization for some males but not others. The mechanisms by which this is achieved include physical ejection of sperm, changes in the biochemistry (e.g., pH levels) of the reproductive track that influence sperm viability, and storage of sperm from multiple males for later fertilization (Neff & Pitcher, 2005).

The last is common in species of insect and bird in which the anatomy of these storage sites can be biased toward the fertilization of sperm with certain characteristics, such as size (G. T. Miller & Pitnick, 2002). MHC molecules are not expressed directly on sperm, but there are other molecules that may signal these gene types, and these in turn may be subject to cryptic choice whereby fertilization is biased toward males with MHC genes that differ from those of the female (Ziegler et al., 2005). As described in the section titled Parasite Resistance (see chap. 2, this volume), *disassortative mating*—choosing a mate that differs from one's self—for MHC genes may provide offspring with an immune system that is well adapted to local parasites. Females may also differentially invest in the eggs fertilized by different males. Gil et al. (1999) found that female zebra finches (*Taeniopygia guttata*) deposited more testosterone in eggs fertilized by highly ornamented, colorful males. The prenatal boost in testosterone increases growth rate, physical size, and later social dominance but may come at a risk of increased susceptibility to parasites. Gil et al. hypothesized, "only chicks sired by highly ornamented males would be able to withstand high concentrations of testosterone" (p. 127).

In some species, female cryptic choice and male–male sperm competition work in concert (Bjork & Pitnick, 2006; G. T. Miller & Pitnick, 2002; Simmons & Kotiaho, 2007). In other species, they work independently, as illustrated by J. P. Evans et al.'s (2003) studies of the guppy (*Poecilia reticulata*). Females of this species prefer colorful males as mating partners, but it is not clear whether the reproductive advantage of these males arises from female choice or sperm competition. In this study, females were artificially inseminated with the same amount of sperm from colorful and less colorful males and thus did not make active mate choices. Assessments of offspring paternity revealed that the most colorful males sired nearly 4 times as many offspring as the drabbest males. Other factors suggested cryptic choice was not the likely cause of this outcome, indicating that colorful males produce more viable sperm. In this species, it appears that sperm competition and female mating preferences may work independently but in the same direction to produce the healthiest offspring. In other cases, males may evolve sperm that not only provide a competitive advantage vis-à-vis other males' sperm but also disable the cryptic choice mechanisms of females (Bernasconi et al., 2004).

Cornwallis and Birkhead (2007) demonstrated that the dynamics of sperm competition can vary with male status and female attractiveness (as indicated by comb size) in the red jungle fowl. Naturally dominant males produce more sperm than subordinate males. Experimentally reversing the status of males changed the amount of sperm produced per copulation; an increase in status resulted in an increase in sperm production, and a decrease in status resulted in a decrease in sperm production. Dominant males produced more sperm and faster sperm when they copulated with attractive females, but the quantity and quality of subordinate males' sperm did not vary across attractive and less attractive females.

Social Context

For some species, female mate choices are also influenced by social information, specifically, through monitoring the results of male–male competition and by imitating the mate-choice decisions of other females. An example of the former is provided by the black-capped chickadee (*Poecile atricapilla*). Both parents' provision offspring in this socially monogamous species, but females will engage in extrapair copulations if their mate is lower quality (e.g., poor health) or subordinate to other males. The result is that about one third of the offspring of these pairs have been sired by dominant extrapair males; dominant males in contrast are almost never cuckolded (Otter, Ratcliff, Michaud, & Boag, 1998). Dominance is determined by the length and complexity of male–male song contests that function to maintain territorial boundaries and keep intruding males at bay. In an experimental study in which the length and complexity of these contest songs were manipulated, Mennill, Ratcliffe, and Boag (2002) demonstrated that females paired with high-status males that lost two of these artificial contests were cuckolded more than 50% of the time for their next brood. Females appear to "eavesdrop" on male–male contests; if their own mate slips in these dominance encounters, they seek extrapair copulations, presumably with the winner!

Copying the mate choices of someone else is another way to cut down the costs of finding the best mate. Female imitation of the mate choices of other females has been most extensively studied in a species of guppy (*Poecilia reticulata*) from Trinidad and in the Japanese quail (*Coturnix japonica*; Dugatkin, 1996; Galef & Laland, 2005). In the studies of guppies, a female watches while another female chooses to mate with one of two males who are matched on a sexually selected trait (e.g., color) and thus would be chosen equally often in natural settings. After watching another female choose, the observer imitated this choice about 85% of the time. Imitation is not random, however. Females will only imitate same-age or older, and presumably more experienced, females (Dugatkin & Godin, 1993). In one experiment, the genetic preferences of the female for orange-colored males—a condition-dependent sexually selected trait in guppies—was pitted against the choice of another female (Dugatkin, 1996). Imitation was assessed under four conditions: The male courted by the model (the model had no choice and was forced to be close to this male by a Plexiglas barrier) was paired with another male with equal orange coloring or with a small (12%), moderate (24%), or large (40%) advantage in the proportion of orange coloration. Under control conditions in which no model was present, females chose the more colorful male about 9 out of 10 times. When the focal female observed the model courting with a less colorful male, she chose the less colorful male about four out of five times when the coloration differences between the two males were small to moderate. With large coloration differences, the focal female did not imitate the model.

In addition to these guppies, at least one other species of fish has shown a similar form of imitation (Schlupp, Marler, & Ryan, 1994). Dugatkin and Godin (1993) suggested that female imitation might reduce the costs associated with finding a suitable mate, such as risk of predation or lost foraging time. Imitation might also result in sexy sons. However, imitation of mate choices has not been found in all populations of guppy (Brooks, 1999) and does not appear to occur in many other species (Clutton-Brock & McComb, 1993; Jamieson, 1995). For instance, female fallow deer (Dama dama) tend to join males with large harems. Such behavior might indicate that the females are imitating the mate choice of other females. Clutton-Brock and McComb, however, demonstrated that this behavior is due to a preference for herding with other females (this reduces predation risks) and not an imitation of mate choice. Male three-spined sticklebacks (Gasterosteus aculeatus) construct the nest and care for offspring; females prefer to deposit their eggs in nests that already contain eggs. This preference is more strongly related to the presence of other eggs than to the imitation of other females (Goldschmidt, Bakker, & Feuth-De Bruijn, 1993). Nonetheless, these behaviors do influence male reproductive success and are an indirect form of mate choice (Wiley & Poston, 1996).

MALE–MALE COMPETITION

Males are not only more ornamented than females in many species, they are often larger and at times sport some type of armament. Male armament of one type or another is in fact found across a wide variety of species ranging from insects (see Figure 3.6) to mammals. Figure 3.7 illustrates the male arma-

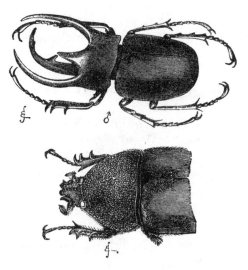

Figure 3.6. Male and female beetles (*Chalcosoma atlas*). From *The Descent of Man, and Selection in Relation to Sex* (Vol. 1, p. 368), by C. R. Darwin, 1871, London: John Murray. In the public domain.

ment for a species of antelope (*Oryx leucoryx*). Two males compete by kneeling in front of each other and then trying to maneuver the points of their horns under the body of their competitor. "If one succeeds in doing this, he suddenly springs up, throwing up his head at the same time, and can thus wound or perhaps even transfix his antagonist" (Darwin, 1871, Vol. 2,

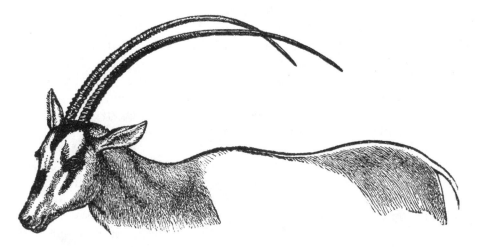

Figure 3.7. The male *Oryx leucoryx.* From *The Descent of Man, and Selection in Relation to Sex,* (Vol. 2, p. 251), by C. R. Darwin, 1871, London: John Murray. In the public domain.

pp. 251–252). As with the *Oryx*, Darwin argued that many of these physical dimorphisms evolved as the result of male–male competition for access to females or as displays that charm these females. Borgia (2006) argued that these traits often serve both functions, first evolving to support male–male competition and then evolving as a trait that signals male condition and through this influences female choice.

Whether or not they are used by females to assess male condition, armaments are almost always used in direct physical competition between males for the establishment of social status or for the direct control of mating territories or mates themselves (Andersson, 1994). Female–female competition over mates occurs in some species, as described for the red-necked phalarope, but it is rare in comparison to the frequency across species of male–male competition. The latter often determines which males will reproduce and which males will not. In the next section, I illustrate physical, behavioral, and cognitive forms of male–male competition.

Physical Competition

Physical male–male competition typically functions to establish social dominance. The losers of these contests often persist in their attempts to mate, but by sneaking rather than fighting.

Fighting for Social Dominance

The dynamics and consequences of physical male–male competition are nicely illustrated with studies of the northern (*Mirounga angustirostris*) and southern (*M. leonina*) elephant seal (C. R. Cox & Le Boeuf, 1977; Haley, Deutsch, & Le Boeuf, 1994; Hoelzel, Le Boeuf, Reiter, & Campagna, 1999; Le Boeuf & Peterson, 1969, 1974; Lindenfors, Tullberg, & Biuw, 2002). As with many mammalian species, the life histories and balance of effort devoted to mating and parenting differ markedly for males and females of these species. Male northern elephant seals provide no parental care, become sexually active around 8 years of age (compared with 3 years of age for females), and show high variability in the number of offspring they sire. In many species, the principle factor governing which males reproduce and which do not is differential access to females (Clutton-Brock, 1988; Le Boeuf & Reiter, 1988). For the northern and southern elephant seal this competition for access to females is one-on-one, although competition can be between coalitions of males, as I illustrate with chimpanzees (*Pan troglodytes*) in chapter 5 (in the section titled Social Dynamics and Coalitions).

During the breeding season, female elephant seals aggregate on relatively confined beaches and their male conspecifics compete physically with

Figure 3.8. Physical competition between two male northern elephant seals (*Mirounga angustirostris*). Rights managed by Publitek, Inc.,dba Fotosearch. Reprinted with permission.

one another for sexual access to these females. One such encounter is illustrated in Figure 3.8 for a pair of northern males.

> These encounters consist of two males rearing up on their foreflippers and trumpeting individually distinct calls . . . at one another. In most cases, one of the males retreats at this stage; if neither male submits, a fight ensues. The two males approach one another and push against each other chest to chest, while delivering open mouth blows and bites at each other's neck, flippers and head. (Haley et al., 1994, p. 1250)

Success in these bouts is related to physical size, age, and duration of residency (i.e., established males as opposed to newcomers) and determines social dominance. Social dominance, in turn, strongly influences reproductive outcomes (Haley et al., 1994; Le Boeuf, 1974; Le Boeuf & Peterson, 1969). For instance, fewer than 1 out of 10 northern males survives to age 8 years, and fewer than one half of these survivors mate at all. For those males that do mate, mating is largely monopolized by socially dominant individuals. On the basis of behavioral observation, Le Boeuf and colleagues (Le Boeuf & Peterson, 1969; Le Boeuf & Reiter, 1988) estimated that the net result of mortality and male–male competition is that fewer than 5% of the males sire between 75% and 85% of the pups, although DNA fingerprinting studies suggest this may be an overestimate (see the discussion that follows; Hoelzel et al., 1999).

In any case, one consequence of intense male–male competition is that selection favors the evolution of characteristics that aid males in their quest for social dominance. Size matters for northern and southern elephant seals (Lindenfors et al., 2002). In both species, mature males weigh between 3 and more than 8 times as much as mature females (Le Boeuf & Reiter, 1988; Lindenfors et al., 2002). Although the physical dimorphism of these seals is on the extreme side, it is by no means uncommon. Sex differences in physical size or armament are common for those species in which males physically compete for social status, territory, or direct access to females (Andersson, 1994; Clutton-Brock, Albon, & Guinness, 1985; Clutton-Brock, Harvey, & Rudder, 1977; Darwin, 1871).

Sneaky Males and Choosy Females

At times, smaller and socially subordinate male elephant seals father offspring by "sneaking" into harems and mating with females. This happens because these subordinate males resemble females (Le Boeuf, 1974). In a study of the relation between mating access and paternity determined by DNA fingerprinting, Hoelzel et al. (1999) confirmed that alpha males in both northern and southern elephant seal colonies tended to monopolize mating access. Among the northern elephant seal, there were on average nine males in and around each harem of females. The alpha male achieved 52% of the copulations, or about 5 times the expected rate if access was egalitarian. Paternity tests revealed something else. Alpha males, on average, only sired 40% of the pups. Some of the remaining pups were sired by a recently displaced alpha male or an alpha male from an adjacent harem, but others were sired by subordinate or "sneaker" males; I provide more information on alternative mating strategies in chapter 4 (in the section titled Intrasexual Competition).

Moreover, C. R. Cox and Le Boeuf (1977) suggested that female choice may influence reproductive dynamics in elephant seals. Northern females will often "protest," through threat vocalizations, the sexual advances of males. These protests, in turn, typically incite male-on-male aggression, effectively disrupting the mating attempt. Females protest more often when approached by low-ranking than by high-ranking males, and their protests are more likely to result in mating disruption for low-ranking than high-ranking males. The net effect of protests is an increase in the likelihood that a socially dominant male will sire her offspring, although the DNA paternity results suggest that females may at times prefer to mate with subordinate males. Scientists do not yet understand the motivations or mechanisms that determine these choices (e.g., whether MHC compatibility is important).

Behavioral Competition

The bower-building activities of the males of most species of bowerbird provide an intriguing example of a complex suite of behaviors that evolved by means of sexual selection (Gilliard, 1969). Bowers are structures that are typically built from twigs and leaves; are decorated with feathers, flowers, shells, bones and other objects; and serve as a courtship arena but not as nests. An example of one such bower is shown in Figure 3.9. The construction of a bower is a behavioral analogy of the bright plumage of the males of many other bird species, the long tail feathers of the barn swallow or the large size of male elephant seals. The bower is the focus of female choice and male–male competition. These two components of sexual selection are intimately related for bowerbirds and are influenced by traits other than the bower. For instance, the aggressive calls used in male social dominance displays are also components of the courtship calls females use in their mate choices (Borgia, 2006; Borgia & Coleman, 2000); female choice is also influenced by intensity of male courtship displays at the bower and by plumage coloration (Coleman, Patricelli, & Borgia, 2004).

In most of these species the males' bower provides a good indicator of overall male quality (Borgia, 1985b, 1995a, 1995b). Larger, healthier males build bowers that are more attractive to females than do other males. Bower quality, as measured by number of female visitations to the bower, is related to overall symmetry of the structure, the types of objects used as decorations, and to bower painting. The latter involves males chewing on vegetation and painting the inside of their bower with the plant-saliva mixture. Females nibble on the paint when visiting the bower (Bravery, Nicholls, & Goldizen, 2006). In an extensive series of observational studies of the satin bowerbird, Borgia found that 16% of the males fathered most of the offspring and that their success in attracting females was strongly related to the symmetry of their bower, the overall density of construction (i.e., number of sticks), and decoration with relatively rare blue flowers and snail shells (Borgia, 1985b); DNA fingerprinting confirms these males sire the vast majority of offspring (S. M. Reynolds et al., 2007).

Figure 3.9. Bower building and behavioral male–male competition and female choice in the bowerbird (*Chlamydera maculata*). From *The Descent of Man, and Selection in Relation to Sex* (Vol. 2, p. 70), by C. R. Darwin, 1871, London: John Murray. In the public domain.

Skill at constructing and maintaining high-quality bowers is related to a number of factors, including age, social learning, and social dominance (Borgia, 1985a; Borgia & Wingfield, 1991; Collis & Borgia, 1992; S. Pruett-Jones & M. Pruett-Jones, 1994). Social dominance is determined by the outcomes of male–male threats and other agonistic behaviors at communal feeding sites and influences an important form of male–male competition— the destruction of one another's bowers and the stealing of colorful objects (Borgia, 1985a; Wojcieszek, Nicholls, Marshall, & Goldizen, 2006). Bower destruction and decoration stealing lower the quality of competitors' bowers and thus reduce the likelihood that these competitors will find mates (S. Pruett-Jones & M. Pruett-Jones, 1994). In studies of the satin bowerbird, Borgia found that socially dominant males were more likely than less dominant males to destroy their neighbor's bowers. The bowers of socially dominant males were just as likely to be attacked as those of their less dominant peers— attacks almost always occur when the male is not at the bower—but attackers spend less time at the bowers of dominant, relative to subordinate, males. "Threat posed by more aggressive males may cause destroyers to avoid long visits at their bowers, thereby reducing the possibility of the destroyer being caught in the act of destruction" (Borgia, 1985a). The net result is that less damage is inflicted on the bowers of socially dominant birds, which, in turn, yields an important advantage in attracting mates.

Sexual reproduction in bowerbirds involves a mix of female choice and male–male competition. The most intriguing feature of these behaviors is that male–male competition is not primarily based on physical prowess, although there is some of that, but rather on skill at constructing relatively complex structures and on strategic raids of competitor's bowers. The studies I have described illustrate clearly that sexual selection can act to create systematic behavioral differences between males and females.

Cognitive Competition

Given the complexity of the behavioral competition of male bowerbirds and female choice, it is not surprising that these species have larger brains than do other species that live in the same habitat but do not build bowers (Madden, 2001). For the family of bowerbirds and especially for males, species with more complex bowers have a larger cerebellum than their less sophisticated cousins (Day, Westcott, & Olster, 2005). The relation between cerebellum size and bower complexity is interesting because this brain region is important for procedural learning through social observation (Leggio et al., 2000); immature male bowerbirds perfect their bower-building prowess through the observation and imitation of older males (Collis & Borgia, 1992, 1993). These patterns suggest that sexual selection will operate on cognitive traits and the supporting brain systems in the same manner as physical and behavioral traits if these competencies covary with reproductive outcomes (G. F. Miller, 2000).

A more specific test of this hypothesis is provided by comparisons of closely related species of monogamous and polygynous vole (Microtus; Gaulin, 1992; Gaulin & Fitzgerald, 1986, 1989; Spritzer, Meikle, & Solomon, 2004, 2005; Spritzer, Solomon, & Meikle, 2005, 2006); sexual selection operates more strongly in polygynous than in monogamous species. In the polygynous meadow vole (M. pennsylvanicus), males compete physically to establish dominance hierarchies and engage in scramble competition. Scramble competition for mates occurs when females are dispersed throughout the habitat and males compete by searching for and locating them. Prairie and pine voles (M. ochrogaster, M. pinetorum), in comparison, are monogamous; males are less aggressive and do not search for additional mates once paired. An illustration of how scramble competition might result in a sex differences in the area of the home range is provided in Figure 3.10. The top panel of the

Male Scramble Competition

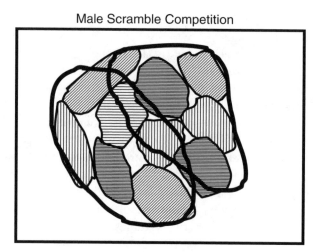

Male Monogamy

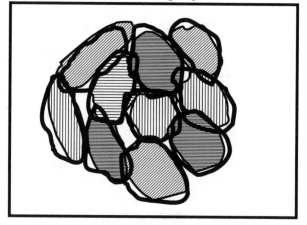

Figure 3.10. Territory size and male scramble competition. With male scramble competition (top panel), males compete by searching for females whose territories (filled shapes) are dispersed throughout the habitat. Male territories (bold open shapes) will encompass that of many females, and males may physically attack one another in those regions in which their territories overlap. With monogamy and male parental investment (bottom panel), the territories of mates largely overlap.

figure indicates that polygynous males will court five or six females. In such situations, competition will in theory favor males who court the most females, which is possible only through an expansion of the home range. The bottom panel shows a rather different situation in that monogamous males and females share the same range.

Field studies of polygynous and monogamous voles indicate that they follow the predicted pattern. In the polygynous meadow vole, males have home ranges that cover 4 to 5 times the area of the home ranges of females but only during the breeding season and only in adulthood (Gaulin, 1992; Gaulin & Fitzgerald, 1986). The latter pattern indicates the sex difference in the size of the home range is related to the reproductive strategy of the male (i.e., searching for females) and suggests that this difference is mediated by the increase in testosterone that occurs during the breeding season. As predicted, the home ranges of male and female prairie and pine voles overlap and do not differ in size.

A corollary prediction is that male meadow voles should have better developed spatial abilities than female meadow voles and male and female prairie and pine voles, and there should be no such sex differences for monogamous prairie and pine voles. A series of laboratory and field studies confirmed these predictions. The polygynous male meadow vole shows better navigational skills than conspecific females and better navigational skills than the males of monogamous species (Gaulin, 1992; Gaulin & Fitzgerald, 1986, 1989). An equally important finding is that this same pattern of differences is found for the overall and relative volume of the hippocampus, which supports spatial cognition, among other cognitive abilities (Jacobs, Gaulin, Sherry, & Hoffman, 1990; Sherry, Vaccarino, Buckenham, & Herz, 1989). The hippocampus of male meadow voles is larger than that of male prairie and pine voles, but comparisons of male and female meadow voles have produced mixed results (Galea, Perrot-Sinal, Kavaliers, & Ossenkopp, 1999; Jacobs et al., 1990).

Studies of individual differences in the reproductive success of male meadow voles, as measured by female mate choices and DNA fingerprinting, tell a complex story. Spritzer et al. (2004) confirmed that males with good spatial abilities have larger home ranges and visit more females in their nests than do their less skilled peers, but the relation between spatial abilities and reproduction is mixed. Socially aggressive and dominant males learn spatial routes more quickly than do other males but do not have a better long-term memory for these routes and are not preferred by females in mate-choice experiments. Females prefer less aggressive males with good spatial abilities (Spritzer, Meikle, & Solomon, 2005; Spritzer et al., 2006). DNA fingerprinting revealed that males with good spatial abilities may visit more females in their nests, but they do not always sire more pups. This finding, however, owed to the high reproductive success of two low-spatial-ability males (Spritzer, Solomon, & Meikle, 2005). Other than these two males, higher spatial abilities were associated with higher reproductive success. Nevertheless, these studies suggest that although the spatial abilities of male meadow voles may have evolved as a result of male–male scramble competition, female choice is also involved. Females sometimes prefer spatially gifted males as mates, but at other times they do not. One trade-off of the ability of these gifted males to find and visit many female nests is that they might spend less time with each individual female; this may reduce their reproductive success because females are less likely to mate with them.

MALE CHOICE AND FEMALE–FEMALE COMPETITION

Darwin (1871) and subsequent naturalists have tended to focus on female choice and male–male competition in the study of sexual selection, which is understandable given the ubiquity of these two components of reproductive dynamics (Andersson, 1994). But males, too, are sometimes choosy when it comes to mates, and females may compete aggressively for access to males. Scientists can now make predictions, consistent with the rich and elegant evolutionary theory of sexual selection, about the conditions under which males might be as choosy as or choosier than females in their mate choices or when females may compete aggressively for mates. As I described in the section titled Parental Care, male choice and female–female competition are predicted to turn on the same mechanisms that govern female choice and male–male competition.

Male Choice

Although male choice has not been found in all species in which it has been studied, discriminating males have been found in dozens of species of insect (Bonduriansky, 2001; LeBas, Hockham, & Ritchie, 2003), many species of fish (Amundsen & Forsgren, 2001; Berglund & Rosenqvist, 2001; Widemo, 2006) and bird (Amundsen & Pärn, 2006; Pizzari, Cornwallis, Løvlie, Jakobsson, & Birkhead, 2003; Roulin, Jungi, Pfister, & Dijkstra, 2000), and in some mammals (M. N. Muller, Thompson, & Wrangham, 2006; Szykman et al., 2001). Across these species, the traits males use to make their mate choices include indicators of female sexual receptivity, the risk of sperm competition, social dominance as determined by female–female competition, female quality, and the quality of parental care the female is likely to provide. An intriguing possibility is that some of these traits may be honest signals of the quantity or quality of eggs the females carry.

The female barn owl (*Tyto alba*) provides one example. Females display a varying number of black spots on their breast plumage, and male mate choice indicates the more the better (Roulin, 1999). Although males do not have as many plumage spots as females, they do have some and, again, the more the better. Sexy females tend to pair with sexy males, and males with sexy mates work harder to provision their offspring. An immune challenge experiment demonstrated that the robustness of the immune response was predicted by the number of black breast spots for females but not for males. These spots are indeed an honest indicator of female but not male health and an apparent indicator of the general health and immunocompetence of her offspring (Roulin, Ducrest, Balloux, Dijkstra, & Riols, 2003; Roulin, Riols, Dijkstra, & Ducrest, 2001).

Pizzari et al. (2003) also found evidence for condition-dependent female ornaments in red jungle fowl as well as for direct and cryptic male choice. Female jungle fowl sport red combs, although smaller and less colorful than those described earlier among males; when females have ornaments, they are typically less conspicuous than those of conspecific males (Amundsen & Pärn, 2006). Females with relatively large combs produce larger eggs with more yolk than their peers, and male mate choices indicate they prefer these females to females with smaller combs. Cryptic male choice was demonstrated by the finding that males transfer more sperm when copulating with females with larger combs; this effect is particularly pronounced for high-status males. Another interesting twist on male choice is found for the paternal pipefish (*Syngnathus typhle*); in this species males copy the mate choices of other males (Widemo, 2006). Copying presumably reduces the costs of finding a mate, but scientists do not know how often this happens in other species.

As I describe in the Paternal Investment section of chapter 4, the conditions associated with male parenting and male choice differ in important ways from female parenting and female choice. My point for now is that when males shift reproductive effort from mating to parenting, they compete less intensely with one another and become choosier when it comes to mates. This is not to say that male choice is always associated with male parenting. Male choosiness can evolve when females vary greatly in the quantity and quality of eggs they carry or when there are limitations—other than parenting—on males' reproductive potential (e.g., as a result of sperm depletion; Sæther, Fiske, & Kålås, 2001).

Female–Female Competition

Female–female competition is less common than male–male competition, in part because of the earlier described sex differences in reproductive rate and parental investment. Less common does not mean rare (Andersson, 1994; Clutton-Brock & Vincent, 1991): Female-on-female aggression over mates and the resources provided by these males was illustrated earlier with a description of the red-necked phalarope (in the section titled Reproductive Rate). Female–female reproductive competition has also been found in other species of bird (Oring et al., 1983; Reynolds & Székely, 1997) as well as in species of insect (Lorch, 2002), fish (Berglund et al., 1997; A. B. Wilson et al., 2003), and mammal (Palombit, Cheney, & Seyfarth, 2001). For some species, such as the cooperatively breeding meerkat (*Suricata suricatta*), female–female reproductive competition is for social dominance, not attracting males. Social dominance is important in this species and at least some other species that breed cooperatively (Engh et al., 2002). The reason is that dominant females suppress the reproduction of subordinates (Clutton-Brock et al., 2006).

I also mentioned that male parenting and female–female competition were common in pipefish and seahorses, but this varies with the ecology of the species (A. B. Wilson et al., 2003). In species in which parental males are clustered in the habitat, females have the potential to be polyandrous, that is, to monopolize the parental investment of more than one male. These are the species in which female–female competition is the most common and intense. When parental males are widely dispersed, monogamy is the most common reproductive outcome, although it is still the males that brood and protect offspring. These ecological constraints on polyandry are the same as those that constrain male polygyny (Emlen & Oring, 1977).

The absence of female–female competition does not mean that female-on-female aggression does not happen; it typically does. The difference is the aggression is related to attempts to gain control of important nonreproductive resources, especially food. This may be achieved through direct competition for the food, or through the formation of social hierarchies, which then influences resource access. Female elephant seals often bite one another or one another's pups, but this form of aggression is largely owing to overcrowding and not to competition over mates (Baldi, Campagna, Pedraza, & Le Boeuf, 1996). As with male elephant seals, male red deer (*Cervus elaphus*) compete physically for social dominance, which in turn influences access to females (Clutton-Brock, 1988; Clutton-Brock, Albon, & Guinness, 1988). Female red deer form dominance hierarchies too, but not to secure access to males. Rather, female dominance hierarchies influence access to food. The feeding of dominant females is less likely to be interrupted by other females; dominant females tend to be better nourished than their subordinates. Better nourishment increases females' year-to-year survival rate and that of their offspring, especially sons. This is because the sex difference in physical size means that poor prenatal nutrition generally affects males more severely than females (Clutton-Brock et al., 1985).

CONCLUSION

The central issue in the life history of individuals among species that reproduce sexually is searching for a mate or mates. In fact, variability in the quality of potential mates sets the stage for the evolution of sex differences and sexual selection (Darwin, 1871). The dynamics of sexual reproduction are typically played out through female choice of mating partners and male–male competition for social dominance, control of resources, or direct control of mates, each of which can influence which males sire offspring and which do not. Female choice and male–male competition vary widely across species and ecologies (Emlen & Oring, 1977), but they follow from well-understood evolutionary principles (Andersson, 1994).

Across species, female choice tends to focus on those characteristics that are an honest—not easily faked—signal of male quality (Zahavi, 1975). These signals in turn are expressed through the male's secondary sexual characteristics, which can range from the brightly colored plumage of the males of many species of birds to male song to the complex suite of behaviors necessary to build and maintain bowers (Amundsen & Pärn, 2006; Borgia, 1985b; W. D. Hamilton & Zuk, 1982). The expression of these characteristics is typically costly for the male. In most cases, it appears that only the fit males can develop the quality of secondary sexual characteristic necessary to attract mates and therefore sire offspring (e.g., Møller, 1994a). The net result of female choice is that in many species only a minority of males sire offspring. Male–male competition typically has the same effect as female choice; a few males sire most of the next generation, and most males leave no offspring. In some cases, males compete for direct access to sexually receptive females, for example, through the attainment of social dominance or through the control of the resources females need to reproduce (Clutton-Brock et al., 1988). In other cases, males compete on those dimensions that females use in their choice of mating partners, as illustrated by the bower-building activities of male bowerbirds (Borgia, 1995a). In many cases, males compete directly with one another and on the dimensions that females use to make their mate choices (Borgia, 2006).

The traditional focus on female choice and male–male competition does not belie their counterparts, that is, male choice and female–female competition. These aspects of sexual selection have now been observed across a wide variety of species (e.g., Berglund et al., 1997) and in response to many of the same social and ecological factors that influence the evolution and expression of female choice and male–male competition (Emlen & Oring, 1977; A. B. Wilson et al., 2003). In species in which males parent, they compete less intensely for mates and are more discriminating in their choices than are nonpaternal males in related species. When males parent, they become an important resource over which females compete, in the same way that males compete over mates in species in which females provide most of the parental effort. In many species, these aspects of sexual selection are expressed less intensely than female choice and male–male competition, but they are expressed nonetheless. Whether sexual reproduction centers on female choice, male–male competition, male choice, female–female competition, or some combination, the result is the evolution of sex differences for those traits that facilitate choice and competition. Any such differences may be more evident in either females or males and may involve physical, behavioral, or cognitive/brain traits.

4

SEXUAL SELECTION AND LIFE HISTORY

Have you ever pondered the reason for your existence and the reasons for the many difficulties in life? When considered through the lens of evolution, the reason you exist is simply to "maximize the likelihood of genic survival through reproduction" (R. D. Alexander, 1987, p. 65), and the trials of life result from pursuit of this difficult task; development, then, is preparation for this pursuit. Stated scientifically, the pace of development, the typical timing of key developmental events such as ages of menarche and first reproduction, and the overall length of the life span are evolved but plastic phenotypes in and of themselves (Allman, Rosin, Kumar, & Hasenstaub, 1998; Gingerich, 2001). Individuals express these phenotypes as a pattern of maturation and reproduction that can be adjusted to current circumstances but within a species-typical range. For instance, delaying maturation increases the risk of dying before reproducing but has the benefits of allowing offspring to get physically larger and juveniles to engage in developmental activities that better prepare them for adult reproduction. The combination of refined social and behavioral skills and larger size pays off because these add to individuals' *reproductive* potential—the suite of traits that allows individuals to compete for and attract mates and to invest in their offspring.

My goals for this chapter are to provide an introduction to life history theory and research and then to weave core features of sexual selection into this perspective. The weaving allows readers to more fully understand why males and females often engage in different types of activities during development, why they often mature at different ages, and why they have different life spans. I keep the focus on aspects of life history that are of particular importance for understanding topics covered in later chapters. These respective topics include the evolutionary function of play, the evolution of parenting and especially paternal investment, and the influence of sex hormones on sex differences in development, behavior, and cognition.

LIFE HISTORY

Life history encompasses the suite of traits that defines a species' maturational and reproductive pattern and the factors that govern the evolution of these traits and their expression during the life span. Scientists must consider a suite of traits because there are trade-offs in the expression of one trait versus another (G. C. Williams, 1957); there is a cost for every expressed benefit. As shown in Figure 4.1, the basic trade-offs involve the allocation of limited resources, such as calories, to somatic effort or to reproductive effort (R. D. Alexander, 1987; G. C. Williams, 1966). Somatic effort includes resources devoted to physical growth and to maintenance of physical systems during development and in adulthood (G. B. West, Brown, & Enquist, 2001); growth can also involve the accumulation of reproductive potential, as in increases in body size needed for male elephant seals (*Mirounga angustirostris*) to successfully compete for mates in adulthood. Reproductive effort is the spending of this potential during adulthood and

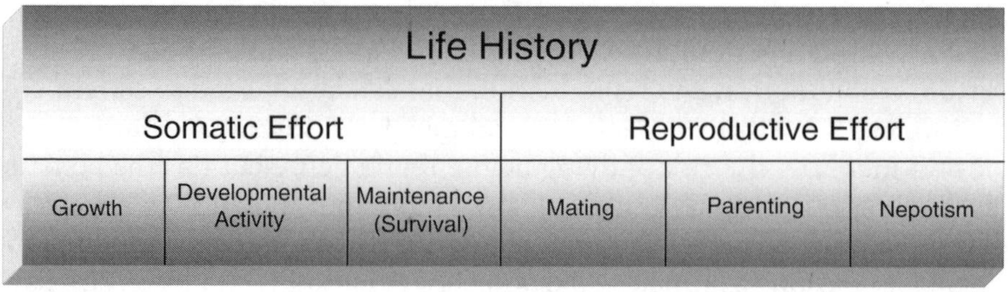

Life History					
Somatic Effort			Reproductive Effort		
Growth	Developmental Activity	Maintenance (Survival)	Mating	Parenting	Nepotism

Figure 4.1. Components of life history. *Developmental activity* refers to social, behavioral, and cognitive activities during juvenility that promote survival and increase the resources that can be invested later in reproductive effort during adulthood.

is distributed between mating, parenting, and in some species nepotism, that is, investment in kin other than offspring (W. D. Hamilton, 1964). In the sections that follow, I illustrate the most basic of these trade-offs as expressed in the pattern of reproduction across the life span, growth and development of offspring, the function of developmental activities, and phenotypic plasticity (see Charnov, 1993; Roff, 1992; Stearns, 1992; West-Eberhard, 2003).

Lifetime Reproductive Pattern

There are two patterns of reproductive timing. With *semelparity*, all reproductive potential is spent in one breeding episode; with *iteroparity*, this potential is spent across multiple episodes. Semelparity is more risky because reproduction during poor ecological conditions, such as a drought, could result in high offspring mortality, with no opportunity to reproduce under better conditions. Selection favors semelparity when adult mortality is high and the probability of surviving to a second breeding season is thus low. Therefore, individuals that devote minimal resources to somatic effort in adulthood and maximal resources to reproductive effort will produce more offspring than individuals that do not. Selection favors iteroparity when juveniles and adults are likely to survive from one breeding season to the next (Roff, 1992). For these species, lifetime reproductive success depends on the trade-off between efforts devoted to the current breeding season balanced against the costs of these efforts with respect to the ability to reproduce in later seasons. When individuals are likely to be successful across many breeding seasons, offspring born in one season are less likely to compete with offspring born in later seasons. Having fewer offspring in one season to have more in a later season is also a good hedge against unpredictable fluctuations in climate, food abundance, and predatory risk. As a result, iteroparous species invest more in maintenance and less in reproduction in any single breeding season than their semelparous cousins.

To illustrate the difference in reproductive pattern, I consider the female Pacific (*Salmo oncorhynchus*) and Atlantic (*S. salar*) salmon. The former experience intense competition for suitable nesting sites and must guard these sites after depositing their eggs (de Gaudemar, 1998). Females that do not pay the costs of competition will not obtain a suitable nesting site or will have their site destroyed by other females and thus will not reproduce at all. The result of this competition has been the evolution of a life history strategy in which these salmon expend resources that could be used for maintenance and survival—females die at the end of the first breeding episode—on behavioral competition for nesting sites and on the development of eggs. The latter results in the production of severalfold more eggs than the iteroparous Atlantic salmon (Roff, 1992). Female Atlantic salmon do not have to compete as intensely for suitable nesting sites and thus devote more resources to maintenance and less to reproduction during each breeding season and thereby survive to reproduce again. Although the female Atlantic salmon produces fewer eggs during any single season than does the female Pacific salmon, the number of viable offspring produced during the reproductive life span of these two species is comparable.

Reznick and Endler's (1982) study of the influence of predation on growth and reproductive patterns in iteroparous guppies (*Poecilia reticulata*) illustrates how and why life history traits can vary within the same species. Three populations of these guppies were studied under high (predators feeding on large adults), medium (predators feeding on juveniles), and low (few predators) predation risk. When risk was high, females matured rapidly and were smaller as adults, two factors that lowered their risk of being eaten before reproducing. In addition, they allocated more reproductive effort to initial breeding episodes, producing 2 to 3 times as many offspring in this first episode than did females in less risky environments. In locales where predation was less severe and adult mortality rates were lower, individuals grew more slowly and attained a larger adult size, and females spread their reproduction over several breeding episodes. Follow-up studies revealed these differences in life history pattern were due to a combination of genetic differences that have emerged between these populations and phenotypic plasticity (e.g., Reznick & Bryga, 1996; Reznick, F. H. Shaw, Rodd, & R. G. Shaw, 1997; Rodd, Reznick, & Skolowski, 1997). Reznick and colleagues' studies also demonstrated that life history patterns in and of themselves are subject to evolutionary change.

The pattern of life history development is also influenced by more proximal reproductive costs, such as those involved in producing eggs, caring for offspring, and competing for mates. These costs can compromise the physical health and often the survival prospects of parents (Clutton-Brock, 1991; Stearns, 1992). The underlying physiological processes governing these trade-offs are not fully understood but include the energetic demands of reproduction (e.g., parental care) and associated hormonal changes (Sinervo & Svensson, 1998). For example, the development of male secondary sexual characteristics needed to compete with other males or to attract females requires an increase in testosterone levels, which in turn can compromise the immune system and survival prospects of unhealthy males, as detailed in the section titled Sex Hormones, Parasites, and Male Quality. There is also evidence for similar trade-offs in females. In the female collard flycatcher (*Ficedula albicollis*), large brood sizes are associated with a reduced production of antibodies for a common parasite and increased infection rates and higher mortality (Nordling, Andersson, Zohari, & Gustafsson, 1998).

Offspring Growth and Development

One might ask why evolution has not resulted in a life history pattern in which females produce a lot of fast maturing offspring that then quickly reproduce themselves (G. C. Williams, 1966). The reason is that producing many quickly maturing offspring results in smaller and less competitive offspring that in turn suffer high mortality (Stearns, 1992). Across species of plant, insect, fish, reptile, and mammal, offspring that are larger at the time of hatching or birth have increased survival rates due, in part, to decreased predation risk and decreased risk of starvation (Roff, 1992). The drawback is that high quality—larger and more competitive—offspring come at a cost of fewer of them during a reproductive life span. Whether a species practices a low-quality/high-quantity or high-quality/low-quantity reproductive pattern is influenced by age-specific mortality risks, population stability or expansion, and intensity of competition with conspecifics, among other factors (Mac Arthur & Wilson, 1967; Stearns, 1992; Roff, 1992).

Species that produce fewer and larger offspring also tend to have slower rates of growth, higher levels of parental care, and a longer life span in comparison with related species that produce smaller but more offspring (Roff, 1992; Shine, 1978), as I describe in the section titled Parenting. This life history pattern is more common in iteroparous than semelparous species and is associated with relatively low juvenile mortality rates and late age of first reproduction (Roff, 1992). Low juvenile mortality is related to larger size at hatching or birth as well as to parental protection and provisioning (Clutton-Brock, 1991; Shine, 1978). As described in the section titled Life History and Sexual Selection, reproductive delay can result from competition with more mature individuals. In this situation, delayed maturation can improve reproductive prospects through, for instance, an increase in body size. Large females can give birth to larger and thus more competitive offspring, and large males often have an advantage in male–male competition (Carranza, 1996; Stearns, 1992). In some species, developmental activity, such as play, may result in improvement in survival and reproduction-related social, behavioral, and cognitive competencies (Pellis & Pellis, 2007). Slow maturation and growth thus allow for the accumulation of more reproductive potential than is possible with faster maturing species.

Developmental Activity

In addition to the traditional somatic and reproductive components of life history, I have included developmental activity as a feature of somatic effort during infancy and juvenility in Figure 4.1. As I elaborate in chapters 10 ("Sex Differences in Infancy and at Play," see Figure 10.1) and 11 ("Sex Differences in Social Development"), much of the research in human development up through adulthood can be easily incorporated into a developmental activity component of life history (Geary, 2002a), and much of the literature reviewed in chapters 6 ("Evolution of Human Fatherhood"), 7 ("Choosing Mates"), and 8 ("Competing for Mates") covers the expenditure of this potential in adulthood. My point for now is that some of these developmental activities promote survival during development (Bjorklund & Pellegrini, 2002), but others may contribute to the accumulation of reproductive potential.

By *accumulation*, I mean that some developmental activities result in the refinement of physical, cognitive, behavioral, and social competencies that enhance reproductive prospects in adulthood (Geary, 2002a; Geary & Bjorklund, 2000) and will presumably result in somatic changes during development. Many developmental activities result in changes that are incorporated into the developing individual, for instance, distribution of slow and fast muscle fibers as related to physical activity (Byers & Walker, 1995), and through this are carried forward into the life span in ways that can contribute to survival and reproductive activities during adulthood. The bottom line is that infancy and especially the duration of the juvenile period evolve only when mortality risks during this period are low and when corresponding activities and growth contribute to the accumulation of reproductive potential.

A straightforward example of the basics of life history development and the accumulation of reproductive potential is found in many species of *Insecta* in which distinct morphs or body types are associated with different life history stages. In the tomato hornworm moth (*Manduca quinquemaculata*) shown in Figure 4.2 and in related species, the behavior of the larvae (caterpillars) is focused on somatic effort—to avoid predation and to grow—but the behavior of the adult moth is focused on reproductive effort. In fact, the caterpillar cannot reproduce, and in some species of *Insecta* the adult morph does not eat; the sole function of the moth or butterfly is to reproduce (R. D. Alexander, 1987). The more successful the caterpillar is at finding food, the larger it grows before its transformation into the adult moth or butterfly. The increased size during the caterpillar stage results in a larger adult that will typically have a reproductive advantage over smaller adults. Although the development of life history traits will sometimes fall neatly into successive stages, as with the tomato hornworm moth, a more continuous pattern of growth and a gradual emergence—sometimes punctuated with a growth spurt and development of secondary sexual characteristics at puberty—into adulthood are more typical.

Phenotypic Plasticity

Plasticity is the potential for phenotypes to change during development and in adulthood in response to social and ecological conditions experienced

Figure 4.2. Two life history stages of the tomato hornworm moth (*Manduca quin-quemaculata*). To the left is the larval stage, during which the caterpillar's behavior is focused on somatic effort, that is, avoiding predation and growth. To the right is the adult stage, during which the moth's behavior is focused on reproductive effort. From *Insects and Mites: Techniques for Collection and Preservation* (p. 75), by the U.S. Department of Agriculture, 1986, Washington, DC: Author. In the public domain.

by the individual and in some cases by the individual's mother (Roff, 1992; West-Eberhard, 2003). Phenotypic plasticity enables a more optimal expression of life history traits as these relate to changing survival and reproductive demands in the local ecology or social group. The mechanisms that support this plasticity are not fully understood (West-Eberhard, 2003) but include hormonal and other endocrine responses to social and ecological conditions (Dufty, Clobert, & Møller, 2002; Lessells, 2008) as well as other circumstances (e.g., water availability) that affect the individual's physical and behavioral condition (McNamara & Houston, 1996; Sinervo & Svensson, 1998). Whatever the mechanisms, plasticity of evolved traits has been demonstrated in many species, from plankton to plants to primates (Alberts & Altmann, 1995; McNamara & Houston, 1996; Roff, 1992; Sultan, 2000). In all of these species, plasticity is expressed within the constraints of norms of reaction (Stearns & Koella, 1986), which represent a genotype whose phenotypic expression varies with ecological conditions but within a constrained range (e.g., age of maturation may vary from age 10 to 14 months, but not outside of this range).

The common field voles (*Microtus agrestis*) shown in Figure 4.3 provide an example of how the expression of life history traits can vary across ecological conditions (Ergon, Lambin, & Stenseth, 2001). Populations of voles in different locales vary significantly in two life history traits, adult body mass and timing of yearly reproduction. It is of course possible that these population differences reflect genetic variance, as with Reznick's guppies. If this is the case,

Figure 4.3. The common field vole (*Microtus agrestis*). From *The Natural History of the Mammalia* (Div. 5, p. 157), by C. Vogt and F. Shecht, 1887, London: Blackie & Son. In the public domain.

individuals transplanted from one population to the other will show the body mass and reproductive timing of their natal group. It is also possible that differences across populations reflect variation in local ecologies, such as quality and availability of food. In this case, individuals moved from one population to the other will, after experiencing local conditions for one breeding season, have the same body mass and reproductive timing of individuals of the local community. This is what Ergon et al. found. Regardless of natal community, voles living in richer ecologies developed a higher wintering body size and thus were able to reproduce earlier. Individuals living in poorer ecologies needed to devote added time to foraging and growth—somatic effort—and thus experienced a delay in the onset of reproduction—reproductive effort.

There is also evidence for cross-generational plasticity whereby the social or ecological conditions experienced by the mother, maternal age at time of pregnancy, and patterns of mother–offspring interactions can influence life history development and trade-offs in offspring (A. S. Fleming, O'Day, & Kraemer, 1999; Mousseau & Fox, 1998; M.-H. Wang & vom Saal, 2000); these are termed *maternal effects*. For example, offspring of nutrient-deprived plants allocate more growth-related resources to root production, whereas offspring of light-deprived plants allocate more resources to leaf production (Sultan, 2000). In mammals, maternal condition during pregnancy and suckling can have lifelong consequences for offspring. Healthy mothers give birth to heavier offspring and they provide more milk, both of which promote early growth that in turn results in larger adult size and higher breeding success (Clutton-Brock, 1991). An example involving social dynamics is provided by one species of baboon (*Papio cynocephalus*): Males born to high-ranking females have accelerated testicular maturation and move quickly up the social hierarchy (Alberts & Altmann, 1995).

Nussey, Postma, Gienapp, and Visser (2005) demonstrated that plasticity itself can be heritable, at least in the great tit (*Parus major*). Females of this species time their egg laying so that chicks hatch when their primary food, caterpillars, is at a peak. The emergence of caterpillars is related to ambient temperature, and warming over the last 2 decades has resulted in caterpillars emerging earlier in the season. As a result, many females lay their eggs too late, resulting in a shortage of food when their offspring hatch. Some females have adjusted their laying dates on the basis of ambient temperature so that their chicks hatch at a more optimal time. In other words, females differ in the plasticity of reproductive timing, such that females that can adjust their laying date on the basis of ambient temperature have more food (caterpillars) available when their chicks hatch. One result is that females that have been able to adjust their reproductive timing have produced more offspring that survive to the next generation. Nussey et al. found that about one third of the variation in this reproductive plasticity is heritable and that there has been a cross-generational increase in the number of females that can alter their egg laying on the basis of temperature.

LIFE HISTORY AND SEXUAL SELECTION

Intrasexual competition and intersexual choice can both influence and be influenced by life history traits (Andersson, 1994; Badyaev & Qvarnström, 2002; Kokko, 1997). As the intensity of competition increases, selection should favor fewer and more competitive offspring (Mac Arthur & Wilson, 1967). The corresponding life history pattern includes iteroparity, a long developmental period, high levels of parental investment, and other traits that add to offsprings' later social competitiveness (Roff, 1992). The empirical link between life history and sexual selection is found with the hormonal mechanisms that influence the expression of life history traits and trade-offs and, at the same time, influence the expression of the secondary sexual characteristics involved in intrasexual competition and intersexual choice (Sinervo & Svensson, 1998). In the next two sections, I illustrate the relation between the evolution and expression of life history traits, trade-offs, and intrasexual competition and intersexual choice, respectively. I close with discussion of the relation between phenotypic plasticity and the dynamics of competition and choice.

Intrasexual Competition

It is not surprising that males have been the focus of research on the relation between intrasexual competition and life history, given that male–male competition is better understood and more common than female–female competition. These studies have been conducted in a variety of mammalian and bird species (Clinton & Le Boeuf, 1993; Harvey & Clutton-Brock, 1985; Wiley, 1974), and in a few others (Stamps, 1995).

Physical Competition

The reader may recall from chapter 3 (in the section titled Parental Care) that males of many species of insect, reptile, fish, and mammal show little or no parental investment and compete intensely for access to multiple females (Andersson, 1994; Clutton-Brock, 1989; Darwin, 1871). One result is only a minority of males reproduce, thereby creating strong selection pressures for the evolution of traits that support competitive ability (Clinton & Le Boeuf, 1993; Plavcan & van Schaik, 1997). Among these traits are physical size and aggressiveness such that larger, more aggressive males are typically more competitive than smaller, less aggressive males. A common developmental pattern for these species is for males to grow at a slower rate and mature later than females and to engage in play fighting during juvenility (P. K. Smith, 1982; Stearns, 1992).

Among primates with intense physical male–male competition, males grow more slowly, have a more pronounced growth spurt before maturing and a longer overall developmental period, and are physically larger in adulthood than females (Leigh, 1996). Comparison of these polygynous species with their monogamous cousins indicates a causal relation between physical male–male competition and life history development. This is because intrasexual competition is less intense in monogamous species, and thus there is no selective advantage for physical size (Clutton-Brock, Harvey, & Rudder, 1977); among monogamous species, the sexes rarely differ in adult size or life history development (Leigh, 1996).

These patterns are not restricted to primates. Among mammals with intense physical male–male competition, males' developmental period can range from moderately longer (e.g., 2.8 vs. 3.5 years in the patas monkey, *Erythrocebus patas*) to more than twice as long as that of females (e.g., 3 vs. 8 years in the elephant seal, *Mirounga angustirostris*; Harvey & Clutton-Brock, 1985; Le Boeuf & Reiter, 1988). Males may weigh slightly more than females (e.g., 19% heavier in colobus, *Colobus angolensis*, a monkey) or in extreme cases, such as elephant seals, may weigh 8 times more than females (Le Boeuf & Reiter, 1988). The low investment in parenting that accompanies intense intrasexual competition is also related to average length of the life span (Allman et al., 1998). The lower investing sex, whether male or female, has a shorter life span on average than does the higher investing sex. The most common pattern is a shorter life span for males, which in turn appears to be a consequence of the nutritional demands needed to grow larger, competition-related injuries, and the immunosuppressive effects of testosterone (Clinton & Le Boeuf, 1993; Clutton-Brock, Albon, & Guinness, 1985).

The evolution of larger males is associated with the evolution of larger but fewer offspring and an accompanying increase in the size of females (Carranza, 1996; Roff, 1992); birthing of larger offspring requires larger females. This does not mean physical male–male competition always results in larger males. It does not. Faster maturing and smaller males often have an advantage for species with scramble competition (see Figure 3.10, chap. 3, this volume) or fight during flight (Andersson, 1994). The magnitude of the sex difference in physical size can also vary within a species; groups living at higher latitudes generally show larger sex differences than their peers living closer to the equator (Isaac, 2005). Although uncommon in mammals, female–female competition is sometimes more intense than male–male competition. An example is the fierce fighting over food among female spotted hyenas (*Crocuta crocuta*; Frank, 1986). These females are larger than and dominate males; female aggression is related in part to prenatal exposure to high levels of androgens (Dloniak, French, & Holekamp, 2006).

Behavioral Competition

To illustrate how intrasexual competition can result in within-sex differences and through this the evolution of between-sex differences, I consider the alternative reproductive strategies of smaller jack and larger hooknose male Pacific salmon (*S. oncorhynchus kisutch*; M. R. Gross, 1985, 1996). For both sexes, fry live the 1st year of their life in the freshwater stream of their hatching and then migrate to the Pacific Ocean. Males that eventually become jacks are larger as fry and spend about 6 months in the ocean before maturing and beginning the journey home to spawn. Hooknose males begin their migration to the Pacific as smaller fry but spend about 18 months in the ocean before maturing and returning to spawn. During this 18-month period, these males grow larger than jacks and develop distinctive secondary sexual characteristics, including hooked upper and lower jaws used in male–male competition, canine-like teeth, red coloration, and a humped dorsal area (back) that provides added defense against attacks by other males. Larger and more aggressive hooknose males are almost always dominant at spawning sites and achieve a disproportionate number of fertilizations. In streams that afford hiding spots, jacks furtively spawn while hooknose males are fighting. The jacks are just as reproductively successful, on average, as hooknose males, and thus early maturity and furtive mating represents a successful life history strategy for males of this species (M. R. Gross, 1985). Female Pacific salmon mature after about 18 months at sea but weigh less and show less exaggerated changes in snouts and body shape than do hooknose males (I. A. Fleming & M. R. Gross, 1994). On average, the females differ from both hooknose and jack males but are especially different from the jacks when it comes to behavioral aggression and maturational timing.

As readers learned in chapter 3 (in the section titled Behavioral Competition), bowerbirds provide an excellent example of the evolution of complex behavioral competition and further illustrate how such competition can result in developmental sex differences. Female satin bowerbirds (*Ptilonorhynchus violaceus*) begin to reproduce at 2 years of age, but males do not produce sperm until 5 years of age and do not achieve an adult male plumage until 6 or 7 years (Vellenga, 1980). Even then, bower-holding males do not mate until 10 years of age, and most never mate. During development, young males watch older males at their bower and imitate bower building and courtship displays when the older males leave to feed (Collis & Borgia, 1992). It takes 5 to 7 years of practice before males can build an adult-like bower (Diamond, 1986). Young males also engage in play fighting, which may provide the experience needed for dominance-related encounters in adulthood, as I describe in the section titled Evolution of Play. In short, the delayed maturation of male satin bowerbirds and related species provides an opportunity for them to practice and refine the bower construction and fighting skills needed for reproductive competition in adulthood.

Intersexual Choice

Lekking species illustrate the influence of intersexual choice (typically female choice) on the life history evolution of the opposite sex (Höglund & Alatalo, 1995; Wiley, 1974). As I described in chapter 3 (in the section titled Ecology of the Mating System), leks can be areas in which males gather together to strut, display plumage, or engage in other activities to attract mates, or they can be more dispersed areas in which single males display. In both situations, females survey a number of males and then mate with one or a few of them. The result is that a minority of males copulate with most of the females; the satin bowerbird is an example of a lekking species. The sex differences in maturational timing and developmental activities are the combined result of male–male competition and female choice. Whatever the relative contribution, female choice has influenced the life history evolution of male bowerbirds.

As I noted in chapter 3 (in the section titled Ecology of the Mating System), peacocks (*Pavo cristatus*) are another lekking species but one with little male–male competition (Höglund & Alatalo, 1995; Petrie, 1994; Petrie, Halliday, & Sanders, 1991). Males develop large tail trains with varying numbers of eyespots, a characteristic that influences female mate choices (Petrie et al., 1991). Peahens begin to reproduce at 2 years of age, whereas males do not develop their full trains until 3 years of age and do not establish a lekking display site until 4 years (Manning, 1989). Some males mate successfully at age 4, but others will not mate until later years, and some will never mate. As with bowerbirds, traits that female peacocks use in mate-choice decisions have resulted in accompanying changes in the life history of male peacocks, including a lengthening of the developmental period and an increase in size at maturity (Wiley, 1974).

Plasticity

Plasticity in life history development can take a fixed and irreversible form once one trajectory is taken or can be highly flexible across breeding seasons, age, prospective mates, and social and ecological context (Badyaev & Qvarnström, 2002; M. R. Gross, 1996; Kemp, 2006; Kokko, 1997). The jack and hooknose Pacific salmon are an extreme illustration of the former. More typically, irreversible trajectories involve change in the timing of major developmental milestones, such as age of reproductive maturity, that are influenced by a combination of genes and proximate conditions (Stearns, 1992; Stearns & Koella, 1986). As described for field voles, physical condition at the beginning of each breeding season can influence the timing of that year's reproduction, and this in turn is related to food availability the preceding winter (Ergon et al., 2001). In other circumstances, resource availability is influenced by social dynamics. In many species of Old World (Africa, Asia) primate (e.g., macaques, *Macaca*), coalitions of female kin compete for control of high-quality food sources, such as fruit trees (Wrangham, 1980). The combination of social dominance and better nutrition results in an earlier age at first reproduction, more offspring surviving to maturity, and higher lifetime reproductive success for females in dominant coalitions (Silk, 1993).

The here-and-now dynamics of intrasexual competition and inter-sexual choice can also influence the age of achieving developmental mile-stones. It is common for males of many species to be physiologically able to reproduce years before they actually do so (Wiley, 1974). The delay can result from competition with older and more dominant males or a female preference for older and thus often more fit—having survived many seasons—males (Kokko, 1997; Selander, 1965). As found with bowerbirds, males in many lekking species must establish and defend a display territory, and the experi-ence of older males typically gives them an advantage over younger males in competition for and at these sites (Höglund & Alatalo, 1995; Wiley, 1974). Competitive dynamics are also dependent on group composition, which changes from one breeding season to the next. As noted previously, Taka-hashi (2004) found that the mating success of low-status, but not high-status, male Japanese macaques (*Macaca fuscata fuscata*) varied across seasons as a result of changes in the operational sex ratio (see the section titled Opera-tional Sex Ratio, chap. 3, this volume). For other species, dominant males can delay the physiological maturation or reduce the reproductive potential (e.g., reduce size of testes) of lower status males through intimidation and behavioral subordination (e.g., Dixson, Bossi, & Wickings, 1993; J. R. Walters & Seyfarth, 1987).

Within-season changes are illustrated by Qvarnström, Pärt, and Sheldon's (2000) study of female choice in the collared flycatcher (*Ficedula albicollis*). These females have a preference for males with a large forehead patch because their offspring are healthier than the offspring of other males (see the section titled Good Taste, chap. 3, this volume). However, these females pay the price of less paternal investment because their "sexy" mates invest more time in attempts to achieve extrapair matings than do other males. Females are thus faced with a trade-off between the genetic benefits provided by large-patched males and the paternal investment provided by small-patched males. Because the benefits of paternal investment decline as the season progresses and nestlings become larger, the trade-offs change during the season. Early in the season, many females prefer paternal, small-patched males. This is when the males' added parental investment, which is feeding of fledglings, provides a benefit to females. As the breeding season progresses, female choice becomes increasingly influenced by the size of the males' patch.

EVOLUTION OF PLAY

Play should of course be embedded in the developmental activity com-ponent of life history, but the topic merits a separate section because of the long developmental period of humans and the sex differences in play activities that I review in chapter 10. Evolutionary accounts of play date back more than a century (Groos, 1898), and the systematic, scientific study of play extends through the latter half of the 20th century. Much is now known about the different forms of play, their distribution across species and the sexes, and the likely evolutionary origins. I can only touch on the surface of this rich literature and refer the interested reader to the many excellent treatments available (Aldis, 1975; Bekoff & Byers, 1998; Burghardt, 2005; Fagen, 1981; Pellegrini & Smith, 2005; Power, 2000).

Play in one form or another is found in many mammalian species and in some species of bird (e.g., many species of parrot, *Psittaciformes*), fish (e.g., great white shark, *Carcharodon carcharias*), reptile (e.g., Komodo dragon, *Varanus komodoensis*), and invertebrate (e.g., octopuses, *Octopus vulgaris, O. briareus*; Burghardt, 2005; Fagen, 1981; Kuba, Byrne, Mather, & Meisel, 2006). Burghardt proposed five common features that define play across species: play is voluntarily, not immediately functional, involves some components—though muted, incomplete, or exaggerated—of more functional activities (e.g., prey capture), is repeated, and occurs only in safe environments. Play is uncommon in small, quickly developing species and is most common in species with relatively large brains, a comparatively long developmental period, and parental care, but the strength of these relations is modest and can vary across and within families of species (Burghardt, 2005).

The three most common classes of play are locomotor, object oriented, and social (Aldis, 1975; Fagen, 1981). The common assumption that these forms of play provide delayed benefits to the individual may or may not be correct (Archer, 1992; Burghardt, 2005; Caro, 1980; J. R. Walters, 1987). It is possible that play simply reflects the spontaneous expression of evolved behavioral repertoires and is not an evolved bias to practice and refine these during development. It is also possible that the early expression of these behaviors is necessary for their maintenance and adaptation to local conditions, including the maintenance and strengthening of the brain systems that support play (Pellis & Iwaniuk, 2000). A mechanism for adapting to local conditions in turn should be important to the extent these conditions are variable across time (Burghardt, 2005; Pellegrini, Dupuis, & Smith, 2007), as is the case for highly social species. Whatever the extent play contributes to adult competencies, it provides a window that allows scientists to view aspects of the social, behavioral, and cognitive evolution of the species.

Locomotor and Object Play

Locomotor play involves running, leaping, jumping, and so forth. It is nearly ubiquitous in mammals and is found in some species of fish and bird and perhaps some reptiles (Burghardt, 2005); locomotor play in a garfish

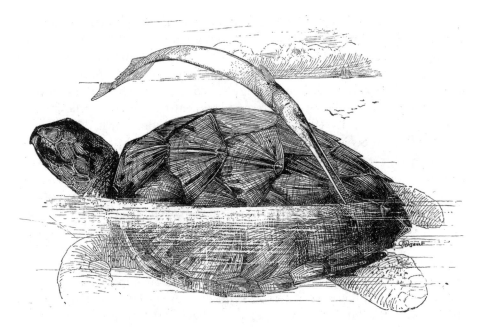

Figure 4.4. Play in the garfish (*Strongylura*). Some species of garfish appear to play by leaping over objects floating on the surface of the ocean, including turtles. From *Along the Florida Reef* (p. 45), by C. F. Holder, 1892, New York: Appleton. In the public domain.

(*Strongylura*) is shown in Figure 4.4. This typically solitary play is found in species that navigate in complex and varied terrains (e.g., mountains) and in species with elaborate predator evasion or prey capture behaviors (Aldis, 1975; Burghardt, 2005; Fagen, 1981; Power, 2000). Byers and Walker (1995) argued that locomotor play results in long-term changes in the synaptic organization of the cerebellum, which is involved in the coordination of complex motor movements and some forms of learning, and in the distribution of fast and slow muscle fibers. In this view, locomotor play results in neural and muscular changes that support complex functional activities in adulthood (Lewis & Barton, 2004); whether these involve the learning and practice of these behavioral repertoires or maintenance and strengthening of preexisting neuromuscular systems remains to be resolved. The Siberian ibex (*Capra sibirica*), a species of mountain goat, illustrates the point: "Social play is equally likely on flat and sloped terrains, but solitary locomotor play was much more frequent on sloped terrain, despite the greater dangers of falling" (P. K. Smith, 1982, p. 142). From Byers and Walker's perspective, the locomotor play of *ibex* kids results in neural and muscular adaptations that facilitate later locomotion in mountainous terrain.

Object play is common in foraging generalists, that is, species that feed on a wide variety of foods and that benefit from learning to manipulate different types of objects, including prey and tools (for a few species), in different ways (Burghardt, 2005; R. Byrne, 1995; Fagen, 1981; Power, 2000). This form of play is found in many species of bird, carnivore, and primate and a few other species (Burghardt, 2005). Object play typically has an exploratory component, especially for novel objects, and includes active object manipulation and for some species combining objects (e.g., placing one object into or on top of another). These activities are more common in juveniles than adults and are similar to prey capture behaviors or behaviors that involve food extraction using a tool (Power, 2000). The assumption that object play provides practice and refinement of prey capture skills has not always been supported (Caro, 1980), however, although it has been experimentally assessed in only a few species (Power, 2000). The assumption that object manipulation allows animals to learn about the different ways in which objects can be used as tools is also in need of further experimental testing (R. Byrne, 1995; P. K. Smith, 1982). Nevertheless, there is an across-species relation between flexible tool use and object manipulation skills in adulthood and the complexity of object play during development.

Sex differences in locomotor and object play are predicted to evolve only to the extent that males and females differ in the corresponding activities in adulthood. Unfortunately, sex differences in these forms of play have not been as extensively studied as the sex differences in social play described in the next section. With respect to locomotor play, the pattern of cross-species sex differences varies considerably; for some species no differences are reported, for other species males are reported as engaging in more locomotor play (Power, 2000), and for still other species females are reported as engaging in more locomotor play (e.g., J. M. Pedersen, Glickman, Frank, & Beach, 1990; Power, 2000). The situation is similar for object play (Power, 2000). It may be that no systematic pattern of sex differences in locomotor and object play exists across species potentially because there are few sex differences in corresponding activities (e.g., predator evasion).

Social Play

Social play is very common in mammals; in many species of bird; and in a few species of fish, reptile, and invertebrate (Burghardt, 2005). The most common form is play fighting, which typically involves chasing and rough and tumble components; the latter can include wrestling, muted biting, pouncing and jumping on partners, pushing, and so forth (Archer, 1992; Panksepp, Siviy, & Normansell, 1984; Powers, 2000; J. R. Walters, 1987). Play fighting typically involves pairs of evenly matched (e.g., in terms of size) individuals and increases in frequency from infancy to the juvenile years and then slowly declines, often merging into serious fighting by reproductive age. Play fighting includes many of the same components of intrasexual fighting or territo-rial defense but differs in enough ways to make a straightforward practice of fighting behaviors unlikely in most species (Pellis & Pellis, 2007). In fact, many of the basic behavioral components of species-specific fighting are evi-dent at birth, but their expression is often better controlled, more nuanced, and more varied for individuals that have engaged in play fighting. By enabling the development of better controlled and more flexible fighting skills, this form of play likely results in later social competitive advantage (Pellis & Pellis, 2007; P. K. Smith, 1982).

Unlike locomotor and object-oriented play, sex differences in play fight-ing are found in a wide range of species, with the form and intensity of this play closely tracking sex differences in the form and intensity of intrasexual com-petition and other agonistic behaviors in adulthood (Maestripieri & Ross, 2004; Power, 2000; P. K. Smith, 1982). Across species of marsupials (e.g., red kangaroos, *Macropus rufus*), pinnipeds (e.g., northern elephant seal, M. *angu-stirostris*), ungulates (S. *ibex*), rodents (Norway rat, *Rattus norvegicus*) and pri-mates (e.g., chimpanzee, *Pan troglodytes*), Power found that males of polygynous species with intense physical male–male competition nearly always engaged in more play fighting during development than did conspecific females; these sex differences are not found in their monogamous cousins with less intense intrasexual competition (Aldis, 1975; P. K. Smith, 1982). Carnivores are the exception that seems to prove the rule. Intense competition over mates or food is the norm for males and females of most of these species, and both sexes tend to engage in play fighting during development. A notable exception among carnivores is the spotted hyena in which females compete fiercely with other females over food, are polyandrous, and are dominant over males (East, Burke, Wilhelm, Greig, & Hofer, 2003). In this species, females engage in more play fighting than males (J. M. Pedersen et al., 1990).

Play parenting is one form of social play that is consistently more com-mon in females than in males, although it can occur in both sexes (Nicolson, 1987; Pryce, 1993, 1995). When presented with an array of children's toys, G. M. Alexander and Hines (2002) found that female vervet monkeys (*Cer-copithecus aethiops sabaeus*) carried and played with dolls much more than their brothers; their brothers engaged in more play with a ball and toy car. Hassett, Siebert, and Wallen (2008) found the same sex difference for rhesus macaques (*Macaca mulatta*). For primates in general, play parenting and gen-eral interest in infants is most frequently observed in young females that have not yet had their first offspring. For many of these species, play parenting (e.g., caring for siblings) is associated with higher survival rates of their first-born, and sometimes later born, offspring (Nicolson, 1987). Across five primate species it was found that first-born survival rates were two to more than 4 times higher for mothers with early experience with infant care obtained through play parenting than for mothers with no such experience (Pryce, 1993). Maternal behavior is also influenced by the hormonal changes that occur during pregnancy and the birthing process, such that a combination of play parenting and these hormones contribute to maternal skill in many primates (Pryce, 1995).

PARENTAL INVESTMENT

Unfortunately, life is not always about play, and in fact for many species the transition to adulthood not only brings reproductive competition and choice, it often brings the cost of parental investment as well. As shown in Figure 4.1, this investment is a key feature of adulthood in these species and an aspect of life history development in which sex differences are common (Clutton-Brock, 1991). There are many associated topics: the effects of maternal age, health, and prenatal and postnatal investment on the development of offspring and grandoffspring (Mousseau & Fox, 1998; M.-H. Wang & vom Saal, 2000). Much remains to be learned about the conflicts of interest, behavioral and genetic, between mothers and fathers and between parents and offspring (Foerster et al., 2007; Haig, 1993; Trivers, 1974). The relative importance of indirect and direct investment also remains to be fully understood (Qvarnström & Price, 2001). Indirect investment is genetic inheritance, which can influence offspring health and development as well as maintain needed variation in an offspring's immune system and other genes, as I reviewed in chapter 2 (in the section titled Why Reproduce Sexually?). Direct investment involves providing offspring with nutrients during gestation or egg production as well as feeding and protecting them from predators postnatally (Clutton-Brock, 1991). For social species, investment can also involve assistance in establishing and navigating social relationships (Alberts & Altmann, 1995; Buchan, Alberts, Silk, & Altmann, 2003). Whatever the form, the most fundamental question is why parents, maternal or paternal, provide direct investment at all given the costs (Clutton-Brock, Albon, & Guinness,1988; Gustafsson & Sutherland, 1988). The answer is simple:

> [in] virtually all species where young are fed by their parents, they do not survive if parents are removed, though where both parents are involved the removal of one is not necessarily fatal. . . . Both across and within species, there is usually a close relationship between feeding rate and the growth rate and survival of young. . . . Early growth may also affect reproductive success in adulthood. In mammals, for example, adult size is commonly related to breeding success and is usually well correlated with early growth, which is affected by birth weight and the mother's milk yield (Clutton-Brock, 1991, p. 25).

In short, parents pay the cost of investing in offspring because these off-spring are more likely to survive and reproduce than are offspring that receive reduced or no direct parental investment. As I described in chapter 3 (in the section titled Parental Care), maternal parenting is much more common than paternal parenting, especially in mammals. This pattern leaves us with a rid-dle when it comes to humans: How did men's parenting evolve, and how is it maintained? I have addressed this issue previously (Geary, 2000, 2005a), and I review and elaborate on these earlier works in chapter 6. To fully understand this forthcoming discussion of human fatherhood, scientists must first under-stand how paternal investment evolved in other species.

Male Parenting

To set the stage for discussion of human fathers in chapter 6, I begin by contrasting obligate and facultative parenting. I follow with discus-sion of the cost and benefit trade-off of male parenting and close with a few implications.

Obligate and Facultative Investment

Although uncommon in mammals, paternal investment is found in many species of bird, fish, and in some species of insect (Perrone & Zaret, 1978; Thornhill, 1976; Wolf, Ketterson, & Nolan, 1988). The study of the attendant cost–benefit trade-offs is complicated by the evolutionary history of the species (Westneat & Stewart, 2003) and by whether the investment is obligately or facultatively expressed (K. E. Arnold & Owens, 2002; Clutton-Brock, 1991). *Obligate* investment means that male care is necessary for the survival of his offspring and will thus favor paternal males. One potential out-come is that all males will show high levels of parenting, independent of prox-imate conditions. For many species, including humans, paternal investment is *facultatively* expressed, that is, it is not always necessary for offspring sur-vival and therefore can vary with here-and-now conditions (Westneat & Sherman, 1993). In these species, male parenting reflects trade-offs between the costs and benefits of this direct investment in the contexts in which the male is situated.

Whether the investment is obligate or facultative, there are often con-siderable benefits to offspring. The benefits have been demonstrated in many bird species by removing fathers from nests. In an analysis across 31 such species, Møller (2000) estimated that 34% of the variability in offspring sur-vival was due to paternal investment. In some species removal of the male results in the death of all nestlings (obligate investment), and in other species male removal has lesser effects because females can often compensate for lost provisions (facultative investment; e.g., Royle, Hartley, & Parker, 2002).

Trade-Offs

The evolution and facultative expression of male parenting is related to a balancing of the benefits to offspring, the cost of lost mating opportunities, and the risk of cuckoldry or paternity certainty, as shown in Exhibit 4.1 (Birkhead & Møller, 1996; Møller & Cuervo, 2000; Perrone & Zaret, 1988). Across species of fish, male parenting is most common when males fertilize eggs externally and defend nesting sites from competitors (Perrone & Zaret, 1988).

EXHIBIT 4.1
Evolution and Facultative Expression of Male Parenting

Offspring survival
1. If paternal investment has little or no effect on offspring survival rate or quality, then selection will favor male abandonment if additional mates can be found (Trivers, 1972; Westneat & Sherman, 1993; G. C. Williams, 1966).
2. If paternal investment results in relative but not an absolute improvement in offspring survival rate or quality, then selection will favor males that show a mixed reproductive strategy. Males can vary in degree of emphasis on mating and parenting, contingent on social (e.g., male status, availability of mates) and ecological (e.g., food availability) conditions (Westneat & Sherman, 1993; Wolf et al., 1988).

Mating opportunities
1. If paternal investment is not obligate and mates are available, then selection will favor
   A. male abandonment if paternal investment has little effect on offspring survival rate and quality (Clutton-Brock, 1991) or
   B. a mixed male reproductive strategy if paternal investment improves offspring survival rate and quality (Perrone & Zaret, 1979; Wolf et al., 1988).
2. Social and ecological factors that reduce the mating opportunities of males, such as dispersed females or concealed (or synchronized) ovulation, will reduce the opportunity cost of paternal investment. Under these conditions selection will favor paternal investment if this investment improves offspring survival rate or quality or does not otherwise induce heavy costs on the male (Clutton-Brock, 1991; Dunbar, 1995; Perrone & Zaret, 1979; Thornhill, 1976; Westneat & Sherman, 1993).

Paternity certainty
1. If the certainty of paternity is low, then selection will favor male abandonment (Clutton-Brock, 1991; Møller, 2000; Westneat & Sherman, 1993).
2. If the certainty of paternity is high, then selection will favor paternal investment if
   A. investment improves offspring survival or quality and
   B. the opportunity costs of investment (i.e., reduced mating opportunities) are lower than the benefits associated with investment (Dunbar, 1995; Thornhill, 1976; Westneat & Sherman, 1993).
3. If the certainty of paternity is high and the opportunity costs in terms of lost mating opportunities are high, then selection will favor males with a mixed reproductive strategy, that is, the facultative expression of paternal investment, contingent on social and ecological conditions (Dunbar, 1995; Westneat & Sherman, 1993).

Note. Reprinted from "Evolution and Proximate Expression of Human Paternal Investment," by D. C. Geary, 2000, *Psychological Bulletin, 126,* p. 60. Copyright 2000 by the American Psychological Association.

Under these conditions, paternity certainty is high and males are able to fertilize the eggs of several females, and thus investment does not reduce mating opportunities. Paternal investment is uncommon in fish with internal fertilization because paternity is not certain and because males can abandon females after fertilization and avoid the cost of investment. Paternal investment does occur in some species with internal fertilization, including most species of bird and a few mammals, mostly carnivores and some primates (Dunbar, 1995; Mock & Fujioka, 1990). Again, the degree of paternal investment varies with potential benefits to offspring, availability of other mates, and paternity certainty.

The trade-offs are illustrated by the across- and within-species relation between level of males' parental investment and the likelihood of paternity (K. E. Arnold & Owens, 2002; Birkhead & Møller, 1996; Møller, 2000). For species in which male investment is obligate, cuckoldry rates are very low; that is, females do not risk losing paternal investment by copulating with other males and risking abandonment by their social partner. For species with facultative paternal investment, cuckoldry rates often vary with male quality (e.g., as indicated by tail length or plumage color); an example is provided by the barn swallow (Hirundo rustica), a species in which females often risk loss of male investment and copulate with healthier and more attractive males if they are paired with a low-quality mate (Møller & Tegelström, 1997). In some cases it is not male quality per se but the degree of genetic difference between the female and prospective mates (J. I. Hoffman, Forcada, Trathan, & Amos, 2007; Rubenstein, 2007) that drives cuckoldry. This makes sense because increased genetic variation can provide multiple benefits to offspring (see the section titled Why Reproduce Sexually?, chap. 2, this volume).

Overall, however, within-species studies of cuckoldry risk and paternal investment are mixed; some studies find a relation (Dixon, Ross, O'Malley, & Burke, 1994), but others do not (Kempenaers, Lanctot, & Robertson, 1998). Some of the inconsistencies may be related to the ability of males to detect their partner's extrapair copulations or extrapair paternity of offspring (Neff & Sherman, 2002). Ewen and Armstrong (2000) studied this relation in the socially monogamous stitchbird (Notiomystis cincta); males provide between 16% and 32% of the food to the nestlings. Extrapair copulations occur in the pair's territory and are easily monitored. Males counter this paternity threat by chasing off intruding males, but extrapair copulations still occur. In this study, as the frequency of female extrapair copulations increased, male provisioning of the brood decreased ($r = -.72$).

Neff (2003) found the same relation between paternal certainty and investment in the bluegill sunfish (Lepomis macrochirus). In this species, parental males defend a territory, externally fertilize, and then fan and protect eggs. One type of cuckolder male hides behind rocks or plants and attempts to sneak into the nest to fertilize the eggs. Before the eggs hatch, threats to paternity can therefore be determined by the presence or absence of cuckolder males. After the eggs hatch, parental males can determine paternity on the basis of olfactory cues from fry urine. As with the stitchbird, parental males reduced fanning and protecting of eggs if cuckolder males were present. Once the fry hatched and parental males could determine paternity, they protected them only if they were the father, whether or not cuckolder males were present before the fry hatched. The results of this and other well-controlled studies (Ewen & Armstrong, 2000) suggest that when males detect risks to paternity, they reduce their level of parental investment and often do so in direct relation to the magnitude of the risk (Møller, 2000). I note, however, that the provisioning and protecting of offspring is not always parental investment. Male provisioning is sometimes an attempt to obtain sexual access to the offspring's mother (Rohwer, Herron, & Daly, 1999; Smuts & Gubernick, 1992); male care of unrelated juveniles often increases the likelihood the mother will choose this parenting male as the sire of her next offspring (Kvarnemo, 2006).

In any case, paternity certainty and an improvement in the survival rate of his offspring are not sufficient for the evolution or facultative expression of paternal investment. The benefits of investment must also be greater than the benefits of siring offspring with more than one female (Dunbar, 1995). For instance, social monogamy and high levels of paternal investment are common in *canids* (e.g., coyotes, *Canis latrens*), which tend to have large litters (Asa & Valdespino, 1998). Large litter sizes, prolonged offspring dependency, and the ability of the male to provide food during this dependency result in *canid* males being able to sire more offspring with a monogamous, high parental investment strategy than with a polygynous strategy. Paternal investment might also evolve if females are ecologically dispersed, and thus males do not have the opportunity to pursue multiple mating partners, as with *callitrichid* monkeys, such as marmosets (*Callithrix*; Dunbar, 1995; Goldizen, 2003). In these species, paternal investment is related to joint male–female territorial defense, which limits the male's ability to expand his territory to include other females; female-on-female aggression that prevents males from forming harems; concealed ovulation, which prolongs the pair's relationship to ensure conception; and the fact that females often have twins, which increases the benefits of paternal care.

Implications

The patterns associated with the facultative expression of paternal investment in nonhuman species and summarized in Exhibit 4.1 provide a critical backdrop for my later (see chap. 6) review of human fathers. Across species, males' reproductive behavior is especially complicated when paternal investment improves offspring survival rate and offspring quality and when the reproductive benefits of seeking additional mates do not always outweigh the reproductive benefits of paternal investment; these dynamics parallel those found in humans. Under these conditions, selection will favor a mixed reproductive strategy, with different males varying in their emphasis on mating and parenting, and individual males varying in emphasis on mating and parenting in their relationship with different females. Individual differences in paternal investment, in turn, are likely to relate to male condition (e.g., social status), ecological factors (e.g., operational sex ratio), female strategies to induce paternal investment, female quality, and to genetically based differences in male reproductive strategy (Krebs & Davies, 1993).

SEX HORMONES AND SEXUAL SELECTION

The field of hormones and behavior has a long history. The corresponding literature is vast, complex, and beyond the scope of this section, but fortunately Adkins-Regan (2005) and Pfaff, Phillips, and Rubin (2004) provided first-rate and evolutionarily informed reviews. My goals are to highlight the influence of prenatal and postnatal exposure to sex hormones on the expression of behaviors associated with sexual selection and with parenting. I address these topics in three sections. The first covers hormonal influences on behaviors discussed earlier in this chapter, such as play and parenting, as well as influences on male–male competition discussed in chapter 3. The second section ties testosterone to the expression of male secondary sexual characteristics and the good genes models of female choice discussed in chapter 3. The third addresses the relation between sex hormones and cognitive and brain systems that have been influenced by sexual selection.

Before beginning, I need to review for the reader some basic concepts and findings. Most generally, prenatal exposure to sex hormones results in *organizational* changes in the central nervous system and in many other areas of the body, whereas postnatal exposure results in *activational* effects. The latter reflect the priming of the behaviors (e.g., copulation) associated with early organizational effects, but these are expressed only in appropriate contexts (Phoenix, Goy, Gerall, & Young, 1959) and sometimes only following related experiences (Balthazart & Ball, 1998). These days, the distinction between prenatal organization and postnatal activation is less rigid than originally proposed. The relative contributions of organizational and activational effects can vary from one species to the next, but the distinction still contributes to scientists' understanding of the influence of hormones on many sex differences (Adkins-Regan, 2005; A. P. Arnold, 2009). I should also note that the relation between sex hormones and sex differences does not follow a single testosterone/male to estrogen/female continuum. The processes that result in the masculinization of behavior do not always result in the defeminization of behavior. In many species, sexual and related behaviors can be masculinized (e.g., showing male copulatory behavior) and feminized (e.g., showing female sexual receptivity), neither, or some combination (Whalen, 1974). Moreover, many of the effects often associated with testosterone result from the transformation of this androgen by an enzyme (aromatase) into an estrogen, which then acts in specific areas of the brain in ways that result in male-typical behavior (e.g., J. T. Watson & Adkins-Regan, 1989).

Many of the sex differences in parenting and mating may be influenced by nonhormonal, genetic effects (A. P. Arnold, 2009), and even hormonal influences can be moderated by genetic sex, physical health, social relationships, and other factors (A. P. Arnold et al., 2004; Morris, Jordan, & Breedlove, 2004; Sapolsky, 2005). For many sexually selected traits, there is both variation within each sex as well as overlap across the sexes, both of which can be influenced by within-sex variation and between-sex similarities in exposure to prenatal and circulating sex hormones (Rhen & Crews, 2002). The link between hormones, behavior, and cognition is not necessarily linear: Some traits may be expressed once a threshold is reached, such that levels just above this threshold or several times higher than it can have the same behavioral effect (Adkins-Regan, 2005). Trait expression is also influenced by the number of hormone receptor sites in different regions of the brain and body, which further complicates the link between circulating hormone levels and behavior and cognition.

Sex Hormones and Life History Development

The relation between sex hormones and sex differences in life history development and sexually selected behaviors and cognitions is more nuanced and complex than I can describe in the sections that follow. Nevertheless, the expression of these behaviors cannot be fully understood without consideration of the influence of sex hormones.

Early Development

As the reader learned in the section titled Social Play, sex differences in rough-and-tumble play tend to track sex differences in intrasexual competition. The relation between sex hormones and the expression of this form of play has been extensively investigated in the laboratory rat (*Rattus norvegicus*) and the rhesus macaque (*Macaca mulatta*), both polygynous species with physical male–male competition (Panksepp et al., 1984; Pellis, 2002; Pellis

& Pellis, 2007; Wallen, 1996). Castration of young male rats results in a level of rough-and-tumble play similar to that found in female rats, and prenatal or early postnatal exposure of females to testosterone results in a level of rough-and-tumble play in between that of typical females and males, at least until puberty (Pellis, 2002). At puberty, increases in testosterone, along with prenatal exposure, contribute to the transition from play fighting to actual fighting in males. But this transition only occurs in females if they are treated with testosterone and their ovaries are removed; that is, ovarian hormones appear to demasculinize the transition to actual fighting at puberty. Lesion and hormone implantation studies reveal that the expression of rough-and-tumble play is related, in part, to prenatal organization of areas of the amygdala, a brain region associated with various social behaviors and emotions (Meaney, Dodge, & Beatty, 1981).

Male rhesus macaques consistently show more rough-and-tumble play than their female cohorts, but the magnitude of this difference varies somewhat with rearing environment (Wallen, 1996). In comparison with males reared in typical male–female social groups, males reared only with other males show more rough-and-tumble play, whereas males reared in isolation show less rough-and-tumble play when introduced to their peers. Neonatal castration and other manipulations that suppress androgens after the male is born have little effect on the frequency of rough-and-tumble play, indicating that prenatal exposure to these hormones is critical. Indeed, prolonged prenatal exposure to androgens significantly increases the frequency of rough-and-tumble play in females, regardless of rearing environment (Wallen, 1996).

The hormonal contributions to play parenting and interest in infants have not been as extensively studied as rough-and-tumble play. In one large study, R. A. Herman, Measday, and Wallen (2003) exposed male and female rhesus macaques to small doses of androgens or chemicals that blocked the action of androgens earlier and later in their prenatal development and studied their engagement with infants (e.g., embracing, grooming) during their 3-year juvenile period. Females showed higher interest than males, especially in the 2nd and 3rd years. During this time, the least interested females showed as much or more interest in infants as the most interested males. These large sex differences varied little across the different hormonal treatments: Prenatal exposure to androgens did not defeminize the females. Maestripieri (2005) found that harsh maternal treatment was associated with higher interest in infants by juvenile female macaques. This heightened interest was related to an increase in the sensitivity of their stress response system, such that mild stressors triggered the release of cortisol—the primary stress hormone in primates—in maltreated females, and this in turn was associated with an increased engagement with infants. Whether interest in infants is related to prenatal exposure to estrogens (Fitch & Denenberg, 1998) or requires higher levels of androgen exposure than used in the R. A. Herman et al. study to be suppressed remains to be determined.

Adulthood

In adulthood, sex hormones coordinate mating behaviors, parenting, and males' trade-offs between mating and parenting. Sex hormones also moderate the dynamics of competition and choice.

Mating. Mating is all about arranging a desirable combination of egg and sperm. The meeting only occurs following a complex coordination of courtship, receptivity, and copulation between the male and female. Sex hormones are well suited for this matchmaking, so to speak, because they circulate throughout the body and can thus coordinate the activation of many diverse systems. To ensure a successful meeting, there must be a close link between the maturational timing of the ova and the females' expression of the cognitive biases (e.g., for a bright plumage) and behaviors that influence their mate choices and thereby ensure sperm are provided by the best male or males. Males, of course, have to be receptive to behavioral and other changes (e.g., sexual swellings, pheromones) that might signal ovulation and must respond in ways that increase the likelihood of being accepted as a mating partner.

The contributions of sex hormones and their metabolites to the orchestration of these mating behaviors have been repeatedly demonstrated through the effects of removal of testes or ovaries on subsequent mating and the reemergence of mating behaviors with the administration of sex hormones. For one well-studied species, the Japanese quail (*Coturnix coturnix japonica*; Balthazart & Ball, 1998), Beach and Inman (1965) noted that for males the

> effects of castration and androgen replacement upon each of the behavior measures was clear-cut and pronounced. In sum, all sexual activity disappeared within 8 days after removal of the testes and returned to normal within 8 days after the implantation of an androgen pellet. (p. 1428)

Similarly, Adkins and Adler (1972) demonstrated that the sexual receptivity of female Japanese quails was strongly influenced by circulating estrogens.

The relation between sex hormones and mating behavior is not always this clear-cut, however, even for the Japanese quail. Subsequent studies have shown that male courtship behaviors (i.e., crowing and strutting) are activated by testosterone or a metabolite, dihydrotestosterone, whereas copulatory behaviors are dependent on transformation of testosterone into estrogens in the brain regions that activate these behaviors (Balthazart & Ball, 1998). In recent decades, it has become clear that the relations between courtship and mating and sex hormones, stress hormones, neurotransmitters, and neuropeptides (small amino-acid-based molecules that are produced by and act in specific brain regions) are nuanced and can vary across species, the sexes, and even individuals within each sex (Goodsori, Saldanha, Hahn, & Soma, 2005; Oliveira, Ros, & Gonçalves, 2005; J. Wade, 2005; Wilczynski, Lynch, & O'Bryant, 2005). Courtship and mating are of course expressed in social contexts that influence these hormonal systems as well as being influenced by them. For species that live and reproduce in large communities with many males and females, the consideration of social context is particularly important, as I discuss in chapter 5 (see the section titled Coalitional Competition).

Parenting. Because parental behavior likely evolved independently in different lineages (Clutton-Brock, 1991), it is unlikely that exactly the same hormonal or social cues underlie these behaviors across species or even across the sexes for species with biparental care (Adkins-Regan, 2005). As an example, two neuropeptides, oxytocin and vasopressin, appear to be involved in promoting and maintaining the long-term social affiliation between male and female prairie voles and their parental care (Carter & Getz, 1993; Winslow, Hastings, Carter, Harbaugh, & Insel, 1993). Vasopressin is particularly important for the expression of parenting in male prairie voles, and oxytocin for its expression in females (Z. X. Wang, Liu, Young, & Insel, 2000). Prolactin stimulates milk production in female mammals, among other effects (de Vlaming, 1979), and appears to promote parental behavior and cooperative social behavior in some socially monogamous birds (e.g., Schoech, Mumme, & Wingfield, 1996). In particular, the research by Schoech, Mumme, and Wingfield (1996) suggests that prolactin promotes male provisioning of resources to the female while she incubates their clutch and later feeding of the nestlings by both parents. Prolactin might also promote parenting in some mammalian fathers (Wynne-Edwards, 2001), including men (see the section titled Hormones and Men's Parenting, chap. 6, this volume).

The hormonal changes that occur during pregnancy and the act of giving birth can also influence maternal behavior, as illustrated with sheep (*Ovis aries*; Kendrick & Keverne, 1991; Lévy, Kendrick, Keverne, Piketty, & Poindron, 1992; see also Lévy, Keller, & Poindron, 2004). In this species, prenatal exposure to estrogen primes oxytocin release when ewes are giving birth. During the birthing process oxytocin is expressed in regions of the hypothalamus and olfactory bulb. The latter leads to a cascade of other neurochemical changes that make ewes very sensitive to the odor of their lamb; exposure to these odors occurs when ewes lick the newborn. These odors are a critical component of maternal bonding, which in turn is necessary for the expression of many maternal behaviors, such as allowing the lamb to suckle. In some species, hormones jump start maternal behavior, but its continuation is dependent on cues provided by offspring, independent of maternal hormones (Adkins-Reagan, 2005).

Mating Versus Parenting. As I described in section titled Parental Investment, there are many species in which trade-offs are made between the amount of effort devoted to finding mates versus caring for offspring. These trade-offs are more common among males than females and tend to occur in species in which male parenting is facultatively expressed. For these species, elevated testosterone in males can result in a shift from parental effort to mating effort (Hirschenhauser & Oliveira, 2006; Ketterson & Nolan, 1992, 1999). An example is provided by an 8-year field study of the dark-eyed juncos (*Junco hyemalis carolinensis*; Reed et al., 2006). For this sample of birds, half of the males were implanted with testosterone over successive breeding seasons, and their survival rate, breeding success, and nestling characteristics were contrasted with those of males that did not receive these implants. Within breeding seasons, the survival rate of testosterone-treated males was about 25% lower than that of other males, but treated males were more likely to be paired with older and thus more successful (in terms of surviving offspring) females and had significantly more extrapair fertilizations. Their nestlings, however, were significantly smaller as a result of lower paternal provisioning and thus likely suffered higher mortality in adulthood than the nestlings of other males.

Competition and Choice. The multiple influences on competition for mates and expression of the traits that influence mate choices make simple relations between sex hormones and the expression of these components of sexual selection unlikely. For some species of bird, for instance, the bright male plumage that attracts the attention of prospective mates is due to the absence of estrogens, whereas in other species it is due to the presence of androgens (Kimball, 2006). There is, nonetheless, a more consistent relation between exposure to androgens, especially testosterone, and the coloration of non-plumage traits, such as the red comb on male jungle fowl (*Gallus gallus*; Kimball, 2006; Zuk, Johnsen, & Maclarty, 1995). Testosterone also influences the expression of sexually selected physical and behavioral traits needed for male–male competition or female choice in species ranging from reptiles (Sinervo, Miles, Frankino, Klukowski, & DeNardo, 2000) to primates (Cavigelli & Pereira, 2000), but these relations can be modified by ecological factors (e.g., latitude), mating system, and current social context (Adkins-Reagan, 2005; Wingfield, Lynn, & Soma, 2001).

As elaborated in the next section, there is a cost to having a lot of testosterone. To lessen these costs, mechanisms have evolved that elevate testosterone and other hormones only at points in the life span or annually when the corresponding physical and behavioral changes are beneficial. Wingfield and colleagues' social challenge hypothesis may capture core aspects of how testosterone levels vary in these adaptive ways (Wingfield et al., 2001; Wingfield, Hegner, Dufty, & Ball, 1990). The gist is that testosterone is low during periods of social stability and rises during periods of instability, particularly when instability results from challenges over control of reproduction-related resources, such as breeding territory or mates. The increase in testosterone and its metabolites (i.e., estradiol and dihydrotestosterone) at the onset of the mating season—triggered in some species by changes in amount of daylight— is associated with a spike in male-on-male aggression, territorial and courtship behavior, and changes in secondary sexual characteristics (Neal & Wade, 2007; B. N. Turner, Iverson, & Severson, 1983). Once territories are established and a mate is found, testosterone levels drop, which protects the male from the ill effects of this hormone. When challenged by another male, testosterone increases to allow the defender to confront the challenge.

The mating system and type of paternal care of the species may also be important in framing scientists' understanding of the relation between sex hormones and reproductive behaviors. For polygynous species with no paternal investment, male–male competition can be continuous throughout the breeding system and thus basal testosterone levels are predicted to remain high but still show modest increases when the male is challenged. For socially monogamous species with paternal care, in contrast, testosterone levels are predicted to drop once the male is mated but rise sharply when defending his territory or guarding his mate. Results from studies that have tested these predictions of the social challenge hypothesis are mixed, however (Demas, Albers, Cooper, & Soma, 2007; Hirschenhauser & Oliveira, 2006; Magee, Neff, & Knapp, 2006), but the hypothesis still provides a useful approach to understanding the complex interactions between sex hormones, intrasexual competition, and paternal investment.

Unfortunately, the social challenge hypothesis has not been widely tested with females, but there is some suggestive evidence. I mentioned the spotted sandpiper (*Actitis macularia*) in chapter 3 (in the section titled Operational Sex Ratio), a polyandrous shorebird in which females compete intensely over parental males (Oring, Lank, & Maxson, 1983). Male sandpipers have higher testosterone levels than females, but the levels converge over the breeding season. In natural settings, testosterone levels drop dramatically (25-fold) as males incubate eggs, whereas female testosterone levels rise (Fivizzani & Oring, 1986). Fivizzani and Oring proposed that these females are more sensitive to testosterone than are males and that the rise in testosterone contributes to and is triggered by female–female competition over nesting sites and mates. Langmore, Cockrem, and Candy (2002) provided more direct evidence for increases in testosterone following social challenge in female dunnocks (*Prunella modularis*). In this species of bird, females can mate monogamously or in multimale, multifemale groups. In the latter situation, females can mate with several males, each of whom invests in one of her clutches, but must compete intensely for this paternal care. An experimental manipulation showed that female–female aggression over mates triggers an increase in testosterone, consistent with the social challenge hypothesis (Wingfield et al., 1990).

For both sexes, aggression is common outside of reproductive competition, for instance, in competition for food or shelter. Outside of the breeding season, testosterone levels tend to be low in males, but behavioral aggression still occurs in many species. The hormonal and neural mechanisms that regulate these forms of aggression differ from those associated with reproduction-motivated aggression (Demas et al., 2007; Soma, 2006). The fascinating implication is that evolution has resulted in multiple systems associated with behavioral and other forms of aggression, each of which is active under different ecological, social, and reproductive conditions.

Sex Hormones, Parasites, and Male Quality

The reader may recall from chapter 3 (the section titled Good Genes) that W. D. Hamilton and Zuk (1982) predicted a relation between parasite resistance and the expression of secondary sexual characteristics. They did not, however, discuss the mechanism by which parasite infestation can affect the expression of these traits, but Folstad and Karter (1992) did; their model is known as the immunocompetence handicap hypothesis. A simplified version of their model is shown in Figure 4.5. At the core is the reciprocal relation between sex hormone levels, especially testosterone, and overall competence

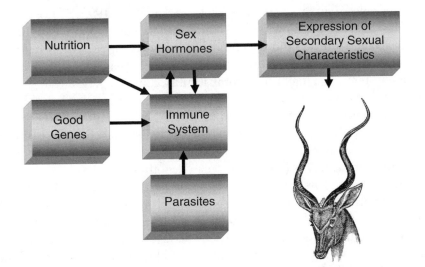

Figure 4.5. Hypothesized relations among sex hormones, immune functioning, parasites, and the expression of secondary sexual characteristics. Male kudu (*Strepsiceros kudu*). From *The Descent of Man, and Selection in Relation to Sex* (Vol. 2, p. 255), by C. R. Darwin, 1871, London: John Murray. In the public domain.

of the immune system. The prediction is that infestation with parasites will lead to an increase in immune system activity, which can suppress the secretion of testosterone (Folstad & Karter, 1992; Saino & Møller, 1994; Zuk et al., 1995). The resulting decline in testosterone will then, in theory, result in poorly developed secondary sexual characteristics, thereby placing the male at a disadvantage in terms of female choice and male–male competition. Moreover, an increase in testosterone levels, as is necessary for the development of males' secondary sexual characteristics, can suppress the effectiveness of the immune system, which then increases risk of disease. The model is also appealing in that it incorporates Zahavi's (1975) handicap hypothesis; specifically, immunosuppression is predicted to be more evident in low-quality than in high-quality males.

Saino and Møller's studies of testosterone levels and immune system competence in the barn swallow were among the first to test the hypothesis (Saino, Bolzern, & Møller, 1997; Saino & Møller, 1994; Saino, Møller, & Bolzern, 1995). As was shown in Figure 3.5 (see chap. 3, this volume), the primary secondary sexual characteristic of these males is length of tail feathers. In natural conditions, long tail feathers are associated with higher testosterone levels and lower rates of parasite infestation (Saino & Møller, 1994), which, at first blush, would appear to be inconsistent with the model. However, testosterone implantation suppressed the immune system of males with shorter tail feathers more severely than it did for males with longer tail feathers. The result was the predicted greater increase in parasite load and mortality in shorter tailed than in longer tailed males (Saino et al., 1995; Saino, Bolzern, & Møller, 1997). Males with long tail feathers can support expensively high testosterone levels and thus more effectively compete with other males without compromising their immune system; these males may have had an immune system (e.g., major histocompatibility complex genes) that was well adapted to local parasites, or they may have been in better general physical condition than males with short tail feathers. These results are also consistent with the view that the expression of secondary sexual characteristics cannot be faked, that is, these characteristics are an honest signal of male quality, in keeping with Zahavi's (1975) handicap hypothesis.

Since Folstad and Karter's (1992) original proposal and these first research efforts, the immunocompetence handicap hypothesis has been the focus of numerous field and experimental studies (Deviche, & Cortez, 2005; Mougeot, Redpath, & Piertney, 2006; Mougeot, Redpath, Piertney, & Hudson, 2005; M. L. Roberts, Buchanan, Hasselquist, & Evans, 2007; Saino, Incagli, Martinelli, & Møller, 2002) as well as theoretical review and revision (Alonso-Alvarez, Bertrand, Faivre, Chastel, & Sorci, 2007; von Schantz, Bensch, Grahn, Hasselquist, & Wittzell, 1999). On the basis of a literature review and meta-analysis, M. L. Roberts, Buchanan, and Evans (2004) concluded that the magnitude of the relation between testosterone and the development of secondary sexual characteristics varies across species and traits, and thus this important link in Folstad and Karter's (1992) model may not apply to all sexually selected traits, although it does apply to many of them. Moreover, the relation between testosterone and other sex hormones and immune functioning is complex and varies across the several components of the immune system and across time within individuals (McEwen et al., 1997). Despite these nuances, combining across species and using only well-designed experimental studies, scientists found that higher testosterone levels were associated with increased infestation with parasites and compromised immune system functions (M. L. Roberts et al., 2004). There was, however, considerable variation in the strength and consistency of these relations across species and different immune system measures (e.g., numbers of white blood cells vs. antibodies).

Following M. L. Roberts et al.'s (2004) review, several studies have provided more thorough and nuanced assessments of Folstad and Karter's (1992) hypothesis. Deviche and Cortez (2005) implanted male house finches (*Carpodacus mexicanus*) with testosterone and monitored change in three components of immune functioning in response to repeated exposures to two different parasites and across 2 months. These males did not differ from a control group of untreated males in terms of initial strength of immune responses. In the days following exposure, however, the males with high testosterone levels were not able to maintain the same level of immune functions as the control group. Even longer term trade-offs have been demonstrated in field studies of the male red grouse (*Lagopus lagopus scoticus*; Mougeot et al., 2006). In this study, males were captured in spring and randomly assigned to testosterone-implant and control groups. The following month, the testosterone-treated males had a larger comb—a sexually selected trait that signals male dominance and influences female choice—but weighed less, possibly because of increased behavioral vigor and aggression during male–male competition for nesting territories. Five months later, during the breeding season, testosterone-treated males were more likely to attract mates than other males and had more offspring but paid the price in terms of slightly higher (12%) mortality, compromised immune functions, and infestation with more intestinal worms (e.g., *Trichostrongylus tenuis*). A related study in which the behavioral changes associated with testosterone implantation were controlled also revealed compromised immune functions and increased infestation with parasites in this same species (Mougeot et al., 2005).

These recent studies and the findings of M. L. Roberts et al. (2004) have provided converging evidence that the increases in testosterone and associated behavioral changes associated with male–male competition and female choice can result in higher male mortality in many species, due in part to compromised immune functions. The pattern is consistent with the gist of Folstad and Karter's (1992) hypothesis, but the mechanisms may be more complex. Another contributing factor shown in Figure 4.5 is nutritional status, which interacts with sex hormone levels, immune system functioning, and the expression of secondary sexual characteristics. Nutritional status is particularly important for males in species with physical male–male competition. This is because attaining and maintaining the larger size associated with this competition can, in and of itself, compromise immune functions and result in increased risk of parasite infestation and early mortality (S. L. Moore & Wilson, 2002). The behavioral aspects of male–male competition and displays associated with female choice included increased risk taking, risk of physical injury and thus infection (K. L. Buchanan, 2000), as well as increases in levels of stress hormones. All of these can further compromise aspects of immune functions (C. J. Grossman, 1985). The combination of these factors typically results in greater within-sex variation for sexually selected traits for males than for females.

Sex Hormones, Brain, and Cognition

Sex hormones influence reproductive behaviors, sensitivity to conditions that influence reproductive outcomes, and the expression of sexually selected traits. In addition, sex hormones have a clear and at times substantial influence on the organization and functioning of the brain systems that support these behaviors and cognitions (Ball & Balthazart, 2004; DeVoogd, 1991; E. Gould, Woolley, & McEwen, 1991). The development of many of these brain regions is sensitive to environmental cues (e.g., amount of daylight) and, at least in some species, involves direct genetic or other influences that are not dependent on exposure to sex hormones (A. P. Arnold, 2009; Gahr, 2003; Kimchi, Xu, & Dulac, 2007).

Gahr (2003) demonstrated that for the male Japanese quail, reproductive development and behaviors are dependent on both the prenatal expression of male genes in specific brain regions and later exposure to male hormones. The expression of many male reproductive behaviors is also related to estrogen, specifically, the transformation of testosterone into estrogen in brain regions that control aspects of sexual behavior. This results in sex differences because the enzyme (aromatase) that enables this transformation is more abundant in these brain regions in males than females (Fusani & Gahr, 2006). There is also evidence that the male brain of some species creates estrogen (from cholesterol) in the absence of testicular hormones (C. C. Holloway & Clayton, 2001). The influences of sex hormones on sex differences in brain structure and functioning are obviously very complex and not fully understood, but their importance for understanding sex differences in the brain and in cognition cannot be underestimated. I illustrate these relations with bird song, the reproductive strategies of monogamous and polygynous voles, and a few other species.

As described in the section titled Male Parenting in this chapter, social monogamy is common in songbirds, but sexual fidelity is not (Birkhead & Møller, 1996; Zeh & Zeh, 1997). In many of these species, extrapair copulations are frequent and largely controlled by female choice, which is influenced by the complexity of the male's song. Males often have two distinct features embedded in their song, one that influences female choice—females tend to prefer males with complex song—and one that signals dominance and territorial control to other males (Ball & Hulse, 1998). In other words, there is little doubt that male song is a sexually selected behavior related to female choice and male–male competition in these species (Andersson, 1994; Saino, Primmer, Ellegren, & Møller, 1997).

Scientists have known for many decades that the development and expression of bird song is controlled by an interconnected system of brain areas and that the sex-typical development and functioning of these areas is dependent in part on exposure to sex hormones (DeVoogd, 1991; Nottebohm, 1970, 2005). In some species, several of these areas—higher vocal control center (HVC) and robustus arcopallium (RA)—are 3 to 8 times larger in the male than the female (Nottebohm & Arnold, 1976). For seasonally breeding species, the magnitude of these differences becomes most pronounced in the breeding season (Nottebohm, 1981). For the canary (*Serinus canarius*), Nottebohm (1980) demonstrated that testosterone implants greatly increase the size of the HVC and RA in females and induces malelike song, whereas male castration reduces the size of these areas and impairs song production. In some species, sex hormones influence the ways in which these sex-dimorphic areas respond to early environmental cues (e.g., father's song) and song expression in adulthood (Ball & Hulse, 1998; DeVoogd, 1991; Marler, 1991). In other words, the learning and later expression of sexually selected song may require early exposure to song (Petrinovich & Baptista, 1987; M. J. West & King, 1980), exposure to male hormones (DeVoogd, 1991), and the expression of estrogens (through transformation of testosterone) in the HVC and RA (C. C. Holloway & Clayton, 2001).

I noted earlier that the hormonal profiles of species with sex-role reversals tend to be sex typical (e.g., higher testosterone in males). Fivizzani and Oring's (1986) hypothesis that females of these species exhibit male-typical behavior as a result of increased sensitivity to testosterone remains to be fully evaluated, but there is at least one supportive study. The African black coucal (*Centropus grillii*) is a bird species in which females mate with multiple paternal males and fight over access to these males. Voigt and Goymann (2007) found that an area of the amygdala that is implicated in various social behaviors responded, in terms of gene expression, more strongly to testosterone in females than males.

The reader may recall that I described in chapter 3 (in the section titled Cognitive Competition) how comparisons of the polygynous meadow vole (M. *pennsylvanicus*) and its monogamous cousins the prairie (M. *ochrogaster*) and pine voles (M. *pinetorum*) have revealed sex and species differences in spatial abilities that are related to reproductive competition. The territorial expansion of male meadow voles during the breeding season is correlated with the seasonal increase in testosterone (B. N. Turner et al., 1983) and is related to an improvement in spatial and navigational abilities in the field and on laboratory tasks (Gaulin & Fitzgerald, 1986). These males show better spatial abilities than female meadow voles and male pine and prairie voles, for whom territory expansion is not found. Although improved spatial cognition and an enhanced ability to find potential mates do not always result in a reproductive advantage because of female choice (Spritzer, Meikle, & Solomon, 2005; Spritzer, Solomon, & Meikle, 2005), they often do and are almost certainly sexually selected traits.

The brain systems that support the enhanced navigation and spatial abilities of male meadow voles, such as the hippocampus, are predicted to be related to prenatal and postnatal exposure to sex hormones, but results of the corresponding studies are mixed. Some studies have found that the volume of the hippocampus is larger for male than female meadow voles and larger in male meadow voles than in male prairie and pine voles (Jacobs, Gaulin, Sherry, & Hoffman, 1990). The research of Galea and colleagues has revealed a more nuanced pattern, at least for meadow voles (Galea, 2008; Galea, Lee, Kostaras, Sidhu, & Barr, 2002; Galea, Perrot-Sinal, Kavaliers, & Ossenkopp, 1999; Ormerod, Lee, & Galea, 2004). Males were not found to have a larger overall hippocampus than females, although males with higher testosterone did have a larger hippocampus than other males (Galea et al., 1999). For females, higher estrogen was associated with a larger hippocampus, but paradoxically also impaired spatial abilities (Galea et al., 2002). To complicate the relations further, the generation of new cells in the hippocampus was highest in females with low estrogen levels, and there was a tendency for higher cell survival for breeding males (Ormerod et al., 2004). Higher cell survival is associated with better spatial memory for males. At this point, it appears there are breeding-season changes in the hippocampus of both male and female meadow voles, and these changes appear to have different effects. The corresponding hormonal changes may enhance the spatial memory of males and suppress that of females.

Studies of the polygynous laboratory rat also suggest a hormonally mediated male advantage in spatial learning (C. L. Williams, Barnett, & Meck, 1990; C. L. Williams & Meck, 1991). C. L. Williams et al. found that normal males and testosterone-treated females outperformed castrated males and normal females on spatial tasks. Moreover, normal males and hormonally treated females relied primarily on the three-dimensional geometry of the environment to navigate, whereas castrated males and normal females used a combination of landmark and geometric cues. The latter finding suggests that, at least in some species, the sex difference in spatial cognition is related to hormonally mediated differences in strategic approaches to navigating. More recent studies have indicated that testosterone contributes to enhanced survival of hippocampal neurons in the rat (Spritzer & Galea, 2007), as it may in voles.

It should be noted, however, that sexual selection does *not* predict that males in all species will have better developed spatial abilities than conspecific females. A sex difference in spatial cognition should be found only when the activities of males and females differ and only when these activities require that males and females have different home ranges or use those ranges differently (Sherry, Vaccarino, Buckenham, & Herz, 1989). Studies of the brown-headed cowbird (*Molothrus ater ater*) nicely illustrate this point (Sherry, Forbes, Khurgel, & Ivy, 1993). Brown-headed cowbirds are brood parasites, that is, females lay their eggs in the nests of other species. The host parents then hatch and feed the cowbird nestlings. Female cowbirds must utilize the home range in more complex ways than male cowbirds because females must locate hosts for their eggs. Many hosts will accept cowbird eggs only after they have started laying eggs of their own. Thus, female cowbirds not only need to locate potential hosts, they must also remember their locations and return at a suitable time. The sex difference in the spatial demands of reproduction should then result in a larger hippocampus in female relative to male cowbirds. This is exactly the pattern found by Sherry et al. (1993). As a control, no sex difference in hippocampal size was found for species of evolutionarily related monogamous birds that do not exhibit sex differences for demands on spatial memory (e.g., red-winged blackbirds, *Agelaius phoeniceus*).

CONCLUSION

Ultimately, the function of growth and developmental activity is to accumulate reproductive potential, that is, to build the type of body and acquire the types of behavioral and cognitive competencies needed to survive to reproductive age and then to successfully reproduce (R. D. Alexander, 1987). As illustrated with the semelparous Pacific salmon, once reproduction has occurred, the gene-carrying body or soma is disposable. The disposable soma is also found with their distant cousin, the Atlantic salmon, but less intense breeding competition results in benefits to spreading reproductive activity over several seasons; selection thus favors the evolution of a lifetime that spans multiple breeding seasons. And so it is with all species: The life span and species-typical activities therein are evolved phenotypes and understandable in terms of the social and ecological selection pressures that resulted in reproductive opportunity and constraint during a species' evolutionary history (Roff, 1992; Stearns, 1992). For species with a relatively long life span, physical development and the expression of developmental and reproductive activities cannot be too tightly constrained. This is because the corresponding social and ecological conditions vary across and within lifetimes. Plasticity in the expression of life history traits represents the evolved potential to physically, behaviorally, and cognitively accommodate, within norms of reaction constraints, variation in these conditions.

The core components of sexual selection, intrasexual competition, and intersexual choice, as well as the intimately related demands of parenting, are key selection pressures in the evolution of life histories and key influences on the here-and-now expression of life history traits. The male–male competition of northern elephant seals results in conditions that favor a longer developmental period during which males gain the weight and physical size needed to compete for mates (Le Boeuf & Reiter, 1988). Female northern elephant seals do not compete for access to mates, and there is no advantage to delaying reproductive maturation; they mature more rapidly and as adults are much smaller than males. Another example is the behavioral competition of male bowerbirds as related to female choice and male–male competition. Males have an evolved and hormonally influenced bias to engage in bower-building activities, but it takes many years of observation of skilled males and practice at bower building before they can build an attractive bower (Collis & Borgia, 1992, 1993).

For slow maturing species, developmental activities include play activities that have no immediate function and mimic to some degree the activities of adulthood (Burghardt, 2005). The extent to which these activities reflect practice of skills needed in adulthood, as with the bower building of young male bowerbirds, or are simply needed to maintain the corresponding brain and behavioral systems until needed in adulthood is debated. In either case, play activities provide a window into the evolutionary history of the physical, behavioral, cognitive, and social competencies needed for successful survival and reproduction in adulthood. Sex differences in play activities are equally informative, as they have been documented across a wide range of species and often track sex differences in adult reproductive strategy (Power, 2000). For species with intense physical male–male competition, rough-and-tumble play is more common in males than females (P. K. Smith, 1982). When both sexes compete physically, both males and females engage in rough-and-tumble play. When females engage in more parenting, play parenting is more common in females than males (Nicolson, 1987).

Play and other aspects of development eventually emerge into adult activities, which, in addition to intrasexual competition and intersexual choice, involve parenting. Of particular interest is male parenting. This is because it is much less common than female parenting, especially in mammals, and is therefore an interesting evolutionary riddle in and of itself. I devote all of chapter 6 to men's parenting and note here that the evolution and proximate expression of paternal parenting in nonhuman species involve trade-offs that follow from the benefits to offspring survival prospects and later competitive abilities and the corresponding costs of lost mating opportunities and risk of cuckoldry. These trade-offs provide the scaffolding for understanding the evolution and expression of men's parenting.

Sex differences in the proximate expression of parental behaviors and in the expression of many other aspects of reproduction, ranging from copulation to intrasexual competition, are moderated by prenatal and postnatal exposure to sex hormones (Adkins-Reagan, 2005). Hormones do not deterministically cause sex differences but rather interact with genetic sex, developmental history, and current conditions to bias males and females to behave in ways that often differ (Wingfield et al., 1990). In fact, sex hormones appear to moderate the expression of many, if not all, of the sex differences described in this chapter and in chapter 3. Included among these behaviors are sex differences in rough-and-tumble play, mating behaviors, parental effort, intrasexual competition, intersexual choice, and health (Balthazart & Ball, 1998; Kimball, 2006). These hormones also influence brain development and functioning and corresponding cognitive and learning biases that support parenting, competition, and choice (Galea, 2008; Lévy et al., 1992; Nottebohm, 1970).

5

SEXUAL SELECTION IN PRIMATES AND DURING HUMAN EVOLUTION

In this chapter, I turn my attention to how the dynamics of sexual selection have unfolded in nonhuman primates and how they likely unfolded during human evolution. By examining sexual selection across primate species, scientists have developed useful constraints on the types of patterns that were likely during the course of human evolution (Foley & Lee, 1989; Rodseth, Wrangham, Harrigan, & Smuts, 1991). The consideration of sexual dynamics in primates also brings scientists one step closer to the human species and demonstrates that many of the reproductive sex differences in modern humans are evident in many other primates. I have organized this chapter into two general sections. The first provides an overview of the dynamics of sexual reproduction in primates, and the second focuses on the implications of these patterns, combined with the fossil record, for drawing inferences about sexual selection during human evolution.

SEXUAL REPRODUCTION IN PRIMATES

The mating systems of primates range from monogamy to polyandry to polygyny to high levels of promiscuous mating by both sexes. Monogamous primates tend to be arboreal (i.e., live in trees) and, unlike humans, show few sex differences in physical size or in the pattern of physical development (C. B. Jones, 2003). Polyandrous reproduction occurs in a few primate species (e.g., *Callitrichids*; Goldizen, 2003), but with the exception of paternal investment, any corresponding sex differences generally do not fall into the same pattern as those found in humans. For these reasons, monogamous and polyandrous primates are not as informative about human sexual selection as species with a polygynous mating system. The most obvious sex differences in these primates are the males' larger body and canine size (Plavcan, 2000; Plavcan & van Schaik, 1997), differences related, at least in part, to male–male competition (Harvey, Kavanagh, & Clutton-Brock, 1978; Plavcan, van Schaik, & Kappeler, 1995). Large body and canine size are particularly important for males with intense one-on-one physical competition and are typically accompanied by sex differences in the pattern of life history development, such as delayed maturation of males (Leigh, 1996). These physical traits are also important, but less so, in species in which competition involves coalitions of males (Manson & Wrangham, 1991; Plavcan, van Schaik, & Kappeler, 1995).

The across-species sex differences in physical size, life history development, and other traits (e.g., paternal investment), allow scientists to make inferences about the mating system and therefore the dynamics of sexual reproduction during human evolution. As an example, human sex differences in physical size and life history development are consistent with an evolutionary history of polygyny and intense male–male competition (R. D. Alexander, Hoogland, Howard, Noonan, & Sherman, 1979; A. R. Rogers & Mukherjee, 1992). Given these parallels, an examination of reproductive dynamics and sexual politics in polygynous primates provides insights into the evolution and current expression of human sex differences. I also consider primates with promiscuous mating systems, even though—as I describe in chapter 6 of this volume (in the section titled Women's Strategies and Men's Mating Opportunities)—women are not generally promiscuous. Consideration of promiscuous mating is nevertheless important because this is the mating system of our two closest relatives, the chimpanzee (*Pan troglodytes*) and the bonobo (*Pan paniscus*; Mountain, Lin, Bowcock, & Cavalli-Sforza, 1993).

I begin with a discussion of male–male competition because this is one of the more intensely studied aspects of primate social behavior, and thus more is known about this feature of sexual selection than female choice (J. P. Gray, 1985; Smuts, 1987). After providing a review of female choice, I move to the dynamics of female–female competition and male choice. These features of sexual selection are not as well understood in primates as male–male competition and female choice but do merit discussion because they are found in humans.

Male–Male Competition

Male–male competition in primates is over control of the mating activities of other males and the activities of sexually receptive females. I begin with consideration of how males' relative success at achieving this control is influenced by social rank or social dominance, and from there I review the relation between dominance and sex hormones, and then the dynamics of coalitional competition. I finish with discussion of the mating strategies of males that have not achieved a high social rank.

Social Dominance

The importance of social dominance for reproductive success is demonstrated by behavioral observation and by DNA finger printing to determine paternity. I highlight both of these literatures for the reader.

Behavioral Research. The northern (*Mirounga angustirostris*) and southern (*M. leonina*) elephant seal provide prototypical examples of how males establish dominance through physical contests (see the section titled Physical Competition, chap. 3). The establishment and maintenance of social dominance is achieved in similar ways in many primates, but the overall relation between dominance and reproductive outcomes is not always as straightforward (L. Ellis, 1995; Goodall, 1986). This is because the social dynamics of reproductive competition are more nuanced and complex than those that emerge with elephant seals. A male's rise to social dominance, or not, can be influenced by the social support of the dominant females within the group, and the relation between social dominance and reproductive outcomes can vary substantially with variation in the operational sex ratio, among other influences (Dunbar, 1984; Takahashi, 2004). The establishment and maintenance of social dominance often has important reproductive consequences for individual males (L. Ellis, 1995).

The mandrill (*Mandrillus sphinx*) provides an excellent example of one-on-one male–male competition in a polygynous primate; as with elephant seals, male mandrills engage in female defense polygyny (see Table 3.1, chap. 3, this volume). Of the mandrill, shown in Figure 5.1, Darwin (1871) proclaimed that

> [no] other member of the whole class of mammals is coloured in so extraordinary a manner as the adult male mandrill. The face at this age becomes of a fine blue, with the ridge and tip of the nose of the most brilliant red. (Vol. 2, p. 292)

In addition to this sexually dimorphic color pattern, males are 3 to 4 times the weight of conspecific females and compete by means of behavioral (e.g., threat grunts) and physical (e.g., lunges) threats and occasional physical

Figure 5.1. The male mandrill (*Mandrillus sphinx*). From *The Descent of Man, and Selection in Relation to Sex* (Vol. 2, p. 292), by C. R. Darwin, 1871, London: John Murray. In the public domain.

attack to establish social dominance over other males (Dixson, Bossi, & Wickings, 1993; Setchell, Lee, Wickings, & Dixson, 2001; Wickings, Bossi, & Dixson, 1993).

The relation between male social dominance and reproductive behavior has been demonstrated in a long-term study of two colonies of free-ranging, captive but living in a seminatural environment, mandrills (Dixson et al., 1993; Setchell, Charpentier, & Wickings, 2005; Setchell, Wickings, & Knapp, 2006; Wickings et al., 1993). Among other traits, Dixson, Wickings, Setchell and their colleagues found that male mandrills mature at about 10 years compared with 6 years for females. Males of this age are more likely to be alpha than younger and oftentimes older males. Dominant and subordinate males do not differ in body weight but differ considerably in degree of facial and sexual organ coloration. Red coloration in particular is a sign of social dominance and physical health, and drabber males are subordinate (Setchell, Smith, Wickings, & Knapp, 2008). Males with similar coloration will proceed through a series of displays that can escalate into a physical confrontation if one does not back down (Setchell & Wickings, 2005). The winners of these confrontations achieve dominance and control sexual activities during females' most fertile time (Setchell et al., 2005), which is signaled by the swelling of sexual organs (Hauser, 1996). In other words, many males copulate with females, but only alpha males copulate when females are most likely to conceive (Wickings et al., 1993). Exceptions occur when several females are simultaneously in estrous. Because alphas cannot mate guard all of them, other high-ranking males may mate and reproduce (Setchell et al., 2005).

As with the mandrill, males form dominance hierarchies in other polygynous and promiscuous species, and position in these hierarchies influences access to estrous females (de Ruiter & van Hooff, 1993; L. Ellis, 1995; Weingrill, Lycett, & Henzi, 2000). However, the relation between dominance and mating success is not always as strong as that found in the mandrill; some studies have found no relation between rank and mating access (e.g., de Ruiter & Inoue, 1993). The differences are related to whether captive, wild, or free-ranging groups have been studied and to social dynamics within these groups. Studies that find little or no relation between dominance and reproductive success are often based on captive groups, with studies of wild and free-ranging groups more consistently finding a positive relation (de Ruiter & van Hooff, 1993). Even in the latter groups, alpha males' access to estrous females can vary within and between species. The reasons include inbreeding avoidance, alternative mating strategies of low-ranking males, fluctuation in the operational sex ratio, female choice, and male coalitions (Alberts, Watts, & Altmann, 2003; Perloe, 1992; Smuts, 1987; Takahashi, 2004; Takahata, Huffman, Suzuki, Koyama, & Yamagiwa, 1999).

Genetic Research. For mandrills, the relation between social dominance and reproductive success has been confirmed using DNA fingerprinting to determine paternity (Dixson et al. 1993; Wickings et al., 1993). During one 5-year period, the two dominant males (of six males) sired all 36 offspring, and the number of offspring fathered in any given year was related to the relative dominance of the two males. During the first 3 years, the alpha male sired 17 of the 18 offspring, whereas the beta (second-ranked) male sired the other 1. During the 4th year, the formerly beta male became alpha, but he sired only 2 offspring during this season, whereas the former alpha male (now the beta) sired 4 offspring. During the 5th year, the new alpha male fathered 9 of the 12 offspring, and the beta male sired the rest. The same pattern was demonstrated over a 20-year period for this and another colony of mandrills (Charpentier et al., 2005). In all, alpha males sired 76% of the offspring born during their tenure, and two of three of the remaining males never reproduced. Two factors predicted when alpha males did not sire offspring, their genetic relation to females and to other adult males. Males avoided copulations with their full sisters, or the females resisted copulations, and were more tolerant of the copulations of closely related males (e.g., brothers). The other predictor was the number of females simultaneously in estrous.

In an 11-year study, Altmann et al. (1996) used DNA fingerprinting and behavioral observation to assess the relation between social dominance and reproductive outcomes in a group of wild savannah baboons (*Papio cyno-cephalus*). Of 20 adult males, a single individual, Radi, sired a disproportionate number of offspring, 44%. Radi sired 81% of the offspring during a 4-year reign as the alpha but only 20% of the offspring during the years before and after his reign. Similar patterns have been reported for groups of wild rhesus (*Macaca mulatta*; Widdig et al., 2004) and long-tailed macaques (*M. fascicularis*; de Ruiter & van Hooff, 1993). Consistent with research described in chapter 3 of this volume (in the section titled Good Genes), variability in major histocompatibility complex genes was the single best predictor of male reproductive success for rhesus macaques. These males may have been more resistant to parasites and recovered more quickly from injuries than other males. Even though chimpanzees mate promiscuously, DNA fingerprinting confirms that socially dominant males sire more offspring than subordinates, but their advantage is not as large as that found for mandrills and baboons (Boesch, Kohou, Néné, & Vigilant, 2006; Constable, Ashley, Goodall, & Pusey, 2001). Constable et al. found that the alpha male sired 36% of offspring, and other dominant males sired another 14%. The remaining 50% of offspring appeared to have been sired through alternative reproductive strategies.

For some species, the maintenance of social dominance affords the alpha male the added benefit of protecting his offspring from infanticide (Böer & Sommer, 1992; Hrdy, 1979). Sometimes when one male or a coalition of males from outside of the group displaces the residing male or males, the new alpha will attempt to kill suckling infants; suckling suppresses ovulation. Females often resist these attacks on their infants, but when infanticide does occur, they often become sexually receptive to the male and may have his offspring (Hrdy, 1979). In these situations, male infanticide is a reproductive strategy at the expense of the recently deposed male, the female, and of course the infant (Borries, Launhardt, Epplen, Epplen, & Winkler, 1999). The threat of infanticide means the maintenance of social dominance can influence the number of offspring sired and, under some conditions, the number surviving to maturity (L. Ellis, 1995).

Status, Hormones, and Health

Injured or sick males typically experience a drop in social rank and presumably in the number of offspring they sire (Goodall, 1986; Sapolsky, 1993). Cause and effect relations between health and status are difficult to determine, however, because status influences and is influenced by health. The relation is further complicated by the multiple influences of sex hormones (Adkins-Reagan, 2005), the typical social pattern of the species (solitary monogamous or multimale, multifemale; Abbott et al., 2003; Sapolsky, 2005), and fluctuation in social conditions within the same species (Whitten & Turner, 2004). Despite these nuances, it is clear that the sex hormones that influence reproductive competition can influence physical health, as discussed in chapter 4 of this volume (in the section titled Sex Hormones, Parasites, and Male Quality).

Setchell and Dixson (2001) documented that rise to alpha status in male mandrills is associated with increases in circulating testosterone and testes size and with the emergence of red coloration. A drop from alpha status results in less dramatic changes; testes size decreases, but testosterone does not drop. The bright red coloration that emerges when males achieve alpha status becomes less pronounced in some males but not others. More striking changes are illustrated by the aftereffects of losing a harem in male gelada baboons (*Theropithecus gelada*; see Figure 5.2):

> Defeated harem-holders literally age overnight. Their chest patches fade from the brilliant scarlet of a harem male to the pale flesh-color typical of juveniles and old animals, their capes lose their luster and their gait loses its bounce. The changes are both dramatic and final. (Dunbar, 1984, p. 132)

A similar pattern is found in many species of New World (South American) monkey (i.e., *Callitrichidae*). When dominated by other males, subordinates experience a severe drop in the hormones responsible for testicular development and the maturation of sperm, resulting in sterility (Abbott, 1993).

There are also more dynamic hormonal fluctuations as males engage in reproductive competition. M. N. Muller and Wrangham (2004) explicitly tested Wingfield, Hegner, Dufty and Ball's (1990) social challenge hypothesis with a group of wild chimpanzees (see the section titled Sex Hormones and Life History Development, chap. 4, this volume). In the presence of estrous females that had previously given birth, the most attractive females for male chimps (see the section titled Male Choice, this chapter), testosterone levels and rates of male–male aggression increased. Alpha males showed the most robust increases in testosterone, which appeared to be directly related to physical fighting for access to females and not to sexual behavior per se. The results are consistent with the social challenge hypothesis as it relates to polygyny with little paternal investment, specifically, high basal testosterone levels and modest increases during direct competition for mates—the same challenge response (Setchell et al., 2008) mandrills show. Muehlenbein, Watts, and Whitten (2004) also found a positive relation between testosterone levels and dominance rank for another community of chimpanzees but did not find a

Figure 5.2. Gelada baboons (*Theropithecus gelada*). The breast of the dominant male at the forefront has a red coloration. From *The Natural History of the Mammalia* (Div. 1, p. 56) by C. Vogt and F. Shecht, 1887, London: Blackie. In the public domain.

testosterone surge when males were competing for access to an estrous female. Further studies will be needed to determine whether a testosterone surge during reproductive competition is the norm for male chimpanzees.

Sapolsky's (1993) and Ray and Sapolsky's (1992) research with wild olive baboons (*Papio anubis*) has revealed that the relations among hormones, health, and immunocompetence are moderated by social stability and behavioral style (e.g., skill at discriminating serious from unimportant threats to status). Dominant males in stable social hierarchies have low levels of stress hormones, are in better physical condition, and appear to have better functioning immune systems than subordinate males. Testosterone levels are not higher than those of subordinates except during agonistic challenges to social position. When this occurs, the testosterone of dominant males rises more quickly than that of subordinates. Once the stressful event is over, testosterone and stress hormone levels quickly return to baseline levels in dominant males, but the stress hormone levels of subordinates remain elevated and are associated with suppression of testosterone. The findings for these baboons and at least some other primates are consistent with the testosterone and immunocompetence hypothesis; specifically, healthy males can tolerate the high levels of testosterone needed to achieve dominance without affecting their health (Muehlenbein, 2006; Muehlenbein & Bribiescas, 2005; see the section titled Sex Hormones, Parasites, and Male Quality, chap. 4, this volume).

Coalitional Competition

Nearly all primates live in complex societies and engage in activities that are familiar to the reader. Among these are maternal care of offspring, sibling rivalry over parental attention, preferential social support and affiliation with friends, preferential treatment of kin, and aggressive conflicts of interest (Altmann et al., 1996; Goodall, 1986; McGrew, 1992; Silk, 2007); a full discussion is beyond the scope of this book, but excellent treatments are available elsewhere (R. Byrne, 1995; de Waal, 1982; Goodall, 1986; S. T. Parker & McKinney, 1999; Russon & Begun, 2004; Smuts, Cheney, Seyfarth, Wrangham, & Struhsaker, 1987; Tomasello & Call, 1997). My focus is on male–male coalitional competition, with an emphasis on the chimpanzee.

The chimpanzee is of interest because of male coalitions and male philopatry. The latter means that males stay with the birth group and females emigrate when they reach adulthood (Manson & Wrangham, 1991; Rodseth et al., 1991). In many human societies, men also tend to stay in their birth group, whereas women often emigrate to the birth group of their husbands (C. R. Ember, 1978; Pasternak, Ember, & Ember, 1997); when men leave their group, it is often to work for their in-laws for the right to marry their daughter (bride price) or because their wife's residence is in the same or a neighboring community as the men's kin (Marlowe, 2004a). Male philopatry is also found in two other close relatives, the bonobo (Eriksson et al., 2006) and the gorilla (*Gorilla gorilla*; Lawson Handley & Perrin, 2007), and a few other primates, such as the hamadryas baboon (*Papio hamadryas*; Colmenares, 1992), but is otherwise uncommon in primates or mammals in general (Greenwood, 1980; Sigg, Stolba, Abegglen, & Dasser, 1982; Wrangham, 1980). I am not arguing that the behavior of chimpanzees is the prototype from which human evolution should be viewed, and in fact I argue otherwise in the section titled Evolutionary Models in this chapter. Nonetheless, discussion of the chimpanzee is useful because it illustrates the combination of one-on-one and coalitional competition.

In theory, male philopatry and kinship will increase the likelihood that a bias toward coalition formation and competition will evolve. However, the evidence for the saliency of within-group kinship ties in male chimpanzees has been mixed (Vigilant, Hofreiter, Siedel, & Boesch, 2001). Males show a preference for forming coalitions with maternal brothers, but they do not consistently do so for paternal brothers (Langergraber, Mitani, & Vigilant, 2007). The best predictors of coalitional behavior are similarities in age and rank and the attendant opportunities such cooperation affords (Mitani & Amsler, 2003; Watts, 1998). Regardless of kinship status, males cooperate when it allows them to move up the dominance hierarchy and to mate guard, hunt, and patrol the group's territorial boundaries (de Waal, 1982, 1993; Goodall, 1986; Mitani & Watts, 2005; Watts & Mitani, 2001; J. M. Williams, Oehlert, Carlis, & Pusey, 2004). The behavior of coalition partners ranges from the mere physical presence of one male while the other threatens or attacks another male, to joint displays, and, occasionally, joint attacks. Goodall (1986) described such an encounter:

> Goliath arrives in camp alone, late one evening. Every so often he stands upright to stare back in the direction from which he has come. He seems nervous and startles at every sound. Six minutes later three adult males appear on one of the trails leading to camp; one is high-ranking Hugh. They pause, hair on end, then abruptly charge down toward Goliath. But he has vanished silently into the bushes on the far side of the clearing. For the next five minutes the three crash about the undergrowth, searching for the runaway . . .
>
> Early the next morning Hugh returns to camp with his two companions. A few minutes later, Goliath charges down, dragging a huge branch. To our amazement, he runs straight at Hugh and attacks him. The two big males fight, rolling over, grappling and hitting each other. It is not until the battle is already in progress that we realize why Goliath, so fearful the evening before, is suddenly so brave today: we hear the deep pant-hoots of David Graybeard. He appears from the undergrowth and displays his slow, magnificent way around the combatants. He must have joined Goliath late the evening before, and even though he does not actually join in the fight, his presence provides moral support. Suddenly Goliath leaps right onto Hugh, grabbing the hair of his shoulders, pounding on his back with both feet. Hugh gives up; he manages to pull away and runs off, screaming and defeated. (p. 313)

These coalitions are a common feature of chimpanzee politics within communities, as is the formation of larger coalitions for patrolling the boarder of their territory and for making incursions into neighboring communities (Mitani & Watts, 2005; Nishida, 1979; Watts & Mitani, 2001; Watts, Muller, Amsler, Mbabazi, & Mitani, 2006).

> A patrol is typified by cautious, silent travel during which the members of the party tend to move in a compact group. There are many pauses as

the chimpanzees gaze around and listen. Sometimes they climb tall trees and sit quietly for an hour or more, gazing out over the "unsafe" area of a neighboring community. (Goodall, 1986, p. 490)

When members of such patrols encounter one another, the typical response is pant-hooting (a vocal call) and physical displays on both sides, with the smaller group eventually withdrawing (M. L. Wilson, Hauser, & Wrangham, 2001). At other times, the meetings can be deadly. Goodall (1986) described a series of such attacks by one community of chimpanzees on their southern neighbors. Over a 4-year period, the southern group was virtually eliminated, one individual at a time, by the northern community, whose members then expanded their territory to include that of the now extinct southern group. As an example of the ferocity of such attacks, consider the fate of Goliath, a member of this southern group, who was attacked 12 years after the just-described incident with Hugh:

> Faben started to attack, leaping at the old male and pushing him to the ground, his functional hand on Goliath's shoulder. Goliath was scream-ing, the other males giving pant-hoots and waa-barks and displaying. Faben continued to pin Goliath to the ground until Satan arrived. Both aggressors then hit, stamped on, and pulled at the victim who sat hunched forward. Jomeo, screaming, joined in. . . . The other males continued to beat up their victim without pause, using fists and feet. . . . Faben took one of his arms and dragged him about 8 meters over the ground. Satan dragged him back again. . . . Eighteen minutes after the start of the attack, Jomeo left Goliath, followed by Satan and Faben. . . . In the attack [Goliath] was, inevitably, very badly hurt. He had one severe wound on his back, low on the spine; another behind his left ear, which was bleed-ing profusely; and another on his head. Like [most other members of the southern group], Goliath, despite intensive searching by all research per-sonnel and field staff, was never seen again (Goodall, 1986, pp. 508–509).

The best available evidence suggests that the primary benefit of winning these conflicts is an increase in territory size, which allows females to expand their individual territories (J. M. Williams et al., 2004). The latter results in more food, shorter interbirth intervals, and thereby a higher reproductive success for the community's females and males. Territory expansion can also result in the recruitment of new females into the community but tends to occur only when all or nearly all of their community's males have been killed (M. L. Wilson & Wrangham, 2003); some males will temporarily isolate females from other communities and hold them "prisoner" to mate with them (Boesch et al., 2008). At the same time, it is important for the reader to know that these descriptions do not mean chimpanzees are continually in conflict. Interindividual and intercommunity aggression are features of chimpanzee social life that reflect extreme ways of resolving conflicts of interest; Kibale males, for instance, patrol only 15 to 35 times a year (Mitani & Watts, 2005). Many conflicts are resolved through display and other social signals, although escalation to physical aggression is more common in chimpanzees than people in traditional societies (Wrangham, Wilson, & Muller, 2006). Nevertheless, these descriptions should not belie the fact that chimpanzees show a suite of social behaviors, including nurturing of young and friendly social affiliation (de Waal, 2000).

Alternative Mating Strategies

Mating and reproductive success for male elephant seals is largely determined by the establishment of social dominance and the maintenance of a harem (see the section titled Male–Male Competition, chap. 3). An alternative mating strategy involves sneaking into harems and attempting to mate with females. This, however, appears to be a strategy that is forced onto subordinates because of the monopolization of females by dominant males. In other cases and as illustrated by jack and hooknose salmon (see the section titled Intrasexual Competition, chap. 4), different mating strategies are true alternatives, that is, each is equally effective in terms of siring offspring. Male primates use a variety of mating strategies, some of which are forced onto subordinate males, but others may be true alternatives to fighting for and achieving social dominance (Dunbar, 1984; Maggioncalda, Sapolsky, & Czekala, 1999; M. N. Muller, Kahlenberg, Emery Thompson, & Wrangham, 2007; Smuts, 1987; Tutin, 1979).

Although chimpanzee sex is largely promiscuous, several alternative mating relationships have been observed (Goodall, 1986; M. N. Muller et al., 2007; Tutin, 1979). The consortship is one such strategy and is more common among lower than higher ranking males. In some cases, the consortship is preceded by male grooming and sharing of food with the female (Tutin, 1979). Once the pair is formed, they separate from the community and spend anywhere from several hours to several weeks in isolation at the community's periphery. The most interesting and potentially most important finding is that different mating strategies may result in different conception rates (Goodall, 1986; Tutin, 1979). Tutin found that 73% of the matings were promiscuous; 25% resulted during mate guarding by dominant males; and 2% occurred during consortships. Despite the low frequency of matings in the last category, it has been estimated that roughly 50% of the offspring were conceived during a consortship; this estimate remains to be confirmed with DNA fingerprinting studies.

M. N. Muller et al. (2007) tested the hypothesis that male-on-female aggression and intimidation are an alternative form of chimpanzee mating strategy. In this study, male-on-female aggression was common and could occur daily for estrous females traveling with a group of males. Estrous females and especially those that had previously given birth—these females are more fertile than other females (see the section titled Male Choice in this chapter)—received the most aggression from males, consistent with the hypothesis that this is reproduction-related coercion. Males copulated twice as often with females against whom they aggressed than with females that were not the targets of aggression. As with the consortship, rates of male-on-female aggression were not related to dominance rank, indicating this is not mate guarding by dominant males but an alternative strategy used by some subordinate males. Whether the consortship and male-on-female aggression and coercion are true alternative mating strategies or strategies adopted by subordinate males that would otherwise mate guard estrous females, as is done by dominant males, is not currently known. The genetic finding that about 50% of offspring are sired by nondominant males suggests that these are or could evolve to become true alternative strategies.

The two reproductive body types of male orangutans (*Pongo pygmaeus*) illustrate a more dramatic alternative strategy (Maggioncalda et al., 1999; Rodman & Mitani, 1987; Setchell, 2003). Socially dominant males are twice the body weight of females and develop large flanges around their face and a large throat sac, as shown in Figure 5.3. These maturational changes, along with others, allow dominant males to produce long calls that attract females and signal their dominance to other males. Females and their offspring live separately from males, but receptive females will seek out dominant males when they are ready to reproduce. Some other males retain the juvenile body type, that is, they remain relatively small and do not develop the flanges and other physical features of socially dominant males. These arrested males are nevertheless fertile and attempt to unobtrusively move through the forest in search of females. If they encounter a female, they will often coerce her to copulate.

Both dominant and arrested males reproduce in the wild (Setchell, 2003), but these alternative morphs are not the same as those of the hooknose and jack salmon (M. R. Gross, 1985). Unlike the smaller jacks, the arrested male orangutan can develop into a flanged dominant male if the dominant male is removed from the area; the presence of a more dominant male appears to suppress testosterone and related hormones needed to develop these secondary sexual characteristics (Maggioncalda et al., 1999). These males, in effect, can adopt alternative strategies at different points in their adult life span, depending on social context.

Female Choice

Although it has received less systematic attention than male–male competition, it is clear that female choice is an influential component of

Figure 5.3. Dominant, fully developed male orangutan (*Pongo pygmaeus*). Copyright by Digital Vision Ltd. Reprinted with permission of Oxford Scientific Library.

reproductive dynamics in many primates (J. P. Gray, 1985; Perloe, 1992). I begin with an overview of the pattern of female choice and then proceed to the bases for these choices.

Pattern of Choice

As the reader will recall from the section titled Female Choice in chapter 3, choice can be behavioral or occur in the reproductive track. I discuss both possibilities for primates.

Behavioral Choice. Females can choose their mating partners directly by soliciting or refusing copulations and can choose them indirectly by inciting male–male competition or by influencing which males can and cannot enter the group (Wiley & Poston, 1996). Female chimpanzees, as an example, can influence the formation of consortships in some social contexts (Tutin, 1979); if a female does not wish to accompany the male, she can alert other males that in turn will disrupt the unwanted male's solicitations. In other cases, as noted, and especially if the female is isolated, males appear to coerce "cooperation" (M. N. Muller et al., 2007).

Despite male coercion, females in many primate species actively rebuff, sometimes quite aggressively, the sexual interests of some males and initiate sex with others (Dunbar, 1984; Kano, 1992; Smuts, 1985). Examples of female-initiated sexual activities are quite clear in our cousin the bonobo: "A female sat before a male and gazed into his face. When the male responded to this invitation, she fell on her back, elevated her buttocks and presented her genitals. In this case they copulated ventro-ventrally" (i.e., *missionary style*; Kano, 1980, p. 255). Smuts (1985) provided other examples from her extensive studies of female–male relationships in the olive baboon. On top of male–male competition for social dominance and access to estrous females, stable female–male relationships are occasionally found. Although female baboons prefer such relationships to be with more dominant males, they often reject the mating attempts of males who have displaced—through male–male competition—a preferred mate, a behavior also found in some other species (Perloe, 1992; Smuts, 1985, 1987). Smuts provided an illustration in her field notes:

> At noon, Delphi, a young adult female, is in consort with Zim, an older, resident male. During an aggressive encounter, Zim loses Delphi to Vulcan, a young natal male about the same age as Delphi. Zim, Alex, and Boz, three older residents, immediately begin to follow the consort pair. Delphi looks back at them and Vulcan nervously herds her away. He tries to groom her, but she pulls away and begins to feed. At 12[:]56 Vulcan approaches Delphi and begins to mount her. She jumps away, and he watches her as she resumes feeding. At 12[:]58 he tries to mount her again, placing his hands on her back. Delphi walks away and Vulcan follows, still holding on to her. He maintains this "wheelbarrow" position for several steps, but then Delphi swerves sharply to one side and he falls off. He approaches her again 1 minute later, but she moves behind a large bush before he reaches her. . . . They circle the bush in alternate directions for several minutes, until finally Vulcan catches Delphi. He tries to mount, but Delphi pulls away. . . . During the 3 hours we followed them Delphi refused 42 copulation attempts. (Smuts, 1985, pp. 170–171)

Females can also at times influence the outcomes of male–male competition. In several species of baboon, for instance, males are more likely to displace a male that is attempting to consort with a female if the female is not responding to the male's gestures (Bachmann & Kummer, 1980; Smuts,

1985). In still other cases, coalitions of females act to influence which males are able to enter their group and which are not. One of the clearest examples is provided by the dynamics of harem acquisition in the gelada baboon (Dunbar, 1984). These baboons are organized into harems consisting of a single male and between 1 and 10 females and their offspring. Males have two general strategies for acquiring a harem. In the first, the male follows the group as a peripheral and subordinate member and begins to develop relationships, through grooming, with the juveniles in the group and gradually with individual females. In some cases, the females will desert, usually as a group, the harem-holding male in favor of the follower.

The other strategy is a hostile takeover attempt, with the intruder provoking and attacking the harem-holding male. The ensuing fights can last for several days, on and off, and can result in severe injury to one or both of the males. In most cases,

> what is crucial to the outcome is the behavior of the females. It is they who decide, by what amounts to a collective decision, whether to desert *en masse* to a new male or to retain their existing harem male. (Dunbar, 1984, p. 132)

Before the final decision is made, the females often fight among themselves as some females attempt to prevent others from interacting with the interloper. Apparently, the females often "disagree" about which male is to be preferred. Each individual female's degree of loyalty to the existing male appears to be determined in large part by the amount of time the male has spent grooming and affiliating with the female.

Sperm Competition. Sperm competition is an important determinant of reproductive outcomes for primates with promiscuous mating (Harcourt, Harvey, Larson, & Short, 1981). Males of these species have larger testes and thus produce more sperm. The production of additional spermatozoa necessarily increases the odds that any one of them will fertilize the egg. An unresolved issue is whether sperm competition has also influenced the evolution of sperm anatomy and physiology, such as the mechanisms that affect swimming speed (M. J. Anderson & Dixson, 2002; Nascimento et al., 2008). Nascimento et al.'s results are among the more intriguing. For promiscuous species, males' sperm swims faster than does the sperm for monogamous species. The issue of postcopulatory cryptic choice (e.g., through sperm retention or rejection) in female primates remains to be fully explored (Engelhardt, Heistermann, Hodges, Nürnberg, & Niemitz, 2006).

Bases for Choice

In comparison with what scientists know about female choice in birds (see the section titled Female Choice, chap. 3), scientists know much less about these choices in primates, except, of course, humans (see the section titled Women's Mate Choices, chap. 7). Scientists do not yet know whether the bright coloration of dominant male mandrills or gelada baboons is a basis for female choice, largely dominance-related signals to other males, or both. Similarly, male control of breeding territories is an important feature of male–male competition in some primates, but it is not clear whether females are choosing the territory or the male (Goodall, 1986; Sigg et al., 1982). Although the male's ability to provide food to the female and her offspring is the basis of female choice in some species, this does not appear to be important for most non-human primates; there are a few minor exceptions, such as male chimpanzees and bonobos sharing food with estrous females in exchange for sex (Goodall, 1986; Kano, 1980). For matrilineal species in which females stay in the birth group, there is a preference for newcomers to avoid incest (Bercovitch, 1997).

For the most part, female choice is driven by the dynamics of social and sexual relationships within the group, especially the frequency and intensity of aggressive encounters (Silk, 2007; Smuts, 1987). In some species, female choice involves selecting males that will provide protection for them and their offspring from other group members (Altmann, 1980; Smuts, 1985; Smuts & Gubernick, 1992), and sometimes female choice is to reduce the threat of infanticide (Beehner, Bergman, Cheney, Seyfarth, & Whitten, 2005; Engh et al., 2006). The reader may recall that infanticide occurs in some species when the group's alpha male is displaced by a new male or coalition of males (L. Ellis, 1995; Hrdy, 1979). Hrdy argued that the promiscuous mating found in many of these species and the tendency of females to mate with unfamiliar males—those at the periphery of the group and therefore candidates to displace resident males—are evolved strategies to counter the threat of infanticide. This is because males are less likely to attack infants if they have copulated with the infant's mother.

There is now good support for Hrdy's (1979) proposal. An illustration is provided by Hanuman langurs (*Semnopithecus entellus*), a species with frequent infanticide by males. In this species, the typically tight synchronization between sexual receptivity and ovulation is disrupted (Heistermann et al., 2001). Although dominant males copulate with estrous females more often than do other males, copulation during this time does not ensure paternity. This is because the timing of ovulation is essentially random across a 3- to 14-day receptive phase, making mate guarding by dominant males difficult to achieve. In the Heistermann et al. study, the dominant male was able to monopolize, to some degree, sex with estrous females but sired only one of five infants typed through DNA fingerprinting. Different males sired each of the other infants, including one male from an adjacent group. The lack of a tight link between cycle phase, ovulation, and sexual receptivity results in a situation in which none of the males or the females can predict paternity.

Even when infanticide is uncommon, females often use sexual relationships to their advantage. These relationships can increase the likelihood that a male will provide some form of investment in her offspring (e.g., carry the infant); at times, the investment is provided even if the male is not likely to be the father, which makes the male's behavior mating effort and not parental effort (Smuts & Gubernick, 1992; Whitten, 1987). For a few species, such as savannah baboons, there is some evidence of paternal recognition of their offspring and protection of these offspring during aggressive encounters and other threats (Buchan, Alberts, Silk, & Altmann, 2003). It is not known whether the bias to protect males' own offspring is the result of copulating with the mother during her estrous phase or whether another recognition mechanism is operating. Either way, these findings suggest true paternal investment in these species.

For highly social species, everyday threat comes from other group members, often males. Male olive baboons direct aggressive displays toward females five times a week, on average, and physically attack females once a week (Smuts, 1985). Individual females are, on average, severely attacked—leaving wounds that require weeks or months to heal—about once a year. Infants are also frequently physically harassed (e.g., pulled out of mother's grasp) or attacked by other group members, both male and female. Female choice of mates in the olive baboon, and at least several other primate species (e.g., rhesus macaques), appears to involve a social strategy to counter these threats (Altmann, 1980; Dunbar, 1984; Sigg et al., 1982). The strategy involves the development of friendships with one or two males (Smuts, 1985). These affiliations can develop into long-term pair bonds, with individual males and females showing preferential treatment of their friends.

The primary benefit to females is the protection that her friend provides to her and her infant. The tendency for females to favor the development of these relationships with more dominant males might reflect the ability of these males to better control the dynamics of social conflicts than their subordinates. In any case, Smuts's (1985) observational studies of group behavior have indicated that when a female or her offspring is attacked and defended, the defender is the female's friend roughly 9 out of 10 times. In more than four out of five female–male friendships, the male spends a considerable amount of time affiliating with her offspring (e.g., grooming, playing)—even if he is not the father—but only rarely affiliates with the offspring of other females (Altmann, 1980; Smuts, 1985; Smuts & Gubernick, 1992). There are costs to the female as well—attacks by friends; nonfriends attack females 3 to 4 times more frequently than do friends, but friends still account for one quarter of all attacks. The reasons for male attacks on their female friends are not clear but appear to involve displaced aggression and jealousy-related mate guarding (Smuts, 1985).

The principal benefits for males are their sexual relationships with female friends and their friends' support during conflicts with other group members. Although the sexual relationship is not exclusive, males copulate with their female friends about twice as often as expected on the basis of overall of sexual activity. Males' preferences for specific females are also evident in gelada baboons; in this species males are 50% more likely to ejaculate when copulating with their preferred partner than when copulating with other females in their harem. These patterns, combined with Tutin's (1979) findings, suggest that males are more likely to sire offspring with female friends than with other females. If so, then in many cases the formation of a friendship increases not only the male's chances of siring offspring but also the chances protection is focused on his own offspring (Buchan et al., 2003). The principal costs to males are the time, energy, and physical risks associated with defending their friends and their friends' offspring.

Female–Female Competition

The earlier section on male–male competition might have given the impression that female primates are not especially aggressive. This is not the case: Female-on-female aggression is quite common, and in fact there is no consistent cross-species sex difference in the frequency of aggressive encounters (Silk, 1987, 1993). In some species, females are relatively more agonistic than males, and in other species males are relatively more agonistic (Smuts, 1987). There are, however, consistent cross-species sex differences in the pattern, severity, and focus of aggressive encounters. Smuts (1987) found that male-on-male aggression results in more severe wounds (e.g., open gashes) than female-on-female aggression in all 16 primate species for which information on intrasexual aggression was available for both sexes. In comparison with female–female aggression, male–male aggression tends to be more ritualized (i.e., it involves more stereotyped social displays) and is more frequently related to mating (Silk, 1993; Smuts, 1987).

When male relationships provide a reproductive benefit to females, such as a reduction in infanticide risk, a bias for females to find these relationships attractive and to compete over them is predicted to evolve. This form of female-on-female aggression is not well understood but has been documented in chacma baboons (*Papio cynocephalus ursinus*; Palombit, Cheney, & Seyfarth, 2001). In this savannah baboon, there is substantial risk of infanticide when a new alpha male emerges. Females counter this risk through the development of friendships with specific high-ranking males. Palombit et al. demonstrated that females compete for these valuable relationships; high-ranking females displace low-ranking females in terms of time spent with these males. There is every reason to believe that similar forms of competition will be found for other species in which males are social and reproductive resources to females.

Female Coalitions

When found, coalitions almost always form among members of the philopatric sex (i.e., the sex that stays in the birth group) and on the basis of kinship, as in mother–daughter coalitions (Ghiglieri, 1987; Wrangham, 1980). With the earlier noted exceptions, females are almost always the philopatric sex in Old World (i.e., African, Asia) primates, and these coalitional species are called *female-bonded*. Unlike the sexual competition associated with male coalitions, female coalitions more typically compete for control of high-quality food sources such as fruit trees (Silk, 1987; Sterck, Watts, & van Schaik, 1997; Wrangham, 1980). Access to these foods has important reproductive consequences for females; specifically, improved nutritional status results in earlier sexual maturation, a longer reproductive life span, shorter intervals between births, and lowered offspring mortality (Silk, 1987; Wrangham, 1980). The result is females in dominant coalitions have a higher lifetime reproductive success than females in subordinate coalitions.

Females also form coalitions as a within-group social strategy to counter male-on-female aggression, for the protection of offspring (e.g., infanticide avoidance), or in response to feeding disputes (Hrdy, 1979). In a study of three captive bonobo populations, Parish (1996) found that female–female affiliations (e.g., sexual contact and cofeeding) were more common than male–male affiliations or male–female affiliations. Coalitions of females were able to dominate individual males and used this domination to control high-quality feeding sites and to refuse male initiated consortships. In these populations, male-on-female aggression was rare, but female-on-male aggression was common. "Most often, the attacks have taken the form of several females holding the male down while biting him in the extremities (fingers, toes, ears, and testicles), although severe attacks by single females have also occurred" (Parish, 1996, p. 77). Female–female affiliations are common in wild populations, and a few instances of female coalitions attacking males have been reported, but male–male aggression is by far the most common form of agonistic behavior (Kano, 1992).

Female Dominance Hierarchies

Female dominance hierarchies—in terms of female kin groups and individuals—are common in female-bonded species and sometimes for individual females for species in which males are the philopatric sex (Parish, 1996; Pusey, Williams, & Goodall, 1997; Silk, 1993; Wrangham, 1980). A female's position within the hierarchy is determined by agonistic interactions, the rank of her mother, and the size and rank of her kin group (Mori, Watanabe, & Yamaguchi, 1989). Pusey et al. demonstrated that high-ranking female chimpanzees have a higher lifetime reproductive success than their lower ranking peers. The offspring of high-ranking females have lower mortality rates and mature more quickly than the offspring of lower ranking females. Although some of the differences in early mortality appear to be due to the tendency of some high-ranking females to kill the infants of lower ranking females, the bulk of the differences are related to access to high-quality food, as with other primates (Silk, 1993).

Dominance-related differences in reproductive success are also related to the dynamics of social behavior: Higher ranking females harass their lower ranking peers. They interfere with copulations, threaten and chase them, disrupt their relationships with male friends, and sometimes injure or kill their offspring (Palombit et al., 2001; Pusey et al., 1997; Vervaecke, Stevens, & Van Elsacker, 2003). The resulting stress can disrupt the hormonal systems associated with ovulation and the maintenance of pregnancy (Smuts & Nicolson, 1989). The most extreme form is found in marmoset and tamarin monkeys (*Callitrichidae*), where dominant females can completely suppress the mating behavior of subordinate females and nearly completely inhibit the secretion of the hormones (e.g., luteinizing hormone) that induce ovulation (Abbott, 1993). This socially induced infertility appears to be related to social conflict and to a chemical signal in the dominant female's urine.

Dominant females better control the dynamics of social interactions than subordinate females, to their reproductive benefit. As an example, in vervet monkeys (*Cercopithecus aethiops*), high-ranking females allow affiliations between offspring and other females more often than do lower ranking females (Fairbanks & McGuire, 1995). This *alloparenting* ("babysitting") reduces the cost (e.g., reduced foraging) of parental care for high-ranking females, which in turn shortens the birth interval. Alloparenting, however, can be risky, as other females will often injure or not protect these infants (Nicolson, 1987). High-ranking vervet females can easily retrieve their infants from allomothers, whereas low-ranking females cannot. Thus, the risks of alloparenting are lower for high-ranking than low-ranking females, and the consequent ability to use allomothers yields reproductive benefits to these high-ranking females.

Male Choice

Males often have individual preferences for specific mates (Dunbar, 1984; Smuts, 1987) but generally prefer to mate when females are the most likely to conceive and with females that are the most likely to successfully rear offspring (Altmann et al., 1996; Dixson et al., 1993; Goodall, 1986; Tutin, 1979). The increases in estrogen and progesterone that result in ovulation also result in pronounced sexual organ swelling and changes in sexual organ coloration (reddening) in many species (Dixson, 1983). Males find these swellings hard to resist and prefer to mate with females during this time in their ovulatory cycle. These swellings are most often found in species that live in multimale, multifemale groups and in species in which females mate with several males; as noted earlier, this helps to confuse paternity (Hrdy, 1979).

In many species, including chimpanzees, males prefer older females that have given birth over younger ones that have not yet done so (Silk, 1987; M. N. Muller, Thompson, & Wrangham, 2006). The older females are more fertile per ovulatory cycle and tend to be more skilled mothers; their infants are more likely to survive (Nicolson, 1987; Smuts & Nicolson, 1989). In some species, males understandably prefer high-ranking to low-ranking females as mating partners (Robinson, 1982), given the relation between female social dominance and reproductive outcomes. Finally, male choice is expected in species in which males provide a considerable level of parental investment at a cost, although the dynamics of these choices and investment are not well understood for many of these species (Goldizen, 2003; Trivers, 1972), with the exception of humans (see chap. 6, this volume).

SEXUAL SELECTION AND HUMAN EVOLUTION

I now turn to physical sex differences, or sexual dimorphisms, found in our hominid ancestors and examine these in light of the dimorphisms found in living primates. This comparison enables inferences to be drawn, albeit with caution, about the nature and evolution of human sex differences (Foley & Lee, 1989; Plavcan, 2001). I begin with the major species in our evolutionary past and follow with descriptions of sex differences in canine size and body size across these species. I follow with a focus on the evolution of brain size and potential evolutionary change in any corresponding sex differences. On the basis of these patterns and those described for primates, I close with inferences about sexual selection during human evolution.

Origins

Despite continuing debate over the number of species composing the genus *Homo* and the most likely predecessor genus *Australopithecus* (Aiello & Collard, 2001; McHenry, 1994b; McHenry & Coffing, 2000; B. Wood & Collard, 1999), there is a consensus on the major hominid species and their likely evolutionary relationships. A simplified family tree is shown in Figure 5.4. The ancestor common to modern humans, chimpanzees, and gorillas existed before the emergence of these species, and genetic analyses and the fossil record suggest a complex divergence (Horai, Hayasaka, Kondo, Tsugane, & Takahata, 1995; Patterson, Richter, Gnerre, Lander, & Reich, 2006). The ancestor common to these three species existed between 8.0 million and

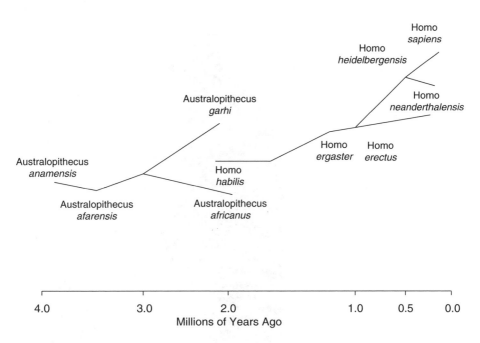

Figure 5.4. Simplified hominid family tree with estimated age of emergence.

6.0 million years ago (MYA; F.-C. Chen & Li, 2001), and separation of the lineages that led to modern humans and chimpanzees may have extended from 6.0 MYA to 4.0 MYA, with potential interbreeding before final speciation (Patterson et al., 2006). To further complicate the issue, there are segments of the human genome that are more similar to that of the gorilla than to that of the chimpanzee, although humans are more closely related to the chimpanzee, overall (Hobolth, Christensen, Mailund, & Schierup, 2007).

The dating of sediments found with australopithecine fossils suggests that *A. anamensis* existed about 4.0 MYA and *A. afarensis* from about 4.0 to 2.8 MYA (Leakey, Feibel, McDougall, Ward, & Walker, 1998; McHenry, 1994b). It has been proposed that *A. africanus* was the link between *A. afarensis*—an illustration of a female of this species is shown in Figure 5.5— and the line that eventually led to humans, but discovery of a contemporaneous species, *A. garhi*, makes this less certain (Asfaw et al., 1999); *A. garhi* is dated at about 2.5 MYA and *A. africanus* from about 3.0 to 2.3 MYA. The alternative is that our direct ancestors were other groups of australopithecines, that is, *Paranthropus boisei* and *P. robustus* (McHenry & Coffing, 2000). Either way, the pattern of sex differences is the same.

H. habilis is also a bit of a puzzle as a result of many features that are more similar to *Australopithecus* than to *Homo* (Dean et al., 2001; B. Wood & Collard, 1999), but in any case, *H. habilis* existed from about 2.5 MYA to

Figure 5.5. Artistic reconstruction of a female *Australopithecus afarensis.* Illustration by Mieke Roth. Printed with permission.

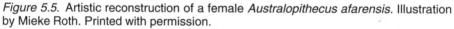

1.5 MYA. *H. ergaster* and *H. erectus* might be earlier and later specimens of the same species, respectively (Asfawet al., 2002), which is hereafter *H. erectus* unless otherwise noted. This species emerged in Africa about 1.8 MYA and began to move into Asia and possibly parts of southern Europe (Gabunia et al., 2000; Stringer, 1992), with separate populations evolving into *H. neanderthalensis* and *H. sapiens* (McHenry, 1994b). The most recent common ancestor of the two latter species appears to have existed about 500,000 years ago (Pääbo, 1999). Genetic analyses suggest that modern humans evolved between 150,000 and roughly 50,000 years ago (Horai et al., 1995; R. Thomson, Pritchard, Shen, Oefner, & Feldman, 2000). There are genetic differences across human populations, but all humans share a common ancestor that emerged from sub-Saharan Africa (Jakobsson et al., 2008; J. Z. Li et al., 2008).

Sexual Dimorphisms

As one might imagine, the study of sex differences based on the fossil record is complicated. Central issues involve determining the sex of the fossil, determining whether the pool of fossils under study represents one or multiple species, and determining the most appropriate method for making body size estimates based on partial remains (Armelagos, & Van Gerven, 1980). These complications often result in disagreements about the magnitude of sexually dimorphic traits. There is, for instance, variability in the estimates of the body weight of male and female A. afarensis but also agreement that males were moderately to considerably larger than females (Aiello, 1994; Richmond & Jungers, 1995).

I focus on sexual dimorphisms in canine size and body size for several reasons. First, reliable sex differences in the architecture of teeth and a variety of bones in living primates provide a means for determining the sex of fossilized bones (Plavcan, 2001). Second, the magnitude of the sex differences in body weight and canine size increases as the intensity of physical male–male competition increases (Plavcan et al., 1995). The combination allows inferences about the likely intensity of male–male competition during human evolution and, more cautiously, inferences about other features of sexual selection.

Canine Size and Body Size

The study of fossilized canines is easier than the study of other bones because teeth are more likely to be preserved as fossils and thus are relatively abundant (M. H. Day, 1994). As noted previously, the determination of sex is based on known sex differences in tooth size and morphology in living primates (Plavcan, 2001) but can still be difficult with fossils, and thus inferences about sex differences must be made with caution (Wolpoff, 1976). In most living primates, males have larger canines than females (Plavcan & van Schaik, 1997), and similar differences are evident in all of the *Australopithecus* and *Homo* species. It has been estimated that male A. afarensis canines were 128% the size of female canines, a degree of dimorphism in between that of living chimpanzees and gorillas. The magnitude of this difference has decreased since the emergence of *Homo*, but a small male advantage is still found (Frayer & Wolpoff, 1985).

The physical size of our ancestors can be estimated on the basis of the relation between the size of certain bones (e.g., the femur) and overall body size and weight in living humans and other primates. The equations used to predict human (or other primate) body weight are then applied to fossil bones to yield estimates of the weight and size of extinct species. Although different methods can yield somewhat different estimates, the pattern of sex differences is the same. For instance, some methods suggest that A. afarensis males were more than twice the weight of A. afarensis females, whereas other methods yield a more moderate sex difference (Richmond & Jungers, 1995; Wolpoff, 1976).

One of the most extensive analyses of these relations suggests a male advantage in body weight in all Australopithecus and Homo species, several of which are illustrated in Figure 5.6 (McHenry, 1992, 1994b; McHenry & Coffing, 2000). On the basis of these estimates, A. anamensis is the most dimorphic, with a sex difference in between that of modern chimpanzees and gorillas and perhaps as large as that found in gorillas (Leakey et al., 1998). A. afarensis and A. africanus were also quite dimorphic, perhaps more so than shown in Figure 5.6 (Richmond & Jungers, 1995). Even if our direct ancestors were Paranthropus, the results do not change (McHenry & Coffing, 2000). I do not show H. habilis in Figure 5.6 because the estimates for the sexual dimorphism vary widely. The estimates of the sex difference for H. erectus are consistent with and similar to that found in modern humans.

The evolutionary pattern is clear: Males were considerably larger than females in our distant ancestors—perhaps as sexually dimorphic as modern gorillas—and this degree of dimorphism decreased substantially with the emergence of H. erectus. The decrease was due to more dramatic increases in the size of our female than male ancestors. McHenry and Coffing (2000) estimated

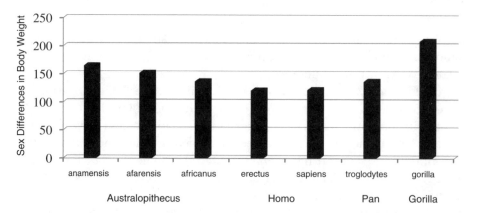

Figure 5.6. Estimated percentage of male body weight to female body weight for various species of *Australopithecus, Homo,* extant chimpanzees (*Pan troglodytes*), and gorillas (*Gorilla gorilla*). The estimated weight of male *A. afarensis* is about 150% that of female *A. afarensis*.

that males of A. *afarensis* were 151 cm in height and 51 kg in weight (i.e., about 4 feet 11 inches and 100 pounds), whereas females were 105 cm in height and 29 kg in weight (i.e., about 3 feet 5 inches and 64 pounds). Modern size for males and females emerged with H. *erectus*, possibly before this.

Brain Size

As I cover in detail in chapter 12 (in the section titled Brain Size and Organization), men's brains are about 15% larger than women's brains, but this declines to about a 10% difference once body size is controlled (Pakkenberg & Gundersen, 1997; Rushton & Ankney, 1996). In other words, about one third of the sex difference in brain size is due to allometry—larger bodies are generally associated with larger brains (Harvey, Martin, & Clutton-Brock, 1987). The allometric relation means that selection that favored an increase in body size might also result in an incidental increase in brain size, an increase in brain size in the absence of direct selection for improved perceptual or cognitive competencies. This is not the whole story, it seems: As I reviewed in chapter 3 of this volume (in the section titled Cognitive Competition), the dynamics of sexual selection can directly lead to the evolution of sex differences in brain size, organization, and in the specific cognitive competencies that facilitate competition and choice; I extend this to human sex differences in brain and cognition in chapters 12 and 13.

As found in our species, the brains of male macaques and male chimpanzees are about 10% larger than the brains of female conspecifics after controlling for body size (Falk, Froese, Sade, & Dudek, 1999; Herndon, Tigges, Anderson, Klumpp, & McClure, 1999). The implication is that the human sex difference may have deep evolutionary roots. Darwin (1871), in fact, speculated that the social components of male–male competition may have contributed to brain and cognitive evolution in primates. The evidence is consistent with this hypothesis but not conclusive. Pawlowski, Lowen, and Dunbar (1998) and Sawaguchi (1997) found a relation between the intensity of male–male competition and size of the neocortex across primate species. Sawaguchi found that the cross-species correlation between relative size of the neocortex (controlling for overall brain size) and indices of the intensity of male–male competition is quite high ($rs = .65–.66$). Lindenfors, Nunn, and Barton (2007) found the relations to be nuanced. For males, brain areas that support the sensorimotor aspects of fighting are larger for species with intense physical male–male competition. For females, the size of the neocortex is larger for female-bonded species than for their more solitary cousins.

The question of whether sex differences in brain size existed in our ancestors after controlling for the sex difference in body size cannot be answered at this time because of difficulties identifying the sex of fossil skulls.

Scientists do know, however, that there have been substantial increases in brain size and changes in organization for both males and females since the emergence of australopithecines. As shown in Figure 5.7, there has been a threefold increase in brain volume since *A. afarensis* (Falk et al., 2000; R. L. Holloway, 1973; McHenry, 1994b; Tobias, 1987; B. Wood & Collard, 1999). These values are potentially confounded by species differences in body size, but the encephalization quotient (EQ) can be used to control for this confound; EQ provides an index of brain size relative to that of a mammal of the same body weight (Jerison, 1973). The EQ of the typical mammal is 1.0 and that of chimpanzees is 2.0. For modern humans, EQ estimates typically range between 5.0 and 6.0 (McHenry, 1994a; Ruff, Trinkaus, & Holliday, 1997). The bottom portion of Figure 5.7 presents EQ values for our ancestors as a percentage of that of modern humans. The EQ of australopithecines is greater than that of chimpanzees but less than 50% that of modern humans. The EQ

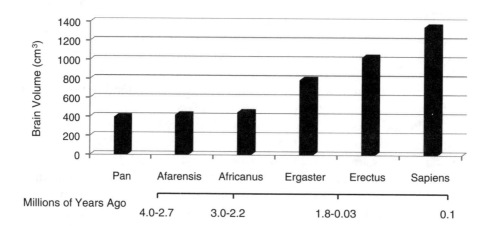

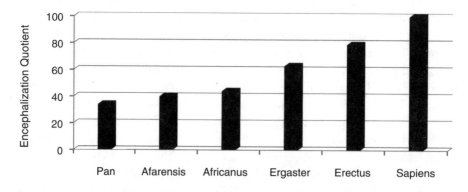

Figure 5.7. Estimated brain volumes (top) and encephalization quotients (EQ, bottom) for chimpanzees (Pan) and selected species of *Australopithecus* and *Homo*. The EQ is represented as a percentage of that of modern humans.

of *H. habilis* was slightly more than 50% of modern humans. Large increases in EQ were evident with the emergence of *H. ergaster* and *H. erectus*.

Although scientists cannot directly estimate the brain volumes of our male and female ancestors, several patterns suggest these differences became smaller during human evolution. First, the more substantial increase in the size of females than males since *A. afarensis* necessarily—as an outcome of the allometry—resulted in a reduction of the sex difference in absolute brain size. Second, there have been substantial reductions in variation in brain size across individuals since *A. afarensis* (R. L. Holloway, Broadfield, & Yuan, 2004). For modern humans, individual differences in brain size vary around the mean of about 1,400 cm³. The variation around the mean for *A. afarensis* is more than double the variation found for modern humans, and the variation for *H. erectus* is about 1.5 times that found for modern humans. In other words, variability in brain volume appears to have decreased since *A. afarensis*, and one corresponding result has almost certainly been a reduction in the magnitude of individual differences as well as sex differences in brain volume.

Evolutionary Models

Reconstructing the evolution of social behavior on the basis of the fossil record is at best an educated guess, and any such model needs to be treated as such. Nevertheless, when scientists take patterns in the fossil record and combine them with what is known about sex differences in living primates, the field of possibilities is substantially narrowed (Foley & Lee, 1989). In the sections that follow, I narrow these possibilities for the main components of sexual selection and end with discussion of the relation between sexual selection and the sexual division of labor.

Male–Male Competition

One of the most striking patterns in our ancestors is the male advantage in physical and canine size. Because these sex differences are found in living primates and other species with physical male–male competition and polygyny (e.g., Plavcan & van Schaik, 1997; Plavcan et al., 1995), these must have been central features of our evolutionary history (R. D. Alexander et al., 1979; Ghiglieri, 1987). Our ancestors' sexual dimorphisms, however, do not explain the intensity of male–male competition (i.e., the degree to which alpha males dominated mating), whether the competition was largely one-on-one, coalitional, or changed during human evolution and whether there was paternal investment. I use current human sex differences in these and other areas—described in chapters 6, 7, and 8—to provide an anchor for making inferences about sexual selection in our ancestors and about evolutionary change in reproductive dynamics.

As I cover in chapter 7 (in the section titled Marriage Systems), in societies in which monogamy is not socially or ecologically imposed, dominant males are polygynous and may have three or more wives (Murdock, 1981). Polygyny occurs with moderate levels of paternal investment and in a modal social context of male philopatry and male kin-based coalitional competition (see the section titled Male–Male Competition, chap. 8, this volume). These are the end points, to date at least, of an evolutionary process that began well before A. anamensis. A common approach to anchoring the beginning point in the evolutionary process is to compare human behavior with the behavior of our closest relatives, the chimpanzee and less frequently the bonobo (de Waal & Lanting, 1997; Kano, 1992; Wrangham, 1999). This is a reasonable starting point in some respects. The EQ of chimpanzees, bonobos (not shown in Figure 5.7), australopithecines, and presumably the common ancestor are very similar. Although bonobo males do not show consistent coalitional aggression, male–male physical aggression is common and presumably a feature of the ancestor common to chimpanzees and bonobos. The most common focus of the human–chimpanzee comparison is coalitional male–male competition, which is rare in primates (e.g., Wrangham & Peterson, 1996).

Coalitional competition aside, there are critical differences between chimpanzees and bonobos and between chimpanzees, bonobos, and humans that call into question the use of these species as the anchor point for understanding sexual selection during human evolution. In terms of physical size, bonobos are about as sexually dimorphic as chimpanzees, but both species are less dimorphic than the estimates for A. anamensis and A. afarensis. The magnitude of the sexual dimorphism for these australopithecines suggests intense one-on-one male–male competition, which in turn is most consistent with either single-male harems or solitary males that controlled territories that encompassed the territories of several females (Ghiglieri, 1987). Unlike men, male chimpanzees and bonobos show little to no paternal investment. And unlike women, female chimpanzees and bonobos show conspicuous estrous swellings and mate promiscuously. On the basis of these and other differences, Geary and Flinn (2001) proposed that modern humans' ancestors might have been more similar to our distant cousin, the gorilla (see also Lovejoy, 1981). This is because moving from a gorilla-like pattern to the current human pattern would require fewer evolutionary changes than needed to move from a chimpanzee-like or bonobo-like pattern to the human pattern.

The modal social organization of gorillas is often described as isolated single-male harems, which typically include one reproductive male, two to four females, and their offspring (Fossey, 1984; A. B. Taylor, 1997). There is, however, considerable variation in this social structure, especially in groups of mountain gorillas (*Gorilla beringei*). Robbins (1999) found that 40% of these groups included several, sometimes related (e.g., brothers), males. Encounters between groups occur about once every 5 weeks and provide females their only opportunity to transfer from one group to another. During these encounters, physical male–male competition over females and male mate guarding are common (Robbins & Sawyer, 2007). Groups of lowland gorillas (*Gorilla gorilla*) maintain single-male harems, but the groups are less isolated. Several families will occupy the same geographical region, and encounters between groups are often friendly, especially among the males (Bradley, Doran-Sheehy, Lukas, Boesch, & Vigilant, 2004; Douadi et al., 2007). DNA fingerprinting indicates that males in neighboring groups are typically related, and females are often related within groups. The kinship organization of male lowland gorillas provides a ready explanation for the lower levels of male–male competition during group encounters in comparison to that found with mountain gorillas.

There are potentially important similarities between families of lowland gorillas and human families. Unlike the unrestricted mating of female chimpanzees (during estrous) or bonobos, and a corresponding low level of paternity certainty (de Waal & Lanting, 1997; Goodall, 1986), adult male and female gorillas often form long-term social relationships. DNA fingerprinting indicates that male lowland gorillas show high levels of paternity certainty (greater than 95%; Bradley et al., 2004). For mountain gorillas in multimale groups, dominant males sire 70% to 80% of the offspring, and other males in the group sire the remaining offspring (Nsubuga, Robbins, Boesch, & Vigilant, 2008). In the absence of intergroup encounters, behavioral observation reveals low levels of male mate guarding (e.g., compared with chimpanzees) and high levels of affiliation with their offspring. "Associated males hold, cuddle, nuzzle, examine, and groom infants, and infants turn to these males in times of distress" (Whitten, 1987, p. 346). Female gorillas do not typically have conspicuous sexual swellings and primarily solicit copulations behaviorally (Harcourt & Stewart, 2007).

The genetic findings indicate that the male-kinship structure for lowland gorillas is close to that currently found with humans (Bradley et al., 2004). The primary difference is the degree of cooperation among adult males as related to coalitional competition. Such coalitions could easily evolve from the social structure described by Bradley et al. The formation of more closely knit male kinships would result in greater proximity of males and through this the creation of the multimale, multifemale communities found in all human societies (Foley & Lee, 1989; Ghiglieri, 1987; Rodseth et al., 1991). Indeed, if gorilla families were placed in closer proximity and if male-kinship bonds were strengthened, the common structure of human families, including polygynous families, in traditional societies would be formed. The formation of male coalitions would lessen the importance of physical size and strength during male–male competition (Plavcan et al., 1995) and place a premium on the brain and cognitive systems that support the formation and functioning of these coalitions. The predicted result is the observed pattern of an evolutionary reduction in physical sexual dimorphisms and an increase in brain size.

Female Choice

The sexual dimorphisms in *Australopithecus* and *Homo* species do not clarify issues related to female choice as well as they do about male–male competition. I believe, nevertheless, that scientists can safely assume that female choice was an important aspect of our ancestors' sexual dynamics. Studies of living primates and traditional societies today (see the section titled Women's Mate Choices, chap. 7) suggest some scenarios for the evolution of female choice are more likely than others. In particular, consideration of female choice in gorillas and in primates that live in multimale, multifemale communities may provide useful insights. I am not proposing that female choice in our ancestors was the same as that found in these species, but rather the pattern in these species provides a range of possibilities for understanding our female ancestors.

Female gorillas emigrate from their birth group when they reach reproductive maturity if the alpha male dies and sometimes during intergroup encounters. The factors that influence female choice include male protection from infanticide by nonpaternal males and large predators, physical qualities of the male, and the results of male–male fights (Caillaud, Levréro, Gatti, Ménard, & Raymond, 2008; Fossey, 1984; Robbins et al., 2004). A male's failure to protect an infant from the attack of another male can result in the mother abandoning this mate and joining the group of the infanticidal male (Robbins, Robbins, Gerald-Steklis, & Steklis, 2007). Caillaud et al. reported lowland males with at least one mate are larger and more muscular than males without mates and that males with larger head crests are more likely to have multiple mates. The head crest is composed of adipose and fibrous tissue and may be an indicator of male health. Once females choose a mate, they tend to maintain a long-term relationship with this male as long as he maintains his health and social status (Harcourt & Stewart, 2007).

An evolved bias to form patrilocal multimale, multifemale communities would have resulted in further complexities in the dynamics of female choice. For females, one potential benefit of being part of a multimale group might have been a reduced risk of infanticide by extragroup males if one of the group's dominant males died. With gorillas, the death of the group's lone silverback makes it necessary for the females and any offspring to transfer to another group, and the new dominant male almost always kills the infants of these females (Harcourt & Stewart, 2007). At the same time, the competitive benefits of a large male coalition likely created pressures to increase within-group cooperation among males and this likely resulted in less polygyny; a male's cooperation in defending the group increases when he has the opportunity to sire offspring. One corresponding cost is that many females would have been paired with lower quality males. In the context of multimale communities, these pairings heighten the potential for extrapair relationships and the potential benefits to females if they cuckold lower quality partners. In this situation, paternity certainty would have been lower than that found in lowland gorillas (i.e., less than 95%) but much higher than that found in chimpanzees or bonobos (near zero). High levels of paternity certainty follow if this paternal investment were maintained by the evolution of mechanisms that strengthened pair bonding, such as continuous female sexual receptivity (K. MacDonald, 1992).

Female–Female Competition and Male Choice

With the formation of multimale, multifemale communities; a corresponding reduction in polygyny; and the maintenance of paternal investment, females would compete more intensely over high-quality mates. A focus on female–female competition and male choice would have almost certainly included female traits that signaled fertility and the likelihood of successfully rearing of offspring. These traits likely included the females' age, whether they had successfully given birth, and their success at raising offspring.

Sexual Division of Labor

As an alternative to sexual selection, some scientists have proposed that many human sexual differences evolved as a result of the sexual division of labor and cooperative child rearing, that is male hunting and female gathering and child care (e.g., H. E. Fisher, 1982; Lovejoy, 1981). Hunting has clearly been an important feature of human evolution (K. Hill, 1982), but it is not likely to be the evolutionary source of many human sexual dimorphisms. The teeth of australopithecines were primarily adapted for eating fruits and seeds (Teaford & Ungar, 2000). Although they may have eaten some meat, the extreme male advantage in physical size preceded the evolutionary emergence, probably with *Homo*, of hunting and meat eating as a major feature of our ancestors' subsistence (Aiello & Wheeler, 1995). Further, a sexual division of labor is common in many species, including many socially monogamous species, in which there are small or no sex differences in physical size (J. M. Black, 1996; Clutton-Brock, 1991; Leighton, 1987).

I propose that sexual selection is the primary source of many human sex differences and that the division of labor emerged later—that the physical, behavioral, and cognitive sex differences many ascribe to the division of labor are in fact due largely to sexual and sometimes natural selection. There is no reproduction-related sexual division of labor in the chimpanzee, but the sex difference in the pattern of hunting and foraging found in many traditional societies is found in this species (Goodall, 1986; McGrew, 1992). Male chimpanzees hunt in a more organized, systematic, and efficient way than do females. Because of their greater size and aggressiveness, male chimpanzees are also able to capture a wider range of prey. As a result of these differences in hunting efficiency, meat represents a relatively larger proportion of males' than females' diet. The female diet, in contrast, consists of a much higher proportion of ants and termites. The ants and termites are found in fixed locations that are frequently surveyed; this is similar to human foraging (Silverman & Eals, 1992).

The reliance of female chimpanzees on ants and termites as sources of protein and their foraging strategies for obtaining these foods has almost certainly been shaped by natural selection, whereas the larger size and aggressiveness of the male chimpanzee is related to male–male competition (Goodall, 1986). The physical and behavioral tendencies of male chimpanzees have been shaped by sexual selection and are co-opted—used for a purpose for which they did not originally evolve—for hunting. Hunting then provides a valuable resource that is used for survival and sometimes to enhance mating opportunities. Once meat is systematically used to enhance mating opportunities, it can potentially become a source of male–male competition and female choice (Symons, 1979) and thus subject to added selection pressures. This is evident today across traditional societies in which the ability of men and women to perform roles associated with the traditional division of labor influences mate selection and retention. In an extensive cross-cultural review of marital relationships, Betzig (1989) noted,

> inadequate support is reported as cause for divorce in 21 societies and ascribed exclusively to the husband in all but one unspecified case. . . . An interesting thing about these economic factors is that they are so clearly segregated according to sex. Husbands are divorced for failing to provide material means, wives for failing to process them. (p. 664)

These cross-cultural results indicate that skill at performing the tasks associated with the sexual division of labor influences mate-choice decisions and is therefore under the influence of sexual selection. Male provisioning is now a component of male–male competition and a feature of female choice in many cultures, but the original evolution of the sex differences that enable males to provide certain resources more efficiently (e.g., meat through hunting) or compete more aggressively than females to obtain these resources did not evolve as a means for cooperative child rearing, even if the net effect today is often cooperative child rearing (Crano & Aronoff, 1978).

CONCLUSION

The dynamics of social relationships within primate communities are strongly influenced by the different ways in which males and females pursue their reproductive interests. In most nonmonogamous species, male–male competition is a very conspicuous feature of these dynamics, and as such, it is not surprising that this competition is one of the better studied features of primate social behavior (Smuts, 1987). Male–male competition is related to the sexual strivings of these individuals, and is based on physical contest and in a few species on the ability to form and maintain coalitions with other males. The prototypical result is larger and more aggressive males than females (Plavcan et al., 1995). Whether they involve one-on-one or coalitional competition, male–male contests result in a dominance hierarchy, and the male's position in this hierarchy has important reproductive consequences (e.g., Dixson et al., 1993). Socially dominant males attempt to control and are often successful at controlling the social and sexual behavior of other group members, particularly estrous females. DNA fingerprints to establish paternity indicate that this mate guarding consistently, but not always, provides dominant males with a reproductive advantage (e.g., Altmann et al., 1996).

Male striving for social dominance is not the whole story. The alternative mating strategies used by less dominant males combined with female choice often undermine the reproductive strivings of dominant males (Perloe, 1992). One such male strategy involves a consortship, one-on-one male–female relationships, and sometimes long-term friendships (Dunbar, 1984; Smuts, 1985; Tutin, 1979). At times, consortships are controlled by subordinate males; these males aggressively coerce females into the relationship (M. N. Muller et al., 2007). At other times, female choice is involved, especially with long-term friendships. For the female, the development of friendships with one or more males appears to be a strategy designed to elicit male support during times of social conflict and to elicit male investment in her offspring (Hrdy, 1979; Smuts & Gubernick, 1992). For the male, the development of such relationships increases the likelihood of siring offspring and sometimes results in direct investment in their own offspring (Buchan et al., 2003).

Females typically develop these friendships with relatively dominant males, presumably because these males are better able to control social dynamics than are subordinates (Robinson, 1982; Smuts, 1985). In other cases, the mating priorities established through male–male competition and female choice conflict, and in many of these cases female choice prevails. Male primates also show preferences in their choice of mating partners, although they are not as choosy as females. Males prefer to mate with females that are the most likely to conceive and the most likely to successfully rear offspring (M. N. Muller et al., 2006). For species in which males provide individual benefits to a female and her offspring, some level of female–female competition over affiliations with such males is predicted and found (Palombit et al., 2001).

By combining the reproductive strategies found in living primates with the pattern of physical sex differences in our ancestors, scientists can draw inferences about the nature of sexual selection during human evolution. The consistent finding of larger males than females indicates that male–male competition was a prominent feature of human evolution and was very likely associated with a polygynous mating system (R. D. Alexander et al., 1979; Ghiglieri, 1987). Following Geary and Flinn (2001), and using the social structure of gorillas as a model, I suggest that the starting point of this feature of sexual selection was one-on-one male–male competition for control of harems, followed by the evolution of male kin-based coalitions. The latter would help to explain the evolutionary reduction in the physical dimorphisms in our ancestors and the corresponding expansion of brain size. The formation of coalitions would reduce the intensity of polygyny; result in the formation of multimale, multifemale communities; and greatly complicate other aspects of sexual selection and male–female relationships. I describe how these social complexities might have contributed to the evolutionary expansion in brain size and EQ in both sexes elsewhere (Geary, 2005b).

The evolution of female choice is more difficult to reconstruct, but patterns in living primates and species that live in multimale, multifemale communities help to narrow the possibilities. Most likely, female choice was influenced by the social and other resources the male could provide (K. Hill, 1982; Smuts, 1985). Social support would have involved some form of protection of the female and her offspring as well as offspring care. A female preference for material support, such as meat provided through hunting, most likely emerged only after the evolution of a female preference for social support. In either case, it has been argued that human sexuality, concealed ovulation and the more or less continuous sexual receptivity of women, evolved as an adaptation to increase the stability of female–male pair bonding and to facilitate paternal investment in offspring (H. E. Fisher, 1982; K. MacDonald, 1992). If the family structure of australopithecines was similar to that found with gorillas (Lovejoy, 1971), then paternal care and long-term male–female relationships have been part of our evolutionary history for millions of years. The formation of multimale, multifemale communities would have resulted in benefits for strengthening (not creating) pair bonding mechanisms that may have already existed.

6

EVOLUTION OF FATHERHOOD

One of the most remarkable features of human reproduction is men's high degree of affiliation with and investment in their children. Such investment might not seem unusual for readers with investing fathers, but it is a riddle in terms of the broader evolutionary picture. Paternal investment is found in less than 5% of mammalian species (see the section titled Parental Investment, chap. 3), and when compared with these species, humans are different. In mammals, high levels of paternal investment tend to be found when family groups are isolated, as with *Callithrix* monkeys (Goldizen, 2003), or when females produce large litters, as with *Canids* (Asa & Valdespino, 1998). Human reproduction occurs in large multimale, multifemale communities, and women have relatively few children during their life span. There is some evidence of paternal protection of males' offspring in one species of savannah baboon (*Papio cynocephalus*) that lives in multimale, multifemale communities (Buchan, Alberts, Silk, & Altmann, 2003), but this level of investment pales in comparison with that usually found in human societies.

I argued in chapter 5 that men's parental investment evolved from a gorilla-like family structure, and an evolved bias to form multimale, multifemale communities around male kin-based coalitions is more recent, though may still date back to *Homo erectus*. The formation of these communities results in many added layers of complexity to human social relationships (Geary, 2005b) and in the potential for humans to form a wide variety of marriage systems and family types (Geary & Flinn, 2001; Pasternak, C. R. Ember, & M. Ember, 1997; see Table 7.1, chap. 7, this volume). The degree to which fathers invest in individual children varies across monogamous and polygynous (described subsequently) marriage systems (Flinn & Low, 1986), and the importance of fathers' investment varies with the extent to which other kin can compensate for the loss or reduction of this investment (Flinn & Leone, 2006; Sear & Mace, 2008).

Regardless of the evolutionary history and specific social dynamics, the maintenance of men's parental investment is subject to the same basic evolutionary trade-offs described for other species in chapter 4. I organize the first section of this chapter around these trade-offs, specifically, benefits to offspring and costs to fathers. In the second and third sections, I focus on sex differences in the level of parental investment and on the many factors that influence the expression (or not) of men's parenting, respectively.

TRADE-OFFS OF MEN'S PARENTING

In a review of child mortality from ancient Greece to modern-day hunter–gatherer societies, Volk and Atkinson (2008) estimated that 50% of children died before reaching adolescence. On the basis of patterns found in other species (see Exhibit 4.1, chap. 4), men's parenting is predicted to have substantively reduced these mortality risks in ancestral environments or otherwise provided children with a social competitive, and thereby a reproductive, advantage over their father-absent peers. Men's parenting also would not have evolved or be maintained without reductions in the costs of lost mating opportunities and the risk of cuckoldry. I therefore examined men's and women's reproductive strategies as they potentially influence these costs.

Benefits to Children

I examined the relation between paternal investment and the physical and social well-being of children in existing populations and throughout the history of Western culture. The results from both sets of reviews support the prediction that men's parental investment substantially improves children's well-being.

Physical Well-Being

Information on whether fathers reduce mortality rates in infancy and childhood is scant in comparison with the literature on the social and psychological correlates of paternal investment. The difficulty stems in part from the very low infant and child mortality rates in modern societies, societies in which most of the research on fatherhood is conducted. Fortunately, there is some information on the relation between paternal factors (e.g., occupation) and childhood mortality rates in preindustrial Europe and the United States, and there are a few studies of this relation in extant developing, hunter-gatherer, and intermediate (e.g., some horticulture) societies; I refer to the latter two as *traditional*. Even when paternal factors correlate with child mortality risks, a strong causal relation cannot be drawn. In species in which males invest in offspring, assortative mating results in higher quality males pairing with higher quality females (Parker & Simmons, 1996). The higher survival rates of these pairs' offspring cannot be due solely to paternal investment but rather to the qualities of both parents. Despite this and other potential confounds, paternal investment does appear to lower infant and child mortality risks in some human groups, but the magnitude of this effect cannot be determined.

Mortality in Traditional Societies. K. Hill and Hurtado's (1996) extensive ethnography and demography of the Ache, a hunter-gatherer society in Paraguay, provides one of the most extensive assessments of the relation between paternal investment and child mortality rates in a traditional society. For forest-dwelling Ache, one out of three children dies before reaching the age of 15 years, with highly significant differences for father-present and father-absent children. Father absence due to death or divorce triples the probability of child death due to illness and doubles the risk of being killed by other Ache men or being kidnapped and presumably killed or sold into slavery by other groups (Hurtado & K. Hill, 1992). Overall, fathers' absence at any point prior to children's 15th birthday is associated with a mortality rate of more than 45% as compared with a mortality rate of about 20% for children whose fathers reside with them until their 15th birthday.

Death due to sickness is related, in part, to the adequacy of the child's diet, and in many traditional societies, paternal provisioning provides an important component of this diet. The Ache share hunting proceeds among all members of the group, and thus fathers do not directly provision their children. Nevertheless, the children of skilled hunters have lower mortality rates than children of less skilled hunters (K. Hill & Kaplan, 1988); this is also true in other hunter-gatherer societies (E. A. Smith, 2004; Wiessner, 2002). It appears that these children are better treated than the children of less skilled hunters. K. Hill and Kaplan indicated that better treatment involves a greater tolerance "of food begging by the children of good hunters" (p. 283), a greater willingness of band members to stay in one location to nurse the ill child of a good hunter, and greater alloparenting of these children. The Ache, however, are not generally willing to invest in the well-being of genetically unrelated children and, as noted, often kill children whose fathers have died or left the group (K. Hill & Hurtado, 1996).

Across a variety of other cultures, Sear and Mace (2008) found no consistent relation between fathers' investment and mortality risks for infants and young children. Sometimes fathers mattered, and sometimes they did not. With the death of the father or following a divorce, other kin, typically maternal grandmothers, are often able to compensate for the lost paternal investment (see also Hrdy, 2005; O'Connell, Hawkes, & Blurton Jones, 1999). As mentioned, even when a father's skill at provisioning his family is related to child mortality risks, a causal link cannot be made (Blurton Jones, Hawkes, & O'Connell, 1997; Borgerhoff Mulder, 1990; Irons, 1979). This is because culturally successful men tend to marry women who have qualities that will improve the well-being of their children, and it may be the mother's contributions that have the strongest effects on child mortality. For the Hadza, a hunter-gatherer group in Tanzania, successful hunters have more surviving children than less successful hunters, but "successful hunters tend to have wives who are more efficient foragers than other women" (Blurton Jones et al., 1997, p. 301).

Protection from other men may be the one area in which other kin may not be able to compensate for loss of a father. As with the Ache, the presence of a stepfather is associated with increased mortality in young children in some human groups (Sear, Steele, McGregor, & Mace, 2002) and is associated with ongoing low levels of conflict and poor health in many other contexts (Flinn, 1992), as discussed in the section titled Physical Health in this chapter. Fathers and other male kin may also be critical for helping young men establish sociopolitical standing within the social world of adult men, and for both men's and women's later marriage prospects. These issues have not been well addressed in studies of parental contributions to their children and adolescents.

Mortality in Developing Societies. As in traditional societies, the importance of fathers varies across developing and preindustrial societies (Sear & Mace, 2008), but the overall pattern indicates that fathers can make a difference. In developing countries in South America, Africa, and Asia there is a consistent relation between marital status and infant and child mortality rates (United Nations, 1985).

> Both univariate and multivariate results show that mortality of children is raised if the woman is not currently married, if she has married more than once or if she is in a polygamous union. . . . Overall, it appears that there is a strong, direct association between stable family relationships and low levels of child mortality, although the direction of causation cannot be inferred from the data. (p 227)

Indonesian children of divorced parents have a 12% higher mortality rate than children of monogamously married couples. The same relation was found in 11 of the 14 developing nations surveyed, but it is possible that the death of a child increases divorce rates rather than paternal absence increasing mortality risks. Death of the father is generally associated with higher infant and child mortality rates than is divorce, suggesting that father absence independent of maternal characteristics directly contributes to these risks.

The same pattern was evident in preindustrial Europe. During the 19th and early 20th centuries in Sweden, infant mortality rates were 1.5 to 3 times higher for children born to unmarried mothers than children born to married couples (Brändström, 1997). The same is true of the Netherlands from 1885 to 1940 (Kok, van Poppel, & Kruse, 1997). The direct importance of fathers is confirmed by the finding that the mortality of these "illegitimate" children was lower if the father provided economic support to the child and mother and by the finding of higher mortality of "legitimate" children if the father died. A relation between paternal provisioning and infant and child mortality risks has in fact been reported throughout preindustrial and industrializing Europe and the United States (Hed, 1987; Herlihy, 1965; Klindworth & Voland, 1995; Morrison, Kirshner, & Molho, 1977; Schultz, 1991).

A. Reid's (1997) analysis of mortality risks in early 20th century England and Wales suggested that "a child's chance of survival was strongly conditioned by who its parents were, or more precisely, by what job its father did" (p. 151). The conclusion was based on a strong relation between socioeconomic status (SES), defined entirely by fathers' occupation, and mortality risks. In comparison to children whose fathers were unskilled laborers, the infants of professional fathers had a 54% lower mortality rate. The children of unemployed fathers, in contrast, had a 38% higher mortality rate than the children of unskilled laborers. If one controlled for SES, environment (e.g., urban vs. agricultural setting), maternal age, and other factors, the children (less than 3 years of age) of working mothers had a 34% higher mortality rate than did children whose mothers did not work. If care was provided to these children while the mother worked (e.g., through kin), the children had a 17% higher mortality rate than did children whose mothers did not work. These effects appear to have been related to whether the infant was consistently breast-fed. In 1900 France, 7% of breast-fed infants died and 37% of bottle-fed infants died (Rollet, 1997). Paternal employment was important because it often increased breast-feeding by allowing the mother to stay at home with the child (A. Reid, 1997).

In an extensive analysis of birth, death, and demographic records from 18th century Berlin, Schultz (1991) found a strong correlation ($r = .74$) between SES and infant and child mortality rates; SES was defined, at least in part, by paternal occupation. Infant (birth to 1 year) mortality rates were about 10% for aristocrats but more than 40% for laborers and unskilled technicians. "A senior official of the welfare authorities (*Armenbehörde*) observed in 1769 that among the poor weavers of Friedrichstadt 75 out of every 100 children borne died before they reached [the age of 12 years]" (Schultz, 1991,

p. 243). During the 1437–1438 and 1449–1450 black plague epidemics in Florence, Italy, child mortality rates increased 5- to 10-fold and varied inversely with SES (Morrison et al., 1977); a similar relation has been found in some traditional societies today (Kiros & Hogan, 2001). In many contexts, the resources provided by fathers also allowed the family to live in healthier environments, provide a more stable food supply, and sometimes hire servants, all of which contributed to the relation between SES and infant and child mortality rates in industrializing Europe (A. Reid, 1997).

In contexts in which food and health care are more or less readily available, child mortality risks drop considerably (K. Hill & Hurtado, 1996; United Nations, 1985). Ache living on reservations have much lower child mortality rates than forest-living Ache. Health care is available on the reservation, and families are able to engage in small-scale gardening, work for wages, and accumulate material resources. Even with lower overall mortality rates, paternal investment is still correlated with the survival rate of children, especially infants. Over the course of about 25 years, a fivefold variation emerged in the net worth of families living on the reservation, and K. Hill and Hurtado (1996) found that "a man's SES is a strong predictor of his offspring's survival to adulthood" (p. 303).

Physical Health. The relation between SES and the physical well-being of children is still found in industrial nations today (I. Reid, 1998). In a review of the literature on the relation between SES—defined as a composite of income, educational level, and occupational status in industrial societies—Adler et al. (1994) concluded that

> individuals in lower social status groups have the highest rates of morbidity and mortality within most human populations. Moreover, studies of the entire SES hierarchy show that differences in social position relate to morbidity and mortality even at the upper levels of the hierarchy. (p. 22)

The relation between SES and health holds for all members of the family, not just the primary wage earner, and is not simply related to access to health care or to differences in health-related behaviors (e.g., smoking). Individuals' SES also influences how well they are treated by other people and the degree to which they can control the activities of everyday life, both of which influence physical health (Marmot, 2004; Sapolsky, 2005). Across industrial societies today, paternal income and occupational status are an important, and sometimes the sole, determinant of the family's SES. Given this, paternal investment is correlated with the physical well-being of a man's children, even in contexts with low infant and child mortality rates.

Flinn and his colleagues have provided clues as to the potential relation between paternal investment and the physical health of children (Flinn & England, 1997; Flinn, Quinlan, Decker, Turner, & England, 1996), although causal relations cannot be drawn from these data. In this multiyear study, the family environment, the stress hormone cortisol, and testosterone were assessed for children and adults in a rural village in the West Indies (Flinn et al., 1996). It was found that fathers' presence or absence was related to the cortisol and testosterone levels of boys but not girls. In comparison with boys residing with their biological father, father-absent boys and boys living with a stepfather had either unusually low or highly variable cortisol levels and weighed less. An analysis of adults who grew up in father-present or father-absent households also revealed significant differences: As adults, father-absent men had higher cortisol levels and lower testosterone levels than did their father-present peers. The endocrine profile of father-absent men suggested chronically high stress levels, which can significantly increase the risk for health problems (e.g., Sapolsky, 2005). Related studies suggested that prolonged parental conflict pre- and postdivorce increases girls' and boys' risk for a variety of health problems in childhood and when they become adults (Troxel & Matthews, 2004). A poor postdivorce relationship with their father is associated with a higher frequency of minor health problems in early adulthood for both sexes (Fabricius & Luecken, 2007).

Reproductive Maturation. As I described in chapter 4 ("Sexual Selection and Life History"), life history is the suite of traits that define the species' reproductive development, the factors (e.g., predation risk) that influence the evolution of this pattern (e.g., fast maturation), and the conditions that can influence variation in the here-and-now expression of one or more of these traits (e.g., age of first reproduction). The core human life history traits include age of sexual maturation, sexual debut, first childbirth, and lifetime number of children. Individual differences in the expression of each of these traits is moderately heritable, and many or all of them may be influenced by a core set of genes that biases individuals toward heavy investment in a few children or lower investment in many children (de Bruin et al., 2001; Figueredo et al., 2006; Kirk et al., 2001). As with other species, human life history development is also influenced by early experiences and current circumstances. My focus is on the potential relation between men's parenting and their children's reproductive development; I describe the relation between early experiences and men's later focus on mating effort or parental effort in the section titled Developmental Correlates in this chapter.

In keeping with predictions of Draper and Harpending (1982) and Belsky and his colleagues (Belsky, 2007; Belsky, Steinberg, & Draper, 1991), paternal absence, marital conflict, and other early stressors are consistently, but not always (Grainger, 2004), associated with overt signs of reproductive maturation (i.e., menarche) in daughters but not sons (Belsky, 2007; Belsky et al., 2007; Bereczkei & Csanaky, 2001; Vigil, Geary, & Byrd-Craven, 2005). Low parental conflict and warm father–daughter relationships are associated with later menarche (B. J. Ellis, McFadyen-Ketchum, Dodge, Pettit, & Bates, 1999) and with monogamy and heavy investment in a small number of children in adulthood (K. MacDonald, 1992). Father absence and the presence of a step-father or maternal boyfriend are not associated with the timing of menarche but are associated with an earlier onset of sexual behavior and younger age of first childbirth (Bogaert, 2005; B. J. Ellis, 2004; B. J. Ellis et al., 1999; Quinlan, 2003). The latter results may be related to reduced involvement by biological fathers. When biological fathers are engaged with the family, they often actively monitor daughters' early romantic relationships (Flinn, 1988b), which may serve to *screen* potential mates and delay the onset of sexual activity (Byrd-Craven, Geary, Vigil, & Hoard, 2007).

Belsky et al. (2007) found that the relation between family background (e.g., maternal and paternal control) and pubertal timing was moderated in complex ways by girls' early emotional and temperamental reactivity. The details of these potential genotype-by-environment interactions remain to be sorted out, but the findings are consistent with Belsky's (1997) prediction of individual differences in children's sensitivity to rearing environment as this potentially influences later reproductive strategy, among other traits. B. J. Ellis and Essex (2007) found that low investment by both parents and higher levels of marital conflict were associated with earlier adrenarche (i.e., production of precursors to testosterone and estrogens by the adrenal glands) in boys and girls. These hormones do not necessarily result in the expression of secondary sexual characteristics but can result in behavioral changes, such as increased aggression, that can bias the dynamics of later reproductive relationships (Del Giudice, 2009b), as I detail in the section titled Developmental Correlates in this chapter.

One other interesting early influence of fathers on their daughters' later reproductive strategy is his age during her childhood. Perrett et al. (2002) found that girls with fathers older than 30 preferred older mates in adulthood. Bereczkei, Gyuris, and Weisfeld (2004) found that adopted daughters married men who looked like their adoptive father but only if they reported a good relationship with him. A similar relation between fathers' facial features and men's facial features that women find attractive has been found for biological father–daughter relationships but again only when these relationships are positive (Bereczkei, Hegedus, & Hajnal, 2009; Wiszewska, Pawlowski, & Boothroyd, 2007).

Social Well-Being

Even when paternal investment can significantly reduce infant and child mortality risks, it is not obligate; many children survive without such investment (Sear & Mace, 2008). When investment is not obligate, men can and often do facultatively shift reproductive effort from parenting to mating (see Exhibit 4.1, chap. 4., this volume). Because some level of paternal investment is found across human societies (described in the discussion that follows), it is almost certain that under some conditions and at some point in our evolutionary past our male ancestors benefited by devoting some portion of their reproductive effort to parenting instead of mating. Human paternal investment is, nonetheless, puzzling when it occurs in contexts with low infant and child mortality. Under these conditions, selection would favor men who reduced or eliminated parental effort in favor of mating effort, but many men still invest in their children. The question is why.

If our ancestors evolved in a gorilla-like family structure, as I suggested in chapter 5, then male parental investment has a very long evolutionary history. If this is true, then there is an inherent bias for men to provide some type of parental investment; on the basis of cost–benefit trade-offs, genetically based individual differences in the degree to which different men are biased toward parenting or mating are also expected. Even with an evolved bias to provide paternal investment, high-investing men may no longer benefit from this investment. All other things being equal, culturally successful high-investing men may be disadvantaged in terms of lost mating opportunities. Another possibility is that paternal investment in low-risk environments provides social competitive advantages to children, investment designed to improve the quality of offspring (J. N. Davis & Daly, 1997), and long-term reproductive benefits (e.g., number of grandchildren) to men. I address these questions in the sections that follow: First, does paternal investment improve social competitiveness? And if so, under what conditions are a smaller number of socially competitive children reproductively better than a larger number of less competitive children?

Paternal Investment and Social Competitiveness. High levels of paternal investment, including income, play time, and support of the mother, are correlated with better social and academic functioning of children as well as higher SES when children reach adulthood (Kaplan, Lancaster, & Anderson, 1998; Pleck, 1997). Despite the consistency of these findings, a causal relation remains to be firmly established (Amato, 1998; Björklund, Ginther, & Sundström, 2007; Parke & Buriel, 1998). Again, the tendency for competent men to marry competent women confounds the interpretation (Luster & Okagaki, 1993).

In keeping with such assortative mating, the strength of the relation between paternal characteristics (e.g., income) and child outcomes is reduced considerably once maternal characteristics are statistically controlled (Amato, 1998). There are, nevertheless, unique relations between paternal investment and some child outcomes. Kaplan and his colleagues found that fathers' investment of time (e.g., helping with homework) and income (e.g., paying for tutoring or college) was associated with the upward social mobility of children when maternal characteristics (e.g., years of education) were controlled (Kaplan et al., 1998; Kaplan, Lancaster, Bock, & Johnson, 1995). Amato (1998) found a similar pattern; paternal investment explained 4 times more variance in educational outcomes than maternal investment. The common finding that withdrawal of paternal investment is associated with decrements in children's later social and cultural success is consistent with these results.

Divorce is the most common reason for reduction or withdrawal of paternal investment. Children from intact families are consistently found to have social and educational advantages over children from divorced families, but again causal relations are difficult to determine. Many of the differences between children from divorced and intact families can be traced to differences in family functioning before the divorce (Cherlin et al., 1991). Still, some differences between children from intact and divorced families are found after controlling for predivorce levels of family conflict and other potential confounds. It appears that divorce results in small to moderate increases in aggressive and noncompliant behaviors in boys, and an early onset of sexual activity and lowered educational achievement for adolescents and young adults of both sexes (Amato & Keith, 1991; Belsky et al., 1991). These findings are consistent with the view that paternal investment can improve children's later social competitiveness, given the strong relation between delayed sexual activity, educational outcomes, and later SES in these societies (Belsky et al., 1991; Parke & Buriel, 1998; Vigil & Geary, 2006).

Fathers also can directly influence the social and psychological well-being of children (Parke, 1995; Parke & Buriel, 1998; Pleck, 1997; Sarkadi, Kristiansson, Oberklaid, & Bremberg, 2008). Paternal involvement in play, especially rough-and-tumble play and play in which the child is able to control or influence the dynamics of the episode, is associated with children's skill at regulating their emotional states and their later social competence. Children with fathers who regularly engage them in physical play are more likely to be socially popular—chosen as preferred playmates by their peers—than are children who do not regularly engage in this type of play (Carson, Burks, & Parke, 1993; Parke 1995). In a longitudinal study, Lindsay, Colwell, Frabutt, and MacKinnon-Lewis (2006) found that boys with a high-quality father–son relationship reported more friends and better relationships with these peers than did other boys. Other qualitative features of fathers' relationships with their children, such as positive emotional tone of the interactions and affection, are also associated with greater social and academic competencies in children (Parke & Buriel, 1998) and with fewer behavioral (e.g., aggression) and psychological (e.g., depression) difficulties (Bronte-Tinkew, Moore, & Carrano, 2006; Pleck, 1997; Sheeber, Davis, Leve, Hops, & Tildesley, 2007).

All of the relations between paternal investment and child outcomes are, however, confounded by genetic and child evocative effects, in addition to maternal effects (Parke & Buriel, 1998; Scarr & McCarthy, 1983). Motivated and intelligent children are more likely to receive education-related paternal investment than are other children (Kaplan et al., 1998), and even these effects might simply be related to shared genes (e.g., for intelligence). It is also possible that the same heritable personality traits (e.g., irritability) that make marital relationships and parenting more conflicted influence children's relationships with peers and in school settings, independent of any direct paternal influences (Rowe, 1994). Studies that incorporate genetic influences and simultaneously assess maternal and paternal effects are needed to more firmly establish a causal relation between paternal investment and child outcomes (Parke & Buriel, 1998; Reiss, 1995). At this point, it seems likely that paternal investment improves children's social competencies and their later cultural success in contexts with low infant and child mortality rates (Nettle, 2008). In fact, it is likely that paternal investment improves the cultural success of children in many contexts, through payment of dowry and bride price and inheritance of wealth and social title (Hartung, 1982; Irons, 1979; Morrison et al., 1977). But the magnitude of this effect is not known, nor is it known whether these effects vary in magnitude across cultures, families, or individual children.

Selection and Social Competitiveness. As noted, high levels of paternal investment in societies with low infant and child mortality risks and with only a small relation between SES and reproductive outcomes might result in disadvantages due to the costs of investment (e.g., lost mating opportunities). However, prior to the dramatic reductions in infant and child mortality rates in modern societies over the past 200 years and in developing and preindustrial societies today, higher SES and cultural success often lowered infant and child mortality rates (Brändström, 1997; Irons, 1979; Hartung, 1982; Hed, 1987; United Nations, 1985). In these contexts, paternal investment could be a viable reproductive strategy if it enabled children to maintain or improve their SES or cultural success in adulthood. Improved social competitiveness would enhance children's ability to acquire socially and culturally important resources in adulthood, such as marrying a competent spouse or generating wealth, which in turn would reduce the mortality risks to their children and the investor's grandchildren.

Paternal investment might have been particularly advantageous in populations subject to frequent but unpredictable population crashes if mortality varied inversely and strongly with SES, as it often did (Perrenoud, 1991). Because fluctuating mortality risks were unpredictable and disproportionately affected low-SES children, selection would have favored men who provided investment that improved their children's social competitiveness even when current mortality risks were low. My proposal and that of others (Boone & Kessler, 1999; Geary & Flinn, 2001; Kaplan et al., 1995, 1998; J. B. Lancaster & C. S. Lancaster, 1987; K. MacDonald, 1997) is that paternal investment reflects an evolved reproductive strategy that results in investment in the physical well-being of children and in their social competitiveness. In environments with intense competition over scarce resources and with fluctuating and therefore unpredictable mortality risks, paternal investment in children's social competitiveness is, in a sense, insurance against unforeseen future risks. Of course, given the uneven distribution of social capital (e.g., intelligence, social title) and wealth in human societies, not all men would have had the means to improve the social competitiveness of their children. Selection would favor a short-term quantity strategy (with one or many wives) for these men.

Costs to Fathers

Reduction of infant and child mortality risks and improvement of children's social competitiveness are not sufficient to explain the evolution and maintenance of men's parental investment. As shown in Exhibit 4.1 (see chap. 4), these benefits have to be balanced against the costs to fathers; specifically, the loss of potential mating opportunities and the risk of cuckoldry.

Women's Strategies and Men's Mating Opportunities

There are several aspects of women's sexual and social behaviors that are potential adaptations that reduce the mating opportunities of men and thereby decrease the opportunity cost of paternal investment. One of these is women's aversion to casual sex (see the section titled Male Choice, chap. 7, this volume; Oliver & Hyde, 1993; Symons, 1979). Men are variable with respect to their desire for casual partners (L. C. Miller & Fishkin, 1997) but nevertheless prefer on average more sexual partners than do women (D. M. Buss & Schmidt, 1993; R. D. Clark & Hatfield, 1989; B. J. Ellis & Symons, 1990). The sex difference results in most men having many fewer partners than they would prefer. The corollary result is most men's mating opportunities, and the attendant opportunity cost of parental investment, are substantially reduced by women's aversion to casual sex (D. M. Buss & Schmidt, 1993). A second facet of women's sexuality is relational aggression (see the section titled Female–Female Competition, chap. 8, this volume). This aspect of female–female competition involves gossiping about and attempting to socially manipulate other girls and women (Archer & Coyne, 2005; A. Campbell, 1995, 1999). One function appears to be to exclude potential competitors (over mates) from the social group (Geary, 2002b). When effective, this strategy reduces the mating opportunities of men and thus lowers the opportunity cost of paternal investment.

Concealed ovulation and continuous sexual receptivity are other features of women's sexuality that may promote paternal investment. To ensure conception, concealed ovulation requires men to maintain a longer relationship with women than is necessary for most other primate males (Dunbar, 1995), but this is not sufficient to ensure paternal investment. Once physical signs of pregnancy are evident, men could easily abandon women and avoid the cost of parenting. As noted, however, abandonment still comes at the cost of increased mortality and health risks to men's children. The combination of concealed ovulation and continuous receptivity may foster another proximate mechanism—pair bonding (L. Campbell & Ellis, 2005; K. MacDonald, 1992; L. C. Miller & Fishkin, 1997)—that maintains men's investment in their partner and children. Pair bonding and women's satisfaction with the relationship are also likely to reduce the risk of cuckoldry; that is, increase paternity certainty.

But paternity is not always certain. One strategy men use to counter the risk of being cuckolded is to vary parental investment on the basis of how much they believe the child looks like them (Burch & Gallup, 2000; Platek, Burch, Panyavin, Wasserman, & Gallup, 2002). The overall results are mixed as to whether infants and young children do in fact resemble fathers more than mothers (Christenfeld & Hill, 1995; McLain, Setters, Moulton, & Pratt, 2000); in the largest study of this kind, unrelated judges determined that newborns resemble their mothers more than their fathers, but as boys grow they resemble their fathers more than their mothers (Alvergne, Faurie, & Raymond, 2007). Regardless, women and their kin often manipulate resemblance information to maintain paternal investment, especially when paternity is ambiguous (Daly & Wilson, 1982; McLain et al., 2000). Daly and Wilson analyzed videos of new parents in maternity wards from two regions in the United States. In both regions, mothers stated that the newborn resembled the father more than the newborn resembled her; many fathers were skeptical. Follow-up studies confirmed the pattern in Canada and Mexico and suggested that it extends to maternal kin (Daly & Wilson, 1982; McLain et al., 2000; Regalski, & Gaulin, 1993). Men are thus biased to invest in children whom they perceive as resembling themselves, and women and their kin either implicitly or explicitly manipulate social information in ways that foster perceived resemblance.

Cuckoldry

The reader may recall that across species females rarely cuckold their partner when male parenting is obligate (see the section titled Parental Investment, chap. 4). When male parenting is not obligate and is facultatively expressed, females sometimes engage in extrapair copulations, especially when paired with lower quality mates. Many of these females risk abandonment and attempt to cuckold their mate to obtain better genes for their offspring or more resources from another male. Given that men's investment is facultative, one would expect the same of some women.

The definitive study of human cuckoldry rates has not been conducted (see also the section titled Sperm Competition, chap. 8); however, the available evidence indicates that it does happen, as with other species with facultative paternal care (Daly & Wilson, 1988a, 1988b; Træen, Holmen, & Stigum, 2007). Essock-Vitale and McGuire (1988) found that about 20% of American women engaged in at least one extramarital affair during their marriage and that some of these relationships resulted in pregnancy. Using a national (U.S.) probability sample, Whisman and Snyder (2007) found that 6% of women reported an affair during the past year. Bellis and Baker (1990) found that when women initiated an infidelity it often occurred around the time of ovulation. For this sample, 7% of the copulations during the time of ovulation were with an extrapair man, and these relationships were less likely to involve the use of contraceptives than were copulations with the woman's social partner. It cannot be stated with certainty, but it appears that men are cuckolded 3% to 10% of the time (K. G. Anderson, 2006; Bellis & Baker, 1990; Bellis, K. Hughes, S. Hughes, & Ashton, 2005; Flinn, 1988a; McBurney, Simon, Gaulin, & Geliebter, 2002). As with other species, cuckoldry rates can vary substantially across contexts and social status. Sasse, Muller, Chakraborty, and Ott (1994) reported nonpaternity rates of 1% in Switzerland, but others have reported rates greater than 20% in low-SES settings (Cerda-Flores, Baron, Marty-Gonzalez, Rivas, & Chakraborty, 1999; Potthoff & Whittinghill, 1965).

It is possible that some of these men are aware of the nonpaternity of the children they are raising and thus have not been technically cuckolded. It remains to be resolved whether women's extrapair relationships are explicitly to cuckold their partners or if cuckoldry results from failed attempts to use the extrapair relationship as a strategy to switch mates. Support for mate switching comes from Banfield and McCabe's (2001) survey of 112 women, 44 of whom were followed longitudinally. Less than 2% of these women had ever engaged in a purely sexual affair, but 12% reported a sexual affair when romantically attached to the extrapair man; romantic attachment suggests the pair-bonding mechanisms that support long-term relationships and biparental care are operating in these women. The issue is further complicated in contexts with high male mortality. As I describe in chapter 7 of this volume (in the section titled Female Choice), women in these cultures often maintain sexual relationships with several men, one of whom is considered to be the primary father and the others secondary fathers (Beckerman et al., 1998; K. Hill & Hurtado, 1996).

Either way, human paternity certainty is at least 90%, if not considerably higher in many populations, in keeping with the gorilla-like model described in chapter 5. The reader may recall that I argued that the formation of male coalitions and the emergence of multimale, multifemale communities would have resulted in an increase in the number of lower quality males entering the reproductive pool. The combination creates greater opportunity for and greater benefits of cuckoldry, especially when women are paired with low-quality or low-investing men. In this situation, paternity rates are predicted to be lower than the 95% found in gorillas—it may be this high in many human populations (K. G. Anderson, 2006; Bellis et al., 2005)—but maintained at a high level by a variety of adaptations, including male mate guarding, sensitivity to potential affairs by their partners, and male–female pair bonding (Andrews et al., 2008; K. MacDonald, 1992). These adaptations, along with a high probability of paternity certainty, are consistent with the gorilla-like social and family structure.

SEX DIFFERENCES IN HUMAN PARENTING

When paternal investment is facultatively expressed but results in significant trade-offs for men, conflict and compromise between parents are predicted (Clutton-Brock, 1991). Conflict results as women attempt to get more paternal investment than men prefer to give and men attempt to reduce investment and focus more on mating effort. Compromise is predicted to result in a level of paternal investment higher than men prefer but lower than women prefer. This is certainly the case for humans: The sex differences in parental investment described in the sections that follow are a common source of marital conflict (Scarr, Phillips, & McCartney, 1989).

Direct Care of Children

More maternal than paternal availability for engagement with children is found in all human cultures (Belsky, Rovine, & Fish, 1989; Eibl-Eibesfeldt, 1989; Konner, 2005; M. M. West & Konner, 1976; B. B. Whiting & Edwards, 1988). Whiting and her colleagues' extensive cross-cultural studies of children's social behavior and development provide numerous examples. In one study, 3- to 6-year-olds in Kenya, India, Mexico, the Philippines, Japan, and the United States were in the proximity of or in contact with their mother 32% to 47% of the time in five of the six cultures and 9% of the time in the sixth (a rural village in Japan); the estimate for the latter is biased because observations were not taken in the household (B. B. Whiting & J. W. M. Whiting, 1975). In these same communities, children were in the proximity of or in contact with their father between 3% and 14% of the time. As shown in Figure 6.1, children were in the presence of their mother 3 to 12 times more frequently than in the presence of their father.

A similar pattern was found for 4- to 10-year-olds in communities in Africa, South Asia, South America, Central America, and North America (B. B. Whiting & Edwards, 1988). Here, children were found to be in the presence of their mother 2 to 4 times more frequently than in the presence of their father. Observation of 5- to 7-year-olds in Kenya, Guatemala, Peru, and the United States indicated that children were much more likely to be directly

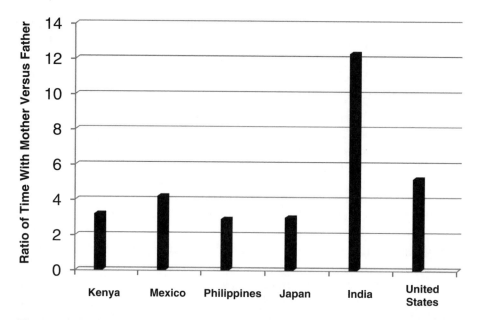

Figure 6.1. Ratio of maternal to paternal care across human societies. For instance, in Kenya, children were in the presence of or engaged in activities with their mother more than 3 times as often as with their father.

engaged in activities with women—mother, grandmother, aunt—than with men. The smallest difference was found in the United States, where children of this age were found to be directly engaged with women 2.5 times more frequently than they were engaged with men. The pattern differed somewhat for boys and girls: Girls spent relatively more time interacting with women, and boys spent relatively more time interacting with men. The extent of these sex differences varies across cultures and is not as pronounced as the overall difference in the frequency with which mothers and fathers interact with their children (Eibl-Eibesfeldt, 1989; M. M. West & Konner, 1976).

The sex difference in parental care is even more pronounced for infants and toddlers (i.e., the first 3 years of life; Crano & Aronoff, 1978). Breast-feeding is, of course, the domain of mothers and in many preindustrial, developing, and traditional societies continues until the child is 2- to 4-years-old (Eibl-Eibesfeldt, 1989; Konner, 2005). Mothers not only breast-feed infants and young children, they provide most of the child's daily care. Observational studies revealed fathers were rarely or never engaged in the care of infants younger than 1 year in Liberia, Kenya, India, Guatemala, or Peru (B. B. Whiting & Edwards, 1988). Fathers in the United States provided more care than did fathers in these other settings, but U.S. fathers still provided considerably less care than the infants' mother.

This sex difference is not because men cannot care for children. When fathers do interact with infants and young children, they show many of the same characteristics as mothers and can provide competent routine care (Belsky et al., 1989; Eibl-Eibesfeldt, 1989; Parke, 1995; Pleck, 1997), although there is some indication that custodial fathers following divorce monitor the activities of their children less diligently, on average, than custodial mothers (C. M. Buchanan, Maccoby, Dornbusch, 1992). Nor can the sex difference be attributed to father absence because he is away hunting or working outside of the home. Belsky, Gilstrap, and Rovine (1984) found that when both parents were present, American (U.S.) mothers spontaneously engaged their infant 1.5 to 2 times more frequently and provided routine care 3 to 4 times more frequently than did their husbands. The same pattern is found in Australia, Belgium, France, Eastern and Western regions of Germany, Great Britain, Israel, and Sweden, (Cooke, 2004, 2007; Lamb, Frodi, Hwang, & Frodi, 1982; Lampert & Friedman, 1992; Parke & Buriel, 1998). In the Swedish study, home observations of maternal and paternal interactions with their infants were conducted for traditional and nontraditional families (Lamb et al., 1982). Fathers in the nontraditional families wanted to be the primary caregiver and had taken leave from work to do so. On a self-report measure, these nontraditional fathers rated parenthood more highly than did nontraditional mothers; the opposite pattern was found for traditional families. These differences in expressed attitudes belied actual caretaking patterns. The mother was the primary caretaker in all of the traditional and nontraditional families. Traditional and nontraditional fathers differed little, except traditional fathers played with their infants more often. In keeping with this finding, Pleck (1997) reported no consistent relation between gender roles and paternal care.

Observation of parental care in the Ache, !Kung San (Botswana), Hadza (Tanzania), Efe (Congo), Aka (Central African Republic), Agta (Philippines), and other societies reveals the same pattern (Flinn, 1992; Konner, 2005). Studies of the !Kung San are particularly interesting because their social customs center on equality among group members. Despite the social norm of equality, observation of caregiving for children younger than 2 years of age indicates !Kung San fathers provide less than 7% of this care; the majority of care is provided by the mother (M. M. West & Konner, 1976). The Aka are a hunter-gatherer society in which fathers provide more direct care to their infants and children than do fathers in any other society that has been studied (Hewlett, 1992). One observational study indicated that when in camp Aka fathers held their 1- to 4-month-old infants 22% of the time, on average. During the course of the day, "the father would on average hold his infant for a total of 57 minutes while the mother would hold the infant 490 minutes" (Hewlett, 1988, p. 268).

Abandonment

Mothers and fathers also differ in how often they abandon their children, such as following a divorce. Although divorced fathers might not be representative of fathers in general, these studies reveal a great deal about the level of paternal investment in a significant portion of men. Studies conducted in modern societies indicate the majority of noncustodial fathers are not actively involved in the day-to-day raising of their children (Amato & Booth, 1996; Furstenberg & Nord, 1985). In one large-scale nationally (U.S.) representative study, it was found that roughly 3 out of 5 children had not seen their noncustodial father during the past year, 4 out of 5 had never slept at his house, and the majority of these fathers exerted little effort to maintain any type of contact, such as through phone calls, with their children (Furstenberg & Nord, 1985). In all, it was found that only 1 out of 6 children had any type of regular contact with their biological father. The same pattern was found in a national (U.S.) longitudinal study of parent–child relationships (Amato & Booth, 1996).

These findings cannot be attributed to the greater likelihood that fathers will be the noncustodial parent (Furstenberg, Peterson, Nord, & Zill, 1983). Furstenberg and Nord (1985) noted that in comparison with noncustodial fathers, noncustodial mothers "tend to maintain a much more active role in childrearing . . . are distinctly more likely to visit with their child on a regular basis, have overnight visits, and have more indirect contact by phone and letter" (p. 896). Amato and Booth (1996) concluded that "divorce does not appear to weaken mothers' affection for their children" (p. 364) but leads to a deterioration in the relationship between fathers and their children. The pattern of relatively less paternal than maternal investment in children is often more evident for children who are born to unmarried couples (Fox, 1995), although many of these fathers do remain in contact with their children (Parke, 1995; Pleck, 1997), especially if the man maintains a good relationship with the children's mother (Fagan & Palkovitz, 2007). In addition to having relatively little direct involvement with their children, about one half of the biological fathers who are not living with the mother do not monetarily support their children, and those who do provide support often invest relatively little in their children in comparison with the mothers and fathers in intact families (Furstenberg, Morgan, & Allison, 1987; Maccoby, Buchanan, Mnookin, & Dornbusch, 1993).

Although these patterns are more prevalent in the United States than in most other modern nations as a result of national differences in divorce rates, the pattern of fathers reducing investment in their children following separation from the children's mother is found in other societies, including traditional ones. Basically, many fathers invest more in their children when they are residing with their children and the children's mother (K. G. Anderson, Kaplan, Lam, & Lancaster, 1999; K. G. Anderson, Kaplan, & Lancaster, 1999; Draper, 1989; Flinn, 1992; Furstenberg et al., 1983; Hewlett, 1992; Hill & Hurtado, 1996). The importance of residence and presumably sex with their children's mother suggests some component of men's parenting is mating effort. In an observational study of parent–child social interactions in a Caribbean village, Flinn found that resident fathers were much more likely to provide some level of care to their children than were nonresident fathers, especially after the nonresident father or the mother remarried (see also Draper, 1989; Furstenberg et al., 1983). A similar pattern of fathers' disengagement with their children following remarriage or mother's remarriage is found in modern societies (Juby, Billette, Laplante, & Le Bourdais, 2007).

Despite the previously described costs to children, many men initiate divorce or reduce their level of investment in the marriage and their children and thus contribute to the likelihood that their wives will initiate divorce. From the man's perspective, divorce or activities that prompt a spouse to initiate divorce (e.g., an affair) can be viewed as an implicit reproductive decision; a reflection of the potential benefits associated with pursuing a new mate balanced against the costs to the current family. Support for this hypothesis is found in studies of divorce, remarriage, and reproduction in modern populations, and in the historical record of Western nations (Hopcroft, 2006; Johanna, Forsberg, & Tullberg, 1995; Käär, Jokela, Merilä, Helle, & Kojola, 1998). Following divorce, men—especially higher status men—are more likely to remarry than are women, and when both remarry men do so more quickly. When men remarry they typically marry women younger than their just-divorced wife and are more likely to have children with the new spouse than are women (Buckle, Gallup, & Rodd, 1996). Moreover, twice (or thrice) married men, but not women, have more children, on average, than their monogamous same-sex peers (Johanna et al., 1995; Käär et al., 1998). In short, a reduction in parental investment in favor of mating effort is a more viable reproductive strategy for men than women.

PROXIMATE EXPRESSION OF MEN'S PARENTING

Given that males provide little if any parental care in the vast majority of mammals (see the section titled Parental Care, chap. 3), the finding of considerably more parental investment by women than men in all regions of the world, across subsistence activities, and independent of social ideology is not surprising. The unique feature of human reproduction is the high level of paternal investment, as I noted at the beginning of this chapter. The facultative expression of men's parenting leads to the expectation of considerable variation in men's parenting, and variation for the same men across different relationships and children (K. MacDonald, 1997; L. C. Miller & Fishkin, 1997; Parke & Buriel, 1998). But what underlies these differences? To address this question, I begin with reviews of the biological, social, and developmental correlates of paternal investment, followed by a review of wider social and ecological correlates of men's parenting.

Biological Correlates

As with other species, sex hormones appear to influence men's bias toward mating effort or parental effort. Heritable influences on parenting are also found, but it is not known if these genetic factors assert themselves through the hormonal mechanisms.

Hormones and Men's Parenting

In species with a facultative expression of male parenting, higher levels of testosterone are associated with a focus on mating competition, and lower levels of testosterone and higher levels of prolactin are associated with a focus on parenting (see the section titled Sex Hormones and Life History Development, chap. 4). Although the research is still in its infancy, trade-offs in men's focus on mating or parenting also appear to be reciprocally related to testosterone and prolactin (Delahunty, McKay, Noseworthy, & Storey, 2007; A. S. Fleming, Corter, Stallings, & Steiner, 2002; P. B. Gray, Parkin, & Samms-Vaughan, 2007; Mazur & Booth, 1998). In North American samples, men in long-term committed relationships have lower testosterone levels than other men (Mazur & Michalek, 1998), consistent with the prediction that these men are allocating less effort to competing for mates (P. B. Gray, Kahlenberg, Barrett, Lipson, & Ellison, 2002). Important tweaks to this relation provide further support: Men in committed relationships who are open to an extrapair affair have higher testosterone levels than their monogamous peers (McIntyre et al., 2006).

In a 10-year longitudinal study (U.S.), Mazur and Michalek (1998) found that men's testosterone levels covary with marital status. The impending breakup of a relationship in the years preceding a divorce and during the mate-search years immediately following a divorce are associated with higher testosterone levels compared with earlier years in the marriage and to the years following a new marriage. P. B. Gray (2003; P. B. Gray, Ellison, & Campbell, 2007) found contradictory relations between testosterone and marriage in two polygynous societies in Kenya, the Swahili (subsistence on fishing, farming, tourism) and the Ariaal (pastoral). Swahili men with two wives had higher testosterone levels than monogamously married men or single men; the two latter groups did not differ from one another. The higher testosterone levels of the polygynously married men might have been related to having multiple simultaneous sexual relationships, as van Anders, Hamilton, and Watson (2007) found for Canadian men who maintained multiple relationships. The failure to find a difference in the testosterone levels of married and single men might be related to the polygynous culture. In these contexts, a first or second marriage does not always mean an end to reproductive competition.

Among the Ariaal, young single men had higher testosterone levels than did young monogamously married men (P. B. Gray et al., 2007). Ariaal men can marry polygynously if they achieve political status and accrue sufficient wealth, but unlike the Swahili, they must wait until they are at least 40 years old. Unlike the Swahili, the testosterone levels of these polygynously married men did not differ from those of the younger monogamously married men. For younger men, their first marriage is dependent in part on their status as a warrior, but later marriages are more strongly influenced by intragroup politics. The nature of the competition for a first wife as compared with later wives may explain the failure to find higher testosterone levels in polygynously married men. The age difference between the polygynously married Swahili and Ariaal men may have also contributed to the differences across these cultures. Moreover, the Ariaal do not officially divorce, and thus many polygynously married men in this culture were only living with a single wife (i.e., they were effectively monogamous).

Men in a committed and monogamous relationship and who wish to become a father may have a different hormone profile than other men, including married men who do not wish to become a father (Berg & Wynne-Edwards, 2001; Hirschenhauser, Frigerio, Grammer, & Magnusson, 2002). The testosterone of prospective fathers fluctuates with the ovulatory cycle of their mate (Hirschenhauser et al., 2002), presumably in response to their wife's heightened interest in sex around the time of ovulation and their mutual interest in becoming parents (see the section titled Female Choice, chap. 7, this volume). Expectant fathers who respond to infant distress cues (e.g., crying) with concern and a desire to comfort the infant have higher prolactin levels and lower testosterone levels than other men (Storey, Walsh, Quinton, & Wynne-Edwards, 2000). "Men with more pregnancy symptoms (couvade) and men who were most affected by the infant reactivity test had higher prolactin levels and greater post-test reduction in testosterone" (Storey et al., 2000, p. 79). Higher paternal (and maternal) cortisol levels are also correlated with more attentive and sensitive parenting of newborns (Corter & Fleming, 1995).

Cause and effect are not certain, however. Lower testosterone levels are associated with greater sensitivity to infant cries among men who are not fathers, suggesting hormone levels may influence tendency toward paternal investment (A. S. Fleming et al., 2002). It is also possible that the lower testosterone associated with a committed relationship makes men more prone to later parenting, that men prone to parental investment are preferred as long-term partners (see the section titled Female Choice, chap. 7, this volume), or some combination. The relation between men's parenting and prolactin is also complex. Close contact with infants appears to result in decreased prolactin levels when fathers hold their first-born but not later born children (Delahunty et al., 2007). A combination of little contact with their infant during the past several hours and stated concern for the infant is related to increasing prolactin levels in men and heightened reactivity to infant crying. On average, men's prolactin levels appear to be more sensitive to development experiences (e.g., having younger siblings) and social context than women's levels (Delahunty et al., 2007), perhaps reflecting the facultative nature of men's parenting.

Heritability of Men's Parenting

Parental behavior can be influenced by heritable biases (e.g., toward warmth or control) in the parent and by heritable traits of their children (e.g., sociability) that evoke parental behavior (Feinberg, Neiderhiser, Howe, & Hetherington, 2001; Kendler, 1996; Neiderhiser, Reiss, Lichtenstein, Spotts, & Ganiban, 2007; Pérusse, Neale, Heath, & Eaves, 1994; Scarr & McCarthy, 1983). Pérusse et al. found modest genetic contributions to individual differences in parental warmth (e.g., sensitivity to emotional state) and protection (e.g., keeping the child close). Genetic models explained 18% to 25% of the individual differences for these facets of men's parenting and 23% to 39% of the variation in women's. Kendler confirmed the finding for warmth, estimating 47% and 63% of the variation among fathers and mothers, respectively, was due to genetic influences. More modest genetic influences were found for parental protection or control and authoritarian parenting (e.g., the parent making decisions for child). There is also evidence that both men's and women's parenting is influenced by heritable traits of their children and adolescents (Feinberg et al., 2001; Neiderhiser et al., 2007) as well as by the unique experiences of mothers and fathers, including in their family of origin.

Firm conclusions cannot yet be drawn, but it appears that heritable influences on maternal behavior are stronger than heritable influences on paternal behavior. Paternal behavior may be more strongly influenced by context, prior experience, and child-evocative effects than maternal behavior, as expected for a facultatively expressed suite of behaviors. Research on heritable and environmental influences on men's basal and reactive (e.g., in presence of children or spouse) testosterone and prolactin levels are needed to more fully understand the proximate biological mechanisms potentially linking genetic and environmental influences to the expression of paternal behavior. Studies of the relation between personality and parenting are also needed. This is because the results reported here could reflect genetic influences on personality that are not directly related to the evolution of paternal care but still influence parenting.

Individual differences in personality traits, such as conscientiousness (i.e., reliability, consistency), are moderately heritable and associated with the stability of long-term spousal relationships and marital quality and could affect responsiveness to children (Graziano & Eisenberg, 1997; Rowe, 2002; Spotts et al., 2005). Although in need of replication, Spinath and O'Connor (2003) found that heritable influences on parental behavior (mothers and fathers combined) were largely independent of heritable influences on personality traits, with one exception. Highly neurotic parents (e.g., anxious) were more rejecting of their children. The relation between a neurotic personality and parental rejection appeared to be due to genes common to both traits as well as unique experiences that influenced both traits. Parents high on the openness to experience dimension of personality (e.g., creative, liking novel experiences and new learning) were less protective and controlling of their children, but this relation was due to experience, not genes.

Social Correlates

The core proximate social correlates on the quality and nature of men's parenting are the quality of the marital relationship and their social status.

Marital Relationship

The quality of the spousal relationship is a key influence on parental behavior (Belsky, 1993; Belsky et al., 1984; Feldman, Nash, & Aschenbrenner, 1983; Lamb, Pleck, & Levine, 1986; J. P. McHale, Kuersten-Hogan, Lauretti, & Rasmussen, 2000). Although the quality of this relationship influences how both parents interact with their children (Amato & Keith, 1991; M. J. Cox, Owen, Lewis, & Henderson, 1989; Davies & Cummings, 1994), "paternal parenting is more dependent on a supportive marital relationship than maternal parenting" (Parke, 1995, p. 37). Observational studies reveal a significant sex difference in the relation between marital satisfaction and parental engagement with children (Belsky et al., 1984; Feldman et al., 1983; Lamb & Elster, 1985): "The quality of the marital dyad, whether reported by the husband or wife, is the one most consistently powerful predictor of paternal involvement [with his infant] and satisfaction [with the parenting role]" (Feldman et al., 1983, p. 1634).

Belsky et al. (1984) and Lamb and Elster (1985) confirmed that fathers' engagement with children was related to the quality of the marital relationship and, at the same time, found little relation between the level of marital interaction (e.g., degree of communication) and mothers' involvement with their children. Marital conflict, for instance, can result in the father's withdrawal, emotional or physical, from his children and his spouse (e.g., Christensen & Heavey, 1990). However, this withdrawal is sometimes more pronounced for daughters than for sons (Kerig, Cowan, & Cowan, 1993) and varies with the nature of the interpersonal dynamics between husband and wife (Gottman, 1998). Fagan and Palkovitz (2007) found that unmarried, nonresident fathers are more engaged with their infants (e.g., visited more frequently) if they have a good relationship with the child's birth mother.

The finding that men with satisfying relationships with their children's mother invest more in parenting suggests women's efforts to maintain an intimate and cooperative relationship with these men is, in part, a strategy to induce more paternal investment. It is also possible that men biased toward paternal investment are more cooperative and prone to monogamy and thus less likely to incite conflict with their wives or seek extrapair relationships than are other men, and that the relation between martial satisfaction and paternal investment reflects genetic and not social effects (K. MacDonald, 1997). One fascinating, though preliminary, study found evidence that the same genetic and neuropeptide (i.e., vasopressin) mechanisms that promote monogamy and parental investment in male prairie voles (see the section titled Sex Hormones and Life History Development, chap. 4, this volume) may influence marital pair bonding in men (Walum et al., 2008). It is most likely that a combination of heritable biases in both parents (e.g., personality; Spotts et al., 2005), reactivity to martial dynamics, and hormonal mechanisms (described previously) influence paternal investment.

Social Status

The extent to which fathers are directly engaged in parenting is also related to the nature of their work and their personal ambition. Fathers in demanding and stressful jobs are less involved in infant caretaking, less playful with their infants, and less engaged with their toddlers than are fathers in less salient occupations (Feldman et al., 1983). Lamb et al. (1986) suggested there is a trade-off between family involvement and commitment to work. In comparison with men who were more focused on work than on family,

> family-oriented accommodators . . . [were] more professionally passive and less successful professionally. They also tended to be in less prestigious jobs . . . although it is not clear whether this was a cause or an effect of the family-oriented accommodative strategies. (p. 79)

A similar relation between a man's success in culturally important endeavors and caretaking of children has been found for Aka pygmies and the Ache (Hewlett, 1988; K. Hill & Hurtado, 1996; K. Hill & Kaplan, 1988). High-status Aka men, those with large kin networks and therefore high hunting success, hold their infants less than half as frequently as men with few kin: Men without male kin hunt either alone or with their wife and are generally less successful hunters than men who hunt in kin-based groups. The less direct care provided by these high-status men appears to be balanced by the provisioning of their families with diets that consist of a high proportion of fat and protein (Hewlett, 1988). As fathers' efforts to obtain income through a job or meat through hunting increases, direct caretaking of children often decreases. It is not clear, however, whether efforts to obtain more income or other indicators of cultural success are components of paternal investment—gaining resources that will be invested in children—or if they are components of mating effort; successful men have more mating opportunities.

Developmental Correlates

Early experiences may bias males toward mating effort or parental effort in adulthood. Draper and Harpending (1982), Belsky and his colleagues (Belsky, 2007; Belsky et al., 1991), and Chisholm (1993) proposed that parents' social experiences (e.g., degree of conflict with other adults) and the availability of resources and risks in the wider community influence parent–child relationships, specifically, the nature of the attachment between parents and their children. In risky, low-resource environments, the psychological and physiological stressors on parents are high and result in less attentive and more conflicted parent–parent and parent–child relationships. These relationships are predicted to increase the risk of insecure parent–child attachments and through this bias the later relationship dynamics of these children. In less risky, high-resource environments, parent–child relationships are warmer, and secure parent–child attachments are more common. Secure attachments are predicted to result in a tendency to form trusting and stable relationships later in life, including the spousal relationship. A history of a warm parent–child relationship during development and a stable spousal relationship is predicted to bias men toward higher levels of parental investment (K. MacDonald, 1992).

The mechanisms linking the form of parent–child attachment to later reproductive strategy has been elaborated by Del Giudice and Belsky (Del Giudice, 2009b; Del Giudice & Belsky, in press). By middle childhood, low-attentive and conflicted parent–child relationships are associated with heightened risk of ambivalent (e.g., emotionally insecure, dependent) attachment styles in girls and women and avoidant (e.g., emotionally distant) styles in boys and men (Del Giudice, 2008). Del Giudice (2009b) proposed the emergence of these sex differences is triggered by earlier adrenarche, which in turn is associated with heightened parent–parent and parent–child conflict (B. J. Ellis & Essex, 2007). An avoidant style may facilitate later male–male competition, which is often related to polygyny and higher mortality (see the section title Male–Male Competition, chap. 8, this volume), and result in an emotionally distant, exploitative view of social relationships. An ambivalent style is hypothesized to result in behaviors that facilitate gaining resources from others, including the women's spouse.

Most of the tests of these predictions have focused on the correlates of an early conflicted home life and stressors and risks in the wider community (Bereczkei & Csanaky, 2001; B. J. Ellis, 2004; Quinlan, 2007). As reviewed by Del Giudice (2009b), the avoidant attachment style is associated with aggression and dominance striving in boys and men, emotionally distant and frequent short-term sexual relationships, as well as little investment in parenting in early adulthood. M. Wilson and Daly (1997) found age of first reproduction, number of children borne per woman, mortality risks, and local resource availability were all interrelated in modern-day Chicago. In neighborhoods with low resource availability, men compete intensely for these resources. The corresponding increase in mortality rates translated into an average life span difference of 23 years (54 years vs. 77 years) comparing the least and most affluent neighborhoods. A shorter life span, in turn, was associated with earlier age of first reproduction for both men and women and nearly twice as many children borne per woman comparing the least and most affluent neighborhoods. In other words, the early and frequent reproduction of women and men in these contexts might be, at least in part, a facultative response to high mortality rates or at least a response to the perception that the future is uncertain and not likely to bring a better life (J. Davis & Were, 2008). In a cross-cultural analysis, Quinlan found that men decrease their parental investment as external mortality risks, those uncontrollable by parents, to children increase; mothers' increase their investment to a point and then decrease it.

In samples of Ache and Mayan (Central America) men, Waynforth, Hurtado, and Hill (1998) found that "measures of family stress and violence were unsuccessful in predicting age at first reproduction, and none of the psychosocial stress indicators predicted lifetime number of partners" (p. 383). Father absence was, however, related to less "willingness to pay time and opportunity costs to maintain a sexual relationship" (Waynforth et al., 1998, p. 383), although this could easily reflect genetic and not psychosocial effects. Other critiques have focused on the tendency for other species, and at times humans, to delay reproduction and reduce parental investment when resources are particularly scarce (Krebs & Davies, 1993; K. MacDonald, 1997). But with intermediate levels of mortality risk and fluctuating resource availability, investment in more rather than fewer offspring is assumed to ensure that at least some of these offspring will survive to adulthood (Chisholm, 1993). Investing limited resources in one or a few offspring might improve their social competitiveness, but if mortality risks are high, such an investment is very risky.

The final word on these issues remains to be heard. The relations between early family stressors and increased risk of insecure attachment and an early onset of adrenarche in both sexes as well as early menarche in girls represent plausible mechanisms linking parent–child relationships to later reproductive strategy. For men, an insecure relationship with one or both parents appears to result in increased risk of detached, exploitative social relationships in adulthood, including sexual relationships, and little investment in parenting (Del Giudice, 2009b). Long-term studies that control for heritable influences and that measure all hypothesized mechanisms (e.g., parent–child attachment) as well as mortality risks and sources of these risks during development are needed to firmly establish causal relations between early developmental experiences and later reproductive activities (see R. Walker et al., 2006).

Cultural and Ecological Correlates

The key cultural and ecological influences on men's bias toward parenting or mating are the social constraints on polygyny and the operational sex ration (OSR; see the section titled Operational Sex Ratio, chap. 3). As I describe in the next section, Draper and Harpending (1988) proposed these social constraints result in father-absent societies and father-present societies. In the section following that, I describe how fluctuations in the OSR can influence men's focus on mating or parenting.

Father-Absent and Father-Present Societies

Father-absent and *father-present* societies refer to men's tendency to focus on mating effort or parental effort, respectively. These are general patterns that are influenced by a host of social and ecological factors, and there are of course individual differences in men's focus on mating or parenting within these societies.

Father Absent. These societies are characterized by aloof husband–wife relationships, a polygynous marriage system, local raiding and warfare, male social displays—verbal and with ornamentation—and little or inconsistent direct paternal investment in children (Draper & Harpending, 1988; Hewlett, 1988; M. M. West & Konner, 1976). These conditions "are particularly prevalent in so-called middle-range societies, i.e., those where agriculture is practiced at a very low level" (Draper & Harpending, 1988, p. 349) and in resource-rich ecologies. In the latter, women and their kin can often provide adequate care to their children, for example, through a dowry of cattle, without substantial direct contributions from the father (Draper, 1989; Sellen, Borgerhoff Mulder, & Sieff, 2000). If men are able to accumulate resources beyond what is needed to attract a single wife, these are conditions and social mores that allow polygyny and provide men with the opportunity to invest time and wealth into either parental investment or mating effort. Most men opt for the latter.

In these societies, men compete with each other for the establishment of social dominance or for the control of those material resources (e.g., land) that women need to raise their children (Borgerhoff Mulder, 1990). The achievement of social or economic dominance, in turn, influences the number of women the man can marry and the number of surviving children (Chagnon, 1988; Hopcroft, 2006; Irons, 1993). Given this, the investment of excess wealth in mating effort is often a successful reproductive strategy for men. An example is provided by Borgerhoff Mulder's (2000) analysis of the reproductive strategies of Kipsigis (Kenya) men and women. In this pastoral society, men are allowed to marry as many women as they can support. The resource they need to support one or more wives is the land controlled by their male-dominated kin group. When men marry, they provide to their wife (or wives) and their children a specific amount of land, which is then used for small-scale agricultural production. The land will be inherited by their sons, who, in turn, will use it in their attempts to marry. Social custom dictates that the land is to be divided evenly among sons. If a woman has too many sons, then none of these men will have enough land to marry and reproduce.

Borgerhoff Mulder (2000) confirmed that the optimal reproductive strategy for women, as indexed by the number of surviving grandchildren, is to invest in a smaller number of sons, that is, to have fewer children than their biological potential. Women who had fewer children than their land could support had more surviving grandchildren than did women who had as many children as their land could support. By having fewer children, each of their sons inherited more land and thus was better able to attract wives. Men in this society are also faced with complex reproductive decisions. If they marry as many women as they can support and thus maximize the quantity of children, then each of their sons will inherit less land than if they married fewer women. Borgerhoff Mulder's analysis indicated that men, on average, did not divert resources from their mating effort to provide their sons with more heritable land. Strassmann (2000) reported a similar strategy among Dogon men (Mali, West Africa).

Polygynous relationships will, on average, result in more distant spousal relationships, more conflict within the wider family (e.g., between cowives), and less direct paternal care. As I described in the section titled Reproductive Maturation and Developmental Correlates in this chapter, these features of family life appear to contribute to early sexual maturation in girls and a tendency for men to engage in emotionally distant and exploitative sexual relationships with little paternal involvement (Del Giudice, 2009b; Kanazawa, 2001).

Father Present. These societies tend to be found in harsh or unstable ecologies and in modern or other relatively large, stratified societies (Draper & Harpending, 1988). These are societies that are sometimes characterized by ecologically or socially imposed monogamy (Flinn & Low, 1986). Under harsh ecological conditions, the vast majority of men are unable to acquire the resources (e.g., meat obtained through hunting) needed to support more than one wife and family. The reproductive aspirations of most men are thus ecologically restricted to monogamy. This is because high levels of paternal investment are often necessary to ensure the survival of a man's children and because these ecologies limit the ability to accumulate excess wealth and thus limit mating opportunities.

In most modern societies, monogamy is socially imposed; formal laws prohibit polygynous marriages. The dynamics that led to the cultural evolution of socially imposed monogamy are not fully understood, but the result is suppression of men's mating efforts and through this, reduced opportunity cost to paternal investment. In these cultures, investing excess wealth in the well-being of children is a viable reproductive strategy for men, especially when child mortality risks fluctuate greatly and vary inversely with level of paternal investment (e.g., during epidemics).

Individual Differences. My description of father-absent and father-present societies does not capture variation within these societies. Even though direct paternal investment tends to be lower in cultures that allow polygynous marriages, most of the men (greater than 80%) in most of these societies are monogamously married (Murdock, 1981). It is nevertheless common for these monogamously married men to divert social and material resources from the family to attempts to attract a second wife (Hames, 1992, 1996). Many men engage in polygynous relationships in monogamous societies through serial marriages or affairs, often to their benefit. In an extensive study of more than 900 Swedish women and men over the age of 40 years, Forsberg and Tullberg (1995) found that men, but not women, who engaged in serial monogamy had more children than their peers who stayed monogamously married.

Under some conditions, high-status polygynously married men are able to invest more material and social resources in their many children than are lower status monogamously married men. On the Ifaluk islands in the Western Pacific, chiefs tend to have more wives (serial monogamy in this case) and children than lower status men but spend twice as much time with their children as these lower status men (Betzig & Turke, 1992). This is possible because high-ranking men receive tributes from other families and receive relatively more food from communal fishing than do low-ranking men. The net result is that chiefs spend less time working and have more material resources and time to invest in their children.

Operational Sex Ratio

As with other species (see the section titled Operational Sex Ratio, chap. 3), the OSR influences men's relative focus on mating effort or parental effort (Guttentag & Secord, 1983; F. A. Pedersen, 1991; Pollet & Nettle, 2008). The OSR is determined by sex differences in birth rates, death rates, and migration patterns.

Sex ratios by themselves do not bring about societal effects, but rather that [sic] they combine with a variety of other social, economic, and political conditions to produce the consequent effects on the roles of men and women and the relationship between them. (Guttentag & Secord, 1983, p. 137)

In modern societies, expanding populations result in an "oversupply" of women because women prefer slightly older marriage partners and men slightly younger ones (Kenrick & Keefe, 1992). With an expanding population, the younger generation of women will be competing for marriage partners from a smaller cohort of older men. The resulting imbalance in the numbers of marriage-age men and women is correlated with changes in divorce rates, sexual mores, and levels of paternal investment (Guttentag & Secord, 1983; F. A. Pedersen, 1991).

During periods when there is an oversupply of women, such as from 1965 through the 1970s in the United States, men's mating opportunities increase. If men, on average, prefer parental effort to mating effort, then the change in mating opportunities should not result in reduction in paternal investment. But it does. These historical periods are generally characterized by liberal sexual mores (i.e., many sexual partners for both men and women), high divorce rates, an increase in the number of out-of-wedlock births and the number of families headed by single women, an increase in female participation in the workforce, and, generally lower levels of paternal investment (Guttentag & Secord, 1983). Although cultural factors play a role as well, the bottom line is that during these periods men are better able to express their preference for a variety of sexual partners and relatively low levels of paternal investment (F. A. Pedersen, 1991).

A different pattern emerges when there is an oversupply of men (Guttentag & Secord, 1983). Here, women are better able to enforce their preferences for a monogamous, high-investing spouse. As a result, these periods are generally characterized by an increase in the level of commitment of men to marriage, as indexed by declining divorce rates and greater levels of paternal investment (F. A. Pedersen, 1991). Pollet and Nettle (2008) illustrated this relation with demographic and marriage data from the U.S. population in 1910. This was an historical period in which there was more migration to western states by men than women, resulting in large across-state differences in the OSR. In all states, wealthier men were more likely to marry than other men, but the strength of this relation increased dramatically as the sex ratio became unbalanced. When there was an oversupply of men, women demanded more in terms of wealth before they would marry. In states with a balanced ORS, a man with a somewhat below-average amount of wealth had a 56% chance of marrying by age 30, and a man with a somewhat above-average amount of wealth had a 60% chance. For states in which there were 110 men to every

100 women, the chance of marrying by age 30 declined for men in both of these wealth categories but much more dramatically for below-average men. These men had a 24% chance of marrying by age 30 as compared with 46% for their wealthier peers. With the unbalanced OSR, women demanded more resources from men and got them.

Hurtado and Hill (1992) found the OSR to be an important influence on marital stability, that is, men's focus on mating or parenting, in the Ache and Hiwi (hunter-gatherers in southwestern Venezuela). Ache men live in a social environment that provides many mating opportunities (because of high male mortality) whereas a large imbalance in the ratio of men to women (more men than women) greatly restricts Hiwi men's mating opportunities.

> Differences in levels of mating opportunities between the Ache and the Hiwi occur alongside marked contrasts in marital stability. Whereas serial monogamy and extra marital promiscuity are very common among the Ache, stable lifetime monogamous unions with almost no extramarital copulation is the normative mating pattern among the Hiwi. (Hurtado & Hill, 1992, p. 40)

These patterns are found despite high infant and child mortality risks associated with paternal abandonment with the Ache and low risks with the Hiwi. Blurton Jones, Marlowe, Hawkes, and O'Connell (2000) confirmed these findings for the Ache and Hiwi and extended them to the !Kung and Hadza. The overall pattern indicates that the reproductive strategy of some men is more strongly influenced by mating opportunities than by child mortality risks.

CONCLUSION

When considered in terms of mammalian reproduction, it is unremarkable that mothers throughout the world show a much greater availability for and engagement with their children than do fathers (Whiting & Edwards, 1988). As I reviewed in chapter 3 of this volume (in the section titled Parental Care), this is because the biology of mammalian reproduction results in higher levels of maternal than paternal investment and creates a faster potential rate of reproduction for males than females. For the vast majority of species with this reproductive biology, females are focused on parental effort and males on mating effort (Trivers, 1972). Given this pattern, the most remarkable feature of human reproduction is that many fathers show some degree of direct and indirect investment in their children. Although the level of paternal care may not always be satisfactory from the perspective of the wives of these men, it is nonetheless remarkable in comparison with the little paternal care found in the two species most closely related to humans and in terms of the more general pattern found with mammals (Clutton-Brock, 1989; Whitten, 1987).

Men's investment or not in their children reflects the same cost–benefit trade-offs found with facultative paternal investment in other species (see Exhibit 4.1, chap. 4). The benefits of paternal investment include reductions in infant and child mortality rates in high-risk environments and improvements in children's later ability to compete for essential social and material resources (Kaplan et al., 1998; A. Reid, 1997). As found with other species with high levels of paternal investment, men's parenting is associated with relatively high—roughly 90% to 95%—levels of paternity certainty and with restricted mating opportunities.

The facultative expression of men's parenting is correlated with many factors, including heritable individual differences, hormonal profile, the quality of the spousal relationship, and child characteristics (Luster & Okagaki, 1993; Neiderhiser et al., 2007; Storey et al., 2000). Childhood experiences may also bias men toward mating effort or parental effort through the nature of the parent–child attachment and the level of parent–parent conflict (Belsky et al., 1991). An insecure, avoidant parent–child attachment and early adrenarche may bias boys and later men to exploit social relationships (Del Giudice, 2009b). Among the consequences are an increased frequency of short-term sexual relationships and little parental investment. Wider social and ecological factors, especially laws against polygynous marriages and the OSR, also influence the degree to which men invest in the well-being of their children (Draper & Harpending, 1988; Flinn & Low, 1986; Guttentag & Secord, 1983). The goal for future studies is to uncover the relative contribution of each of these factors in general and to better understand individual differences in men's responsiveness to factors such as marital quality and the OSR.

7

CHOOSING MATES

Men's parenting greatly complicates the dynamics of sexual selection. In addition to male–male competition and female choice, female–female competition and male choice are central features of human reproductive dynamics. I review the dynamics of male–male and female–female competition in chapter 8 and focus here on how and why women and men are selective in their mate choices. Both female and male choice follow from the cross-species relation between parenting and choosiness (see the section titled Parental Care, chap. 3). At the same time, the sex differences in the quantity and forms (e.g., pregnancy) of investment in children and the facultative nature of men's investment result in different cost–benefit trade-offs for women and men when it comes to choosing mates. The trade-offs shown in Table 7.1 provide a framework for thinking about the costs and benefits of short-term and long-term sexual relationships.

The most fundamental sex difference is that the cost of reproduction is higher for women than for men because of pregnancy and the sex difference in postnatal parental investment. Women are, therefore, predicted to be more careful than men in their mate choices for both short-term and long-term relationships. Women, in fact, are predicted to largely avoid short-term relationships because the potential costs often outweigh the potential benefits. A

TABLE 7.1
Potential Costs and Benefits of Short-Term and Long-Term Mate Choices

Cost	Benefits
Women's short-term mating	
Risk of sexually transmitted disease	Some resources from mate
Risk of pregnancy	Good genes from mate
Reduced value as a long-term mate	
Women's long-term mating	
Restricted sexual opportunity	Significant resources from mate
Sexual obligation to mate	Paternal investment
Men's short-term mating	
Risk of sexually transmitted disease	Potential to reproduce
Some resource investment	No parental investment
Men's long-term mating	
Restricted sexual opportunity	Increased paternity certainty
Heavy parental investment	Improved social competitiveness of children
Heavy relationship investment	Sexual and social companionship

Note. From "Evolution of Human Mate Choice," by D. C. Geary, J. Vigil, and J. Byrd-Craven, 2004, *Journal of Sex Research, 41,* p. 29. Copyright 2004 by The Society for the Scientific Study of Sexuality. Reprinted with permission.

different pattern is predicted for men because the potential benefits of short-term relationships will often outweigh the potential costs. When men do commit to a long-term relationship, their level of choosiness is predicted to increase as a result of the costs of parental care and lost mating opportunities. Before I move to a discussion of the details of women's and men's mate preferences and choices in the second and third respective sections, I provide a primer on marriage systems; a culture's marriage system places constraints on and affords opportunities for the expression of mate-choice preferences.

MARRIAGE SYSTEMS

I argued in chapter 5 (in the section titled Evolutionary Models) that a gorilla-like family structure emerged during hominid evolution, specifically, a male and one or several females and their offspring embedded in a larger male-biased kin group. Although this is indeed a common form of family constellation across cultures (Brown, 1991; Pasternak, C. R. Ember & M. Ember, 1997), the unpredictable nature of social dynamics and variation in the ecologies and cultures in which families are situated result in a range of marriage systems and family types (Murdock, 1981). The most common variations of mating systems in other species were described in chapter 3 of this volume (see Table 3.1) and include polygyny, polyandry, and monogamy (R. D. Alexander, 1979). Each of these forms of marriage system is found in humans, though to varying degrees, as described in Table 7.2.

The social and ecological conditions that account for this variation are not fully understood, but there are general patterns (Flinn & B. S. Low, 1986). Key ecological variables include the quantity, type, and distribution of food and other material resources and whether these resources (e.g., cows) can be monopolized by male kin-based coalitions (e.g., sparse hunted game). Key social variables include rules for marriage, the extent of intragroup competition and warfare, and paternity certainty (White, 1988; White & Burton, 1988). A majority of traditional societies have marriage rules that allow polygynous or polyandrous unions, although the former are many times more common than the latter (Murdock, 1981). In these societies, coalitions of related men cooperate to gain access to and maintain control of the resources women need to rear their children or to control reproduction-related social dynamics. Control of material resources, such as land or cattle, results in resource-based polygyny (Borgerhoff Mulder, 1990), whereas control of social dynamics results in social power polygyny (Chagnon, 1988).

The material and social resources that are controlled by kin-based coalitions are not simply related to these men's mating efforts, they also are often used to influence the social and reproductive interests of their children. With resource-based polygyny, younger men in the coalitions are often dependent on the wealth of their father, uncles, and other relatives to pay the bride price, such as cattle paid to the prospective bride's parents, needed to marry (e.g., Borgerhoff Mulder, 2000). At the same time, a young woman's parents and other relatives will often use their wealth and social power to facilitate her marriage to a wealthy or socially powerful man and kin group, and to influence her treatment by the man and his kin after she has married. A similar pattern is found with social power polygyny, whereby men's coalitions engage in negotiations to influence the reproductive prospects of their sons and daughters. In both forms of marriage system, women almost always marry, some monogamously and some into polygynous unions (Hartung, 1982). High-status men typically have several wives; other men marry monogamously; and some men never marry (Murdock, 1981). Polyandry is found in less than 1% of human societies and is also related to resource control (E. A. Smith, 1998); land tends to be inherited by sons but cannot be subdivided into smaller functional plots (i.e., plots that can support a family). To keep this resource in the family and to provide sufficient resources to support children, brothers will marry the same woman and work the same land.

Monogamous marriages and families consisting of a husband, wife, and their children who reside in the same household are common in societies in

TABLE 7.2
Marriage Patterns and Family Formation

Marriage system	Variations of the system
Polygyny	*Resource-based polygyny.* In resource rich environments and cultures in which polygyny is not legally prohibited, male kin-based coalitions compete for control of these resources (e.g., land, cows), and dominant men in successful coalitions marry polygynously. A common family structure is a husband who lives separately (e.g., in a different hut) from his wives and their children (e.g., Borgerhoff Mulder, 1990; Draper, 1989). *Social power polygyny.* In ecologies in which resources are abundant but not easily controlled by coalitions and in which polygyny is not prohibited, male kin-based coalitions compete for social dominance and power (e.g., through warfare). Dominant men in successful coalitions marry polygynously. A common family structure is a husband, two or three wives and their children (e.g., Chagnon, 1988). Family units consisting of a husband, wife, and their children are common as well (e.g., Hames, 1996).
Polyandry	*Fraternal polyandry.* Although rare, in societies in which land is of low fertility and thus yields poor crops, families tend not to divide inherited land (E. A. Smith, 1998). In these societies, brothers share the land, which can only support a small number of children, and marry polyandrously. In these cases, the family consists of two husbands, one wife, and their children. If one brother acquires additional wealth, he will often marry another woman, who does not become the wife of his brother.
Monogamy	*Ecologically imposed.* In environments with sparse and widely distributed food sources, high levels of both maternal and paternal investment are needed to successfully raise offspring and thus polygyny is rare. Monogamy and family units that consist of a husband, wife, and their children are common (Flinn & B. S. Low, 1986). *Socially imposed.* Legal prohibition of polygamy in Western culture suppresses the male tendency to form polygynous marriages in resource rich ecologies. Monogamy and family units consisting of a husband, wife, and their children are thus more common than would otherwise be the case. Serial monogamy and single parent (typically mother) families are also common in these societies. *Serial.* In resource rich ecologies with socially imposed monogamy, men and women often have a series of legal marriages, although this pattern is sometimes found in other cultures as well (e.g., K. Hill & Hurtado, 1996). Men, but not women, who marry serially have, on average, more children than do men who stay monogamously married to one person (Buckle et al., 1996; Johanna et al., 1995).

Note. From "Evolution of Human Parental Behavior and the Human Family," by D. C. Geary and M. V. Flinn, 2001, *Parenting: Science and Practice, 1,* p. 33. Copyright 2001 by the Lawrence Erlbaum Associates. Adapted with permission.

which monogamy is ecologically or socially imposed, as I reviewed in chapter 6 (in the section titled Father-Absent and Father-Present Societies). The result is a suppression of polygynous marriages in higher status men, although serial monogamy is common in these societies, as are single-parent families (typically headed by mothers and aided by maternal kin). These societies are also unusual in that nuclear families are often physically isolated from the wider kin network, although kin are still a source of social and economic support; this isolation is more common in the professional classes in which jobs often require moving away from kin (Argyle, 1994). In societies with socially imposed monogamy, kin-based negotiations for marriage partners are uncommon, but intergenerational transfer of wealth from parents to children, as related to children's later marriage prospects or the well-being of the donor's grandchildren, is common (Gaulin & Boster, 1990).

As readers know from chapter 6, both men and women are involved in family formation and parental investment, but the dynamics of these processes vary across differing physical and social ecologies (see the section titled Cultural and Ecological Correlates, chap. 6). When it is not prohibited, men attempt to acquire the resources needed to marry polygynously, but they must do so through cooperation with their male kin and often through the cooperation of prospective brides (e.g., Chagnon, 1997). The combination of male coalitions, men's status within the coalition, and the distribution of resources in the wider ecology influences men's reproductive strategies and patterns of family formation, spousal warmth, paternal investment, and men's and women's mate choices. In some cultures, women influence these patterns, from attempting to bias men's negotiations for marriage of their daughters (e.g., Borgerhoff Mulder, 1990) to negotiating the nature of the spousal relationship. In other cultures, the mate choices of men but especially women are constrained because their spouses are often chosen by their parents or other kin (Apostolou, 2007). As I have described elsewhere (Geary, 2005b) and as I review in chapter 9 of this volume, all of these dynamics are variations on the same theme: Humans form complex kinship networks that cooperate to control social dynamics and to gain access to resources in the wider community.

WOMEN'S MATE CHOICES

In terms of evolutionary logic, an ideal situation for many women is predicted to be marriage to a long-term partner who has good genes (e.g., looks healthy), social influence, and material resources (B. S. Low, 2000). It is important that any such prospective husband has to be willing to invest in her and her children. Stated differently, women prefer marriage to men who are culturally successful, men who have social influence and control of material resources (Irons, 1979). Putting one's preferences into practice, however, is more easily said than done. The previously described cultural and ecological influences on marriage systems place constraints on women's and men's mate choices, as do kin. I describe the ubiquity of kin influences in the next section. In the section following that, I focus on the importance of men's cultural success when women and their kin choose the woman's marriage partner. In the third and fourth respective sections, I review research on the behavioral and physical traits that women prefer in prospective partners. I close with discussion of alternative mating strategies.

Who Chooses Whom?

Apostolou (2007) analyzed marriage types across 190 hunter–gatherer societies. The marriages were classified into four categories on the basis of who made the decision, specifically, parental arrangement, kin arrangement (e.g., brother, uncle), courtship with parental approval, and courtship. Each society was classified in terms of the most common or primary marriage type and whether any of the other marriage types occurred; these were classified as secondary. As shown in Figure 7.1, parents arranged most of the marriages in 70% of these societies, and courtship—in which women and men make their own decisions about whom to marry—was the primary marriage type in only 4% of the societies. Courtship without parental approval was a secondary marriage type in 14% of the societies. Unconstrained mate choices (primary or secondary) were not reported for four out of five of the hunter–gatherer societies.

Conflicts of interest between women and their kin over marriage partners are especially evident in societies in which young women are an economic asset to their families: societies in which bride price (i.e., material resources) or bride service (i.e., labor) are required of prospective suitors. In an analysis of the dynamics of marriage across 860 societies, Daly and Wilson (1983) found that the bride's kin required a substantial bride price or bride service in 500, or 58%, of them and a less substantial bride price in 53 others. In another 27 societies, men from different kin groups often acquire wives through a direct exchange of daughters, thus circumventing female choice. In only 205, or fewer than 1 out of 4, of these societies are the woman's marriage preferences relatively unencumbered by the priorities of her kin. Even in these societies, kin monitor the romantic relationships of their children and often attempt to influence their children's marriage choices (Faulkner & Schaller, 2007; Flinn, 1988b).

Culturally Successful Men

All else being equal, female primates prefer sexual and often longer term relationships with dominant males (see the section titled Female Choice,

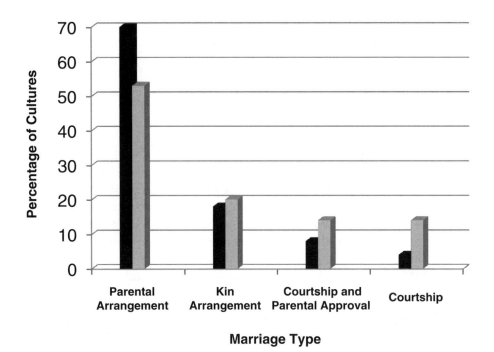

Figure 7.1. Primary (black bar) and secondary (gray bar) marriage types in hunter–gatherer societies. *Primary* refers to the most common way in which marriage partners are chosen, and *secondary* refers to whether an alternative type ever occurs. Data from Apostolou (2007). Courtesy of the author.

chap. 5). These males are able to protect females and their offspring and often provide better access to high-quality foods. The same is true for humans, although the consistency of these advantages is not always obvious when examined across cultures because men's dominance and status can be achieved in different ways from one culture to the next (Irons, 1979). Regardless of how cultural success is defined, women and their kin prefer culturally successful men as marriage partners. These men wield social influence and often have control over more reproductively useful resources than do other men. Women's marriage and mating preferences indicate they are motivated to capture and use these resources for their own reproductive ends.

As described previously, few women (or men) always get what they want, because of the competing interests of kin, competition with other women over desirable mates, and the preferences of these mates. This does not mean that preferences, as are often measured in psychological studies, do not provide useful information about the evolution of human mate choices. As I describe in chapter 9 (in the section titled Conscious–Psychological), these preferences are components of mental representations of the *perfect world*. This is a world in which one has social influence and control of culturally important resources.

The fantasized world provides a goal to achieve, and the associated components of these fantasies are hypothesized to represent resources that improved social and reproductive prospects during human evolution. In short, preferences and fantasies provide a glimpse into evolutionarily salient motivations and desires that are not constrained by the competing interests of others.

Actual Choices

The marriage patterns of the Kipsigis provide an example of how kin can influence women's actual mate choices and the benefits of marrying a culturally successful man (Borgerhoff Mulder, 1990, 2000). As with many of the hunter–gatherer societies represented in Figure 7.1, choice of marriage partners is made by the young woman's parents. In most cases, however, the parents' decision is influenced by their daughter's preferences. These joint decisions are strongly influenced by the amount of land made available to her and her future children. Land and cattle are controlled by men, and gaining access to these has important reproductive consequences for women.

> Land access is correlated with women's reproductive success, and may be an important causal factor contributing to reproductive differentials, given the greater availability of food in the homes of "richer" women and the lower incidence of illness among them and their offspring. (Borgerhoff Mulder, 1990, p. 256)

The benefits continue to the next generation. As I described in chapter 6 (in the section titled Father-Absent and Father-Present Societies), land is divided among a woman's sons, who eventually use it to attract wives. Thus, women who gain access to large land plots (through marriage) have more surviving grandchildren than do women with small plots (Borgerhoff Mulder, 2000). Given these relations, it is not surprising that across an 18-year period, Borgerhoff Mulder (1990) found that the two men offering the most land were chosen as husbands by 13 of 29 brides and their families, and either one or both of these men were married in 11 of the 15 years in which one or more marriages occurred. The two lowest ranking men were chosen as husbands in only 1 of these 15 years. The pattern clearly follows the evolutionary prediction: Women and their parents prefer culturally successful men because these men provide the resources women need to keep their children alive and healthy.

Even when men share the proceeds of successful hunts with everyone in their group, these good hunters are desirable as mates above and beyond the calories they provide through hunting. These men are higher status, and their children have lower mortality risks (Hawkes, O'Connell, & Blurton Jones, 2001; E. A. Smith, 2004; Wiessner, 2002). Marlowe (2003) found that good Hadza hunters were also more successful than other men at locating and securing honey; honey is not shared and provides substantial calories when their wives are nursing. A woman's decision to stay married or not is also influenced by the quantity and quality of resources provided by her husband (Betzig, 1989; Buckle, Gallup, & Rodd, 1996; A. Campbell, 2002). In the most extensive cross-cultural study of the pattern of marital dissolution ever conducted, Betzig (1989) found that "inadequate support is reported as cause for divorce in 21 societies and ascribed exclusively to the husband in all but one unspecified case" (p. 664).

Preferred Choices

Because preferences cannot always be put into practice, a woman's preferred marriage partner and her actual marriage partner are not typically the same. Social psychological studies of explicit and implicit preferences—for instance, preference for an attractive face without conscious awareness of why it is attractive—are thus an important adjunct to research on actual marriage choices. These preferences are less constrained by the competing interests of other people and capture the processes associated with the social and psychological mechanisms that can influence reproductive decisions and behaviors (Kenrick, Sadalla, Groth, & Trost, 1990). Preferences can nevertheless be influenced by social and sexual dynamics in the local community (Kenrick, N. P. Li, & Butner, 2003), by wider economic and social conditions, and by the individual woman's attractiveness as a mate; attractive women demand more from their mates (Pawlowski & Jasienska, 2008). To complicate matters further, not all preferences are equal; some are necessities and others are luxuries (N. P. Li, Bailey, Kenrick, & Linsenmeier, 2002). To examine this further, I begin with a discussion of the sex difference in preference for a culturally successful mate and then turn to mate-choice trade-offs and wider influences.

Culturally Successful Men. Women throughout the world indicate that men's cultural success or attributes that are likely to lead to success (e.g., ambition) are necessities when it comes to their preferred marriage partners (D. M. Buss, 1989b; N. P. Li et al., 2002). One of the largest studies ever conducted on women's and men's preferences included more than 10,000 people in 37 cultures across six continents and five islands (D. M. Buss, 1989b). Women rated "good financial prospect" higher than did men in all cultures. The pattern is illustrated for different parts of the world in Figure 7.2. The magnitude of the sex difference was smallest in Eastern Europe, but even here two out of three women rated good financial prospect as more important in a prospective marriage partner than did the average man. For the remaining regions of the world, from three out of four to five out of six women rated good financial prospect more highly than did the average man. In 29 samples, the "ambition and industriousness" of a prospective mate were more important for women than for men, presumably because these traits are indicators of his

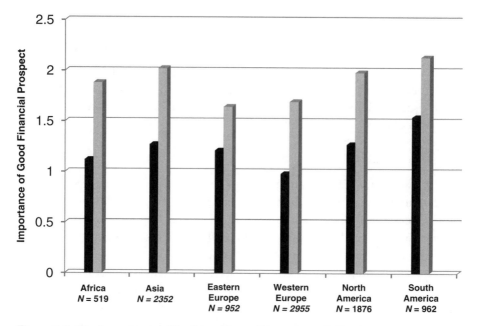

Figure 7.2. The importance of the "good financial prospects" of a prospective marriage partner on a 0 (unimportant) to 3 (indispensable) scale for men (black bar) and women (gray bar). Data from D. M. Buss (1989b). Courtesy of the author.

ability to eventually achieve cultural success. In only one sample were men's ratings significantly higher than those of women, the Zulu of South Africa; this may reflect the high level of physical labor (e.g., house building) expected of Zulu women.

Hatfield and Sprecher (1995) found the same pattern for college students in the United States, Japan, and Russia. In each of these nations, women valued a prospective mate's potential for success, earnings, status, and social position more highly than did men. A meta-analysis of research published from 1965 to 1986 revealed the same sex difference (Feingold, 1992a). Across studies, three out of four women rated socioeconomic status as more important in a prospective marriage partner than did the average man. Studies conducted prior to 1965 showed the same pattern (e.g., R. Hill, 1945), as did a survey of a nationally representative sample of unmarried adults in the United States (Sprecher, Sullivan, & Hatfield, 1994). Across age, ethnic status, and socioeconomic status, women preferred husbands who were better educated than they were and who earned more money than they did. Buunk, Dijkstra, Fetchenhauer, and Kenrick (2002) found the same pattern for women ranging in age from their 20s to 60s.

Women's preference for culturally successful men is also found in studies of singles ads and popular fiction novels. In a study of 1,000 "lonely hearts" ads, Greenlees and McGrew (1994) found that British women were 3 times more likely than British men to seek financial security in a prospective partner. Oda (2001) found that Japanese women were 31 times more likely than Japanese men to seek financial security and social status in a long-term partner. Muslim women sought educated and financially secure partners who were tall, emotionally sincere, and socially skilled (Badahdah & Tiemann, 2005). Young women (younger than 40 years) in Spain wanted both financial success and physical attractiveness in a prospective mate (Gil-Burmann, Peláez, & Sánchez, 2002); older women retained their desire for financial success but valued physical attractiveness less highly than did the younger women. Whissell (1996) found the same themes across 25 contemporary romance novels and 6 classic novels that have traditionally appealed to women more than men, including two stories from the Old Testament written about 3,000 years ago. In these stories, the male protagonist is almost always an older, socially dominant, and wealthy man who ultimately marries the woman.

As in traditional societies, marriage to a culturally successful man can have reproductive consequences for a woman in modern societies. Bereczkei and Csanaky (1996) studied more than 1,800 Hungarian men and women who were 35 years of age or older and thus not likely to have more children. They found that women who had married men who were older and better educated than themselves had, on average, more children, were less likely to get divorced, and reported higher levels of marital satisfaction than did women who married younger and/or less educated men.

Trade-Offs. Women's preference for a culturally successful partner is highlighted when they must make cost–benefit trade-offs between a partner's cultural success versus other important traits, such as his physical attractiveness (N. P. Li, 2007; N. P. Li et al., 2002). When their "mate dollars," so to speak, are limited, women spend more of them on the social status and resources of a long-term partner than on other traits. When they have additional mate dollars, they spend proportionally less on status and resources and more on the personal traits of this mate (e.g., his friendliness). Figure 7.3 highlights the sex difference in the importance of cultural success across different mate dollar budgets (N. P. Li et al., 2002). Unmarried women on a tight budget allocate more mate dollars to the resources or social standing of a prospective mate than do men, but the magnitude of this sex difference declines as budgets become flush. In yet another study, college women reported the minimally acceptable earning potential of a prospective husband was the 70th percentile; on the basis of earning potential alone, 70% of men were eliminated from the pool of potential marriage partners. The corresponding figure for college men was the 40th percentile (Kenrick et al., 1990).

Once a prospective mate has achieved the minimal social standing, additional resources and status yield diminishing results. Kenrick, Sundie,

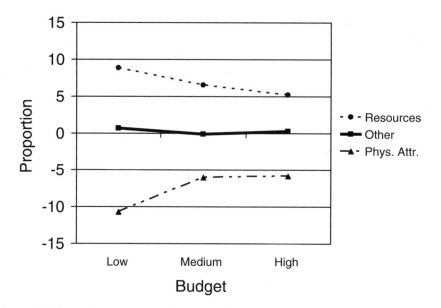

Figure 7.3. Sex differences in allocation of mate dollars on a prospective marriage partner's resources (including social standing) and physical attractiveness across low to high budgets. From "The Necessities and Luxuries of Mate Preferences: Testing the Tradeoffs," by N. P. Li, J. M. Bailey, D. T. Kenrick, and J. A. W. Linsenmeier, 2002, *Journal of Personality and Social Psychology, 82,* p. 951 (Panel B, Figure 1). Copyright 2002 by the American Psychological Association. Reprinted with permission of Norman P. Li.

Nicastle, and Stone (2001) found that the desirability of man as a marriage partner increased sharply as his income rose from low- to an upper-middle-class level (about $100,000) and then leveled off. An increase in a man's income from $25,000 per year to $75,000 per year resulted in a substantial increase in his desirability, but increasing his income from $100,000 per year to $300,000 per year had little effect.

Wider Cultural Wealth and Mores. Wider economic or cultural influences may influence stated preferences and the magnitude of some but not all of the sex differences in these preferences (D. M. Buss, 1989ab Eagly & Wood, 1999; Lippa, 2007). In Figure 7.2 and D. M. Buss's 1989b study, the reader can see that both women and men rated the financial prospects of a prospective mate as less important in Europe than in other regions of the world. At the time of the study, central governments in Eastern Europe provided many basic necessities (e.g., housing, health care), and there were constraints on earned income. To a lesser degree, the central governments in Western Europe provide similar economic supports, and high taxes constrain income differences. The same pattern is found when responses in China are compared with those of the rest of Asia (not shown in Figure 7.2).

Eagly and Wood (1999) found that the magnitude of the sex difference in the value of a prospective mate's financial prospects, from D. M. Buss's study (1989b), was smaller in nations in which women had political and social influence and when they had some financial independence. The gist is that when economic supports are provided by sources outside of the marital relationship, both women and men downgrade the importance of a prospective mate's financial prospects and presumably focus more on luxuries. Despite this cultural variation, the sex difference in the importance of a would-be partner's cultural success remains.

Personal and Behavioral Attributes

A preference for a culturally successful marriage partner is not enough in and of itself to constitute a successful reproductive strategy for women. Culturally successful men are often arrogant, self-serving, and better able to pursue casual sex than are other men. When situated in a wealthy country with large numbers of men who make a sufficient income, women do not have to tolerate the competing interests of the most culturally successful men; Eagly and Wood's (1999) findings suggest just this. Women can focus on luxuries that will make a long-term relationship satisfying. These traits provide information on the willingness of the man to cooperate in a long-term relationship and to invest in children.

Interpersonal Luxuries

In addition to traits that signal cultural success, women often rate the emotional stability and the family orientation of prospective marriage partners more highly than do men (e.g., Oda, 2001). D. M. Buss (1989b) found that women rated a prospective husband who was kind, understanding, and intelligent more highly than a prospective husband who was none of these but had the potential to become culturally successful. In his Internet survey of more than 200,000 people, Lippa (2007) found that women valued a prospective mate's sense of humor, honesty, kindness, dependability, and communication skills more highly than did men. These are traits that enable women (and men) to form stable long-term marital relationships. Preferences for these traits are a luxury that can be expressed in wealthy, individualistic Western nations and especially in the middle- and upper-middle classes of these societies (Argyle, 1994).

In less wealthy, more collectivistic societies (e.g., Latin America) women weight a prospective mate's social respectability, competence, and responsibility more heavily than his interpersonal traits (e.g., humor, kindness) and more heavily than do women in individualistic societies (Lippa, 2007).

Emotional satisfaction is central to white middle-class Euroamerican marriages because the Euroamerican family is so mobile, nucleated, isolated, and far away from relatives so that emotionally close relationships are hard to come by. . . . Husband–wife emotional satisfaction is not as critical for the Aka as it is for Euroamericans. (Hewlett, 1992, p. 170)

Hadza women report wanting "nice" husbands, but in this society nice means these men do not hit them (Marlowe, 2004b). In the Hadza, Ache, Yanomamö, and many other traditional societies, wives and husbands spend much of their time in sex-segregated groups, with sometimes emotionally distant and tense spousal relationships (Chagnon, 1997; Hawkes et al., 2001; K. Hill & Hurtado, 1996; Pasternak et al., 1997).

This is not to say that women in these societies do not prefer emotional satisfaction, but rather that it is a luxury that cannot be realized as easily as it can in wealthy Western nations. When women must focus on keeping their children alive and healthy, luxuries such as the man's attentiveness to her emotional needs cannot be substituted for the resources controlled by culturally successful men or the potentially less desirable characteristics of these men. Even if they cannot indulge in these luxuries, they would still like to have them in a mate, as illustrated in this interview with an Ache woman (Hill asked Achipura, but another woman named Achipuragi responded; K. Hill & Hurtado, 1996, p. 228).

> *Kim Hill* : Achipura, what kind of man could get many women, what kind did women love, the kind who could easily find a wife?
>
> *Achipuragi* : He had to be a good hunter.
>
> *Kim Hill* : So if a man was a good hunter he could easily find a wife?
>
> *Achipuragi* : No, not just a good hunter. A good hunter could find a wife, but a man needed to be strong.
>
> *Kim Hill* : When you say strong, do you mean a man who could beat up others in a club fight?
>
> *Achipuragi* : No, women don't like those men. Women don't like men who love to hit others. I mean a strong man. One who would walk far to hunt, one who would carry heavy loads. I mean a man who would work hard when everyone was tired, or build a hut when it was cold and rainy. I mean a man who was strong. A man who could endure and not get tired.
>
> *Kim Hill* : Did women love big men then [i.e., men of large body size]?
>
> *Achipuragi* : No, they would love a small man or a large man, but he had to be strong.

Kim Hill : What other men would be able to acquire a wife easily?

Achipuragi : A man who was "a good man."

Kim Hill : What does it mean, "a good man?"

Achipuragi : A good man is one who is handsome [attractive face]. One whom women love. One who is nice and smiles and tells jokes. He is a man who is handsome.

Emotional Commitment and Jealousy

As mentioned previously, many women find emotional intimacy with a partner to be an attractive part of their relationship. It follows that seeing another woman receive this emotional resource from a partner or prospective partner will evoke jealousy. But why?

Daly, Wilson, and Weghorst (1982) hypothesized that men's risk of cuckoldry (see the section titled Cuckoldry, chap. 6, this volume) heightened the benefits of mate guarding and sexual jealousy in men more than women and resulted in an evolved sex difference in response to sexual infidelity. D. M. Buss, Larsen, Western, and Semmelroth (1992) hypothesized that women, in contrast, may experience jealousy more intensely than men when a mate or prospective mate develops an emotional attachment to another woman. This emotional attachment may signal risk of abandonment and thus risk of losing the man's resources. Intimacy is, in effect, a cue to relationship stability and continued investment. The finding that many women require intimacy before the development of a sexual relationship is another indicator of a link between intimacy and women's reproductive psychology (Oliver & Hyde, 1993); the delay discourages men who are primarily interested in casual sex (D. M. Buss, 2003; Paul & Hirsch, 1996).

The proposal that women become more jealous than men with threats to the intimacy of their relationship has created considerable debate and resulted in much empirical research (Buunk, Angleitner, Oubaid, & Buss, 1996; DeSteno & Salovey, 1996; C. R. Harris, 2000, 2003; C. R. Harris & Christenfeld, 1996; Sabini & Green, 2004). When women and men are forced to choose the lesser of two evils—whether a partner's sexual or emotional infidelity is more upsetting—more women than men report their partner's emotional infidelity as more upsetting, and more men than women choose their partner's sexual infidelity. This pattern has been found in the vast majority of studies and in samples from the United States, China, Japan, Korea, Germany, Holland, Austria, and Sweden (e.g., C. R. Harris, 2003; Sabini & Green, 2004). Marlowe (2003) reported that Hadza women become jealous when their husbands court other women. Schützwohl and Koch (2004) found that women were more likely to remember (1 week later) cues of a partner's potential emotional infidelity than his potential sexual infidelity; men's memory was better for cues to a partner's sexual infidelity. A brain imaging study of people's reactions to their partners' infidelity revealed sex differences for scenarios of emotional infidelity (Takahashi et al., 2006). Brain regions associated with detection of social intent and deception (e.g., the superior temporal sulcus) were activated in women but not men.

These sex differences are more consistently found for younger and naïve adults than for older adults with more relationship experience and when distress is measured without having to choose one or the other form of infidelity as being more distressful (DeSteno & Salovey, 1996; Sabini & Green, 2004; Shackelford et al., 2004). As with the expression of nearly all other traits, the magnitude of the sex difference in emotional responses to threats to valuable relationships is influenced by many factors, ranging from cultural mores to partner characteristics to intrapersonal variables (e.g., self-esteem; D. M. Buss & Shackelford, 1977; Geary, Rumsey, Bow-Thomas, & Hoard, 1995). The point is that women value emotional intimacy and, regardless of how men react, are sensitive to and intensely distressed if their partners become emotionally intimate with other women. These are strong indications that jealousy and attendant emotional and behavioral reactions have a long evolutionary history in women, as expected if the development of long-term relationships with men provides benefits to them and their children (see the section titled Benefits to Children, chap. 6, this volume).

Physical Attractiveness and Good Genes

In classical literature and romance novels, the male protagonist is almost always socially dominant, wealthy, and handsome (Whissell, 1996). As I described in chapters 3 (in the section titled Behavioral Precopulatory Choice) and 4 (in the section titled Sex Hormones, Parasites, and Male Quality) of this volume, a preference for a handsome husband (or short-term partner) makes biological sense (Fink & Penton-Voak, 2002; Gangestad & Buss, 1993). This is because the physical traits that women find attractive in men are very likely to be indicators of the man's physical and genetic health (Gangestad & Simpson, 2000)—especially in contexts with extensive health risks (B. S. Low, 1990a)—in the same way that the long tail feathers of the hummingbird shown in Figure 3.3 (see chap. 3, this volume) are an indicator of the male's genetic and physical quality. The take home message is that handsome husbands should not only sire children who are attractive and thus sought out as mating and marriage partners in adulthood, these men and their children are also predicted to be physically healthier than other men and their children (Gangestad, Thornhill, & Yeo, 1994; Grammer & Thornhill, 1994; Singh, 1995b; Thornhill & Gangestad, 1993).

Body and Facial Attractiveness

What makes a man handsome? On the basis of women's preferences, these are men who are taller than average (but not too tall) and have an athletic (but not too muscular), symmetric body shape with a 0.8 to 0.9 waist-to-hip ratio (WHR) and 0.7 waist-to-chest ratio; these men have a muscular V shape (Barber, 1995; Beck, Ward-Hull, & McClear, 1976; Fan, Dai, Liu, & Wu, 2005; Gangestad et al., 1994; Hatfield & Sprecher, 1995; Singh, 1995b). Men with these traits are, as predicted, physically fit (Hönekopp, Rudolph, Beier, Liebert, & Müller, 2007). Women choose them as short-term and long-term mates more often than they choose other men; in some contexts, but not others, these men sire more children (Hönekopp et al., 2007; Kurzban & Weeden, 2005; N. P. Li & Kenrick, 2006; Nettle, 2002; Pawlowski, Dunbar, & Lipowicz, 2000; Sear, 2006; M. D. Taylor et al., 2005). The facial features that women generally rate as attractive include somewhat larger than average eyes, a large smile area, prominent cheekbones and chin and overall facial symmetry (Barber, 1995; Cunningham, Barbee, & Pike, 1990; Scheib, Gangestad, & Thornhill, 1999).

These facial features and the V shape may be good indicators of genetic variability, which is important for disease resistance and suggest a healthy developmental period (Barber, 1995; Langlois et al., 2000; Lie, Simmons, & Rhodes, 2009; S. C. Roberts et al., 2005; Thornhill & Gangestad, 1993). S. C. Roberts et al. found that women rated the faces of men with more variable immune-system genes (i.e., major histocompatibility complex [MHC]) as more attractive and healthy than the faces of men with less variation in these genes. The development of prominent cheekbones and a masculine chin is related to testosterone levels and testosterone/estrogen ratios during puberty (Fink & Penton-Voak, 2002; Tanner, 1990). Chronic illness or poor nutrition during adolescence can suppress testosterone secretion, resulting in less prominent cheekbones and a more feminine-looking chin (Thornhill & Gangestad, 1993). Shackelford and Larsen (1997) found that men with less symmetric facial features were less physically active, manifested more symptoms of depression and anxiety, and reported more minor physical problems (e.g., colds, headaches) than their peers with more symmetric faces. Men with asymmetric faces and body features also have higher basal metabolic rates, somewhat lower IQs, and fewer sexual partners (Furlow, Armijo-Prewitt, Gangestad, & Thornhill, 1997; Manning, Koukourakis, & Brodie, 1997).

Other analyses conducted in wealthy populations with modern medical care, however, do not always support a relation between men's facial and body traits and overall physical health (Weeden & Sabini, 2005). In these populations, there may be a relation between health and height at the extremes of height (Nettle, 2002) and within the middle range of attractiveness; people overestimate the health of very attractive men and underestimate that of unattractive men (Kalick, Zebrowitz, Langlois, & Johnson, 1998). Men who are overweight and especially with upper body fat (e.g., large waists) in middle age are also more like to suffer from premature death (Yusuf et al., 2005). These relations aside, the modern world is not the context in which women's preferences for handsome mates evolved. In today's world, the relation between health and attractiveness is most likely to emerge in populations with lower quality medical care, wider variation in access to food, and with a high number of parasites. As I covered in chapter 3 of this volume (in the section titled Good Genes), a consistent condition-dependent relation between attractiveness and health may only emerge in stressful conditions.

Studies by B. S. Low (1988, 1990a) and Gangestad and D. M. Buss (1993) provide support for the condition-dependent relation between attractiveness and health. B. S. Low hypothesized that men living in environments with many parasites would be more variable, as a group, in terms of health and physical attractiveness than men living in more benign regions of the world. Greater variation in men's health and attractiveness in parasite-ridden environments would reduce the number of acceptable male marriage partners and thereby increase the degree of polygyny. Across 186 cultures, as the number of parasites in the local environment increases, the number of unmarried men increases (B. S. Low, 1990a). Gangestad and D. M. Buss found that women and men in these same regions of the world rated the importance of the physical attractiveness of a prospective mate more highly than did individuals living in regions of the world with fewer parasites.

Immune-System Genes

The reader may recall that genes of the MHC are involved in immune-system responses to parasites and other pathogens (see the section titled Parasite Resistance, chap. 2). Mates with highly similar MHC genes may produce offspring with resistance to fewer parasites, whereas mates with highly dissimilar MHC genes may produce offspring with increased risk of autoimmune disorders (Milinski, 2006). Women's choice of mates with MHC genes moderately different from their own might then result in the best immune system for their children. Women are not aware of these genetic differences, but they can smell indications of them: Immune-system genes are signaled through pheromones, and women are sensitive to and respond to these scents. They are especially sensitive to these scents when they are ovulating (Garver-Apgar, Gangestad, Thornhill, R. D. Miller, & Olp, 2006; Thornhill & Gangestad, 2008) and to scents associated with MHC genes inherited from their fathers (Jacob, McClintock, Zelano, & Ober, 2002).

The prediction that women will prefer mates with dissimilar MHC genes has been supported by many (Garver-Apgar et al., 2006; Thornhill & Gangestad, 2008; Wedekind, Seebeck, Bettens, & Paepke, 1995) but not all of the corresponding mate-choice studies (Thornhill et al., 2003). In the first of these, Wedekind et al. (1995) found that women who are not taking oral contraceptives—these can change sensitivity to pheromones—rated the scents of men with dissimilar immune-system genes as more pleasant and sexy than the scents of men with similar immune-system genes. Thornhill et al. (2003) did not, however, find that women preferred the scent of men with highly dissimilar MHC genes, but there was a tendency for women to prefer the scent of men with moderately dissimilar genes.

In a long-term fertility study, Ober, Elias, Kostyu, and Hauck (1992) found that couples with dissimilar immune-system genes conceived more quickly (2 months vs. 5 months) and had fewer spontaneous abortions than did couples with more similar genes. Hedrick and Black (1997a), in contrast, found no evidence of MHC-based disassortative mating in 194 couples from 11 South Amerindian tribes. As is common in hunter–gatherer societies (see Figure 7.1), these women may not have had complete freedom in their choice of marriage partners, and thus the negative results are difficult to interpret. In a study of more than 500 offspring of these and other South Amerindian couples, Hedrick and Black (1997b; F. L. Black & Hedrick, 1997) found much more variation in MHC genes than would be expected on the basis of the degree of MHC-gene similarity between their parents. Greater MHC variation in children than in parents could result from a high frequency of spontaneous abortions of fetuses with too little MHC variation, as found by Ober et al. (1997).

The subtlety and importance of MHC genes are illustrated further by Garver-Apgar et al. (2006). In their study, 48 exclusive couples (11 married or cohabiting) were assessed using multiple measures of satisfaction with the personal and sexual relationship with their partner across high- and low-fertility points in the ovulatory cycle. Varieties of several MHC genes were also assessed. There was a tendency for couples to be more dissimilar on MHC genes than would be expected by chance. A more intriguing finding was that as the degree of MHC similarity increased, women reported decreased sexual attraction to and arousal (confirmed by their partners) by their partners; MHC similarity was not related to satisfaction with other aspects of their relationship. Women with MHC-similar partners also reported more extrapair relationships, as Potts, Manning, and Wakeland (1991) found for female mice (see the section titled Parasite Resistance, chap. 2, this volume).

Even when women do not have complete control over their marriage partner or choose partners on the basis of other traits, their sexual behavior and the likelihood of bringing a pregnancy to term indicate that at least a moderate degree of dissimilarity between their MHC genes and those of their partners results in the best outcome for their children, at least with respect to variation in immune-system genes.

Eye of the Beholder

Although women agree on the general body and facial features that they find attractive in men, women's current and past relationships, as well as other male traits, can influence their judgment of any particular man's physical attractiveness. When other women negatively evaluate a man, women rate this man as less physically attractive than they would have rated him otherwise (Graziano, Jensen-Campbell, Shebilske & Lundgren, 1993). Socially dominant men are rated as more physically attractive than subordinate men (e.g., Townsend, Kline, & Wasserman, 1995). As I described in chapter 6 of this volume (in the section titled Reproductive Maturation), the nature of a woman's relationship with her father and his age and facial features can bias her to rate men with similar features as attractive or unattractive.

To make matters more confusing, women's ratings of whether relatively masculinized or relatively feminized male facial features are more attractive vary across the ovulatory cycle (see the section that follows). Women with masculine partners (DeBruine et al., 2006), women who perceive themselves as physically attractive (Little, Burt, Penton-Voak, & Perrett, 2001), and women who mature at an earlier age (Cornwell et al., 2006) show a strong preference for masculinized faces.

Ovulatory Cycle

The reader is almost certainly aware that women's reproduction-related hormones vary across the 28-day cycle (on average) shown in Figure 7.4. The estrogen (e.g., estradiol) surge begins about Day 8 or 9 in a typical cycle and in combination with other hormones (not shown) contributes to ovulation. There is a corresponding window of fertility that is 5 days before and the day of ovulation (Wilcox, Weinberg, & Baird, 1995). The increase in testosterone corresponding to the estrogen peak may increase women's desire for sex, contingent on other conditions (van Anders, Hamilton, & Watson, 2007). The progesterone increase contributes to the preparation of the uterus for implantation of a fertilized egg. For scientists, the central questions are whether there is a shift in mate preferences during the fertile window and whether any such shift reflects a heightened sensitivity to traits that are indicators of men's genetic fitness (see the section titled Good Genes, chap. 3, this volume). If this is the case, are there complementary psychological changes that increase the chances that women will seek an extrapair relation-

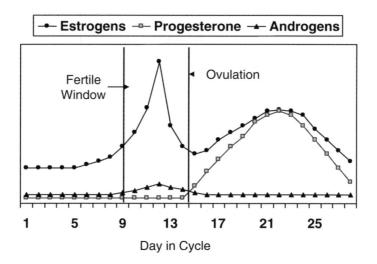

Figure 7.4. Hormonal changes across women's ovulatory cycle. Estrogens (e.g., estradiol) begin to increase at about Day 8 or 9 in a typical cycle and contribute to ovulation. The corresponding increase in androgens (e.g., testosterone) may increase women's desire for sex. The progesterone increase contributes to the preparation of the uterus for implantation of a fertilized egg. Illustration by Melanie Sheldon. Printed with permission.

ship with such a man during this window (Gangestad & Thornhill, 2008; Gangestad, Thornhill, & Garver-Apgar, 2005a)?

Good Genes

Women's ratings of men's attractiveness change as they approach and enter the 6-day window of high fertility. During this window, many women are more attentive to physically attractive men (Gangestad & Thornhill, 1998; Thornhill & Gangestad, 1999), and some women are more easily aroused by sexually explicit images (Slob, Bax, Hop, Rowland, & van der Werff ten Bosch, 1996), but others are not (Meuwissen & Over, 1992). During this window, women show increased attraction to taller men (Pawlowski & Jasienska, 2005), the scents of men with symmetrical body features (Thornhill & Gangestad, 1999), masculine faces (Penton-Voak et al., 1999), deeper voices (Puts, 2005), assertive and dominant behavior and personality (Gangestad, Garver-Apgar, Simpson, & Cousins, 2007), and high creativity (Haselton & Miller, 2006).

Nearly all of these studies indicate that when women's preferences shift it is for short-term and not long-term mates (Cárdenas & Harris, 2007; Puts, 2006), and particularly if she is paired with a physically unattractive long-term mate (Gangestad, Thornhill, & Garver-Apgar, 2005b; Haselton & Gangestad,

2006). Bressan and Stranieri (2008) found that women preferred men with these traits if the men were single and thus presumably more available for a short-term encounter. Roney and Simmons (2008) found that women's preference for masculine faces was directly related to their estrogen levels; women with higher circulating estrogen showed a stronger preference for these faces. During the low-fertility phase of their cycle, women's preference for these physical and behavioral traits declines, and their preference for traits that signal men's emotional sensitivity and parental investment increases (Penton-Voak et al., 1999).

The pattern found with these studies is similar to that found in other species with the facultative expression of male parenting. As I discussed in chapter 4 (in the section titled Male Parenting), females of these species often engage in extrapair copulations if they are paired with lower quality males and if the males' investment is not obligate: Male investment is not absolutely needed for offspring survival, which lowers the cost of male abandonment if the extrapair partner is detected. The extrapair copulations are with males that are more attractive than their mate—they are more colorful, have longer tail features, and so forth—or with males with dissimilar immune-system genes (e.g., Hoffman, Forcada, Trathan, & Amos, 2007). The combination results in healthier offspring (see the section titled Good Genes, chap. 3, this volume). The implication for humans is that some women engage in strategic mating (Gangestad & Simpson, 2000). When they are paired with an unattractive husband or do not want to pay the cost of maintaining a relationship with a sexually attractive man (these men may require more mate guarding), some women seek good genes from a short-term mate and paternal investment from a long-term mate.

Social and Psychological Change

If there is a bias for women paired with unattractive men to at least consider a short-term affair, then there should be social and psychological changes that accompany the shift in mate preferences. These changes are indeed found. During the window of high fertility, women spend more time in mixed-sex social settings and flirt more with attractive men in these settings (Haselton & Gangestad, 2006); they report heightened interest in extrapair men and fantasize about these men (Gangestad, Thornhill, & Garver, 2002); they report less attraction to their current partner (Gangestad et al., 2005b); they wear more revealing clothing when they are not with their partner (Durante, N. P. Li, & Haselton, 2008; Grammer, Renninger, & Fischer, 2004; Schwarz & Hassebrauck, 2008); and they appear to be less emotionally jealous and less concerned about intimacy as a motive for sex (Geary, DeSoto, Hoard, M. S. Sheldon, & Cooper, 2001; M. S. Sheldon, Cooper, Geary, Hoard, & DeSoto, 2006).

The last change suggests an emotional disengagement from a woman's primary partner, which, in turn, would make a short-term relationship less emotionally difficult for the woman. The gist is that a woman who engages in a short-term affair may be generally attentive to the relationship with her social partner and thus maintain his investment, and become sensitive to the cues of a more fit man only during the 6-day fertility window. In this way, the risk of a woman's partner detecting an affair is reduced, given the brief period during which she is attracted to and potentially sexually responsive to other men.

Not that all women are biased to have an affair around the time they ovulate. Women paired with attractive husbands and partners do not show heightened attraction to extrapair men during the fertility window (Haselton & Gangestad, 2006), and most women with less attractive mates do not act on their fantasies. If they did, the cuckoldry rate would not be strongly related to the man's social status (see the section titled Cuckoldry, chap. 6, this volume). This is because higher status men are less likely to be cuckolded than are lower status men, but many high-status men are not physically attractive. Women are less likely to cuckold high-status men because of the potential costs to them and their children if they were caught cheating and lost his investment. As I described in chapter 6 of this volume (in the section titled Women's Strategies and Men's Mating Opportunities), pair bonding should also reduce the risks of an affair by both partners, even if intimacy dips during the fertile window for some women (M. S. Sheldon et al., 2006). It is also unclear whether some women's extrapair relationships are failed attempts to switch mates rather than cuckoldry per se.

Along with the potential benefits of having a child sired by an attractive man come the risks of pregnancy by an unwanted man (Thornhill & Palmer, 2000). During the window of high fertility, women are particularly sensitive to men's potential to be sexually coercive (Petralia & Gallup, 2002) and are more cautious about their surroundings (Chavanne & Gallup, 1998). Chavanne and Gallup found that normally cycling women, but not women using hormonal contraceptives, reported engaging in less risky behaviors (e.g., going to bars) around the time of ovulation than at other times in their cycle. Women are also more likely to rate assertive men as "creepy," "frightening," or potentially coercive during the fertility window (Garver-Apgar, Gangestad, & Simpson, 2007). These women may be overestimating the risks of assault, but it is better to err on the side of caution given the costs of pregnancy and maternal care.

Alternative Mating Strategies

There are many contexts in which women are unable to obtain the type of relationship described in romance novels: a long-term monogamous relationship with a handsome, socially dominant, and high-investing man. And there is more to these situations than implied by my earlier discussions of cuckoldry (see chap. 6) and interest in short-term mates (discussed earlier in this chapter). D. M. Buss and Schmitt (1993) hypothesized and Regan and Dreyer (1999) confirmed that women sometimes engage in short-term sexual relationships as a means to attract the attention of and attempt to develop a longer term relationship with a desired man. In these relationships, the traits women find attractive in a long-term partner are the same as those used to select a short-term partner (Vigil, Geary, & Byrd-Craven, 2006), unlike during the ovulatory shift described previously.

In a study of 460 women, the majority of whom were living in impoverished circumstances (e.g., more than half received government assistance), Vigil et al. (2006) found considerable individual differences in the trade-offs women make when choosing short-term and long-term mates. Almost 2 out of 5 of these women reported significant differences in the traits they desired in a long-term and short-term mate; the remaining women were similar in their preferences across long-term and short-term mates, consistent with D. M. Buss and Schmitt's (1993) prediction. The women who reported differences in the preferred traits of long-term and short-term mates clustered into 2 groups. One group focused on the physical attractiveness of a short-term mate, as predicted by good genes models (Gangestad & Simpson, 2000), but the other group focused on the potential financial gains of such a relationship. These women were more likely to be dependent on government assistance, had more children, and were less conscientious. In other words, some women used their sexuality and men's desire for short-term mates and sexual variety for financial or other material gains (Brewer et al., 2000). I am not saying this was their preference, but rather their circumstances pressed them to use this strategy.

In many parts of the world, there are large numbers of men who do not have the material or social resources to support a family. To adapt to this circumstance, some women develop a successive series of relationships with a number of these men or several simultaneously, each of whom provides some investment during the course of the relationship (Campbell, 2002; Lancaster, 1989). These women are practicing serial monogamy and sometimes polyandry. In recounting a study conducted in the Dominican Republic, Lancaster (1989) noted that in comparison with women monogamously married to men with low incomes,

> women who excluded males from the domestic unit and maintained multiple liaisons were more fecund, had healthier children with fewer pre- and post-natal mishaps, were able to raise more children over the age of five, had better nourished children (as measured by protein per capita), and had better psychological adjustment (as measured by self-report and lower maternal blood pressure). (pp. 68–69)

In several South Amerindian societies, such as the Ache and Barí, women engage in sexual relations with men who are not their social partner, especially after becoming pregnant (Beckerman et al., 1998; K. Hill & Hurtado, 1996). By tradition, these men are called *secondary fathers* and are socially obligated to provide material resources and social protection to the woman's child, although not all of them do so. The result seems to be a confusion of paternity such that both primary and secondary fathers invest in the child. The mortality rate of Ache children with one secondary father is about half that of children with no secondary father or two or more secondary fathers. With more than one secondary father, paternity is too uncertain, and thus these men do not invest in the child. The benefit of a secondary father cannot be attributed to qualities of the mother; Beckerman et al. found that 80% of Barí children with a secondary father survived to adulthood, compared with 61% of their siblings without a secondary father.

MEN'S MATE CHOICES

Men differ from women in terms of their enthusiasm for casual sex and in terms of the traits they prefer in short-term and long-term mates. I describe all of the corresponding sex differences and men's preferences in sections that follow. But I ask the reader to first reflect on how these follow from the sex difference in parental investment and from the facultative expression of men's parenting (see chap. 6). Men may not invest as much in children as women do, but they do invest considerably more than nearly all other mammalian males (Clutton-Brock, 1989). Because of this, men are predicted to show more selectivity in their choice of long-term mates and marriage partners than is evident in most other mammals, and this is indeed the case. Men's enthusiasm for casual sex also follows logically from the biological fact that they can potentially reproduce without paying the cost of pregnancy and the longer term investment in children, whereas women do not have this option. When men expect to invest little or nothing in any resulting children, their mate-choice standards are predicted to drop, and they do.

After describing the sex difference in preference for short-term relationships, I move to a description of the personal and behavioral attributes that men prefer in marriage partners, followed by respective reviews of the physical attributes of women that men find attractive and the relation between these attributes and women's fertility. Before moving to these reviews, I note that individual men vary in their mate preferences and choices, such as the importance they place on a mate's attractiveness. Desirable men devote more time and effort to obtaining short-term sexual relationships and have a stronger preference for physically attractive short-term and long-term mates than do other men (B. C. Jones et al., 2007; Pérusse, 1993; Pratto & Hegarty, 2000; Surbey & Brice, 2007).

Casual Sex

As I noted in the section titled Alternative Mating Strategies earlier in this chapter, women sometimes pursue short-term sex as a means to secure material or other resources for themselves or their children and occasionally to cuckold their partner. Many men, in contrast, pursue short-term sex as an end in and of itself (D. M. Buss & Schmitt, 1993; Symons, 1979). Men who are culturally successful (Pérusse, 1993), have the physical traits that women find attractive (Gangestad, Bennett, & Thornhill, 2001), are open to new experiences and are sexually liberal (Schmitt et al., 2004), or are would-be alpha males—young men who are driven to achieve cultural success (Pratto & Hegarty, 2000)—are more likely than other men to succeed in attracting short-term mates. At the same time, there are also men, including some who might be successful in attracting short-term mates, who are not especially interested in casual relationships (e.g., L. C. Miller & Fishkin, 1997), a finding that ignited debate as to whether there is in fact an overall sex difference in the preferred number of sexual partners.

In D. M. Buss and Schmitt's (1993) review and studies, young men reported, on average, a desire for 18 sexual partners over their lifetime compared with women's desire for 4 or 5 partners. W. C. Pedersen, Miller, Putcha-Bhagavatula, and Yang (2002) reanalyzed these data and with new data of their own confirmed the mean sex difference reported by D. M. Buss and Schmitt. When median scores—50% of the people reported a lower number of preferred partners and 50% a higher number—were examined, however, there was no sex difference in one study and a small difference in another; "women ideally wanted a median of 1 of these [casual] relationships before settling down with one mutually exclusive sexual partner, whereas men wanted a median of 2" (W. C. Pedersen et al., 2002, p. 159). Analyses of data reported in both studies using techniques appropriate to simultaneously analyzing means, medians, and extreme values, McBurney, Zapp, and Streeter (2005) found at "all comparable locations on curves showing cumulative number of desired partners, men report preferring more than three times as many partners as women do" (p. 271). Schmitt et al. (2003) found the same sex difference for samples of 6,822 men and 9,466 women from nearly all regions of the world, and confirmed that many more men than women in all of these regions, married or not, were actively seeking short-term mates and sexual variety.

Men's preference for short-term mates and the correlated preference for sexual variety are not typically realized because of women's desire for more committed relationships. But they are nevertheless real: The best window on the strength of these preferences comes from studies that release the brakes of female choice, specifically, research on sex differences in sexual attitudes and fantasies and in the use of prostitutes and pornography.

Sexual Attitudes and Fantasy

In a meta-analysis of 177 studies of sexuality conducted in the United States and Canada representing the responses of more than 125,000 people, Oliver and Hyde (1993) found large sex differences in attitudes toward casual sex and the frequency of masturbation; the latter reflects a disparity between sexual appetite and the number of sexual partners. About 4 out of 5 men were more enthusiastic about the prospect of casual sex than the average woman, and about 6 out of 7 men reported masturbating more frequently than the average woman. Women more strongly endorsed the double standard—premarital sex is less acceptable for women than men—and they reported more anxiety and guilt over sex than did men, but these were small differences. The sex difference in attitudes toward casual sex did not differ across the 1960s, 1970s, or 1980s, but other attitudes changed. The largest change regarded opinions of sexual relationships for couples who were engaged to be married. Women were more likely to endorse this type of relationship in the 1980s than in the 1960s.

Thus, as social prohibitions against women's sexuality lessened in the United States, the attitudes of women toward sexual relationships showed only selective changes. The tendency to avoid casual sex remained, but women's willingness to engage in sex with a man committed to a long-term relationship increased greatly. The selectivity of these changes is supported by another meta-analysis that included 530 studies and 269,649 people from the United States. From 1943 to 1999, B. E. Wells and Twenge (2005) found that the age of first sexual experience dropped; the percentage of young women engaging in premarital sex increased; and attitudes became more lenient with regard to this behavior. There were changes for young men as well, but these were less dramatic (see Baumeister, 2000). At the same time, the number of reported sexual partners did not increase across these decades, indicating that women remained discriminating and restrictive in their choice of mates.

Men's reported attitudes about casual sex are not simply talk to impress peers: When given the opportunity, most men will put this desire into practice. R. D. Clark and Hatfield (1989) demonstrated as much in a set of studies in which undergraduates approached attractive but unfamiliar members of the opposite sex and asked them for a date, to go to their apartment, or to engage in casual sex. When asked for a date, 1 out of 2 men and 1 out of 2 women accepted. When asked to engage in casual sex, 3 out of 4 men agreed, but none of the women agreed. In his classic work on the evolution of human sexuality, Symons (1979) illustrated the sex difference in enthusiasm for casual sex with a contrast of the sexual and intimate lives of gay men and lesbians. This contrast is telling because these individuals do not have to deal with the often competing interests and motivations of the opposite sex.

Fundamental male–female differences also are apparent in variety-seeking. The search for new sexual partners is a striking feature of the male homosexual world: the most frequent form of sexual activity is the one-night stand in which sex occurs, without obligation or commitment, between strangers . . . In one-night stands and in longer liaisons the basis of the male homosexual relationship usually is sexual activity and orgasm. . . . But lesbians form lasting, intimate, paired relationships far more frequently and easily than male homosexuals do; stable relationships are overwhelmingly preferred to any other, and monogamy is the ideal. (Symons, 1979, pp. 293–298)

There are also extensive differences in the quantity and nature of men's and women's sexual fantasies. G. D. Wilson (1997) found that men were 2.5 times more likely to fantasize about group sex than were women, and Trudel (2002) found an even larger difference (40% of men, 13% of women) in a random sample of nearly 1,000 married adults. Ellis and Symons (1990) found that men were twice as likely as women to report having sexual fantasies at least once a day and were 4 times as likely to report having fantasized about sex with more than 1,000 different people (32% of men, 8% of women). Although there were no sex differences in feelings of guilt over sexual fantasies, men and women differed considerably in the content of their fantasies. Women were 2.5 times as likely to report thinking about the personal and emotional relationship with their partner, whereas men were nearly 4 times as likely to report focusing on their partner's physical characteristics. Moreover, women were twice as likely to report fantasizing about someone they were currently romantically involved with or had been involved with, whereas men were 3 times as likely to fantasize about having sex with someone they were not involved with and had no intention of becoming involved with.

Prostitution

By definition, prostitution involves a short-term sexual relationship. Thus, if there is a sex difference in the preference for short-term mates, then this difference should manifest itself in the use of prostitutes. It does: The demand for prostitutes is almost entirely male driven. The focus of this demand can be other men (i.e., male prostitutes) but is predominantly women (Brewer et al., 2000; C. F. Turner et al., 1998). Across two national (U.S.) surveys of 9,066 adults between the ages of 18 and 59 years, Brewer et al. found that men, on average, reported between 1.5 and 2.5 times as many sexual partners during the past year and 5 years, respectively, as did the average woman. On the basis of prostitution arrest and re-arrest records, surveys, interviews, and other techniques, Brewer et al. further estimated that a typical female prostitute in the United States has, on average, 700 male sexual partners a year. This number was then combined with the estimated prevalence rate of 22 prostitutes per 100,000 adults and used to determine whether the sex difference in the reported number of sexual partners might be due to use of prostitutes. It was: Once the estimated use of prostitutes was controlled, there was no sex difference in the reported number of sexual partners.

It is difficult to estimate the number of men who have visited a prostitute because men are reluctant to admit to this behavior (Brewer et al., 2000). In a survey of 1,729 adolescents between the ages of 15 and 19, 2.5% reported having had sex at least once with a prostitute (C. F. Turner et al., 1998). Given the age range in this sample, the percentage of men who visit a prostitute at some point in their lifetime must be considerably higher. For a random sample of 852 Danish and Swedish adults between the ages of 23 and 87, 16% of the men, but none of the women, reported having visited a prostitute at least once (Bonnerup et al., 2000). Monto and McRee (2005) compared sexual attitudes and behavior of 1,672 men arrested for soliciting a prostitute with those of more than 3,800 men across two nationally (U.S.) representative samples. The would-be "Johns" were less likely to be married (40% vs. 50%), and those who were married were more likely to be unhappy in this relationship (22% vs. 3%). The men in the representative samples were more conservative in their sexual attitudes and were less likely to have bought sexually explicit material during to past year. But "[most] differences were small, indicating customers as a category differ from other men in degree rather than quality" (Monto & McRee, 2005, p. 505).

Personal and Behavioral Attributes

Whether or not they pursue casual sex, nearly all men want a marriage partner. These are long-term reproductive relationships in which men have committed to investing in children. Given the attendant costs of investment, it is not surprising that men are careful in their choice of marriage partners. When it comes to the personal and behavioral attributes of a prospective bride, men are particularly choosey if they are culturally successful and living in societies with socially imposed monogamy. These are societies in which men's marriage opportunities are legally restricted and thus the opportunity cost of marriage is higher for these men than it is for similarly successful men in societies in which polygyny is legal. As described in Table 7.2, families in societies with socially imposed monogamy tend to be more independent of kin group influences, and as a result the husband–wife relationship is more central to men's social life than it is in many other societies (Pasternak et al., 1997).

For wealthy Western cultures with socially imposed monogamy (e.g., United States, Canada, Western Europe), Lippa (2007) found few differences in the personal attributes men and women preferred in a long-term mate. As I described for women in the section titled Personal and Behavioral Attributes earlier in this chapter, these men prefer a marriage partner with traits (e.g., agreeable, sense of humor) that facilitate a long, cooperative interpersonal relationship (Kenrick et al., 1990; N. P. Li et al., 2002). Across a wider range of cultures, however, there was considerable variation in the personal attributes of men's and women's preferred marriage partners. Men in Latin America, Malaysia, India, Singapore, and Japan rated interpersonal traits, such as agreeableness, as less important than did women in these nations and, with the exception of Japan, rated them as less important than did men in Western nations. Even in Western nations, men place a higher priority on a prospective marriage partner's physical appearance than on these personal and behavioral attributes (N. P. Li et al., 2002; Lippa, 2007).

Sexual Fidelity and Jealousy

In all areas of the world, men are more concerned about their partner's sexual fidelity than are women; of course, this is a matter of degree and not an absolute sex difference. Men's concern for fidelity is an evolutionarily coupled feature of the cuckoldry risks described in chapter 6 (in the section titled Cuckoldry) and the attendant costs of investing in the child of another man. It is not simply about sex: Sagarin, Becker, Guadagno, Nicastle, and Millevoi (2003) found that men were distressed by the prospect of their partner having an affair with another man and thus risking pregnancy but were not distressed by the prospect of their partner having an affair with a woman. The social and psychological manifestation is sexual jealousy, which has a near universal influence on the dynamics of men's and women's relationships, including male-on-female aggression and men's attempts to control the social and sexual behavior of their partners (Daly & Wilson, 1988a, 1988b; Daly et al., 1982; Flinn, 1988a). Although the associated sexual proprietary behavior of men and the sex differences in jealousy patterns have been questioned (see the section titled Emotional Commitment and Jealousy in this chapter), men's actual behavior and their behavior as reported by their partners is consistent with the evolutionary prediction and may be especially pronounced in men who strive for social dominance (Pratto & Hegarty, 2000).

The dynamics of men's sexual jealousy are illustrated by Flinn's (1988a) observational study of mate guarding in a rural Trinidadian village. In this village, "13 of 79 (16.4%) offspring born . . . during the period 1970–1980 were putatively fathered by males other than the mother's coresident mate. Clearly, mate guarding could have significant effects on fitness" (Flinn, 1988a, p. 10). Mate guarding by men but not women was found to be a common feature of long-term relationships but varied with the woman's risk of pregnancy. Men monitored the activities less diligently and had fewer conflicts with pregnant and older wives than they did with younger and nonpregnant wives. As described in the section titled Ovulatory Cycle in this chapter, Gangestad et al. (2002) found that women reported an increase in their partner's mate guarding during the fertility window, and during this time women reported more sexual fantasies about and interest in other men. Sexual jealously is also implicated in the dissolution of many relationships. After sterility, adultery is the most common cause of marital dissolution across cultures.

> In 25 societies, divorce follows from adultery by either partner; in 54 it follows only from adultery on the wife's part and in 2 only from adultery on the husband's. If marriage qualifies as near universal, so must the double standard. (Betzig, 1989, p. 658)

On a darker note, Daly and Wilson's (1988b) seminal study of homicide revealed that a common motive for a man killing his wife is her sexual infidelity, her suspected sexual infidelity, or her desertion of him. In an analysis of the circumstances surrounding a man's attempt to kill his partner, 22 of 30 attempts occurred when she attempted to end the relationship (Nicolaidis et al., 2003). "Twenty-five of the 30 women (83%) described examples of their partners using stalking, extreme jealousy, social isolation, physical limitations, or threats of violence" (Nicolaidis et al., 2003, p. 790). In an analysis of 844 FBI cases in which a man killed his wife, 345 (41%) involved a lover's triangle (Shackelford, Buss, & Weekes-Shackelford, 2003). In keeping with Flinn's (1988a) findings, younger wives were much more likely to be murdered as a result of infidelity than were older wives, independent of the husbands' age. Takahashi et al.'s (2006) imaging study revealed that brain areas associated with sexuality and aggression (i.e., amygdala, hypothalamus) were activated when men, but not women, imagined their partner engaging in a sexual infidelity.

These are serious examples of male-on-female aggression and attempts by men to control the sexual behavior of their partners. In the United States, physical aggression that is directed toward a romantic partner does not typically escalate to this level, due in part to legal consequences. Women are as likely to hit men as men are to hit women for minor physical disputes, but women are more likely to be seriously injured in these disputes (Archer, 2000). The pattern is different in societies in which women's social, political, and economic opportunities are limited and families live among male kin. In these societies, men are more likely than women to physically assault their spouse or partner (Archer, in press).

Physical Attributes and Fertility

People of both sexes prefer physically attractive partners, but this preference is consistently found to be more important—a necessity and not a luxury—for men than for women (D. M. Buss, 1989b; Feingold, 1990; Hatfield

& Sprecher, 1995; N. P. Li et al., 2002; Lippa, 2007). Indeed, the largest sex difference in Lippa's study regarded the importance of good looks in a prospective mate. In each of the 53 nations with large sample sizes, men valued a good looking mate more highly than did women, confirming D. M. Buss's (1989b) earlier results from another multinational study. The overall magnitude of the sex difference in Lippa's study indicated that 7 out of 10 men rated a partner's good looks as more important than did the average woman. But what makes a woman good looking? Are these traits related to her reproductive fitness, especially to her fertility?

Young, Attractive Women

Men find women with the following traits physically attractive: a WHR (recall, waist-to-hip ratio) of about 0.7, facial features that signal a combination of sexual maturity but relative youth, symmetric body and facial features, proportionally longer legs, larger than average breast size and symmetry, small abdomen and waist, and youth (Cunningham, 1986; Fan, Liu, Wu, & Dai, 2004; Guéguen, 2007; D. Jones, 1995; Møller, Soler, & Thornhill, 1995; Rilling, Kaufman, Smith, Patel, & Worthman, 2009; Singh, 1993a, 1993b, 1995a). The key facial features are large eyes, prominent cheekbones, and a large smile area. A brain imaging study revealed that viewing attractive faces of the opposite sex resulted in heightened activation of a core reward center (nucleus accumbens) in both sexes, but only men showed concurrent activation of areas of the frontal cortex that are associated with reward-driven social behaviors and motivations (orbital frontal cortex; Cloutier, Heatherton, Whalen, & Kelley, 2008). Both women and men find viewing attractive faces of the opposite sex rewarding and pleasurable, but men also appear to be more easily primed to act on these feelings especially when their testosterone levels are high (Welling et al., 2008).

Body mass index (BMI)—a measure of leanness to obesity independent of height—is also associated with rated attractiveness and maybe more so than WHR (Cornelissen, Hancock, Kiviniemi, George, & Tovée, in press); the normal BMI range is between 18 and 24. For a sample of young Canadian adults, Hume and Montgomerie (2001) found that for women, but not men, higher BMI values were associated with lower rated attractiveness. K. L. Smith, Cornelissen and Tovée (2007) found the same relation for young adults in the United Kingdom using a more direct measure of body fat. In both studies, leaner women (BMI less than 22) were rated as more attractive than heavier women. A preference for relatively slender (i.e., a BMI in the average range) women is not universal, however: Across 62 cultures, J. L. Anderson, Crawford, Nadeau, and Lindberg (1992) found that relatively slender women were preferred in 12 (19%) cultures, moderately fat women in 23 (37%) cultures, and "plump" women in 27 (44%). The latter are preferred and considered beautiful in cultures in which the food supply is unreliable. Average weight to somewhat slender women are preferred in some societies in which food is readily available and in which lower status women are heavier, on average, than higher status women.

Why is age so important in men's ratings of women's attractiveness? It is simple: Men's mate preferences evolved to be sensitive to indications of a woman's age because age and fertility are tightly linked in women. Women's fertility is low in the teen years, peaks at about age 25, and then gradually declines to near zero by age 45 (Menken, Trussell, & Larsen, 1986). Teenage mothers experience more complications during pregnancy (e.g., ectopic pregnancy, stillbirth) than do women in their 20s (Andersen, Wohlfahrt, Christens, Olsen, & Melbye, 2000). Risks begin to increase in the 30s and increase sharply after age 35. Spontaneous abortion is the most common cause of fetal loss, with the risk of loss at 9% for a 22-year-old woman, 20% for a 35-year-old, 40% for a 40-year-old, and 84% for a 48-year-old.

D. M. Buss's (1989b) 37-culture study and many other studies confirm that men prefer and marry mates younger than themselves—younger brides have more reproductive years ahead of them than do older brides—and mates in the age range of high fertility (e.g., Buckle et al., 1996; D. M. Buss & Shackelford, 1997; Kenrick & Keefe, 1992; Kenrick, Keefe, Gabrielidis, & Cornelius, 1996; Sprecher et al., 1994). Across cultures, D. M. Buss found that brides were, on average, 3 years younger than their grooms. Kenrick and Keefe demonstrated this same pattern across samples from the United States, Germany, Holland, and India. Marriage patterns across the 20th century in the United States and Poro, a small Philippine island, also revealed that men marry younger women. As men get older, they tend to marry younger and younger women (Buckle et al., 1996; Kenrick & Keefe, 1992). For instance, in 1923 the typical American man in his 20s married a woman who was about 3 years younger than himself, as did the typical Filipino man between 1913 and 1939. The typical man in his 60s married a woman who was about 15 years younger than himself in the United States and 20 years younger in Poro. These patterns cannot be attributed to a social norm that "men should marry younger women, and women should marry older men." Kenrick et al. found that the most attractive dating partner for teenage males was a woman about 5 years older than they were—a woman with higher fertility than girls of the same age or younger than these adolescent boys.

Attractiveness and Health

The assessment of the relation between traits that men find attractive in women and women's actual health and fertility is plagued by the same confound described for men: Most of the studies have been conducted with relatively wealthy samples with access to modern health care. As I noted earlier, in these circumstances the relation between attractiveness and health is likely to be much weaker than any such relation during our evolutionary history.

Even in these populations, women with BMI values and facial features that men find attractive tend to be healthier than other women (Langlois et al., 2000; Weeden & Sabini, 2005). Women's WHR may also be important, especially as the ratio becomes greater than 0.85. Women with ratios above this value are at risk of a number of physiological disorders and appear to have greater difficulty conceiving than do women with lower ratios (Singh, 1993a; Zaadstra et al., 1993). A study of nearly 15,000 Australian women between 18 and 23 years of age revealed that heavier women (above average BMI values) had an increased risk of a variety of health problems and very thin women menstruated infrequently (W. J. Brown, Mishra, Kenardy, & Dobson, 2000). The health risks associated with deviations from average weight, especially excess weight, continue throughout the life span (Ferrie et al., 2007; Yusuf et al., 2005).

In a study of 119 healthy 30-year-old women, estradiol and progesterone levels at the time of ovulation (see Figure 7.4) were significantly related to WHR and breast size (Jasienska, Ziomkiewicz, Ellison, Lipson, & Thune, 2004). The hormone profile of women with a combination of a narrow waist (WHR = 0.69) and large breasts indicated "an approximate three-fold increase in the probability of conception" (Jasienska et al., 2004, p. 1215) relative to women with a higher WHR and smaller breasts. Singh (1995a) found that women with asymmetric breasts were rated as less attractive by men than women with symmetric breasts; Møller et al. (1995) found that women with significant breast asymmetry had fewer children, on average, than did other women in samples from Spain and the United States. Manning, Scutt, Whitehouse, and Leinster (1997) found the same pattern for women in England.

The relation between women's attractiveness and health may extend to their children. Pawlowski and Dunbar (2005) examined the relation between WHR and BMI in 374 first-time mothers and the birth weight of their child; only healthy neonates were included in these analyses. Birth weight is a critical health outcome because low birth weight is associated with increased risk of death during infancy and poor health outcomes at later ages (Moyo et al., 2007). For women of average or heavier prepregnancy weight, smaller (i.e., closer to 0.70) WHRs were associated with higher birth weights for their children, and Lassek and Gaulin (2008) found the children of women with lower WHRs have higher intelligence scores. For smaller women, a slightly larger than average BMI (i.e., greater than 21) was associated with a heavier birth weight for their children.

Ovulatory Changes

Behavioral and physical changes that occur during the 6-day window of fertility make women more attractive to men and thereby better able to influence men's behavior. G. Miller, Tybur, and Jordan (2007) found that the earnings of normally cycling lap dancers almost doubled during their fertile window relative to when they were menstruating; compared with the days following ovulation but before menstruation, the dancers earned 40% more than when they were menstruating. The change in the attractiveness of these women and other women is related, at least in part, to changes in their physical appearance. Compared with other days in their cycle, during the fertile window women's faces are rated as more attractive, feminine, and healthy looking (Law Smith et al., 2006; S. C. Roberts et al., 2004); breast symmetry increases (Scutt & Manning, 1996); WHR decreases (Kirchengast & Gartner, 2002); their voices are rated as more attractive (Pipitone & Gallup, 2008); they self-groom more often and dress in more fashionable and revealing clothing (Durante et al., 2008; Haselton, Mortezaie, Pillsworth, Bleske-Recheck, & Frederick, 2007; Schwarz & Hassebrauck, 2008); and are more responsive to men (Guéguen, in press).

Women may also produce olfactory cues that signal ovulation (Singh & Bronstad, 2001). Singh and Bronstad asked women to wear T-shirts during the time of ovulation and during a nonovulatory phase of their cycle. Men then rated the T-shirt odors in terms of pleasantness, sexiness, and intensity. Shirts worn during the ovulatory phase were rated as more pleasant and sexy than shirts worn by the same women during the nonovulatory phase. Havlicek, Dvoráková, Bartoš, and Flegr (2006) replicated this finding.

CONCLUSION

There is little question that human mate preferences and choices are products of our evolutionary history and reflect many of the same mechanisms—sexual selection—that influenced the evolution of and the proximate expression of mate choices in other species (Darwin, 1871). To be sure, human mate choices are complicated by men's parental investment and variation in customs from one culture to the next. Within this variation are invariants that are only understandable in terms of evolved biases in women's and men's mate preferences. The bottom line is that the preferred mates and attendant cognitions and behaviors (see chap. 12, this volume) of both sexes evolved to focus on and exploit the reproductive potential and reproductive investment of the opposite sex. Reproductive potential is the genetic or other resources (e.g., ability to have children) an individual can potentially invest in children, whereas investment is the actual use of resources to promote the well-being of children. When it comes to choosing mates, women and men prefer traits that signal reproductive potential and a bias to invest this potential in children.

Although the details vary from one setting to the next, culturally successful men have higher reproductive potential than do less successful men (Irons, 1979; B. S. Low, 2000). Culturally successful men are men who wield social influence and control the resources—money, land, cattle—that women would prefer to have invested in themselves and their children. When men invest resources in parenting, the mortality rates of their children drop, and these children's social competitiveness is enhanced (see the section titled Benefits to Children, chap. 6, this volume). It is not surprising that women and their kin throughout the world prefer these men as marriage partners. This preference is expressed in social psychological studies, reading materials, lonely hearts ads, and other measures (Lippa, 2007; Oda, 2001) and in their actual mate choices (e.g., Borgerhoff Mulder, 1990, 2000). In short, most women prefer monogamous marriages to wealthy, socially dominant, and physically attractive men—healthy men with good genes—and want these men to be devoted to them and their children. For most women, this preference is not achieved, and thus they have to make trade-offs. These typically involve trading his physical attractiveness for his cultural success. Some women attempt to achieve a compromise of sorts through relationships with several men. The implicit goal appears to be getting the best material investment from one man and the best genetic investment from the other (Bellis & Baker, 1990).

The reproductive effort of most mammalian males (see the section titled Male–Male Competition, chap. 3, this volume) is largely or exclusively focused on mating (Andersson, 1994). Men's parental investment changes this dynamic and results in a more mixed reproductive strategy (D. M. Buss & Schmitt, 1993; Gangestad & Simpson, 2000). As with other mammals, men can reproduce with little investment in parenting or the relationship. More unique to humans and in keeping with the gorilla-like model I described in chapter 5 of this volume, men can also reproduce with an exclusive, long-term monogamous or polygynous relationship with heavy parental investment. Or men can reproduce with a mixture of these strategies. The approach men take is influenced by their ability to attract (or not) short-term mates, by social mores, and by partner characteristics. When men invest in long-term relationships, they are similar to women in many mate-choice criteria, especially in wealthy societies with socially imposed monogamy (Lippa, 2007). Men consistently differ from women, regardless of where they are in the world, in terms of their enthusiasm for casual sex and in terms of the importance of the physical attractiveness of a potential mate. Men's enthusiasm for casual sex follows simply and logically from the sex difference in the costs of reproduction. The physical traits (e.g., age, WHR) men find attractive are readily understood because these traits are predictive of women's fertility (Jasienska et al., 2004) and perhaps the health of their children (Pawlowski & Dunbar, 2005).

8

COMPETING FOR MATES

In chapter 3 (in the section titled Parental Care), I discussed how sex differences in reproductive rate and parental investment result in more intense male–male than female–female competition in the vast majority of mammalian species. Humans are no different, despite men's comparatively high level of parental investment (see chap. 6). Men do differ from other mammals in the many creative ways in which they compete (Griskevicius, Cialdini, & Kenrick, 2006; G. F. Miller, 2000), but underneath these various forms of creative competition is a very real and often deadly struggle for social influence and control of cultural resources. The combination of social influence and resource control determines men's cultural success (Irons, 1979), which in turn influences their desirability as a mate (see the section titled Culturally Successful Men, chap. 7, this volume). Irons's concept of cultural success allows one to understand how ecology, cultural history, and current conditions influence how men express an evolved desire for social status. Pastoral raiders who steal another tribe's cattle to pay bride price and Wall Street raiders who seek hostile takeovers of competitor's companies may seem different on the surface, but they are not: Each of these activities is an expression of men's desire for control of the resources that affect their reproductive prospects and general well-being. A Wall Street raider does not, of course, need that extra $10 million to attract a bride or live well, but as long as there are other raiders who make more than this, the ambitious raider will continue the struggle.

It is not simply the absolute level of resource control vis-à-vis what it takes to raise a family that underlies men's competitive behavior; it is the level of influence, control, and status relative to other men in the communities and niches in which they compete. I described the importance of relative status in chapter 6 (in the section titled Benefits to Children) and elaborate in chapter 9 (in the section titled Motivation to Control). In modern, industrial societies, high status confers better health and a longer life span for men, women, and their children (Marmot, 2004). In these same societies but before the emergence of modern health care, sanitation, and so forth, parental status often determined which children survived to adulthood and which did not (see the section titled Benefits to Children, chap. 6, this volume). Relative status matters for women as well as for men, but more so for men. As I detailed in chapter 5 (in the section titled Sexual Reproduction in Primates), the relation between social dominance and reproductive success is stronger for male than for female primates, and this sex difference has almost certainly been the case throughout human evolution. Low status for men results in heightened risk of not reproducing at all, whereas high status increases mating opportunities, especially when polygyny is not illegal.

In the next section, I describe how the corresponding motivations for social dominance, status, and resource control are expressed as male–male competition in traditional and in modern societies. When men differ from one another in status and resource control and in what they can potentially invest in children, women view higher status men as a resource (see the section titled Women's Mate Choices, chap. 7). In the second section, I describe female–female competition, that is, how women compete with one another for these desirable mates and for other resources. I close the chapter with a brief discussion of the factors that contribute to the different ways in which male–male and female–female competition are expressed across cultures and historical periods.

MALE–MALE COMPETITION

Male–male competition and female choice are in some respects different sides of the same coin. Women's mate-choice preferences and how they relate to male–male competition were discussed in chapter 7. As with many other species (see the section titled Female Choice, chap. 3, this volume), men often compete on those dimensions that women desire in marriage partners (e.g., social status) or in short-term mates (e.g., physical attractiveness; N. P. Li, 2007). Although men will attempt to enhance those traits (e.g., income) that women use in their mate choices—especially in cultures with relatively few restrictions on female choice—there is much more to men's mating effort.

More broadly, men are focused on their status and success relative to other men as defined by the extent to which they have social influence and direct control of the forms of resource—money, cows, land, and so on—that enhance their well-being in the wider culture. As noted previously, the extra $10 million earned by a Wall Street raider would not at first blush seem to enhance his survival prospects. His drive to continue to earn money is an expression of the relation between *relative* status and health and longevity at all levels of the social hierarchy (Marmot, 2004; see the section titled Benefits to Children, chap. 6, this volume). In short, social competition during human evolution is predicted to have resulted in evolved social comparative processes (Festinger, 1954) that result in a focus on relative status and control, not simply the acquisition of sufficient resources for survival and reproduction (R. D. Alexander, 1989; Flinn, Geary, & Ward, 2005; Geary, 2005b). Women's preference for high-status partners has contributed to the evolution of the social comparative processes that focus men on their relative status, but the desire for status and control often takes on a life of its own. Many men are focused on the attainment of sociopolitical power and, where possible, resource control. When successful, many of these men use this power to control the sexual behavior of women and other men, independent of female choice (e.g., Betzig, 1986).

I begin with a description of how male–male competition is expressed in traditional societies and then move to its expression in modern ones. Again, Irons's (1979) concept of cultural success pulls together all of these different ways of competing and ties them to the underlying motive for social status and resource control vis-à-vis that of other men in their communities (Betzig, 1986; Irons, 1979; Hopcroft, 2006; Klindworth & Voland, 1995). I then move to reviews and discussions of male–male competition and testosterone, risk taking, and sperm competition. I close with a discussion of genetic studies as these relate to the issues of male philopatry and male–male competition during human evolution.

Competition in Traditional Societies

Men are similar to male chimpanzees in that they have the capacity for intense and often deadly one-on-one and coalitional competition (Wrangham & Peterson, 1996). Although these forms of male-on-male violence may have an evolutionary history, they are not always expressed (Daly & Wilson, 1988b). The social dance that leads to men's physical aggression follows the same pattern found in other species in which males compete physically: Physical aggression is used only when social displays or other social rituals fail to resolve issues of social dominance or other social conflicts (Chagnon, 1997; Maynard Smith & Price, 1973).

> Furthermore, even the most bellicose societies did not award the best warriors or captains their highest positions of status or leadership. Instead, these rewards were reserved for men who, although they were often expected to be brave and skilled in war, were more proficient in the arts of peace—oratory, wealth acquisition, generosity, negotiation, and ritual knowledge. The six desired characteristics of a western Apache headman, for instance, were industriousness, generosity, impartiality, forbearance, conscientiousness, and eloquence; not one of these pertains directly to warfare. Cheyenne "peace chiefs" had more political influence, material wealth, and wives than the chiefs who led war parties. (Keeley, 1996, p. 144)

When the ritualized social dynamic escalates to violence it can be expressed within the man's kin or social group or in the context of group-level politics. At times, the latter can be related to natural disasters or other factors (e.g., drought) that diminish the ability of social groups to survive in their current ecology. These groups then move into the territory of neighboring groups, which can lead to deadly conflict over territorial control (Keeley, 1996; D. W. Read & LeBlanc, 2003). Under these conditions, male aggression is influenced more by natural than by sexual selection. More typically, male-on-male aggression, whether one-on-one or coalitional, is related to the establishment and maintenance of social dominance, the acquisition of the resources needed to support reproduction, or the direct capture of women. These conflicts often have reproductive consequences for both men and women and are often an expression of social power polygyny or resource-based polygyny (see Table 7.2, chap. 7, this volume).

Polygyny

Social power polygyny is common in societies in which material resources are not easily controlled, as illustrated by the Yanomamö who live in the Amazon jungle in Venezuela (Chagnon, 1997). Social dynamics among Yanomamö men include within-group one-on-one social displays and physical aggression to resolve disputes (e.g., over sexual infidelity) and to establish social dominance. Within-group aggression ranges from chest pounding to club fights to machete fights (using the flat part of the blade). The goal is not to kill the opponent but to cause sufficient injury to make him withdraw from the duel. The clubs used in club fights are 8 to 10 feet long, and the fights involve repeated blows to the top of the opponent's head as well as taking blows from the opponent. The welts that accumulate over many years of such fights become a status badge because they indicate courage and the ability to survive these fights.

The fights do not typically result in death, but they can: K. Hill and Hurtado (1996) found that 8% of Ache men die as a result of similar club fights.

The dynamics between groups include political intimidation of smaller groups by larger ones and frequent raiding of neighboring villages. The raids are often for blood revenge—to avenge harm inflicted on kin—and when opportunity permits, capture of brides (Chagnon, 1988, 1997). In this social climate, men who are skilled at political negotiations or are fierce warriors enjoy a higher social status than do other men, but they do not have more material wealth (Hames, 1996). Fierce warriors are men who have participated in the killing of a man from a rival village. In the Yanomamö villages studied by Chagnon (1997), two out of five men have participated in at least one such killing. These men marry sooner and more often. They have 2.5 times as many wives as men who have not participated in a killing and 3 times as many children. Overall, about one out of four Yanomamö men die violently, largely during the course of between-villages raids. Chagnon concluded male-on-male violence is ultimately about reproductive competition, but this has been challenged. Ferguson (1995), for instance, argued that much of the violence is the direct result of the introduction of Western manufactured goods (e.g., steel machetes) into Yanomamö society; that is, much of the fighting is over control of these goods.

However, Chagnon's (1988, 1997) findings for Yanomamö men are consistent with the pattern of male–male competition I reviewed in chapter 5 of this volume for other primates and human ancestors, and Chagnon's findings are not an isolated case. One-on-one and coalitional male-on-male aggressions are common features of hunter–gatherer, horticultural, pastoral, and agricultural societies. Keeley (1996) reported that ambushes and raids occur nearly continuously or frequently in about 70% of hunter–gatherer societies and even more frequently in agricultural and pastoral societies (see also Ember, 1978; White & Burton, 1988). Many of the more peaceful societies are relatively isolated or politically subjugated to larger groups (Keeley, 1996). Across hunter–gatherer societies, about 30% of men die as a result of some form of raid, ambush, or larger scale conflict. Examples of mortality rates resulting from these forms of male–male competition are shown in Figure 8.1; women are not immune from the effects of this violence but still have consistently lower mortality than men. Figure 8.2 shows the motives reported in ethnographies of North American Indian tribes for initiating between-groups conflicts (Keeley, 1996). These motives are similar to those reported in other regions of the world and include blood revenge, economic gain (e.g., land, booty, and slaves), the capture of women, and personal prestige. The last involves the accumulation of culturally important trophies, such as the heads of competitors, that influence the man's reputation and social status within the community, which in turn influence his desirability as a marriage partner.

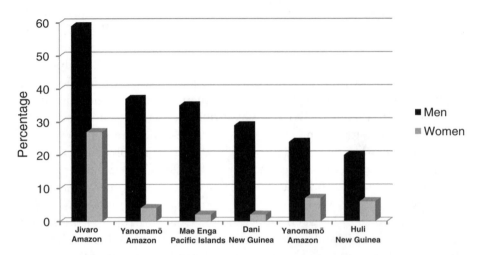

Figure 8.1. Estimated mortality rates resulting from ambushes, raids, or larger scale warfare for six traditional societies. The values for the Yanomamö are from two different groups, the Shamatari (left) and Namowei (right). Data from Keeley (1996). Courtesy of author.

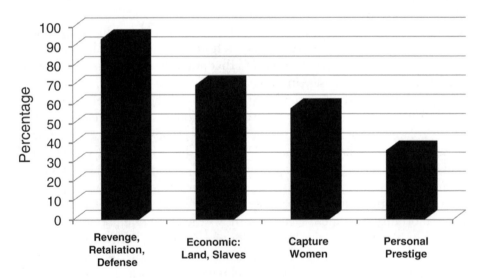

Figure 8.2. Reported motives for warfare for North American Indian tribes. Data from Keeley (1996). Courtesy of author.

Deadly male-on-male violence is also found in societies without explicitly designated status differences among men. The Gebusi of New Guinea, for instance, are described as being primarily a gatherer society (with some hunting) with male social life "markedly devoid of male status rivalry. Instead, there is a pronounced aura of diffuse male friendship and camaraderie" (Knauft, 1987, p. 460). Yet, the Gebusi have one of the highest per capita murder rates in the world, including a precontact (by Westerners) homicide rate that was estimated to be more than 10 times that found in most major U.S. cities. Although Knauft (1987) argued that the proximate causes of Gebusi murders are superstition—sorcery (e.g., casting of a magic curse)—and other psychological factors, not reproduction, he nonetheless concluded that "sorcery homicide is ultimately about male control of marriageable women" (pp. 465–466). Similar patterns are found in other so-called peaceful societies (Daly & Wilson, 1988b; C. R. Ember, 1978; Keeley, 1996; Knauft, 1987).

Contra Ferguson's (1995) argument, the pattern of intergroup aggression among Yanomamö tribes is unlikely to be due to interference from modern societies because warfare is typically less frequent after contact with these societies (Keeley, 1996). Nor is this aggression a relatively recent phenomenon, as archaeological evidence suggests frequent intergroup aggression over at least the past 20,000 to 30,000 years:

> For example, at Crow Creek in South Dakota, archaeologists found a mass grave containing the remains of more than 500 men, women, and children who had been slaughtered, scalped, and mutilated during an attack on their village a century and a half before Columbus's arrival (ca. A.D. 1325). The attack seems to have occurred just when the village's fortifications were being rebuilt. All the houses were burned, and most of the inhabitants were murdered. This death toll represented more than 60 percent of the village's population, estimated from the number of houses to have been about 800. The survivors appear to have been primarily young women, as their skeletons are underrepresented among the bones; if so, they were probably taken as captives. (Keeley, 1996, p. 68)

The capture of women and the murder of competitors have nothing to do with female choice; rather, these practices show men pursuing their reproductive interests at the expense of other human beings (White & Burton, 1988). The potential for coalitional violence is heightened in populations with a high proportion of young men (15 to 30 years of age) who do not have sufficient resources to attract a wife (Mesquida & Wiener, 1996). In these circumstances, the reproductive potential (e.g., desirability as a marriage partner) of many young men drops, and as a result, the costs of risky aggression decrease and the potential benefits increase (M. Wilson & Daly, 1985). In traditional societies, expansion into neighboring territories to acquire resources or to capture women is one potential and apparently common response to these conditions (Mesquida & Wiener, 1996). The ability to expand territory and the corresponding level of male–male competition and violence can reach extreme levels in agricultural and other large political states (Keeley, 1996). In these societies, coalitions of men can practice resource-based polygyny, which includes elements of social power polygyny. Betzig (1986, 1993), in fact, argued that in each of the first six civilizations—ancient Mesopotamia, Egypt, the Aztec and Inca empires, and imperial India and China—"powerful men mate with hundreds of women, pass their power on to a son by one legitimate wife, and take the lives of men who get in their way" (Betzig, 1993, p. 37). The population genetic studies described in the section that follows confirm that these social dynamics have occurred many times during recent human evolutionary history and in many parts of the world.

Reproductive Skew

The reader may recall that male–male competition results in *reproductive skew*; specifically, successful males sire a disproportionate number of offspring, and many males sire no offspring (see the sections titled Male–Male Competition, chaps. 3 and 5). The same is true of men in traditional societies. Among the Yanomamö studied by Chagnon (1977, 1997), the most successful man, nicknamed Shinbone, had 11 wives and 43 children, compared with 14 children for the single most successful woman. Shinbone's father "had 14 children, 143 grandchildren, 335 great grandchildren and . . . 401 great-great grandchildren" (Chagnon, 1979, p. 380); the third and fourth estimates are low because many of the descendants of Shinbone's father are still in their reproductive years. At the same time, many low-status Yanomamö men never marry or reproduce (Jaffe et al., 1993).

More typically, the reproductive differences across men in societies with social power polygyny are not this extreme, but they can still be substantial. There are, of course, individual differences in the number of children women successfully raise to adulthood, but the differences are 2 to 3 times larger among men than women (Archer, in press). An example is provided by the Xavante of Brazil (Salzano, Neel, & Maybury-Lewis, 1967). In this traditional society, women had on average 3.6 surviving children, and variation among women (i.e., standard deviation) was 3.9. The average number of children for men who reproduced was necessarily the same as that of women, but the variation among men was 12.1, a ratio of just over 3:1. With resource-based polygyny, the differentials can become many orders of magnitude larger than that reported for Shinbone versus other Yanomamö men or the Xavante. Betzig (1986, 1993) provided many historical examples, and I describe supporting evidence in the section titled Population Genetics in this chapter.

Competition in Modern Societies

In comparison with the mortality rates shown in Figure 8.1, male-on-male physical violence is low in modern societies (Daly & Wilson, 1988b; Keeley, 1996). The decline in the frequency with which men kill one another is likely related to the emergence of central governments that suppress kin-based violence, such as blood revenge, and institute social controls that reduce male reproductive skew and thereby reduce the benefits of extreme violence. In Western culture, socially imposed monogamy (described subsequently) necessarily reduces, but does not eliminate, the benefits of intense male–male competition. Fewer restrictions on women's reproductive behavior and mate choices in these societies almost certainly change the flavor of men's competition, shifting it toward traits that reflect women's preferences. When male-on-male aggression does escalate to homicide in modern societies, the precipitating events are often centered on sexual jealousy or male status competition, as in traditional societies (Daly & Wilson, 1988b).

Industrializing Societies

I described the relation between men's social status and their children's mortality risks in industrializing Europe and the United States in chapter 6 (in the section titled Benefits to Children). The children of higher status men were healthier and more likely to survive to adulthood than the children of lower status men (Hed, 1987; Schultz, 1991). However, if lower status men had many children, their reproductive success may have been equal to or better than that of their higher status peers, even if many of these children did not survive to adulthood; this was sometimes the case (Korpelainen, 2000). More typically, higher status men had more children survive to adulthood for a combination of reasons. Higher status men were more likely to marry, and in comparison with lower status men who did marry, higher status men often married earlier, married younger brides, were more likely to remarry following divorce or death of a spouse, and were more likely to sire illegitimate children (Käär, Jokela, Merilä, Helle, & Kojola, 1998; B. S. Low & Clark, 1992). Higher status men were also less likely to die prematurely and thus had a longer reproductive life span (Boone, 1986; B. S. Low, 1990b).

The pattern is illustrated by extensive parish and government birth, marriage, and death records between 1760 and 1810 for Krummhörn men in northwest Germany. Using these records, Klindworth and Voland (1995) were able to reconstruct the relation between social status and long-term reproductive outcomes. Information from tax records indicated that there were large differences in the wealth—land and cattle—held by different families. Relative to other men, the wealthiest men sired more children primarily because they married younger wives and had more children survive to adult-hood. Across generations lower status men were 4 times more likely than wealthy men to experience an extinction of their lineage, that is, reach a point at which there were no surviving direct descendants. Men's relative status influenced their reproductive success even among the privileged classes. The majority of these men had a single legal wife with whom they sired legitimate heirs, but those of the highest status (e.g., king being higher than duke) were more likely to have one or many concubines (e.g., Betzig, 1986; Boone, 1986). For some groups within Western culture (e.g., early Mormons), polygynous marriages remained common and resulted in reproductive advantages for high-status men (Mealey, 1985).

Although the children of the wives of high-status men had lower mortality risks, higher status women did not always have a lifetime reproductive advantage over lower status women and sometimes had fewer surviving children (Boone, 1986; B. S. Low, 1990b). Higher status women were less likely to "marry down" than were higher status men, and thus the pool of available mates was smaller for higher than for lower status women. Boone, for instance, found that about 40% of Portuguese noblewomen in the 15th and 16th centuries lived their adult years in convents and thus never reproduced, compared with about 28% of lower status women. The decline in family size that followed reductions in child mortality in Western culture began earlier with higher status than lower status women. Despite great wealth and access to servants, the typical British noblewoman had an average of 2.3 children during her lifetime in 1500, declining to an average of 1.5 children by 1850 (Westendorp & Kirkwood, 1998); the smaller number of children may have resulted in the benefit of a longer life span for these women.

Modern Society

In modern societies, the relation between men's social status and their reproductive success is more nuanced than that found in traditional societies or in earlier centuries of modern societies. Many studies have found that men with higher earnings and all the trappings of cultural success do not sire more children than their less successful peers (Kaplan, Lancaster, Bock, & Johnson, 1995). Findings such as these led Vining (1986) to dismiss the importance of men's status striving in modern societies, but this dismissal seems to have been premature. Scientists do not yet fully understand all of the nuances at play in these societies, but they do know that a complete understanding of the relation between cultural and reproductive success will require assessment of men who have completed fertility (i.e., they are not likely to have more children) and are at their peak earning years (i.e., 45 to 55) as well as the simultaneous consideration of potential confounding variables, such as their wives' income and status (Kaplan & Lancaster, 2000; Weeden, Abrams, Green, & Sabini, 2006).

Scientists also have to consider the influence of socially imposed monogamy and contraceptive use in these societies. These may reduce reproductive skew among men, but they may not decouple, so to speak, the relation between status and men's ability to attract sexual partners. Pérusse (1993) studied the relation between socioeconomic status (SES) and the sexual behavior of more than 400 men from Québec and indeed found a relation between status and mating success. Here, cultural success was defined in terms of income, educational level, and occupational status (i.e., SES) and sexual behavior in terms of the number of reported sexual partners and the overall frequency of intercourse. The two latter factors were used to derive an estimate of the likelihood of paternity in the absence of birth control. For unmarried men 30 years of age and older, higher SES was associated with more sexual partners and more overall sexual activity. The combination explained as much as 63% of the individual differences in the likelihood of paternity in the absence of birth control. This relationship was somewhat lower, but still positive, in younger unmarried men, as might be expected given the length of time needed to acquire indicators of cultural success in modern societies (e.g., higher education).

Hopcroft (2006) confirmed this pattern using a series of large, nationally (U.S.) representative surveys of adults. Men with higher incomes reported more sexual activity than men with lower incomes and women at any income level. Hopcroft also found that intelligence, as measured by performance on a vocabulary test, was inversely related to sexual activity; intelligent men reported less sex than their more average peers. Her findings suggest that composite measures of SES may obscure the relation between men's status and sexual opportunity because income and intelligence work against each other. The same result emerged for number of biological children. The highest income men, on average, had about 2.5 children, compared with an average of 1.4 children for the lowest income men. These results are likely to underestimate the actual relation because institutionalized men were not included in these surveys and the highest income group included men collapsed across a very wide range of incomes. Again, men's intelligence worked against their reproductive success, except to the extent it influenced their income.

Some of the previous research on this question failed to include childless men in the analyses and thereby excluded a critical group: men excluded entirely from the reproductive pool. Fieder and Huber (2007) addressed this confound using a sample of 7,000 Swedish men who were 45- to 55 years old. When childless men were excluded, men in the lowest 25% of income had the most children, followed by men in the highest 25% of income. When childless men were included, however, men higher in the income hierarchy had more children than did men lower in the hierarchy, as also found by Hopcroft (2006). The different patterns emerged because about 1 out of 3 men in the lowest income category were childless by age 45 to 55 and thus likely to remain so, whereas about 1 out of 9 men in the highest category were childless. For a national sample of 45- to 55-year-old men in the United States, Weeden et al. (2006) also found that men with higher incomes had more children and were less likely to be childless than men with lower incomes. The same was found among Harvard graduates. Independent of their wives' incomes, the most successful graduates had more children than their less successful peers. A similar relation between status and number of children was found for 2,693 university employees (Fieder et al., 2005).

The relation between status and the reproductive success of men in modern societies is almost certainly muted relative to the strength of this relation in traditional and industrializing societies. Nevertheless, status still matters for men, even in this situation. Of the various contributors to a man's cultural success (i.e., SES), income emerges as the most consistent predictor of lifetime reproductive success, as measured by average number of children and by the risk of dying childless. Other factors, such as educational level and intelligence, appear to be important to the extent that they contribute to income, and too much intelligence may interfere with men's reproductive prospects once income is controlled.

Testosterone

In chapter 4, I discussed some of the cost–benefit trade-offs between testosterone and males' relative focus on mating or on parenting (in the section titled Sex Hormones and Life History Development) and on the potential for high testosterone levels to compromise the health of some males (in the section titled Sex Hormones, Parasites, and Male Quality). I also described Wingfield, Hegner, Dufty, and Ball's (1990) social challenge hypothesis. To recap, the gist is that testosterone levels will be low during seasons when competition for mates is not necessary and rise (e.g., triggered by changes in daylight) during the breeding season, that is, when males must compete for mates or other resources that females need to reproduce (e.g., nesting sites). For species without a clear breeding season, testosterone levels are predicted to remain at moderate levels throughout the year but spike during potential sexual encounters and during male–male competition. The lack of a breeding season in humans results in the expectation that men's testosterone will be at detectable levels throughout the year and will influence and change in response to sexual opportunity and to challenges to social status.

Archer (2006) provided a thorough review of the relation between men's and women's testosterone levels and predictions derived from Wingfield et al.'s (1990) challenge hypothesis. Women were included because female–female competition over men's parental investment is predicted and found (in the discussion that follows). Although few of the human studies have taken advantage of the challenge hypothesis, the patterns revealed in Archer's review provide some support. The predicted trade-off between testosterone and parenting—high investment in a monogamous relationship and children is associated with lower testosterone—was described in chapter 6 of this volume (in the section titled Hormones and Men's Parenting). In addition, at least tentative support was found for the predictions that little to no relationship exists between testosterone and aggression during puberty, that status-related competitive situations can result in a testosterone surge for men, that testosterone increases further for the winners and decreases for the losers of these competitions, that there are higher testosterone levels among men (and women) who are motivated to achieve social dominance (this is not necessarily related to physical aggression), and that bidirectional influences of testosterone on sexual desire and activity are found. The magnitude of most of these relations is modest and moderated by contextual and psychological factors. I illustrate and elaborate on a few of these findings in the sections that follow.

Puberty and Aggression

There are increases in both testosterone and the potential for lethal male-on-male violence during puberty and early adulthood (e.g., M. Wilson & Daly, 1985), but most adolescents in modern societies do not engage in lethal or even harmful physical aggression. Studies of developing adolescents indicate that the testosterone increases associated with puberty do not, in and of themselves, result in an increase in male-on-male physical aggression (Archer, 2005; C. T. Halpern, Udry, Campbell, & Suchindran, 1993) as they do in some other species. These boys do, however, frequently engage in less intense physical confrontations, but this male-on-male aggression is evident before the onset of puberty (R. B. Cairns, Cairns, Neckerman, Fergusson, & Gariépy, 1989). The high prepubertal levels of aggression might be related to androgen increases associated with adrenarche (i.e., production of precursors to testosterone and estrogens by the adrenal glands) during childhood (Del Giudice, 2009a), and testosterone changes during puberty might be expressed as other forms of dominance and status-related behaviors, such as risk taking (Vermeersch, T'Sjoen, Kaufman, & Vincke, 2008).

In any case, a direct increase in competition-related aggression is not predicted to occur because these males are not yet ready to compete with adults for cultural success. As I described in chapter 4 (in the section titled Life History and Sexual Selection), male–male competition is often associated with an extended developmental period during which males become larger, stronger, and better able to compete with mature males. The human developmental period (see the section titled Physical Development, chap. 10, this volume) is especially long, with puberty lasting throughout much of the teen years for women and into the early 20s for men (Tanner, 1990). Men's muscle size and strength, skeletal development, and cardiovascular capacity all increase through the early 20s (Bogin, 1999; Tanner, 1990) as do some aspects of brain development (Giedd et al., 1999). The function of testosterone during this time is to promote these and many other aspects of physical development and not to prompt developing boys to engage in the intense forms of physical male–male competition that is common among adult men in traditional societies. Developing adolescents are not ready for adult competition.

I also described in chapter 4 (in the section titled Plasticity) how the presence of mature and established males can suppress the reproductive activities of developing males. The same dynamic occurs in many traditional societies. However, the potential for older men to suppress the aggressive, status striving, and sexual activities of adolescents is disrupted to some extent in modern societies. In high schools, for instance, adolescent males do compete for girlfriends and are interested in and some engage in sex. These types of dynamics are less likely to emerge in more traditional societies because of parental monitoring of girls' sexual relationships and the marriage of adolescent girls to older men (United Nations Children's Fund, 2005). One implication is that the disruption of male kin groups and the ability of older men to monitor adolescent males in modern societies may have the unintended effect of prematurely releasing social constraints on potentially lethal physical male–male aggression.

Competition and Social Challenge

Assessing the relation between testosterone and male–male competition in adulthood is considerably more difficult in humans than in other species. Men can achieve cultural success in a variety of ways, many of which do not include the one-on-one physical aggression that is common in other species; of course, this type of aggression does frequently occur in some traditional societies, as described in the section titled Competition in Traditional Societies earlier in this chapter. The importance of coalition formation and the political competence needed to rise in the dominance hierarchy make a direct comparison of competition found in many other primates, such as mandrills (*Mandrillus sphinx*), with humans unfruitful, especially in modern societies. To be certain, the general relation between dominance and reproductive outcomes is the same in men and male mandrills, but the achievement of dominance is a more socially nuanced and a longer term process in humans. In modern societies, men prone to physical aggression have modestly higher testosterone levels than do other same-age men (Archer, Graham-Kevan, & Davies, 2005), but these aggressive men are also more likely to be in jail: Successful men in modern societies have instituted cultural rules that remove many physically aggressive men from the mating pool. Men with higher testosterone levels may simply be more attracted to competitive activities (Carré & McCormick, 2008), with only a subset of these men engaging in criminal aggression.

The many niches in which men can achieve cultural success in modern societies also make tests of the challenge hypothesis difficult to conduct. A challenge to one man may not be important to another, depending on how closely the activity matches the man's interpretation of how the event influences position in his status-relevant niche. Laboratory and field studies are generally consistent with this view; the relation between testosterone and competition-related challenges depends on the relation between the event and status in niches that are important to men, on how men interpret the outcomes of the event (D. Cohen, Nisbett, Bowdle, & Schwarz, 1996; Gonzalez-Bono, Salvador, Serrano, & Ricarte, 1999; Salvador, 2005), and on their social confidence (Maner, S. L. Miller, Schmidt, & Eckel, 2008).

Despite these complications, Archer's (2006) meta-analysis revealed that men show small to moderate increases in testosterone in anticipation of a competitive sporting contest and small increases during the event. During sporting events, there is a tendency for winners' testosterone to increase and losers' to decrease. A similar pattern is found for laboratory tasks, although the postcompetition differences between winners and losers is larger than for physical contests; the physical exertion during sporting events may mask some of these effects. In a pair of small-scale studies, Bernhardt, Dabbs, Fielden, and Lutter (1998) found that the testosterone of basketball and soccer fans increased if their team won and decreased if it lost. Watching movies with competition and aggression can also increase testosterone levels in men but not women (Schultheiss, Wirth, & Stanton, 2004). There is also evidence for an influence of testosterone on the home field advantage in competitive sports, that is, the home team has an increased chance of winning. Neave and Wolfson (2003) found larger pregame increases in testosterone when soccer teams played in their "territory" (home field) than when they played in another team's territory; the increase in testosterone may provide home team players with a modest physiological advantage.

Among actual competitors, postevent changes in testosterone are influenced by their contributions to their teams' victory or loss and their attributions about whether the victory or loss was due to factors under their control (e.g., poor relative skills) or not (e.g., poor referee calls). Gonzalez-Bono et al. (1999) assessed testosterone levels in professional basketball players before and after a National Basketball Association (Spain) game. In comparison with pregame levels, the testosterone of the players on the winning team increased and that of the losing team decreased, but these changes did not reach statistical significance, probably because of the small number of players. Players on the winning team who thought the result was due to luck or to mistakes made by the referees did not show an increase in testosterone, but players who contributed the most points to their team's win had significantly higher pre- to postgame increases in testosterone than did other players. Oxford, Ponzi, and Geary (in press) found the same pattern when teams of young men competed while playing video games.

Schultheiss and his colleagues have shed further light on the source of variation in men's testosterone and other hormonal responses to competition (e.g., Schultheiss, Dargel, & Rohde, 2003; Schultheiss & Rohde, 2002; Schultheiss et al., 2005; Wirth, Welsh, & Schultheiss, 2006). Men's response to winning and losing a competition varies with their implicit—evident in fantasy and stories, but not explicitly acknowledged—motivation for personal power and the desire to dominate other people (see also R. T. Johnson, Burk, & Kirkpatrick, 2007). Men with this motivation show pronounced increases in testosterone after winning a competition and declines after losing. The increase in testosterone following a win is associated with improved learning on the competition-related task, whereas losing disrupts this learning. In contrast, men with a prosocial power motive—a desire for social power and influence through prosocial behavior—show declines in testosterone after winning a one-on-one contest and sometimes increases following a loss. Wirth et al. found that losing a contest resulted in increased stress hormone (i.e., cortisol) levels in men with a high personal power motivation as well as higher stress hormone levels for winners with a low personal power motivation.

I concur with Archer's (2006) conclusion that, in total, studies in this area are consistent with the social challenge hypothesis (see also Mazur & Booth, 1998). Men differ from males of other species in terms of the wider variety of niches in which they compete and in their ability to mentally discount (e.g., bad refereeing) losses or to enhance victories (Salvador, 2005). When the contest is important and the method of competing is consistent with men's social strategies and their desire for power, they respond in ways similar to those shown by other species. Men with a desire for personal power show predicted testosterone changes when they personally win, whereas men whose social strategy involves seeking influence through prosocial acts do not. The latter are still seeking social influence, but the direct competition used to assess the challenge hypothesis has not assessed their social style (i.e., their use of prosocial behavior to gain social influence). These men may show testosterone increases when, for instance, they have successfully organized a protest for world peace—a strategy that would suppress the power dominance aspirations of men with personal power motives.

Sexual Interest

To complete this discussion, I consider the extent to which men's testosterone increases when they are presented with a sexual opportunity, or at least an imaginary one, and whether testosterone in and of itself is sufficient for sexual arousal. The reader may recall that men who are in monogamous relationships, and especially men interested in children, have lower testosterone levels than their peers (see the section titled Hormones and

Men's Parenting, chap. 6). Men in monogamous relationships who are open to an extrapair affair and married men in polygynous societies do not show this reduction in testosterone (P. B. Gray, 2003; P. B. Gray, Ellison, & Campbell, 2007). These men are still primed, so to speak, to compete for mates and to quickly respond to novel mating opportunities. These patterns are not surprising because testosterone can influence sexual behavior and can increase in response to sexual opportunity in many species.

Several studies have found that men's testosterone increases when viewing erotic material (e.g., Redouté et al., 2000). Redouté et al. found that viewing these materials activates a distributed network of brain regions that may contribute to attentiveness to women's physical attractiveness and regions associated with erectile functions and more basic reward centers; these are preliminary findings, because viewing these materials also involves emotional components that may be distinct from those controlling the sexual responses per se (Walter et al., 2008). Whatever brain networks are engaged, Roney, Mahler, and Maestripieri (2003) found testosterone increases in young men after they interacted with a young woman, but only for men with prior sexual experience and primarily for men whom the woman rated as "displaying" (e.g., showing off). Van der Mey, Buunk, van de Sande, and Salvador (2008) found that same effect for socially dominant men; women's testosterone may also increase when they interact with an attractive man.

Experimental manipulations of testosterone levels in normal men also reveal nuanced effects that can vary from man to man. In a well-designed study, O'Connor, Archer, and Wu (2004) administered testosterone to normal men such that their levels of this hormone reached about the 98th percentile. Following the increase in testosterone levels, these men reported less fatigue and more anger and hostility—in the normal range—but no increase in aggressive or sexual behavior. In remains unclear, however, whether these men would have showed an increase in sexual behavior with a novel partner. R. A. Anderson, Bancroft, and Wu (1992) found little change in sexual behavior following administration of testosterone to normal men, but there was an increase in sensitivity to sexual cues. Men with low testosterone levels (e.g., due to aging), in contrast, tend to show increased interest in sex and heightened sexual arousability when administered testosterone, but whether the frequency of intercourse increases depends on prior sexual experience and on the nature of the relationship with their partner (Bancroft, 2005).

Risk Taking

When individuals make decisions or engage in behaviors that are risky—that is, involving a potential cost—they are typically focused on the potential benefits and discounting the risks; individuals who tend to avoid risks focus on the potential costs (C. R. Harris, 2003; Zuckerman & Kuhlman, 2000). Men are predicted to engage in more status-oriented risks than are women (M. Wilson & Daly, 1985) because of the reproductive costs and benefits of succeeding or not in the male dominance hierarchy and because many women are attracted to men who engage in risky activities (Kelly & Dunbar, 2001). Because competition always entails some degree of risk, the likelihood of success in male–male competition will be, in theory, higher for men who focus on potential gains and lower for men who are risk avoidant and thus do not compete.

A sex difference in risk taking is predicted to emerge largely for domains that are tied to cultural indicators of success and when engagement in risky behavior can result in reputation enhancement—for instance it is viewed by other males and by females—or attainment of cultural resources (e.g., money, cows). Developmental sex differences are predicted as well. As I describe in chapters 10 (in the section titled Play) and 11 (in the section titled Cultural Divide) and in keeping with the life history perspective described in chapter 4 (in the section titled Developmental Activity), the developmental period is predicted to include evolved biases to engage in behaviors that prepare boys and girls for activities that provide survival and reproductive advantages in adulthood. Boys are predicted to engage in more risk taking than girls, to the extent these behaviors result in lower risks—due to better developed skills—in adulthood and to the extent boys' reputations can carry over into adulthood, as they likely will in traditional societies (Del Giudice, 2009a).

Almost none of the psychological research on sex differences in risk taking has been designed to test these evolutionary hypotheses. In one exception, Ermer, Cosmides, and Tooby (2008) confirmed that men, but not women, make more risky decisions when resources are at stake and when competing against an equal status rival; the latter is important because most status contests are between individuals of similar rank. Other research is summarized by Byrnes, Miller, and Schafer's (1999) meta-analysis of 150 studies of sex differences in risk taking from the preschool years to adulthood and across hypothetical scenarios, self-report measures, and observation by others. Across all of these ages and measures, there is a small sex difference favoring boys and men in risk taking. There were no sex differences in engagement in some risky behaviors, such as self-reported smoking, but moderate differences in some observed behaviors, including engagement in intellectual and physical risks; about two out of three men engage in these behaviors more often than the average woman. Across ages, risk taking appears to be much more common when an audience is present (Morrongiello & Dawber, 2004; Pawlowski, Atwal, & Dunbar, 2008).

As an example, D. C. Miller and Byrnes (1997) examined the social and personality factors associated with risk taking in 3rd-, 5th-, and 7th-grade boys and girls in the United States; in this study, risk taking involved making decisions about engaging in activities that had a high chance of failure but provided extra benefits if successful. In keeping with previous studies of children (Ginsburg & Miller, 1982), boys engaged in more risky activities than did girls but only when peers were present. Girls' decisions were more conservative than boys' decisions, whether or not their peers were aware of their choices. A second study revealed that children who are high in risk taking tend to be competitive, enjoy engaging in physical activities that entail some risk of injury, and are usually boys. Morrongiello and Dawber (2004) found the same pattern in another sample of children, as did Zuckerman and Kuhlman (2000) for adults. C. R. Harris, Jenkins, and Glaser (2003) found that women focus more on the potential costs of risky behaviors, and men focus more on the benefits and enjoyment of the activity; men understand the potential costs but rate these as less severe and less likely to happen than do women.

The reader will not be surprised to learn that the cost–benefit trade-offs associated with risk taking have been linked to testosterone (Apicella et al., 2009; Booth, Johnson, & Granger, 1999; Coates & Herbert, 2008). Coates and Herbert measured the testosterone levels of a group of male financial traders in London for 8 days of expected market volatility. In keeping with the earlier described winner and loser effects, traders' testosterone levels were higher at the end of profitable days compared with days when their returns were average or they lost money. Traders who started the day with higher than their typical levels of testosterone made more money than they did on their average days, possibly because they took more risks on these days or they were confident about their planned trading strategy for that day. Other studies, in contrast, have found higher testosterone levels to be associated with impulsive and thus poor decision making (Reavis & Overman, 2001). It may be that testosterone levels interact with the man's skill and experience, such that increased risk taking is more likely to be rewarded in domains of expertise. Testosterone may also influence women's risk taking. Reavis and Overman found that women with naturally higher testosterone levels reported more sensation seeking, a form of risk taking. Administering testosterone to healthy women decreases their fear responses (Hermans, Putman, Baas, Koppeschaar, & van Honk, 2006) and increases the frequency of risky choices in a decision-making task (van Honk et al., 2004).

Although much remains to be learned, the overall sex difference in risk taking—one consequence is a sex difference in accidental injury (see Geary, 1998b)—and the contexts in which it is expressed support evolutionary predictions. Boys and men engage in risk taking only when they have an audience to impress, that is, when this behavior can enhance their standing relative to peers of about the same status and as a display to attractive girls and women. The psychological mechanisms that promote risky decisions and behaviors include a focus on potential gains (higher in men) and a discounting of potential costs (lower in women). Testosterone appears to influence risk taking by shifting the focus from the potential costs of failure to the potential rewards of success. The testosterone surge after a success may improve skill development in the domain, resulting in a feedback mechanism whereby successful males are both more likely to compete in this domain again and are more skilled when they compete. Unsuccessful males are likely to withdraw from this form of competition and focus on a different cultural niche.

Sperm Competition

Although paternity is never certain, it is unusually high in humans given our multimale, multifemale communities (Geary & Flinn, 2001). As I covered in chapter 6 (in the sections titled Women's Strategies and Men's Mating Opportunities, Cuckoldry), women sometimes cuckold their partners. For the deception to work, the woman must, of course, maintain a sexual relationship with her primary partner. And she may time intercourse with her primary partner so that it coincides with intercourse with her extrapair partner (Baker, 1996). In this way, her partner cannot detect nonpaternity on the basis of the timing of any pregnancy.

Bellis and Baker (1990) found that when women initiate an infidelity it often occurs during the time of high fertility; in their study, 7% of the copulations during the time of ovulation were with an extrapair man. A national probability survey of the sexual behavior of adults in Britain revealed that 15% of 16- to 24-year-old women and 8% of 25- to 34-year-old women engaged in concurrent sexual relationships during the past year (A. M. Johnson et al., 2001). These relationships set the stage for sperm competition (see the section titled Cryptic Postcopulatory Choice and Sperm Competition, chap. 3, this volume). The occasional finding of dizygotic (two ova) twins being fathered by two different men leaves no question that sperm competition occurs in humans (W. H. James, 1993; Wenk, Houtz, Brooks, & Chiafari, 1992). In these cases, it appears the competition was a draw! W. H. James estimated that among White women in the United States, about 1 in 400 dizygotic twins are fathered by different men. Wenk et al. reported that bipaternity is found in 1 in 42 cases in which the paternity of dizygotic twins has been questioned by one of the fathers.

Although these findings confirm that sperm competition occurs, its extent and its importance in shaping the evolution of human reproductive behavior are debated (Pound, 2002; Shackelford & Goetz, 2006). A common approach to the reconstruction of this evolutionary history is to first identify physical (e.g., testicle size) and behavioral (e.g., female promiscuity) traits across species in which sperm competition is common and then compare and contrast these traits with species in which it is uncommon (Baker & Bellis, 1993; Dixson & Anderson, 2004; Gallup & Burch, 2004; Shackelford & Goetz, 2006). A contrast of the chimpanzee (*Pan troglodyte*) and gorilla (*Gorilla*

gorilla) provides an apt illustration. The intense sperm competition in chimpanzees is associated with large (relative to body size) male testicles and conspicuous estrous swelling in females; the latter incites male sexual interest and copulation with multiple males. The lack of sperm competition in gorillas, which is due to single-male harems, is associated with small male testicles and minor estrous swelling in females (R. L. Smith, 1984). In terms of testicle size, men fall in between the values for chimpanzees and gorillas, but closer to the gorilla.

Consistent with my argument in chapter 5 of this volume (in the section titled Evolutionary Models), R. L. Smith (1984) proposed that the reproductive behavior of our australopithecine ancestors was similar to that found in modern gorillas and that sperm competition was not a significant factor in human evolutionary history until the emergence of *Homo*. R. L. Smith's focus was on males' use of hunted meat to entice female copulations and on the separation of couples when males hunted; separation provides opportunity for extrapair sex. I also believe that sperm competition is comparatively recent, but I propose here that the key change was the formation of male kin-based coalitions and the corresponding emergence of multimale, multifemale groups. As I detailed in chapter 5, the formation of these groups likely increased the number of females that were mated with lower quality males and, at the same time, increased the opportunity for these female to seek higher quality extrapair mates. If this is correct, inciting sperm competition is not the primary reproductive strategy of women and never has been. It can occur in situations in which the woman is attempting to switch mates and thus maintaining multiple relationships before the switch or cannot switch mates but is nonetheless having extrapair sex with a man of higher quality than her social partner (see the section titled Cuckoldry, chap. 6, this volume).

Population Genetics

Advances in scientists' understanding of genetic variation and in the ease of measuring this variation have shed a clarifying light on the study of sexual selection. Studies of the distribution of these genetic variations within and across populations provide insights into larger scale aspects of human social dynamics, including migration patterns (Seielstad, Minch, & Cavalli-Sforza, 1998) and patterns of social competition (Wyckoff, Wang, & Wu, 2000; Underhill et al., 2000). Of particular importance is the geographic distribution and variability of mutations in mitochondrial DNA (mtDNA) genes and genes on the Y chromosome. Children inherit mtDNA genes only from their mother, and boys inherit the Y chromosome from their father. Because of this, the geographic distribution and variability of mtDNA and Y-chromosome genes can be used to make inferences about the migration patterns and reproductive dynamics of our maternal and paternal ancestors, respectively.

Philopatry

Scientists can test the hypothesis that males were the philopatric sex during human evolutionary history through examination of the distribution of mtDNA and Y-chromosome genes across and within populations. In addition to male-based kin groups in many traditional societies, and among our three closest relatives, males tend to stay in their birth group and females migrate to other groups (see the section titled Coalitional Competition, chap. 5). As with these species, most of the population genetic studies reveal that men in local communities tend to be more closely related to one another than are women, but women have more kin ties to other communities in the region (R. S. Wells et al., 2001; J. F. Wilson et al., 2001). Neither genetic nor ethnographic studies indicate that male philopatry was always the case, nor would one expect it to be (Marlowe, 2004a); male-biased philopatry should be most evident in groups with a long history of frequent between-groups warfare. The pattern of less diversity for the Y-chromosome genes is not always found (Wilder, Kingan, Mobasher, Pilkington, & Hammer, 2004), and some populations are matrilocal with a corresponding decrease in variability of mtDNA genes (G. Hamilton, Stoneking, & Excoffier, 2005); women are more closely related to each other in these groups than are men. The overall direction of these genetic footprints is, nonetheless, consistent with an evolutionary history of male philopatry; a contrast of X-chromosome and Y-chromosome genes from populations ranging from southern Africa to southeastern Asia to northern Europe also supports this conclusion (Balaresque, Manni, Dugoujon, Crousau-Roy, & Heyer, 2006).

Male–Male Competition

The genetic footprints revealed by studies of mtDNA and the Y-chromosome lead to insights about the nature of male–male competition and long-distance migrations. I cover the gist of these findings in the sections that follow.

Replacement. If male–male competition has been more intense than male choice and female choice more selective than female–female competition during our evolutionary history, then it follows that there will be less variation in Y-chromosome genes than in mtDNA genes. In a monogamous society, 10 of Shinbone's 11 wives would have each reproduced with a different man, resulting in male descendants with Y-chromosomes from 11 men rather than only from Shinbone. The results from population genetic studies indicate that Shinbone is not alone. We have fewer male than female ancestors throughout the world (Underhill, Jin, Zemans, Oefner, & Cavalli-Sforza, 1996; Underhill et al., 2000; R. S. Wells et al., 2001; J. F. Wilson et al., 2001; Zerjal et al., 2003).

The most extreme example of reproductive domination comes from Zerjal et al.'s (2003) analyses of the Y-chromosome genes of 2,123 men from regions throughout Asia. They found that 8% of the men in this part of the world have a single common ancestor who emerged from Mongolia and lived about 1,000 years ago. The geographic distribution of these genes fits well with the historic boundaries of the empire of Genghis Khan (c. 1162–1227), who was known to have had hundreds of wives and many hundreds of children. They estimated that Genghis Khan and his close male relatives are the direct ancestors of 16 million men in Asia, ranging from northeast China to Uzbekistan, and the ancestors of about 0.5% of the world's total population. Underhill et al.'s (2000) analysis of Y-chromosome genes from 1,062 men from all over the world indicates a repeating pattern of one population of men replacing another in Africa, Europe, and Asia (J. F. Wilson et al., 2001; Xue et al., 2005).

The extent of replacement can vary from one region to the next and from one historical time period to the next (e.g., Capelli et al., 2003). Some analyses also suggest an overall increase in Y-chromosome variation over the past 5,000 to 10,000 years (Dupanloup et al., 2003). The implication is that despite evidence for extensive resource-based polygyny, as with Genghis Khan, population expansions and the advent of agriculture and urban settlements may have resulted in an increase in the proportion of men reproducing monogamously.

Distant Migration. Although women tend to migrate to the group of their husbands, genetic and historical records suggest that more distant migrations are initiated by men in search of material resources, social status, and reproductive opportunity (Carvajal-Carmona et al., 2000; Semino et al., 2000). An example is provided by Carvajal-Carmona et al.'s assessment of mtDNA and Y-chromosome patterns in a Colombian (South America) population that was established by European settlers in the 16th and 17th centuries. The results revealed that the maternal ancestry is largely (more than 90%) Amerindian, whereas the paternal ancestry is largely (94%) European. When combined with the historical record of this population, these genetic patterns paint a picture of male–male competition in which European men displaced Amerindian men to the reproductive benefit of the former and at a large cost to the latter. Related studies have found similar though less extreme patterns in other Amerindian populations (Merriwether et al., 1997) as well as in Melanesia, South Asia, the Middle East, and southern China (Kayser et al., 2003; Quintana-Murci et al., 2004).

FEMALE–FEMALE COMPETITION

As discussed in chapter 5 (in the section titled Female–Female Competition), female-on-female aggression is common across primate species, but it is rarely as intense—inflicting serious injury and death—as male-on-male aggression (Silk, 1993; Smuts, 1987). The competition is typically over access to high-quality food but can be over the attention of males that have something to contribute to the well-being of females and their offspring (Palombit, Cheney, & Seyfarth, 2001). Men's potential to contribute to the well-being of children was documented in chapter 6 of this volume (in the section titled Benefits to Children), and this potential makes many men a resource over which women compete; these men are "resource objects" to women (D. M. Buss, 2003). Women are not, however, predicted to compete as intensely as men because of women's higher level of parental investment (see the section titled Sex Differences in Human Parenting, chap. 6, this volume) and the sex difference in reproductive skew. The latter means that in many traditional societies, men who are unsuccessful in terms of intrasexual competition are often eliminated from the reproductive pool, but this risk is much lower for women. In fact, young women almost always marry, even if it is not always to the man they prefer. Whereas women can gain some benefits from multiple mates, they do not typically gain as much as men do (see the section titled Alternative Mating Strategies, chap. 7, this volume). The gist is that because they have more to lose and less to gain, women's intrasexual competition is predicted to be more subtle and less risky than that of men (A. Campbell, 1999, 2004; Geary, 2002a).

These dynamics can be expressed as competition among single women in monogamous societies or among cowives in polygynous marriages. The competition can range from the enhancement of traits that men find attractive to the social manipulation and exclusion of potential competitors to physical violence. In societies with socially imposed monogamy, women's financial contributions to the marriage (e.g., dowry) can be another form of female–female competition. I begin with the different ways women compete and close with discussion of the influence of sex hormones on this competitiveness.

Dressed to Kill

When marriage choices are not tightly constrained by kin influences, people have to find and compete for marriage partners largely on their own. In these contexts, many people put considerable effort into enhancing the traits that members of the opposite sex find attractive (N. P. Li, 2007). Among women, this competition involves enhancing or bringing attention to physical traits that influences men's mate choices (see the section titled Men's Mate Choices, chap. 7, this volume) as well as the derogation of these traits in potential competitors (D. M. Buss, 1988; Cashdan, 1993; Jonason, 2007; Schmitt & D. M. Buss, 1996; S. Walters & Crawford, 1994). Women's corresponding sensitivity to the physical attractiveness of potential competitors has been demonstrated in several different ways (D. M. Buss, Shackelford, Choe, Buunk, & Dijkstra, 2000; Försterling, Preikschas, & Agthe, 2007; Gutierres, Kenrick, & Partch, 1999).

D. M. Buss et al. (2000) asked young adults in Korea, the Netherlands, and the United States to rate the traits of a same-sex rival from most to least distressing. A rival with an attractive face or attractive body was rated as more distressing to women than to men in all three cultures. About 2 out of 3 Korean women rated a same-sex rival with an attractive face as more distressing than did the average Korean man, whereas 17 out of 20 Dutch women rated a rival with an attractive body as more distressing than did the average Dutch man; the magnitude of each of the remaining sex differences was in between these extremes. Gutierres et al. (1999) asked young women and men to rate same-age peers on several desirability dimensions. These peers varied in terms of social success, as conveyed by high- and low-success vignettes (e.g., editor of a university newspaper vs. writing letter to editor), and physical attractiveness, as conveyed in facial photographs. These young adults then completed self-assessments. Women who viewed photographs of attractive same-sex peers rated themselves as less desirable as a marriage partner than did women who read vignettes of socially successful peers; men showed the opposite pattern. Overall, about 2 out of 3 women rated themselves as less desirable as a marriage partner after brief exposure to a physically attractive woman.

D. M. Buss and Shackelford (1997) found that the same tactics used by single women to attract mates were often used to keep them. Women married to culturally successful men (e.g., ambitious men with relatively high incomes) use more mate retention tactics, including enhancing their appearance and monitoring his activities, than do women married to less successful men.

Women's Aggression

The ways in which women compete with one another vary across cultural and social contexts, as with men's competition. I begin with an overview of common forms of female–female competition in modern societies and then turn to competition among cowives in polygynous marriages. The section ends with discussion of women's striving for cultural success.

Modern Society

Women and girls may not injure and kill one another as frequently as men and boys, but they manipulate relationships and spread malicious gossip at least as frequently if not slightly more often (Archer & Coyne, 2005; Björkqvist, Osterman, & Lagerspetz, 1994; Card, Stucky, Sawalani, & Little, 2008; Feshbach, 1969; Grotpeter & Crick, 1996; R. Martin, 1997; Rose & Rudolph, 2006). These social tactics are called *indirect, social,* or *relational aggression* (Archer & Coyne, 2005); hereafter, *relational aggression.* Children and adolescents who engage in relational aggression also tend to engage in more overt aggression (e.g., hitting, yelling), and when overt aggression is controlled, girls engage in more relational aggression than boys (R. L. Smith, Rose, & Schwartz-Mette, 2009). These behaviors involve the use of gossip, rumors, and lies to sully the reputation of, manipulate the friendships of, and socially ostracize potential competitors. Although this form of aggression emerges during the preschool years, it becomes especially prominent for girls during early adolescence and midadolescence and increasingly focused on competition with other girls over romantic relationships (Bond, Carlin, Thomas, Rubin, & Patton, 2001; Crick, Casas, & Mosher, 1997). As these adolescents move into adulthood, they become increasingly skilled at using relational aggression to manipulate and to control social relationships and groups in self-serving ways.

Although both sexes engage in and are the targets of relational aggression, little is known about the different ways men and women use this form of aggression. I suspect that boys and men use it politically, that is, to influence their standing in a wider group's dominance hierarchy, whereas girls and women use it to manipulate and disrupt the relationships of specific competitors. In any event, relational aggression can be particularly pernicious among women and girls. This is because they reveal more personal and potentially more embarrassing information to their best friends than do men and boys and are more dependent on these forms of intimate same-sex relationships (see the section titled Peer Relationships, chap. 11). The heightened interpersonal intimacy among women and girls comes at a cost of greater vulnerability to social manipulation and other forms of relational aggression should the relationship dissolve (Bond et al., 2001; Murray-Close, Ostrov, & Crick, 2007), as it often does (Benenson & Christakos, 2003). In prospective study of more than 2,500 adolescents, Bond et al. found that girls who are the victims of relational aggression are 2.6 times more likely to suffer from depression or anxiety (for elaboration see Geary, 1998b) than are girls who are not victims or boys who are victims. The risk for girls is particularly high if they lack social support from friends or family; this vulnerability continues into adulthood (Kendler, Meyers, & Prescott, 2005).

In a study of 2,319 high school students, Leenaars, Dane, and Marini (2008) confirmed higher levels of depression in victims of relational aggression and that physically attractive girls, but not boys, were victimized more often than their less attractive peers; "a one standard deviation increase in physical attractiveness increased the odds of females being indirectly victimized by 35% . . . and decreased the odds of males being victimized by 25%" (p. 410). These findings follow from the patterns described in the section titled Dressed to Kill earlier in this chapter. Women compete on the basis of physical attractiveness, and those with an advantage are targeted for social and reputational attacks.

Harm to victims is the predicted, evolved function of relational aggression. Women who are anxious, depressed, and socially ostracized are not likely to be strong competitors for mates or other forms of resource (e.g., job promotion). The other side of this prediction is that women (and men) who can manipulate the social relationships and reputations of competitors and, at the same time, hide this aggression in the guise of rationality, advice, and casual comments should be at a competitive advantage. Unfortunately, most of the research on this topic has been on the victims of relational aggression, and thus firm conclusions cannot be reached at this time. Preliminary studies of perpetrators reveal mixed outcomes (Archer & Coyne, 2005). Many perpetrators are at risk of exclusion from the very groups they are trying to control, but others appear to be more successful. LaFontana and Cillessen (2002) found that as children move into adolescence, the use of relational aggression becomes associated with peer popularity, specifically, social visibility and influence. Socially aggressive and popular peers, however, are not well liked, especially by other girls. For adolescents, R. L. Smith et al. (2009) found that relationally aggressive girls, directed largely toward other girls, were more popular among boys than were other girls. One might speculate that these aggressive girls used different social tactics in their relationships with other girls compared with their relationships with boys.

Although girls and women attempt to mask their relational aggression, they are not always successful at doing so. If the victim discovers the source of the rumor, especially in contexts in which there are few successful or attractive men and thus the competition over these men is stiff, female-on-female aggression can escalate to physical violence. A. Campbell (1995) described how in many of these contexts, being called a *slut* is "fightin' words":

> She started spreading rumors about me saying that I used to sneak out in the middle of the night in my night-dress and meet ten boys or something, really stupid. . . . Well we were arguing with each other about the rumor mainly and she was saying she didn't say it . . . and then she started calling me names like that and then she started to walk off across the road and she said "I'll get you some time, you fucking bitch." And that made me mad because if she was going to get me she was going to get me there and then, I mean there was no point in getting me later and so I kicked her in the back and she fell flat on her face . . . and we started fighting. (pp. 115–116)

A. Campbell (1995) also noted that in

> China and Zambia . . . female aggression is principally driven by competition over resources and often includes men. The degree of female economic and social dependence on men is related to the intensity with which women are prepared to fight to secure high-status men. (p. 116)

Polygynous Societies

Social manipulation and an occasional slap fight over a would-be boyfriend or husband is one thing, but competition among cowives or with other women (e.g., sister- or mother-in-law) in polygynous households or compounds is at another level of seriousness. As I described in the section titled Competition in Traditional Societies in this chapter and in chapter 7 (see Table 7.2), polygyny is common across human societies and has been an important feature of human evolution (see the section titled Sexual Selection and Human Evolution, chap. 5). One result is that women often have to contend with the competing interests of the other wives of their husbands, as well as their husbands' female kin if they move into his village. The level of competition will likely vary with whether a cowife is a sister and the extent to which cowives must cooperate to produce food (White 1988). Whatever the specifics, polygynously married women typically have less healthy children and fewer surviving children than do monogamously married women, although the reasons are not fully understood (Josephson, 2002; Strassmann, 1997; Strassmann & Gillespie, 2002).

Strassmann (1997; Strassmann & Gillespie, 2002) provided one of the more thorough assessments of this pattern with her study of the lifetime reproductive success of monogamously and polygynously married Dogon, an agricultural society in western Africa, women. For women, the reproductive disadvantage of polygyny was largely due to a sharply higher mortality rate for their children; even with increased mortality, men still benefited (reproductively) from polygyny. After controlling for the age and sex of the child, the number of children in the family compound, and the overall economic well-being of the family, the odds of premature death were 7 to 11 times higher for children from polygynous than from monogamous marriages (Strassmann, 1997). The premature mortality was not due to diminished resources per child but may have been related to less paternal investment and competition from cowives. "In addition to neglect and mistreatment, it was widely assumed that cowives often fatally poisoned each other's children. . . . Cowife aggression is extensively documented in Malian court cases with confessions and convictions for poisoning" (Strassmann, 1997, p. 693).

Murdering the children of cowives not only increases immediate resources available to women's own children but also reduces the number of heirs to their husbands' land. As with the Kipsigis (see the section titled Father-Absent and Father-Present Societies, chap. 6), sons inherit and divide the land of their father, and therefore the sons of cowives are direct competitors for the land each woman's sons will need to attract wives. This competition may explain why the mortality of Dogon boys is 2.5 times higher than that of their sisters. The extent to which overt acts of aggression, such as poisoning, or more subtle mistreatment contributes to the high mortality rates of children from polygynous unions remains to be determined. Nonetheless, it is clear that competition among these women can be intense and sometimes deadly, and likely illustrates the contexts in which female–female competition evolved in humans.

Resources and Cultural Success

Although bride price and bride service are common in traditional societies, the bride's family provides a dowry to the couple or to the groom's family in less than 6% of societies (Daly & Wilson, 1983; Dickemann, 1981; Gaulin & Boster, 1990; Murdock, 1981). Dowries are primarily found in highly stratified societies with socially imposed monogamy. These are societies in which wealthy men invest the bulk of their resources in a single woman and their children, rather than in many wives and families. The net effect is the mate value of wealthy men is much higher in societies with socially imposed monogamy than in polygynous societies. Gaulin and Boster argued that dowry is a form of female–female competition to attract these high-status men as marriage partners. In societies without a traditional dowry but with socially imposed monogamy, a woman's financial prospects contribute to her attractiveness as a marriage partner. In the United States, men rate the financial prospects of a potential marriage partner as important, but not as important as her physical attractiveness and not as highly as women rate the financial prospects of men (Kenrick, Sadalla, Groth, & Trost, 1990).

But do women's financial and other forms of cultural success translate into reproductive success, as they do for men? In traditional and developing societies, including those in which dowry was once common (e.g., Western Europe), the SES of the family substantially influenced children's risk of premature mortality (see the section titled Benefits to Children, chap. 6). All else being equal, a woman's contribution to the income of her family should then result in a reproductive advantage in terms of more surviving children. All else is not equal, however, because attaining cultural success in the modern world results in different life history trade-offs for women than for men (B. S. Low, Simon, & K. G. Anderson, 2002). Using a nationally (U.S.) representative sample of 3,902 women age 45 years and older, B.S. Low et al. found a trade-off between years of education and thus earnings potential and number of children. Across generations, women with a high school diploma had, on average, 2.8 children, whereas women with a graduate degree had 1.8 children. The pattern for childlessness is the opposite that described for men in the section titled Competition in Modern Societies in this chapter: Compared with high school graduates, 3 times as many women with postgraduate degrees never had children (9% vs. 27%). The same pattern is found in other large-scale U.S. studies (Hopcroft, 2006; Weeden et al., 2006) and less dramatically in Sweden (Fieder & Huber, 2007). These SES differences in lifetime number of children are largely due to the delay in childbirth commonly associated with obtaining a higher education in modern societies.

These patterns do not necessarily mean that trading reproductive success for cultural success is a poor choice for women (B. S. Low et al., 2002). As with other evolved trade-offs, the costs and benefits vary with social and ecological conditions. When there is low risk of premature mortality and with an increasing population, women who reproduce early and often will necessarily have more descendants in later generations. For stable and declining populations in which mortality risks decrease as one moves up the social ladder, a delay in childbirth to obtain additional education and resources and to attract a better mate makes evolutionary sense (B. S. Low et al., 2002). Although these culturally successful women will have fewer children in their lifetime, they are likely to have more children survive to adulthood and more descendents in later generations than less culturally successful women.

Hormones and Women's Competitiveness

The social challenge hypothesis has not been widely tested for species in which female–female competition is intense (see the section title Sex Hormones and Life History Development, chap. 4). In these species, males and females show sex-typical (e.g., higher testosterone in males) hormone levels, but there is preliminary evidence that prenatal exposure to androgens, circulating testosterone levels, and perhaps a heightened sensitivity to testosterone contribute to the aggressiveness of these females (e.g., Fivizzani & Oring, 1986; Langmore, Cockrem, & Candy, 2002). As with men, the many different ways in which women can compete complicate the analogy between the physical female–female competition in these nonhuman species and the more subtle forms of competition among women. There is, nevertheless, evidence that testosterone (produced by the adrenal glands in women), estrogens, and other hormones can influence women's assertiveness and competitiveness and how these are expressed (Archer, 2006; Cashdan, 1995, 2003; Schultheiss et al., 2003), with both similarities and differences in relation to hormones and men's competitiveness (Kivlighan, Granger, & Booth, 2005; Stanton & Schultheiss, 2007; Wirth et al., 2006).

Archer's (2006) meta-analysis revealed that the positive relation between testosterone and overt behavioral assertiveness was at least as high in women as in men; other studies suggest that women's use of behavioral aggression and social assertiveness may also be influenced by prenatal exposure to androgens (Berenbaum & Resnick, 1997). Testosterone in women, as noted in the section titled Risk Taking earlier in this chapter, is correlated with decreased fear responses (Hermans et al., 2006), more sensation seeking (Reavis & Overman, 2001), and more risky decision making (van Honk et al., 2004). Women with higher testosterone levels also tend to overrate their status among their same-sex peers but are rated as lower status and less liked by these peers (Cashdan, 1995). The social assertiveness of these women may not be an effective way of influencing other women, consistent with women's use of the more subtle relational aggression to orchestrate relationships. Van Goozen, Cohen-

Kettenis, Gooren, Frijda, and Van de Poll (1995) found that male-to-female transsexuals who were administered antiandrogens and estrogens reported a decrease in overt aggression and an increase in relational aggression after 3 months of hormonal treatments. Female-to-male transsexuals, in contrast, were administered testosterone and showed an increase in overt aggression.

Unlike those in men, women's testosterone levels do not show a post-win increase and postloss decrease, suggesting this hormone may not be as central to female–female competition as it is to male–male competition (Kivlighan et al., 2005; Schultheiss et al., 2005). A core estrogen, estradiol, may be the key hormone. Schultheiss et al. (2003) and Stanton and Schultheiss (2007) found higher estradiol levels were associated with stronger implicit social power motives for single, but not romantically involved, women. As a parallel to the winner–loser effect found with men's testosterone, women with strong social power motives had an increase in estradiol following a competitive victory and a decrease following a loss. These findings are in need of replication, but make theoretical sense, given the relations among estradiol, fertility, and reproductive behaviors described in chapter 7 of this volume (in the section titled Ovulatory Cycle).

Similar to men, women with high implicit social power motives show an increase in stress hormone (cortisol) levels when they lose a competition (Wirth et al., 2006). Cortisol, however, may have different competition-related effects for women and men. Kivlighan et al. (2005) found that cortisol levels increased in both women and men athletes prior to a rowing competition. High cortisol in men was associated with social withdrawal and mental focus and preparation for the competition, but for women high cortisol was associated with an increased interest in bonding and affiliating with teammates; the latter finding is a common stress response in girls and women (S. E. Taylor et al., 2000), as I elaborate in chapter 11 (in the section titled Peer Relationships).

CONCLUSION

Humans compete in a variety of creative and seemingly evolutionarily novel ways (G. F. Miller, 2000), but careful consideration of this variation reveals a core structure. As with the males of most other species, the core issue for men is their status relative to other men. Status can be achieved in many different ways, from the intimidation and murder of competitors to the control of the ecological (e.g., land) and biological (e.g., cattle) resources that women need to reproduce to the attainment of a college degree and the securing of a well-paid job. The reason is simple: Status matters. Men at the top of their society's hierarchy are better able to realize their mating preferences, and men at the bottom are at serious risk of being completely shut out of the reproductive pool. Unlike most other species, men need other men to achieve and maintain status; men compete in coalitions and strive for status within their coalition. Men, of course, vary in the risks they are willing to take and the costs they are willing to pay to achieve status. Some men are satisfied with being in the middle of the pack, having enough status to marry but not enough to incur the wrath of the most competitive men. Other men want absolute control and dominance; fortunately, most would-be despots do not achieve this goal.

In societies characterized by kin-based or ideological coalitions, men cooperate with one another to control the social and material resources of the society. If any such coalition gains control, the men that compose the coalition use the society's resources and their social power to actualize their reproductive preferences. These are situations that give rise to despotic regimes (Betzig, 1986). In many of these societies, coalitions of high-status men achieve social control by means of violence or threats of violence and use this control to reproduce at the expense of lower status and middle-status men and with little regard for the preferences of women. These societies stand in sharp contrast to societies in which monogamy is ecologically or socially imposed (Betzig, 1986; Flinn & B. S. Low, 1986); the latter are often democratic. However it is imposed, monogamy reduces reproductive skew among men—differences in the number of children sired by elite and low-status men are substantially reduced—and changes the cost–benefit trade-offs of male–male competition. The reproductive benefits of achieving high status are reduced, as is the willingness of many men to pay the costs to achieve this status. As a result, monogamous mating systems are generally associated with less intense and deadly male–male competition. Men's competition in these societies essentially shifts from the use of physical violence for controlling the behavior of other people to the accumulation of indicators of cultural success (Keeley, 1996; Irons, 1979). Achieving cultural success is simply another means of achieving control and increasing one's ability to exercise one's reproductive preferences, but this influence is not achieved by force.

Monogamous societies are also characterized by a fuller expression of female choice and more exacting male choice. As I described in chapter 7 (in the section titled Men's Mate Choices), when men are restricted to one wife—at least one at a time—they become choosy when it comes to a marriage partner and invest more in parenting (see the section titled Cultural and Ecological Correlates, chap. 6). As Trivers (1972) predicted, men's parental investment results in women competing in monogamous societies for the more desirable bachelors. Women also compete in polygynous societies but with their husband's other wives. Competition among women can be as creative and variable as that found among men and can range from the enhancing of their appearance to the spreading of lies about the sexual fidelity of other women to the murder of the children of cowives (A. Campbell, 2004; Strassmann, 1997). The last of these aside, female–female competition is typically more subtle than male–male competition. The corresponding tactics are relational aggression, that is, the use of gossip, rumors, and lies to manipulate and control social relationships in self-serving ways. The subtlety of relational aggression in comparison with physical aggression follows from the sex difference in the cost–benefit trade-offs of competition. Most women will have the opportunity to marry and reproduce, whether or not they are culturally successful. To be sure, it is better to be successful for both women and men, but is it not as critical for women's reproductive success as it is for men's.

9

EVOLUTION AND DEVELOPMENT
OF THE HUMAN MIND

In this chapter, I provide a framework for linking sex differences in parenting, intrasexual competition, and intersexual choice to sex differences in motivational focus, affective expression, life history development, cognitive biases, and brain organization. I cover sex differences in motivation and affect as integral to a basic framework for linking reproductive behaviors with psychological and cognitive evolution. As introduced in the first edition of this book (Geary, 1998b) and elaborated in *The Origin of Mind: Evolution of Brain, Cognition, and General Intelligence* (Geary, 2005b), the framework states that the mind is composed of functional systems that result in a bias to attend to and process evolutionarily significant forms of information that include corresponding behavioral, affective, and motivational biases. The focus of these systems is to attempt to gain social influence and access to and control of the forms of biological and physical resources that enhanced survival and reproductive prospects during our evolutionary history. In this and subsequent chapters, I use this framework to interpret the pattern of developmental, brain, and cognitive sex differences that researchers have long observed.

The apex of the triangle in Figure 9.1 represents this fundamental motivation to achieve control. The midsection shows the supporting affective, conscious–psychological, and working memory mechanisms that support the

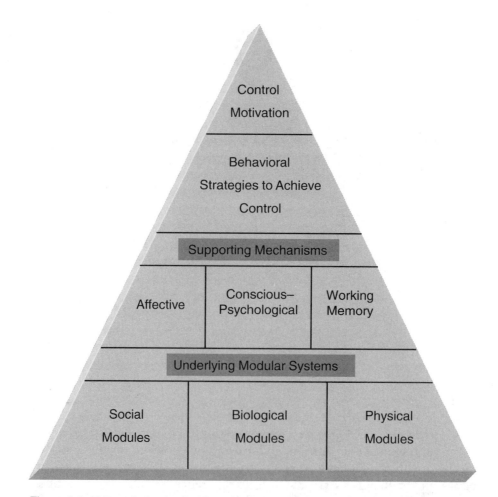

Figure 9.1. Human behavior is driven by the motivation to control the social, biological, and physical resources that have tended to covary with survival and reproductive outcomes during human evolution. The midsection shows the supporting affective, conscious–psychological (e.g., attributional biases), and cognitive (e.g., working memory) mechanisms that support the motivation to control and operate on the modular systems shown at the base. From *The Origin of Mind: Evolution of Brain, Cognition, and General Intelligence* (p. 74), by D. G. Geary, 2005, Washington, DC: American Psychological Association. Copyright 2005 by the American Psychological Association.

corresponding behavioral attempts to gain social influence and resource control. The base represents the classes of cognitive modules that have evolved to facilitate the processing of evolutionarily salient social, biological, and physical information (discussed subsequently). The general structure shown in Figure 9.1 should provide a useful conceptual frame for studying behavior and cognition across species, although the specifics (e.g., the types of information processed by the social modules) will differ from one species to the next, as I have elaborated elsewhere (Geary, 2005b). I assume that men and women and boys and girls are more similar than different when it comes to the basic structure of these functional systems, for instance, both women and men have cognitive modules for processing facial expressions, and that these systems have been largely shaped by natural selection. Sex differences in parenting and in the patterns of intersexual choice and intrasexual competition are predicted to result in sex differences in the degree to which the associated competencies such as the ability to interpret facial expressions are elaborated in one sex or the other. I begin with an overview of affective, conscious–psychological, and working memory mechanisms and then move to the folk domains that correspond to the base of the triangle. I close with a focus on the ways in which functional systems become elaborated during development.

MOTIVATION TO CONTROL

For all species, selection has favored the evolution of traits that enable individuals to attempt to achieve some level of access to and control of the types of resources that have supported survival and reproduction during the species' evolutionary history. I do not mean an explicit desire to control. Rather, I mean that many adaptive traits result in resource control and social influence. The point can be illustrated by returning to beak evolution in Darwin's finches (see the section titled Natural Selection, chap. 2). Recall that the beak size and shape evolved to allow the different species of finch to exploit different sources of food (P. R. Grant & B. R. Grant, 2002). Beak structure and presumably a perceptual sensitivity to food sources that can be handled by the beak, along with behavioral foraging for these foods, are all encompassed under the motivation to control. This functional constellation of adaptations results in the ability of these birds to identify the right type of food and to control or use these foods for their survival, with no conscious or explicit motivation to do so. When conceptualized in this way, the behavioral, affective, conscious–psychological, and cognitive (i.e., working memory and folk modules) adaptations described in the next section enabled our ancestors to monitor and influence social dynamics and to gain access to the biological (e.g., food) and physical (e.g., territory) resources that enhanced their survival and reproductive prospects (Geary, 2005b). Stated somewhat differently, Darwin's conceptualization of natural selection as resulting from a "struggle for life" (Darwin, 1859, p. 115) is more precisely defined as a struggle for control of the resources that support life and allow one to reproduce.

Benefits of Control

Whatever the species, male–male competition is all about gaining access to reproductive females or control of the resources females need to reproduce. This is achieved by controlling others males' access to females and resources and by limiting the expression of female choice. The same is true for female–female competition and competition over the resources needed for survival. Broadly, these resources are social, biological, and physical. For us, biological resources include food and medicine, and physical resources include the territories that contain biological resources and that support homes, pastures, and so on. Although humans have attributional mechanisms that obscure the fact that they often use social relationships for their own ends (Fiske & S. E. Taylor, 1991), use them they do: Other people are resources if they have reproductive potential, social power, or access to the resources that define cultural success.

History's despots illustrate the theme, as their behavior provides a glimpse into how some people use social influence and resource control in the absence of social and affective (e.g., guilt) constraints. As I noted in chapter 8 (in the section titled Competition in Traditional Societies), successful despots and their coalitions gained control of the first six human civilizations—ancient Mesopotamia, Egypt, the Aztec and Inca empires, and imperial India and China (Betzig, 1986). These men did not share their wealth and power but diverted the material and social resources of the culture to themselves and to their kin and used these resources in ways consistent with evolutionary predictions. The men, for instance, almost always had exclusive sexual access to scores of women, often many more. I am not proposing that deep down everyone is a would-be despot, as most of these individuals end up in an early grave; this cost constrains the evolution of extreme despotic motivations. The result is individual differences in the intensity of the motivation to dominate and control others as well as individual differences in the how social influence is gained (Pratto, 1996).

Nevertheless, gaining some level of control over the activities of daily life, important social relationships, and material resources affords many of the same benefits, albeit on a much smaller scale, as those enjoyed by despots. In the section titled Benefits to Children in chapter 6, I covered a wealth of studies that demonstrated, time after time, how social influence and access to material resources substantially affect mortality risks in traditional and developing societies and affect physical health in modern societies. Although my focus was on children, the relation between social status and resource control and physical and psychological (e.g., risk of depression) health also holds for adults (Adler et al., 1994; Marmot, 2004). A fundamental motivation to control has evolved in humans and all other species because success at achieving social influence and control of biological and physical resources very often meant the difference between living and dying or reproducing or not.

Sex Differences

Women as well as men benefit by having some level of influence in social relationships, access to material resources, and status within their community (Marmot, 2004), and thus the sexes are more similar than different when it comes to wanting some degree success in these endeavors. I predict that sex differences will be found in the foci of control-related activities and in the strategies used to achieve control; examples of the latter are use of physical violence (more common in men) or relational aggression (used at least as often by women as men) to influence social dynamics. For any species, humans included, the emergence of sex differences is predicted to mirror the relative emphasis of males and females on parental effort and mating effort and the ways in which the latter is expressed. In polygynous mammals, for instance, the functional systems of males, in comparison with females, are predicted to be more strongly focused on the activities that enhance mating opportunities, whereas for females these systems are predicted to be more strongly focused on the activities that enhance offspring survival.

Sex differences in the social motives of women and men illustrate the point; these motives reflect how individuals would prefer, in the absence of constraints, to organize their social relationships and community. Studies of personal values and interests reveal a consistent pattern of social sex differences, with women, more than men, valuing the development of altruistic, reciprocal relationships with other people and men, more than women, being "interested primarily in power, competition, and struggle," that is, politics (Willingham & Cole, 1997, p. 144); four out of five women value the development of reciprocal social relationships more than does the average man, whereas three out of four men value political activities more than does the average woman. These sex differences are found across historical periods, across cultures, and in the social relationships of chimpanzees (*Pan troglodytes*; de Waal, 1993; Tiger & Shepher, 1975; Willingham & Cole, 1997). As discussed earlier, male chimpanzees share men's taste for coalitional competition and politics (see the section titled Coalitional Competition, chap. 5, this volume).

Politics is essentially about gaining control of other people and their resources and across human cultures is largely a manifestation of competition between coalitions of men, coalitions that include women in democratic societies. As noted previously, gaining control over the group's resources enhances the reproductive success of men in winning coalitions (Betzig, 1986). Socially dominant men in these coalitions have more wives and mistresses and more children than do subordinates or members of losing coalitions (Betzig & Turke, 1992; Chagnon, 1988; Fieder & Huber, 2007; Hopcroft, 2006). The bottom line is that men usually have more to gain reproductively than women by engaging in political activities. The corresponding sex difference in interest and engagement in the political arena is a reflection of a more basic, in my opinion, sex difference in orientation toward social dominance and comfort with an unequal distribution of the group's resources versus social equality in decision making and resource distribution (Sidanius, Pratto, & Bobo, 1994); I elaborate in chapter 12 of this volume (in the section titled Ingroups and Outgroups).

Across nations, generations, political ideologies, and income levels, men have a stronger social dominance orientation and women a social equality orientation (Pratto & Hegarty, 2000; Sidanius et al., 1994); about two out of three men endorse the importance of social dominance more strongly than the average woman, and almost three out of four women endorse the importance of social equality more strongly than the average man. Men who are high in the desire to achieve social dominance also express a desire for multiple mating partners and show less interest in parental investment, in keeping with the prediction that the motivation to achieve dominance is implicitly related to reproductive interests. Socially dominant women, in contrast, are more interested in marrying high-status men than in finding multiple mates (Pratto, 1996; Pratto & Hegarty, 2000). Tiger and Shepher's (1975) study of the social egalitarian Kibbutzim revealed greater voluntary participation of men than women on politically influential committees and more extramarital affairs by dominant men on these committees but not by dominant women on the same committees.

The tendency of women to value social equality and reciprocal social relationships more so than men might reflect, in part, a stronger preference for reducing conflict through nonviolent means and maintaining stability within the social community. Despots can and often do maintain stability but through violence and intimidation. Violence and intimidation are "necessary" because there will always be coalitions of men who are not in power but wish to be, and thus they and their kin are often targets of suppression. In other words, coalitions of men have the most to gain through the use of violence, but these coalitional struggles for control can disrupt entire communities. A United Nations report concluded that from 1985 through 1996, 2 million children were killed worldwide and 6 million were seriously injured during large-scale wars to smaller scale ethnic conflicts, and millions more suffered from malnutrition and illness, among other deleterious consequences (Machel, 1996). Of course, millions of women are similarly affected during these male–male conflicts.

Even relatively subtle levels of social instability can have adverse effects on the physical well-being of children (Flinn, 2006; Flinn & England, 1997;

Flinn, Quinlan, Decker, Turner, & England, 1996), which is of greater concern for women than for men. Children living in unstable social environments tend to have abnormal (elevated or highly variable) stress hormone (i.e., cortisol) profiles, are ill more frequently, and weigh less than children living in more stable households and communities. Growing up in a socially unstable environment increases health and mortality risks in adulthood and, as a result, can shorten the life span (Marmot, 2004). Within relatively small communities, stable social relationships can be achieved by suppressing male–male competition, enforcing a more or less equal distribution of resources, and promoting cooperative child care and economic interdependence of women and men (Hewlett, 1992).

These are, of course, relative and not absolute sex differences. Not all men are politically active or politically motivated, and many men in many cultures are more concerned with the well-being of their family than with achieving social power. In societies in which men do not actively suppress the political activities of women, many women seek and obtain political power. Even in societies in which the overt political activities of women are suppressed by men, women may be able to achieve social power by influencing the political activities of their husbands or male kin. However, on average, the political interests and activities of women and men tend to differ. Consistent with their social dominance orientation, men are more inclined to advocate political policies associated with group dominance, such as military spending. Consistent with their social equality orientation, women are more inclined to advocate political policies that result in a more equitable distribution of social resources (e.g., higher taxes to pay for social welfare) and a greater investment in children (e.g., public day care; Pratto, 1996).

There are consistent sex differences in the ways in which men and women prefer to organize their social worlds and in the strategies (e.g., physical violence) they use to achieve this organization. These sex differences are reflected in social motives and political interests and activities and are consistent with the relative focus of men on mating effort and women on parental effort. Men seek to achieve social dominance and are more concerned with social status—cultural success—than women because today and throughout our evolutionary history the achievement of dominance and status results in more wives and more children. Women, in contrast, cannot improve their reproductive success by gaining additional husbands, but they can improve their reproductive success by organizing the social community in a way that would enhance the well-being of their children; sometimes this involves enlisting a secondary father (see the section titled Alternative Mating Strategies, chap. 7). These communities are socially stable, with sufficient material and social resources to provide a safety net for families and children who are in difficult circumstances. I suspect that the strength of this preference varies with the level of available resources. As I described in chapter 8 (in the section titled Women's Aggression), when women compete for a limited and valuable resource, they can be vicious.

My point is that men are more likely to benefit from substantial increases in status and wealth, especially in polygynous societies, and the relative benefits to women are mitigated by the costs associated with male coalitional conflicts over the distribution of this wealth. By advocating social policies that suppress male–male competition (e.g., political opposition to warfare), women might be able to reduce the overall level of socially disruptive violence in the society, including male-on-female aggression; male primates and men often displace aggression stemming from male–male competition onto conspecific females and women (Smuts, 1985). From this perspective, women's focus on social equality is just as functionally self-serving as the dominance-oriented social motives of men. As do men, women work to organize and control social relationships and dynamics, but the sexes do so in different ways.

Mechanisms

I turn now to the middle sections of Figure 9.1, conscious–psychological, working memory, and affective mechanisms that support control-related behavioral strategies. I describe the modular systems in the section titled Folk Domains in this chapter.

Conscious–Psychological

I start with a brief definition of conscious–psychological mechanisms; see Geary (2005b) for a more complete description. I then turn to sex differences in the use of these mechanisms.

Mechanisms. The core of the conscious–psychological mechanism is the human ability to form a conscious, explicit mental representation of situations that are centered on the self and one's relationship with other people or one's access to biological and physical resources. The representations often involve a form of mental time travel, specifically, mental simulations of past, present, or potential future states, which can be cast as images, in language, or as episodic memories (i.e., memories of personal experiences; Suddendorf & Corballis, 1997; Tulving, 2002). Following R. D. Alexander (1989) and integrating the work of Suddendorf and Corballis, Tulving, and Johnson-Laird (1983), I proposed that the ability to construct a self-centered conscious–psychological representation of past, present, and potential future states and the ability to engage in effortful reasoning and problem solving on the content of these representations are uniquely human and evolved as a result of the fluidity of social dynamics and social competition (see Geary, 2005b). A key component is the ability to create a mental representation of a desired or fantasized state and to compare this with a mental representation of one's current situation. This might involve, for instance, fantasizing about developing a relationship with a potential romantic partner and strategizing about ways to bring about this outcome.

Explicit beliefs and attributions about the self, others, or group dynamics can also be components of these representations. Attributions about favored ingroup members and disfavored members of an outgroup are an example of the form of bias that would be expected to evolve if there has been an evolutionary history of coalitional competition in humans; these biases are particularly salient during times of intergroup competition and hostilities (J.-K. Choi & Bowles, 2007; Fiske, 2002; L. T. Harris & Fisk, 2006). Horowitz's (2001) seminal analysis of ethnic conflict in the real world is consistent with laboratory studies and with the prediction that conflict is invariably over resource control and competitive advantage. In these situations, unfavorable attributions about the character and intentions of members of the outgroup often include rumors of an intended outgroup attack or conspiracy to, for instance, poison the ingroup's food supply or attack the women. These attributional biases justify, facilitate, and precede violence in many instances of ethnic conflict. The result is often deadly and often results in the self-serving elimination of economic or social competitors. The attributional biases not only justify this self-serving violence, they also protect individuals from the affective consequences, such as guilt, that could result if the violence were directed against members of the ingroup.

People also have a system of attributional biases that support attempts to achieve some level of control (Heckhausen & Schulz, 1995). These control mechanisms are important because the failure of these mechanisms appears to result in depression and behavioral inhibition, that is, a cessation of attempts to achieve control (Shapiro, Schwartz, & Astin, 1996). One important function of these mechanisms is to maintain control-oriented behaviors in the face of failure (Heckhausen & Schulz, 1995). These mechanisms include attributions that allow people to interpret personal failure in ways that maintain their sense of self-efficacy, their belief that they can achieve the goal in question. Such interpretations might involve attributing failure to external causes ("It wasn't my fault") or maintaining an illusion of control by interpreting the outcome as predictable ("I knew that this would happen"). These same mechanisms are engaged with rituals, belief in psychic powers, and so on and serve the function of attempting to predict and control potentially significant life events (e.g., finding a mate, the health of kin) and to mollify the fear and anxiety associated with not having complete control over these events.

Sex Differences. The sex differences in sexual fantasy, in the content of personal ads, and in preferred fiction, described in chapter 7 (in the sections titled Preferred Choices, and Sexual Attitudes and Fantasy), illustrate evolutionarily salient content represented in the conscious–psychological control system. Ellis and Symons's (1990) finding that nearly 1 out 3 young men but fewer than 1 out of 10 young women report having fantasized—generated mental representations in the conscious–psychological system—about sexual relationships with more than 1,000 members of the opposite sex reflects the sex difference in the motivation to seek multiple sex partners, which evolved as a result of the sex difference in the reproductive benefits of multiple partners (Symons, 1979). Fantasizing about multiple sexual relationships is not only a reflection of this motive but also may provide a means for rehearsing strategies for achieving these relationships. In the absence of birth control, men who have such fantasies and seek multiple relationships will, per force, leave more descendants than their less imaginative peers.

In this view, the reproductive motivation of despots and young college men is the same, although they clearly differ in the ability to realize their fantasies and in the strategies used during the pursuit of this reproductive goal. Similarly, the content of popular fiction stories that women find more appealing, on average, than men mirrors the sexual fantasies of many women, as I described in chapter 7 (in the section titled Female Choice). The realization of such a fantasy would result in the woman developing a long-term relationship with a physically attractive, socially dominant, and wealthy man. The development of such a relationship, in turn, would not only provide good genes to her offspring but also allow her to create a stable and resource-rich social and material environment within which to raise her children.

Working Memory

Working memory is the ability to explicitly form and maintain mental representations of information (e.g., a visual image, a word) and to manipulate these representations. The component skills include attentional control, the ability to inhibit the automatic processing of folk-related information (see the section titled Folk Domains in this chapter), and the ability to inhibit behavioral reactions (Baddeley, 1986; Bjorklund & Harnishfeger, 1995; Cowan, 1995). These representations can be systematically manipulated in working memory through problem solving and reasoning (J. St. B. T. Evans, 2002; Stanovich & West, 2000). Working memory and associated attentional and inhibitory control are the evolved *content-free* mechanisms that enable the integration of a current conscious–psychological state with memory representations of related past experiences and the generation of mental models or simulations of potential future states (R. D. Alexander, 1989; Johnson-Laird, 1983).

More precisely, the motivation to control is facilitated by the ability to mentally simulate potential future social scenarios (R. D. Alexander, 1989; Humphrey, 1976), to use problem solving to generate a variety of potential responses to these situations, and to mentally rehearse these responses (Geary, 2005b). All of these processes require working memory. The basic idea is that an evolutionary history of complex and ever-changing patterns of social cooperation and competition has resulted in a high level of social unpredictability. The resulting evolutionary solution is to mentally generate potential variations of these conditions in working memory and then to rehearse behavioral strategies for controlling outcomes associated with each of these variations. Although not a focus of this book (see Geary, 2005b), I note here that working memory is a core component of general fluid intelligence (Kane & Engle, 2002) and that I discuss associated sex differences in Geary (1998b) and the afterword of this volume.

Affective

I begin with a brief definition of affective mechanisms and then turn to sex differences in the two corresponding components—emotions and feelings.

Mechanisms. Affective mechanisms are separated into emotions— observable behaviors (e.g., facial expressions)—and feelings—nonobservable conscious representations of an emotional state (Damasio, 2003). Among other benefits, emotions provide observable feedback to others (e.g., frowns signal disapproval) and feelings provide unobservable feedback to the individual (J. J. Campos, R. G. Campos, & Barrett, 1989). Feelings are a useful indicator of the effectiveness of control-related behavioral strategies and an indicator of the potential benefits of a simulated behavior. Positive feelings provide reinforcement when strategies are resulting in the achievement of significant goals, or at least a reduction in the difference between the current and desired state, and negative feelings provide punishment and promote disengagement when behaviors are not resulting in this end (J. A. Gray, 1987). The supporting brain systems, such as the amygdala, function in part to amplify attention to evolutionarily significant forms of information, such as facial expressions, and to produce emotions, feelings, and corresponding behavioral biases that are likely to automatically (see the section titled Folk Heuristics in this chapter) reproduce outcomes that have covaried with survival or reproduction during human evolution (Lazarus, 1991; Öhman, 2002). Kensinger (2007) described how memories for emotionally threatening or potentially harmful objects or events engage the amygdala and the hippocampus, which is involved in forming long-term memories, more strongly than neutral or positive events.

> Although emotional memories are susceptible to distortion, negative emotion conveys benefits on memory for detail. These benefits make sense within an evolutionary framework. Because a primary function of

emotion is to guide action and to plan for future occurrences (Lazarus, 1991), it is logical that attention would be focused on potentially threatening information and that memory mechanisms would ensure that details predictive of an event's affective relevance would be encoded precisely. (p. 217)

Positive emotions are evolutionarily functional as well. For instance, happiness is strongly related to the strength of reciprocal and romantic relationships (Diener & Seligman, 2002), the former being sources of social support and the latter related to reproductive goals. Negative and positive affective reactions may shape niche-seeking activities, such that individuals pursue evolutionarily significant goals in ways that are most adaptive for them (Rowe, 1994; Scarr & McCarthy, 1983). Adaptive niche seeking would require individuals to pursue goals in ways that capitalize on their social, cognitive, or behavioral strengths, that is, by using competencies for which they have a relative advantage over other people (Lubinski & Dawis, 1992). The use of these strengths is more likely to result in success, and the corresponding affective reactions reinforce use of these competencies (Izard, 1993).

Sex Differences. Emotions and feelings are predicted to have guided women and men to attempt to organize their social world and their pursuit of other resources in ways that have been adaptive throughout human evolution. Although they are rarely studied from this perspective, sex differences in affective responses are often found for behaviors that are related to the different reproductive motives of men and women, specifically, the relative focus of men on mating effort and women on parental effort (D. M. Buss, 1989a; Vigil, in press). Women's and men's reactions to casual sex provide a theoretically potent example. In these relationships, more women than men develop unwanted feelings of social dependency and anxiety about their partner's emotional investment in them (Townsend, Kline, & Wasserman, 1995); 2 out of 3 of the young women in this study reported these feelings as compared with 1 out of 5 of the young men. Women also report more negative feelings, such as guilt and disgust, following a 1-night stand than do men (A. Campbell, 2008). These feelings make evolutionary sense because of the higher costs paid by women if there is an unwanted pregnancy and because of the risks to women's social reputation. In theory, feelings of social dependency, anxiety, and disgust prompt women to evaluate whether their partner is likely to provide long-term investment in them and any resulting children and to avoid men who are not likely to make such an investment.

With a few exceptions, such as Townsend et al.'s (1995) study of casual sex, the vast majority of studies of sex differences in affective responses have been conducted in laboratory settings and using stimuli (e.g., films that elicit happiness or fear) that are not explicitly designed to test evolutionary predictions. These studies have nevertheless revealed intriguing sex differences and similarities in emotions and feelings.

Expressed Emotions. Although there are a few exceptions, the majority of studies reveal that women express emotions more frequently and intensely (e.g., wider smile) than men (Buck, Savin, Miller, & Caul, 1972; J. J. Gross & John, 1998; Kring & Gordon, 1998; Vigil, in press), although women's and men's expressiveness is moderated by social context (Buck, Miller, & Caul, 1974; M. L. Hoffman, 1977). Gross and John identified five affective facets or subdomains that are common across the many measures of emotions and feelings: expressive confidence (the ability to act out emotions without feeling them), positive expressivity (the expression of positive emotions), negative expressivity, impulse intensity (intensity of feelings and difficulty controlling their expression), and masking (suppression of feelings). There were no sex differences in expressive confidence, but about 3 out of 4 women reported more positive expressivity than the average man, and 2 out of 3 women reported more negative expressivity than the average man.

There do not appear to be sex differences in proneness to anger (Archer, 2004), but men are more likely than women to express aggression physically (A. Campbell & Muncer, 2008; Knight, Guthrie, Page, & Fabes, 2002; Verona & Curtin, 2006). In a meta-analysis of 122 samples of children to young adults, Knight et al. found that, independent of age, about 2 out of 3 boys and men behaved more aggressively (e.g., hit another person) across a variety of settings than did the average same-age girl or woman. These sex differences were most pronounced following mild to moderate provocations (e.g., subtle insults), when 7 out of 10 boys or men responded more aggressively (e.g., administering shocks to another person) than did the average girl or woman. Under conditions of low or high provocation, the sex differences were much smaller. When women are directly provoked *and* there is little risk of retaliation, they can behave nearly as aggressively as men. Men also tend to be more overtly aggressive in stressful situations, even when they are not directly provoked (Verona & Curtin, 2006).

These sex differences are due in part to boys' and men's tendency to use aggression instrumentally, that is, to control social dynamics and to get what they want (e.g., A. Campbell & Muncer, 2008). The instrumental use of aggression follows readily from an evolutionary history of physical male–male competition and, in fact, is necessary to achieve cultural success in many traditional societies (see the section titled Competition in Traditional Societies, chap. 8, this volume). Girls and women, in contrast, tend to inhibit the expression of physically aggressive behavior to avoid the risks of escalation or retaliation (Bjorklund & Kipp, 1996). As I described in the section titled Reproductive Skew in chapter 8 of this volume, women have less to gain and more to lose, reproductively, by allowing conflicts to escalate to the point of risk of physical injury or death. In addition, I explained that the administration of testosterone decreases fear (Hermans, Putnam, Baas, Koppeschaar, & van Honk, 2006) and increases risk taking (van Honk et al., 2004) in women (see the section titled Risk Taking, chap. 8, this volume). These findings are consistent with an influence of male–male competition on the sex differences in emotional expression, given that testosterone is one of the mechanisms that influences the proximate expression of sexually selected traits.

Feelings. Whether women or men have more intense *feelings*—that is, unobservable personal experience of an emotion—is not clear. The phenomenon is obviously more difficult to study than observable emotions, but it has nonetheless been assessed using self-report, physiological reactivity, and brain imaging methods. Women typically report more intense feelings than men (Buck, Miller, & Caul, 1974; M. Grossman & Wood, 1993). Using diary methods, Barrett, Robin, Pietromonaco, and Eyssell (1998) found that women and men reported a similar range of emotions during day-to-day social interactions, but women rated the intensity of their accompanying feelings higher than did men. In their analysis of multiple emotions and feelings scales, Gross and John (1998) found that 6 out of 7 women reported more intense emotional impulses—difficulty inhibiting the expression of feelings—than did the average man, whereas 2 out of 3 men reported more masking than did the average woman.

The physiological and brain imaging studies reveal a much more nuanced picture. Sometimes women show more intense physiological reactivity (e.g., sweating) than men to affect-eliciting situations (e.g., viewing an injury), consistent with their reports of more intense feelings, but sometimes they do not (Eisenberg & Lennon, 1983; Gard & Kring, 2007; Wager, Phan, Liberzon, & S. F. Taylor, 2003). Buck et al. (1974) found disconnections between expressed emotions, reported intensity of accompanying feelings, and physiological indicators of affective reactivity. In situations designed to elicit a range of affective reactions, more women than men expressed emotions, reported intense reactions, but showed little physiological indication of reactivity. In support of Grossand John's (1998) finding that men report more masking, Buck et al. found more men than women inhibited emotional expressions, reported less intense feelings, but at the same time showed strong physiological reactivity to the situation. But there were also women who reported intense feelings and had intense physiological reactions, just as there are men who reported little emotional reactivity and showed little physiological reactivity. These sex differences were confirmed by Kring and Gordon (1998).

In a meta-analysis of brain imaging studies in this area, Wager et al. (2003) found no evidence for more overall brain activation in women than in men during the processing of affective information (e.g., car accident), but there were sex differences in the pattern of activation. The brain activity of men suggested that they focus more on the "sensory aspects of emotional stimuli and tend to process them in terms of implications for required actions, whereas [women] direct more attention to the feeling state engendered by the emotional stimuli" (Wager et al., 2003, p. 527). If Wager et al. are correct, many women experience feelings in a more personally intense way than men.

Men's masking of their feelings is consistent with both socialization and the dynamics of male–male competition. In chapter 10 (in the section titled Rough and Tumble Play), I describe how socialization practices can vary with the intensity of male–male competition in the wider society and how boys are expected to suppress fear, pain, empathy, and other feelings that may interfere with their ability to compete in these contexts. The disconnection between emotions and feelings in many women is intriguing and suggests some women are using emotional expressions strategically. These women are not experiencing the corresponding feelings but are expressing the emotion for social effect. My predictions are these emotional expressions are largely used in the context of female–female relational aggression, although they might also be used to better manage relationships with men and in their relationships with same-sex friends.

FOLK DOMAINS

I focus now on the base of the triangle in Figure 9.1. The corresponding folk domains are shown in Figure 9.2 and provide a way to organize the understanding of evolved biases in human cognition, such as language, and to differentiate these from cognitive competencies, such as reading, that are dependent on culturally specific practices (e.g., schooling; Geary, 1995a, 2007, 2008). In other words, folk domains represent cognitive competencies that are found in people across human cultures, not just modern ones (e.g., reading). Much of the research in psychology has focused on sex differences in culturally specific forms of cognition, such as reading and mathematics. My goal in differentiating folk cognition from these culturally specific forms of cognitive competence is to provide a more nuanced examination of sex differences than has been the norm for much of the research and theory on sex differences in brain and cognition. I provide reviews of sex differences in folk psychological domains in chapter 12 of this volume and cover folk biological and folk physical domains in chapter 13. I touch on a few sex differences in modern academic domains (e.g., reading) in the afterword of this volume and in Geary (1998b). My task for now is to provide an overview of the basic structure of folk domains as a means to organize these later reviews.

As shown in Figure 9.2, the classes of evolved cognitive domains are organized around the areas of folk psychology, folk biology, and folk physics

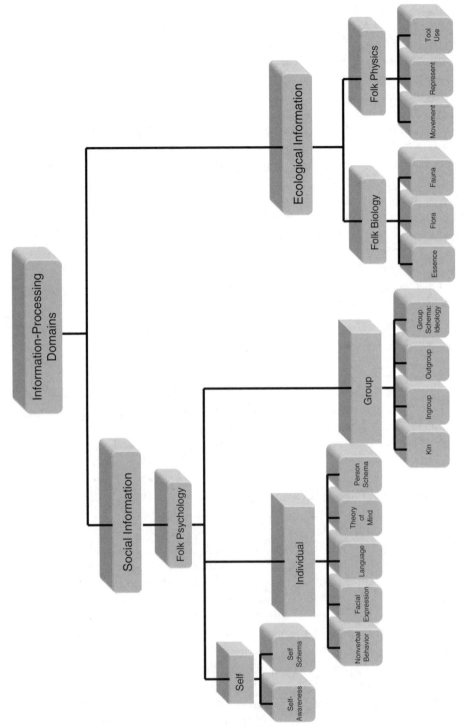

Figure 9.2. Evolutionarily salient information-processing domains and associated cognitive modules that compose folk psychology, folk biology, and folk physics. From *The Origin of Mind: Evolution of Brain, Cognition, and General Intelligence* (p. 129), by D. G. Geary, 2005, Washington, DC: American Psychological Association. Copyright 2005 by the American Psychological Association.

(e.g., Baron-Cohen, 1995; Medin & Atran, 1999; Pinker, 1997; Spelke, Breinlinger, Macomber, & Jacobson, 1992). I assume these modular (but plastic) systems support the motivational disposition to attempt to gain access to and control of the types of social, biological (e.g., food), and physical (e.g., territory) resources that have tended to covary with survival and reproductive outcomes during human evolutionary history. The second level of the figure—social and ecological information—reflects the evolutionary salience of other people and their behavior (Brothers, 1990; Brothers & Ring, 1992; Geary & Flinn, 2001; Humphrey, 1976) and the biological and physical ecologies that support survival and reproductive activities (Kaplan, Hill, Lancaster, & Hurtado, 2000). The third level represents the functional modules that encompass key folk domains.

Functional means that different combinations of modules, and underlying perceptual and neural mechanisms, can be put together in building block form to meet current social or ecological demands (Geary, 2005b; Marcus, 2004). A functional constellation of modules is goal related and represents the dynamic engagement of underlying neural, perceptual, and cognitive systems and an integration of the associated processing with affective and motivational systems. The individual-level functional system, as an example, is engaged during one-on-one social interactions and integrates systems for processing and responding to nonverbal behavioral cues, language, and so forth. These cognitive systems are integrated with affective and motivational systems and function to direct behavioral strategies toward the achievement of social goals.

Folk Psychology

The taxonomy of folk psychological modules shown in Figure 9.2 accommodates forms of competitive and cooperative social dynamic that are common in humans and, for some domains, in other species (Bugental, 2000; Caporael, 1997; Hauser, 1996; Hrdy, 2005; Pinker, 1994; Tulving, 2002). Although I have separated these in terms of self-, individual-, and group-level systems, simultaneous activation of multiple systems is common in day-to-day life. One's sense of self, for instance, is influenced by one's group memberships, such as ethnicity or political affiliation (Ashmore, Deaux, & McLaughlin-Volpe, 2004).

Self

Self-awareness is the ability to consciously represent the self as a social being, is integrally related to the ability to mentally time travel (Suddendorf & Corballis, 1997; Tulving, 2002), and may be unique to humans (Suddendorf & Busby, 2003). Self-awareness is also integral to the explicit representations of past and present states and the ability to create self-centered mental simulations of potential future states, as described in the section titled Conscious–Psychological earlier in this chapter. Associated with self-awareness is the *self-schema* (Fiske & S. E. Taylor, 1991; Markus, 1977), which is a long-term memory network of information that links together knowledge and beliefs about the self, including positive (accentuated) and negative (discounted) traits (e.g., friendliness), episodic memories, and self-efficacy—a self-referenced appraisal regarding the likelihood of success in various endeavors (Bandura, 1997)—in various domains, among other aspects of the self. During most day-to-day activities, this knowledge is implicit; it is not something most people explicitly think about. Explicit awareness of the self and information represented in the self-schema can occur when one's typical ways of coping are not working; see the section titled Folk Heuristics in this chapter.

Although the evidence is mixed, self-schemas can regulate goal-related behaviors, specifically, where one focuses effort and whether one will persist in the face of failure (Sheeran & Orbell, 2000). Self-regulation results from a combination of implicit and explicit processes that influence social comparisons, self-efficacy, valuation of different forms of ability and interests, and the formation of social relationships (Drigotas, 2002). When evaluating the competencies of others, people focus on attributes that are central features of their self-schema and prefer relationships that provide feedback consistent with their self-schema. Athletes implicitly compare and contrast themselves with others on dimensions that involve physical competence, whereas professors focus more on intellectual competence (Fiske & S. E. Taylor, 1991). People value competencies on which they excel and discount those for which they are at a competitive disadvantage (S. E. Taylor, 1982). The combination may facilitate niche seeking and the development of niche-relevant competencies.

Individual

There are several types of universal one-on-one relationships in humans, including attachment between a parent and a child and friendships (Bugental, 2000; Caporael, 1997). Despite motivational and affective differences across these relationships, they all appear to be supported by the same suite of cognitive competencies, including the ability to read nonverbal communication signals, facial expressions, language, and theory of mind (Adolphs, 1999; Brothers & Ring, 1992; Humphrey, 1976; Leslie, 1987; Pinker, 1994). *Theory of mind* represents the ability to make inferences about the intentions, beliefs, emotional states, and likely future behavior of other individuals and may be especially developed in humans (Baron-Cohen, 1995; Leslie, Friedman, & German, 2004). The functional individual-level system is also engaged during the dynamics of one-on-one social interactions, providing cues to the online feeling states and intentions of other people.

The integration of these modular systems with motivational and affective systems provides the basis for the development and maintenance of long-term relationships. In these relationships, the *person schema* becomes important. People develop such schemas of familiar people and people for whom future social relationships are expected (Fiske & S. E. Taylor, 1991). The schema is a long-term memory network that includes representations of the other person's physical attributes, especially race, sex, and age, as well as memories for specific behavioral episodes and more abstract trait information. The trait information typically varies across two continuums, sociability (warm to emotionally distant) and competence (Schneider, 1973). The person schema also includes information about the person's theory of mind (Adolphs, 1999; Leslie, 1987). This includes memories and trait information about how the person typically makes inferences, responds to social cues, his or her social and other goals, and so forth. The person schema is also likely to include affective dimensions, including memory representations that elicit a sense of familiarity and specific feelings based on episodic memories (Brothers, 1990).

Group

People readily demarcate their world into social groups that reflect the evolutionary significance of kin, the formation of ingroups and outgroups, and ideologically based social identification (R. D. Alexander, 1979; Dunbar, 1993; Eagly, 1987; K. MacDonald, 1988). An evolved bias to differentially favor kin over nonkin is found in all species (W. D. Hamilton, 1964) and is illustrated by the section titled Parental Investment in chapter 4 of the volume and by men's and women's investment in their children (see chap. 6, this volume). In the following discussion, I outline the basics of the evolution and social psychology of ingroups and outgroups and group schemas. I highlight the importance of group schemas with a discussion of the ideology of gender.

Ingroups and Outgroups. As I discussed in chapter 8 (in the section titled Competition in Traditional Societies), group-level coalitional competition is common across human societies and almost certainly has a deep evolutionary history. As I described in chapter 5 (in the section titled Coalitional Competition), coalitional competition is found in some other primates and among other species and is characterized by cooperation among members of the ingroup to more effectively compete against outgroups for control of survival-related (e.g., fruit trees) or reproduction-related (e.g., mates) resources. Contrasting species that form coalitions to their more solitary cousins provides a means to test the hypothesis that the cognitive competencies and brain systems that govern coalition formation have evolved. Such contrasts have consistently revealed that species in which coalitions form have a larger neocortex and more complex social–cognitive competencies than do evolutionarily related solitary species (D. A. Clark, Mitra, & Wang, 2001; Dunbar, 1993; Dunbar & Bever, 1998).

My hypothesis is that the initial evolutionary bases for large-scale human coalitions is male philopatry and the formation of kin-based coalitions among men, as I reviewed in chapters 5 (in the section titled Coalitional Competition) and 8 (in the sections titled Competition in Traditional Societies, Population Genetics); there are of course many other human kin-based biases, as reflected in the formation of families of one type or another in all human societies (D. E. Brown, 1991; Geary & Flinn, 2001). In traditional societies, group size varies in response to the opportunities and demands of the local habitat that supports the group (R. D. Alexander, 1990; Chagnon, 1997) but usually does not exceed 150 to 200 individuals (Dunbar, 1993). The individuals who constitute these groups are typically kin and share beliefs, such as origin myths, that not only distinguish them from other groups but often, if not always, assign special significance to their group (D. E. Brown, 1991). Under conditions in which a group's status or resources are threatened by the activities or perceived hostile intentions of other groups, the basic tendency of humans to form ingroups and outgroups and to process information about members of these groups in ways that are favorably biased toward the ingroup and negatively biased against the outgroup is exacerbated (Hewstone, Rubin, & Willis, 2002; Horowitz, 2001). Hewstone et al. concluded that "threat is a central explanatory concept in several of the theories . . . and literature on intergroup bias" (p. 586). Ingroups and outgroups are defined by differing social and moral ideologies that favor ingroup members—kin and friends—and devalue outgroup members (L T. Harris & Fiske, 2006; Hartung, 1995).

One key condition for effective competition against an outgroup is the disengagement of the affective and moral mechanisms that appear to be designed to reduce conflict and foster cooperation within ingroups (Haidt, 2007). Although some level of ingroup conflict is anticipated—especially when there are no current competing outgroups—it appears that feelings such as guilt and empathy moderate this conflict in the service of mutually beneficial cooperative exchanges (Baumeister & Leary, 1995; Trivers, 1971), as does the belief that reciprocal relationships are often in one's best interest (Baron, 1997). When directed toward outgroups, these same moderating affective reactions result in a competitive disadvantage. In other words, when the competition between groups affected reproduction and survival—and it likely did in many instances throughout the course of human evolution (R. D. Alexander, 1990; Chagnon, 1988; Hartung, 1995; Keeley, 1996)—individuals who were able in extreme cases to dehumanize outgroups were likely at a competitive advantage.

My basic point should be clear: The implicit and explicit cognitive and behavioral processes involved in the formation of ingroups, outgroups, and social identification are readily interpretable in terms of social selection pressures. These social psychological phenomena are the proximate mechanisms—elaborated in chapter 12 (in the section titled Ingroups and Outgroups)—that facilitate the formation of cooperative coalitions that, in turn, function to gain access to or control of the social and ecological resources that enhance the well-being of ingroup members. Enhancement is essentially about control of the resources that facilitate the health and well-being of the individual and his or her kin and about improving reproductive options, as with other species. When viewed in terms of mental models and the motivation to control, explicit representations of group-level dynamics allow for the simulation of potential future relationships among groups as well as competitive strategies. These simulations are at the heart of military strategy and many competitive games (e.g., chess, many video games that appeal to boys).

Group Schema. Social psychologists have studied group identification—group schema in Figure 9.2—for much of the 20th century and have a considerable understanding of group dynamics at a cognitive and behavioral level (Fiske, 2002; Fiske & S. E. Taylor, 1991; Hewstone et al., 2002). The theories and literature focus on, among other things, the identification with members of a perceived ingroup under conditions of threat and competition. The shared beliefs of members of the ingroup are central to the social identification processes underlying group formation and competition (Abrams & Hogg, 1990).

The social psychology of ingroup and outgroup cognitions likely evolved in kin-based groups, and these cognitions may have provided the foundation for the evolution of social identification mechanisms (R. D. Alexander, 1990; K. MacDonald, 1988). The initial pressure for the evolution of these mechanisms might have been ancestor worship and the cross-generational transfer of myths about these ancestors that in turn promoted cooperation among distantly related kin (Palmer, Ellsworth, & Steadman, 2009). A tendency to organize cooperative groups around ancestor myths may have provided the foundation for use of ideologies to form even larger groups that in turn had a competitive advantage vis-à-vis other groups (R. D. Alexander, 1990). These ideologies are the basis for the formation of large nation-states, the social organization of individuals who have never met and never will and thus are unable to develop one-on-one reciprocal relationships. Such ideologies define the perceived mutual self-interest of individuals who compose groups that are larger than functional villages in traditional societies and are the basis for the intragroup cooperation that facilitates large-scale between-groups conflict and reduces freeloading within the ingroup (Norenzayan & Shariff, 2008). Supporting evidence comes from experimental results that show that enhancing mortality cues, as well as less severe threats, increases people's endorsement of ingroup ideologies and results in harsher evaluations of outgroup members (Arndt, Greenberg, Pyszczynski, & Solomon, 1997). People rally around ideologies when they are threatened, although some people are more easily threatened than others (Oxley et al., 2008).

Ideology of Gender. There is no question that humans socially categorize each other on the basis of biological sex and begin to do so very early in life (Maccoby, 1988; C. L. Martin, Ruble, & Szkrybalo, 2002). Kujawski and Bower (1993), for instance, showed that infants as young as 10 months can distinguish—as measured by looking patterns—the sex of other infants; they did not categorize other infants as boys or girls, as far as we know, but responded to differences in the other infants' behavior. Cognitive and brain imaging studies reveal that people can categorize others' sex in less than 1 s on the basis of a few facial features, and when they do so they engage different brain regions than when they process other facial information (e.g., familiarity; Cabeza & Nyberg, 1997; Schyns, Bonnar, & Gosselin, 2002).

Humans also have a system of beliefs termed *gender roles* that reflect the behaviors, attitudes, social expectations, and social position of men and boys and women and girls in most societies (Eagly, 1987); see the section titled Gender Schema in chapter 10 of this volume. Eagly and her colleagues proposed that these beliefs include *descriptive* and *injunctive* norms (Eagly, 1987; Eagly & Karau, 2002; W. Wood & Eagly, 2002). The former are descriptions of stereotypical sex differences, such as men are more physically aggressive than women, and the latter are expectations about how boys and girls and men and women ought to behave. Both types of norms are organized, in part, in terms of communion and agency. Eagly (1987) contended that women are, on average, more communal than men, as "manifested by selflessness, concern with others, and a desire to be at one with others" (p. 16), whereas men are, on average, more agentic than women, as manifested by "self-assertion, self-expansion, and the urge to master" (p. 16).

Eagly and colleagues argue further that sex differences in communion and agency are influenced by the different social and economic roles that men and women occupy in most if not all societies to varying degrees, in particular, women's greater involvement in domestic activities such as child care and men's greater involvement in paid employment (e.g., Eagly, 1987; W. Wood & Eagly, 2002). These roles in turn are influenced by a combination of physical sex differences (e.g., larger men than women), contextual factors, and modes of economic activity (e.g., agriculture). In addition to the greater communal demands of domestic activities and the greater agency demands of employment-related activities, women and men tend to differ in social status, including a greater frequency of men than women in high-status occupations and in key political positions. The greater social status of men than women not only further reinforces the communal and agency roles of women and men, respectively, but influences the emergence of sex differences through injunctive norms in those social behaviors associated with dominance and submission (Eagly & Karau, 2002). Whereas Eagly (1987) acknowledged that many factors contribute to these sex differences, "the requirements of the economy and social structure interact with the biological attributes of women and men and with the political ideologies of societies to produce differential role occupancy" (p. 31), the gist of the theory is that most sex differences are caused by injunctive norms.

In theory, women and men use these norms to evaluate their own social behavior and that of other people, and in fact, social psychological studies confirm these evaluations (e.g., Eagly & Karau, 2002). It is not simply that boys and girls internalize injunctive norms, but in addition, other people mete out rewards and punishments for adherence to and violations of these norms. I cannot do complete justice to the nuances of the social role model but argue that scientists do not fully understand the cause and effect of these relations. The normative stereotypes are found in all cultures in which they have been studied (Best & Williams, 1983), and some of these reflect biologically influenced sex differences; for example, men are in fact more physically aggressive than women, and women do in fact invest more in children. The extent to which sex differences are caused by injunctive norms and other social processes, as contrasted to or interacting with biological biases in these behaviors, cognitions, and so on is not well understood. These theorists have, in my opinion, downplayed the potential importance of sexual selection for understanding human sex differences (W. Wood & Eagly, 2002), and some theorists have incorrectly characterized evolved biases as deterministic, that they cannot be expressed (or not) in different ways in different contexts (Bussey & Bandura, 1999).

From the lens of my motivation-to-control model, the argument that sex differences are largely the result of injunctive norms is appealing to many people because such theories create an illusion of control, which, as described in the section titled Conscious–Psychological in this chapter, is of fundamental importance to human beings. If gender-role theories are largely correct, then all sex differences in social status, social behavior, and so on can be potentially eliminated by modifying the social expectations for women and men. Although appealing, strong versions of this view are almost certainly wrong (Archer, 1996). The communal versus agency distinction can be applied to nearly all of the sex differences I described in chapter 5 for nonmonogamous primates and in other chapters for many other species. As I discussed, male–male competition to establish social dominance, or agency, is a salient feature of nearly all of these primate societies, as is the fact that most "domestic" activities, in particular the care of offspring, are the domain of females (Andersson, 1994; Whitten, 1987).

Furthermore, the social roles of women and men differ in consistent ways across societies, including societies where there are no explicit gender roles, such as the Batek of Malaysia (Endicott, 1992; Murdock, 1981). The same general pattern of sex differences emerges in societies that are socially isolated from one another, and thus similarities across these societies cannot be explained in terms of shared cultural ideologies about the gender roles of women and men (D. E. Brown, 1991; Eibl-Eibesfeldt, 1989). In a review of sex differences in the division of labor across 224 societies, among many other differences, Daly and Wilson (1983) reported that weapon making—an agentic activity—was an exclusively male activity in 121 of the 122 societies in which information on this activity was available (women assisted men in the 1 remaining society), whereas cooking—a communal activity—was an exclusively female activity in 158 of the 201 societies surveyed; in 38 of the 43 remaining societies men did some of the cooking.

Pratto and her colleagues have also shown that a combination of factors influence the occupational differences that are prominent in Eagly's (1987) theory (Pratto, 1996; Pratto, Stallworth, Sidanius, & Siers, 1997). In addition to stereotypes about the relative communal and agentic orientations of women and men, which can influence hiring practices (Eagly & Karau, 2002), the distribution of women and men into different status-related occupations is related to self-selection; for further discussion, see Geary (1998b) and Browne (2002). When given a choice, men, on average, prefer *dominance-oriented* occupations, those emphasizing hierarchical social relationships and the control of other people. Women, on average, prefer to work in *hierarchy-attenuating* jobs, those that involve working with people, especially the disadvantaged and underprivileged (Pratto et al., 1997). These differences are in keeping with the ways in which men pursue cultural success in modern societies and with the tendency for women to avoid direct competition and to have a more communal orientation. This orientation, as I noted, is a reflection of women's higher investment in children and families and an implicit desire to suppress male–male competition within their ingroup.

Social ideologies can influence human behavior, and there is no reason to expect that gender will be immune from such influence; there is much to be learned here. The construction of gender ideologies is at times an attempt at social and political manipulation. The tendency of some writers to describe girls and women as passive and boys and men as active might represent an implicit attempt to suppress female choice and maintain the status quo, that is, male control of social and material resources (Smuts, 1995); there is a sex difference favoring males in physical activity levels (see the section titled Physical Development, chap. 10, this volume), but both men and women actively pursue their self-interests. Similarly, the ideological prescriptions of some feminist scholars appear to be implicitly designed to disrupt the formation of male coalitions, suppress male–male competition (i.e., suppress the establishment of dominance hierarchies), and at the same time, increase female choice and female control of essential resources (e.g., G. C. H. Hall & Barongan, 1997). These prescriptions reflect the expression of sexual politics—conflict over the different reproductive preferences of men and women—through human language.

Folk Biology

As with beak specialization in Darwin's finches (see the section titled Ecological Selection Pressures, chap. 2, this volume), there is evidence for species-specific brain, cognitive, behavioral, and physical specializations that enable the location and manipulation (e.g., raccoons, *Procyon lotor*, cleaning of food) of edible plants, fruits, and nuts as well as the location and capture of prey species (Barton & Dean, 1993; Huffman, Nelson, Clarey, & Krubitzer, 1999). The folk biological modules shown in Figure 9.2 represent the most rudimentary cognitive specializations that support humans' ability to learn about, identify, and secure biological resources in the wide range of ecological niches occupied by our species (Atran, 1998; Caramazza & Shelton, 1998; Malt, 1995; Medin & Atran, 2004). Although the extent to which these specializations are the result of evolved biases or experience and learning is debated (Keil, Levin, Richman, & Gutheil, 1999), the functional competencies are manifested as hunting, gathering, and horticulture in traditional societies.

Analogous to both variation in the surface structure of human languages and a universal grammar (Pinker, 1999), there is cross-cultural variation in the extent and organization of folk biological knowledge but also a universal core. As a reflection of this core, humans throughout the world are able to categorize the flora and fauna in their local ecologies and show similar categorical and inferential biases when reasoning about these species (Atran, 1998; Berlin, Breedlove, & Raven, 1966; Diamond, 1966). Through ethnobiological studies, "it has become apparent that, while individual societies may differ considerably in their conceptualization of plants and animals, there are a number of strikingly regular structural principles of folk biological classification which are quite general" (Berlin, Breedlove, & Raven, 1973, p. 214). Bailenson, Shum, Atran, Medin, and Coley (2002) asked groups of novices and bird experts from the United States and Itza' Maya Amerindians (Guatemala) to classify about 100 birds from their region and from the region of the other group. There were similarities and differences in the classifications of all three groups. The classification system of U.S. experts and the Itza' Maya was more similar to the scientific taxonomy of these species than was the classification system of the U.S. novices.

> The Itza' data are dramatic in that despite not being exposed to either western science in general or formal taxonomy in particular, their consensual sorting agrees more with (western) scientific taxonomy than does the consensual sort of US non-experts. This difference held for both US birds and Tikal birds. (Bailenson et al., 2002, p. 24)

Bailenson et al.'s (2002) findings for novices are not unique; without sufficient experience with the natural world, as with Western college students or children living in modern urban areas, only rudimentary aspects of folk biology develop (Median & Atran, 2004). With sufficient experience, people develop at least a three-level organization to their knowledge of the biological world. The most general level—corresponding to the kingdom level in the scientific classification—is shown in Figure 9.2. People further subdivide flora and fauna into groups of related species corresponding to the class level, such as birds, mammals, and trees, and then more specific species, such as bluebirds (*Sialia*) and robins (*Turdus*). Cross-cultural variation is largest for knowledge of species that are specific to the local ecology and that are of functional importance to the local population (Atran, 1998; Malt, 1995). This species-specific knowledge can then be used to make inferences about the behavior, growth, and so forth of less familiar but related species.

Knowledge of the species' morphology, behavior, growth pattern, and ecological niche (e.g., arboreal versus terrestrial) helps to define the *essence* of the species (Atran, 1994; Malt, 1995). The essence is a species schema that includes knowledge of salient and stable characteristics, including the species' relationships with other species in the wider ecology (e.g., Medin et al., 2006). Biological essence may also be analogous, in some respects, to people's theory of mind. This is because mental models of flora and fauna would be well suited for representing and predicting the likely behavior of these organisms (e.g., seasonal growth in plants). The combination of folk biological categories, inferential biases, and knowledge of the species' essence allows people to use these species in evolutionarily significant ways (Figueiredo, Leitão-Filho, & Begossi, 1993, 1997).

Folk Physics

At the most basic level, natural selection should favor the evolution of mechanisms that allow species to detect food, shelter, or mates and to move to these fitness-enhancing resources and away from threats to their well-being (Dyer, 1998). My conceptualization of physical modules in terms of movement and representation, as shown in the rightmost portion of Figure 9.2, is based on Milner and Goodale's (1995) analysis of the functional and anatomical organization of the visual system. They argued that for the visual system, the systems for movement and representation are functionally and anatomically distinct, although they can interact.

Consistent with a modular approach, Milner and Goodale (1995) provided examples of distinct visuomotor pathways for a variety of movement-related functions, such as predator avoidance and navigating around obstacles. Barton and Dean (1993) hypothesized that the function of one particular visual pathway is prey capture. They tested this hypothesis by examining the relations among the number of neurons in this pathway, the size of the corresponding cell bodies, and predatory behaviors within four groups of mammals, *Rodentia, Primates, Carnivora,* and *Marsupiala.* Within each of these groups, species were classified as more (i.e., their diet was largely based on prey capture) or less (e.g., heavy reliance on fruits) predatory. Predatory species had more and larger neurons in this visual pathway than did their less predatory cousins, but there were no cross-species differences in the volume of adjacent visual pathways not related to prey capture. Across species, a strong relation was found ($r = .92$) between the percentage of diet based on prey and the number of pathway neurons.

The search for prey, shelter, and other resources requires systems for navigating in three-dimensional space (Gallistel, 1990; Shepard, 1994). Studies of a variety of mammalian species reveal that organisms have egocentric and allocentric views of this space (P. Byrne, Becker, & Burgess, 2007; Maguire et al., 1998). The *egocentric* representation is what the organism sees, including objects and locations with respect to itself, and is dependent on areas of the parietal cortex (P. Byrne et al., 2007). The *allocentric* system codes for large-scale geometric relations and positioning of objects in space independent of the organism and is dependent on the hippocampus and adjacent areas of the temporal cortex (O'Keefe & Nadel, 1978). Both systems work conjointly to enable the organism to remain oriented and goal focused while moving in space. The allocentric representation may result in an implicit three-dimensional analog map that codes the geometric relations among features of the environment and enables navigation by means of dead reckoning, movement from one place to another on the basis of geometric coordinates (Gallistel, 1990).

Human navigation involves both the egocentric and allocentric systems, but for different aspects of navigation (P. Byrne et al., 2007). Of particular importance for discussion in chapter 13 of this volume (in the section titled Folk Physics) is the use of landmarks as opposed to allocentric representations during navigation (see also Jacobs & Schenk, 2003). In a series of neuroimaging studies, Maguire, Frackowiak, and Frith (1996, 1997) contrasted the brain regions involved in navigating a complex route through London—taxi drivers imagined and described these routes while being imaged—with the brain regions involved when drivers imagined highly salient landmarks. The route and landmark tasks engaged many of the same areas of the parietal cortex, but the route task also engaged the hippocampus, the allocentric system, whereas the landmark task did not.

A few species can also generate explicit, conscious–psychological representations of egocentric and allocentric physical space in working memory. Kuhlmeier and Boysen (2002) demonstrated that many chimpanzees (*Pan troglodytes*) can form a correspondence between the location of a miniature object in a scale model of an enclosure and the location of the actual object in the enclosure, suggesting that some chimpanzees are able to generate an explicit mental representation of the location of objects that are not currently being viewed. Other experimental manipulations suggested that these chimpanzees form a mental representation of the location of objects on the basis of both landmark information (e.g., the object is next to another object) and geometric coordinates (e.g., the object is northeast of another object). However, as I discuss in chapter 13 of this volume (in the section titled Folk Physics), humans are exceptional in both regards; human competence appears to greatly exceed that of other primates.

Tool use is found in one form or another in all human cultures and enables people to more fully exploit biological resources in the local ecology (Murdock, 1981). The neural, perceptual, and cognitive systems that support tool use have not been studied as systematically as have the systems that support movement and representation in space. On the basis of brain imaging and cognitive deficits following brain injury, Johnson-Frey (2003) concluded that homologous brain regions are involved in basic object grasping and manipulation in humans and other primates. At the same time, it is clear that humans have a much better conceptual understanding of how objects can be used as tools (Povinelli, 2000), and their definition of how these objects can be used is influenced by the inferred intentions of potential tool users (Bloom, 1996). At the core, human tool use involves the ability to mentally represent an object as a potential tool, to manipulate this mental representation to explore the different ways in which the object might be used, and finally to integrate such representations with active tool use (Lockman, 2000).

Foley and others have detailed the relation between advances in the sophistication of tools used for food extraction (e.g., digging sticks) and hunting with the appearance of species since *Australopithecus afarensis* (Foley, 1987; Foley & Lahr, 1997). There is evidence that *Homo habilis* used simple stone tools and that increases in the complexity of stone tools and their geographic distribution coincided with the emergence and migration patterns of *H. erectus*. Further increases in the complexity of stone tools and again their geographic distribution coincided with the emergence and migration patterns of early modern humans. The most complex stone tools are found in archeological sites dating back less than 50,000 years ago and are found with the fossils of modern humans and *H. neanderthalensis* (Foley & Lahr, 1997). The pattern of tool "evolution" and the likely function of these tools, including hunting and other forms of food extraction (e.g., digging up edible roots), appear to be consistent with an increase in reliance on hunting during recent human evolutionary history. I remind the reader that the recent emergence of hunting contrasts sharply with the sex difference in physical size—a strong indicator of physical male–male competition—that extends back at least 4 million years (see the section titled Sexual Division of Labor, chap. 5, this volume).

Folk Heuristics

I mention explicit mental representations in both the conscious–psychological and working memory systems at the center of Figure 9.1 as well as implicit knowledge represented in folk modules; I extensively discussed both types of knowledge and their relation in Geary (2005b). Implicit knowledge is inferred by regularities in the behavior of organisms, but the principles governing these regularities cannot always be explicitly articulated (Gigerenzer, Todd, & ABC Research Group, 1999; Karmiloff-Smith, 1992; Rozin, 1976; Simon, 1956). To illustrate the point, I turn again to Barton and Dean's (1993) analysis of the visuomotor pathway in mammals as related to prey capture. Cells in this system are likely to be sensitive to the movement patterns of prey species and enable the coordination of the behaviors necessary to capture this prey; the functioning of this module reflects an implicit understanding of how to catch prey. The organization of prey-catching behavior indicates a form of knowledge that is represented in the structure and functioning of the underlying neural systems.

Mate-choice decisions provide another illustration. With the possible exception of despots, it is not possible for any individual to attract and evaluate all potential mates and only then make the optimal choice or choices. Once a potential mate is rejected, the option of choosing that mate at a later time has typically evaporated. In addition, the costs of searching for and evaluating all potential mates make the evolution of motivational, cognitive, and behavioral systems that result in optimal choices unlikely. The trade-offs inherent in evolved traits result in the evolution of systems that achieve good enough outcomes (Simon, 1956).

Barnacle geese (*Branta leucopsis*) demonstrate how the process works. Pairs of geese bond for many breeding seasons and choose mates on the basis of similarities in age and size (J. M. Black, Choudhury, & Owen, 1996). Smaller females are reproductively better off when paired with smaller than with larger males, and larger females are reproductively better off when paired with larger than with smaller males. Some mates are thus better than others, which in turn creates conditions that will favor the evolution of brain, cognitive, and behavioral mechanisms that will guide mate-choice decisions. These mechanisms must enable the birds to assess the relative age and size of potential mates, and there must be a mechanism to stop searching once a good enough mate is found. J. M. Black et al. found individuals that sampled many potential mates and switched mates if a marginally better one was found had a 50% reduction in the probability of successfully breeding during that season. The cost of mate switching and the cognitive demands of comparing several potential mates on one or more dimensions (e.g., size) place serious limits on the potential for optimizing mechanisms to evolve.

A good enough choice can be made with limited sampling and perceptual-cognitive mechanisms (or stimulus-unconditioned responses; Timberlake, 1994) that cue into specific features of other geese, such as size, coloration, and movement patterns (e.g., Blythe, Todd, & Miller, 1999). Geese of similar age, health, and size should more readily synchronize the mating dance than other pairs. Synchronization may thus serve as a simple mechanism for assessing other geese and a mechanism for stopping the mate search. Thus, what appears to be a complex mate-choice decision may be achieved by implicit neural and perceptual folk mechanisms that are sensitive to a few cues (e.g., size), and a mechanism that stops the mate search when a compatible (e.g., as determined by synchronized movements) partner is found.

Much of human behavior is influenced by these implicit, *intuitive* mechanisms. Children, for example, form and maintain friendships based on reciprocity, without having read Trivers's (1971) seminal article on the evolution of reciprocal altruism. Despite not having read this article, the social behavior of children indicates they understand implicitly the reciprocal core of long-term social relationships; children who do not reciprocate are socially rejected (Youniss, 1986). Reciprocity results from the organization of folk psychological modules, the pattern of affective reactions to social relationships, and more or less automatically results in an implicit understanding of the costs and benefits of friendships and in mechanisms for their formation, maintenance, and in many cases dissolution. The explicit understanding of these same principles, in contrast, was only achieved through considerable scientific effort.

The explicit representation of social and other forms of information in working memory and the formation of a conscious–psychological and self-centered mental simulation of the world are only necessary when the folk systems do not result in the desired outcome or when there is a mismatch between knowledge implicit in these systems and experience (Geary, 2005b). During social interactions, the knowledge represented in the person schema is implicit, that is, there is no conscious representation of this information (e.g., where the person is on the sociability trait), but it nonetheless influences the dynamics of the interaction (Fiske & S. E. Taylor, 1991). However, when the behavior of this other person is inconsistent with the schema, then attention is drawn to the inconsistency and the behavior is explicitly and consciously represented in working memory. The explicit representation allows inferences about the likely source of the inconsistency and facilitates incorporation of the behavior into the person schema.

The person schema is also related to the use of mental simulations—called the *simulation heuristic* by Kahneman and Tversky (1982)—to make judgments about how the person might react in various situations. For instance, the individual's traits, such as warm to emotionally distant, influence how easy it is generate one type of behavioral sequence or another. It is easier to imagine—mentally simulate the dynamics—a socially warm friend making a good impression when first meeting one's family than it is to imagine the same outcome with an emotionally distant friend. The person schema allows for seamless interactions in most situations. When the dynamics or outcomes are not certain, the combination of the person schema and the conscious–psychological system allows one to simulate how other people will respond in potential future situations and thus enables better predictions of other people's behavior and the rehearsal of related social strategies.

DEVELOPMENT OF FUNCTIONAL SYSTEMS

I turn again to several of the life history topics discussed in chapter 4, specifically, the evolved functions of experiences during development, phenotypic plasticity, and play. Consideration of the developmental period is critical for understanding humans and human sex differences. The length of this period appears to have nearly doubled since *H. erectus* (Dean et al., 2001) and has almost certainly coevolved with the plasticity of folk modules and with the corresponding ability to transmit cultural information (e.g., Darwin's natural selection, Mozart's 25th symphony) across generations. The plasticity of folk modules, the ability to explicitly problem solve to cope with social dynamics and to modify the ecology in self-serving ways (e.g., build shelters), and a corresponding ability to create cultural scenarios that support large-scale societies enable humans to adapt to an unusually wide range of ecological and social niches. At the same time, and as every parent knows, there are limits on adults' ability to influence developing children. This is because children have built-in biases to seek certain types of experiences and to build their own social and cultural niches.

Children's Niche Seeking

All of us desire to exert some level of control over the social and other environments within which we live and develop (Heckhausen & Schulz, 1995), but the specifics of these environments vary considerably from one culture and context to the next. Social and ecological variability in turn results in pressures for the evolution of cognitive systems that can adapt to changing circumstances (Siegler, 1996; Tooby & Cosmides, 1990). The ontogenetic adaptation of an evolved cognitive system to local conditions appears to reflect the operation of what Mayr (1974) called an *open genetic program*. A *closed genetic program* results in a perceptual, cognitive, or behavioral trait that cannot be affected by experience. With an open program "new information acquired through experience is inserted into the translated program in the nervous system" (Mayr, 1974, p. 651), although an "open program is by no means tabula rasa; certain types of information are more easily inserted than others" (p. 652).

> The longer the life span of an individual, the greater will be the selection premium on replacing or supplementing closed genetic programs by open ones. . . . A subsidiary factor favoring the development of an open program is prolonged parental care. When the young of a species grow up under the guidance of their parents, they have a long period of opportunity to learn from them—to fill their open programs with useful information on enemies, food, shelter, and other important components of their immediate environment. (Mayr, 1974, p. 657)

Mayr's (1974) description of an open program is consistent with research in the developmental sciences. It is now known that many of the early competencies of infants and young children reflect innate but skeletal knowledge (R. Gelman, 1990; S. A. Gelman, 2003; Karmiloff-Smith, 1992; Spelke et al., 1992). *Skeletal* means that the underlying brain and perceptual systems provide the initial structure of evolved cognitive competencies, which are then fleshed out during the developmental period (R. Gelman, 1990; Keil, 1992; Spelke et al., 1992). For these epigenetic processes to operate, early attentional, perceptual, and cognitive biases must be coupled with a motivational bias for children to engage the ecology and social world in ways similar to those in which the biases originally evolved (Bjorklund & Pellegrini, 2002; Scarr, 1992). Behavioral engagement is predicted to generate evolutionarily expectant experiences that provide the feedback needed to adjust the architecture of folk systems to nuances in evolutionarily significant domains (Greenough, Black, & Wallace, 1987), such as allowing the individual to discriminate one face from another (e.g., Pascalis, de Haan, & Nelson, 2002). These behavioral biases are expressed as common childhood activities, such as social play and exploration of the ecology, as I described in chapter 4 of this volume (in the section titled Evolution of Play) and elaborate for boys and girls in chapter 10 (in the section titled Play).

The interaction between infants' language perception and their early exposure to language illustrates how early experiences can shape the architecture of an evolved module. Infants born into all cultures respond to the same basic phonemes, including those that are not in their parents' native language, and can discriminate these language sounds from other categories of sound, such as musical notes (Kuhl, 1994; Molfese, Freeman, & Palermo,

1975). The neural, perceptual, and cognitive systems that allow infants to respond to the phonemes of all languages are part of the skeletal structure of the language domain. In this case, language exposure during the 1st year of life results in a trimming of the range of phonetic sounds to which the system responds (Kuhl et al., 1997). The net result is that the functional features of the system, that is, the language sounds that can be comprehended and produced, correspond to the local language.

Parents and Culture

It is an all too common and rather naïve assumption that parents, social injunctions, and other cultural information drive children's experiences and thereby shape their cognitions, motivations, and even their brain architecture (Hyde, 2007; W. Wood & Eagly, 2002). As I described in chapter 6 of this volume (in the section titled Benefits to Children), parents can have a profound influence on the well-being of children, but the relation between parenting and the social, psychological, and cognitive development of children is considerably weaker than many people assume (J. R. Harris, 1995; Lytton & Romney, 1991; Rowe, 1994; Scarr, 1992). Nevertheless, cross-cultural comparisons do suggest that parents and other socializing influences can affect the social and psychological development of children, although the magnitude of these effects appears to be small to moderate (B. S. Low, 1989). In fact, children are predicted to have some degree—within limits because of the conflicting interests between parents and offspring (Trivers, 1974)—of receptivity to parental and socializing influences; this follows for a species with an unusually long developmental period and the cross-generational transmission of cultural knowledge.

When viewed from a cross-cultural perspective, parenting practices appear to provide an adaptive link between the demands of the adult world and children's developing competencies. My assumption is there are universal demands, such as finding a mate, obtaining resources, and developing a social network, that can be addressed in a variety of ways. Cultural factors, such as the economic and social systems of the society, determine the most adaptive way in which these demands can be approached, and parental practices might be one means of fine-tuning the competencies their children will need to meet these demands (K. MacDonald, 1988, 1992).

These child-rearing practices appear to be a reflection of parental knowledge of the demands of adult life as well as more subtle, implicit influences. In Western culture, for instance, parents in secure bureaucratic jobs tend to have relatively permissive child-rearing practices and lay "greater stress on the development of interpersonal skills; by contrast . . . (parents) working in entrepreneurial settings were found to be more concerned with individual achievement and striving" (Bronfenbrenner, 1986, p. 728). More subtle influences might include the degree of job-related stress, which appears to influence parental responsiveness to children and the parent–child attachment (Belsky, Steinberg, & Draper, 1991).

Parent–child warmth, a component of this attachment, may vary in ways that prepare children for adult life (B. S. Low, 1989; K. MacDonald, 1988; B.. B. Whiting & J. W. M. Whiting, 1975). K. MacDonald proposed that the degree of parental warmth modifies the neurobiological systems that underlie affective reaction to social dynamics, much like early language exposure modifies aspects of the language system. These modifications result in children becoming more or less sensitive to other people, influencing the extent to which their behavior is relatively self-serving or cooperative. Harsh treatment, such as physical beatings, may "shut down" the systems that generate the feelings that facilitate empathy and social cooperation, resulting in a relatively self-serving social style. As with many traits, the cost–benefit trade-offs associated with a relatively cooperative or self-serving approach to social relationships depend on context and cannot be known ahead of time (K. MacDonald, 1988). In short, K. MacDonald hypothesized that parental warmth moderates the sensitivity of the affective systems associated with at least some of the social modules shown in Figure 9.2; there are almost certainly genetic influences on the sensitivity of these modules as well.

CONCLUSION

My thesis in this chapter and elsewhere (Geary, 2005b) is that humans and all other organisms have evolved traits that allow them to attempt to achieve some level of control over the social, biological, and physical resources that support survival and allow them to reproduce. The motivation to control is a heuristic rule of thumb that I use to attempt to better understand how human behavior and other traits are organized and how they may have evolved. If gaining some level of control over the dynamics of social discourse, for instance, provided survival and reproductive benefits during human evolution, then selection would favor the emergence of social–cognitive competencies that process associated information, such as facial expressions. The processing of this information is necessary but not sufficient to ensure adaptive responses to local conditions, however. To be functional, the systems must also include affective and behavioral components. Affective components provide feedback to others (emotions) and to the self (feelings) about relative success at gaining some level of control (Damasio, 2003), and behavioral components are needed to actually achieve corresponding goals.

As an illustration, consider that one-on-one social discourse is typically imbued with affective tone that in turn moderates the dynamics of the social engagement. Such discourse is not possible without the dynamic processing of social information (e.g., facial expressions, body language), the development of a mental model of the feeling state, intentions, and likely future behavior of the individual, as well as attempts to elicit information from other people or to change their behavior (Baron-Cohen, 1995; Ekman, 1992). The attempt to change behavior is often achieved through language, which is a behavioral as well as a cognitive competency; language is considered a behavioral competency to the extent it can affect the social environment (Pinker & Bloom, 1990). The individual-level modules shown in Figure 9.2 thus constitute a functional system that regulates one-on-one social discourse and enables the pursuit of social strategies.

The specific architecture of the cognitive components of such functional systems is not completely clear, although it is likely that many of these modules are the product of open genetic programs, to use Mayr's (1974) term. An open program allows the neurobiological systems that support the cognitive modules to be influenced by contextual factors, particularly during childhood (Karmiloff-Smith, 1992). If language perception is representative of the architecture of cognitive modules in general, then an open program determines the types of experiences to which the system responds and how early experience modifies the system such that it is adapted to local conditions (Geary, 2005b). It is unlikely that all modules are constrained to the same extent as is apparently the case with phoneme perception. Such constraints would require the skeletal structure of the flora and fauna modules shown in Figure 9.2, for instance, to include the representation of all plants and animals found throughout the world, which is not the case.

It is more likely that many modules consist of skeletal features that guide the processing of domain-relevant information and bias the ways in which this information is categorized and represented but are otherwise relatively open systems (R. Gelman, 1990). For instance, early in development, such skeletal structures would result in infants implicitly categorizing objects as alive and not alive and gradually developing complex representations of the essence of those objects that are categorized as alive (S. A. Gelman, 2003). When these skeletal constraints are combined with a general motivation for children to seek information about the biological world, the result is predicted to be regularities in folk taxonomies across cultures, but at the same time, cross-cultural variation that is well suited to local conditions; in the case of the restricted experiences of urban Western children, this results in an underdeveloped folk biology (Medin & Atran, 2004).

A core function of development is to provide the experiences needed to adapt open folk modules and corresponding affective and behavioral components to local conditions. Children's play and exploratory behavior are predicted to be self-directed and focused on providing the experiences needed to elaborate and adapt the social, biological, and physical modules to local conditions. The play and exploratory biases in the behavior of boys and girls are predicted to provide the experiences necessary for the emergence of those cognitive and other sex differences associated with the different reproductive strategies of men and women that I described in chapters 6, 7, and 8. In chapters 10 and 11, I place human developmental sex differences in this evolutionary context and turn to sex differences in brain and cognition as organized around the folk systems shown in Figure 9.2 and in chapters 12 and 13.

10

SEX DIFFERENCES IN INFANCY
AND AT PLAY

In this chapter, I integrate what is known about human sex differences in physical development, during infancy, and at play with the life history perspective reviewed in chapter 4 and with sex differences in parenting, mate choice, and mate competition. I complete the integration in chapter 11 with a focus on the social development of boys and girls and the influence of parents and culture on the expression of sex differences. Figure 10.1 provides an organizing frame. The figure expands the developmental activity component of Figure 4.1 (see chap. 4) and embeds research on human sex differences into the broader theories of life history and sexual selection. I begin with physical development because the well-known relation between sexual selection and physical development for other species can be easily tied to our own species. From there, I move to infancy. As Darwin (1871) observed, sex differences are often expressed with the approach of reproductive maturation, with smaller or no differences early in development. This is generally true for humans, but there are some intriguing sex differences in infancy. I close this chapter with children's play, which is of particular interest because it is an area in which I can evaluate the prediction that children's self-directed activities result from our evolutionary history, regardless of whether this is a direct preparation for the adulthood of our ancestors or maintenance of evolved behavioral biases.

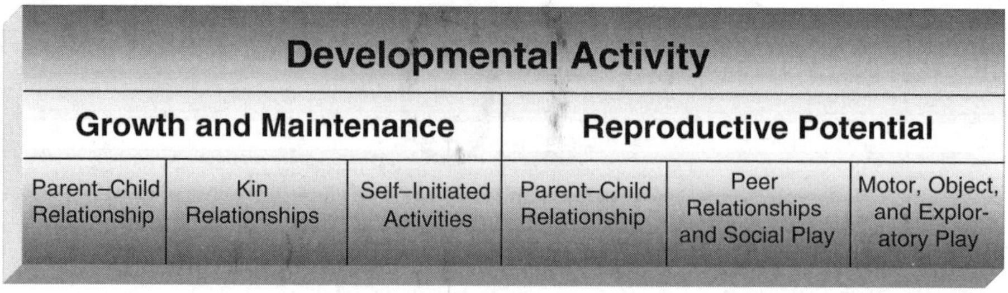

Developmental Activity					
Growth and Maintenance			Reproductive Potential		
Parent–Child Relationship	Kin Relationships	Self–Initiated Activities	Parent–Child Relationship	Peer Relationships and Social Play	Motor, Object, and Exploratory Play

Figure 10.1. Components of developmental activity within the context of life history. Parent–offspring relationships emerge from parents' reproductive efforts and the efforts of offspring to obtain parental resources; kin relationships represent investment from the wider kin group in the child; self-initiated activities refer to the child's foraging and related behaviors that contribute to physical growth and maintenance; the parent–child relationship can also contribute to the child's reproductive potential (e.g., through educational and cultural success); peer relationships and the various forms of play provide experiences that flesh out evolved biases and adapt them to local circumstances.

PHYSICAL DEVELOPMENT

For this chapter and chapter 11, I assume the key functions of developmental experiences are to tailor evolved cognitive competencies (see Figure 9.2, chap. 9, this volume) to local conditions (R. Gelman, 1990; Mayr, 1974), and to refine the associated physical, behavioral, and social skills needed to function in adulthood. By *adulthood*, I mean that of our ancestors; I provide discussion of the relation between development and preparation for adulthood in modern societies elsewhere (Geary, 1995a; 2007, 2008). In the first section, I address the issue of evolutionary change in the length of the human developmental period, and in the second, I provide a review of sex differences in physical development and physical competencies.

Evolution of Childhood and Adolescence

Several methods can be used to estimate the developmental trajectory of our ancestors, including the tight link between the timing of molar eruption and timing of other life history milestones (Bogin, 1999; Dean et al., 2001; McHenry, 1994a). Across primate species, the age of first molar eruption is strongly correlated with age of weaning, age of sexual maturation, and adult brain size (Bogin, 1999; Kelley, 2004); the brain approaches adult size about the time the first molar erupts. On the basis of such relations, McHenry and Bogin estimated the age of maturation for A. *afarensis* and A. *africanus* to have been similar to that found in the modern chimpanzee (Pan *troglodytes*), 10 to 12 years. There is disagreement about the specific age of maturation for species of Homo, but the general evolutionary pattern can be estimated with some certainty. As shown in Figure 10.2, Bogin estimated gradual increases in the length of the developmental period from *H. habilis* to *H. erectus* to modern humans. Of particular interest are differences in the evolved pattern of human development compared with that of our ancestors, specifically, the unique and qualitatively different periods of childhood and adolescence (Bogin, 1999).

Chimpanzees and our early ancestors—to the best of our knowledge—had three relatively distinct developmental periods, as do other mammals. *Infancy* is the time of suckling, and *juvenility* is the time between weaning and *reproductive maturation;* reproductive maturation is the final development period, when reproductive competition, choice, and parental investment begin in earnest. For most primates, the juvenile period is initiated with the eruption of the first molar and independent feeding. Unlike most other primates, chimpanzees have a 12- to 18-month delay between the age of first molar eruption and weaning. During this time they learn, through observation and imitation, how to "fish" for termites, crack open nuts, and perform other survival-related skills (Goodall, 1986). Bogin (1999) proposed that human childhood emerges between infancy and juvenility and extends from 2 to 3 years of age (weaning

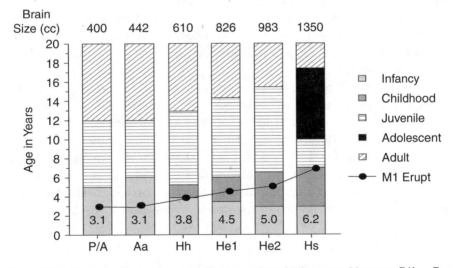

Figure 10.2. The evolution of hominid life history from birth to age 20 years. P/A = *Pan troglodytes* (i.e., chimpanzee) and *A. afarensis;* Aa = *A. africanus;* Hh = *H. habilis,* He1 = early *H. erectus;* He2 = late *H. erectus;* Hs = *H. sapiens.* Mean brain sizes are given at the top of each histogram. Mean age at eruption of the first permanent molar (M1) is graphed across the histograms and given below the graph. From *Patterns of Human Growth* (2nd ed., p. 185), by B. Bogin, 1999, Cambridge, England: Cambridge University Press. Copyright 1999 by Cambridge University Press. Reprinted with permission of Cambridge University Press and Barry Bogin.

in traditional societies) to the age of eruption of the first molar at 6 to 7 years. Weaning is typically followed by a new pregnancy in traditional societies, leaving the 3-year-old dependent on a wider range of adults for food preparation, feeding, and care. As I described in chapter 6 of this volume (in the section titled Physical Well-Being), this community of adults often includes grand kin (e.g., maternal mother) and the father.

As noted, age of first molar eruption is also tightly related to adult brain size and brain development (Kelley, 2004). The human brain in particular is very large and is expensive to build and maintain. In most primates, the brain consumes 8% to 9% of resting metabolic calories, but this jumps to 20% to 25% in humans (W. R. Leonard & Robertson, 1994). The share of calories devoted to the developing brain is still larger. A 5-year-old, for instance, devotes 44% of basal metabolic calories to brain development and functioning (Bogin, 1999). Although it does not get much larger in terms of volume, the human brain continues to develop by generating axonal connections between regions that are used together through adolescence and into early adulthood (Giedd et al., 1999).

The juvenile period is the same as that found in other primates and lasts from age 7 to the onset of the hormonal changes that begin reproductive maturation. Boys and girls show marked skeletal growth following the onset of puberty, along with increases in muscle mass and fat tissue. The growth spurt in other primates is different in that it is largely due to increased muscle mass (Bogin, 1999; Leigh, 1996). These differences in physical development and the social behavior of teenagers mark the evolutionarily novel human adolescence.

My points are that the human developmental period coevolved with the increase in brain size described in chapter 5 (in the section titled Sexual Selection and Human Evolution) and with a corresponding increase in the complexity of social relationships, including intrasexual competition (Joffe, 1997; Sawaguchi, 1997). The 15- to 20-year period between weaning and reproduction in traditional societies, compared with 5 to 7 years in chimpanzees and our early ancestors, is intriguing and indicates that activities during this developmental period are of critical evolutionary significance.

Sex Differences

For extensive reviews of sex differences in physical development, I refer the reader to the first-rate contributions of Tanner (1990) and Bogin (1999). My goals in this section are to examine the general pattern of sex differences in physical development as potentially related to sex differences in parenting and sexual selection, and to discuss boys' heightened vulnerability to illness and developmental difficulties.

Development Pattern

As mentioned previously, the development of secondary sexual charac-teristics can be costly, especially for males (see the section titled Sex Hormones, Parasites, and Male Quality, chap. 4). The costs include potential suppression of immune functions, increased risk of predation (e.g., for brightly colored males), and increased aggression from conspecifics, among others. These costs create pressures favoring the delayed emergence of reproductive maturation and any corresponding physical sex differences until the individual has gained the physical (e.g., weight), social, behavioral, or cognitive competencies needed for successful intrasexual competition or intersexual choice. Darwin described this pattern nearly than 140 years ago:

> There is . . . a striking parallelism between mammals and birds in all their secondary sexual characteristics, namely in their weapons for fighting with rival males, in their ornamental appendages, and in their colours. In both classes, when the male differs from the female, the young of both sexes almost always resemble each other, and in a large majority of cases resemble the adult female. In both classes the male assumes the charac-ters proper to his sex shortly before the age for reproduction. (Darwin, 1871, Vol. 2, p. 297)

Consider again the northern elephant seal (*Mirounga angustirostris*) and the satin bowerbird (*Ptilonorhynchus violaceus*). Male elephant seals mature at around 8 years of age, compared with 3 years for females (Clinton & Le Boeuf, 1993). Among other benefits, the males' relatively long matu-rational period allows them to gain the body mass and reproductive poten-tial (see Figure 10.1) needed to compete for a harem. Male satin bowerbirds do not achieve full adult blue plumage until they are 7 and do not typically reproduce until 10 years, compared with 2 years for females (Collis & Borgia, 1992, 1993). Prior to this point, young males maintain a green plumage and do not differ significantly in appearance from young and adult females. During their juvenile period, "young males spend a great deal of time observing older males at their bower, and practice bower building and display behaviors when the owner is absent from the bower site" (Collis & Borgia, 1992, p. 422). Young males also engage in fighting with their same-age peers, which provides experience needed for serious dominance-related encounters in adulthood. In short, delayed maturation allows males to grow larger and gain the social and behavioral competencies needed to compete for and attract mates.

Humans are no different. Many sex differences in physical development do not emerge until puberty and adolescence, and many of those that are found during childhood and juvenility are comparatively small (Bogin, 1999; Tanner, 1990). Overall, girls grow up faster than boys: that is, they reach 50% of their adult height at an earlier age . . . , enter puberty earlier and cease earlier to grow. . . . At birth the difference corresponds to 4 to 6 weeks of maturation and at the beginning of puberty to 2 years. (Tanner, 1990, p. 56)

The slower maturation of boys (see Garai & Scheinfeld, 1968; Hutt, 1972) appears to heighten their risk of early mortality but contributes to their adult height; later puberty results in longer legs in men than in women, relative to overall height. The most prominent sex differences to emerge during puberty are a widening of the hips and pelvis in girls, which is not complete until about age 17 (Bogin 1999), and a widening of the width of the shoulders in boys. Boys also

develop larger hearts as well as larger skeletal muscles, larger lungs, higher systolic blood pressure, lower resting heart-rate, a greater capacity for carrying oxygen in the blood, and a greater power of neutralizing the chemical products of muscular exercise. . . . In short, the male becomes more adapted at puberty for the tasks of hunting, fighting and manipulating all sorts of heavy objects. (Tanner, 1990, p. 74)

The changes in lean muscle mass are dramatic. At 9 years, boys have about 8% more muscle than girls (J. Kim et al., 2006). During the next 6 years, girls' lean muscle mass increases about 50%, but muscle mass more than doubles for boys. At this age (15 years), boys have, on average, about 70% more muscle tissue than girls, and nearly all boys have more muscle mass than the average girl. These differences increase over the next several years because muscle growth is complete in girls and continues for at least 3 more years in boys (Tanner, 1990); by young adulthood, only 1 out of 50 women have more muscle than the average man. At age 9, girls have about 25% more fat than boys, but this increases to 60% by age 15 (J. Kim et al., 2006). The facial features that women find attractive in men (see the section titled Physical Attractiveness and Good Genes, chap. 7, this volume) also emerge during this time, but there are less marked changes in girls' faces; "in some girls scarcely any detectable spurt in face dimensions occurs at all" (Tanner, 1990, p. 68). The minor changes result in the retention of the youthful appearance that men find attractive in women's faces.

As with other species, these physical changes are the result of the increase in sex hormones that occurs during puberty (Tanner, 1990). The hormonal changes also influence the expression of a wide range of social, behavioral, and sexual differences (Hayward, 2003). As examples, the hormonal changes influence the emergence of sexual fantasy described in chapter 7 of this volume (in the section titled Sexual Attitudes and Fantasy), but a direct link to testosterone per se is sometimes found (Udry, Billy, Morris, Groff, & Raj, 1985) and sometimes not (B. C. Campbell, Prossinger, & Mbzivo, 2005). For boys, there is a marked increase in sexual behavior, especially masturbation, although most males do not reproduce until their 20s or later (Bogin, 1999); delayed reproduction is expected (see the section titled Puberty and Aggression, chap. 8, this volume).

Physical Competencies

There are a few sex differences in physical competencies prior to puberty, but these are not as marked as those that emerge during adolescence. During childhood there are small to moderate differences favoring boys in tasks such as grip strength, jumping distance, and running speeds, with large differences emerging during adolescence (Thomas & French, 1985); by 17 years of age, more than 9 out of 10 boys outperform the average girl in these areas. From near parity during childhood and juvenility, substantial sex differences emerge in lower and especially upper body strength during adolescence and early adulthood (Pheasant, 1983). From 10 to 16 years of age, boys' raw upper body strength increases nearly fourfold and their lower body strength nearly threefold (Carron & Bailey, 1974), compared with much more modest changes in girls (Round, Jones, Honour, & Nevill, 1999). Activity levels differ as well: Boys are more physically active in infancy than girls; about three out of five boys are more active than the average girl and become more so over time. By adolescence, about 7 out of 10 boys are more active than the average girl (Eaton & Enns, 1986).

As a result of the sex difference in leg length, muscle mass, and cardiovascular capacity, men can run faster, on average, than women (Deaner, 2006). By far, the largest differences in physical competencies are for throwing distance and throwing velocity (Thomas & French, 1985). Between the ages of 4 and 7 years, 9 out of 10 boys have higher throwing velocities than the average same-age girl. By 12 years of age, the most skilled girls have throwing velocities that are comparable to those of the least skilled boys. The sex difference is even larger for throwing distance: By 2 to 4 years of age, more than 9 out of 10 boys can throw farther than the average girl, and by 17 years only the most skilled girls can throw as far as the least skilled boys. By early adulthood, men also have moderate to large advantages in visual acuity, throwing accuracy, and in the ability to track and block objects thrown at them; about three out of four men outperform the average woman in these areas (Jardine & Martin, 1983; N. V. Watson & Kimura, 1991).

The sex differences in throwing skills are related to differences in the structure of the supporting skeletal system. Relative to overall body height, boys have a longer ulna and radius (i.e., forearm), on average, than do girls (Gindhart, 1973). For neonates, the radii of three out of four boys are longer than the radii of the average girl, and for 18-year-olds, the radii of more than 19 out of 20 men are longer than the radii of the average woman. There are also sex differences in the timing and pattern of skeletal ossification in the elbow and in the length and robustness of the humerus (i.e., upper arm; Benfer & McKern, 1966; Tanner, 1990), all of which contribute to men's throwing advantage.

These differences in skeletal structure and associated throwing competencies, combined with the large male advantage in arm and upper body strength, indicate strong selection pressures for these traits in men. These sex differences, in fact, provide support for the hypothesis that the evolution of male–male competition in humans was influenced by the use of projectile (e.g., spears) and blunt force (e.g., clubs) weapons (Keeley, 1996); see chapter 8 of this volume (in the section titled Competition in Traditional Societies). During puberty and adolescence, when these physical sex differences are emerging or becoming larger, a sex difference in sensitivity to pain and risk of pain-related disorders also emerges (Greenspan et al., 2007). Men have a higher threshold and greater tolerance for physical pain than do women, on average, especially when their tolerance is gauged against that of other members of their ingroup (A. H. Buss & Portnoy, 1967).

Nonetheless, some theorists have argued that the physical differences evolved from the division of labor, including men's hunting, rather than male–male competition (e.g., Kolakowski & Malina, 1974). I described in chapter 5 of this volume (in the section titled Sexual Division of Labor) and elaborate in chapter 13 (in the section titled Movement) why I do not believe the division of labor hypothesis is correct. In addition to the reasons outlined in these sections, sex differences in pubertal development are closely tied to sex differences in intrasexual competition and the corresponding sex differences in physical size. Across polygynous primates with intense male–male competition, there is a characteristic pattern of female and male growth. When it occurs, the female growth spurt begins at an earlier age, reaches the peak more quickly, and lasts for a shorter period than that of males (Leigh, 1996). The human sex differences fit this pattern (Leigh, 1996; Tanner, 1990).

Of course, some physical sex differences, such as the wider pelvic region in women, have evolved through natural rather than sexual selection. Once the large pelvis evolved, the waist-to-hip ratio that men find attractive emerged and began to be shaped by male choice (see the section titled Physical Attributes and Fertility, chap. 7). Girls are also more physically flexible than boys and have an advantage in fine eye–motor coordination. Unlike many of the advantages shown by boys, the advantages of girls in these areas do not change substantively during adolescence, suggesting they are not related to sexual selection; about three out of five girls outperform the average boy in these areas (Thomas & French, 1985). Kimura (1987) argued that the advantage of girls and women might be related to manipulating objects "within personal space, or within arm's reach, such as food and clothing preparation and child care" (p. 145). Coss and Goldthwaite (1995) argued that the greater flexibility of girls and women, among several other traits, are evolutionarily old adaptations related to an arboreal life that have never completely disappeared. As found in orangutans (*Pongo pygmaeus*), the smaller female australopithecines appear to have had adaptations (e.g., greater flexion in ankle joints) that facilitated movement in trees; this predator avoidance strategy is more difficult for large males.

Vulnerable and Variable

As noted previously, the expression of many sexually selected traits is condition dependent; their expression is an indicator of the genetic and physical health of the individual (see the section titled Good Genes, chap. 3). Only fit individuals are able to fully express these traits, especially under difficult circumstances. Sexual selection also results in the evolution of greater trait complexity, such as more coloration or larger size, for one sex or the other. Greater complexity suggests more genes underlying trait expression, the need for a longer developmental period, better conditions (e.g., higher quality food), or some combination for full expression (Pomiankowski & Møller, 1995). The bottom line is that more can go wrong for the sex that has undergone intense intrasexual competition or intersexual choice (see the section titled Mate-Choice Trade-Offs, chap. 3, this volume). As a result, individuals of this sex are more vulnerable to social and ecological disturbances and more variable as a group. The vulnerable and variable sex is typically males but, in theory, could also include sexually selected traits in females. My focus here is on boys' vulnerability to illness and variability in health and related outcomes.

Vulnerability. There are several potential evolutionary and biological reasons for the human sex difference in vulnerability (J. C. K. Wells, 2000), but I favor sexual selection. Related to the need to grow larger and stronger than girls is slower growth, beginning prenatally: Boys are born "premature" relative to girls. They have higher activity levels and higher basal metabolic rates than girls, resulting in higher caloric requirements for normal development. The increase in testosterone needed to fully develop sexually selected traits during adolescence places these males at risk of suppression of immune functions. Among other social and behavioral sex differences is higher risk taking and accidental injury in boys. The prediction is that boys will be more sensitive—suffer more physical, social, and cognitive deficits—than girls when growing up in poor conditions, including poor nutrition, inadequate health care, or poor social stimulation (Stinson, 1985). The vulnerability of boys, however, is not always obvious in well-nourished populations with good health care and attentive parents. As with other species, underlying vulnerability becomes most apparent in less than optimal conditions.

In 1956 and 1957, the health of 22,873 infants to 6-year-olds from lower socioeconomic (SES) families was assessed in New York City (Jacobziner,

Rich, Bleiberg, & Merchant, 1963). These thorough examinations revealed that 64% of the girls were in good health—showing no evidence of congenital, chronic, or acute (e.g., infection) disease— compared with 58% of the boys. About 8% of the boys had multiple disorders, compared with 1% of the girls. Brothwood, Wolke, Gamsu, and Cooper (1986) followed 141 and 130 very low-birth-weight boys and girls, respectively, for 2 years. During the 1st year, 41% of the boys died, as did 19% of the girls. Among surviving infants, boys were twice as likely as girls to have a variety of medical and development problems. Donaldson and Kohl (1965) controlled for prenatal environment by assessing the health of 840 sets of opposite-sex twins. During the 1st month of life, 45 boys died, compared with 17 girls. W. J. Martin (1949) documented the secular decline in infant mortality from 1900 to 1947 in Great Britain and found that at

> the beginning of the century the infant mortality of males was about 20% greater than the rate for females. The subsequent decline has been greater for girls than for boys, and now the male infant mortality is about 30% in excess of the female rate. (p. 439)

An analysis of 16,000 infant deaths in the United States between 1983 and 1987, inclusive, revealed that boys had a 38% higher mortality rate due largely to infectious disease during the 1st year of life (J. S. Read, Troendle, & Klebanoff, 1997).

Mortality rates decline as children grow older, but boys remain overrepresented for mild to serious medical and physical problems (Kitange et al., 1996; Van den Bosch, Huygen, Van den Hoogen, & Van Weel, 1992). For 5- to 9-year-olds, Van den Bosch et al. found boys had more acute ear (i.e., otitis media) and lower respiratory infections than girls and suffered many more accidental injuries; girls had more infections of the urinary tract. Kitange et al. tracked adult mortality for 3 years in a sample of more than 150,000 urban and rural Tanzanians. Maternal complications resulted in increased mortality rates among women of childbearing age (infant mortality ranged from 25% to 30%), but risks were otherwise higher for men. There is no need to continue: The same pattern is found across ethnicity, in modern and traditional societies, and in urban and rural settings.

Variability. Poor early physical development, exposure to parasites, frequent illness, poor nutrition, and inadequate social and cognitive stimulation have been shown to be related to poor long-term cognitive, academic, and social outcomes, even after controlling for SES and other confounds (S. P. Walker, Chang, Powell, & Grantham-McGregor, 2005). Sex differences are not typically reported in these studies, but boys' risk of poor early growth and development is likely to result in an overrepresentation of boys and men with poor long-term outcomes.

The best evidence comes from a randomized experimental trial of the effectiveness of a nutritional supplement for low-birth-weight neonates (Lucas, Morley, & Cole, 1998; Lucas et al., 1989). The supplement was designed to facilitate brain development during the critical 1st month after birth; however, not just any supplement would be effective (S. P. Walker et al., 2005). If boys are more sensitive to early environmental conditions—poor nutrition in this case—then they should gain more than girls from this intervention. The study included four groups: supplements contrasted with typical bottle formula and across mothers who breast fed and those who did not. In terms of reaching normal developmental milestones during infancy, both boys and girls benefited from the supplement, but boys showed larger gains. The longer term results were particularly striking.

Breast-fed infants of both sexes had normal IQ scores at age 8 years, but boys who received a standard formula and were not breast fed had verbal IQ scores that were 12 to 14 points lower than boys who were not breast fed but were given the supplement; about 4 out of 5 boys in the former group had IQ scores lower than did the average boy in the latter group. For the two groups that were not breast fed, the risk of cerebral palsy or other significant cognitive impairments was 5 to 6 times higher for boys who received standard formula compared with boys who received the supplement. The risk was not elevated for girls. In fact, the mean IQ of girls was in the average range and did not vary across conditions. There was also evidence that the enriched supplement not only eliminated the risks of poor early nutrition for boys but also may have enhanced outcomes. Although the results were not statistically significant and are in need of follow-up, boys who received the most supplement during infancy had higher IQ scores than boys who received less supplement and higher scores than girls. Stated somewhat differently, the impact of poor nutrition on intellectual development is substantially higher for boys than for girls, and there is a hint that boys may gain more from nutritional enrichment.

Martorell, Rivera, Kaplowitz, and Pollitt (1992) followed the physical, intellectual, and educational development of 249 rural Guatemalans from early childhood up to 26 years of age. Growth failure at age 3 years, due to an inadequate diet and high rates of infection, was related to stunted physical and educational development for both men and women in adulthood. However, as a group, men were more severely affected than women on a number of dimensions, including the proportion of lean muscle mass, years of education, and literacy scores. For instance, of those individuals showing early growth failure, nearly 1 out of 3 men but only 1 out of 10 women exhibited reading difficulties in adulthood. For individuals showing normal growth at age 3 years, more men than women passed the literacy test.

Implications. The developmental period is a time of risk for both sexes, but boys are especially vulnerable. As noted earlier, competition and choice can influence life history development (see the section titled Life History and Sexual Selection, chap. 4). As with other species, the benefits of larger size and other physical traits that provide men with an advantage when physically competing with other men and in terms of women's mate choices come at a cost of a protracted period of development and the immunity costs of exposure to testosterone, among others. When times are tough, only the fittest boys survive. Among those who survive to adulthood, only the healthiest men develop the physical skills needed for the oftentimes intense male–male competition in traditional societies and to express the traits women prefer in a mate.

The flip side of boys' greater vulnerability may be an enhanced potential to benefit more than girls from an enriched environment. This hypothesis has not been tested, although there were hints of such an effect in the Lucas et al. (1998) study. Either way, one important consequence of the sex difference in vulnerability is greater variation within groups of boys and men as compared with groups of girls and women on many traits. It remains to be determined, however, if boys and adolescent males are particularly sensitive in terms of vulnerability, potential, and variability when it comes to the development of traits specifically related to male–male competition and female choice. Are boys generally vulnerable across traits or is their vulnerability and potential heightened for sexually selected traits, as it is for other species (see the section titled Good Genes, chap. 3, this volume)? Are girls more vulnerable when it comes to the development of traits related to female–female competition and male choice? Is girls' advantage in many folk psychological domains (see chap. 13, this volume) related to female–female competition, and does this heightened sensitivity to social information put them at risk for social stress and corresponding increases in anxiety and depression? I think so.

INFANCY

To recap Darwin's (1871) observation: For most species, the sexes are more similar than different early in life, and this include humans. There are, however, several intriguing patterns in the infancy literature that suggest the skeletal structure of later sex differences is evident in the first year or 2 of life and possibly in the first few days of life. G. M. Alexander (2003) hypothesized that some of the early sex differences in orientation toward people (more in girls) or things (more in boys) reflect the evolved skeletal structure of the visual system, specifically, biases in the *what* and *where* visual pathways. Prenatal and early postnatal exposure to androgens may enhance development of the latter and result in attentional and perceptual biases for processing spatial location and object motion. The former is enhanced in the absence of these hormones and results in an attentional and perceptual bias for processing faces and color variation in the green to red spectrum. As I discuss subsequently, many of the early sex differences are consistent with this hypothesis. These early biases in turn result in experiences that selectively maintain or prune the corresponding neural pathways, leading to a developmental increase in the magnitude of the corresponding sex differences.

Attention to People

Studies of infants' brain activity while they view social information, such as faces, confirm that the skeletal structures of the folk psychological systems are in place very early in life and become fine-tuned (e.g., in discriminating one face from another) with development and social experience (Grossmann & Johnson, 2007). The use of a variety of behavioral measures also reveals this early social bias and that girls orient to other people more frequently than do boys (Connellan, Baron-Cohen, Wheelwright, Batki, & Ahluwalia, 2001; Freedman, 1974; Garai & Scheinfeld, 1968; Haviland & Malatesta, 1981; McClure, 2000; McGuinness & Pribram, 1979). Orientation toward other people is measured in terms of the duration of eye contact, empathy for others' distress, and time spent looking at faces, among other behaviors.

Individuals and Groups

In a review of sex differences in nonverbal behavior, Haviland and Malatesta (1981) noted that "there is no doubt that girls and women establish and maintain eye contact more than boys and men. The earliest age for which this is reported is one day" (p. 189). Connellan et al. (2001) assessed the amount of time 102 newborns—average age of 37 hours—spent looking at a face and at a mobile. Girls attended longer to the face, and boys attended longer to the mobile. The sex difference in time spent looking at the face was small but consistent with studies of older infants (McClure, 2000). Boys and men also gaze avert more frequently than do girls and women, a sex difference that has been found as early as 6 months of age. By this age, girls might also have a better memory for faces and might be more skilled in discriminating two similar faces (e.g., J. F. Fagan, 1972); these sex differences, however, are not found as consistently in infants as they are in older individuals (J. A. Hall, 1984; Haviland & Malatesta, 1981). In all, McClure's (2000) meta-analysis of sex differences in face processing—the social modality for which scientists have the most information—yielded conservative to liberal estimates of the magnitude of this difference in infants. On the assumption that the actual difference is between these extreme values, I estimate about two out of three infant girls are more attentive to human faces than the average infant boy.

The typical study in this area presents infants with a single face, voice, or movement pattern or with a pair of individuals. These types of stimuli reveal infants' interest in other people but may not capture an important aspect of male sociality. As I describe in the section titled Rough-and-Tumble later in this chapter, boys organize themselves into larger groups than do girls and engage in competitive play in the context of these groups. Boys' group-level play is consistent with preparation for the coalitional male–male competition described in chapter 8 (in the section titled Competition in Traditional Societies).

Benenson and her colleagues tested the corresponding hypothesis that the sex difference in social organization will manifest in the attentional interests of boy (i.e., a focus on groups) and girl (i.e., a focus on individuals) infants. In the first study, 6- to 8-month-olds were presented with a series of video clips of a single puppet or a group of three puppets (Benenson, Duggan, & Markovits, 2004). Both girls and boys looked longer at the group than at the individual, but the bias were larger in boys (83% and 63% of the boys and girls, respectively). The same procedure was used in the second study, but the infants watched film clips of groups of six 6-year-old boys and girls or individual 6-year-old boys and girls (Benenson, Markovits, Muller, Challen, & Carder, 2007). Again, both girls and boys looked longer at the groups of children, but the difference was larger in boys. The sex difference emerged because the boy infants watching the groups of boys looked significantly longer than did the girl infants, but there was no difference in the amount of time spent watching the groups of girls. About 3 out of 4 of these 6- to 8-month-old infant boys watched the boys' groups longer than did the average girl. These fascinating results are consistent with a skeletal structure to the group-level folk psychological models shown in Figure 9.2 (see chap. 9, this volume) and may be the seeds of the corresponding sex difference in coalition formation.

Empathy and Social Responsiveness

Infant girls may react with greater empathy than infant boys to the distress of other people (M. L. Hoffman, 1977). Simner (1971) found that infant girls cried longer than infant boys when exposed to the cry of another infant, but there was no sex difference in reflexive crying when the infants were exposed to artificial noise of the same intensity. Girls 12 to 20 months old respond to the distress of other people with greater empathic concern than boys. Zahn-Waxler, Radke-Yarrow, Wagner, and Chapman (1992) defined this as "emotional arousal that appears to reflect sympathetic concern for the victim . . . manifested in facial or vocal expressions (e.g., sad looks, sympathetic statements . . .) or gestures" (p. 129). Girls also tend to respond to distressed individuals with more prosocial behavior (e.g., comforting) and engage in more information-seeking behaviors (e.g., "what's wrong") than boys. Boys, in contrast, are more frequently unresponsive or emotionally indifferent to the victim's distress. These differences, however, are only found for distress that is witnessed and not caused by the child; girls do not show more empathy than boys when they cause the distress. At 20 months of age, about three out of five girls respond with greater empathic concern to the distress of another person than the average boy, whereas two out of three boys show more affective indifference than the average girl.

Studies of the quality of social interactions between parents and infants also reveal that girls are more responsive, and perhaps more sensitive, to social cues than boys (Freedman, 1974; Gunnar & Donahue, 1980; W. D. Rosen, Adamson, & Bakeman, 1992). W. D. Rosen et al. found that in ambiguous situations, 12-month-olds of both sexes would approach a potentially risky unfamiliar object if their mother signaled positive emotions (e.g., smiling) in reference to the object. When mothers signaled fear through their facial expressions, girls tended to withdraw, but boys still approached the object. Independent coders rated the intensity of the mothers' fear signal and judged that these signals were more intense when directed toward boys, suggesting the sex difference was not due to the behavior of their mothers. Rather, the tendency of boys to approach unfamiliar objects more frequently than do girls might be an early manifestation of the sex difference in risk taking (see the section titled Risk Taking, chap. 8, this volume), and mothers' more intense signaling may reflect prior experiences with unresponsive sons.

In a related study with 6- to 12-month-olds, Gunnar and Donahue (1980) found that mothers were just as likely to attempt to initiate social interactions with their sons as with their daughters, but daughters were much more responsive; Whiting and Edwards (1988) reported the same pattern with older children across cultures. For instance, 12-month-old girls responded to 52% of their mother's verbal requests to engage in some form of social interaction, compared with a 25% response rate in same-age boys. Boys and girls were equally responsive to their mother, in contrast, when she used a toy to attempt to initiate a social interaction. Girls also initiated about 30% more social interactions with their mother than did boys. Gunnar and Donahue's results suggest that the occasional finding that mothers sometimes interact more with their daughters than with their sons (e.g., Klein & Durfee, 1978) might stem from a sex difference favoring girls in social responsiveness and the degree to which social interactions are initiated by girls, rather than a maternal preference for girls per se (Freedman, 1974). These early dyadic differences, in turn, may set in motion patterns of relating between mothers and daughters and mothers and sons that exaggerate these differences during childhood and beyond.

Social Dynamics

Many of the average sex differences in infancy (and later) are dynamic, moderated by context and social relationship, and do not capture within-sex variation. K. A. Buss, Brooker, and Leuty (2008) found that 2-year-old girls sought contact with and stayed closer to their mother than did boys in a fear-eliciting situation, for example, the approach of a stranger. In this situation, girls maintained high levels of contact with their mother, whether or not they were observably distressed (e.g., crying). Boys who showed little observable distress did not seek out their mother, but highly distressed boys did. In fact, boys who were very distressed showed contact seeking and proximity that were almost as high as those found in the most distressed girls. Kiel and K. A. Buss (2006) found that mothers could predict the fear responses of their daughters more accurately than the responses of their sons but could predict both their sons and daughters responses in most other situations. Even young boys may attempt to "hide" their fears.

In an intensive naturalistic study of mother–infant interactions from birth to 3 months, Lavelli and Fogel (2002) found that girls spent more time in face-to-face communication with their mothers than did boys. The sex difference may have been due to boys' greater fussiness and irritability, which disrupted these interactions; newborn boys are more irritable and less consolable (Osofsky & O'Connell, 1977) than newborn girls, but these differences disappear by 3 months (Else-Quest, Hyde, Goldsmith, & Van Hulle, 2006). Lavelli and Fogel's findings are important because they suggest that some of the early sex differences in engagement with mothers may be due to factors other than an evolved bias to attend to people or to things.

Attention to Things

The sex difference in attentiveness to different forms of social information is complemented by a sex difference in orientation to some types of physical information, such as shapes and some aspects of mechanical motion (L. B. Cohen & Gelber, 1975; Freedman, 1974; McGuinness & Pribram, 1979). Sex differences are not always found for interest in these types of folk physical information (Spelke, 2005), but when they are found, they favor boys. In Connellan et al.'s (2001) study of newborns, the sex difference in looking time was larger for the mobile than for the face. Boys not only looked longer at the mobile than at the face, on average, but about 7 out of 10 boys looked longer at the mobile than did the average girl. Lutchmaya and Baron-Cohen (2002) presented 12-month-olds with videos of a moving car or a moving face. Nearly 4 out of 5 boys (79%) spent more time watching the car than the face, compared with less than half as many girls (37%). Only 18% of the boys spent more time watching the face than the car, compared with 56% of the girls.

On the basis of a review of early sex differences in perception, McGuinness and Pribram (1979) concluded that when "differences are found, males from 4–6 months onwards respond preferentially to blinking lights, geometric patterns, colored photographs of objects and three-dimensional objects" (p. 19). A similar conclusion was drawn by L. B. Cohen and Gelber (1975) on the basis of a review of research on infants' visual memory:

> Males and females are processing and storing different kinds of information about repeatedly presented [visual] stimuli. Males appear to be more likely to store information about the various components of a repeatedly presented stimulus, for example, its form and color. . . . [while] females, unlike males, are more likely to store information about the consequences of orienting. (p. 382)

It appears that by about 4 months of age, boys selectively attend to the physical properties of objects, such as shape, whereas girls selectively attend to the consequences of orienting to objects in their environment, rather than to the objects themselves (except when these objects are people); consequences refer, for instance, to how the objects might be related to the behavior of other people.

In all, there are probably more similarities than differences in infant girls' and boys' attention to and processing of folk physical information (Spelke, 2005). An intriguing possibility, however, is that boys' relative focus on nonhuman objects and object motion may be related to an early sex difference in the what and where components of the visual system (G. M. Alexander, 2003), and these in turn may lay the foundation for the later described sex differences in object-oriented play and implicit knowledge of tool use as well as men's advantage in tracking and responding to objects in motion (see the section titled Movement, chap. 13, this volume).

Prenatal Hormones

As discussed earlier, sex hormones have both organizational and activational effects on brain and behavior (see the section titled Sex Hormones and Sexual Selection, chap. 4). The organizational effects primarily occur prenatally but may also be influenced by the postnatal surge in testosterone that is common to male primates; this surge starts soon after birth and lasts for several months (Mann & Fraser, 1996). Baron-Cohen and his colleagues have been studying how prenatal exposure to testosterone influences sex differences in infancy and in older children (Baron-Cohen, Lutchmaya, & Knickmeyer, 2004; Lutchmaya, Baron-Cohen, & Raggatt, 2002a, 2002b). They estimated the fetus's exposure to testosterone by obtaining amniotic fluid from the mother about halfway through the pregnancy, that is, during the prenatal surge in testosterone. Testosterone gets into the amniotic fluid by diffusion through the fetus's skin and through urination.

Lutchmaya et al. (2002a) examined the relation between prenatal testosterone levels and the frequency with which 12-month-olds made eye contact with their mother. As an experimenter presented the infant with a series of toys, the location of the infants' gaze was videotaped. Analyses of these tapes revealed that girls made more eye contact than boys, as is commonly found. The level of prenatal testosterone was of course much lower in girls than in boys and was unrelated to how often the girls made eye contact. Prenatal testosterone levels were, however, related to how often the boys made eye contact but not in a straightforward way. Boys with the lowest and highest levels of prenatal testosterone had the lowest frequency of eye contact. In a related study, Lutchmaya et al. (2002b) assessed the vocabulary of boys and girls at 18 and 24 months. At 18 months, the vocabulary of girls was more than double that of boys. At 24 months, the typical girl knew 40% more words than did the typical boy. At this age, higher prenatal testosterone levels were associated with lower vocabulary scores but only when both sexes were assessed together; there were no within-sex effects.

The procedure used in these studies likely underestimated the quantity and duration of prenatal exposure to testosterone. The potential influence of the postnatal surge in testosterone on earlier and later sex differences also remains to be assessed. For these and other reasons, the findings should be considered preliminary, but they nonetheless point to potential hormonal influences on the expression of sex differences in infants.

PLAY

As I reviewed for other species in chapter 4 (in the section titled Play), sex differences in play activities are a universal aspect of children's behavior. Burghardt (2005) identified five common features that define play: it is voluntary, not immediately functional (but may have delayed benefits), involves some components of more functional activities, is repeated, and occurs in safe environments. Humans also engage in more organized games that can involve elements of play (e.g., voluntarily organized by children) but are also constrained by rules and have a specific objective. I include them here because children's engagement in culture-specific games may provide important practice for later functional activities. The study of sex differences in play has focused on three relatively independent components: gender schemas, child-initiated activities, and the formation of same-sex play groups (D. E. Brown, 1991; Lever, 1978; Maccoby, 1988; Maccoby & Jacklin, 1974; Pitcher & Schultz, 1983; Sandberg & Meyer-Bahlburg, 1994; Whiting & Edwards, 1973, 1988). I begin with a brief discussion of gender schemas and then move to child-initiated social play, followed by discussions of their locomotor, exploratory, object-oriented, and sociodramatic play. Children's segregation into same-sex play groups is discussed in chapter 11 of this volume (in the section titled Segregation).

Gender Schema

Infants begin to make sex-based discriminations (e.g., between male and female voices) as early as 6 months of age (C. L. Martin, Ruble, & Szkrybalo, 2002). By 18 months, they are beginning to categorize some activities as male typical and others as female typical (Eichstedt, Serbin, Poulin-DuBois, & Sen, 2002), and they talk about these as 2-year-olds (S. A. Gelman, Taylor, & Nguyen, 2004). The corresponding studies of these emerging gender schemas— beliefs about the core or essential features of *girls* and *boys*—reveal that children are often more stereotyped than their parents and other adults (e.g., S. A. Gelman et al., 2004). Gender schemas are important because they are one mechanism through which injunctive norms and other social–psychological processes might influence the expression of behavioral sex differences (Eagly & Karau, 2002; W. Wood & Eagly, 2002).

Explicit knowledge of gender schemas, however, is only weakly related to the actual play and social activities of girls and boys (Turner & Gervai, 1995). Girls and boys segregate into same-sex groups whether or not they are engaging in sex-typed activities (Maccoby, 1988), and children raised by egalitarian parents—those who actively discourage sex typing—have less stereotyped beliefs about sex differences than do children raised in other types of families, but their toy and play preferences are the same as these other children (Weisner & Wilson-Mitchell, 1990). This does not mean that children's emerging gender schemas do not influence sex differences in behavior. Rather, they do not appear to do so in straightforward ways. More implicit and subtle processes may be operating. The details of these processes are a source of continuing theoretical debate and remain to be fully demonstrated empirically (see Bussey & Bandura, 1999; C. L. Martin et al., 2002).

I leave these studies and debates to others but note here that gender schemas are not an alternative theory to the influence of sexual selection on human sex differences. In fact, gender schemas are highly compatible with an evolutionary history of sexual selection in our species. I have previously discussed Irons's (1979) cultural success and the many different ways in which male–male competition, for example, can be expressed across cultures and historical periods (see the section titled Male–Male Competition, chap. 8, this volume). There must be here-and-now mechanisms that enable children to modify the expression of inherent biases so they are expressed in culturally useful ways; this was the point of the section titled Development of Functional Systems (see chap. 9, this volume). Gender schemas may be one of these mechanisms.

Social Play

My focus here is on the forms of child-initiated social play. Rough-and-tumble play is more common among boys and play parenting is more common among girls. Sociodramatic play is also child-initiated and social but appears to be unique to humans, and thus it is discussed in a separate section.

Rough-and-Tumble

In chapter 4 (in the section titled Social Play), I noted that play fighting is found in many species of mammal and is more common for males than for females when male–male competition is intense and physical (Power, 2000). Many of the actual fighting behaviors (e.g., biting) are evident at birth, but engagement in this form of play makes their expression more flexible and nuanced (S. M. Pellis & Pellis, 2007). The evidence for an evolutionary history of one-on-one and coalitional male–male competition in our species was laid out in chapters 5 (in the section titled Sexual Selection and Human Evolution) and 8 (in the section titled Male–Male Competition) of this volume. In the sections that follow, I detail the evidence that strongly supports the corresponding predictions that boys will engage in more one-on-one and coalitional rough-and-tumble play fighting than will girls.

One-on-One. Rough-and-tumble play is not exclusive to boys, but it occurs much more frequently, with more vigor, and with greater zest among boys than among girls. This sex difference is found in all modern societies in which it has been studied and in many traditional ones (Eibl-Eibesfeldt, 1989; Maccoby, 1988; Whiting & Edwards, 1973, 1988). The sex difference is most evident with groups of three or more children and in the absence of adult supervision (Maccoby, 1988); adults in societies with less intense physical male–male competition often discourage this type of play. In these situations, groups of boys engage in various forms of playful physical assaults and wrestling 3 to 6 times more frequently than do groups of same-age girls (DiPietro, 1981; Maccoby, 1988). In an analysis of the activities of triads of same-sex 4-year-olds, DiPietro found that boys engaged in playful hitting, pushing, and tripping 4.5 times more frequently than did girls.

The sex difference in rough-and-tumble play emerges by age 3 years (Maccoby, 1988) and peaks between the ages of 8 and 10 years, at which time boys spend about 10% of their free time in these activities (Pellegrini & Smith, 1998). As boys move from juvenility (see Figure 10.2) to puberty and adolescence, the roughness of the play intensifies and the line between play and outright physical aggression begins to blur. As for the males of many other species, a relation between boys' physical roughhousing, physical aggression (e.g., bullying), and social dominance begins to emerge in early adolescence. Pellegrini and Bartini (2001) found that between the ages of 10 and 12 years, bullying among boys increased at the beginning of the school year and then decreased later in the school year; the decrease likely resulted from the establishment of a dominance hierarchy. Unlike younger boys for whom physical aggression is often associated with social rejection, physical bullying in adolescent boys is associated with the achievement of social dominance, as defined by peers and teachers, and with a higher frequency of dating and higher rated attractiveness by girls (Bukowski, Sippola, & Newcomb, 2000). This does not mean these boys are liked, but they do have social presence and influence (Berger, 2007). Other studies suggest that dominant adolescents use a mix of coercive (e.g., bullying) and prosocial (e.g., taking charge) behaviors to achieve dominance, depending on context and the relationship (Hawley, 1999).

The intensity and nature of boys' rough-and-tumble play varies with the intensity of physical male–male competition—especially between-groups warfare—in their social world (C. R. Ember & M. Ember, 1994). In societies characterized by high levels of male-on-male physical aggression among adults, the play fighting of boys is rougher than the play fighting in more peaceful societies. The intense male-on-male aggression described for the Yanomamö in chapter 8 of this volume (in the section titled Competition in Traditional Societies) is complemented by young Yanomamö boys' play fighting with clubs. In this society and others like it, parents (often fathers) encourage the escalation of rough-and-tumble play and inculcate aggression and emotional indifference in their sons (C. R. Ember & Ember, 1994); socialization tends to be harsh for girls as well (Barry, Josephson, Lauer, & Marshall, 1976). Loy and Hesketh (1995) provided a number of other examples in their analysis of the war-related games of the Native American warrior societies of the Central Plains.

> Evidence suggests that all Plains Indian tribes were, to greater or lesser degrees, involved in a wide range of warring activities . . . confined primarily to small war parties, raids, forays; that is, conflicts which were brief and usually indecisive. (p. 80)

For the Sioux and many other Indian tribes the activities of young boys were designed to encourage aggression, both one-on-one and coalition based, and physical endurance:

> Games for the Sioux frequently were contrived life-situations in miniature. They ran the gamut from the more complex diversion of the Moccasin Game enjoyed by adults to the raucously rough Swing-Kicking game played by young boys. . . . The Swing-Kicking Game took first place as a rugged conditioner, and there was no pretense at horseplay. Here two rows of boys faced each other, each holding his robe over his left arm. The game was begun only after the formality of the stock question, "Shall we grab them by the hair and knee them in the face until they bleed?"

Then using their robes as a shield, they all kicked at their opponents, endeavoring to upset them. There seems [sic] to have been no rules, for the boys attacked whoever was closest, often two boys jumping one. Kicking from behind the knees was a good way of throwing an opponent, and once down he was grabbed at the temples with both hands and kneed in the face. Once released, the bloody victims would fight on, kicking and kneeing and bleeding until they could fight no longer. . . . As Iron Shell explained, "Some boys got badly hurt, but afterwards we would talk and laugh about it. Very seldom did any fellows get angry. . . . Throw at Each Other with Mud was a slightly more gentle spring pastime where teams of boys attacked [each other] with mud balls which they threw from the tips of short springy sticks. Each boy carried several sticks and an arsenal of mud as he advanced. "It certainly hurt when you got hit, so you must duck and throw as you attack." Sometimes live coals were embedded in the mud balls to add zest to the game. (Hassrick, 1964, pp. 127–130)

Good times! Boys engage in play fighting and aggressive games, though rather tempered in comparison with the Sioux, even in societies in which the majority of men do not engage in intergroup aggression or physical one-on-one competition (Rose & Rudolph, 2006). Boys in these societies are often discouraged from engaging in play fighting and games that get too rough, but they do so anyway, at least when adults are not around.

Coalitions. The sex difference in infants' interest in groups (Benenson et al., 2004) continues into childhood and beyond. These studies confirm that boys organize themselves into much larger social groups than do girls, engage in intergroup competition once such groups are formed, form within-group dominance hierarchies, and show within-group role differentiation and specialization when engaged in group-level competition (Eder & Hallinan, 1978; Lever, 1978). Boys begin to show a preference for group-level activities over dyadic ones as early as 3 years of age, show a strong bias against members of competing groups by 5 years of age, and consistently form larger groups than girls by 6 years (Benenson, 1993; Rose & Rudolph, 2006).

The sex difference is illustrated by Lever's (1978) study of children's play and engagement in games. She asked 181 ten- and eleven-year-old children to record their after-school activities during the course of 1 week, resulting in 895 cases of social play. During this week, boys participated in group-level competitive activities, such as football and basketball, 3 times as frequently as did girls. Observation of these children's spontaneous (i.e., not organized by adults) play activities and games confirmed the pattern noted in their diaries and indicated that boys' social play involves larger groups and greater role differentiation within these groups.

More often, boys compete as members of teams and must simultaneously coordinate their actions with those of their teammates while taking into account the action and strategies of their opponents. Boys interviewed expressed finding gratification in acting as a representative of a collectivity; the approval or disapproval of one's teammates accentuates the importance of contributing to a group victory. (Lever, 1978, p. 478)

A questionnaire-based assessment of the play activities of 355 six- to ten-year-old girls and 333 same-age boys revealed the same pattern (Sandberg & Meyer-Bahlburg, 1994). For 6 year olds, 44% of the boys regularly played American football, compared with 2% of the girls. For 10 year olds, 70% of the boys regularly played football, compared with 15% of the girls. The magnitude of the sex difference was smaller, though still substantial, for basketball; 85% and 86% of the 6- and 10-year-old boys, respectively, played regularly, compared with 25% and 36% of the same-age girls. With respect to child-initiated—not including adult-organized—play, these sex differences have changed little from one decade to the next and are evident whether observations, questionnaires, interviews, or diaries of leisure activities are used to assess play behavior (Rose & Rudolph, 2006; Sutton-Smith, Rosenberg, & Morgan, 1963). The process of coalition formation is described in the section titled Peer Relationships in chapter 11 of this volume.

Hormones and Gender Schemas. Collaer and Hines (1995) concluded that the "clearest evidence for hormonal influences on human behavioral development comes from studies of childhood play. Elevated androgen in genetic females . . . is associated with masculinized and defeminized play" (p. 92). This and similar conclusions (see Cohen-Bendahan, van de Beek, & Berenbaum, 2005) are largely based on all of the different forms of sex-typed play activities (described in later sections) taken together. When these are combined, the sex differences are very large and consistent with a substantive influence of male hormones. The results related to rough-and-tumble and coalitional play are less clear, however, because most of the studies have not targeted these specific activities.

Berenbaum and Snyder (1995) provided some evidence for an influence of prenatal hormones on engagement in group-level competitive play. These researchers administered the same questionnaire used by Sandberg and Meyer-Bahlburg (1994) to boys and girls who were prenatally exposed to excess levels of androgens (i.e., affected by congenital adrenal hyperplasia [CAH]), children unaffected by CAH, and their parents. On the basis of self-report and parental report, girls affected by CAH engaged in more athletic competition than their unaffected peers; between 7 and 8 out of every 10 girls affected by CAH engaged in athletic competition more frequently than did the average unaffected girl. A follow-up study revealed these differences persist into adolescence (Berenbaum, 1999). The difference between the play of girls affected with CAH and other girls (often their sisters in these studies) was not as large as the difference between unaffected boys and unaffected girls; more than 9 out of 10 unaffected boys reported engaging in athletic competition more frequently than the average unaffected girl.

In an observational study, Hines and Kaufman (1994) found that girls affected by CAH engaged in more playful physical assaults, physical assaults on objects, wrestling, and rough-and-tumble play in general than did unaffected girls, but none of these differences were statistically significant. The lack of significance may have been the result of the testing arrangements. Specifically, most of the girls affected by CAH were observed as they played with one unaffected girl, a situation that would not typically result in rough-and-tumble play; what happens when three girls with CAH play together? In a larger scale study, parents reported more physical aggression for daughters with CAH than for unaffected daughters (Pasterski et al., 2007); 4 out of 5 girls with CAH were reported as being more aggressive than the average unaffected girl. Knickmeyer et al. (2005) did not find a relation between the amniotic measure of testosterone described in the section titled Infancy in this chapter and the frequency with which 5- to 6-year-olds engaged in boy-typical or girl-typical play. There were large sex differences in these play activities, but they did not vary systematically with individual differences in prenatal testosterone, as measured in amniotic fluid. These scientists did not, however, specifically measure one-on-one rough-and-tumble play, and the children were too young to assess the sex difference in coalitional play.

Evidence for potential social influences on these sex differences comes from a longitudinal study of change in girls' engagement in male-typical and female-typical leisure activities from juvenility to adolescence (McHale, Shanahan, Updegraff, Crouter, & Booth, 2004). Girls' interest in masculine activities (e.g., competitive sports) and their mothers', but not their fathers', sex-typed attitudes predicted girls' relative engagement in masculine or feminine activities 2 years later. Engagement in feminine activities was also related to circulating testosterone levels. Girls with feminine interests and low testosterone spent more time engaged in girl-typical activities (e.g., dance, handicrafts) than did other girls.

Overall, the sex differences in one-on-one and coalitional play are robust and consistent with the basics of the evolutionary prediction. However, the prediction is nuanced and involves an interaction between early and later hormonal influences and cultural patterns of warfare and other forms of male-on-male violence as these are related to the socialization of children (e.g., C. R. Ember & Ember, 1994). I assume socialization involves a relative suppression or amplification of evolved biases through parenting, social learning, and related processes (B. S. Low, 1989). The available evidence does not allow strong tests of such an interaction, but, consistent with S. M. McHale et al.'s (2004) study, does suggest a combination of biological and social influences on the expression of these sex differences (see also S. M. McHale, Kim, Dotterer, Crouter, & Booth, 2009).

Skill Development. I hypothesized in chapter 9 (in the section titled Development of Functional Systems) that one evolved function of the developmental period is to enable children to adapt folk systems to the nuances of the local social group and ecology. In this view, play fighting allows boys to assess their physical competencies and skills relative to those of their peers and allows them to practice the social skills needed for coalition-based intergroup warfare (Geary, Byrd-Craven, Hoard, Vigil, & Numtee, 2003; S. M. Pellis & Pellis, 2007). The bias for men to stay in their birth group is particularly likely to be expressed during periods of intergroup warfare (Pasternak, Ember, & Ember, 1997). Under these conditions, boys' coalitional play groups form the core of actual competitive coalitions in adulthood. The dozen or so years in which these boys have competed together in play coalitions provide a substantive opportunity to learn about each others' strengths and weakness and how to organize their group into an effective coalition; this is elaborated in chapter 11 of this volume (in the section titled The Cultural Divide). It is also likely that the intensity of the play fighting results in changes in the sensitivity of the associated affective systems (K. MacDonald, 1988). The physical pain that was associated with playing the Swing-Kicking Game almost certainly resulted in more aggressive boys than would otherwise have been the case as well as boys who were less sensitive to the distress of other people and better able to suppress their own fear and reactions to physical pain.

A contrast of the game of baseball played in the modern United States and the game of Throw at Each Other with Mud played by Sioux Indians 200 years ago—similar games were common throughout Native American tribes and in many other parts of the world (Eibl-Eibesfeldt, 1989)—further illustrates my point. Both games require many of the same physical, social, and cognitive competencies involved in coalitional warfare in traditional societies (Geary, 1995b). Both require the formation of ingroups and outgroups, the strategic coordination of the activities of ingroup members as related to competition with the outgroup, the throwing of projectiles (baseballs and mud balls) at specific targets, and the tracking and reacting to the movement of these projectiles. The latter activities mesh well with the earlier described advantages of boys and men in throwing distance, velocity, and accuracy and with their skill at intercepting thrown objects (Thomas & French, 1985; Watson & Kimura, 1991). These component skills, along with the male advantage in upper body strength and length of the forearm (Tanner, 1990), are the same competencies involved in the use of and in the avoidance of being hit by projectile weapons.

In short, the rough-and-tumble play and fighting games of boys appear to provide the activities needed to fine-tune the competencies associated with physical one-on-one competition and coalition-based male–male competition as these are often expressed during periods of conflict in traditional societies. Cultural factors are expected to influence the magnitude of any corresponding sex differences, but the early physical differences in the arms and later the upper body of boys and girls and the sex differences in physical size of our ancestors (see the section titled Sexual Selection and Human Evolution, chap. 5) make it all but impossible to deny an evolutionary history of male–male competition. My point is that these physical sex differences, the sex differences in children's self-organized play, and their openness to social influences on the intensity and form of this play are all interrelated; play provides a means to adapt biologically biased sex differences to the nuances of what it takes to achieve cultural success as adults.

Play Parenting

Before turning to human sex differences, I revisit several points from the section titled Social Play in chapter 4. For primate species in which females provide more parenting than males, juvenile females are more attentive to and engage in more alloparenting (e.g., holding a younger sibling) than their brothers (Nicolson, 1987). When provided the opportunity to play with a doll or other plush toys or with wheeled toys (e.g., a car), female vervet monkeys (*Cercopithecus aethiops sabaeus*) and female rhesus macaques (*Macaca mulatta*) carried and played with the dolls or similar plush toys relatively more than did their brothers (G. M. Alexander & Hines, 2002; Hassett, Siebert, & Wallen, 2008). The male vervets interacted with all of the toys more often than did their sisters, and so the sex difference emerged in terms of the proportion of all time spent with the toys (e.g., percentage of toy time that involved a doll). The testing for the rhesus monkeys was similar to that used with children, and the sex difference emerged as a result of the indifference of males to the plush toys; 30% of the females showed a preference for the plush toys, compared with 9% of the males. In some species, play parenting increases the survival rate of firstborns (Pryce, 1993), in keeping with a skill development component of play.

Throughout the world, girls are assigned child-care roles, especially for infants, more frequently than are boys (Whiting & Edwards, 1988). Girls also seek out and engage in child care, play parenting, and other domestic activities (e.g., playing house) with younger children or child substitutes such as dolls more frequently than do same-age boys (Pitcher & Schultz, 1983). Sandberg and Meyer-Bahlburg (1994) found that nearly 99% of 6-year-old girls frequently played with dolls, compared with 17% of same-age boys (it was not clear whether this included play with "action figures"). By 10 years of age, 92% of girls frequently played with dolls, compared with 12% of same-age boys. Similar differences were found 30 years earlier, despite significant changes in the social roles of men and women in the United States (Sutton-Smith et al., 1963). These sex differences have also been documented across many traditional societies, such as the Yanomamö, the !Ko Bushman of the central Kalahari, the Himba of southwest Africa, and the Baka of the Congo Basin in central Africa (Eibl-Eibesfeldt, 1989; Kamei, 2005).

The magnitude of these differences varies across age and context (Berman, 1980; Whiting & Edwards, 1988). Both girls and boys are responsive to infants prior to the juvenile stage (i.e., until about 6 years of age), but after this age and continuing into puberty, adolescence, and adulthood, girls and women are more responsive, on average, to infants and younger children than are boys and men (Berman, Monda, & Myerscough, 1977; Whiting & Edwards, 1973). The emergence of this sex difference is due to a significant drop in the frequency with which juvenile and older boys attend to and interact with infants and younger children and an increase in girls' interest during puberty (Goldberg, Blumberg, & Kriger, 1982). The latter finding and more recent studies suggest that girls' interest in infants and children is heightened as a result of the increases in estrogen during puberty (Sprengelmeyer et al., 2009), as is the case with many other species of primate (Nicolson, 1987).

Research on children affected by CAH suggests play parenting is also influenced by prenatal exposure to androgens (Berenbaum & Hines, 1992; Berenbaum & Snyder, 1995; Collaer & Hines, 1995). Direct observation of the play activities of 5- to 8-year-old boys and girls affected with CAH and unaffected same-sex relatives revealed that unaffected girls played with dolls and kitchen supplies 2.5 times longer than did girls affected by CAH (Berenbaum & Hines, 1992). These girls, in turn, played with boys' toys (e.g., toy cars) nearly 2.5 times longer than unaffected girls. The same pattern was found in a follow-up study 3 to 4 years later (Berenbaum & Snyder, 1995). In this follow-up study, the children were also allowed to choose a toy to take home after the assessment was complete. Unaffected girls most frequently chose a set of markers or a doll to take home, whereas girls affected by CAH most frequently chose a transportation toy (e.g., toy car) or a ball to take home; 7% of the girls affected by CAH chose a doll, compared with 28% of the unaffected girls.

In sum, a sex difference in play parenting favoring girls is found in both modern and traditional societies and in fact most other species of primate (Eibl-Eibesfeldt, 1989; Nicolson, 1987). These patterns do not rule out social influences on these sex differences but nonetheless provide strong support for the evolutionary prediction: Play parenting is predicted to be expressed in the sex that provides the majority of the parental investment. Further support is provided by Tiger and Shepher's (1975) study of sex differences in the socially egalitarian kibbutzim. Their study revealed a change to traditional sex roles after the first generation and a stronger push by women than by men for a family-centered rather than communal-centered social organization. It remains to be determined, however, whether girls' play parenting contributes to their later child-rearing competencies.

Locomotor and Exploratory Play

As I covered in chapter 4 (in the section titled Locomotor and Object Play), locomotor play is found in a wide variety of species and mirrors evolutionarily salient activities such as predator evasion. The extent to which these activities fine-tune motor and muscular systems to the nuances of the local ecology or maintain them while the animal is developing remains to be determined (Burghardt, 2005; Byers & Walker, 1995). Across species, sex differences in locomotor play are not found as consistently as those found for rough-and-tumble play and play parenting (Power, 2000). This is probably because females and males are more similar than different in terms of locomotor demands—catching prey, avoiding predators, migrating. In this section, *exploratory play* refers to exploration of the ecology, as contrasted with objects, and is thus linked with some aspects (e.g., traveling) of locomotor play.

Across traditional societies, men travel farther from the home village than do women for many reasons, including finding mates, developing alliances with the men of neighboring villages, hunting, and intergroup warfare (Chagnon, 1997; K. Hill & Hurtado, 1996; K. Hill & Kaplan, 1988). To engage in these activities, men have to be aware of and travel in larger and often more novel ecological ranges than women. Women's foraging, in contrast, typically occurs within the group's territory, and when women leave their birth group to migrate to the group of their husbands, they do not make this journey on their own. Studies of men's hunting in traditional societies indicate that mastery of some competencies, such as shooting a bow and arrow, are dependent on physical growth, with some learning. The combination of skills needed to identify (e.g., through smell, tracks), track, and ultimately kill prey can take 10 to 20 years to master (Gurven, Kaplan, & Gutierrez, 2006). The complexity and risks are no doubt higher when the prey includes other people. Unlike women's foraging for fruit or tubers, hunting requires an ability to track and predict the movements of evasive prey, human and nonhuman.

Developmental sex differences in locomotor and exploratory play are theoretically important because they are predicted to provide the experiences in the local ecology that better prepare men for raiding, hunting, and so forth. Sex differences in exploration of the ecology are also predicted to contribute to some of the cognitive sex differences described in the section titled Folk Physics in chapter 13.

Sex Differences

The greater activity level of infant boys than girls continues into childhood and beyond and is expressed as a sex difference in gross locomotor play (Eibl-Eibesfeldt, 1989; Whiting & Edwards, 1988). The sex difference is related in part to the sex difference in group-level competitive play and to a greater engagement of boys than girls in solitary running (Eaton & Enns, 1986; Lever, 1978). If Byers and Walker (1995) are correct about locomotor play resulting in neuromuscular changes to suit the local ecology, then these early sex differences will result in men being better adapted for running and traveling long distances on foot than women. In addition to any neuromuscular adaptations, the sex difference in gross locomotor activities results in larger play ranges for boys than for girls. This sex difference is related to more parental restrictions on the ranges of girls than boys but is also found when there are no such restrictions.

Matthews (1992) found that both boys and girls in suburban England played within close proximity of one or both of their parents during childhood. During juvenility and beyond, boys have a larger play range than girls; girls stay closer to their home during play. For 8- to 11-year-olds, boys' unrestricted play range covered from 1.5 to nearly 3 times the area of girls' unrestricted play range. Whiting and Edwards (1988) reported a similar sex difference for juveniles in Peru, Guatemala, and for three separate groups in Kenya. For the Ache, who live in dense tropical rain forest, the size of the range of boys and girls does not typically diverge until adolescence (K. Hill & Hurtado, 1996). Whenever it emerges, boys not only engage in more locomotor activities over a larger range than girls but also explore and manipulate (e.g., build things, such as forts) the ecology much more frequently (Matthews, 1992).

Skill Development

The overall relation between play activities and children's cognitive development is uncertain; sometimes play is associated with enhanced cognitive competence, and sometimes it is not (e.g., Matthews, 1987; R. H. Munroe, Munroe, & Brasher, 1985; Rubin, Fein, & Vandenberg, 1983). It appears that the relation between play experiences and children's developing cognitive competencies is very specific and thus difficult to assess. For instance, ecological exploration is correlated with the ability to generate mental maps of the physical layout of the ecology but is not consistently related to other forms of spatial cognition, such as the ability to copy geometric figures (R. H. Munroe et al., 1985). Most of these relations are based on correlational studies and thus cause and effect is not well understood. Do good spatial skills make it easier to range widely in the ecology, or does exploration enhance spatial skills, or is there an interaction (Newcombe & Huttenlocher, 2006)?

Scientists do know that 4-year-old boys, and perhaps even infant boys (D. S. Moore & Johnson, 2008; Quinn & Liben, 2008), have an advantage over same-age girls on some spatial tasks (Levine, Huttenlocher, Tayler, & Langrock, 1999) and that this advantage grows during juvenility, puberty, and adolescence (Matthews, 1992; D. Voyer, Voyer, & Bryden, 1995). I review these differences in chapter 13 of this volume (in the section titled Folk Physics). I consider here whether there is a link between sex differences in the frequency and complexity of ecological exploration and the development of sex differences in some forms of spatial and navigational (e.g., understanding maps) cognition as well as whether the development of these competencies is condition dependent in males.

Exploration and Spatial Cognition. A potential link between exploratory experience and the sex difference in spatial cognition is illustrated by Matthews's (1987) study of the relation between exposure to a novel environment and children's ability to later generate a spatial representation of this environment. Here, 8- to 11-year-olds were taken on a 1-hour tour of an unfamiliar area. In one condition, the children were given a map of the entire area and were then taken on the tour, with the guide pointing out various landmarks. In the second— memory demanding—condition, another group of children was given a map of one half of the area and their tour was interrupted for 30 minutes at the halfway point; the same landmarks were pointed out. At the end of the tour, the children were asked to draw a map of the entire area. The maps were analyzed in terms of the inclusion of key landmarks and the clustering and relative orientation of these landmarks. The maps of boys and girls did not differ in the overall amount of information provided, but sex differences did emerge for other features.

Of the group taken on the uninterrupted tour, girls included more landmarks in their maps and boys included more routes (e.g., roads), but there were no other sex differences. Of the group taken on the memory-demanding tour, boys outperformed girls on a number of map features. At all ages, but especially for 10- and 11-year-olds, "boys showed a keener appreciation of the juxtaposition of places" (Matthews, 1987, p. 84). Boys were better at integrating clusters of landmarks in ways that reflected their actual topographical positions and showed significantly fewer topographical distortions than girls. Moreover, "some of the older boys . . . managed to show a euclidean grasp of space" (Matthews, 1987, p. 86). In other words, under conditions with fewer supports boys were better able than girls to mentally reconstruct an allocentric representation of the topography of an unfamiliar environment (see the section titled Folk Physics, chap. 9, this volume), retaining general orientation, clustering, and euclidean (e.g., relative direction) relations among important landmarks. Under conditions with many supports—an entire map of the area and an uninterrupted tour—girls remembered more landmarks and boys remembered more routes; the same sex difference is found in adults (see the section titled Representation, chap. 13, this volume).

The study, however, did not demonstrate that boys' exploratory experience enhanced their spatial abilities but rather demonstrated that boys implicitly—without the intention to learn—develop more accurate allocentric memories of large-scale ecological space during exploration. In an experimental study, J. F. Herman and Siegel (1978) constructed a replica of a small town and assessed kindergarten, second-, and fifth-grade children's ability to reconstruct this town after walking through it or watching someone else walk through it three times. When the "town" was placed in a large space, a gymnasium, boys were more accurate at reconstructing it in second and fifth grades, but not in kindergarten; all of the kindergarten children had difficulty with the task. The boys' advantage was found after their first and second walks through, but the sex difference disappeared after the third. In all, girls required three walks to reach the level of accuracy obtained by boys after two walks. This study indicates that during exploration in a large-scale space, boys learn the geometric relations among landmarks more rapidly than do girls.

Condition-Dependent Development. Several studies have suggested that restricted exploration of the ecology can affect the development of spatial competencies but more so for boys than for girls (e.g., Levine, Vasilyeva, Lourenco, & Huttenlocher, 2005; Parameswaran, 2003). Levine et al. assessed 547 children from high-, middle-, and low-income backgrounds across second and third grades on two spatial tasks—map reading and two-dimensional mental rotation—and a syntax comprehension test. No sex differences were found on the syntax test, but boys from high- and middle-income families had an advantage on both spatial tasks. There was no sex difference on either spatial task for children from low-income families. In other words, low family income was associated with lower scores for both boys and girls on all three tests. In relation to same-sex peers, the spatial competencies of boys were more strongly affected by poverty than were the competencies of girls. The features of these environments that influenced spatial development are not known. One possibility offered by Levine et al. is that the activities of both boys and girls were severely restricted in the low-SES group because of potential risks in some of these neighborhoods. Another possibility is that the children from higher income families were provided with experiences (e.g., extracurricular sports) that facilitated boys' development of spatial skills.

Either way, these results suggest that some aspects of the developing spatial competencies of boys are more dependent on exploratory experiences than are those of girls. This is the same pattern I described in the section titled Vulnerable and Variable earlier in this chapter, specifically, that boys' development is more sensitive to environmental conditions than girls' development. It remains to be determined whether boys' spatial and especially navigational competencies are condition-dependent traits related to sexual selection in the same ways described in chapter 3 (in the section titled Good Genes) for sexually selected traits in other species. The relation between exposure to sex hormones and the sex differences in spatial abilities and their development is also nuanced and discussed in chapter 13 (in the section titled Folk Physics).

Object-Oriented Play

The reader may recall that object play is common in species that feed on a variety of foods and that have to manipulate different types of objects, including prey and tools, in different ways (see the section titled Locomotor and Object Play, chap. 4). Object play typically has an exploratory component and includes object manipulation that is similar to prey capture behaviors or behaviors that involve tool use. Evidence for the hypothesis that these are developmental activities that provide practice and refinement of prey capture and tool use skills is mixed (Caro, 1980; Power, 2000). The alternative is these play activities maintain, but do not refine, evolved competencies that involve object manipulation. In either case, human sex differences in children's object manipulation play are predicted, to the extent men and women differed in corresponding behaviors during our evolutionary history. With respect to tool use, they almost certainly did.

Support for my assertion comes from anthropological studies showing that men work with a wider range of objects than do women across traditional societies (Daly & Wilson, 1983; Murdock, 1981). The activities that are performed exclusively or primarily by men include metal work; weapon making; the manufacture of musical instruments; work with wood, stone, bone, and shells; boat building; the manufacture of ceremonial objects; and net making (Daly & Wilson, 1983). Across cultures, nearly 92% of those activities that appear to be most similar to the likely tool-making activities of *H. habilis* and *H. erectus*—weapon making and work with wood, stone, bone, and shells—are performed exclusively by men; just over 1% of these activities are performed exclusively by women, and about 7% are performed by both sexes (Daly & Wilson, 1983; Gowlett, 1992). At the same time, there are no object-working activities that show the same degree of exclusivity for women, although across cultures women engage in pottery making, basket making, and weaving much more frequently than do men (Murdock, 1981). To the extent that some tools, such as stones used as projectile weapons or spears, provided an advantage in male-on-male aggression, their use, along with any associated play patterns, is a component of sexual selection.

Sex Differences

Boys engage in much more object-oriented play than do girls (Eibl-Eibesfeldt, 1989; Freedman, 1974; Sandberg & Meyer-Bahlburg, 1994; Sutton-Smith et al., 1963). The sex difference in this form of play cannot simply be described as play with things versus play with people, however. Girls engage more frequently than boys in the broader category of construction play, including play with puzzles, markers, clay, and so on (Christie & Johnson,

1987; Rubin et al., 1983). Boys engage in a more restricted category of play with inanimate mechanical objects (e.g., toy cars) and construction play that involves building (Garai & Scheinfeld, 1968). Boys also engage in the experimental manipulation of these objects, such as taking them apart and trying to put them back together, more frequently than do girls (Hutt, 1972).

The degree to which boys are interested in play with inanimate mechanical objects is illustrated by the previously described Sandberg and Meyer-Bahlburg (1994) study. It was found that 97% of 6-year-old boys frequently played with toy vehicles (e.g., cars), compared with 51% of same-age girls. At 10 years of age, 94% of boys frequently played with toy vehicles, but only 29% of girls did so. Sutton-Smith et al. (1963) found the same sex difference 30 years earlier, and Eibl-Eibesfeldt (1989) described a similar pattern with !Ko children. Here, an analysis of 1,166 drawings revealed that boys drew technical objects, such as wagons and airplanes, 10 times more frequently than did girls (20% vs. 2%). An analysis of the drawings of 5- to 6-year-old Japanese children revealed that 94% of the boys but only 5% of the girls drew these types of objects, all of which moved (Lijima, Arisaka, Minamoto, & Arai, 2001). The same pattern has been found in the drawings of children in China, Bali, Ceylon, India, and Kenya (Freedman, 1974). The basis for choosing one toy or another appears to be what the child can do with them (Eisenberg, Murray, & Hite, 1982); specifically, boys prefer toys that can be put in motion (e.g., toy train) or can be used to build (e.g., blocks), whereas girls prefer toys that can be nurtured (e.g., stuffed animals).

Skill Development

The first issue for this section is whether object-oriented play results in enhanced competence in using tools. The evidence is mixed, but suggestive. Jennings (1975), for instance, found that the free play activities of preschool children could be classified as largely people oriented or largely object oriented. An analysis of the relation between the focus of play activities and the pattern of cognitive abilities indicated that children whose play was object oriented "performed better on tests of ability to organize and classify physical materials" (Jennings, 1975, p. 515), as assessed by tests of spatial cognition (e.g., the ability to mentally represent and manipulate geometric designs) and the ability to sort objects on the basis of, for example, color and shape. Results such as these suggest that object-focused play may contribute to the elaboration of aspects of the folk physical cognitive abilities described in chapter 9 of this volume (in the section titled Folk Physics), but this cannot be stated with certainty at this time.

The second issue is whether there are sex differences in the ability to use tools, and if so, whether these differences are related to the sex differences in object-oriented play. As I review elsewhere (Geary, 1998b), there are sex differences in interest in and pursuit of careers that involve designing and working with mechanical objects, as in engineering and computer technology. The immediate issue is whether there is an early sex difference in interest in using objects as simple tools and in the ease with which boys and girls learn to use objects as tools. Again, scientists do not know, but there are some intriguing differences. Z. Chen and Siegler (2000) found that as early as 18 months of age, boys have small to moderate advantages over girls in several aspects of early tool use, as in using a hooked stick to retrieve a desired toy. Boys were better at applying tool-related knowledge learned in one setting to another setting, were more consistent in the use of tools across settings, and were more successful in the use of tools in problem solving. Without any hints from an adult, 79% of the boys and 31% of the girls were able to use such tools to retrieve the toy. For 3-year-olds, Gredlein and Bjorklund (2005) found that engagement in boy-typical forms of object-oriented play was associated with skilled tool use during problem solving for boys but for not girls.

These results are in need of replication and further study, but they give rise to the hypotheses that young boys' implicit understanding of how to use simple objects as tools is more advanced than that of girls and that boys' knowledge of tool use benefits more from object-oriented play. The combination is consistent with the model laid out in chapter 9 (in the section titled Development of Functional Systems), specifically, that the early skeletal structure of folk domains is enhanced during children's self-initiated social and play activities. In this case, sex differences in some folk physical abilities described in chapter 13 (in the section titled Folk Physics) may be accompanied by early sex differences in sensitivity to corresponding forms of information (e.g., attending to objects and implicitly framing them as potential tools).

Prenatal Hormones

Studies of children affected by CAH indicate that prenatal hormone exposure influences children's object-oriented play (Berenbaum & Hines, 1992; Berenbaum & Snyder, 1995). As noted earlier, girls affected by CAH played with boys' toys—a helicopter, two cars, and a fire engine—nearly 2.5 times longer than did unaffected girls and played with these boys' toys more than 3 times longer than they played with girls' toys, such as a doll. When given an opportunity to take a toy home, 43% of the girls affected by CAH chose a toy car or airplane, but none of the unaffected girls chose these items; boys affected by CAH and unaffected boys chose these items 57% and 61% of the time, respectively. As described for boys' drawings, Lijima et al. (2001) found that the drawings of girls with CAH often included mobile vehicles; overall, the drawings of girls with CAH included a mix of boy-typical and girl-typical features.

The results from several small-scale studies of prenatal exposure to testosterone and children's later sex-typed behavior are mixed (Hines, Golombok, Rust, Johnston, & Golding, 2002; Knickmeyer et al., 2005). The largest study of this kind examined the relation between prenatal amniotic testosterone levels and sex-typed play in 212 six- to ten-year-olds (Auyeung et al., 2009). For both sexes, higher prenatal testosterone levels were associated with more frequent boy-typical play. All of these studies are difficult to interpret, however, because the researchers did not assess the relation between testosterone and specific types of play but rather used a composite of all sex-typed activities. The result for the Knickmeyer et al. study, for instance, was that only 3 of the 30 items assessed object-oriented play.

The toy preference studies of vervet and rhesus monkeys shed some light on the potential biological contribution to the sex difference in object play (G. M. Alexander & Hines, 2002; Hassett et al., 2008). Vervet males frequently interacted with both a doll and a toy car but spent relatively more time playing with the car. Rhesus males showed a much stronger bias; 79% of these males preferred wheeled over plush toys, and only 9% preferred plush over wheeled toys. Although rhesus females showed an overall—averaged across individuals—bias toward plush toys, as I noted earlier, there was much more variation among females than males. In fact, 30% of the females showed no preference for either type of toy.

These findings are noteworthy because the testing procedure (making a wide range of toys available) was similar to that used with children and because the findings mirror those found with children: Boys are more strongly sex-typed in their play activities than are girls; girls are more likely to engage in *cross-over* play than are boys (Sandberg & Meyer-Bahlburg, 1994). In all, there is no question that the majority of boys are fascinated with objects that produce mechanical motion (e.g., cars, trucks, trains), as contrasted with biological motion, and engage in other forms of object-oriented play (e.g., building) much more frequently than do girls. Prenatal hormones appear to contribute to these biases, but much remains to be learned.

Sociodramatic Play

Sociodramatic play involves groups of children enacting some social episode—often with great flair and emotion—centered on an everyday or imaginary theme, such as dinner or a dragon slaying (Rubin et al., 1983). This form of play appears to involve the rehearsal and development of social and social–cognitive (e.g., theory of mind) competencies (Leslie, 1987) and by the end of childhood (see Figure 10.2) includes a fantasy element; fantasy play in general emerges at about 2 years of age and peaks at about 6 to 7 years (Pellegrini & Bjorklund, 2004). Both boys and girls regularly engage in sociodramatic play but differ in the associated themes and the roles they tend to adopt, as noted by Pitcher and Schultz (1983):

> Boys play more varied and global roles that are more characterized by fantasy and power. Boys' sex roles tend to be functional, defined by action plans. Characters are usually stereotyped and flat with habitual attitudes and personality features (cowboy, foreman, Batman, Superman). Girls prefer family roles, especially the more traditional roles of daughter and mother. Even at the youngest age, girls are quite knowledgeable about the details and subtleties in these roles. . . . From a very early age girls conceive of the family as a system of relationships and a complex of reciprocal actions and attitudes. (p. 79)

In other words, the sociodramatic play of boys focuses, more often than not, on themes associated with power, dominance, and aggression. The sociodramatic play of girls focuses, more often than not, on interpersonal relationships, including those among family members, such as a parent taking care of children. These activities, of course, reflect the same sex differences found in rough-and-tumble play and play parenting, respectively.

Stated differently, sociodramatic fantasy play involves the practice of the roles and behaviors associated with intrasexual competition and parenting, and engages the conscious–psychological control mechanisms described in chapter 9 (in the section titled Motivation to Control). Children's fantasies are mental representations of social scenarios organized by the evolutionarily salient motives to compete and reproduce. Of course, children are not ready for these activities, but they need to prepare for them. Part of this preparation is learning how to mentally simulate and think about social situations. My hypothesis is that the fantasy component of sociodramatic play provides practice at using mental simulations to rehearse later social strategies and provides a vehicle for the expression of the motivational and affective mechanisms associated with adult activities.

CONCLUSION

The length of the developmental period has increased considerably during human evolution (Bogin, 1999), corresponding with an increase in the complexity of human social systems (Dunbar, 1993; Flinn, Geary, & Ward, 2005). The complexity of these systems is related, in part, to the dynamics of cooperation and competition that emerges in and among human groups and in reproductive dyads (Chagnon, 1988; Geary, 2002a; Symons, 1979). I described the many ways in which sexual selection is an important part of this dynamic mix in chapters 6 (i.e., parenting), 7 (i.e., intersexual choice), and 8 (i.e., intrasexual competition) of this volume. Folding sex differences described in these chapters into those described in this one makes sense if one important function of the developmental period is to provide the experiences needed to refine and adapt evolved competencies to the nuances of local conditions. The experiences emerge, in part, through children's attentional biases, through their self-initiated play and social activities, and through wider cultural factors (e.g., Greenough, Black, & Wallace, 1987; Scarr, 1992). The seeds of children's self-initiated activities appear to be found in the attentional biases of boy and girl infants. The question is the extent to which the magnitude of these sex differences reflects human evolutionary history or more proximate social learning mechanisms, such as selective imitation. These, of course, are not mutually exclusive mechanisms and almost certainly interact in many ways. However, I ask the reader to consider the evidence for the importance of sexual selection for understanding the evolution and expression of human developmental sex differences.

The delayed physical maturation of boys relative to girls and the sex difference in the timing, duration, and intensity of the pubertal growth spurt follow the same pattern found in other polygynous primates (Leigh, 1996). Across these species, sex differences in the pattern of physical maturation are more consistently related to the intensity of physical male–male competition than to alternative explanations, such as a sex difference in foraging strategy (Mitani, Gros-Louis, & Richards, 1996). Many of the human sex differences in physical traits and competencies (e.g., a longer forearm and greater upper body strength in men) are also readily explained in terms of selection for male-on-male aggression, specifically, selection that involved the use of projectile and blunt force weapons (Keeley, 1996). Stated more directly, the sex differences in physical development and physical competencies have almost certainly been shaped by sexual selection to a significant degree. Of course, some physical sex differences, such as the wider pelvis in women, have been shaped primarily by natural selection but further exaggerated by sexual selection, that is, male choice, in this example.

The sex differences in rough-and-tumble play, exploratory behavior, size of the play range, and the tendency of boys to form competitive coalitions and within-coalition dominance hierarchies are also consistent with an evolutionary history of one-on-one and coalitional male–male competition. In this view, these features of boys' play and social behavior involve a preparation for later within-group dominance striving and coalition formation for intergroup aggression. Through parenting practices such as degree of physical discipline, the selective imitation of competitive activities, gender schemas, and actual experiences within same-sex groups (see the section titled The Cultural Divide, chap. 11), boys learn how to best achieve within-group social dominance and practice the competencies associated with male–male competition in their particular culture. They learn how to achieve cultural success (e.g., by leading raids on other villages or becoming a star football player).

My focus on boys and male–male competition is not to downplay the importance of our evolutionary history for understanding girls' development but rather to make a point: Sexual selection is a powerful set of mechanisms that allows scientists to incorporate children's behavior and development into a wider evolutionary framework that simultaneously allows for social and other experiential influences on emerging sex differences. As the reader knows, the dynamics of sexual selection are influenced by more fundamental differences in the potential rate of reproduction and in parental investment, and there are human sex differences here as well. Girls' more frequent engagement in play parenting follows readily from women's greater investment in children and is consistent with sex differences found in other species in which females invest more heavily in offspring than do males.

11

SEX DIFFERENCES IN SOCIAL DEVELOPMENT

I continue my discussion of the world of boys and girls in this chapter but now turn my attention to the nuances of their social behavior and development as it is expressed in the contexts of peer groups and dyadic relationships. The sex differences that unfold in these contexts are, at least in part, a continuation of children's self-directed preparation for engaging in the reproductive activities described in earlier chapters. Their preparation accelerates during the juvenile years as they segregate into same-sex peer groups and create very different boy and girl cultures. I begin with this segregation and the processes that underlie it. From there, I provide an evolutionary framework for conceptualizing differences in the peer relationships of boys and girls and men and women and how these fit with sex differences described in previous chapters. The framework is followed by the reviews of peer relationships in group and dyadic contexts and of other sex differences in social motives and behaviors. I tie these sections together with a broader discussion of social development and evolution and close with consideration of potential parent influences on the expression of social sex differences.

BOYS' AND GIRLS' CULTURES

In this section, I discuss why boys and girls self-segregate into same-sex groups and the different cultures that they create within these groups.

Segregation

The formation of same-sex play and social groups is one of the most consistently found features of children's behavior (Maccoby, 1988, 1998; Strayer & Santos, 1996; Whiting & Edwards, 1988). Children begin to form these groups before the age of 3 years and do so with increasing frequency throughout the juvenile years. In a longitudinal study of children in the United States, Maccoby and Jacklin (1987) found that 4- to 5-year-olds spent 3 hours playing with same-sex peers for every single hour they spent playing in mixed-sex groups. By the time these children were 6 to 7 years old, the ratio of time spent in same-sex versus mixed-sex groups was 11:1. The same pattern has been documented in Canada, England, Hungry, Kenya, Mexico, the Philippines, Japan, and India (Strayer & Santos, 1996; P. J. Turner & Gervai, 1995; Whiting & Edwards, 1988), although the degree of segregation varies across these societies. The social segregation is most common in situations that are not monitored by adults, that is, when children are free to form their own groups (Maccoby, 1988; Strayer & Santos, 1996).

The different play and social styles of girls and boys contribute to the segregation (Maccoby, 1988; Serbin, Powlishta, & Gulko, 1993). Girls and boys not only play differently, as described in chapter 10 of this volume (in the section titled Play), but also use different social strategies to attempt to gain control over desired resources (e.g., toys) and to influence group activities. In situations in which access to a desired object, such as a movie viewer that can be watched by only one child at a time, is limited, boys and girls use different strategies, on average, for gaining access to this object (Charlesworth & Dzur, 1987). More often than not, boys gain access by playfully shoving and pushing other boys out of the way, whereas girls gain access by means of verbal persuasion (e.g., polite suggestions to share) and sometimes verbal commands (e.g., "It's my turn now!").

Maccoby (1988, 1998) concluded that the sex differences in play and social styles contribute to segregated social groups because children are unresponsive to the styles of the opposite sex. Boys sometimes try to initiate rough-and-tumble play with girls, but most girls withdraw from these initiations, whereas most other boys readily join the fray. Girls often attempt to influence the behavior of boys through verbal requests and suggestions, but boys, unlike other girls, are generally unresponsive (Charlesworth & LaFrenier,

1983); many readers are probably wondering whether boys ever become responsive—they do by adulthood, somewhat (Maccoby, 1990). In short, the differences in play and social styles, as well as the sex differences in play interests (see the section titled Play, chap. 10, this volume), result in children forming groups on the basis of mutual interests and the ability to influence group activities, and one result is sex segregation. Other peer influences that contribute to segregation include teasing about acquiring "cooties" (an early sexually transmitted disease, apparently) if one interacts with a member of the opposite sex (Maccoby, 1988).

The sex difference in play interests is related to prenatal exposure to male hormones (see the section titled Social Play, chap. 10). Exposure to these hormones also influences the social styles that contribute to segregation, as revealed by studies of children, juveniles, and adolescents affected by congenital adrenal hyperplasia (CAH) and by studies of the social correlates of amniotic testosterone levels (Knickmeyer, Baron-Cohen, Raggatt, & Taylor, 2005; Knickmeyer, Baron-Cohen, Raggatt, Taylor, & Hackett, 2006). The studies also suggest a role for gender schemas, specifically, explicit knowledge of one's sex, the categorization of other children as boys or girls, and the tendency to congregate with children in the same social category (Berenbaum & Snyder, 1995). The same-sex segregation occurs before many children consistently label themselves and other children as a boy or a girl, indicating that the explicit categorization of children as boys and girls is not a sufficient explanation for segregation but nonetheless likely exaggerates its expression.

Evidence comes from the finding that most girls affected by CAH prefer other girls—children in the same social category as themselves—as playmates, even though their play activities tend to be masculinized (Berenbaum & Hines, 1992). At the same time, many girls affected by CAH prefer boys as playmates, consistent with Maccoby's (1988) position: Children with masculinized play interests and styles (boy or girl) will congregate into play groups that differ from those formed by children with feminized interests. Of the girls affected by CAH in the Hines and Kaufman (1994) study, 44% indicated that their most frequent playmates were boys, compared with 11% of their unaffected peers and compared with more than 80% of the boys affected by CAH and unaffected boys. Girls affected by CAH thus show a pattern intermediate to that found in unaffected boys and unaffected girls. Some adult women (31% in this study) with CAH report dissatisfaction with their gender identity and report more frequent engagement in male-typical activities while growing up than do other women with CAH (Hines, Brook, & Conway, 2004). Whether this variability among girls and women with CAH is due to different levels or timing of prenatal exposure to androgens, to individual differences in the influence of gender schemas, or to explicit knowledge of gender roles remains to be determined.

The Cultural Divide

The net result of sex segregation is that boys and girls spend much of their childhood in distinct peer cultures (J. R. Harris, 1995; Maccoby, 1988). It is in the context of these cultures that differences in the social styles and preferences of girls and boys become larger and congeal (C. L. Martin & Fabes, 2001). I begin with an evolutionary frame that places boys' and girls' cultures in the context of male–male competition and male philopatry and situates women's relationships in these social groups. I then move to descriptions of peer relationships in the context of groups and in dyads.

Evolution of Social Styles

In keeping with the model described in chapter 9 of this volume (in the section titled Development of Functional Systems), Geary, Byrd-Craven, Hoard, Vigil, and Numtee, (2003) proposed that children's attentional, behavioral, and social systems are inherently biased such that they will recreate the forms of relationship (e.g., as in mother–infant attachment) and experience that help them navigate the developmental process and that prepare them for the survival and reproductive demands of our adult ancestors (Caporael, 1997). These reproductive demands are captured by parental investment (see chap. 6, this volume), intersexual choice (see chap. 7, this volume), and intrasexual competition (see chap. 8, this volume). To provide an anchor for an evolutionary analysis of children's social development, my colleagues and I decomposed male–male coalitional and one-on-one competition as expressed in traditional societies. These dynamics allowed us to make predictions about the nuances of these forms of competition and how they would be expressed during boys' social development, as contrasted with that of girls. The details are laid out in Table 11.1. Many of the features described in the table have been discussed previously, including men's coalition formation and dominance hierarchies (see the section titled Competition in Traditional Societies, chap. 8, this volume), muted expression of emotions (see the section titled Affective, chap. 9, this volume), and physical traits associated with male–male competition (see the sections titled Sexual Selection and Human Evolution, chap. 5, and Physical Development, chap. 10, this volume), among others.

My goal here is to outline a theoretical perspective that places the process of group formation and the nuances of dyadic relationships in the context of the reproductive demands described in previous chapters. Specifically, Geary et al. (2003) proposed that girls and women and boys and men have different styles of social relationship in the context of groups and dyads in part because of the cost–benefit trade-offs associated with the formation of large competitive coalitions as contrasted with emotionally supportive dyads. When it comes to coalitional competition, size matters: Across species, larger coalitions

TABLE 11.1
Social Dynamics and Supporting Mechanisms
of Boys' and Men's Social Behavior

Ultimate selection pressures	Proximate selected forms
Group formation and maintenance	

1. Male–male competition for
  a. Control of local ecology and resources contained therein
  b. Control of reproductive dynamics
	1. Coalition formation
	  a. Warfare over control of ecologies (e.g., land) and reproductive opportunities (e.g., raiding)
	  b. Hunting for individual survival and provisioning of kin and family and to enhance cultural success and through this, mating prospects
	  c. Protection of kin and family from other male coalitions
	2. Intragroup dynamics
	  a. Dominance hierarchy to facilitate coordinated activity
	  b. Low threshold to form emotional and social bonds with group members to facilitate group size
	  c. Role specialization and differentiation
	  d. Shared goals and attentional and behavioral focus on ecological problems (e.g., building a fort) or group competition

One-on-one dynamics	

1. Male–male competition for
  a. Dominance and influence within the coalition
	1. Focus on dominance indicators
	  a. Physical: size, musculature, skill
	  b. Social and cognitive: leadership and other competencies that facilitate group performance
	  c. Emotional: aggression, lack of fear
	2. Individual relationships
	  a. Easily formed with shared activities, especially cooperative competition
	  b. Formed more strongly among individuals of similar status (to facilitate greater reciprocity)
	  c. Dominance contests are constrained
	  d. Tolerance of interpersonal conflict to allow for dominance contests while maintaining coalition cohesion

Note. From "Evolution and Development of Boys' Social Behavior," by D. C. Geary, J. Byrd-Craven, M. K. Hoard, J. Vigil, and C. Numtee, 2003, *Developmental Review, 23,* p. 453. Copyright 2003 by Elsevier. Reprinted with permission.

have a competitive advantage over smaller ones (Wrangham, 1999). The coalitions are of course fluid because the gains of victory are distributed—often unequally according to dominance rank—among coalition members. The result is a balance between the benefits of having a large enough ingroup coalition to be competitive against the costs of having to share gains with ingroup members. As I noted in chapter 5 of this volume (in the section titled Coalitional Competition), male philopatry and kinship increase the likelihood that a bias toward coalition formation will evolve in men and will mitigate—because of the genetics of kinship—the costs of sharing reproductively valuable resources among coalitionary confederates (W. D. Hamilton, 1964).

The features of girls' and women's dyadic relationships are described next. My point for now is that the time commitment, emotional support, and social risks associated with these relationships are high and thus limit the number that can be maintained. The trade-offs are shown in Figure 11.1, where the x-axis represents the number of friendships and the y-axis the costs

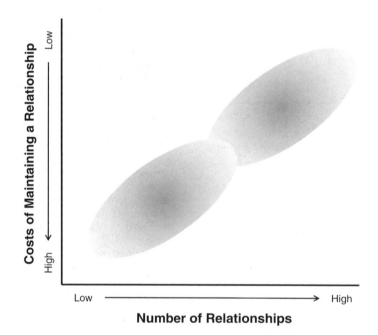

Number of Relationships

Figure 11.1. Cost–benefit trade-offs in same-sex relationships. Same-sex friendships entail cost–benefit trade-offs such that high levels of intimacy and emotional support limit the number of such relationships. The left oval represents a theoretical distribution of girls and women (darker areas equal more people); most have a few close friendships that involve high levels of intimacy, personal disclosure, and interpersonal support. The right oval represents a theoretical distribution of boys and men; most have a large number of friendships that can be maintained with lower levels of investment than is found in girls' and women's friendships.

of maintaining each of them: The many benefits of girls' and women's friendships are traded for fewer of them (Rose & Asher, 1999; Rose & Rudolph, 2006; S. E. Taylor et al., 2000). The trade-offs are represented by the lower left area of Figure 11.1. The left oval represents the theoretical distribution of girls and women (darker areas equal more people) and shows that most have a few close friendships that involve high levels of intimacy, personal disclosure, and interpersonal support. The right oval represents the theoretical distribution of boys and men, and shows a large number of friendships that can be maintained with lower levels of investment than is found in girls' and women's friendships. The distributions overlap such that some women have more male-typical forms of friendships and some men have more female-typical forms of friendships. The cost–benefit trade-offs associated with interpersonal intimacy do not mean that boys and men do not form dyadic friendships; many do (J. G. Parker & Asher, 1993; Rose & Rudolph, 2006). What the trade-offs mean is that the cost of maintaining the same style of interpersonal relationship as is common in girls' and women's friendships would place severe constraints on the ability of boys and men to form large, well-functioning, and competitive coalitions (Geary & Flinn, 2002).

In comparison with girls and women, boys and men are predicted to have a lower threshold for forming cooperative same-sex social relationships; their relationships are predicted to be more easily maintained (e.g., with less time-intensive disclosure) and evince a greater tolerance for interpersonal conflict. The results from studies of peer relationships support all of these predicted sex differences (Benenson & Christakos, 2003; Benenson et al., 2009; Eder & Hallinan, 1978; Rose & Rudolph, 2006; Whitesell & Harter, 1996). Tolerance for conflict is necessary to maintain the coalition and at the same time compete for within-coalition status. Dominance striving must, at the same time, be balanced against the cost of potentially losing the coalitional support of other boys and men, and thus social and psychological mechanisms that restrict dominance-related differentials between ingroup members are predicted to evolve, as cogently argued by Boehm (1993). In other words, the capacity to form high-quality bonds exists in both sexes, but the mechanisms that support the development and maintenance of these bonds and the social contexts, especially group-level competition, in which they are expressed differ (Geary & Flinn, 2002; S. E. Taylor et al., 2000).

On the assumption of an evolutionary history of male philopatry, I proposed that the pattern in girls' and women's friendships (described in the discussion that follows) is a reflection, in part, of social and emotional mechanisms that evolved to support relationships among nonkin (Geary, 2002b). These mechanisms are captured by Trivers's (1971) *reciprocal altruism*, specifically, psychological mechanisms (e.g., warmth, guilt) that promote long-term friendships based on a strict equality of the give-and-take in the relationship. I am not arguing that girls and women do not develop close relationships with their parents, children, and other kin, as they clearly do. What I am arguing is that male philopatry and the need to maintain relatively large male coalitions created different social ecologies, or cultures, for our male and female ancestors and different patterns of cost–benefit trade-offs in their same-sex relationships. If girls' and women's relationships are more heavily dependent on reciprocal altruism than those of boys and men, then the former will involve more monitoring of the give-and-take of the relationship and a lower threshold for dissolving the relationship when strict reciprocity is not achieved (Geary, 2002b; Trivers, 1971). This does not mean that boys and men are not reciprocal in many of their friendships but rather that girls and women are predicted to be less tolerant of nonreciprocal relationships and that the maintenance of any such relationships is predicted to be more strongly dependent on equalitarian reciprocity among girls and women than among boys and men (de Waal, 1993).

The principle benefit for girls and women is a core set of relationships that provide social, emotional, and interpersonal stability, particularly support during times of interpersonal conflict with other individuals, such as a spouse (S. E. Taylor et al., 2000). At the same time, the high investment of time, disclosure of personal information, and near constant availability for social support place severe constraints on the possible number of these relationships. The level of personal disclosure that is common in these relationships can also leave the girl or woman vulnerable to social manipulation and other forms of relational aggression by their friends, should the relationship dissolve (Bond, Carlin, Thomas, Rubin, & Patton, 2001; Murray-Close, Ostrov, & Crick, 2007). The risk of relational aggression and girls' and women's sensitivity to this form of aggression place further constraints on the number of such friendships; see the section titled Women's Aggression (chap. 8, this volume).

Peer Relationships

Peer relationships or friendships are a critical part of both girls' and boys' social development. The number and nature of these relationships differ considerably between the sexes and can be placed in the context of groups and dyads.

Forming Groups. In the section titled Rough-and-Tumble in chapter 10, I touched on the sex difference in coalition formation and engagement in between-groups competition. This brief overview did not provide insights into the process of group formation, contrast this process with that of girls, or detail the strategies used to gain social influence and dominance in the context of these groups. Generally, higher status juveniles and adolescents adaptively use a mix of physically coercive behaviors (e.g., bullying), prosocial behaviors, and relational aggression to gain control of desired resources and to gain social influence (Hawley, 1999; Hawley, Little, & Card, 2008). Girls and boys can use any or some combination of these social strategies but often put them into practice with different frequencies and in different ways.

The process of group formation and the social strategies used during the corresponding dynamics are nicely illustrated by Savin-Williams's (1987) ethological study of adolescents. Social relationships that developed during the course of a 5-week summer camp were documented for groups of 12- to 16-year-old boys and girls who were assigned to the same cabin. Within these same-sex groups, both boys and girls formed dominance hierarchies and frequently used ridicule to establish social dominance, such as name calling ("homo," "perverted groin") or gossiping; social displays that are easily observed by many people (e.g., anger) are common for both boys and girls in group settings (Benenson et al., 2002). For both sexes, the establishment of social dominance resulted in greater access to desired resources (e.g., larger desserts) and greater control over the activities of the group relative to lower status peers.

At the same time, there were important differences in boys' and girls' groups; specifically, with respect to the stability and integration (i.e., degree to which all group members became friends) of social hierarchies, the degree to which dominance displays were direct or indirect, the coercive use of physical strength and skills to establish dominance, and the benefits of achieving dominance (see also Hawley, 2003; J. G. Parker & Seal, 1996; Rose & Rudolph, 2006). In some groups, boys began their bid for dominance within hours of arriving in the cabin, whereas most of the girls were superficially polite for the first week and then began to exhibit dominance-related behaviors. Boys' dominance-related behaviors included ridicule, as noted previously, as well as directives ("Get my dessert for me."), counterdominance statements ("Eat me."), and physical assertion (e.g., play wrestling, pillow fights, sometimes actual physical fights). More than 90% of the time these behaviors were visible to all group members, were clearly directed at one other boy, and were attempts to establish dominance over this individual.

Girls used ridicule, recognition, and verbal directives to establish social dominance but used physical assertion only one third as frequently as did boys. In contrast to boys' blatant behaviors, more than one half of the girls' dominance behaviors were indirect. A girl might suggest to another girl that she "take her napkin and clean a piece of food off of her face," whereas under the same conditions a boy would simply call his less kempt peer a "pig" and then try to enlist other boys in a group-wide ridicule session; once "down" lower status boys would typically use this opportunity to attempt to establish individual dominance over their ridiculed peer. Girls, in contrast, often overtly recognized the leadership of another girl. Recognition was the second most common form of dominance-related behavior with girls but occurred infrequently with boys (23% vs. 6% of the dominance-related behaviors for girls and boys, respectively). In these cases, less dominant girls would approach their more dominant peers for advice, social support, grooming (e.g., having her hair combed), and so on.

As documented in other studies (J. G. Parker & Seal, 1996), Savin-Williams (1987) found that by the end of summer camp boys' groups showed greater stability and cohesiveness relative to the 1st week of camp. Most of the girls' groups, in contrast, were on the verge of splintering or had already split into "status cliques based on popularity, beauty, athletics, and sociability" (Savin-Williams, 1987, p. 124). Some of the dominant girls disengaged from the cabin group and spent most of their free time with one or two friends. Dominant boys never disengaged, and they spent most of their free time directing the group in competitive athletic activities against other groups. In short, dominant boys more actively and more successfully controlled group activities than did dominant girls, as illustrated by the following flag making exercise:

> Andy [the alpha male] immediately grabbed the flag cloth and penciled a design; he turned to Gar for advice, but none was given. Otto [low ranking] shouted several moments later, "I didn't say you could do it!" Ignoring this interference, Andy wrote the tribal name at the top of the flag. Meanwhile, Delvin and Otto were throwing sticks at each other with Gar watching and giggling. SW [the counselor] suggested that all should participate by drawing a design proposal on paper and the winning one, as determined by group vote, would be drawn on the flag. . . . Andy, who had not participated in the "contest," now drew a bicentennial sunset; it was readily accepted by the others. Without consultation, Andy drew his design as Gar and Delvin watched. Gar suggested an alteration but Andy told him "Stupid idea," and continued drawing. Otto, who had been playing in the fireplace, came over and screamed, "I didn't tell ya to draw that you Bastard Andy!" Andy's reply was almost predictable, "Tough shit, boy!" (Savin-Williams, 1987, p. 79)

Andy's mode of domination was more physically assertive and verbally aggressive than that of the dominant boys in other cabins. The result was the same, however. The dominant boys got first choice of what to eat (e.g., they almost always got the largest desserts), where to sleep, and what to do during free time. Across cabins, dominant girls also differed in their social styles. Although some girls were physically assertive and direct in their attempts to dominate other girls, the most influential girls (over the course of the 5 weeks) were much more subtle, as exemplified by Ann:

> [Her] style of authority [was] subtle and manipulative, she became the cabin's "mother." She instructed the others on cleanup jobs, corrected Opal's table manners ("Dottie, pass Opal a napkin so she can wipe the jelly off her face."), and woke up the group in the morning. . . . Ann became powerful in the cabin by first blocking Becky's [the beta female] dominance

initiations through refusing and shunning and then through ignoring her during the next three weeks. By the fifth week of camp Ann effectively controlled Becky by physical assertion, ridicule, and directive behaviors. (Savin-Williams, 1987, p. 92)

For both boys and girls, the achievement of social dominance was related to athletic ability, physical maturity, and leadership. Dominant girls were more socially popular than were many of the dominant boys—Andy was not well liked by his cabin mates, but they followed his directives—and physical attractiveness was more important for achieving social dominance within boys' groups than within girls' groups. In all, the boys described ideal leaders as instrumental,

> determined and tries hard at what he does, considerate in tolerating underlings, organizes activities, and knows what to do and makes the right decisions. The [girls'] groups emphasized expressive attributes: relates to my problems, friendly, outgoing, patient, considerate in respecting the needs and feelings of others. (Savin-Williams, 1987, p. 127)

Ethological and other studies indicate that these social patterns congeal as adolescents approach adulthood (Ahlgren & Johnson, 1979; Savin-Williams, 1987). Ahlgren and Johnson found that at about the time of puberty, girls' social motives become more cooperative and less competitive than those of their younger peers. Savin-Williams found that by the end of adolescence, there was a significant reduction in ridicule, "backbiting, bickering, and cattiness" (p. 150) in girls' interpersonal relationships, compared with early adolescence. By late adolescence, girls' dyadic relationships (described in the section that follows) also showed greater stability (i.e., less changing of *best friends*), more recognition, greater sensitivity to the needs and emotions of their friends, more helping behavior, and fewer attempts at establishing dominance than was found during early adolescence.

Boys' relationships changed as well. By late adolescence, boys' group-level games were characterized by greater focus and organization, with fewer negative criticisms and more encouragement directed toward ingroup peers than was found with younger boys (Savin-Williams, 1987). During their dominance-related encounters, older boys used physical assertion less frequently and recognition more frequently than their younger peers. Under some conditions, however, male dominance encounters could become physically aggressive (Berger, 2007) and even deadly by late adolescence (M. Wilson & Daly, 1985).

Dyads. Whereas the typical boy is engaged in some form of activity that involves groups of his friends, the typical girl is talking with one of her friends (Eder & Hallinan, 1978; Lever, 1978; Rose & Rudolph, 2006). Boys of course have one-on-one friendships, but they spend less of their social time with peers in exclusive dyadic encounters than do girls. In fact, boys' dyadic relationships tend to be embedded in the network of friends described previously. Over time, all of the boys in the ingroup are likely to become friends with one another to varying degrees, but girls' friendships are more likely to be exclusive (Eder & Hallinan, 1978). J. G. Parker and Seal's (1996) study of peer relationships during a 4-week summer camp illustrated the process of embedding dyadic friendships into larger social networks; the outcome is termed *network density*. During the 1st week of camp, there were no sex differences in network density. However, 3 to 4 weeks later, nearly 9 out of 10 boys were embedded in a more cohesive social network—all network members knew and liked each other—than was the average girl.

There are also important qualitative differences in the nature of girls' and boys' dyadic friendships. As they move into the juvenile years and beyond, girls' relationships become more exclusively focused on one or two best friends. In comparison with boys' friendships, girls' friendships are characterized by higher levels of emotional support and more frequent intimate exchanges (e.g., talking about their problems) and are a more central source of help and guidance in solving social and other problems (Maccoby, 1990; J. G. Parker & Asher, 1993; Rose & Asher, 1999; Savin-Williams, 1987). Girls are more interpersonally engaged in the relationship, and as a result they know more about their best friend than do boys (Markovits, Benenson, & Dolenszky, 2001). During discussions, girls are more sensitive to the social and emotional cues of their partner (Buck, Savin, Miller, & Caul, 1972) and work harder to minimize perceived inequalities in the give-and-take of the relationship and in outcomes (e.g., having a boyfriend) that are important to both girls (Ahlgren & Johnson, 1979; Winstead, 1986).

Conflicts of interest are common among friends of both sexes, but girls invest more in resolving these conflicts and attempt to do so through accommodation, compromise, and other socially constructive means; boys tend to use more direct and confrontational strategies (J. G. Parker & Asher, 1993; Rose & Asher, 1999). Despite the more subtle approach to managing conflicts, girls are more sensitive to personal slights on the part of their best friend and respond with more initial and lingering negative affect (e.g., sadness, anger) than do boys (Whitesell & Harter, 1996). As predicted, their friendships are also more fragile; they are much more likely to permanently dissolve as a result of conflict, betrayal, or other stressors on the relationship (Benenson & Christakos, 2003; Lever, 1978).

Social Motivations and Personality

On top of the sex differences in the tendency to embed same-sex relationships within larger groups and in the dynamics of dyadic friendships, there are broader sex differences in social motives, behaviors, and personality; these differences can manifest in many different types of relationships, not just those with same-sex peers. Specifically, boys' and men's concerns about social dominance and their relative hierarchical position and girls' and women's social agreeableness and tendency to nurture is found across modern and traditional societies (e.g., Del Giudice, 2009a; Feingold, 1994; Whiting & Edwards, 1988). In their study of the social development of children in Liberia, Kenya, India, Mexico, the Philippines, Japan, and the United States (with less extensive observations in Peru and Guatemala), Whiting and Edwards concluded,

> Of the five major categories of interpersonal behavior explored in [these studies]—nurturance, dependency, prosocial dominance, egoistic dominance, and sociability—two emerge as associated with sex differences. Across the three older age groups (knee, yard, and school-age children) girls on average are more nurturant than boys in all dyad types . . . while boys are more egoistically dominant than girls. (p. 270)

These findings are consistent with Eagly's (1987) description of men and women as being agentic and communal, respectively, and are consistent with many other studies of adolescents and adults. Feingold (1994) examined sex differences on personality tests normed in the United States; analyses of test norms are especially informative because they are based on large (105,742 people in this study) and typically nationally representative samples. He found moderate to large sex differences for "tender-mindedness" (i.e., nurturance and empathy), favoring women, and assertiveness (e.g., dominance-related activities), favoring men; about 6 out of 7 women scored higher than the average man on measures of tender mindedness, and about 7 out of 10 men scored higher than the average woman on measures of assertiveness. The magnitude of these differences did not vary much for samples assessed from the 1940s to the 1990s and varied little across groups of adolescents and younger and older adults (see also L. B. Lueptow, Garovich-Szabo, & M. B. Lueptow, 2001). Multiple (i.e., more than one) studies of sex differences in personality were also available for adults from Canada, Finland, Germany, and Poland and confirmed the pattern found in the United States, but the magnitude of the differences varied across cultures. Across two large-scale studies that spanned 57 nations and included 40,668 individuals, these differences were found to be the largest in cultures with the fewest social restrictions on personal expression (Costa, Terracciano, & McCrae, 2001; Schmitt, Realo, Voracek, & Allik, 2008).

Ahlgren and Johnson (1979) found a similar pattern in the social motives of 2nd to 12th graders. The social motives of these juveniles and adolescents were captured by two salient themes, cooperation (e.g., "I like to learn by working with other students") and competition (e.g., "I like to do better work than my friends"). At all grade levels, girls endorsed cooperative social behaviors more frequently did than boys, whereas boys endorsed competitive social behaviors more frequently than did girls. A study of 250 fourteen-year-olds revealed the same pattern: Boys' social goals were relatively more focused on the achievement of dominance and leadership, whereas girls' social goals were relatively more focused on the establishment of intimate and nurturing relationships (Jarvinen & Nicholls, 1996). The largest sex differences were for the establishment of intimacy; more than 4 out of 5 girls rated this goal as being more important than the average boy. For the establishment of dominance, 3 out of 4 boys rated this goal as being more important than the average girl.

Knight and Chao (1989) found the same pattern in the rules that 3- to 12-year-olds use to distribute a valuable resource amongst themselves and their social group (money in this case). These studies were designed to determine whether the children had preferences for *equality* (minimizing differences between oneself and others), *group enhancement* (enhancing the overall resources of the group, regardless of how this effects one's own resources), *superiority* (trying to maximize one's resource relative to other group members), or *individualism* (enhancing one's resources independent of peer resources). Self-interest was evident in the resource distributions of younger boys and girls, as about one half of them showed an individualism preference. At the same time, 1 out of 4 girls but not one of the boys showed an equality preference, whereas 1 out of 5 boys but only 1 out of 20 girls showed a superiority preference. By 6 years of age, the majority of boys showed a superiority preference, whereas the girls were largely split between the individualism and equality preferences. For 9- to 12-year-olds, 3 out of 4 boys showed a superiority preference compared with 1 out of 5 girls. The remaining girls were split evenly (40% each) between the individualism and equality preferences; only 7% of the boys showed an equality preference.

Parallel sex differences are often, but not always, found in the moral judgments of boys and girls and men and women. Gilligan (1982) found that girls and women consistently endorse a moral ethos that espouses equality in social relationships and an avoidance of the harm of others. Her findings were confirmed by Graham, Haidt, and Nosek's (2009) research on the components of people's moral intuitions, that is, the rules and expectations for social living. The components include avoidance of harm, fairness and equity in the treatment of and resources made available to group members, loyalty to the ingroup, respect for authority, and the purity and sanctity of cultural symbols and rituals (Haidt, 2007). Women endorsed the harm avoidance, fairness and equity, and purity components of morality more strongly than did men; surprisingly, there were no sex differences for ingroup loyalty or respect for authority. There are other sex differences in social motives and personality, specifically, in terms of risk taking and emotional expressiveness, but I have already discussed these (see the sections titled Risk Taking, chap. 8, and Affective, chap. 9, this volume).

SOCIAL DEVELOPMENT AND EVOLUTION

In this section, I integrate the just-described sex differences into the framework laid out in the section titled Evolution of Social Styles earlier in this chapter and the life history approach discussed in the section titled Development of Functional Systems in chapter 9. The reader may recall that, in theory, children's self-generated niche seeking and the nature of their peer relationships provide the experiences needed to elaborate and adapt the individual- and group-level folk psychological cognitive modules and corresponding motivational and affective components to their community's social structure and customs (see the section titled Folk Domains, chap. 9). Peer relationships within girls' and boys' cultures also allow them to practice and refine the specific social and other skills they will use later in the contexts of adult reproductive and broader social relationships. During development, among other things, they learn which social strategies work well for them and which do not (e.g., social persuasion vs. attempts to physically dominate; K. MacDonald, 1996).

As I reviewed in chapter 10 (in the section titled Rough-and-Tumble), boys' play fighting is readily understood in terms of an evolutionary history of one-on-one male–male competition. The process of coalition formation during boys' social development and the embedding of their friendships into the wider ingroup network are readily understood in terms of an evolutionary history of male philopatry and coalitional competition, as predicted in the section titled Evolution of Social Styles earlier in this chapter (see also Geary et al., 2003) and as described in chapters 5 (in the section titled Evolutionary Models) and 8 (in the section titled Philopatry) of this volume. In this view, the social culture that emerges within boys' groups provides a context for refining individual-level dominance-related competencies and an opportunity to develop the competencies necessary to form and maintain cohesive and effective large-scale coalitions. The speed and ease with which boys form these ingroups are particularly telling, as are the social support and role differentiation that emerge as boys' groups congeal into an integrated coalition (J. G. Parker & Seal, 1996; Savin-Williams, 1987). In cultures with male philopatry, the boys and adolescents who compose these play groups become the leaders and warriors of their generation. By adulthood, they will have spent 10 to 15 years engaging each other in play fighting and coalitional games, and through this, they will have had ample opportunity to prepare for the rigors of male–male competition described in chapter 8 of this volume (in the section titled Competition in Traditional Societies).

As found in other species with male philopatry, girls and women do not form coalitions to compete against groups of other girls and women—bonobo females sometimes form coalitions but not for the purpose of intergroup aggression (de Waal & Lanting, 1997)—nor are they as concerned as boys and men about establishing social dominance. This does not mean girls and women are not concerned about their relative status; they are and should be. Status results in more social influence and greater access to important resources and through these status often has survival and reproductive consequences (e.g., the section titled Benefits to Children, chap. 6, this volume). Relational and sometimes physical aggression over romantic partners, as predicted for a species with paternal investment, is common and clearly illustrates that girls and women can be very competitive with one another (see the section titled Women's Aggression, chap. 8, this volume). In work or other settings in which girls and women are in frequent contact, they develop subtle dominance relationships (Björkqvist, Osterman, & Lagerspetz, 1994; A. Campbell, 2002). The reader may recall, however, that women's dominance struggles are predicted to remain relatively subtle in comparison with those of men because the reproductive trade-offs (i.e., the reproductive skew) are severalfold higher for men than for women in many traditional societies and presumably during our ancestral history (see the section titled Competition in Traditional Societies, chap. 8, this volume).

With the exception of research on relational aggression, much of the peer relationship literature has focused on the positive characteristics and benefits of girls' and women's relationships with their close friends. The depictions of these relationships are correct but leave unaddressed the deeper questions of why girls and women form these intense friendships and why they differ from the friendships of boys and men. The question of why girls and women are more superficially friendly and socially outgoing in many social contexts also remains to be answered. My proposal is that these aspects of girls' and women's relationships and social behaviors are a reflection of the social ecology that would emerge in the context of an evolutionary history of male philopatry. Again, this does not mean our female ancestors always immigrated into the group of their mate—this is not always the case in traditional societies—but rather this was the most common (not exclusive) reproductive pattern. In traditional societies, this pattern is common during periods of intergroup hostilities when cohesive male coalitions are most needed. If these circumstances are similar to those of ancestors, our female ancestors likely found themselves in a social world in which they were more isolated from close kin than their husbands.

I suggest that the greater attentiveness of girls and women to social cues (e.g., facial expressions), their more frequent and positive social signaling (e.g., smiling), their skill at strategically using emotional cues (see the section titled Affective, chap. 9, this volume), and their general motivation to develop a few intimate social relationships as an end in itself rather than as a means to compete as with boys and men are adaptations to the social conditions described in the preceding paragraph (Bjorklund & Kipp, 1996; Freedman, 1974). I elaborate on some of these sex differences in chapter 12 of this volume (in the section titled Individual), but as an example, about 7 out of 10 women smile more frequently in noncompetitive social situations than does the average man and direct these smiles more frequently to other women than to men (J. A. Hall, 1984). S. E. Taylor et al. (2000) provide a *tend-and-befriend* explanation for these and related social sex differences:

> Specifically, we propose that women's responses to stress are characterized by patterns that involve caring for offspring under stressful circumstances, joining social groups to reduce vulnerability, and contributing to the development of social groupings, especially those involving female networks, for the exchange of resources and responsibilities. We maintain that aspects of these responses, both maternal and affiliative, may have built on the biobehavioral attachment–caregiving system. (pp. 421–422)

I agree that women's relationships are a critical source of support that aids in their ability to care for children—they are more heavily dependent on these relationships for social and emotional support than are men (Strough, Berg, & Sansone, 1996)—and that some aspects of girls' and women's social motives and behaviors are consistent with engagement of the attachment–caregiving system. Whiting and Edwards's (1988) finding that girls are more socially nurturing than are boys is consistent with this hypothesis. However, girls' friendships develop with same-age peers and not younger children, as might be expected if these friendships are engaging parenting and parent–child attachment systems. Girls' social motives and behaviors with their friends differ from their play parenting described in chapter 10 of this volume (in the section titled Play Parenting), and women's friendships differ from their relationships with their children. These differences suggest girls' and women's friendships are not simply engaging the attachment–caregiving system—this does not preclude engagement of some underlying neurobiological components of this system—but some other mechanisms must be involved.

Geary and Flinn (2002) and Geary (2002b) suggested these other mechanisms are Trivers's (1971) social and emotional processes that underlie reciprocal altruism, that is, long-term relationships with nonkin. We suggested that these processes became more elaborated in the context of women's than men's friendships because of the different social ecologies that result from male philopatry. If we approach the issue from another direction, being embedded in a network of male kin would more or less automatically provide males with a system of social support that does not need to be repeatedly confirmed, but no such extensive kin-based support system would be available for immigrant females. In this situation, intimate relationships would provide an important resource in a potentially hostile social environment, but relationships would be based more on reciprocal altruism than on kin-based attachment systems. Several core aspects of girls' and women's friendships are consistent with reciprocal altruism: In comparison with those of boys and men, girls' and women's friendships are more fragile and more heavily dependent on equality, as described in the section titled Dyads earlier in this chapter. This is not the whole story, no doubt. Girls' and women's endorsement of an ethos of harm avoidance, for instance, follows from the sex difference in the cost–benefit trade-offs associated with the escalation of intrasexual competition; men have more to gain and women more to lose.

PARENTING

There is no question that children's survival and development are critically dependent on the care provided by their parents and kin (see the section titled Benefits to Children, chap. 6). My concern is about more subtle effects of parenting on children's emerging social and cognitive competencies. Similarities between parental characteristics and those of their children are often assumed to be due to parental socialization but might well result from the overlapping genes between parents and children, socialization, or differences in the ways in which children with different genes react to similar rearing environments (Belsky, 2005; Scarr, 1992). Indeed, behavioral genetic and other studies suggest that parental influences on individual differences in children's personality, social behavior, and cognition are much weaker than many people believe or would like to believe (J. R. Harris, 1995; Plomin, Fulker, Corley, & DeFries, 1997; Rowe, 1994).

As a complement to children's niche seeking described in chapter 9 (in the section titled Development of Functional Systems), most parents provide an evolutionarily expected rearing environment (e.g., exposure to language, synchronized parent–child interactions) that provides the experiences that begin to flesh out the skeletal competencies of folk modules (Kuhl et al., 1997; K. MacDonald, 1993). In cultures with sufficient resources, experiences that go above and beyond the evolutionarily expected ones do not appear to have a strong, long-lasting influence on the developing child (Scarr, 1992). Of course, behaviors outside of the range that naturally occurs in parent–child relationships, such as neglect, can adversely affect children's development (Scarr, 1992), just as neglectful parenting can adversely affect offspring development in other primates (Goodall, 1986). Most parents, however, provide a level of investment that allows for normal development, and variations in parental behaviors within this normal range do not appear to be systematically related to variations in most child outcomes. Regardless, I provide an overview of some of the explanations of how parents and other socializing agents can create or exaggerate developmental sex differences.

Parental Treatment of Boys and Girls

Lytton and Romney (1991) provided an exceptionally comprehensive assessment involving 172 studies and 27,836 participants of the parental treatment of boys and girls. In this meta-analysis, parental treatment was assessed across eight broad socialization areas, including amount of interaction, achievement encouragement, warmth and nurturance, encouragement of dependency, restrictiveness, disciplinary strictness, encouragement of sex-typed activities, and clarity of communication directed toward the child.

For studies conducted in North America, there were very few differences in the ways in which parents treated girls and boys, as assessed by observation, parental report, and child report. One exception was for encouragement of sex-typed activities, although the difference was small; for about two out of three boys, parents encouraged sex-typed activities more frequently than they did with the average girl. This result appeared largely to reflect an active discouragement of boys, especially by fathers, from playing with girls' toys, such as dolls; doll play in boys often prompts concerns of homosexuality (Maccoby & Jacklin, 1974). Studies conducted in Western nations outside of North America indicated that boys received more physical discipline than girls, but again the difference was small. Another meta-analysis revealed mothers talked more and provided more encouraging speech to their daughters than to their sons (Leaper, Anderson, & Sanders, 1998), but this may be related to the greater social responsiveness of daughters than sons and to more mutual concern between mothers and daughters than between mothers and sons (R. Butler & Shalit-Naggar, 2008).

Selective Imitation

It is not likely that the sex differences described in this chapter and in chapter 10 are due simply to children's selective imitation of the same-sex parent or other same-sex people. On the basis of a review of 23 studies of children's imitative behavior, Maccoby and Jacklin (1974) tentatively concluded "that early sex typing is not a function of a child's having selectively observed, and selectively learned, the behavior of same-sex, rather than opposite-sex, models" (p. 299). Barkley, Ullman, Otto, and Brecht (1977) reached the same conclusion after reviewing 81 relevant studies. In an empirical study of their own, they found that girls tended to imitate traditionally feminine behavior—such as playing house—whether these behaviors were enacted by a male or female model and boys tended to imitate traditionally masculine behavior—such as play fighting—regardless of the sex of the model. It is not likely that these findings result from children only imitating behavior that is considered to be sex appropriate, at least not in any straightforward way.

As I discussed previously (see the section titled Gender Schema, chap. 10, this volume), children's explicit knowledge of gender roles is only weakly related to the actual behavioral differences that are observed in boys and girls (Serbin et al., 1993; P. J. Turner & Gervai, 1995). This does not preclude more subtle influences of social learning and knowledge of gender roles on the expression of developmental sex differences (Bussey & Bandura, 1999; C. L. Martin, Ruble, & Szkrybalo, 2002). As I described in the section titled Gender Schema in chapter 10 of this volume, this knowledge may be one sociocultural mechanism that provides information to children on how to be successful in their particular culture. Slaby and Frey (1975), for instance, found that young boys who label themselves as *boys* and who understand that they will someday be *men* do attend to men more frequently than do boys who do not yet understand that one's biological sex is constant through time. Another contributing factor to selective imitation is differences in what captures the attention of girls and boys. Also, as I discussed in the section titled Infancy in chapter 10 of this volume, there is evidence that girls and boys selectively attend to (e.g., people vs. objects) and find more attractive and engaging behaviors that are traditionally defined as sex typed. Endicott (1992) illustrated the selective attention of boys with her description of the play of Batek children in Malaysia. The Batek are a relatively egalitarian hunter–gatherer society in which "no gender distinctions are made in the terms for children, siblings, cousins, and grandchildren" (Endicott, 1992, p. 282):

> Playgroup activities range from pretending to move camp to imitating monkeys to play-practicing economic skills such as blowpipe-hunting, digging tubers, collecting rattan, and fishing. Fathers sometimes intervene in the activities of children to offer advice about how to perform these skills. For example, when several children were pretending that they were harvesting honey by smoking bees out of a hive high in a tree in the middle of camp, a father who often participated in honey collecting showed the children how to properly construct rattan ladders to use for climbing up to the hive. It was the older boys, in the 10- to 12-year-old range, *who paid closest attention to this informal lesson* [italics added]. (p. 288)

Parenting Across Cultures

Although studies conducted in Western nations suggest that parental behavior does not strongly influence individual differences in children's personality and social behavior, cross-cultural comparisons do find a relation between parenting and child outcomes (Barry, Josephson, Lauer, & Marshall,

1976; B. S. Low, 1989; K. MacDonald, 1992). These seemingly contradictory findings are due, in part, to differences in how the relation between parenting and child outcomes is measured. For within-culture studies, such as those reviewed by Lytton and Romney (1991), individual differences in children's behavior are related to individual differences in parenting style, whereas cross-cultural studies involve comparisons of average differences across groups of people from different societies. On top of this methodological difference, within- and cross-culture studies may yield different results because the range of parenting behaviors is larger when assessed across than within cultures (MacDonald, 1992).

To illustrate, in societies characterized by high levels of intergroup aggression, parenting practices for both boys and girls tend to be harsher—including more physical discipline, less responsiveness to the child's emotional state and so on—than parenting practices found in more peaceful societies (Barry et al., 1976; K. MacDonald, 1993). One apparent result is a cross-cultural difference in the average level of aggression found in societies with relatively harsh as opposed to relatively warm parenting (C. R. Ember & Ember, 1994; K. MacDonald, 1992). At the same time, the pattern of sex differences remains within cultures, even when girls or women from one culture might be described as more aggressive, on average, than boys and men from another culture. The cross-cultural patterns suggest that parenting can accentuate or attenuate the expression of certain social behaviors (e.g., frequency of physical aggression), but these effects largely result in cross-cultural differences in the behavior of same-sex children and not the creation of sex-differences in one culture but not another.

B. S. Low (1989) analyzed child-rearing practices across 93 cultures as they related to social structure (i.e., stratified vs. nonstratified societies and group size) and marriage system (i.e., polygynous vs. monogamous). In *nonstratified* polygynous societies, societies in which men can improve their social status and thus increase the number of women they can marry (see the section titled Competition in Traditional Societies, chap. 8, this volume), the socialization of boys focuses on fortitude, aggression, and industriousness, traits that likely influence cultural and thus reproductive success in adulthood. For these nonstratified societies, there was a very strong linear relation between the socialization of competitiveness in boys and the maximum number of wives allowed within the society. The more women a man can marry, the more competitiveness was emphasized in parental socialization of sons.

In *stratified* societies, in which men cannot improve their social status, boys are not strongly socialized to exhibit aggression and fortitude, although industriousness is still important. For girls, there was a relation between the amount of economic and political power held by women in the society and socialization practices. In societies in which women could inherit property and hold political office, girls were socialized to be less obedient, more aggressive, and more achievement oriented in comparison with girls who lived in societies in which men had more or less complete control over economic and political resources. B. S. Low (1989) concluded that "there is thus some evidence that patterns of child training across cultures vary in ways predictable from evolutionary theory, differing in specifiable ways between the sexes, and varying with group size, marriage system, and stratification" (p. 318); these results are consistent with cross-cultural variation in the trade-offs women and men make in their mate choices (e.g., see the section titled Preferred Choices, chap. 7, this volume).

CONCLUSION

As I discussed in chapter 10, the length of the development period has as much as doubled during the course of hominid evolution (Dean et al., 2001). Also, as noted in chapter 4 of this volume (in the section titled Life History), changes in the pattern of development can result from changes in social (e.g., intrasexual competitors), ecological (e.g., food availability), and other demands (e.g., risk from predators) that influence survival during each developmental period and later reproductive prospects. The mechanisms that resulted in the change in the human developmental period are not yet fully understood, but much of this change likely resulted from the increasing complexity of social dynamics (R. D. Alexander, 1989). My assumption is that many of the social sex differences described in this chapter stem from changes in human life history development that evolved to allow boys and girls to learn the nuances of their local culture and to prepare for the forms of reproductive demands described in chapters 6 (i.e., parenting investment), 7 (i.e., intersexual choice), and 8 (i.e., intrasexual competition) of this volume.

Sex differences in interests, play patterns, and styles of social influence result in the segregation of boys and girls into different cultures (Maccoby, 1988, 1998), especially during the juvenile years but continuing into adolescence. The culture that girls and boys create for themselves amplifies and congeals sex differences that begin to emerge by 3 years of age. The sex differences in rough-and-tumble play, the process of friendship formation among boys, and the embedding of these dyadic relationships into a larger ingroup flow easily with an evolutionary history of coalitionary male–male competition and the formation of dominance hierarchies within the coalition. From a life history perspective, these features of boys' play and social behavior involve a preparation for later within-group dominance striving and coalition formation for intergroup aggression. Through a combination of parenting practices, such as degree of physical discipline, the selective imitation of competitive activities, and actual experiences within same-sex peer groups, boys learn how to best achieve within-group social dominance and congeal into a role-differentiated and effective coalition by early adulthood.

Girls' peer relationships are a critical part of their social development and form the core of their social support from the juvenile years onward (Strough et al., 1996). Girls' friendships differ in many ways from boys' friendships. Girls spend more of their peer time in dyadic interactions with their best friend; they disclose more about themselves and rely more on this friend for help solving social and other problems (J. G. Parker & Asher, 1993; Rose & Asher, 1999). These relationships are much more socially demanding and time intensive than those of boys, and thus girls can only maintain one or two of them at a time (J. G. Parker & Seal, 1996). Ironically, despite high levels of intimacy, personal disclosure, and support from their friends, girls' relationships are more fragile than are boys' and are more strongly dependent on equality in the give-and-take of the relationship and equality of outcomes that are important to them (Benenson & Christakos, 2003; Rose & Rudolph, 2006; Whitesell & Harter, 1996). My proposal is that these relationship dynamics are, in part, a reflection of an evolutionary history of male philopatry and our female ancestors emigrating to the group of their mate. In this circumstance, distantly related or unrelated women are a potential source of social support, but the establishment of such relationships is predicted to be based more strongly on reciprocal altruism (Trivers, 1971) than on kin-based systems (cf. S. E. Taylor et al. 2000).

12

SEX DIFFERENCES IN FOLK PSYCHOLOGY

Throughout the 20th century and continuing into the 21st, the issue of human sex differences in the brain and in cognition has captured the attention of the general public and that of many scientists (Baron-Cohen, 2003; Blum, 1997; L. Ellis et al., 2008; D. F. Halpern, 2000; Kimura, 1999). There is no longer any question whether men and women differ in patterns of cognitive abilities or in aspects of brain organization; today scientists are focused on the origin, magnitude, and practical importance of these differences. In this chapter and in chapter 13, I turn my attention to these differences and do so using the taxonomy of folk domains introduced in chapter 9 (in the section titled Folk Domains). In chapters 12 and 13, I focus on the origin of sex differences in the brain and cognition from the clarifying light of sexual selection. As I reviewed in the section titled Sex Hormones, Brain, and Cognition in chapter 4, there are many examples of sex differences in reproductive behaviors, cognitions, and brain organization that are influenced by hormonal mechanisms and that can be placed within the broader framework of sexual selection. I assume humans are no different and begin with a brief introduction to sex differences in brain size and organization. From there I move to consideration of sex differences in folk psychology and then cover differences in folk biology and folk physics in chapter 13.

BRAIN SIZE AND ORGANIZATION

Sexual selection can result in sex differences in brain size, organization, and functioning in the same way the corresponding processes of intrasexual competition and intersexual choice have resulted in the evolution of sex differences in physical size, coloration patterns, and behavioral biases in the many species I discussed in chapters 3, 4, and 5. The best documented examples are for the sexually dimorphic nuclei that underlie male bird song, the brain systems that allow males to sing in courtship of females and to issue territorial warnings to other males (Ball & Hulse, 1998; Nottebohm, 1970, 2005). As I described in chapter 5 of this volume (in the section titled Brain Size), only a general relation between brain size and sexual selection has been established for primates, and this suggests that intense male–male competition is associated with a larger neocortex for males (Pawlowski, Lowen, & Dunbar, 1998; Sawaguchi, 1997). However, the relation between the nuances of the selection pressures facing male and female primates and sex differences in the patterns of brain size and organization remain to be determined (Falk, 2001; Lindenfors, Nunn, & Baron, 2007). In the sections that follow, I review general findings on human sex differences in brain size, organization, and functioning but do not discuss any potential relations to sexual selection until I discuss specific folk psychological sex differences in later sections.

Relative Size and Organization

The reduction in the sex difference in physical size since the australopithecines and the corresponding reduction in the variability across hominid brain volumes make it very likely that the average brain size of our male and female ancestors has converged since the emergence of *Homo* (see the section titled Sexual Dimorphisms, chap. 5). Sex differences persist, nevertheless: In a detailed analysis of sex differences in brain volume, neuron numbers, and neuronal density, Pakkenberg and Gundersen (1997) found that in comparison with women's brains, men's brains, on average, are 13% heavier, occupy 15% more volume, and contain 16% more neurons, among other differences. In a study of young adults, C. M. Leonard et al. (2008) found that the overall brain size of more than 9 out of 10 men was larger than that of the average woman. These sex differences are consistent across the four major lobes of the neocortex—frontal, temporal, parietal, and occipital (see Figure 12.1)—but are reduced to about a 10% male advantage once the sex difference in body size is controlled (Falk, Froese, Sade, & Dudek, 1999; Herndon, Tigges, Anderson, Klumpp, & McClure, 1999; Rushton & Ankney, 1996, 2009). The 10% male advantage in brain size is found in newborns and continues into childhood, juvenility, and adolescence; there are, however, sex differences in

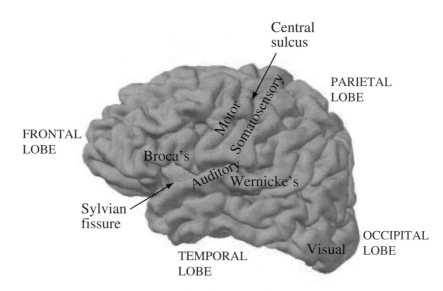

Figure 12.1. Outer surface of the left hemisphere of the human neocortex. From *Words and Rules: The Ingredients of Language* (p. 244), by S. Pinker, 1999, New York: Basic Books. Copyright 1999 by Steven Pinker. Reprinted with permission.

the pace with which some brain regions develop (Giedd et al., 1999; Gilmore et al., 2007).

There are also more subtle differences, especially when the size of one particular brain region is taken as a percentage of total brain volume (L. Cahill, 2006; Goldstein et al., 2001; R. C. Gur, Gunning-Dixon, Bilker, & Gur, 2002; R. C. Gur et al., 1999; Sowell et al., 2006). Overall, men have more gray matter (neuronal cell bodies and dendrites that collect information from other cells) and white matter (neuronal axons that transmit information to other cells) than women. Once brain size is adjusted, women are often but not always found to have proportionally more gray matter than men and men to have proportionally more white matter than women (R. C. Gur et al., 1999). There are also sex differences in neocortical thickness and in the distribution of gray matter and white mater throughout the neocortex (e.g., Goldstein et al., 2001; Good et al., 2001). Sowell et al., for instance, found that men have especially large areas in both hemispheres at the tip of Area 10 (see Figure 12.2) and in Areas 17 and 18, whereas women—even without adjustment for overall brain size—have thicker cortices in parts of the temporal and parietal lobes of the right hemisphere.

The areas of enhanced thickness in women are associated with language skills and correspond to the Wernicke's label in Figure 12.1 and to areas below this and slightly to the right as well as parts of Areas 20, 21, 22, and 37 in Figure 12.2. Many other studies, but not all of them, have also

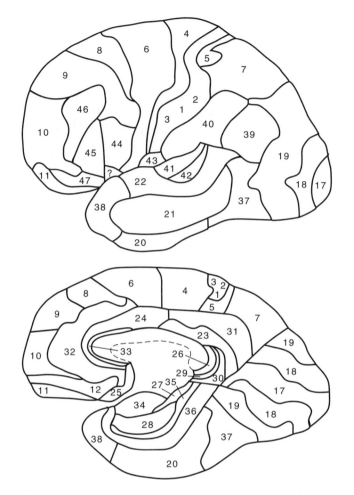

Figure 12.2. Maps of Brodmann's (1909) areas of the human neocortex. The top section is a lateral (outer) view of the cortex, whereas the bottom section is a medial (center, between the two hemispheres) view. Many of these areas can be subdivided into specialized subregions that may process different forms of information. Very generally, Areas 1, 2, 3, 5, 31, 39, 40, and 43 are part of the parietal cortex and support a variety of functions including sense of body position, attention, and spatial competencies; Areas 17, 18, and 19 are part of the occipital cortex and support simple and complex visual perception; Areas 22, 41, 42, and subregions of Areas 40 and 38 are part of the temporal cortex and support simple and complex auditory and speech perception; Areas 20, 21, 26–28, 34–37, and 52 are also part of the temporal lobe but support a variety of complex visual competencies; Areas 4, 6, and 8 are involved in complex motor movements and are part of the frontal cortex; Area 44 and subregions of Area 45 are involved in speech generation and are part of the frontal cortex; Areas 9, 10, 11, 25, 46, 47, and subregions of 45 are part of the prefrontal cortex and support behavioral control, executive functions, and many complex social competencies; Areas 23, 24, 30, (parts of 31), 32, and 33 are part of the cingulate and support attentional and emotional functions. Illustration by Mark Dubin. Printed with permission.

found proportionally larger language-related areas in women than in men (Harasty, Double, Halliday, Krill, & McRitchie, 1997; C. M. Leonard et al., 2008). In the first of these studies, Witelson, Glezer, and Kigar (1995) conducted a detailed analysis of the neuronal architecture of the planum temporale, which is a core region for the processing of language sounds; the region is buried within the Sylvian fissure just above the Wernicke's label in Figure 12.1. They found that women have a higher density of neurons in the input layers of this region, but there was no sex difference for the output layers. It cannot be known with certainty from this study, but the sex difference in the input layers might provide women with an advantage in discriminating nuances in language sounds. In any case, there is also evidence for sex differences in the ways in which different brain regions are interconnected (R. C. Gur et al., 2002; Kilpatrick, Zald, Pardo, & Cahill, 2006; Kimura, 1987; McGlone, 1980).

One of the more controversial findings concerns the corpus callosum, the bundle of axons that allows communication across the left and right hemispheres. De Lacoste-Utamsing and Holloway (1982) reported that the back portion of the callosum was shaped differently in men and women and that relative to overall brain weight was larger in women. They speculated "that the female brain is less well lateralized—that is, manifests less hemispheric specialization—than the male brain for visuospatial functions" (p. 216). This particular finding, and the implication that some cognitive sex differences have a neural basis, has been debated, refuted, and revived ever since (e.g., Bishop & Wahlsten, 1997). With a large sample of women and men and using sensitive neuroimaging techniques, Dubb, Gur, Avants, and Gee (2003) confirmed de Lacoste-Utamsing and Holloway's original finding and reported that men have a proportionally larger anterior callosum. More subtle differences have been found in other brain imaging studies (e.g., Shin et al., 2005), but the functional significance remains to be determined.

The evolutionary significance of these and other neural sex differences also remains to be determined and must be approached with caution. As an example, the sex difference in the proportion of gray matter and white matter might be a reflection of the overall difference in the average size of women's and men's brains and not evolved traits per se. Larger brains tend to have proportionally more white matter as a result of the necessity of transmitting information across farther distances (Falk, 2001). The absolutely and proportionally higher white matter in men's brains might be due to the larger overall size and not a direct result of sexual selection or other selection pressures. The best candidates for brain regions that have been shaped by sexual selection are those that not only exhibit sex differences but are disproportionally large in relation to other brain regions and are functionally linked to cognitive sex differences that may contribute to intrasexual competition or intersexual choice, as I discuss in later sections.

Hormones and Gene Expression

The reader may recall from chapter 4 (in the section titled Sex Hormones, Brain, and Cognition) that prenatal exposure to sex hormones can organize areas of the brain that support sexually selected behaviors and cognitions, and postnatal exposure to these hormones can activate them (A. P. Arnold & Gorski, 1984; Ball & Balthazart, 2004). I also noted in chapter 4 that the relation between sex hormones and prenatal organization and postnatal activation of brain systems is nuanced and not fully understood (Adkins-Reagan, 2005). To further complicate matters, there may be genetic influences on sex differences in brain organization and functioning that are independent of hormones, and these too remain to be fully explored (A. P. Arnold, 2009). In other words, scientists' understanding of these influences on human brain organization is still in its infancy, but some insights have been achieved.

Inferences about the influence of prenatal hormones on human sex differences in brain organization are dependent, in large part, on studies of individuals with medical conditions that result in sex-atypical hormone exposure—as described in chapter 10 of this volume (in the section titled Social Play) for girls with congenital adrenal hyperplasia (CAH)—or individuals who have been prenatally exposed to these hormones in other ways (e.g., through maternal medication; Collaer & Hines, 1995). These studies have focused on whether prenatal exposure to testosterone or estrogens (which can be converted to testosterone) results in male-typical patterns of brain organization or functioning. Determining whether this is the case is difficult, however, because direct measures of prenatal hormone exposure are not typically available. Indirect measures of prenatal hormone exposure are degree of lateralization of cognitive abilities and handedness; handedness and the lateralization of language and visuospatial functions often go together, differ systematically across the sexes, and may be related to prenatal exposure to testosterone (Annett, 1985; Geschwind & Galaburda, 1987).

More men than women are left-handed, and language and spatial functions tend to be more strongly localized in the left and right hemispheres, respectively, in men and distributed across both hemispheres in women (McGlone, 1980; Witelson, 1976, 1991). Kelso, Nicholls, Warne, and Zacharin (2000) found more left-handers and better nonverbal than verbal abilities for girls and women with CAH, consistent with an effect of prenatal exposure to male hormones on laterality and the pattern of cognitive abilities. These girls and women did not, however, differ from other girls and women on a task that assessed whether the right or left hemisphere was more sensitive to language sounds, inconsistent with an effect of prenatal hormone exposure on brain lateralization. The results from similar studies of individuals with CAH or other forms of atypical exposure to sex hormones are also mixed (e.g., Hines & Shipley, 1984; L. L. Smith & Hines, 2000); there are indications of male-typical brain organization associated with prenatal exposure to sex hormones in some areas but not others. Results using alternative approaches to this question are also inconclusive but do suggest prenatal hormones influence sex differences in human brain organization (Baron-Cohen, Knickmeyer, & Belmonte, 2005; Cohen-Bendahan, Buitelaar, van Goozen, & Cohen-Kettenis, 2004), as is the case for other species.

An intriguing example is provided by a brain imaging study of amygdala activation, which is involved in the processing of emotionally and sexually laden information, when individuals with CAH viewed facial expressions that conveyed neutral and negative affect (i.e., fear or anger; Ernst et al., 2007); L. Cahill and his colleagues discovered that the right amygdala is more active when men process and form memories of emotional scenarios, whereas the left amygdala is more active for women (L. Cahill, 2006; Kilpatrick et al., 2006). Ernst et al. found the male-typical pattern of amygdala activation for adolescent girls with CAH. Other studies have revealed a larger amygdala in men than in women (Goldstein et al., 2001), and Neufang et al. (2009) found that this sex difference emerged only during the later stages of pubertal maturation and that a higher level of circulating testosterone but not estrogens was associated with a larger amygdala.

Evidence for activational effects of sex hormones comes from studies of changes in brain functioning across the ovulatory cycle (Dreher et al., 2007; Goldstein et al., 2005). Dreher et al. assessed women at two points in their cycle, specifically, during Days 4 to 8 when estrogen levels are rising and Days 6 to 10 when both estrogen and progesterone levels are rising (see Figure 7.4, chap. 7, this volume). The degree of activation of the brain systems that influence sensitivity and response to rewards, including the amygdala, was influenced by the levels of circulating estrogen and progesterone. When only estrogen was rising, higher levels were associated with stronger reward-related brain responses, whereas progesterone drove these responses when both hormones were circulating. There are also sex differences in the distribution of neurotransmitters and other biochemicals throughout the brain and in the experiences that trigger their release (e.g., Grachev & Apkarian, 2000).

Reinius et al. (2008) compared the pattern of gene expression in the visual cortex of two polygynous primates, humans and a species of macaque (*Macaca fascicularis*), with that of the monogamous marmoset (*Callithrix jacchus*). This is an intriguing analysis because, as noted previously, polygyny is associated with sexual selection in general and with intense male–male competition in particular, whereas these evolutionary processes are less intensely expressed in monogamous species. There were few sex differences in gene expression in the marmoset, but considerable differences in humans and macaques. These genes were more highly expressed in the brain than in other tissues, suggesting they are important for brain functions. It is too soon to know with certainty, but there was suggestive evidence that a subset of these genes may be important for the development of sex hormone receptors in the visual cortex. In any case, the similarity in the pattern of neural gene expression in the human and macaque suggests that some of these genes were present in the ancestor common to these species; that is, these sex differences were likely present in our lineage dating back at least 25 million years. Future studies will, no doubt, reveal further similarities as well as differences in the pattern of gene expression in humans and related species. Many interesting questions remain to be explored; for example, will sex differences in gene expression be found for the human amygdala?

FOLK PSYCHOLOGY

My goal for the preceding section was to show there are sex differences in brain size, organization, distributions of neurotransmitters, and patterns of gene expression as well as hormonal influences on brain structure and functional activation. My goals for this section are to review sex differences in the folk psychological domains shown in Figure 9.2 (see chap. 9), to explore whether any of these differences might be related to sexual selection, and where possible to tie these to sex differences in brain organization and functioning.

Self

The reader may recall that my model of folk domains includes self-awareness (awareness of oneself as a social being) and self-schema (knowledge of one's traits; see Figure 9.2, chap. 9). Self-awareness is also a core element of the conscious–psychological mechanisms I proposed in chapter 9 of this volume (in the section titled Motivation to Control) and elsewhere (Geary, 2005b), specifically, to explicitly generate self-centered mental models of past, present, and potential future situations as a means to strategize about how to better achieve control over desired relationships or other resources. In the context of these simulations, self-knowledge is particularly important for traits that one can use to better achieve these outcomes or traits that might influence the corresponding social dynamics, for instance, traits that influence how one is perceived by others and thus one's relative influence over others. I predict sex differences in self-knowledge of and reflection on traits that have influenced the outcomes of intrasexual competition and intersexual choice during human evolutionary history. I note that the importance of these traits and how they might be expressed can be exaggerated, attenuated, or modified across cultures and historical periods.

When reflecting on or describing themselves (e.g., completing "I am . . . "), women are more likely than men to view themselves in terms of close relationships with family members or friends, whereas men are more likely to view themselves as members of groups or teams (Gabriel & Gardner, 1999). These sex differences follow the developmental patterns described in chapter 11 of this volume (in the section titled Peer Relationships) and are consistent with the sex differences described in the sections titled Ingroups and Outgroups. In keeping with the sex differences in emotional expressivity and reported intensity of feelings (see the section titled Affective, chap. 9, this volume), girls and women appear to be more aware of nuances in their feelings and emotions than boys and men and have better memories for the details of emotionally charged personal experiences (Barrett, Lane, Sechrest, & Schwartz, 2000). In a brain imaging study, McRae, Reiman, Fort, Chen, and Lane (2008) found that women's awareness of feelings is related to activation of the anterior cingulate cortex (see Area 24, Figure 12.2), an area of the brain that triggers engagement of explicit, conscious–psychological representations of various forms of information (Botvinick, Braver, Barch, Carter, & Cohen, 2001). My interpretation is that girls and women are better able to use awareness of their feelings as a social barometer, that is, as information in their evaluation of and strategizing about personal relationships and other goals. I predict that reflection on feelings will be particularly likely in the context of potential reproductive relationships, including relationships with men and as related to competition with other women over desired men. Unfortunately, currently available studies do not allow for a strong evaluation of these predictions.

It is easier to evaluate the potential relation between sexual selection and sex differences in self-awareness and self-reflection for physical traits than for psychological ones. This is because physical traits are more easily measured than feelings, for instance, and because we know what traits have likely evolved under the influence of sexual selection. The usefulness of this approach is illustrated by several corresponding predictions, specifically, that boys and men will show greater awareness and valuation of their physical strength and athletic ability (related to male–male competition) as well as traits that influence female choice. Women are predicted to show greater awareness and valuation of facial features, weight, and breasts, traits that influence men's mate choices and are thereby a focus of female–female competition. Women's evaluation of their physical traits has been the subject of sociological and social psychological debates and studies, including hypotheses about the sexual objectification of women:

> Sexual objectification occurs whenever people's bodies, body parts, or sexual functions are separated out from their identity, reduced to the status of mere instruments, or regarded as if they were capable of representing them . . . when objectified, individuals are treated as bodies and, in particular, as bodies that exist for the use and pleasure of others. (Fredrickson, Roberts, Noll, Quinn, & Twenge, 1998, p. 269)

The issue here is the emphasis on women's bodies as sexual objects, which in turn relates to the stronger preference of men than women for casual sex, and men's focus on women's physical traits when making mate choices. The dynamic has, however, become exaggerated in Western culture for girls and women who compare themselves with images of other women presented in the mass media (e.g., Cusumano & Thompson, 2000) and as a result of a heightening of female–female competition in the context of socially imposed monogamy; see the discussion of eating disorders in Geary (1998b) and the afterword of this volume. The goal here is to consider whether existing research supports the predictions that girls and women focus more than boys and men on the physical traits that influence male choice and female–female competition and that boys and men focus more on the physical traits that influence physical male–male competition and female choice.

In general, girls and women tend to reflect on their behavior and traits more frequently than do boys and men across many domains (Fejfar & Hoyle, 2000), and their bodies are a common area of reflection and appraisal (K. A. Phillips, Menard, & Fay, 2006). In comparison with young men, young college women in the United States are more concerned about their relative thinness, are more aware of and monitor their weight more frequently, and feel shame if they do not meet their internalized standard for thinness (Mintz & Betz, 1986). In a study of body dysmorphic disorder (BDD), a psychiatric problem that involves preoccupation with an imagined bodily defect (American Psychiatric Association, 1994), K. A. Phillips et al. found more similarities than differences in the symptoms of women and men but also found a sex difference in the areas of preoccupation: "Women were more likely to obsess about the appearance of their skin, stomach, weight, breast/chest, buttocks, thighs, legs, hips, and toes" (p. 83). Similar concerns have been found in women without BDD or eating disorders (Dolan, Birtchnell, & Lacey, 1987). Bacchini and Magliulo (2003) found that body image was a much more salient concern for adolescent girls in Italy than for same-age boys. Several brain imaging studies have revealed greater activation of the amygdala in women than in men when processing unflattering body-image information, consistent with women's more intense negative feelings and greater shame about their bodies (S. Cahill & Mussap, 2007; Kurosaki, Shirao, Yamashita, Okamoto, & Yamawaki, 2006; Shirao, Okamoto, Mantani, Okamoto, & Yamawaki, 2005).

There is less research on the physical traits that are the foci of boys' and men's self-reflections, but the results are also in line with predictions. Men are more likely to consider themselves to be underweight and to explicitly focus on and sometimes obsess about their muscularity (Mintz & Betz, 1986; K. A. Phillips et al., 2006). Men's concern about muscularity is as great and may be slightly greater than women's concern about thinness. In a sample of college students, Smolak and Murnen (2008) found that more than 9 out of

10 men were more focused on their muscularity than was the average woman—a similar sex difference is found among individuals with BDD (K. A. Phillips et al., 2006)—whereas 4 out of 5 women were more focused on their thinness than was the average man. T. J. Wade (2000) found that young men with higher self-rated physical fitness and competence (e.g., strength, reflexes) and with facial features associated with social dominance had higher a self-esteem and considered themselves to be more sexually and physically attractive than did other men.

Individual

As I reviewed in chapter 9 (in the section titled Folk Psychology), the individual-level modules are hypothesized to support one-on-one dyadic interactions and relationships. Following the organization shown in Figure 9.2 (see chap. 9), I begin with sex differences in sensitivity to nonverbal behavior and to nuances in reading facial expressions. I follow with respective reviews of sex differences in language competencies, and theory of mind and person schemas. My hypothesis is that most of these systems will be more highly elaborated in women than in men as a result in part of sexual selection. Although both men and women engage in relational aggression (see the section titled Women's Aggression, chap. 8), when women are aggressive it is almost always relationally. With the onset of puberty and beyond, the focus of this aggression is other girls and women and more often than not over romantic partners (i.e., female–female competition over prospective mates). Female–female competition is not the only potential source of sex differences in individual-level folk competencies. The sex differences in parental investment and in the need to monitor potentially predatory men may also have resulted in conditions that would favor the evolution of more sensitive competencies in women (Hampson, van Anders, & Mullin, 2006).

If female–female competition has contributed to an enhanced sensitivity in girls and women to the social cues of other people, then the sex difference in sensitivity to these cues should be larger when girls and women view cues from same-sex others than when they view the same cues from men. In contrast, if monitoring of potentially predatory men has been important, women should be particularly sensitive to the social cues of men (Garver-Apgar, Gangestad, & Simpson, 2007). Finally, if the sex difference in parental effort is the source of sex differences in sensitivity to social information, then girls and women should be more sensitive to the social cues of infants and children than to the cues of adolescents and adults. There may, of course, be a more nuanced pattern of sex differences. Garver-Apgar et al. (2007) found that women's ratings of men's assertive and flirtatious behaviors varied across the ovulatory cycle. They were more likely to view these behaviors as sexually coercive when ovulating than when the same behaviors were rated during other days of the cycle. Whether women are more sensitive to subtle changes in men's nonverbal cues, vocal intonation, and so forth across the cycle remains to be fully explored.

Nonverbal Behavior and Facial Expressions

My review of sex differences in these folk psychological domains is organized in terms of cognition, brain, and hormones. I make links to sexual selection in each section, as warranted.

Cognition. Girls and women are better than boys and men at interpreting and sending nonverbal social messages, including skill at reading emotional states conveyed in facial expressions, gesture, and body language and in generating nuance in the social use of these forms of communication (Buck, Savin, Miller, & Caul,1972; J. A. Hall, 1978, 1984; J. A. Hall & Matsumoto, 2004; McClure, 2000; Rosenthal, Hall, DiMatteo, Rogers, & Archer, 1979; van Beek & Dubas, 2008; Wagner, Buck, & Winterbotham, 1993). Rosenthal et al. (1979) conducted one of the most ambitious and comprehensive assessments of sex differences in this area with the development of a standardized test— Profile of Nonverbal Sensitivity (PONS)—for the assessment of sensitivity to nonverbal emotion cues. These cues are visual (e.g., facial expressions, body posture), auditory (e.g., emotional tone conveyed in utterances), and combined (i.e., including both visual and auditory information). The test involves watching a film of 220 short segments of a woman's nonverbal behavior, including facial expressions, body posture, and content-filtered speech (i.e., speech in which the individual words cannot be identified but the emotional tone can), as well as segments that include combinations of cues. The PONS was initially administered to 492 high school students and in follow-up studies to more than 4,000 elementary to college students and to older adults from a variety of occupations. Assessments were done on three or more samples from Australia, Canada, Israel, and New Guinea and smaller samples from Northern Ireland, Mexico, New Zealand, Hong Kong, West Germany, and Singapore.

Girls and women were more accurate than boys and men when judging emotion cues on the basis of facial expressions, body posture, and vocal intonation (Rosenthal et al., 1979); these sex differences were found in all nations in which three or more samples were obtained—Australia, Canada, the United States, Israel and New Guinea—and were of the same general magnitude in all of these nations (J. A. Hall, 1984). J. A. Hall concluded that the advantage of girls and women in the decoding of nonverbal messages "is most pronounced for facial cues, less pronounced for body cues, and least pronounced for vocal cues" (p. 27). When all nonverbal cues were provided— offering a more accurate assessment of nonverbal decoding skills in the real world—about 17 out of 20 girls and women were more accurate at decoding the emotion cues of another individual than was the average same-age boy or man (J. A. Hall, 1978).

Buck et al. (1972) found that dyads of women are more effective in expressing and reading the emotion cues of the other member of the pair, as signaled by changes in facial expression, than are dyads of men, and Wagner et al. (1993) found that women are more accurate in judging the emotion cues of other women than the emotion cues of men. Rehnman and Herlitz (2006) found that 9-year-old girls have a better memory for faces than do 9-year-old boys and that girls have an especially large advantage in recognizing the faces of other girls and women over the faces of boys and men; Rehnman and Herlitz (2007) confirmed this sex difference in a follow-up study with adults. These findings appear to reflect a combination of girls and women allocating more attention to the processing of same-sex faces than boys and men (Herlitz & Rehnman, 2008), the greater sensitivity of girls and women to the emotion cues signaled by facial expressions and other nonverbal behaviors, and a greater expressiveness on the part of women than men; roughly 17 out of 20 women are judged to convey more information in their facial expressions than does the average man, and nearly 3 out of 4 women engage in social smiling and maintain eye contact more consistently than does the average man (J. A. Hall, 1984). Some men are so poor at reading the nonverbal cues of women that they often misperceive sexual interest on the part of women as friendliness (Farris, Treat, Viken, & McFall, 2008); many misperceive friendliness as sexual interest (Haselton & Buss, 2000).

Men's sensitivity to negative cues signaled by other men, such as an angry facial expression, is an intriguing exception to women's overall advantage in reading nonverbal cues; men are more sensitive to these cues than to the same ones signaled by women (N. G. Rotter & Rotter, 1988; Wagner et al., 1993; M. A. Williams & Mattingley, 2006). In two large-scale studies involving more than 1,100 people, N. G. Rotter and Rotter found that women are more accurate than men in judging disgust, fear, or sadness in the facial expressions of other women and of men. Women are also more accurate than men in detecting an angry expression on the face of other women. Men, in contrast, are more accurate in detecting an angry expression on the face of other men (N. G. Rotter & Rotter, 1988). Dimberg and Öhman (1996) concluded that men are more sensitive to the angry expressions of other men than they are to the angry expressions of women, especially when these anger-signaling cues are expressed in adult men as contrasted with adolescents and when the expressions are directed toward the individual (e.g., with eye contact). Women, in contrast, appear to be equally sensitive to angry expressions in men and other women. At the same time, men are less accurate in detecting disgust, fear, and sadness in other men's facial expressions than in detecting these cues in women's facial expressions.

The finding that men might be especially sensitive to angry expressions in other men is consistent with Rosenthal et al.'s (1979) finding that men are particularly sensitive to negative dominance-related cues. In other words, women are more sensitive than men in detecting nonverbal indicators of negative emotional states, but the gap is smaller and sometimes reversed for aggression- and dominance-related themes, such as jealous anger or other social threats. Rehnman and Herlitz's (2006, 2007) finding that girls and women are especially sensitive to the nonverbal cues of other girls and women is consistent with an influence of female–female competition on the evolution of these sex differences.

Brain. As described in the section titled Hormones and Gene Expression earlier in this chapter, the amygdala is among the core brain systems involved in the processing of emotion-laden information and is structurally and functionally different in women and men (e.g., Goldstein et al., 2001; Kilpatrick et al., 2006). The ventral (bottom) and medial (center) areas of the prefrontal cortex are also critical for processing, evaluating, and responding to social-emotional information; these regions include Areas 10, 11 12, and 25 in Figure 12.2 (see also Adolphs, 1999). After correcting for the sex difference in brain size and size of the frontal cortex, the social–emotional processing areas of the prefrontal cortex are larger in women than in men (Goldstein et al., 2001; R. C. Gur et al., 2002); Area 11 may be especially large in women (J. L. Wood, Heitmiller, Andreasen, & Nopoulos, 2008). The amygdala and ventromedial areas of the prefrontal cortex, along with the anterior cingulate cortex (see Area 24, Figure 12.2), are richly interconnected and operate to balance the emotional and rational components of social decision making and behavioral responding (Adolphs, 1999).

In addition to the sex differences in proportional size of the amygdala (larger in men) and ventromedial prefrontal cortex (larger in women), these regions are interconnected differently in women and men (Kirkpatrick et al., 2006; Tranel, Damasio, Denburg, & Bechara, 2005). There appears to be greater functional connectivity between these regions in the right hemisphere for men and the left hemisphere for women. The right hemisphere may be disproportionately important for inhibiting men's behavioral responses in emotional and sexual contexts and the left hemisphere for inhibiting women's responses. The combination of overall differences in proportional size and connectivity may contribute to women's advantage in inhibiting behavioral responses, especially aggression, in emotionally charged situations (Gur et al., 2002) and may contribute to their better memory for details of emotional episodes; vivid memory for details of personal experiences is associated with activation of the left amygdala, whereas memory for overall gist is associated with activation of the right amygdala (L. Cahill, 2006).

These studies indicate sex differences in the brain systems that support the processing of and responding to emotion cues, but the magnitude and consistency of the functional differences across different emotion cues and social contexts remain to be determined (e.g., Fischer, Sandblom, Nyberg, Herlitz, & Bäckman, 2007). Moreover, few of the studies provide direct tests of the hypothesis that women and men will be particularly sensitive to emotion cues associated with intrasexual competition. McClure et al. (2004) demonstrated that women have greater activation than men in areas of the ventromedial prefrontal cortex and amygdala during the processing of angry facial expressions but did not test whether this varied with the sex of the sender. Do men show faster and heightened brain responses to the angry faces and other dominance cues of men? Do women show faster and heightened brain responses to emotion cues of other women as related to relational aggression, such as dismissive facial expressions or gestures?

Although uncommon, evolutionarily informed studies of this type are doable. I covered one such study in chapter 7 (in the section titled Young, Attractive Women). Cloutier, Heatherton, Whalen, and Kelley (2008) found that both women and men showed activation of the nucleus accumbens, which is associated with feelings of pleasure and reward, when viewing attractive faces of the opposite sex, but only men showed activation of areas of the ventromedial prefrontal cortex that are associated with reward-driven social behaviors and motivations. Women and men find viewing attractive faces of the opposite sex pleasurable, but men appear to be more ready, in terms of brain activation, to consider how they might act on these feelings. While viewing visually erotic pictures, men show stronger activation of the amygdala than do women, consistent with use of visual cues in male choice (Hamann, Herman, Nolan, & Wallen, 2004). Aleman and Swart (2008) provided another theoretically driven study with their assessment of men's and women's responses to facial expressions of disgust and contempt. Both facial expressions signal disapproval and negative emotion, but the latter signals social superiority and dominance. Men showed stronger brain activation in the prefrontal areas involved in social evaluations in response to the contemptuous facial expressions of both sexes. Women, in contrast, showed stronger responses to facial expressions that signaled disgust. The results are consistent with men's greater emphasis on dominance relations than women but suggest these concerns are not simply related to intrasexual competition because they can be provoked by both sexes, not just other men.

Hormones. As described in the section titled Hormones and Gene Expression earlier in this chapter, prenatal exposure to male testosterone may bias the later functioning of the amygdala (Ernst et al., 2007), and men's larger amygdala may be due to the pubertal increase in testosterone (Neufang et al., 2009). Other studies have confirmed the latter finding and suggest further that the sex differences in the ventromedial prefrontal cortex do not consistently emerge before puberty (McClure et al., 2004; J. W. Wood, Murko, & Nopoulos, 2008). Circulating sex hormones can also influence the functioning of these systems and the corresponding sex differences in sensitivity and responses to social–emotional information (Dreher et al., 2007; Goldstein et al., 2005; Heister, Landis, Regard, & Schroeder-Heister, 1989; van Honk et al., 1999; Wirth & Schultheiss, 2007).

Higher basal levels of testosterone are associated with greater attentiveness to and of processing of angry facial expressions, especially those of same-sex individuals. Wirth and Schultheiss (2007) found that higher testosterone in the morning—levels tend to be highest at this time—in both men and women were associated with faster implicit processing of angry facial expressions but not other facial expressions. The same pattern was found by van Honk et al. (1999) when men and women processed the angry faces of same-sex others. Unfortunately, the design of these studies does not provide an ideal test of the challenge hypothesis (see the section titled Testosterone, chap. 8, this volume) because it is not known whether the men with higher testosterone levels were more actively competing for mates during the time of the study and thus more sensitive to dominance-related social cues in other men. It is nevertheless plausible that these men were more actively competing, given the relation between testosterone and marriage—having a mate is associated with lower testosterone (see the section titled Hormones and Men's Parenting, chap. 6, this volume)—but an explicit test of this hypothesis awaits further study. The relation between testosterone and women's sensitivity to the angry facial expressions of other women is fascinating, but the meaning is not clear because it is estrogens rather than testosterone that appear to be central to female–female competition (Schultheiss, Dargel, & Rohde, 2003; Stanton & Schultheiss, 2007).

Indeed, there is consistent evidence that estrogen levels influence women's processing of facial features, but unfortunately, most of these studies have not been framed to test the various evolutionary reasons for this relation (e.g., parenting vs. female–female competition). Yonker, Eriksson, Nilsson, and Herlitz (2003) found that women's advantage in the recognition of children's faces (adult faces were not used as a contrast)—nearly 3 out of 4 women had a better memory than the average man—was associated with higher circulating estrogen levels; women with higher levels had better memory for faces than other women. Estrogen was not, however, related to women's overall advantage in episodic memory, that is, memory for personal experiences. Goldstein et al. (2005) demonstrated that the influence of stressors on sensitivity of the amygdala, ventromedial prefrontal cortex, and anterior cingulate cortex, among other brain regions, varies across women's ovulatory cycle. Specifically, exposure to stress when estrogen levels are rising and fertility is high is associated with heightened responsiveness of these brain regions to exposure to unpleasant events (e.g., a photo of a threatening person) but with damped responsiveness during menstruation.

Heister et al. (1989) examined speed of facial processing across the ovulatory cycle and when the faces were presented to the left or right hemisphere. Women were tachistoscopically presented a series of pictures of normal faces and pictures in which the major features of the faces were scrambled; for instance, the mouth was placed on the forehead. The tachistoscope was used to briefly present the faces to the right or left visual field, which effectively results in the information being initially presented to the left or right hemisphere, respectively. The task was simply to determine whether the presented face was real or scrambled. Consistent with other studies, faces initially presented to the right hemisphere were processed faster and more accurately than were faces initially presented to the left hemisphere, except during the premenstrual phase, that is, when estradiol and progesterone levels are declining. At this point, the processing of faces was relatively slow and inaccurate, whether the faces were initially presented to the left or the right hemisphere. The results also showed that whether they were initially presented to either the left or to the right hemisphere, the processing of faces was the fastest and most accurate around the time of ovulation.

The results from subsequent studies suggest the preovulatory surge in estrogen, or possibly testosterone, which also surges at this time, enhances the speed of processing men's facial features (Macrae, Alnwick, Milne, & Schloerscheidt, 2002) and of detecting fearful facial expressions in both sexes (Pearson & Lewis, 2005). Heightened sensitivity to fear in others' facial expressions is consistent with an increase in risk avoidance around the time of ovulation (Chavanne & Gallup, 1998), but the Macrae et al. study did not assess the corresponding prediction that women's identification of men's faces would be particularly fast for potentially threatening or coercive facial expressions (Garver-Apgar et al., 2007). Progesterone, in contrast, may disrupt women's ability to discriminate angry and fearful facial expressions from facial expressions signaling other negative emotions, such as disgust (Derntl, Kryspin-Exner, Fernbach, Moser, & Habel, 2008). In all, it is clear that the sex differences in the processing of nonverbal social cues is influenced by the hormonal changes that occur during puberty and by circulating hormones in adulthood, but a tight link to the nuances of intrasexual competition, intersexual choice, and parenting remains to be forged.

Language

As in the previous section, I cover sex differences in language competencies in terms of cognition, brain, and hormones. Links to sexual selection are made where and when the evidence is sufficient to do so.

Cognition. Girls and women do not have an advantage on all tests of verbal ability (D. F. Halpern, 2000), such as the verbal section of the Scholastic Assessment Test (Hyde & Linn, 1988); these types of tests are not good measures of evolved language abilities. Nor do women talk more: A large-scale study of the conversations of college students revealed no sex difference in the number of words spoken throughout the day, although there was 18% more variation among the men than the women, suggesting some men talked quite a bit and others not so often (Mehl, Vazire, Ramírez-Esparza, Slatcher, & Pennebaker, 2007). Girls talk more than boys during the first 2 years of life and during the juvenile period (about 10–13 years), but boys may talk more during adolescence (Leaper & Smith, 2004). At the same time, sex differences are consistently found in aspects of language production, language comprehension, and the pragmatics of language (K. J. Anderson & Leaper, 1998; D. F. Halpern, 2000; Hyde & Linn, 1988; Kimura, 1999; Majeres, 2007; B. A. Shaywitz et al., 1995).

Pragmatics refers to the use of language in social contexts. Boys and men tend to use language to attempt to assert their social dominance, a form of status display, in their interactions with other males, as was illustrated by Andy in chapter 11 of this volume (in the section titled Peer Relationships).

> Boys in their groups are more likely than girls in all-girl groups to interrupt one another; use commands, threats, or boasts of authority; refuse to comply with another child's command; give information; heckle a speaker; . . . top someone else's story; or call another child names. (Maccoby, 1990, p. 516)

The magnitude of the sex difference in this social style varies with age and social context (K. J. Anderson & Leaper, 1998; Leaper & Smith, 2004). During development, the largest differences emerge when boys are in one-on-one interactions with an unfamiliar peer. In these contexts, three out of five boys use more directives ("Go do this . . . ") than does the average girl, but there are no sex differences on other aspects of assertive language, such as making generally negative comments (Leaper & Smith, 2004). In adulthood, men use intrusive, dominance-oriented interruptions somewhat more frequently than women, except in group settings. These are contexts in which dominance displays convey information to a wide audience (Vigil, in press), and here almost three out of four men intrusively interrupt others as a means of displaying dominance (e.g., superior knowledge), which is more often than the average woman.

As discussed in the section titled Peer Relationships (see chap. 11), language is more central to the development and maintenance of intimate and reciprocal relationships for girls and women than for boys and men, and this is reflected in their dialogues. Girls and women more frequently show socially enabling language, language that provides equal time to all members of the group and allows other girls and women to express their thoughts and feelings. In all-girl groups, they

> are more likely than boys to express agreement with what another speaker has just said, pause to give another girl a chance to speak, or when starting a speaking turn, acknowledge a point previously made by another speaker. . . . Among girls, conversation is a more socially binding process. (Maccoby, 1990, p. 516)

Again, the magnitude of these differences varies with age and context (Leaper & Smith, 2004).

Language is also a relatively more central feature of female–female competition than it is of male–male competition. Girls' and women's aggression and social competitiveness is more likely to be expressed relationally than physically, that is, through the manipulation and disruption of the social relationships of their competitors. As described in the section titled Women's Aggression (see chap. 8), relational aggression is conveyed through language, specifically, gossiping about other girls, spreading lies and rumors about their sexual behavior, telling secrets, and attempting to control other girls' social behavior. The use of language in relational aggression combined with the importance of language for the development and maintenance of reciprocal same-sex relationships sets the stage for selection to elaborate basic language competencies more in women than in men, in much the same way that physical male–male competition has resulted in larger and physically stronger men than women.

The cognitive and brain evidence supports this evolutionary prediction. Relative to boys and men, girls and women have advantages for many basic language-related skills, including the length and quality of utterances (e.g., in their utterances women show standard grammatical structure and a correct pronunciation of language sounds more frequently than do men), the ease and speed of articulating complex words, the ability to generate strings of words, the speed of retrieving individual words from long-term memory, and skill at discriminating basic language sounds from one another (R. A. Block, Arnott, Quigley, & Lynch, 1989; D. F. Halpern, 2000; Hampson, 1990a; Hyde & Linn, 1988; Majeres, 2007). Girls and women also show many fewer pauses (e.g., filled with "uhh") in their utterances than do boys and men (J. A. Hall, 1984), and at the same time, boys and men manifest language-related disorders, such as stuttering, 2 to 4 times more frequently than do girls and women (Tallal, 1991). There is also evidence that women process the prosody (e.g., emotional tone) of language more quickly and with less allocation of attention than do men (Schirmer, Kotz, & Friederici, 2005).

The relative advantage of girls and women in these areas ranges from small to very large, depending on the skill and the complexity of the task. For simple speech tasks, as in speed of producing or remembering related words (e.g., types of furniture), about 2 out of 3 women outperform the average man (Hyde & Linn, 1988). Similarly, about 3 out of 4 women commit fewer speech errors (e.g., retrieving the wrong word) than does the average man (J. A. Hall, 1984). One study found that 9 out of 10 women outperformed the average man in the ability to discriminate basic language sounds (R. A. Block et al., 1989), and an analysis of sex differences across many different studies indicated that nearly 9 out of 10 men have more pauses in their utterances than does the average woman (J. A. Hall, 1984). These latter findings represent some of the largest cognitive sex differences ever documented.

Brain. As I noted in the section titled Brain Size and Organization earlier in this chapter, debate continues as to whether there are sex differences in the corpus callosum (Bishop & Wahlsten, 1997; de Lacoste-Utamsing & Holloway, 1982). Studies suggest that subtle sex differences do in fact exist (Dubb et al., 2003), but their relation to the sex differences in language competencies remains to be determined. As I also mentioned, cognitive competencies tend to be more lateralized—situated largely in one hemisphere and not the other—in men than in women, and this is the case for language.

In a now classic study, Geschwind and Levitsky (1968) demonstrated that the planum temporale, which processes speech sounds, is physically larger in the left temporal cortex than the comparable area in the right cortex for about two out of three people. This asymmetry (i.e., left larger than right) is less pronounced or sometimes reversed in more women than men (McGlone, 1980; Wada, Clark, & Hamm, 1975). These findings, among other factors—including fewer language disorders associated with damage to the left hemisphere in women than in men (Kimura, 1999)—led McGlone (1980) to conclude that language functions are differentially represented in the left and the right hemispheres (i.e., left and right cortex) for women and men. Specifically, many basic language skills are represented in both hemispheres for many women but are largely represented in the left hemisphere for most men; these sex differences are most evident with comparisons of right-handed men and women (Annett, 1985; Hampson, 1990a). Brain imaging studies are not yet conclusive, but some are consistent with these differences and have revealed several important details.

In one of these studies, B. A. Shaywitz et al. (1995) found that women's and men's Broca's areas (see Area 44 and parts of Area 45, Figure 12.2), which are involved in language production and related competencies, were differentially engaged across the two hemispheres during the processing of language sounds. These differences were evident when men and women were asked to determine whether a pair of words read off of a computer screen rhymed (e.g., GOOZ–REWS), that is, they had to base their judgments on the sounds associated with the words. In this study, about one half of the women showed a strong activation of both the left and right hemispheres while processing these sounds, but none of the men showed any significant activation of the right hemisphere; all of the men's processing was confined to the left hemisphere. Several follow-up studies confirmed this pattern for the processing of language sounds, but others suggested smaller sex differences or no sex differences for some processes (Jaeger et al., 1998; Kansaku & Kitazawa, 2001; Sommer, Aleman, Bouma, & Kahn, 2004). The finding of small or no sex differences included the processing of single words, which may occur too quickly and automatically for the sharing of information across the two hemispheres. In any event, women also showed more bilateral activation of the temporale regions during language comprehension tasks than did men (Kansaku, Yamaura, & Kitazawa, 2000).

Kimura's (1987) analysis of the relation between brain injury (e.g., stroke) and patterns of language-related disorders (i.e., aphasia) suggests sex differences in the regions supporting language competencies within the left hemisphere. Damage to many different regions of the left hemisphere, including the frontal, temporal, parietal, and occipital cortices, could produce aphasia in men. For women, in contrast, only damage to the frontal and temporal cortices, corresponding roughly to Broca's and Wernicke's areas, resulted in aphasia. The highest incidence of aphasia was associated with damage to the frontal cortex for women and the parietal and temporal cortices for men. On the basis of these patterns, Kimura concluded that language functions were diffusely represented in the left hemisphere for men but focally represented in women. A preliminary but related study suggested that women's and men's sensitivity to the emotional tone of spoken language is dependent on different areas of the right hemisphere, frontal areas for women and subcortical areas for men (Rymarczyk & Grabowska, 2007).

As I indicated in the section titled Relative Size and Organization earlier in this chapter, women have several disproportionally large—after controlling for overall brain size—areas of the brain that support language processing (Good et al., 2001; C. M. Leonard et al., 2008; Sowell et al., 2006; Witelson et al., 1995). This is a critical finding because it is consistent with the predicted evolutionary enlargement and elaboration of specific brain regions that underlie the cognitive competencies—language in this case—involved in intrasexual competition or intersexual choice. The important point is that these selection pressures result in the enlargement or elaboration of some brain regions but not others, just as female choice has resulted in the evolution of larger and redder combs in male red jungle fowl (*Gallus gallus*) but not in other male traits (Zuk, Thornhill, & Ligon, 1990; see also the section titled Good Genes, chap. 3, this volume). The best available evidence for sex-specific elaboration of brain regions supporting language is for the planum temporale; in the right hemisphere, the regions corresponding to the planum temporale and those nearby are important for identifying specific people on the basis of their voice (Formisano, De Martino, Bonte, & Goebel, 2008).

In a brain imaging study of 100 men and 100 women, C. M. Leonard et al. (2008) found that the planum temporale was not only disproportionately larger in women than in men but also large in women independent of overall brain size. For men, larger overall brain size was associated with larger areas throughout the cortex, including the planum temporale, but this was not the case for women. The raw size of this brain region was maintained in women, regardless of overall brain size. This suggests a selection pressure that acts more strongly in women than in men and involves the use of language. In other words, maintaining the language systems, independent of body and brain size, has been more important for our female than our male ancestors. The dynamics of female–female relational aggression and the use of language to maintain same-sex relationships are candidates for the corresponding selection pressures.

Hormones. The relation between sex hormones and language has been studied for some competencies (e.g., verbal fluency or speed of word articulation) but not others (e.g., grammatical structure of utterances). The results for the domains that have been studied provide tentative but not conclusive support for the prediction that prenatal and postnatal exposure to sex hormones contributes to the sex differences in language competencies. The complexity stems in part from the finding that some of the relations between sex hormone levels and language competencies, as well as other cognitive functions, are nonlinear—performance is at its best when specific hormone levels are at their lowest or their highest—and from the finding that the same hormone may affect women's and men's language competencies differently (Kimura, 2002; O'Connor, Archer, Hair, & Wu, 2001; Schattmann & Sherman, 2007; Thilers, MacDonald, & Herlitz, 2006). To muddy the theoretical waters further, sex hormones, such as estradiol (an estrogen), can have general effects on attentional control and working memory that provide women with an advantage on some language-based memory tasks but may not be specifically related to language. This advantage fluctuates across the ovulatory cycle, making comparisons of women's and men's competencies a moving target. Similarly, men's testosterone is highest in the morning, and thus any influence on cognitive functioning could vary across the day (Moffat & Hampson, 1996).

Despite these complications, it has been hypothesized that prenatal exposure to testosterone suppresses the development of the brain systems that later support language competencies (Baron-Cohen et al., 2005; Geschwind & Galaburda, 1987; Witelson, 1991), but the evidence is mixed. The basic architecture of the planum temporale appears to be largely set prenatally (Wada et al., 1975), and as I indicated in chapter 10 of this volume (in the section titled Prenatal Hormones), exposure to higher prenatal testosterone levels may slow vocabulary development during infancy (Lutchmaya,

Baron-Cohen, & Raggat, 2002b) and may adversely influence a wider range of language and other social–cognitive competencies (Baron-Cohen et al., 2005; Cohen-Bendahan et al., 2004). Inconsistent with the prediction of prenatal influences on language functioning is the finding that girls and women affected by CAH do not differ, on average, from their unaffected peers on measures of verbal fluency (Collaer & Hines, 1995), but these girls and women have not been systematically compared with their unaffected peers on all of the language competencies for which sex differences are found.

Circulating hormone levels appear to influence the expression of some but not all language competencies (Hampson, 1990a), and estrogen (e.g., estradiol) and testosterone may affect these competencies differently in women and men (Gouchie & Kimura, 1991; Moffat & Hampson, 1996; O'Connor et al., 2001; Thilers et al., 2006). The approach described in the section titled Ovulatory Cycle in chapter 7 of this volume can be applied to changes in the strengths and weaknesses of women's cognitive competencies at different points in their cycle, and this allows scientists to assess whether sex hormones influence these competencies. Figure 7.4 (see chap. 7, this volume) shows that estrogen (i.e., estradiol) is at its lowest level during menstruation, increases rapidly, peaks a few days prior to ovulation, and then declines rapidly; the estrogen peak is accompanied by a small increase in testosterone. Following ovulation, both estrogen and progesterone levels increase and then decline just prior to the onset of menstruation.

Hampson (1990a, 1990b) found that the speed of articulating words is at its highest when estradiol and progesterone levels are relatively high; not all studies have found this relation, however (Mordecai, Rubin, & Maki, 2008). Skill at generating words (e.g., a list of mammals) has also been found to vary across the ovulatory cycle, but this pattern is found less consistently than the pattern for verbal fluency. L.-F. Low and Anstey's (2006) review of the relation between hormone therapy and cognitive functioning yielded mixed results for verbal memory. For postmenopausal women, estrogen replacement may improve performance on simple verbal memory tasks (e.g., holding a list of numbers in mind) but not on more complex tasks (e.g., remembering a story).

Van Goozen, Cohen-Kettenis, Gooren, Frijda, & Van de Poll (1994, 1995) studied change in social behavior and cognition for female-to-male transsexuals and for male-to-female transsexuals before and during hormonal treatments. The female-to-male transsexuals were treated with testosterone, and the male-to-female transsexuals were treated with a combination of androgen suppressing drugs and estrogens. Following 3 months of hormonal treatments, the female-to-male transsexuals scored 30% to 34% lower on two measures of verbal fluency, one assessing the ability to generate words and the other the ability to generate sentences. For the male-to-female transsexuals, performance on the word fluency test decreased slightly (6%) but improved significantly (22%) for the sentence fluency test. The results for male-to-female transsexuals have not been replicated, however (Slabbekoorn, van Goozen, Megens, Gooren, & Cohen-Kettenis, 1999).

In a nicely controlled study, O'Connor et al. (2001) demonstrated that increasing testosterone levels beyond normal levels enhances men's verbal fluency. Related studies have confirmed this relation and have suggested that the mechanism may involve the biochemical change of testosterone into estradiol (G. M. Alexander et al., 1998). On the basis of these and related studies, O'Connor et al. proposed that more typical testosterone levels may suppress some language competencies in men in favor of spatial abilities, resulting in high verbal fluency for men with significantly lower or significantly higher than average testosterone levels. The results are more straightforward for women: Thilers et al. (2006) found that higher levels of naturally circulating testosterone are associated with lower verbal fluency (speed of generating words), and Schattmann and Sherwin (2007) found that a medical treatment that reduced women's testosterone levels resulted in improved verbal fluency.

One final twist is provided by Newman, Sellers, and Joseph's (2005) study showing that manipulating status can influence the relation between testosterone and verbal fluency. On the basis of Wingfield, Hegner, Dufty, and Ball's (1990) challenge hypothesis (see the section titled Testosterone, chap. 8, this volume), men and women with higher and lower than average testosterone levels for their sex were assigned to lower status (follower) or higher status (leader) positions for a group project. Their verbal fluency and spatial abilities were then assessed. Status did not affect the cognitive performance of individuals with low testosterone but did affect that of their high-testosterone peers. Specifically, the performance of these would-be leaders dropped for both sexes on the fluency and spatial task when they were in a low-status position. I agree with Newman et al.'s conclusion that this effect was found because the individuals with high testosterone levels were probably preoccupied by their low-status assignment, which in turn likely disrupted their ability to focus on these tasks.

All of this leaves at least as many questions as answers. It is almost certain that prenatal exposure to testosterone has some organizational effects on the brain systems that later support language, but the details remain to be sorted out. Circulating estrogen (i.e., estradiol) appears to facilitate the processing of language sounds and may speed up the retrieval of words from long-term memory and the speed of speaking them. Circulating testosterone appears to suppress verbal fluency in women but may enhance it in men with higher than average levels of testosterone. Newman et al. (2005) conducted one of the few theoretically motivated—from an evolutionary perspective—studies in this area and found important interactions between testosterone, status, and cognitive performance. More of these types of studies are needed to fully understand the relations between sex hormones and language competencies. For instance, are girls and women more likely to engage in relational aggression against other girls and women when estrogen levels peak, and are they more successful at using their language competencies to achieve their aggressive goals during this phase of their ovulatory cycle? Are girls and women with higher than average levels of testosterone more likely to engage in physical competition and aggression and less likely to engage in language-based relational aggression?

Theory of Mind and Person Schema

As discussed in chapter 10 (in the section titled Empathy and Social Responsiveness), girls typically express more empathy for the distress of other people than do boys. In the section titled Nonverbal Behavior and Facial Expressions earlier in this chapter, I focused on girls' and women's advantage in the ability to perceive corresponding social cues, such as sensitivity to the emotions signaled by others' facial expressions. Theory of mind goes at least one step beyond these sex differences. The empathetic responses may or may not indicate an understanding of the internal state of the distressed individual and certainly do not for infant girls who cry when hearing the distress of other infants (Simner, 1971). Likewise, many responses to facial expressions and other social cues occur rapidly and without a conscious awareness of the internal state of the person sending the signals (Öhman, 2002). Theory of mind represents the critical ability to make inferences about the intentions of other people and their beliefs and to infer whether the emotions signaled by facial expressions or other cues are or are not an accurate reflection of the actual feelings of the individual (Baron-Cohen, 1995; Leslie, 1987).

Girls and women have advantages in most other individual-level social competencies, and one might then expect them to have an advantage for at least some aspects of theory of mind (see also Baron-Cohen, 2003). From the viewpoint of intrasexual competition, however, I predict that girls and women will have advantages when it comes to understanding other girls and women and especially as this relates to these others' thoughts, intentions, and feelings about significant relationships, especially romantic relationships and same-sex friendships. I predict that boys and especially men will be focused on competitors' thoughts and intentions as they relate to larger scale groups and politics. Rather than a focus on what the competitor is intending with respect to a few specific relationships, the focus is on how a potential competitor intends to organize larger competitive groups or convince many others to vote for them in an election. These predictions follow from my discussion in chapter 9 of this volume (in the section titled Benefits of Control) of sex differences in how men and women prefer to organize their social worlds. Unfortunately, little of the theory of mind research has focused on sex differences, and the work that has does not address my predictions.

Studies that have contrasted the sexes suggest either no sex difference on the currently available theory of mind tasks (Lucariello, Durand, & Yarnell, 2007) or that girls and women have a small advantage (Banerjee, 1997; Bosacki, 2000; Bosacki & Astington, 1999; Charman & Clements, 2002; S. Walker, 2005); one study found an advantage for men on one theory of mind task (Russell, Tchanturia, Rahman, & Schmidt, 2007). In one of the more comprehensive of these studies, Banerjee (1997) administered two theory of mind tests to 3- to 5-year olds. The first assessed how well the children understood that the expression of emotion cues could differ from the individual's actual feelings; children who do not understand this distinction believe, for instance, that if another individual "looks happy," then he or she must feel happy. The second test assessed the children's understanding of social display rules: that emotion signals should be suppressed in certain situations so as, for example, not to "hurt another person's feelings." Both of these competencies were assessed by presenting the children with a series of stories in which the child character was motivated to hide his or her emotional state, as illustrated by the following:

> Diana has a brother named Bill. Bill wasn't very nice to Diana today so Diana wants to hide his favorite toy. That's what she does—she hides his favorite toy. When Bill comes home he can't find his toy anywhere. Diana is really happy because Bill can't find his toy anywhere. But, Diana doesn't want Bill to see how she feels, because then Bill will shout at her. So, Diana tries to hide how she feels. (Banerjee, 1997, p. 115)

After hearing each story, the children were asked a number of questions to ensure that they remembered and understood the story plot. They were then presented with a series of facial drawings depicting happy, sad, and neutral expressions and were asked "Show me the picture for how Diana really feels. How does Diana really feel when Bill can't find his favorite toy?" (Banerjee, 1997, p. 116). After this, they were asked to point to the picture for how Diana was trying to look. A similar procedure was used to assess their understanding of display rules. The results showed that many 3-year-olds have some understanding of the difference between emotion cues (e.g., facial expressions) and internal feelings and some understanding of display rules, although both of these competencies were more fully developed in 5-year-olds. Girls had a better understanding than boys of the difference between emotions and feelings, especially for stories associated with a positive feeling. Both boys and girls understood that emotion signals should be suppressed in some situations (e.g., so as not to "hurt someone's feelings"). In situations in which it is appropriate to display positive emotions, boys more frequently than girls stated that emotion displays should be suppressed. The overall results suggest that preschool girls understand better than boys that others' emotion cues can differ from their feelings. In terms of display rules, girls "seem more attuned to the social context" (Banerjee, 1997, p. 127) than boys. Charman and Clements (2002) replicated Banerjee's findings of an advantage for young girls, but this sex difference disappeared by age 6 years. Using a more complex theory of mind task, Bosacki (2000; Bosacki & Astington, 1999) found that three out of four 12-year-old girls were more skilled than the average same-age boy at making inferences about the thoughts, feelings, and social perspective of their peers.

Other studies suggest different relations between theory of mind competence and the dynamics of boys' and girls' peer relationships (Bosacki & Astington, 1999; Dunn, Cutting, & Demetriou, 2000). S. Walker (2005) found that young girls with good theory of mind skills engaged in more prosocial behavior (e.g., cooperating, sharing) than did less competent girls or boys in general. Boys with good theory of mind skills engaged in more aggressive, disruptive, and attention-seeking behaviors than did less competent boys or girls in general. Dunn et al. found that girls were more likely than boys to focus on the internal feelings of friends during potential conflicts of interest, whereas boys were more likely to focus on emotionally neutral mental states (e.g., what the friend was thinking). Whether these sex differences in focus reflect an underlying difference in theory of mind competence is not known, however.

The person schema is related to theory of mind but is focused on knowledge about specific significant others, rather than the more general ability to make inferences about the internal states of others. As described in chapter 11 of this volume (in the section titled Peer Relationships), girls' friendships involve more frequent discussions of social and personal problems than do boys' friendships (J. Parker & Asher, 1993; Rose & Asher, 1999), and thus girls often know more personal information about their friends (Markovits, Benenson, & Dolenszky, 2001; Swenson & Rose, 2003). Should the relationship turn sour, this personal information could then be used in the context of relational aggression. Knowledge about the feelings and vulnerability of one's friend is, in theory, less central to boys' relationships because this is not information that is directly relevant to male–male competition. Further research will be needed to test the corresponding prediction that boys and men are more attuned to the physical, athletic, and leadership traits of their peers.

In all, girls may have a small advantage over boys on some theory of mind tasks, but it is not known whether these simply reflect a difference in the developmental emergence of these competencies or if they represent longer term differences. Moreover, the tasks used in these studies focus on dyadic interactions or relationships and thus do not allow for a test of the prediction that boys and men will be better at inferring the political or other large-scale social strategizing (e.g., military strategy) of potential opponents.

The relation between person schema knowledge and accuracy of theory of mind inferences is also in need of elaboration.

Brain and Hormones. The question of which brain regions support theory of mind remains to be resolved. Brain imaging studies suggest that regions that correspond roughly to Areas 32 and 9 in the prefrontal cortex, portions of Areas 38 and 22 in the temporal cortex, or the junction of Areas 22 and 40 of the temporal cortex (see Figure 12.2) may support theory of mind (Gallagher & Frith, 2003; Saxe & Kanwisher, 2003). The first two areas appear to be involved in the mental construction—representation in the conscious–psychological system (see the section titled Conscious–Psychological, chap. 9, this volume)— of the internal states (e.g., feelings, thoughts) of others, whereas the others (e.g., Area 22) support representations of people in general and the retrieval of specific memories of others, presumably related to the person schema. Unfortunately, sex differences are not typically assessed in these studies. In one study that did provide such an assessment, Fukushima and Hiraki (2006) found that women engaged prefrontal regions more strongly than did men when a competitor experienced a negative outcome and emotion; women but not men appeared to automatically register this feeling state in the competitor.

Similarly, there are only a few studies of the relation between prenatal exposure to androgens and postnatal circulating hormone levels and performance on theory of mind tasks (DeSoto, Bumgardner, Close, & Geary, 2007; Knickmeyer, Baron-Cohen, Raggatt, Taylor, Hackett, 2006). Knickmeyer et al. found that girls and women with CAH performed more poorly on a social skills inventory than did other girls and women, but they did not explicitly test theory of mind competencies. DeSoto et al. found that higher testosterone levels in men were associated with poorer performance on one theory of mind task. The few men with extremely high testosterone levels, however, performed very well on this task. Whether there is a nonlinear relation between circulating testosterone and men's theory of mind competencies, as O'Connor et al. (2001) found for men's verbal fluency, remains to be determined.

Group

In comparison with research on individual-level social competencies, there is much less work on sex differences in the cognitive and brain systems that underlie the parsing of the social world into kin, ingroups and outgroups, and ideologically. I cover what is known, beginning with kin, then moving to ingroups and outgroups, and finally discussing group schemas.

Kin

Preferential treatment of kin is ubiquitous across species, and one would expect the same of women and men (W. D. Hamilton, 1964; Kurland &

Gaulin, 2005). The critical evolutionary tests come from the pattern of kin preferences. On the basis of the sex differences in potential rate of reproduction and the cost–benefit trade-offs of focusing reproductive effort on mating or on parenting (see the section titled Parental Care, chap. 3, this volume), women are predicted to invest more in their children than are men, as is the case for mammals in general (Clutton-Brock, 1991). Ample support for this prediction was provided in chapter 6 of this volume. In chapter 10 (in the section titled Play Parenting), I touched on the prenatal and postnatal hormonal influences on girls' and women's interest in children, which almost certainly contribute to the sex difference in parental investment.

A less obvious prediction is that men will show a bias for male kin, especially when their group is engaged in frequent intergroup conflict; this appears to be the case. In societies characterized by intense physical male–male competition and frequent intergroup conflict, the activities of men tend to be relatively more centered on relationships among adult male kin than on relationships with their wives and children (Draper & Harpending, 1988; Pasternak, Ember, & Ember, 1997). In fact, relatively cohesive male kin groups are often found in traditional societies that are frequently engaged in intergroup conflict, although this pattern is most common in economically midlevel societies, such as agricultural ones without a central government (Pasternak et al., 1997). The reader may recall that the population genetic research touched on in chapter 8 of this volume (in the section titled Population Genetics) also supports this prediction, specifically, the evidence for male philopatry and frequent reproductive replacement of one male kin group by another (e.g., Underhill et al., 2000; Zerjal et al., 2003). In societies with ecologically or socially imposed monogamy, in contrast, men tend to focus more on their wives and children than on the larger network of male kin (Flinn & Low, 1986; K. MacDonald, 1988). This is because central governments and professional police forces suppress male-on-male violence (Daly & Wilson, 1988b) and disrupt kin-based coalitional competition and because the reproductive benefits of violent male–male competition are reduced when men's opportunity for polygyny is suppressed.

The perceptual and cognitive systems that enable people to discriminate kin from nonkin are not well understood but appear to be influenced by experiences during development and by physical similarity (Kurland & Gaulin, 2005). People avoid marrying others with whom they grow up and thus avoid inbreeding risks (Tal & Lieberman, 2007); people implicitly assume that others with whom they grow up are siblings or other close relatives. When processing the faces of unfamiliar others (e.g., those of a different race), the amygdala and fear are often quickly and automatically triggered, resulting in caution with or avoidance of these others (Wheeler & Fiske, 2002). In other words, we have brain systems and feeling states that alert us when we see people who differ from those who are familiar to us. During human evolution, the most familiar people would have been kin. The preferential treatment of kin may also be influenced by feelings of emotional closeness (Korchmaros & Kenny, 2001) and the expectation that kin are likely to provide assistance during times of need (Kruger, 2003). In the context of mate choices (see the section titled Immune System Genes, chap. 7, this volume), women may detect genetic relatedness on the basis of major histocompatibility complex genes signaled through olfactory cues (i.e., odor).

Much remains unresolved when it comes to kin detection in humans. One critical question, for instance, concerns whether there are sex differences favoring men in sensitivity to physical similarity to others of the same sex, as would follow from a male bias for male kin, especially during times of intergroup competition.

Ingroups and Outgroups

When it comes to the cognitive and behavioral processes that support ingroup and outgroup dynamics, there are probably more similarities than differences between boys and girls and men and women (L. E. Davis, Cheng, & Strube, 1996; M. Rogers, Hennigan, Bowman, & Miller, 1984; Towson, Lerner, & de Carufel, 1981); individuals of both sexes readily form ingroups and outgroups and make judgments about ingroup members that are more favorable than their judgments about outgroup members. Sex differences in some aspects of these dynamics follow from an evolutionary history of coalitional male–male competition (see the section titled Male–Male Competition, chap. 8, this volume) and are predicted to become exaggerated during periods of intergroup conflict. The more theoretically important findings are sex differences in the level of bias against and desire to dominate outgroups (Sidanius & Ekehammar, 1983; Sidanius, Pratto, & Mitchell, 2001) and in the level of intragroup cooperation during competitive situations (Gaertner & Insko, 2000; Van Vugt, De Cremer, & Janssen, 2007).

As mentioned in chapter 11 (in the section titled Peer Relationships) in the context of intergroup competition, such as competitive sports, boys form larger same-sex groups than do girls. One dynamic is that boys' groups are better integrated than are girls' groups (J. G. Parker & Seal, 1996) and are more accessible to boys who might otherwise be considered members of an outgroup. M. Rogers et al. (1984) showed that under some conditions Black boys and White boys were more likely to play together than were Black girls and White girls, who showed a strong tendency to self-segregate into same-race groups. The greater integration of boys' groups was largely due to competitive play, that is, "because black and white boys need each other to form complete sports teams" (M. Rogers et al., 1984, p. 215). Even so, the formation of mixed-race teams is to compete against another group of boys, who, by definition, form an outgroup. The mixed-race permeability of boys' groups in the service of outgroup competition should be considered against the backdrop of stronger racism, when mixed-race cooperation is not necessary, among men than among women (Sidanius & Ekehammar, 1983).

Once competitive groups have formed, boys and men show higher levels of ingroup reciprocal cooperation than do girls and women (Gaertner & Insko, 2000; Savin-Williams, 1987; Van Vugt et al., 2007)—girls and women are more reciprocal in dyadic relationships (see the section titled Peer Relations, chap. 11, this volume)—and exert more social pressure on ingroup members to conform to group-sanctioned activities. Both boys and girls exert this pressure on their same-sex peers, but it is relatively stronger within boys' groups than within girls'. Boys, for instance, show a greater concern for and teasing about "cooties" than do girls (Maccoby, 1988). Adults' attitudes toward gay men show the same sex difference. Men and women have similar attitudes toward lesbians, but "men's attitudes toward homosexuality are particularly negative when the target is a gay man rather than a lesbian" (Whitley & Kite, 1995, p. 147); about 7 out of 10 men had more negative attitudes toward gay men than did the average woman. A similar pattern is found with the Ache (Hill & Hurtado, 1996). In this society, men who take on a feminine role and behaviors are called *panegi* (*pane* means unlucky in hunting).

> Men who are *panegi* generally do not hunt, but instead collect plant resources and insect larvae. They weave baskets, mats . . . and other female handicrafts. [These men] were low status and not always treated well. They were forced to do menial chores . . . and were also often the butt of jokes and off-color sexual humor. (Hill & Hurtado, 1996, pp. 276–277)

I assume gay men are discriminated against by other men because of an implicit assumption that gay men's contributions to male–male coalitional competition will be limited; whether this is the case remains to be determined.

The results from several experimental studies also indicate sex differences in the dynamics of ingroup and outgroup relationships, particularly when these relations involve direct competition or the distribution of resources (L. E. Davis et al., 1996; Van Vugt et al., 2007; Van Vugt & Spisak, 2008). In one study, fifth- and sixth-grade children watched videos of boys and girls working in low- (working to meet individual goals) and high-competition settings (Towson et al., 1981). In the high-competition setting, the workers were described as being members of a boys' team or a girls' team, thus creating a same-sex ingroup and an opposite-sex outgroup. The task was to determine each worker's pay. In the low-competition setting, both boys and girls paid the more productive worker more than her or his less productive peer (60% vs. 40%), regardless of the worker's sex. When the more productive worker was a girl in the high-competition setting, boys paid her significantly less than when she was the more productive worker in the low-competition setting. Girls, in contrast, showed the opposite pattern. Girls paid productive boys the same amount in the high- and low-competition settings but substantially favored productive girls in the high-competition setting. In short, during periods of competition, boys discriminated against the outgroup, and girls "boosted" the ingroup.

L. E. Davis et al. (1996) studied the behavior of same-sex groups that differed in racial composition, thus implicitly creating a same-race ingroup and other-race outgroup. Each group was composed of 4 individuals: 2 White and 2 Black or 3 of one race and 1 of the other. Each group was provided with a brief description of 10 people (no information was provided on race) and was then "given the hypothetical scenario that war had been declared and that an existing fallout shelter could support only six individuals. Thus, four individuals must be excluded from the shelter so that six could live to rebuild a new society" (L. E. Davis et al., 1996, p. 159). The task was to reach a consensus about which 4 people would be excluded from the shelter. The contentiousness allowed for the testing of several hypotheses about group relationships, one of which is that intergroup tensions increase when ingroups and outgroups are of equal size, and indeed this was the case. Both men and women rated the group atmosphere as relatively cold and unpleasant for groups that contained 2 individuals of each race. For women, however, the racial composition of the group did not influence their overall satisfaction with the final decision; most women were satisfied. Men's highest levels of satisfaction were found for groups in which one race was the majority and lowest levels when the group consisted of 2individuals from each race. The pattern suggests that women were able to reach a consensus that was supported by all of the group members, regardless of group composition. Men reached a consensus when the ingroup had a numerical majority but did not reach a satisfactory consensus when the ingroup and outgroup were equal in size; intergroup cooperation was lower for men but not for women when the ingroup and the outgroup were equally matched (L. E. Davis et al., 1996).

Sidanius and his colleagues have repeatedly demonstrated that men—across ethnic group, social class, education level, religion, nationality, and political party—have a stronger group-related social dominance orientation than do women (Sidanius et al., 2001; Sidanius, Pratto, & Bobo, 1994; see also the section titled Benefit of Control, chap. 9, this volume). Men are more likely than women to view groups, however defined (e.g., nationality, ethnically, arbitrarily), as hierarchically arranged in terms of social status and distribution of resources and to endorse policies (e.g., military spending) that will strengthen the ingroup vis-à-vis the competitive abilities of other groups. Across these studies, about two out of three men endorsed group-based inequality more strongly than did the average woman. Moreover, individual differences in men's social dominance orientation were weakly related, if at all, to their scores on tests of their desire for ingroup dominance (Pratto, Sidanius, Stallworth, & Malle, 1994). Even men who are low on the ingroup status hierarchy can have a strong identification with their ingroup and strong attitudes about the hierarchical position of their group relative to other groups.

In sum, individuals of both sexes form ingroups and outgroups and generally favor ingroup members over outgroup members. However, relative to girls and women, boys and men form larger ingroups, exert more intense social pressures on ingroup members to adhere to group ideologies, are more cooperative within the ingroup during times of intergroup competition, and regardless of their ingroup status have more hierarchical and prejudicial attitudes about intergroup relationships. All of these sex differences result in cohesive all-male groups and groups that are easily provoked into coalition-based competition, in keeping with the pattern of male–male competition found in traditional societies (see the section titled Male–Male Competition, chap. 8).

Brain and Hormones. In addition to the previously noted activation of the amygdala when processing the faces of members of an outgroup (Wheeler & Fiske, 2002), areas of the medial prefrontal cortex involved in processing social information (e.g., see Area 32, Figure 12.2) and sometimes the insula (not shown in Figure 12.2) may be activated (L. T. Harris & Fiske, 2006). The insula is associated with feelings of disgust (Murphy, Nimmo-Smith, & Lawrence, 2003), and the combination suggests that under some conditions members of outgroups can evoke strong feelings of anger and disgust. When combined with little or no activation of the prefrontal cortex, that is, no explicit, conscious evaluation of these individuals, the result can be an emotional dehumanization of the outgroup (L. T. Harris & Fiske, 2006); in contrast, areas of the prefrontal cortex (Area 47) may contribute to favorable evaluation of ingroup members (Van Bavel, Packer, & Cunningham, 2008). Unfortunately, scientists do not know whether there are sex differences in the pattern of brain activation when processing outgroup information or whether any such differences are moderated by levels of intergroup competition or individual differences in social dominance orientation.

As I described in chapter 8 (in the section titled Testosterone), there is some evidence for changes in men's testosterone levels in the context of group-level competition. As a reminder, Bernhardt, Dabbs, Fielden, and Lutter (1998) found that sports fans' testosterone increased if their team won and decreased if it lost. Neave and Wolfson (2003) found larger pregame increases in testosterone when men's soccer teams played on their home field—defending their "territory"—than when they played on another team's home field. These effects are also influenced by each man's individual contribution to his team's victory or loss and his subjective interpretations about any such contribution (Gonzalez-Bono, Salvador, Serrano, & Ricarte, 1999; Salvador,

2005). Future studies will be needed to test the predictions that men's testosterone and other hormonal responses to group-level competition will differ from those associated with ingroup competition (Oxford, Ponzi, & Geary, in press) and are moderated by their social dominance orientation.

Group Schema

Social–psychological studies have yielded a wealth of information on the processes that contribute to group and social identification (Fiske, 2002; Hewstone, Rubin, & Willis, 2002). *Social identification theory*, as an important example, refers to the categorizing of oneself and others on the basis of a personal identification with a socially defined category, such as nationality or religion (Tajfel & Turner, 1979). Self-evaluations and evaluations of others as well as the ingroup and outgroup biases described previously are influenced by the social groups (e.g., sex, race, nation) that contribute to one's identity. Some scholars have argued that the sex differences in social dominance orientation actually reflect social identification processes, specifically, the extent to which men and women identify with the social groups of male and female, respectively, and their attitudes toward perceived inequalities in the social privileges of these two groups (e.g., M. S. Wilson & Liu, 2003).

From an evolutionary perspective, social dominance orientation and social identity theory are not competing, but rather complementary, processes. As detailed in chapter 9 (in the section titled Group), social identification enables the formation of larger and therefore more competitive social groups, and one of the core selection pressures for the establishment and maintenance of large competitive groups is coalitional male–male competition. In this situation, men are predicted to identify with male-based social competitive groups and to organize these groups hierarchically. If this hypothesis is correct, then social identification with competitive groups (e.g., a sports team, a nationality) should be more easily instantiated in men than in women, and men should show a stronger tendency to organize themselves around these social competitive identities than women.

As with ingroup and outgroup dynamics, there are probably more similarities than differences in women's and men's social identification processes. Under conditions that implicitly or explicitly provide a reminder of one's mortality (e.g., being exposed to issues associated with death), both women and men show a marked increase in their endorsement of the ingroup's social ideology and more negative attitudes toward people who question this ideology (Arndt, Greenberg, Pyszczynski, & Solomon, 1997). These findings, however, were confounded by the use of the ingroup category (e.g., America) along with the mortality cue manipulation. In a series of experiments in which mortality risk was explicitly (e.g., writing about one's death) or implicitly (e.g., subliminal presentation of the word *death* during a computer-based task) presented without reference to an ingroup social category, Arndt, Greenberg, and Cook (2002) found that men and women differ in their subsequent thoughts. Men thought more about group-related ideologies, as such nation, whereas women thought more about romantic relationships (see also Bugental & Beaulieu, 2009). These results provide preliminary support for the just-mentioned hypotheses, but many questions remain to be answered. For instance, do competition-related increases in testosterone make these ingroup social ideologies more accessible in men?

CONCLUSION

There is no question that men and women differ in many respects, in terms of brain size and organization and the corresponding pattern of cognitive competencies. The debate is now focused on the origins of these differences, in particular, the contributions of biology and culture. As is discussed throughout this book, an exclusive focus on one type of explanation or the other creates a false dichotomy because evolved biases are expressed in cultural contexts that can exaggerate, suppress, or distort the expression of the corresponding behaviors or cognitive competencies. The real debate is with regard to the relative contributions of biology and culture and the extent to which the former is modifiable by the latter. The debate will no doubt continue for some time to come. My goal for this chapter was to consider whether existing sex differences in brain and folk psychological cognitions are consistent with what has been discussed about intrasexual competition and intersexual choice in previous chapters.

The evolutionary history of cognitive sex differences is more readily apparent than is the evolutionary history of sex differences in brain size and organization. This is because few of the associated studies were specifically designed to test predictions related to sexual selection. As an example, the finding that men have a larger brain, on average, than women, even after controlling for body size, is consistent with findings for other species of primate (Sawaguchi, 1997); more intense male–male competition in social primates is associated with larger brain size in males than females. However, the relation between gross size differences and male–male competition or female choice remains to be determined (but see G. F. Miller, 2000). A more definitive case for the importance of sexual selection comes, in my opinion, from sex differences in brain regions that support cognitive and behavioral competencies directly related to intrasexual competition or intersexual choice.

Strong candidates are the planum temporale and other language-supporting brain areas. More precisely, women's size and organizational advantages in these areas (C. M. Leonard et al., 2008) fit well with their advantages on many dimensions of language competence (R. A. Block et al., 1989). If language is more central to female–female competition than to male–male competition, then these regions have been elaborated more in women than in men as a result of women's intrasexual competition. Other strong candidates include the amygdala and ventromedial areas of the prefrontal cortex and the interconnections between them (Gur et al., 2002; Kilpatrick et al., 2006), as related to the processing of nonverbal social information (e.g., facial expressions) and reacting to social dynamics. As noted earlier, men's larger amygdala is related to hormonal changes during puberty (J. L. Wood et al., 2008) and may result in lower thresholds for behaviorally reacting in sexual and aggressive contexts. The lower threshold would contribute to men's disproportionate use of physical aggression (R. C. Gur et al., 2002), especially as directed toward other men (Daly & Wilson, 1998b). The use of physical aggression is of course a common feature of male–male competition (see the section titled Male–Male Competition, chap. 8, this volume).

In any case, there are sex differences in all three core areas of folk psychology, specifically, the processing of information related to the self, other individuals, and with respect to group dynamics. The combination of sexual selection and cultural influences provides a vantage point for understanding these differences that cannot be captured by either process alone. Social psychological theories regarding the sexual objectification of women have captured a real phenomenon (e.g., Fredrickson et al., 1998) but leave unanswered the more basic question as to why women would be objectified more than men. The answer can be found with the sex differences in parental investment and the cost–benefit trade-offs associated with casual sex. It is not a coincidence that many of the physical traits that are objectified in women are the same traits that men use in their mate choices and the same traits that are cues to women's fertility (see the section titled Physical Attributes and Fertility, chap. 7, this volume). The combination of male choice and thus female–female competition makes some traits (e.g., facial features, breasts) more central to women's sense of self than others, but cultural factors can exaggerate this focus and has in Western mass media (Cusumano & Thompson, 2000).

The sex differences in the individual-level cognitive competencies (e.g., reading body language, facial expressions) indicate that girls and women have a much more nuanced approach to relationship dynamics than do boys and men. As I mentioned in chapter 8 (in the section titled Women's Aggression), female–female competition often involves subtle, at least in comparison with male–male competition, manipulation of social relationships, especially when the competition is over a romantic partner (Crick, Casas, & Mosher, 1997; R. L. Smith, Rose, & Schwartz-Mette, 2009). Women are not predicted to escalate to physical competition over mates because the benefits are lower than for men; in traditional societies noncompetitive men risk elimination from the gene pool (see the section titled Competition in Traditional Societies, chap. 8, this volume). Because they are smaller and not as physically strong as men, women's subtlety also provides advantages in their relationships with men. A key folk psychological domain in which men are predicted to have an advantage is in the formation of ideologically based ingroups. This follows from an evolutionary history of male–male competition and the competitive advantage of large ingroups; ideologies allow for the formation of larger ingroups than would otherwise be the case. There is much to be learned, but boys and men do show a different pattern of ingroup and outgroup dynamics than do girls and women, especially during intergroup competitions (e.g., Van Vugt et al., 2007), and they think more in terms of group ideologies than do girls and women in threatening circumstances (Arndt et al., 2002; Bugental & Beaulieu, 2009).

13

SEX DIFFERENCES IN FOLK BIOLOGY AND FOLK PHYSICS

I continue my discussion of sex differences in brain and cognition but now turn my attention to the folk biological and folk physical systems described in chapter 9 (in the section titled Folk Domains). The reader—as a member of a highly social species and situated in circumstances that are almost certainly far removed from those experienced by people in traditional societies—may not fully appreciate the importance of folk biological and folk physical competencies. The combination is critical for survival in traditional cultures and provided our ancestors with the ability to modify and control the ecology in ways that are uniquely human. Without the corresponding ability to dominate the ecology (R. D. Alexander, 1989), the modern world as we know it would not exist and would not be maintainable. I addressed R. D. Alexander's concept of ecological dominance and the evolution of the associated brain and cognitive systems in *The Origin of Mind: Evolution of Brain, Cognition, and General Intelligence* (Geary, 2005b) but did not address sex differences in these systems. I do so here.

FOLK BIOLOGY

I introduced the fundaments of folk biology in chapter 9 (in the section titled Folk Biology) and argued in chapter 5 (in the section titled Sexual Division of Labor) that the sexual division of labor and its evolution are not the primary sources of human sex differences. This does not mean that the sexual division of labor, in particular, hunting and gathering, did not result in the evolution of sex differences in some forms of folk biological and folk physical competence (Silverman & Eals, 1992), but some of these followed from sex differences that emerged earlier in our evolutionary history; for instance, coalitional male–male competition likely preceded cooperative hunting. Those aspects of the sexual division of labor that influence women's and men's mate choices (Betzig, 1989) are now components of natural as well as sexual selection; as reviewed in chapter 7 of this volume (in the section titled Actual Choices), women prefer good hunters as mates. Folk biological knowledge is also important for the preparation of traditional medicines, including use of animal parts and native plants for the treatment of a wide array of common ailments (Mahawar & Jaroli, 2008).

To the extent that folk biological knowledge influenced skill at gathering, hunting, and treating illness and to the extent that women and men differed in these activities, sex differences evolved in the cognitive and brain systems that support ease of learning about and interest in other species (Barbarotto, Laiacona, Macchi, & Capitani, 2002; Caramazza & Shelton, 1998). A sex difference in folk biological interests, for instance, is predicted to manifest during development, following the argument laid out in chapters 9 (in the section titled Development of Functional Systems) and 10 (in the section titled Play) of this volume. Boys are predicted to show greater interest in potentially hunted species and to engage in early play activities, such as selective imitation of men's and older boys' hunting, that prepare them to become hunters in adulthood. Girls are predicted to show a bias for flora and interest in their potential uses in foods and medicines. Unfortunately, sex differences in folk biological knowledge have not been systematically assessed by either ethnobiologists who study classification systems in traditional societies or developmental psychologists who study children's intuitive understanding of the behavior and growth of plants and animals (Berlin, Breedlove, & Raven, 1966; Keil, 1992). On the basis of the available research, it appears that the folk biological knowledge of boys and girls and men and women is more similar than different, but some differences in knowledge of flora and fauna have been found as well as hints of a sex difference in the brain systems that support this knowledge.

Folk Biological Knowledge

Figure 9.2 (see chap. 9) shows that folk biological knowledge is categorized in terms of flora, fauna, and essence. Sex differences in an understanding of the essence of these species have not been explicitly assessed, but they are implied by sex differences in knowledge of flora and fauna.

Flora

Berlin, Boster, and O'Neill (1981; Boster, 1985) conducted one of the more extensive assessments of sex differences in folk biological knowledge with their study of the Aguaruna, a forest-dwelling tribe in northern Peru. Their subsistence activities include gardening, fishing, hunting, and collecting foods in the forest. Among other assessments, women and men were asked to name and classify (i.e., put related species together) species of plants grown in local gardens and were interviewed to determine their depth of knowledge about these different species and their growth (Boster, 1985). As a group, women showed more agreement among themselves about the classification of these species, showed greater complexity in their overall classification system, and had more nuanced knowledge about individual species. In a study of the Paniya and Kuruma tribes in India, Cruz García (2006) found that mothers were more knowledgeable of local plants than fathers and passed this folk biological knowledge to their children; children also learn from other adults and from peers (Setalaphruk & Price, 2007).

Both women and men can be healers in traditional cultures (e.g., Ankli, Sticher, & Heinrich, 1999), but use of plants to treat illness appears to be more common among women than among men (Begossi, Hanazaki, & Tamashiro, 2002; Monteiro, Albuquerque, Lins-Neto, Araújo, & Amorim, 2006; Nolan & Robbins, 1999); in some cultures, however, only men are healers (Teklehaymanot & Giday, 2007). Figueiredo, Leitao-Filho, and Bergossi, (1993, 1997) found that for groups of South Amerindians residing at the Sepetiba Bay region of Brazil, women showed greater knowledge of medicinal plants than did men. J. M. Nolan and Robbins (1999) described women healers in the rural Ozark Mountains (Arkansas and Missouri, United States):

> In Ozark communities, women play pivotal roles in the delivery of health care. For example, it is mostly women who gather wild plants from forests and herbs from garden patches to prepare medicinal concoctions, provide treatment to the sick, and assist in natal events . . . Known among the hill folks as *granny women*, these practitioners are especially experienced in childbirth management . . . yet are knowledgeable in using plant-based medicines for treating illnesses. (p. 68)

The potential usefulness of this folk biological knowledge was demonstrated in a study of the Tsimané, a horticultural and foraging society in the Amazon (Bolivia; McDade et al., 2007). The activity of the immune system—indicating current infection—and indices of adequate nutrition and growth were assessed for 330 children across 13 Tsimané villages. Mothers' and fathers' folk biological knowledge was assessed and used to predict their children's health. After controlling for multiple other factors (e.g., age, years of formal education), these researchers found that mothers with more diverse folk biological knowledge had children with fewer infections and children who were at lower risk of poor nutrition and stunted growth. Mothers in the bottom 15% to 20% of folk biological knowledge had children who were 50% more likely to be in poor health in comparison with children whose mothers had average folk biological knowledge. Fathers' folk biological knowledge was also considerable but did not contribute to their children's health beyond the contributions of their wives' knowledge. McDade et al. suggested "women may be experts in using plants to prevent and treat infectious disease, whereas men may possess more knowledge relevant to construction or habitat management" (p. 6137).

Fauna

Given men's greater participation in hunting in traditional societies, it is not surprising that they have more complex knowledge of local fauna than do women. Berlin et al. (1981) asked groups of Aguaruna men and women to name and classify more than 150 specimens of local species of bird, some of which men hunt with blowguns. The classification system of men was more highly differentiated and showed more consistency across raters than did the classification system of women. For many species, the men's classification system was very similar to the corresponding taxonomy developed by Western biologists. Atran (1994) found a similar sex difference in the folk biological knowledge of the Itza-Maya (Guatemala). Men and women showed similar taxonomies for local animals but differed considerably in their level of expertise. In their classifications, women were more likely to rely on static morphological features of the animal, such as color or body shape, than were men, whereas men relied "more on complexly related features of behavior, habitat, diet, and functional relationship to people" (Atran, 1994, p. 331) than did women.

In support of the predicted developmental sex difference, there is some indication that boys attend to potentially dangerous and wild animals more often than do girls and know more about these animals (Blurton Jones, Hawkes, & O'Connell, 1997; Eibl-Eibesfeldt, 1989; Setalaphruk & Price, 2007). For instance, Eibl-Eibesfeldt noted that boys growing up in a kibbutz (Israel) "often identified in their symbolic games with animals, such as horses, dogs, snakes, frogs, and wolves, and not with those surrounding them, like cows, lambs, sheep or chickens" (Eibl-Eibesfeldt, 1989, p. 282). He also found that the drawings of

!Ko boys (central Kalahari) depicted domestic and wild animals about 3 times more frequently than did girls' drawings. Blurton Jones et al. (1997) documented a related sex difference in the self-initiated activities of Hadza (Tanzania) children older than 10 years of age. Before this age, both boys and girls forage. After this age, boys generally restrict their activities to hunting, despite the fact that their hunting returns—in terms of calories—are much lower than would be the case if they continued to forage.

Brain and Hormones

Although the evidence is not conclusive, because of a meager research base, there are hints of sex differences in the brain systems that support folk biology. There is very little research on the relation between folk biological knowledge and exposure to sex hormones, but I review what is known.

Brain. Scientists' understanding of the brain systems that support people's folk biological knowledge comes largely from studies of brain injury (e.g., stroke) or disease (e.g., encephalitis) as these affect the ability to categorize, discriminate, and describe (e.g., the function of a saw) plants, animals, and man-made objects (Farah, Meyer, & McMullen, 1996; Laws & Neve, 1999; A. Low et al., 2003). In these studies, an individual who suffered from a stroke might be asked to point to the carrots or airplane in Figure 13.1. The results provide support for distinct perceptual, cognitive, and brain mechanisms for the categorization of living and man-made things (Capitani, Laiacona, Mahon, & Caramazza, 2003; Farah et al., 1996) and some evidence for distinct systems for the categorization of and knowledge about plants and animals (Hart & Gordon, 1992). Because injury and disease typically result in damage to multiple brain regions, these studies have not allowed for the localization of this knowledge to specific regions. These studies do suggest, at the very least, involvement of the left temporal cortex (e.g., see Area 22, Figure 12.2, chap. 12, this volume), as do some brain imaging studies. A. Low et al. (2003) found evidence that different but adjacent regions of the left temporal cortex represented categories of plants, animals, clothes, and furniture.

In any case, a more interesting pattern is that men are overrepresented by a factor of 3 to 1 among patients with difficulties identifying and describing fruits and vegetables following some forms of brain damage (Laiacona, Barbarotto, & Capitani, 2006). These findings are preliminary but do not appear to be related to women's advantage in verbal fluency (see the section titled Language, chap. 12, this volume), which would provide them with an advantage on some of these assessments (e.g., number of vegetables that can be named in one minute), or their greater familiarity with vegetables. The categorization and naming of animal species has not been as extensively assessed, but existing results suggest no sex differences for identifying and describing animals following brain injury (Laiacona et al., 2006). For normal

Figure 13.1. Items used to assess people's ability to discriminate plants, animals, and man-made objects. Certain forms of brain injury can make it difficult for the individual to point to items in one category (e.g., man-made) but not others (e.g., fruits).

adults, McKenna and Parry (1994) found that women were better at naming fruits and vegetables and men were better at naming animals, but other studies have not found this sex difference (Barbarotto et al., 2002); men are better at naming tools, however (see the section titled Tool Use later in this chapter). Unfortunately, the key prediction that men will be more attuned to wild animals as contrasted with pets has not been assessed in these studies.

Hormones. A strong link between fluctuating hormone levels and sex differences in folk biological knowledge is not expected because fruits and vegetables must be gathered daily and animals hunted regularly in traditional societies. Prenatal exposure to testosterone and hormonal changes associated with puberty may bias boys and girls and men and women to focus on different features of the biological world and to have different interests (e.g., wild animals vs. flowers), but this remains to be demonstrated.

Sex hormones may have less direct influences on folk biological competencies. As described in the section titled Representation later in this chapter, Silverman and Eals (1992) hypothesized that women's advantage in object location memory is the result of the sexual division of labor, specifically, women's gathering. The sex difference does not emerge until puberty, suggesting a potential influence of sex hormones on this form of memory (Voyer, Postma, Brake, & Imperato-McGinley, 2007). As described in chapter 10 of this volume (in the section titled Locomotor and Exploratory Play), some hunting competencies (e.g., use of bow and arrow) improve as a result of physical growth during puberty, but it is not known whether there is a corresponding improvement in folk biological knowledge and related interests and cognitive competencies. One possibility, for instance, is that these hormonal changes also result in improved detection of movement in large-scale space, as would be important for the detection of potential prey at long distances.

Origin

At this point, scientists do not know enough to draw firm conclusions about the origin of the sex differences in folk biological competencies. The differences found in traditional societies could result from the different subsistence activities of men and women. These activities could result in a sex difference in knowledge of flora and fauna without any inherent differences in the ways in which women and men organize or learn about the biological world (e.g., Boster, 1985). This explanation is less likely for sex differences that have emerged in modern societies, however (Laiacona et al. 2006). I suspect the differences arise from the combination of sex differences inherent in attentional and interest biases and corresponding sex differences in engagement with the biological world. The tendency of boys to attend to wild and potentially dangerous animals more frequently than girls might reflect such an attentional bias, and their play hunting, a corresponding activity that would eventually result in a sex difference favoring men, might result in knowledge of local fauna (Blurton Jones et al., 1997; Eibl-Eibesfeldt, 1989).

FOLK PHYSICS

The review of sex differences in folk physics follows the organization shown in Figure 9.2 (see chap. 9), that is, in terms of movement, representation, and tool use. *Movement* refers to our ability to act on and respond to the physical world, and *representation* is our ability to remember and mentally reconstruct this world. *Tool use* is our ability to modify objects and use them to gain control of biological resources (e.g., weapons used in hunting), change the physical world or our exposure to it (e.g., build shelters, damns), and influence human social dynamics (e.g., weapons used in warfare).

Movement

I review sex differences in movement-related competencies in terms of cognition, brain, and hormones and as potentially related to sexual selection and the sexual divisions of labor.

Cognition

I return to G. M. Alexander's (2003) hypothesis about the development of the *where* as contrasted with the *what* stream of the visual system (see the section titled Infancy, chap. 10, this volume), specifically, that prenatal and early postnatal exposure to testosterone may enhance aspects of the development and functioning of the where system and result in a sex difference favoring boys in interest in object motion. This framework and the early sex difference in attentional focus on object motion may provide the seeds for later sex differences in the detection of objects obscured in a complex visual scene, detecting and tracking the movement of objects in physical space, and skill at behaviorally reacting to these moving objects (Law et al., 1993; Peters, 1997; Schiff & Oldak, 1990). A related question is whether boys' and men's advantage in throwing accuracy is supported by a sex difference in the where and coordinated systems? This question addresses the hypothesis that men's use of projectile weapons in male–male warfare and in hunting resulted in an evolutionary elaboration of the supporting cognitive and brain systems.

Detecting Objects. Men show several advantages in the visual system, even though women have more sensitive sensory systems in the areas of touch, smell, taste, and some aspects of hearing (Velle, 1987). Men have sharper vision than do women and are better at detecting the orientation of objects relative to a background and seeing individual objects embedded in a complex montage of objects. The male advantages in these areas are sometimes found before puberty and appear to be similar to skill at detecting the movement of animals or other people in a forest or at a distance against a natural background; before puberty about three out of five boys show better skills in these areas than does the average girl, whereas in adulthood about 7 out of 10 men outperform the average woman (Linn & Peterson, 1985; Velle, 1987; D. Voyer, S. Voyer, & Bryden, 1995). These sex differences might be related to the where visuospatial system combined with a heightened sensitivity of the primordial—early evolution—vision system. The primordial vision system results in sensitivity to colors in the yellow–blue spectrum and is often accompanied by insensitivity to color variation in the red–green spectrum (G. M. Alexander, 2003).

About 8% of men have varying degrees of *color blindness*, that is, they are poor at discriminating colors in the red–green spectrum; about 2% of men cannot discriminate red from green at all (Nathans, Piantanida, Eddy, Shows, & Hogness, 1986). Discrimination of red from green appears to be an evolved feature of the primate visual system that supports the detection of fruit and other colorful foods (Shyue et al., 1995), and thus these men should be at an evolutionary disadvantage. However, sensitivity to variation in color in the red–green spectrum comes with a cost or insensitivity with an advantage. Men who are color-blind have an advantage in detecting camouflaged objects, especially objects in dappled light (M. J. Morgan, Adam, & Mollon, 1992). In other words, the evolution and expression of systems that enable the detection of, for example, red objects against a green background comes at a cost to the ability to detect camouflaged objects embedded in a varied background and vice versa.

The extent to which this ability extends to men without obvious color blindness and relates to sex differences on tests of spatial cognition that require identification of objects embedded in a complex background is not known. The hypothesis that these men will be especially advantaged in detecting motion of camouflaged objects also remains to be tested. Whether or not all men can detect visually camouflaged objects, they also have, on average, an advantage in detecting the location of sounds and in identifying a specific sound against background noise (McFadden, 1998).

Tracking Objects. Men also show advantages in the ability to judge the velocity and trajectory of a moving object, generate visual images of a moving object, estimate when an object moving directly toward them will hit them, and hit a moving object with a thrown projectile (Pavio & Clark, 1991; Schiff & Oldak, 1990). In a set of experiments, Law, Pellegrino, and Hunt (1993) asked men and women to judge the relative distance traveled by two objects and their relative velocity. No sex differences were found in the ability to judge which object had traveled farther, but men are more accurate in estimating distance at longer distances than those assessed by Law et al. (Deregowski, Shepard, & Slaven, 1997). Men showed a moderate to large advantage in the ability to judge object velocity. In one of the studies, more than 4 out of 5 men were more sensitive to relative velocity than was the average woman. Practice and feedback improved the performance of both men and women, but the magnitude of the men's advantage did not change; practice does, however, reduce or eliminate men's advantage on some less complex tracking tasks and for some visual attention tasks (Feng, Spence, & Pratt, 2007; Joseph & Willingham, 2000).

In another series of experiments, Schiff and Oldak (1990) demonstrated that men were more accurate than women in judging time of arrival, that is, judging when an object moving toward them would either hit them or pass by. For objects that could only be seen, about 3 out of 4 men were more accurate at judging time of arrival than was the average woman. Men were also more accurate, on average, at judging time of arrival for objects that could only be heard. Judging time of arrival may have a practical function: N. V. Watson and Kimura (1991) found that about 3 out of 4 men could block targets that were thrown at them— tennis balls shot from launching devices—

with both their right and their left hands with greater skill than could the average woman. As a group, men successfully blocked an average of 26 of the 30 tennis balls shot at them, suggesting that the task was too easy for men and thus likely underestimated the magnitude of the sex difference in blocking skill.

Intercepting Objects. As I mentioned in chapter 10 of this volume (in the section titled Physical Competencies), boys and men have a very large advantage over same-age girls and women in throwing distance, velocity, and accuracy (Thomas & French, 1985). Jardine and Martin (1983), as an example, found that about 7 out of 8 adolescent boys threw more accurately at a non-moving object than did the average same-age girl, whereas 9 out 10 of their fathers threw more accurately than their mothers. Peters (1997) assessed men's and women's accuracy at hitting a moving target with a thrown object. Men were more accurate, especially as the speed of the moving object increased, and their accuracy was related to better estimation of the velocity of the target and better timing of the release of the thrown object vis-à-vis the velocity of the target; men's advantage on this task was not related to their reported participation in sports that involved throwing objects. On top of advantages in these component competencies, such as estimating target velocity, Peters hypothesized that men's overall advantage in throwing accuracy was related to the coordination of the where system with a *when* system.

Brain

Detecting and behaviorally reacting to objects moving in space involve coordination of the where and spatial attention regions of the parietal cortex (e.g., see Areas 7, 40, Figure 12.2, chap. 12, this volume) with areas of the visual (e.g., Area 19) and motor (e.g., Area 4) cortices along with contributions from several subcortical (cerebellum, not shown in Figure 12.2) areas (Milner & Goodale, 1995; Posner, 1994; Scott, 2004). There are subtle sex differences in the architecture of most of these brain regions (Amunts et al., 2007; Goldstein et al., 2001; Sowell et al., 2006), but their relation to the previously described sex differences has not been fully explored. There are a few intriguing links, nonetheless.

Amunts et al. (2007) found that men had absolutely and proportionally more volume and surface area in the motion detection region of the right hemisphere (parts of Areas 19, 37, and 39, Figure 12.2, chap. 12, this volume) than did women. The elaboration of men's motion detection brain regions is specific to the right hemisphere and is contrasted with more uniform—because of the sex difference in brain size—sex differences in adjacent areas of the visual cortex. The right motion detection region might also have more connections to other brain regions in men than women. The spatial attention areas of the right parietal cortex, which is dominant over the left in terms of initiating attention shifts (Posner, 1994), may be among these regions, and these in turn are linked with other regions that support behaviorally responding to and acting on the external world (Milner & Goodale, 1995). These sex differences are exciting and potentially analogous to the sex-specific enlargement of the planum temporale related to language processing (C. M. Leonard et al., 2008; see the section titled Language, chap. 12, this volume). Whether these brain regions are organized by prenatal exposure to testosterone given the apparent influence of prenatal hormones on targeting accuracy (see the section that follows) and related to men's advantage in tracking and hitting moving targets remains to be determined.

Moreover, detecting a movement and reacting to this movement may depend on whether the object is at a distance or within arm's length; men typically excel in the latter and women in the former (Ecuyer-Dab & Robert, 2004a). Weiss and colleagues found that attention to objects in *far space* was associated with neural activation of the what visual stream, whereas attention to objects in *close space* was associated with activation of the where visual stream (Weiss et al., 2000; Weiss, Marshall, Zilles, & Fink, 2003). These findings appear to be inconsistent with elaboration of the where visuospatial system in men (G. M. Alexander, 2003), but the results are difficult to interpret with respect to this hypothesis. This is because far space in these studies was less than 6 feet and thus might not engage the space-distance mechanisms involved in the identification of more distant targets and the use of projectile weapons; 6 feet is a range in which blunt force weapons are more likely to be used.

Hormones

Evidence for an influence of hormones on these sex differences comes from targeting tasks and from prenatal exposure (J. A. Y. Hall & Kimura, 1995; Hines et al., 2003; van Goozen, Slabbekoorn, Gooren, Sanders, & Cohen-Kettenis, 2002). Hines et al. found that about 3 out of 4 women affected by congenital adrenal hyperplasia (CAH) were more accurate than the average woman at hitting targets about 10 feet away. For one of the throwing tasks, the accuracy of these women was comparable to that of men, and on the other task their accuracy was in-between that of unaffected women and men. To control for the sex difference in the structure of the arm and shoulders, which can affect throwing competence, J. A. Y. Hall and Kimura compared the throwing accuracy of gay men with that of heterosexual men and women; sexual orientation is likely to be influenced in part by prenatal exposure to sex hormones (e.g., Breedlove, 2000). Heterosexual men were more accurate than heterosexual women, as is typically found, but the targeting accuracy of gay men did not differ from that of heterosexual women (see also van Goozen et al., 2002).

Potential hormonal influences on most of the other sex differences covered in this section have not been assessed as systematically, but influences are likely. Men's advantages in locating objects on the basis of sound and in identifying specific sounds against background noise may be related to prenatal exposure to testosterone (McFadden, 1998) as may their advantage in detecting the geometric orientation of objects (Collaer, Reimers, Manning, 2007; van Goozen et al., 2002). Studies of the relation between circulating hormones and the visuospatial abilities assessed in this section are mixed, however; some studies find a relation (Hampson, 1990a; Hampson & Kimura, 1988), but others do not (Liben et al., 2002; van Goozen et al., 2002). The inconsistent results for circulating hormones may result from larger prenatal than postnatal effects or from subtle and fluctuating effects of circulating hormones. I noted previously that the control of spatial attention is dominated by the parietal cortex of the right hemisphere (Posner, 1994). Circulating testosterone may enhance the functional integration of this brain region with areas of the left hemisphere (Schutter, Peper, Koppeschaar, Kahn, & van Honk, 2005), and estradiol (an estrogen) and progesterone may disrupt it (Hausmann & Güntürkün, 2000). If circulating hormones subtly influence the spatial attentional systems of the right parietal cortex, then detecting an influence of circulating hormones on spatial performance may be difficult given that men's testosterone levels vary across the day and women's sex hormones vary across their ovulatory cycle, as previously discussed.

Representation

In the preceding section, I focused on sex differences in the ability to act on and respond to change in the physical environment, and in this section I focus on sex differences in the ability to form mental representations (e.g., images of the local ecology) of and to remember this environment. Sex differences in these representational and memory skills have been studied for many decades, and the pattern is complex. Men typically outperform women on tests that involve the representation and mental rotation of images in three-dimensional space (see Figure 13.2), and women outperform men on some memory tasks (see the section titled Object Location Memory later in this chapter), but there are often small or no sex differences for other visuospatial tasks (Herlitz, Nilsson, & Bäckman, 1997; Linn &

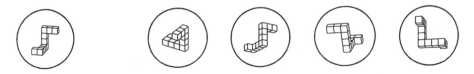

Figure 13.2. A sample item from the Mental Rotation Test (Vandenberg & Kuse, 1978). When rotated, two of the items to the right (first and third items) are identical to the target comparison on the left, and two are different (second and last items).

Petersen, 1985; Silverman & Eals, 1992; Voyer et al., 2007). Moreover, tasks of the same name can produce different results from one study to the next because of differences in task complexity. Men typically outperform women on complex versions of the task (e.g., three-dimensional virtual mazes), but there are no sex differences on less complex versions (e.g., two-dimensional mazes; Coluccia & Louse, 2004). The pattern is complicated further because some visuospatial abilities vary for right- and left-handers and even for right-handers with and without left-handed parents (e.g., Casey & Brabeck, 1989).

Despite these complications, a consistent pattern of sex differences has emerged for representational and memory abilities that are potentially related to the different reproductive and foraging activities of men and women in traditional societies. These competencies include the ability to generate mental representations of the large-scale physical environment, which appears to be related to skill at navigating within this environment; the ability to mentally manipulate or transform three-dimensional representations, which may engage the same cognitive systems used to represent and navigate in three-dimensional space (Just & Carpenter, 1985; Shepard, 1994) or may be useful for tool construction; and memory for the location of specific objects in the environment.

Navigation

As I mentioned in chapter 10 of this volume (in the section titled Locomotor and Exploratory Play), boys have larger home ranges than girls (Matthews, 1987, 1992). The same sex differences are found in adults in traditional and modern societies. Men travel farther than women in traditional societies because of differences in hunting contrasted with foraging, to find mates, and sometimes simply to explore. Across five traditional societies, D. H. MacDonald and Hewlett (1999) reported that men traveled roughly 2 to 4 times farther than women during their typical ranging activities. Ecuyer-Dab and Robert (2004b) asked women and men in Montreal to record their daily personal and professional travel in a diary. Men ranged farther than women for both personal and professional travel in and around Montreal, and men's personal travel range was 1.8 times larger than women's range; D. H. MacDonald and Hewlett found the same 1.8:1 ratio of men's to women's travel ranges for the Aka.

When asked to generate a map after exploring a novel environment, boys' maps showed more accurate clustering of environmental features and more accurate representations of the geometric relations—cardinal direction (e.g., Building A is northwest of Building B)—among these features (Matthews, 1992). Boys and girls also differed in the extent to which they focused on landmarks (e.g., specific buildings) or routes (e.g., roadways) in their maps. In this study and others, girls have been found to attend more to landmarks and relative direction (Building A is left of Building B) and boys to routes and cardinal direction (see also J. Choi & Silverman, 2003). The same pattern is found in adults (C. S. Holding & D. H. Holding, 1989). Galea and Kimura (1993) asked men and women to study a map of an unfamiliar fictitious town and tested their ability to learn a route within this town. Men learned the route in less time with fewer practice trials and made fewer errors during learning. A follow-up task revealed that women remembered more street names and the locations of landmarks, whereas men had a better recall of the geometric relations among the landmarks. Men also show advantages in route learning and navigation when drawing maps (Coluccia, Iosue, & Brandimonte, 2007), navigating in virtual mazes (Moffat, Hampson, & Hatzipantelis, 1998), and finding their way (Silverman et al., 2000). In the Silverman et al. study, women and men were led on a circuitous 410-m walk through an unfamiliar wooded area that did not have obvious external landmarks to aid in navigation. The participants were stopped at four locations, and their sense of cardinal direction was assessed by asking them to place an arrow pointing in the direction of the start location. At a fifth location, they were asked to lead the experimenter back to the start location as quickly and directly as possible. Men's arrow placements and their return walk indicated they had a better sense of cardinal direction than did the women.

Saucier, Bowman, and Elias (2003) found that women tend to use verbal labels for remembering landmarks and relative direction when navigating, whereas men are more likely to rely on a nonverbal visuospatial strategy, consistent with Silverman et al.'s (2000) findings for sense of cardinal direction; the tilt toward use of a verbal versus visuospatial strategy may have a genetic component (W. Johnson & Bouchard, 2007). Men's enhanced sense of large-scale space and geometric relations among landmarks is expressed in other ways. In five experiments, Beatty and Tröster (1987) found that young college men in all regions of the United States had more geographic knowledge (e.g., location of U.S. cities on a map) than did women of the same age and region. Men also had advantages on measures of egocentric and allocentric spatial orientation, but this did not contribute to their geographic knowledge nor did travel history, geography or related coursework, or other potential factors. Men are more interested in and attend more to maps and, as a result, know more about geography.

The potential relation between performance on navigation tasks and skill at mentally rotating three-dimensional images is theoretically important because skill at rotating these images represents one of the larger sex differences in spatial cognition favoring men (Linn & Petersen, 1985; Vandenberg & Kuse, 1978; Voyer et al., 1995). The advantage of boys and men in the ability to generate and rotate three-dimensional images is found at the earliest age at which the test can be reliably administered, early adolescence, and is found at every age thereafter (Linn & Petersen, 1985; Voyer et al., 1995). Between 15 and 20 years of age, about 4 out of 5 boys and men are better able to generate and mentally manipulate three-dimensional images than the average girl or woman, and between 20- and 35-years-of-age about 6 out of 7 men outperform the average woman (Linn & Petersen, 1985). In an extensive analysis of the cognitive processes supporting the ability to generate and rotate these images, Just and Carpenter (1985) concluded that "the cognitive coordinate system within which the figures are represented is the standard environmentally defined one" (p. 165). Stated differently, it appears that the ability to generate and rotate three-dimensional images is dependent to some extent on the same cognitive system involved in generating three-dimensional representations of large-scale physical space (Shepard, 1994), although there is not a perfect one-to-one relation between these competencies (Galea & Kimura, 1993).

Object Location Memory

Boys' and men's advantages in the ability to generate representations of novel environments and to mentally manipulate three-dimensional images stand in sharp contrast to girls' and women's advantages in certain forms of visuospatial memory (Eals & Silverman, 1994; T. W. James & Kimura, 1997). As noted, Silverman and Eals (1992) proposed

> spatial specializations associated with foraging should have . . . evolved in females. Food plants are immobile, but they are embedded within complex arrays of vegetation. Successful foraging, then, would require locating food sources within such arrays and finding them in ensuing growing seasons. (p. 535)

In this view, women should have an advantage over men in the ability to remember objects and their locations.

To test this hypothesis, women and men were given 1 minute to examine the objects in an array similar to that shown in Figure 13.3 and were then presented with two additional sheets of objects (Silverman & Eals, 1992). The first included the same objects shown in the original array and several additional items; the second included the same items shown in the original but some of them were moved to a different location. The first test assessed object memory by asking participants to circle all of the items that were on the original sheet and crossing out new ones, and the second test assessed object location memory by asking participants to circle the objects that were in the same location and crossing out objects that moved. Women outperformed men on both tests. Three additional studies confirmed this pattern and found that 8- to 13-year-old girls outperformed same-age boys on object memory tests but not on location memory tests. The latter finding suggests the sex difference in object location memory does not emerge until puberty.

Figure 13.3. An example of a stimulus array used for tests of object memory and location memory.

Follow-up studies confirmed these basic sex differences, with some nuance for object location memory (Eals & Silverman, 1994; Ecuyer-Dab & Robert, 2007; T. W. James & Kimura, 1997). In a meta-analysis, Voyer et al. (2007) found a modest but highly consistent advantage for girls and women on various object memory tests; about 11 out of 20 girls and women have a better memory for viewed objects than the average same-age boy or man. In the same meta-analysis, they confirmed that there is not a sex difference in object location memory before age 13 years. After this age, girls' and women's advantage on object location tests varies with test and item type. Their most consistent advantages are for familiar items under incidental learning conditions and when asked to recall rather than recognize item location. With incidental learning, the participants are exposed to an array of objects (e.g., randomly placed on a desk) but not explicitly asked to attend to them and then later asked to recall where each object was located. Under these conditions, at least 7 out of 10 girls and women recall more locations than does the average boy or man. There are no sex differences, however, when participants are explicitly asked to learn the location of each object for later testing.

The combination of women's advantages in location memory under incidental learning conditions when asked to recall object location rather than recognize location and their enhanced memory for landmarks provides strong support for Silverman and Eals' (1992) hypothesis. The latter is important because some edible foods, such as tubers (roots), can only be located on the basis of their position relative to local landmarks (Ecuyer-Dab & Robert, 2007). Additional support is provided by the enhanced ability of many women to discriminate subtle variation in natural colors (Jameson, Highnote, & Wasserman, 2001), which, as noted in the section titled Movement earlier in this chapter, appears to have evolved in primates to aid in the detection of fruits (Shyue et al., 1995). With the exception of color-blind dichromatic men, it has long been thought that human eyes contained three types of retinal photopigment, but this might not be the case for a large percentage of women. In a series of genotyping and color perception studies, Jameson et al. found that 23 of 38 women appeared to have four types of photopigment and perceived much greater variation in color than did the remaining 15 women or any of the men. Because the corresponding genes are situated on the X chromosome, about 50% of women may have this enhanced sensitivity to color variation but very few men will (M. Neitz, Kraft, & J. Neitz, 1998).

For most domains, women have a better memory for personal experiences than do men (Herlitz et al., 1997), and this could provide an alternative explanation for women's advantage on object memory and object location tasks. Their advantage is not found on all tasks, however, and in fact men have a considerable advantage on episodic memory tasks that require incidental recall of routes (Herlitz & Rehnman, 2008). The latter is of course consistent with the sex differences reviewed in the section titled Navigation earlier in this chapter but also suggests that women's advantage in episodic memory is not found for all visual arrays. Another possibility is that women's advantage on many episodic memory tasks is related, in part, to evolved advantages in object memory and object location memory, as proposed by Silverman and Eals (1992).

Brain

In chapter 9 (in the section titled Folk Physics), I briefly touched on the brain systems involved in navigation and object location memory. To recap and elaborate, areas of the right hippocampus (not shown in Figure 12.2, chap. 12, this volume) and right parietal cortex (see Area 7, Figure 12.2, chap. 12, this volume) are particularly important for allocentric (e.g., bird's eye view) representations of large-scale space and for navigating in this space (Maguire, Frackowiak, & Frith, 1996; O'Keefe & Nadel, 1978; Spiers et al., 2001). Locating objects in space also engages parts of the parietal cortex as well as left and right parahippocampal areas (areas surrounding the hippocampus; e.g., see Area 27, Figure 12.2, chap. 12, this volume) and part of the fusiform gyrus (see Area 37, Figure 12.2, chap. 12, this volume; see also Ekstrom et al., 2003); the fusiform gyrus is engaged in object identification and naming. Ekstrom et al.'s research illustrates differences in the brain regions involved in navigation and object location. Electrodes were placed in the hippocampus and adjacent brain regions to determine the foci of seizures for patients with severe epilepsy. These individuals then navigated in a computer-generated virtual town. Cells in the hippocampus selectively responded to geometric location, whereas cells in the parahippocampal region responded to specific landmarks; the parahippocampal area is also important for recognizing familiar scenes (Epstein & Higgins, 2007).

At issue is whether anatomical or functional sex differences in these regions are related to the sex differences in spatial navigation and object location memory; sex differences in the anatomy of the hippocampus have been found in several nonhuman species (Jacobs & Schenk, 2003). As noted in chapter 12 of this volume (in the section titled Relative Size and Organization), Sowell et al. (2006) found that women have thicker cortices in some regions of the parietal lobe of the right hemisphere, but men may have more volume, corrected for overall brain size, in other parietal regions (Goldstein et al., 2001). The absolute size of men's hippocampus and anterior parahippocampal areas is larger than that of women, but women's is larger when overall brain size is adjusted (Goldstein et al., 2001). The absolute size of the posterior portions of the parahippocampal region, those likely involved in scene recognition and landmark memory, is about the same in women and men, even though men have larger brains overall. Whether this is a region-specific enlargement for women, similar to that described for the planum temporale (see the section titled Language, chap. 12, this volume), is not currently known. If so, these regions should show preferential activation in women during object location tasks.

Some functional brain imaging studies have revealed sex differences in the regions engaged during navigation, mental rotation, and spatial perspective taking (Grön, Wunderlich, Spitzer, Tomczak, & Riepe, 2000; Kaiser et al., 2008; Schöning et al., 2007). Unfortunately, the use of different types of spatial tasks and the failure to control for ovulatory cycle phase complicate the interpretation of these results. Despite these complications, there are some intriguing, albeit preliminary, findings. For instance, Grön et al. (2000) examined brain activity while women and men navigated through a virtual maze. Although there were many similarities in the brain regions engaged by women and men during navigation, there were several important differences. Men showed greater activation of the left hippocampus, whereas women showed greater activation of the right prefrontal-parietal network. Men's activation patterns suggested an automatic bottom-up processing of geometric coordinates of the maze to aid in navigation, whereas women's suggested use of a more explicit and effortful top-down strategy. In other words, men seemed to cruise through the maze with less cognitive effort than did women as would be expected if the brain and cognitive systems that support navigation have been more highly elaborated during human evolution for men than for women.

Women also appear to engage in more cognitive effort during the mental rotation of three-dimensional images such as those shown in Figure 13.2 (Jordan, Wüstenberg, Heinze, Peters, & Jäncke, 2002). During the mental rotation of these images, T. Butler et al. (2006) found that women showed greater activation of prefrontal areas associated with cognitive effort than did men, whereas men showed greater activation in an area of the parietal cortex, the precuneus (see Area 7, Figure 12.2, chap. 12, this volume), associated with mental imagery (Cavanna & Trimble, 2006). Using a similar task, Schöning et al. (2007) found more activation in the parietal cortex in men than in women in a different area of the parietal cortex than found by T. Butler and colleagues and that the pattern of women's brain activation varied across their ovulatory cycle. For instance, women showed stronger activation in Broca's area when their progesterone and estrogen levels were at their highest, suggesting some women may use a language-based approach to solving mental rotation problems more frequently at midcycle than at other times. Jordan et al. (2002), in contrast, did not find enhanced activation of this language area in women, but they did not control for ovulatory phase.

In all, the existing evidence is consistent with anatomical and functional sex differences in the brain regions engaged during navigation, three-dimensional mental rotation, and object location memory. The results, however, are not consistent enough or most of the tasks specific enough to draw firm conclusions about the potential relation between the sex differences described in the sections titled Navigation and Object Location Memory earlier in this chapter and the sex differences in brain anatomy and functional activity described here. The potential relation between sex differences in spatial experiences and sex differences in the brain regions—hippocampus, parahippocampal regions, parietal cortex—that support navigation and object location memory also remains to be addressed because experience may affect their structure and functioning (Maguire, Woollett, & Spiers, 2006).

Hormones

As with other cognitive and brain systems discussed in other sections of this chapter and in chapter 12, I consider the potential influences of prenatal and circulating hormones on the sex differences reviewed in this section.

Prenatal. As discussed previously, the comparison of individuals affected by CAH with their unaffected same-sex peers is often used to explore the influence of prenatal sex hormones on human sex differences. When it comes to the spatial abilities covered in this section, results from the associated studies have been mixed (Hines et al., 2003) in part because of small sample sizes and potentially because of individual differences in the severity of CAH (Mueller et al., 2008). Meta-analyses can of course correct for the sample size issue, and this has been done for studies of the ability to mentally rotate three-dimensional images (Puts, McDaniel, Jordan, & Breedlove, 2008). The resulting sample provided information on 128 girls and women with CAH and 61 boys and men with CAH. In comparison with unaffected individuals, almost 7 out of 10 women affected by CAH outperformed their unaffected peers on three-dimensional (or closely related) mental rotation tasks, whereas nearly 3 out of 4 affected men performed more poorly than their unaffected peers; the latter result suggests that higher than normal levels of prenatal androgens may disrupt the organization of this spatial system.

Mueller et al. (2008) constructed a virtual water maze in which individuals had to, in first-person (egocentric) perspective, "swim" to an underwater platform when placed in random locations in the maze. The participants included a comparatively large sample of 57 individuals with CAH who varied in terms of the severity of the disease and thus in level of prenatal androgen exposure. Whether they were in the control group or one of the CAH groups, men swam faster and more directly to the platform and had significantly fewer trials on which they failed to find the platform than did women in all but one group. This group was the women with the severest form of CAH and thus the highest prenatal exposure to androgens among the women. These women swam as quickly to the platform as the men. Their path lengths were shorter, and they had fewer failures to find the platform than did the other women, but the differences were not statistically significant. Although CAH is typically detected at birth and treated, the treatments do not always completely suppress adrenal androgens. The result can be higher than normal exposure to androgens during childhood and juvenility, which results in faster bone maturation. Individuals with CAH and indications of premature bone maturation swam to the platform more quickly and with fewer failures than did individuals with CAH and normal bone maturation, suggesting prepubertal postnatal exposure to androgens can also affect the development of spatial competence. The implications for understanding boys' surge in testosterone in the first few months of their life and the sex differences in spatial cognition (see the section titled Prenatal Hormones, chap. 10, this volume) remain to be explored.

In any case, sexual orientation and sexual identity appear to be influenced by prenatal exposure to sex hormones (Breedlove, 2000; Collaer & Hines, 1995; Hines, Brook, & Conway, 2004) and thus should be related to spatial abilities. This is often the case. Lesbians score higher on many tests of spatial abilities, including three-dimensional mental rotation, than do heterosexual women (Rahman & Wilson, 2003; van Anders & Hampson, 2005), whereas gay men score lower than heterosexual men (Hassan & Rahman, 2007; Rahman,

Anderson, & Govier, 2005; Rahman & Koerting, 2008; Rahman & Wilson, 2003). Using the previously described water maze task, Rahman and Koerting found that gay men had longer swim times than heterosexual men and swim times similar to that of heterosexual women. As is the case for heterosexual women, gay men use more landmarks during navigation (Rahman et al., 2005) and have better object location memories than do heterosexual men (Hassan & Rahman, 2007). Van Goozen et al. (2002) administered a battery of spatial ability measures to transsexual women (female-to-male transsexuals) and men (male-to-female transsexuals) who were also homosexual (some transsexuals are heterosexual) and to heterosexual women and men. Heterosexual women had the lowest scores on three mental rotation tasks, followed by the transsexual women, transsexual men, and heterosexual men. In other words, the performance across groups tracked the likely levels of prenatal exposure to androgens or sensitivity to androgens.

Circulating. As previously discussed, prenatal hormones may contribute to sex differences in brain organization, and circulating hormones may activate these brain regions (see the section titled Sex Hormones and Sexual Selection, chap. 4). If this is the case with spatial cognition, then circulating testosterone may enhance performance or estrogens may inhibit performance on spatial tasks. One of the more consistent findings in this literature is that women's performance on difficult (e.g., three-dimensional mental rotation; see Figure 13.2) but not easy (e.g., two-dimensional rotation) spatial tests is highest during the menstrual phase of the ovulatory cycle and lowest around midcycle when estrogen and progesterone levels are rising (Hampson, 1990a, 1990b; Hausmann, Slabbekoorn, van Goozen, Cohen-Kettens, & Güntürkün, 2000; K. Phillips & Silverman, 1997). In one of the better controlled of these studies, Hausmann et al. measured 8 women's hormone levels every 3 days for 6 weeks, which allowed these scientists to precisely plot the ovulatory cycle. Although the results are in need of replication because of the small sample, performance on a three-dimensional mental rotation test but not two easier spatial tests was higher for 7 of the 8 women during menstruation than at midcycle. The results from these studies suggest estrogen (specifically estradiol) or progesterone might dampen some forms of spatial ability (Sherry & Hampson, 1997) but leave unanswered the potential effect of testosterone.

With the exception of the ovulatory cycle effects on three-dimensional spatial cognition, studies of the relation between estrogen, testosterone, and several other hormones and performance on spatial tests have yielded such mixed results—sometimes a relation is found and other times it is not—that a straightforward hormonal activation or inhibition of the supporting brain regions is unlikely (Gouchie & Kimura, 1991; Hampson & Kimura, 1988; Liben et al., 2002; McKeever, 1995; Moffat & Hampson, 1996; van Goozen, Cohen-Kettenis, Gooren, Frijda, & Van de Poll, 1994). Most of these studies involved a one-time snapshot assessment of hormones and spatial abilities, which may not capture more subtle relations between circulating hormones and these abilities. Specifically, sex hormones may influence spatial learning, bias the individual to use of one type of strategy or another, or interact with individual differences in prenatal exposure to sex hormones or sensitivity (e.g., through number of cell receptor sites) to these hormones.

Burkitt, Widman, and Saucier (2007) examined the relation between testosterone level and women's and men's performance on a mental rotation task and the virtual water maze. The most interesting finding was that women with low testosterone levels showed no improvement on the water maze task across six attempts, but women with high testosterone levels did, as did men regardless of their testosterone levels. A similar study also revealed that higher testosterone was associated with faster learning on the water maze task but only for men (Driscoll, Hamilton, Yeo, Brooks, & Sutherland, 2005). A well-controlled experimental study suggested a learning effect for mental rotations (Aleman, Bronk, Kessels, Koppeschaar, & van Honk, 2004). Here, women took a three-dimensional mental rotation test on separate days, once after taking a testosterone pill and once after taking a placebo (*sugar pill*). Taking testosterone was associated with improved scores but only if the women took the placebo on an earlier day; that is, the benefit of testosterone was only evident if they had prior practice on the test. The results from other studies of hormone administration and change in spatial abilities with learning or repeated testing are mixed, however (Liben et al. 2002; C. Miles, Green, & Hines 2006; Slabbekoorn, van Goozen, Megens, Gooren, & Cohen-Kettenis, 1999; van Goozen et al., 1994; van Goozen, Cohen-Kettenis, Gooren, Frijda, & Van de Poll, 1995; van Goozen et al., 2002).

Performance on these spatial tasks and most other cognitive tasks involves multiple brain regions and many different cognitive processes. The final score results from the adding up of all of these processes and thus may obscure sex differences on one or several of them (Ho, Gilger, & Brink, 1986). G. M. Alexander and Son (2007) used a device that bounced an infrared beam off of the back of people's retinas while they performed the mental rotation task shown in Figure 13.2. This method allowed for the tracking of eye movements during the task and through this a fine-grained analysis of how people were solving these problems. Women and men showed similar eye-tracking patterns, but men allocated relatively more attention to correct alternatives (e.g., the first item in Figure 13.2) and less attention to incorrect ones (e.g., the second item) than did women. Men quickly rejected figures that differed from the target and attended closely to figures that matched the target. For women, higher testosterone was associated with closely attending to correct matches, but testosterone was unrelated to men's attentional patterns.

To further confuse matters, the tendency of one system of brain regions or another to be engaged during spatial tasks may be influenced by circulating hormone levels (Hausmann & Güntürkün, 2000; Schöning et al., 2007). Schöning et al. found that men with higher testosterone levels showed stronger engagement of the parietal cortex while engaged in three-dimensional mental rotations than did other men, whereas women with higher estrogen (i.e., estradiol) levels showed stronger activation in multiple brain regions than did other women (Schöning et al., 2007); the latter effects might be because estrogen can dilate blood vessels and thus increase blood flow throughout the brain. As noted, Schöning et al. found that women at midcycle showed enhanced engagement of language areas relative to men, but sex differences in activated brain regions were smaller during menstruation, suggesting use of more similar spatial strategies for men and women during this phase of the ovulatory cycle (Halari et al., 2006). A shift from a language bias to a spatial bias is consistent with the increase in women's spatial abilities during menstruation. The gist of these results is that scientists will not understand the potential activational effects on women's and men's spatial cognition until they better understand how hormones bias engagement of one brain system or another and the corresponding biases in strategic approaches to spatial tasks; hormone-biased fluctuations in the strategic approaches to these tasks may explain the mixed results in this literature.

Tool Use

As I discussed in chapter 10 of this volume (in the section titled Object-Oriented Play), tool construction is much more common among men than women across traditional societies (Daly & Wilson, 1983; Murdock, 1981); boys have a better intuitive sense of how to use objects as tools and learn how to use tools more quickly than do girls (Z. Chen & Siegler, 2000; Gredlein & Bjorklund, 2005); also, prenatal exposure to androgens results in more frequent engagement in the object-oriented play that appears to facilitate this learning (Collaer & Hines, 1995). The brain systems that support tool use in humans include areas of the parietal cortex that are involved in mental rotation and mental imagery and the coordination of these regions with those that support object grasping and manipulation (Johnson-Frey, 2003).

Witelson (1976) asked 200 six- to twelve-year-old right-handed girls and boys to physically manipulate meaningless objects one at a time; the children could not see the objects. They were then asked to identify the shape from a visual display containing the manipulated object and five others. Because the perception of objects manipulated by the left hand is largely mediated by the right hemisphere and the perception of objects manipulated by right hand is largely mediated by the left hemisphere, this procedure provides an assessment of whether the right hemisphere (left hand) or the left hemisphere (right hand) is more sensitive to shape perception. The results indicated that at all ages, boys were significantly better at identifying shapes with their left hand (right hemisphere) than with their right hand (left hemisphere). Girls, in contrast, were equally skilled with their left and right hands. Boys and girls did not differ in overall identification accuracy, although the boys' use of their left hand resulted in the highest overall accuracy scores, whereas the use of their right hand resulted in the lowest overall accuracy scores; the left-handed and right-handed scores of girls fell in-between these extremes. On the basis of this pattern, Witelson concluded "that for boys of at least 6 (years of age) the right hemisphere is more specialized than the left for spatial processing; in girls, however, there is a bilateral representation at least until adolescence" (p. 426). This finding is in need of follow-up but suggests sex differences in the brain systems that support object manipulation and presumably ease of learning to use objects as tools.

CONCLUSION

As with my discussion of sex differences in folk psychology, my inferences about the natural history of sex differences in folk biology and folk physics need to be made with some caution but with an eye on sex differences in intrasexual competition, intersexual choice, and the division of labor. In comparison with scientists' knowledge of sex differences in folk psychology, little is known about sex differences in folk biology. What is known, however, is consistent with the division of labor found in traditional societies, specifically, women's foraging and men's hunting (Murdock, 1981).

When differences are found in these societies, women know more about local plants than men and use this knowledge for food gathering and preparation and for folk medicines. McDade et al.'s (2007) finding that Tsimané women's but not men's knowledge of folk medicines is associated with better health and developmental for their children is in need of replication in other traditional societies but is important. This is the type of reproductive outcome (offspring survival) that would result in the evolution of modular folk biological cognitive domains (see the section titled Folk Domains, chap. 9, this volume) and in this case a sex difference for knowledge of flora. Modular does not necessarily mean a fixed, hardwired brain system but rather soft constraints that result in early attentional biases and ease of learning in the domain. Scientists do not yet know whether girls and women learn about flora more easily than boys and men. While awaiting such studies, scientists gather additional evidence from the advantage of women in the detection of subtle variation in color in the green–red spectrum (Neitz et al., 1998), color vision that evolved in fruit-eating primates (Shyue et al., 1995), and from Silverman and Eals's (1992) hypothesis and corresponding results: Adolescent girls and women have better object location memories than do same-age boys and men as would be expected if the benefits of foraging were higher for women than for men during our evolutionary history.

Evidence for a corresponding specialization for men's hunting is also found in the folk biological literature, their greater knowledge of local fauna, and in the sex differences in detection of camouflaged objects, tracking object motion at a distance, hitting moving objects with projectiles, and navigating in and mentally representing novel large-scale environments (e.g., Moffat et al., 1998; M. J. Morgan et al., 1992; Peters, 1997). Whether these sex differences initially emerged from hunting or male–male competition that involved the use of projectiles—I favor the latter—is debated. Evidence that men are also better than women at judging when an object thrown at them will hit them and at blocking such objects (Schiff & Oldak, 1990; N. V. Watson & Kimura, 1991) implicates male–male competition as a core selective pressure; these are defensive competencies that would not be necessary for hunting. Even if male–male competition was the initial selection pressure for the evolution of these competencies, once they evolved, their use in hunting would reinforce the corresponding sex differences, especially given that women prefer successful hunters as mates (see the section titled Women's Mate Choices, chap. 7, this volume). Much remains to be learned about the proximate hormonal and experiential processes that create these sex differences during development, and much remains to be learned about sex differences in the brain and cognitive systems that support tool use. I suspect that answers will emerge in coming decades.

AFTERWORD

To close my discussion, I offer some thoughts on how biases that have evolved by means of sexual selection may be expressed in the modern world. I noted in the Introduction that space considerations do not allow me to fully address how our evolutionary history asserts itself in our daily lives, but I provide a few glimpses in this afterword. I do so by following the organization of the chapter titled "Sex Differences in Modern Society" in the first edition of this book, specifically, sex differences in academic competencies, behavioral and psychological sex differences, and sex differences in occupational interests and achievement. Of course, much of what we observe day-to-day is expressed in a cultural and historical context that differs in important ways from the evolutionary contexts of our ancestors; nevertheless, my discussion provides some clear implications for our understanding of sex differences in modern society.

SEX DIFFERENCES IN ACADEMIC COMPETENCIES

L. Ellis et al. (2008) identified 21 studies published in the past 7 decades of children's and adolescents' liking of school. In every nation in which it has been assessed and without exception, girls report liking school more than do boys. Although the skew is not quite so imbalanced, girls generally get better grades than do boys from elementary school through college in North America, Latin America, Europe, Asia, and Oceania. This is nothing new as the earliest study of this kind was published 100 years ago (W. R. Miles, 1910). These differences emerge because the social organization of schools is better suited to girls and because in relation to boys, girls are more compliant with teacher requests, miss fewer school days, and turn in their assignments with greater frequency. At the same time, there is no sex difference in overall academic competence (Willingham & Cole, 1997), but there are consistent differences in some specific academic areas, including reading, writing, mathematics, and the sciences (Hedges & Nowell, 1995).

The largest differences favoring girls are for components of writing, including spelling and the correct use of grammar; about 7 out of 10 girls outperform the average boy in overall writing performance. Girls also have a small but cross-nationally consistent advantage in reading achievement (Machin & Pekkarinen, 2008) with about 3 out of 5 girls outperforming the average boy. The largest differences favoring boys are for the physical sciences, mechanics, and technology (Hedges & Nowell, 1995; Stumpf & Stanley, 1998); in some of these areas, more than 9 out of 10 boys outscore the average girl. Boys' advantage in mathematics is small and varies from one nation to the next, but there are more consistent sex differences in some areas of mathematics (D. F. Halpern et al., 2007). The sex differences in the pattern of academic achievement are interesting and important but at first blush appear to be far removed from the cognitive domains I covered in chapters 12 and 13 of this volume.

I have argued that the folk abilities described in chapters 12 and 13 and in chapter 9 provide the foundation for the construction of culturally specific abilities and knowledge (Geary, 1995a). I term these culturally dependent abilities *biologically secondary* to distinguish them from biologically primary folk abilities. I do not believe there is always a sharp distinction between these forms of ability, but I do believe that acknowledging that some abilities are universal (e.g., language) and that others (e.g., reading) can be built from them, but only as a result of cultural practices (e.g., schooling), is essential for an understanding of modern education (Geary 2005b, 2007, 2008). The distinction is important because it allows for a framing of sex differences in achievement outcomes as they might relate to differences described in chapters 12 and 13. I cannot detail here the mechanisms needed to construct secondary abilities from primary ones but I note that intelligence is among them. After a brief tour of sex differences in intelligence, I use reading and mathematics to illustrate how this approach can be used to link evolved cognitive sex differences to sex differences in secondary abilities.

General Intelligence

General intelligence, or *g*, is typically measured using IQ tests and, as noted in the section titled Working Memory in chapter 9, consists of the ability to focus attention on the matter at hand and to use working memory resources to reason and problem solve about this matter; the evolution of *g* is covered elsewhere (Geary, 2005b). General intelligence is important for this discussion because it influences the ease of learning in school and thus contributes to outcomes on academic achievement tests.

In the first edition of this book, I concluded that there is no sex difference or only a small advantage for boys and men in average IQ. Since that time, the issue has resurfaced to considerable rancor and debate (Blinkhorn, 2005; Irwing & Lynn, 2005). In a meta-analysis of sex differences in the IQs of young adults, Irwing and Lynn found a 3- to 5-point advantage for men, as did Jackson and Rushton (2006). Other recent studies have found about a 1-point advantage for boys (Dykiert, Gale, & Deary, 2009), a 1-point advantage for girls (Strand, Deary, & Smith, 2006), or no sex differences for children or adults (van der Sluis et al., 2006, 2008). If there are sex differences in average IQ scores, they are small and favor boys and men, but the issue remains to be settled.

A more consistent but not universal finding (e.g., Irwing & Lynn, 2005) is that there are more boys and men than girls and women at the high and low ends of IQ scores (Deary, Irwing, Der, & Bates, 2007; Deary, Thorpe, Wilson, Starr, & Whalley, 2003; Feingold, 1992b; Lubinski & Humphrey, 1990). In a study of about 80,000 eleven-year-olds, Deary et al. (2003) found no sex difference in average IQ, but as scores moved away from the average, the ratio of boys to girls increased; 55% and 56% of the children in the top and bottom 2% of IQ, respectively, were boys. In a unique study that controlled for many aspects of the prenatal and postnatal environments, Deary et al. (2007) compared the IQs of 1,296 pairs of opposite-sex twins. There was only a small male advantage for average IQ, but again there were more brothers than sisters at the high and low ends. For the top 2% of scores, brothers outnumbered sisters 2 to 1.

Consideration of this variation is important practically because these differences can contribute to sex differences in the extremes of academic and occupational achievement and important theoretically because this variation is consistent with sexual selection. As discussed in chapter 10 (in the section titled Vulnerable and Variable), boys as a group are more sensitive to social and environmental conditions than are girls, and this sensitivity may extend to the development of the brain systems that later support IQ (Lucas, Morley, & Cole, 1998; Lucas et al., 1989). Whether this is a consequence of more intense intrasexual competition and intersexual choice during our evolutionary history is not known, but these results are certainly consistent with such a hypothesis. If so, then the variability among boys and men and the sex difference in average IQ may vary from one culture to the next and historically. When conditions are good, boys and men may have an advantage, but when times are bad, girls and women may have an advantage, on average; the sex difference in variability is predicted to remain across conditions.

Academic Patterns

I have argued elsewhere that the working memory and attentional components of IQ contribute to people's ability to modify evolved folk systems to learn how to read, write, do geometry, and master other culturally specific academic competencies (Geary, 2007). Even with similar average IQs, sex differences can emerge in academic domains to the extent there are sex differences in the primary folk systems on which the academic competences are built.

Reading

Girls and women have a modest but consistent advantage on reading tests across historical periods and nations (Hedges & Nowell, 1995; Machin & Pekkarinen, 2008; Willingham & Cole, 1997). The sex differences I reviewed in chapter 12 for language and some other folk psychological domains may be the source of these differences. In particular, the advantage of girls and women in the mechanics of language production and in language comprehension may provide them with an advantage when learning how to read and in comprehending text that involves nuanced social relationships.

As noted previously, there is a bias for women to engage both hemispheres during the processing of some language sounds and during language comprehension (see the section titled Language, chap. 12, this volume). Pugh et al. (1997) found that the representation of language sounds in both the left and right hemispheres was strongly associated with skill at making correspondences between letters and the associated sounds. In other words, individuals (more women than men) who process language sounds in both the left and right hemispheres may be more skilled at matching letters to their correct English pronunciations, a critical skill for decoding unfamiliar words during reading. Women's richer input layers in Wernicke's area, as potentially related to the discrimination of language sounds, may be an important source of this advantage, but this remains to be determined. To further complicate the matter, an advantage in language processing may give girls a boost during the early phases of reading acquisition when phonemic decoding is particularly important and may be less important for skilled readers. In other words, the relation between the sex differences in language processing and reading achievement may differ depending on the skill level of the sample and the reading competence being assessed.

Independent of brain anatomy, sex differences in reading interests contribute to the sex difference on reading comprehension tests (Asher & Markell, 1974). Girls and women read more than do boys and men and read more about romance and other interpersonal relationships than do boys and men, whereas boys and men read more about politics, competition (e.g., sports), and technical matters (e.g., Benton, 1995; Willingham & Cole, 1997). These sex differences mirror some of the sex differences described in the section titled Cultural Divide in chapter 11 as well as many other sex differences I have covered, for example, those related to object use (see the section titled Folk Physics, chap. 13, this volume). In short, I am proposing that the sex differences in reading interests, and through this reading comprehension (i.e., girls' advantage in novels that involve social relationships), reflect deeper sex differences that are a reflection of our evolutionary history. Girls and women are more interested in the details and nuances of their actual social relationships than are boys and men, and this interest is expressed in their leisure reading.

Mathematics

Mathematics is considered a gateway to employment in well-paying and prestigious science, technology, engineering, and mathematics (STEM) professions, and because of this the issue of sex differences in mathematical competence is a continuing source of review, conjecture, and heated debate (Ceci & Williams, 2007; Ceci, Williams, & Barnett, 2009; D. F. Halpern et al., 2007). I have written on this topic several times in the past, but I have to assert that the entire debate has become tiresome and in many ways unproductive. As noted previously, there are small or no average sex differences for many mathematical domains, and there are some areas in which girls and women outperform boys and men (Geary, 1996). Nonetheless, boys and men have advantages in several areas—for instance, some areas of geometry and in solving word problems—especially for problems that are novel or difficult and when visuospatial representations can be used to aid in problem solving (e.g., Johnson, 1984; Penner, 2003).

In a 1996 target article in *Behavioral and Brain Sciences* (Geary, 1996), I argued that these differences are related, at least in part, to the advantage of boys and men in the spatial abilities that support navigation in large-scale space (see the section titled Folk Physics, chap. 13, this volume) as well as to the sex difference in interest in people versus things; the latter is associated with greater interest in STEM fields. I also proposed that the sex differences in variability in mathematical ability and achievement—there are more boys and men at the high and low ends of these tests—can be linked to sexual selection, as I noted earlier for IQ. I do not see any reason to change the gist of my earlier proposal, although this is not the full story. There are clearly multiple influences on the development of mathematical and other STEM competencies and multiple biological and social influences on the sex differences in these domains (Ceci et al., 2009). Important social influences are suggested by recent changes in the ratio of boys and men to girls and women at the very high end of performance on mathematical tests; the ratio has dropped from about 13:1 in 1983 to roughly 3:1 today (Benbow & Stanley, 1983; Ceci et al., 2009). Even so, I am staying with my original proposal that boys' and men's advantages in spatial abilities and their greater interest in things (vs. people) contribute to the sex differences in some mathematical domains.

BEHAVIORAL AND PSYCHOLOGICAL SEX DIFFERENCES

I have covered numerous behavioral and psychological sex differences throughout this volume. In the sections that follow, I touch on behavior and psychological issues that are considered to be pathological in modern societies. The behavioral section focuses on activities directed toward the outer world, including other people, whereas the psychological section focuses on processes (e.g., depression) and activities that largely involve the individual.

Behavioral Sex Differences

On the basis of what was discussed in chapter 8 (in the sections titled Competition in Traditional Societies and Risk Taking) and chapter 10 (in the section titled Rough-and-Tumble) and just through life experiences, it is not surprising that boys and men outnumber girls and women when it comes to violence and accidental injuries (L. Evans, 2006; B. N. Rosen & Peterson, 1990; Rushton, 1996).

Violence

As is consistent with an evolutionary history of physical one-on-one and coalitional male–male competition, there "is no known human society in which the level of lethal violence among women even approaches that among men" (Daly & Wilson, 1988b, p. 146). As discussed in chapter 8, murder sometimes results in increased social status and marriage prospects for the perpetrator, although this is not typically the case in the modern world. In an analysis of same-sex homicide rates across industrial and preindustrial societies, including homicide records dating from more than 700 years ago, Daly and Wilson found that male-on-male homicide occurs between 30 and 40 times more frequently than does female-on-female homicide. Male-on-male homicide occurs most frequently during the initial mate-finding stage of the life span (i.e., late teens through mid 20s) and more frequently among unmarried than married men (M. Wilson & Daly, 1985). Moreover, roughly two out of three male-on-male homicides occur as a result of social conflict rather than being crime-specific (e.g., during the course of a robbery), and more than one half of the homicides are associated with "matters of status competition and the maintenance of face" (Daly & Wilson, 1988b, p. 175).

Men not only kill each other much more frequently than do women, they also kill women more frequently than women kill men. This form of male-on-female violence as well as serious nonlethal assaults often stems from mate guarding and sexual jealousy, as I reviewed in the section titled Sexual Fidelity and Jealousy (see chap. 7). I am not, of course, excusing these forms of violence but rather noting that one can better understand them and perhaps address them by placing them within an evolutionary context. Even if male violence was once effective and adaptive, it no longer is and should not be in the modern world.

Accidents

When successfully executed, a risky behavior can result in fame and sometimes fortune, but it is often just a boost in status within an individual's peer group. When unsuccessful, risky behavior often leads to accidental injuries. In a comprehensive assessment of childhood injuries and deaths in the United States, B. N. Rosen and Peterson (1990) documented a much higher frequency of accidental death and injury in boys than in girls. Boys experience near drowning nearly twice as frequently as girls and die as a result of drowning almost 4 times as frequently as girls. Boys are injured and killed more frequently than are girls while riding bicycles, playing on recreational equipment, and during unorganized (i.e., not supervised by adults) sports activities. For every girl who is injured on a playground, four boys are injured. For every girl who sustains a serious burn, three boys sustain an equally serious burn (e.g., while playing with fireworks).

B. N. Rosen and Peterson (1990) concluded that the sex differences in accidental injury and death rates were related to the sex differences in activity levels, risk taking, and the frequency of engagement in rough-and-tumble and competitive play. L. Evans (2006) reached a similar conclusion based on the finding that the sex difference in traffic fatalities, including pedestrians who are killed, peaks in the late teens and early 20s. In preceding chapters, I have made it clear why it is not a coincidence that the sex difference in risk taking and accidental death and injury peaks during the period of initial reproductive competition.

Psychological Sex Differences

Whereas boys and men are more likely to act on their feelings, sometimes to their detriment and sometimes to that of others, girls and women are more likely to internalize their social and psychological issues. As a result, girls and women outnumber boys and men when it comes to anxiety, depression, and eating disorders.

Anxiety and Depression

From adolescence and continuing through adulthood, almost twice as many girls and women experience socially important levels of anxiety and depression as same-age boys and men (e.g., Kessler et al., 2005; Nolen-Hoeksema, 1987). The question is, why? I suggest that the sensitivity of girls and women to the nuances of social relationships that often provides advantage may also result in increased risk of internalizing disorders. This is analogous to the cost–benefit trade-offs associated with boys' and men's risk taking.

I covered aspects of these trade-offs in chapter 8 (in the section titled Women's Aggression) with a discussion of girls' and women's use of relational aggression to socially maneuver for access to desired resources, especially romantic partners. Sensitivity to nuances of this maneuvering, as well as disclosure in interpersonal relationships and thus risk of social manipulation by former best friends, appears to make girls more vulnerable to anxiety and depression than boys when girls are victimized by same-sex peers (e.g. Bond, Carlin, Thomas, Rubin, & Patton, 2001). It is not that boys and men are completely clueless when it comes to this form of competition, but rather for them it does not have the same degree of social and thus emotional potency that it does for girls and women. The greater intimacy in girls' and women's close same-sex relationships provides important social support but also comes with risks. Girls and women who co-ruminate too often—that is, repeatedly discuss unsolvable and emotional personal issues—are at risk of later depression (Rose, Carlson, & Waller, 2007); co-rumination also results in increased stress hormone levels (Byrd-Craven, Geary, Rose, & Ponzi, 2008). Girls and women also react more strongly—they are more likely to become depressed—to conflict with important people in their life, especially "threats to intimacy and closeness in relationships" (Leadbeater, Blatt, & Quinlan, 1995, p. 12). Adolescent girls, for instance, are 4 times more likely than same-age boys to experience anxiety and depression following a lost relationship. On top of this, girls and women often experience symptoms of depression when negative life events affect their family or friends, whereas boys and men typically do not.

Relational female–female aggression and the risks involved in establishing and maintaining close interpersonal relationships with family members and a few friends are not the only sources of the sex difference in risk for anxiety and depression; other risks include childhood trauma and poor parent–child attachment, among other factors (e.g., Zahn-Waxler, Shirtcliff, & Marceau, 2008). I mention these risks here because they are understandable in terms of the sex differences I have covered in previous chapters. If adolescent girls are at risk of anxiety and depression in part because of a spike in female–female relational aggression during puberty, then psychologists should be aware of the potency of this form of aggression on girls and take measures to reduce it. Socially isolated girls (and women) are particularly vulnerable and in need of additional social and psychological support.

Eating Disorders

As I discussed in chapter 7 (in the section titled Young, Attractive Women) "plump" women are considered more attractive than slender women in 44% of human cultures compared with 19% of cultures in which slender women are considered more attractive (J. L. Anderson, Crawford, Nadeau, & Lindberg, 1992). The preference for heavier women is strongest in cultures with unpredictable food supplies and is thus a wise preference in these societies. Even in societies in which men prefer slender women as romantic partners, men's preferences are still for women with an average body mass index, not the very slender women portrayed in fashion magazines (Rozin & Fallon, 1988). With these facts in mind, why do some women in modern societies develop severe eating disorders? For every adolescent boy or man with anorexia nervosa (i.e., self-starvation to stay thin) or bulimia nervosa (i.e., binge eating, followed by fasting or vomiting) there are nine same-age girls and women with a similar disorder (American Psychiatric Association, 1994).

I suggest that the combination of men's focus on women's physical traits, women's focus on these same traits, and mass media presentations of increasingly thin fashion models creates a sometimes deadly mix for some women. Specifically, women's motivation to compete for romantic partners is based, in part, on enhancing the traits that men find attractive (see the section titled Dressed to Kill, chap. 8, this volume). For some women, however, this competitive motivation is being expressed in unchecked and unhealthy ways, especially among perfectionist and competitive women (Bardone-Cone et al., 2007). When these women are exposed to unusually thin fashion models, there appear to be modest increases in their dissatisfaction with their bodies and distortions of their beliefs about eating (e.g., Bardone-Cone & Cass, 2007; Grabe, Ward, & Hyde, 2008). The combination can result in extreme female–female competition and develop into anorexia nervosa if a woman views thin models as symbolic competitors and focuses on her physical appearance as a means to compete, as many women do (see the section titled Self, chap. 12, this volume). In such circumstances, a woman's inherent motivational bias is the same as that of other women but has spun out of control because of a combination of personality, media portrayals of "attractive" women, and other factors, no doubt.

SEX DIFFERENCES IN OCCUPATIONAL INTERESTS
AND ACHIEVEMENT

In the modern world occupational success means cultural success, and as I covered in chapter 8, cultural success means reproductive success for men but not for women. In traditional societies, men were much more focused than women on attaining social and culture status because success in these cultural spheres often meant the difference between reproducing or not. To be sure, social status is important to women and their children, but the consequences of not achieving some modicum of success are not as severe as they are for low-status men. It follows from these patterns that men will have an inherent motivational bias to devote time and effort to achieving success in their cultural niche. On the basis of the sex difference in parental effort (see the section titled Sex Differences in Human Parenting, chap. 6, this volume), women in turn are predicted to trade time and effort that would otherwise be focused on attaining cultural success for time and effort to devote to their families. As I covered in chapter 8 (in the section titled Resources and Cultural Success), women who do not make this trade-off pay the cost of having fewer children on average.

All of these predicted patterns are found in the modern workplace (Browne, 2002): Across occupations "evidence consistently suggests that despite comparable educational qualifications, tenure, and occupational attitudes, women have not achieved occupational status comparable to that of men" (Phillips & Imhoff, 1997, p. 46). I am not arguing that bias does not sometimes contribute to these differences, but I am saying that bias is not a sufficient explanation for all of them. In addition to motivational differences, there are cognitive and social factors that are proximate mechanisms that contribute to the sex differences in occupational attainment as well as differences in occupational interests. In the sections that follow, I illustrate these differences for STEM fields because these are often a source of social and political contention (National Academy of Sciences, 2006).

Cognitive Influences

More men than women enter high-paying STEM occupations, and this pattern contributes to the overall wage advantage enjoyed by men (Paglin & Rufolo, 1990). The attainment of the educational credentials that allow access to a high-paying STEM career, such as engineering, is made easier by a number of cognitive factors, specifically, above average general intelligence and above average spatial, mathematical, and mechanical competencies (Gottfredson, 1997; Humphreys, Lubinski, & Yao, 1993; Paglin & Rufolo, 1990). Sex differences in the latter competencies contribute to the sex difference in the proportion of men and women entering STEM fields. Individuals who enter these fields tend to have scores on the mathematics section of the Scholastic Assessment Test and the quantitative section of the Graduate Record Examination that are in the 600 to 800 range (500 is average, and 800 is the top score), and the ratio of men to women with scores in this range is between 2:1 to more than 5:1 (Paglin & Rufolo, 1990). The ratio of top-scoring men to women on physics tests is nearly 3:1 and on chemistry texts about 2.5:1 (Stanley, 1993). A similar pattern is found for advanced placement tests, including tests in all areas of physics and chemistry (Stanley, Benbow, Brody, Dauber, & Lupkowski, 1992). In other words, many more men than women have the minimal spatial, mathematical, and mechanical competencies needed to succeed in many STEM fields. This said, I note that women who enter STEM careers are similar to their male colleagues in many ways (Lubinski, Benbow, Shea, Eftekhari-Sanjani, & Halvorson, 2001); there just are not as many of these women as men.

As I mentioned earlier, at least some of these sex differences appear to be related to the sex difference favoring boys and men in evolved spatial navigational competencies and are thus indirectly related to sexual selection. It is also likely that the sex difference favoring boys and men in object-oriented interests and activities contributes to some of these sex differences (e.g., in mechanical competencies).

Social Influences

I suspect that social sex differences may be relatively more important than cognitive ones for understanding why more men than women enter and stay in STEM fields. When women and men are free to choose their own careers, their occupational interests and choices consistently differ. On interest tests, "young women [score] higher than young men on domestic, artistic, writing, social service, and office service vocational interests and young men [score] higher than young women on business, law, politics, mathematics, science, agriculture, athletics, and mechanical interests" (Willingham & Cole, 1997, p. 178). The sex difference in vocational interests is especially striking among the mathematically gifted. Among students in their 20s, for every mathematically gifted woman who is working toward or who aspires to earn an advanced degree in a STEM field, there are eight equally talented men (Lubinski & Benbow, 1994).

For these gifted individuals, the sex difference in the pursuit of an advanced education in STEM areas cannot be attributed to cognitive factors because all of these women have the mathematical and intellectual competencies necessary to succeed in these careers, nor can the difference be attributed solely to a bias against women; gifted women as a group do not view mathematics as a "male" occupation and are not discouraged from pursuing math-intensive careers (e.g., Raymond & Benbow, 1986). Rather, the sex difference in the pursuit of STEM careers is driven in part by the occupational and social interests of these gifted men and women.

People who enter STEM fields tend to have a relatively "low need for people contact" (Lubinski, Benbow, & Sanders, 1993, p. 701) and tend to prefer work environments that provide many theoretical and investigative activities. Mathematically gifted men who enter these fields do indeed show this pattern of occupational and social interests. As a group, mathematically gifted women "are more socially and esthetically oriented and have interests that are more evenly divided among investigative, social and artistic pursuits" (Lubinski et al., 1993, p. 702). In short, proportionally few of these women enter STEM fields because they have broader social and occupational interests than their male peers. The gifted women who do enter these fields are very successful in them, but as they move from graduate school to their mid-30s, more of these women than their male peers make trade-offs that likely affect their career development; specifically, women—but not men—who have children shift their priorities so they can devote more time to their families and to the wider community (Ferriman, Lubinski, & Benbow, 2009; see also Pinker, 2008). There is no need for me to point out why the sex differences in these occupational- versus family-time trade-offs make biological sense.

FINAL THOUGHTS

I hope to have convinced many readers that Darwin's (1871) theory of sexual selection represents a powerful set of processes that has shaped and will continue to shape the evolution of all sexually reproducing species, including our own. To be sure, there is much to be learned, especially how the expression of evolved biases are influenced by developmental experience and cultural context. We will never fully understand the developmental and cultural influences on the many sex differences covered in this book and the many differences that were not covered without placing them in the context of evolution in general and sexual selection in particular. I ask those readers who remain unconvinced to reflect on the theory of evolution, of which sexual selection is one set of pressures. Evolution is not just another psychological, sociological, or anthropological theory; it has proven to be the unifying meta-theory for all of the biological sciences. Eventually, all psychological, sociological, and anthropological models will need to be reconciled with the principles of natural and sexual selection. One can choose to be part of the discovery process or one can let these forthcoming scientific advances pass one by.

REFERENCES

Abbott, D. H. (1993). Social conflict and reproductive suppression in marmoset and tamarin monkeys. In W. A. Mason & S. P. Mendoza (Eds.), *Primate social conflict* (pp. 331–372). Albany: State University of New York Press.

Abbott, D. H., Keverne, E. B., Bercovitch, F. B., Shively, C. A., Mendoza, S. P., Saltzman, W., et al. (2003). Are subordinates always stressed? A comparative analysis of rank differences in cortisol levels among primates. *Hormones and Behavior, 43*, 67–82.

Abrams, D., & Hogg, M. A. (Eds.). (1990). *Social identity theory: Constructive and critical advances*. New York: Springer-Verlag.

Adams, K. F., Sueta, C. A., Gheorghiade, M., Schwartz, T. A., Koch, G. G., Uretsky, B., et al. (1999). Gender differences in survival in advanced heart failure: Insights from FIRST study. *Circulation, 99*, 1816–1821.

Adkins, E. K., & Adler, N. T. (1972). Hormonal control of behavior in the Japanese quail. *Journal of Comparative and Physiological Psychology, 81*, 27–36.

Adkins-Regan, E. (2005). *Hormones and animal social behavior*. Princeton, NJ: Princeton University Press.

Adler, N. E., Boyce, T., Chesney, M. A., Cohen, S., Folkman, S., Kahn, R. L., & Syme, S. L. (1994). Socioeconomic status and health: The challenge of the gradient. *American Psychologist, 49*, 15–24.

Adolphs, R. (1999). Social cognition and the human brain. *Trends in Cognitive Sciences, 3*, 469–479.

Agrawal, A. F. (2001, June 7). Sexual selection and the maintenance of sexual reproduction. *Nature, 411*, 692–695.

Ahlgren, A., & Johnson, D. W. (1979). Sex differences in cooperative and competitive attitudes from the 2nd to the 12th grades. *Developmental Psychology, 15*, 45–49.

Aiello, L. C. (1994, March 31). Variable but singular. *Nature, 368*, 399–400.

Aiello, L. C., & Collard, M. (2001, March 29). Our newest and oldest ancestor? *Nature, 410*, 526–527.

Aiello, L. C., & Wheeler, P. (1995). The expensive-tissue hypothesis: The brain and digestive system in human and primate evolution. *Current Anthropology, 36*, 199–221.

Ajie, B. C., Estes, S., Lynch, M., & Phillips, P. C. (2005). Behavioral degradation under mutation accumulation in *Caenorhabditis elegans*. *Genetics, 170*, 655–660.

Alberts, S. C., & Altmann, J. (1995). Preparation and activation: Determinants of age at reproductive maturity in male baboon. *Behavioral Ecology and Sociobiology, 36*, 397–406.

Alberts, S. C., Watts, H. E., & Altmann, J. (2003). Queuing and queue-jumping: Long-term patterns of reproductive skew in male savannah baboons, *Papio cynocephalus*. *Animal Behaviour, 65*, 821–840.

Aldis, O. (1975). *Play fighting*. New York: Academic Press.

Aleman, A., Bronk, E., Kessels, P. R. C., Koppeschaar, P. F., & van Honk, J. (2004). A single administration of testosterone improves visuospatial ability in young women. *Psychoneuroendocrinology, 29*, 612–617.

Aleman, A., & Swart, M. (2008). Sex differences in neural activation to facial expressions denoting contempt and disgust. *PLoS One, 3*. Retrieved November 6, 2008, from http://www.plosone.org/article/info:doi/10.1371/journal.pone.0003622

Alexander, G. M. (2003). An evolutionary perspective of sex-typed toy preferences: Pink, blue, and the brain. *Archives of Sexual Behavior, 32*, 7–14.

Alexander, G. M., & Hines, M. (2002). Sex differences in response to children's toys in nonhuman primates (*Cercopithecus aethiops sabaeus*). *Evolution and Human Behavior, 23*, 467–479.

Alexander, G. M., & Son, T. (2007). Androgens and eye movements in women and men during a test of mental rotation ability. *Hormones and Behavior, 52*, 197–204.

Alexander, G. M., Swerdloff, R. S., Wang, C., Davidson, T., McDonald, V., Steiner, B., & Hines, M. (1998). Androgen-behavior correlations in hypogonadal men and eugonadal men: II. Cognitive abilities. *Hormones and Behavior, 33*, 85–94.

Alexander, R. D. (1979). *Darwinism and human affairs*. Seattle: University of Washington Press.

Alexander, R. D. (1987). *The biology of moral systems*. Hawthorne, NY: Aldine de Gruyter.

Alexander, R. D. (1989). Evolution of the human psyche. In P. Mellars & C. Stringer (Eds.), *The human revolution: Behavioural and biological perspectives on the origins of modern humans* (pp. 455–513). Princeton, NJ: Princeton University Press.

Alexander, R. D. (1990). *How did humans evolve? Reflections on the uniquely unique species* (Museum of Zoology Special Publication No. 1). Ann Arbor: University of Michigan.

Alexander, R. D., Hoogland, J. L., Howard, R. D., Noonan, K. M., & Sherman, P. W. (1979). Sexual dimorphisms and breeding systems in pinnipeds, ungulates, primates, and humans. In N. A. Chagnon & W. Irons (Eds.), *Evolutionary biology and human social behavior: An anthropological perspective* (pp. 402–435). North Scituate, MA: Duxbury Press.

Allman, J., Rosin, A., Kumar, R., & Hasenstaub, A. (1998). Parenting and survival in anthropoid primates: Caretakers live longer. *Proceedings of the National Academy of Sciences USA, 95*, 6866–6869.

Alonso-Alvarez, C., Bertrand, S., Faivre, B., Chastel, O., & Sorci, G. (2007). Testosterone and oxidative stress: The oxidation handicap hypothesis. *Proceedings of the Royal Society London B, 274*, 819–825.

Altmann, J. (1980). *Baboon mothers and infants*. Cambridge, MA: Harvard University Press.

Altmann, J., Alberts, S. C., Haines, S. A., Dubach, J., Muruthi, P., Coote, T., et al. (1996). Behavior predicts genetic structure in a wild primate group. *Proceedings of the National Academy of Sciences USA, 93*, 5797–5801.

Alvergne, A., Faurie, C., & Raymond, M. (2007). Differential facial resemblance of young children to their parents: Who do children look like more? *Evolution and Human Behavior, 28*, 135–144.

Amato, P. R. (1998). More than money? Men's contributions to their children's lives. In A. Booth & A. C. Crouter (Eds.), *Men in families: When do they get involved? What difference does it make?* (pp. 241–278). Mahwah, NJ: Erlbaum.

Amato, P. R., & Booth, A. (1996). A prospective study of divorce and parent–child relationships. *Journal of Marriage and the Family, 58*, 356–365.

Amato, P. R., & Keith, B. (1991). Parental divorce and the well-being of children: A meta-analysis. *Psychological Bulletin, 110*, 26–46.

American Psychiatric Association. (1994). *Diagnostic and statistical manual of mental disorders* (4th ed.). Washington, DC: Author.

Amundsen, T., & Forsgren, E. (2001). Male mate choice selects for female coloration in a fish. *Proceedings of the National Academy of Sciences USA, 98*, 13155–13160.

Amundsen, T., & Pärn, H. (2006). Female coloration: Review of functional and nonfunctional hypotheses. In G. E. Hill & K. J. McGraw (Eds.), *Bird coloration: Vol. 2. Function and evolution* (pp. 280–345). Cambridge, MA: Harvard University Press.

Amunts, K., Armstrong, E., Malikovic, A., Hömke, L., Mohlberg, H., Schleicher, A., & Zilles, K. (2007). Gender-specific left-right asymmetries in human visual cortex. *Journal of Neuroscience, 27*, 1356–1364.

Andersen, A.-M. N., Wohlfahrt, J., Christens, P., Olsen, J., & Melbye, M. (2000, June 24). Maternal age and fetal loss: Population-based register linkage study. *BMJ, 320*, 1708–1712.

Anderson, J. L., Crawford, C. B., Nadeau, J., & Lindberg, T. (1992). Was the Duchess of Windsor right? A cross-cultural review of the socioecology of ideals of female body shape. *Ethology and Sociobiology, 13*, 197–227.

Anderson, K. G. (2006). How well does paternity confidence match actual paternity? Evidence from worldwide nonpaternity rates. *Current Anthropology, 47*, 513–520.

Anderson, K. G., Kaplan, H., Lam, D., & Lancaster, J. (1999). Paternal care by genetic fathers and stepfathers II: Reports from Xhosa high school students. *Evolution and Human Behavior, 20*, 433–451.

Anderson, K. G., Kaplan, H., & Lancaster, J. (1999). Paternal care by genetic fathers and stepfathers: I. Reports from Albuquerque men. *Evolution and Human Behavior, 20*, 405–431.

Anderson, K. J., & Leaper, C. (1998). Meta-analyses of gender effects on conversational interruption: Who, what, when, where, and how? *Sex Roles, 39*, 225–252.

Anderson, M. J., & Dixson, A. F. (2002, April 4). Motility and the midpiece in primates. *Nature, 416*, 496.

Anderson, R. A., Bancroft, J., & Wu, F. C. (1992). The effects of exogenous testosterone on sexuality and mood of normal men. *Journal of Clinical Endocrinology & Metabolism, 75*, 1503–1507.

Andersson, M. (1994). *Sexual selection*. Princeton, NJ: Princeton University Press.

Andersson, M. (2004). Social polyandry, parental investment, sexual selection, and evolution of reduced female gamete size. *Evolution, 58*, 24–34.

Andersson, M., & Simmons, L. W. (2006). Sexual selection and mate choice. *Trends in Ecology and Evolution, 21*, 296–302.

Andrews, P. W., Gangestad, S. W., Miller, G. F., Haselton, M. G., Thornhill, R., & Neale, M. C. (2008). Sex differences in detecting sexual infidelity: Results of a maximum likelihood method for analyzing the sensitivity of sex differences to underreporting. *Human Nature, 19*, 347–373.

Ankli, A., Sticher, O., & Heinrich, M. (1999). Yucatec Maya medicinal plants versus nonmedicinal plants: Indigenous characterization and selection. *Human Ecology, 27*, 557–580.

Annett, M. (1985). *Left, right, hand and brain: The right shift theory*. Hillsdale, NJ: Erlbaum.

Apanius, V., Penn, D., Slev, P. R., Ruff, L. R., & Potts, W. K. (1997). The nature of selection on the major histocompatibility complex. *Critical Reviews in Immunology, 17*, 179–224.

Apicella, C. L., Dreber, A., Campbell, B., Gray, P. B., Hoffman, M., & Little, A. C. (2009). Testosterone and financial risk preferences. *Evolution and Human Behavior, 29*, 384–390.

Apostolou, M. (2007). Sexual selection under parental choice: The role of parents in the evolution of human mating. *Evolution and Human Behavior, 28*, 403–409.

Archer, J. (1992). *Ethology and human development*. Savage, MD: Barnes & Noble Books.

Archer, J. (1996). Sex differences in social behavior: Are the social role and evolutionary explanations compatible? *American Psychologist, 51*, 909–917.

Archer, J. (2000). Sex differences in aggression between heterosexual partners: A meta-analytic review. *Psychological Bulletin, 126*, 651–680.

Archer, J. (2004). Sex differences in aggression in real-world settings: A meta-analytic review. *Review of General Psychology, 8*, 291–322.

Archer, J. (2006). Testosterone and human behavior: An evaluation of the challenge hypothesis. *Neuroscience and Biobehavioral Reviews, 30*, 319–345.

Archer, J. (in press). Does sexual selection explain human sex differences in aggression? *Behavioral and Brain Sciences*.

Archer, J., & Coyne, S. M. (2005). An integrated review of indirect, relational, and social aggression. *Personality and Social Psychology Review, 9*, 212–230.

Archer, J., Graham-Kevan, N., & Davies, M. (2005). Testosterone and aggression: A reanalysis of Book, Starzyk, and Quinsey's (2001) study. *Aggression and Violent Behavior, 10,* 241–261.

Argyle, M. (1994). *The psychology of social class.* New York: Routledge.

Armelagos, G. J., & Van Gerven, D. P. (1980). Sexual dimorphism and human evolution: An overview. *Journal of Human Evolution, 9,* 437–446.

Arndt, J., Greenberg, J., & Cook, A. (2002). Mortality salience and the spreading activation worldview-relevant constructs: Exploring the cognitive architecture of terror management. *Journal of Experimental Psychology: General, 131,* 307–324.

Arndt, J., Greenberg, J., Pyszczynski, T., & Solomon, S. (1997). Subliminal exposure to death-related stimuli increases defense of the cultural worldview. *Psychological Science, 8,* 379–385.

Arnold, A. P. (2009). The organizational–activational hypothesis as the foundation for a unified theory of sexual differentiation of all mammalian tissues. *Hormones and Behavior, 55,* 570–578.

Arnold, A. P., & Gorski, R. A. (1984). Gonadal steroid induction of structural sex differences in the central nervous system. *Annual Review of Neuroscience, 7,* 413–442.

Arnold, A. P., Xu, J., Grisham, W., Chen, X., Kin, Y.-H., & Itoh, Y. (2004). Sex chromosomes and brain sexual differentiation. *Endocrinology, 145,* 1057–1062.

Arnold, K. E., & Owens, I. P. F. (2002). Extra-pair paternity and egg dumping in birds: Life history, parental care and the risk of retaliation. *Proceedings of the Royal Society of London B, 269,* 1263–1269.

Asa, C. S., & Valdespino, C. (1998). Canid reproductive biology: An integration of proximate mechanisms and ultimate causes. *American Zoologist, 38,* 251–259.

Asfaw, B., Gilbert, W. H., Beyene, Y., Hart, W. K., Renne, P. R., WoldeGabriel, G., et al. (2002, March 21). Remains of *Homo erectus* from Bouri, Middle Awash, Ethiopia. *Nature, 416,* 317–320.

Asfaw, B., White, T., Lovejoy, O., Latimer, B., Simpson, S., & Suwa, G. (1999, April 23). *Australopithecus garhi:* A new species of early hominid from Ethiopia. *Science, 284,* 629–635.

Asher, S. R., & Markell, R. A. (1974). Sex differences in comprehension of high- and low-interest reading material. *Journal of Educational Psychology, 66,* 680–687.

Ashmore, R. D., Deaux, K., & McLaughlin-Volpe, T. (2004). An organizing framework for collective identity: Articulation and significance of multidimensionality. *Psychological Bulletin, 130,* 80–114.

Atran, S. (1994). Core domains versus scientific theories: Evidence from systematics and Itza-Maya folkbiology. In L. A. Hirschfeld & S. A. Gelman (Eds.), *Mapping the mind: Domain specificity in cognition and culture* (pp. 316–340). New York: Cambridge University Press.

Atran, S. (1998). Folk biology and the anthropology of science: Cognitive universals and cultural particulars. *Behavioral and Brain Sciences, 21,* 547–609.

Auyeung, B., Baron-Cohen, S., Ashwin, E., Knickmeyer, R., Taylor, K., Hackett, G., & Hines, M. (2009). Fetal testosterone predicts sexually differentiated childhood behavior in girls and boys. *Psychological Science, 20,* 144–148.

Bacchini, D., & Magliulo, F. (2003). Self-image and perceived self-efficacy during adolescence. *Journal of Youth and Adolescence, 32,* 337–350.

Bachmann, C., & Kummer, H. (1980). Male assessment of female choice in hamadryas baboons. *Behavioral Ecology and Sociobiology, 6,* 315–321.

Badahdah, A. M., & Tiemann, K. A. (2005). Mate selection criteria among Muslims living in America. *Evolution and Human Behavior, 26,* 432–440.

Baddeley, A. D. (1986). *Working memory.* Oxford: Oxford University Press.

Badyaev, A., & Qvarnström, A. (2002). Putting sexual traits into the context of an organism: A life-history perspective in studies of sexual selection. *Auk, 119,* 301–310.

Baer, B., & Schmid-Hempel, P. (1999, January 14). Experimental variation in polyandry affects parasite loads and fitness in a bumble-bee. *Nature, 397,* 151–154.

Baglione, V., Canestrari, D., Marcos, J. M., & Ekman, J. (2003, June 20). Kin selection in cooperative alliance of carrion crows. *Science, 300,* 1947–1949.

Bailenson, J. N., Shum, M. S., Atran, S., Medin, D. L., & Coley, J. D. (2002). A bird's eye view: Biological categorization and reasoning within and across cultures. *Cognition, 84,* 1–53.

Baker, R. R. (1996). *Sperm wars: The science of sex.* New York: Basic Books.

Baker, R. R., & Bellis, M. A. (1993). Human sperm competition: Ejaculate adjustment by males and the function of masturbation. *Animal Behaviour, 46,* 861–885.

Balaresque, P., Manni, F., Dugoujon, J. M., Crousau-Roy, B., & Heyer, E. (2006). Estimating sex-specific processes in human populations: Are XY-homologous markers an effective tool? *Heredity, 96,* 214–221.

Baldi, R., Campagna, C., Pedraza, S., & Le Boeuf, B. J. (1996). Social effects of space availability on the breeding behavior of elephant seals in Patagonia. *Animal Behaviour, 51,* 717–724.

Ball, G. F., & Balthazart, J. (2004). Hormonal regulation of brain circuits mediating male sexual behavior in birds. *Physiology & Behavior, 83,* 329–346.

Ball, G. F., & Hulse, S. H. (1998). Birdsong. *American Psychologist, 53,* 37–58.

Balthazart, J., & Ball, G. F. (1998). The Japanese quail as a model system for the investigation of steroid-catecholamine interactions mediating appetitive and consummatory aspects of male sexual behavior. *Annual Review of Sex Research, 9,* 96–176.

Bancroft, J. (2005). The endocrinology of sexual arousal. *Journal of Endocrinology, 186,* 411–427.

Bandura, A. (1997). *Self-efficacy: The exercise of control.* San Francisco: Freeman.

Banerjee, M. (1997). Hidden emotions: Preschoolers' knowledge of appearance-reality and emotion display rules. *Social Cognition, 15,* 107–132.

Banfield, S., & McCabe, M. P. (2001). Extra relationship involvement among women: Are they different from men? *Archives of Sexual Behavior, 30,* 119–142.

Barbarotto, R., Laiacona, M., Macchi, V., & Capitani, E. (2002). Picture reality decision, semantic categories and gender: A new set of pictures, with norms and an experimental study. *Neuropsychologia, 40,* 1637–1653.

Barber, N. (1995). The evolutionary psychology of physical attractiveness: Sexual selection and human morphology. *Ethology and Sociobiology, 16,* 395–424.

Bardone-Cone, A. M., & Cass, K. M. (2007). What does viewing a pro-anorexia website do? An experimental examination of website exposure and moderating effects. *International Journal of Eating Disorders, 40,* 537–548.

Bardone-Cone, A. M., Wonderlich, S. A., Frost, R. O., Bulik, C. M., Mitchell, J. E., Uppala, S., & Simonich, H. (2007). Perfectionism and eating disorders: Current status and future directions. *Clinical Psychology Review, 27,* 384–405.

Barkley, R. A., Ullman, D. G., Otto, L., & Brecht, J. M. (1977). The effects of sex typing and sex appropriateness of modeled behavior on children's imitation. *Child Development, 48,* 721–725.

Barluenga, M., Stölting, K. N., Salzburger, W., Muschick, M., & Meyer, A. (2006, February 9). Sympatric speciation in Nicaraguan crater lake cichlid fish. *Nature, 439,* 719–723.

Baron, J. (1997). The illusion of morality as self-interest: A reason to cooperate in social dilemmas. *Psychological Science, 8,* 330–335.

Baron-Cohen, S. (1995). *Mindblindness: An essay on autism and theory of mind.* Cambridge, MA: MIT Press/Bradford Books.

Baron-Cohen, S. (2003). *The essential difference: The truth about the male & female brain.* New York: Basic Books.

Baron-Cohen, S., Knickmeyer, R. C., & Belmonte, M. K. (2005, November 4). Sex differences in the brain: Implications for explaining autism. *Science, 310,* 819–823.

Baron-Cohen, S., Lutchmaya, S., & Knickmeyer, R. (2004). *Prenatal testosterone in mind: Amniotic fluid studies.* Cambridge, MA: MIT Press.

Barrett, L. F., Lane, R. D., Sechrest, L., Schwartz, G. E. (2000). Sex differences in emotional awareness. *Personality and Social Psychology Bulletin, 26,* 1027–1035.

Barrett, L. F., Robin, L., Pietromonaco, P. R., & Eyssell, K. M. (1998). Are women the "more emotional" sex? Evidence from emotional experiences in social context. *Cognition and Emotion, 12,* 555–578.

Barry, H., III, Josephson, L., Lauer, E., & Marshall, C. (1976). Traits inculcated in childhood: Cross-cultural codes 5. *Ethnology, 15,* 83–106.

Barton, R. A., & Dean, P. (1993). Comparative evidence indicating neural specialization for predatory behaviour in mammals. *Proceedings of the Royal Society of London B, 254,* 63–68.

Bateman, A. J. (1948). Intra-sexual selection in *drosophila. Heredity, 2,* 349–368.

Baumeister, R. F. (2000). Differences in erotic plasticity: The female sex drive as socially flexible and responsive. *Psychological Bulletin, 126,* 347–374.

Baumeister, R. F., & Leary, M. R. (1995). The need to belong: Desire for interpersonal attachments as a fundamental human motivation. *Psychological Bulletin, 117,* 497–529.

Beach, F. A., & Inman, N. G. (1965). Effects of castration and androgen replacement on mating in male quail. *Proceedings of the National Academy of Sciences USA, 54,* 1426–1431.

Beatty, W. W., & Tröster, A. I. (1987). Gender differences in geographical knowledge. *Sex Roles, 16,* 565–590.

Beck, S. P., Ward-Hull, C. I., & McCLear, P. M. (1976). Variables related to women's somatic preferences of the male and female body. *Journal of Personality and Social Psychology, 34,* 1200–1210.

Beckerman, S., Lizarralde, R., Ballew, C., Schroeder, S., Fingelton, C., Garrison, A., & Smith, H. (1998). The Barí partible paternity project: Preliminary results. *Current Anthropology, 39,* 164–167.

Beehner, J. C., Bergman, T. J., Cheney, D. L., Seyfarth, R. M., & Whitten, P. L. (2005). The effect of new alpha males on female stress in free-ranging baboons. *Animal Behaviour, 69,* 1211–1221.

Begossi, A., Hanazaki, N., & Tamashiro, J. Y. (2002). Medicinal plants in the Atlantic forest (Brazil): Knowledge, use, and conservation. *Human Ecology, 30,* 281–299.

Bekoff, M., & Byers, J. A. (Eds.) (1998). *Animal play: Evolutionary, comparative, and ecological perspectives.* Cambridge, England: Cambridge University Press.

Bell, G., & Maynard Smith, J. (1987, July 2). Short-term selection for recombination among mutually antagonistic species. *Nature, 328,* 66–68.

Bellis, M. A., & Baker, R. R. (1990). Do females promote sperm competition? Data for humans. *Animal Behaviour, 40,* 997–999.

Bellis, M. A., Hughes, K., Hughes, S., & Ashton, J. R. (2005). Measuring paternal discrepancy and its public health consequences. *Journal of Epidemiology and Community Health, 59,* 749–754.

Belsky, J. (1993). Etiology of child maltreatment: A developmental–ecological analysis. *Psychological Bulletin, 114,* 413–434.

Belsky, J. (1997). Attachment, mating, and parenting: An evolutionary interpretation. *Human Nature, 8,* 361–381.

Belsky, J. (2005). Differential susceptibility to rearing influence. In B. J. Ellis & D. F. Bjorklund (Eds.), *Origins of the social mind: Evolutionary psychology and child development* (pp. 139–163). New York: Guilford Press.

Belsky, J. (2007). Experience in childhood and the development of reproductive strategies. *Acta Psychological Sinica, 39,* 454–468.

Belsky, J., Gilstrap, B., & Rovine, M. (1984). The Pennsylvania infant and family development project, I: Stability and change in mother–infant and father–infant interaction in a family setting at one, three, and nine months. *Child Development, 55,* 692–705.

Belsky, J., Rovine, M., & Fish, M. (1989). The developing family system. In M. R. Gunnar & E. Thelen (Eds.), *Systems and development: The Minnesota symposia on child psychology* (Vol. 22, pp. 119–166). Hillsdale, NJ: Erlbaum.

Belsky, J., Steinberg, L. D., & Draper, P. (1991). Childhood experience, interpersonal development, and reproductive strategy: An evolutionary theory of socialization. *Child Development, 62,* 647–670.

Belsky, J., Steinberg, L. D., Houts, R. M., Friedman, S. L., DeHart, G., Cauffman, E., et al. (2007). Family rearing antecedents of pubertal timing. *Child Development, 78,* 1302–1321.

Benbow, C. P., & Stanley, J. C. (1983, December 2). Sex differences in mathematical reasoning ability: More facts. *Science, 222,* 1029–1031.

Benenson, J. F. (1993). Greater preference among females than males for dyadic interaction in early childhood. *Child Development, 64,* 544–555.

Benenson, J. F., & Christakos, A. (2003). The greater fragility of females' versus males' closest same-sex friendships. *Child Development, 74,* 1123–1129.

Benenson, J. F., Duggan, V., & Markovits, H. (2004). Sex differences in infants' attraction to group versus individual stimuli. *Infant Behavior & Development, 27,* 173–180.

Benenson, J. F., Maiese, R., Dolenszky, E., Dolensky, N., Sinclair, N., & Simpson, A. (2002). Group size regulates self-assertive versus self-deprecating responses to interpersonal competition. *Child Development, 73,* 1818–1829.

Benenson, J. F., Markovits, H., Fitzgerald, C., Geoffroy, D., Flemming, J., Kahlenberg, S. M., & Wrangham, R. W. (2009). Males' greater tolerance of same-sex peers. *Psychological Science, 20,* 184–190.

Benenson, J. F., Markovits, H., Muller, I., Challen, A., & Carder, H. P. (2007). Explaining sex differences in infants' preferences for groups. *Infant Behavior & Development, 30,* 587–595.

Benfer, R. A., & McKern, T. W. (1966). The correlation of bone robusticity with the perforation of the coronoid-olecranon septum in the humerus of man. *American Journal of Physical Anthropology, 24,* 247–252.

Benton, P. (1995). Conflicting cultures: Reflections on the reading and viewing of secondary-school pupils. *Oxford Review of Education, 21,* 457–470.

Bercovitch, F. B. (1997). Reproductive strategies of rhesus macaques. *Primates, 38,* 247–263.

Bereczkei, T., & Csanaky, A. (1996). Mate choice, marital success, and reproduction in a modern society. *Ethology and Sociobiology, 17,* 17–35.

Bereczkei, T., & Csanaky, A. (2001). Stressful family environment, mortality, and child socialisation: Life-history strategies among adolescents and adults from unfavourable social circumstances. *International Journal of Behavioral Development, 25,* 501–508.

Bereczkei, T., Gyuris, P., & Weisfeld, G. E. (2004). Sexual imprinting in human mate choice. *Proceedings of the Royal Society of London B, 271,* 1129–1134.

Bereczkei, T., Hegedus, G., & Hajnal, G. (2009). Facialmetric similarities mediate mate choice: Sexual imprinting on opposite-sex parents. *Proceedings of the Royal Society of London B, 276,* 91–98.

Berenbaum, S. A. (1999). Effects of early androgens on sex-typed activities and interests in adolescents with congenital adrenal hyperplasia. *Hormones and Behavior, 35,* 102–110.

Berenbaum, S. A., & Hines, M. (1992). Early androgens are related to childhood sex-typed toy preferences. *Psychological Science, 3,* 203–206.

Berenbaum, S. A., & Resnick, S. M. (1997). Early androgen effects on aggression in children and adults with congenital adrenal hyperplasia. *Psychoneuroendocrinology, 22,* 505–515.

Berenbaum, S. A., & Snyder, E. (1995). Early hormonal influences on childhood sex-typed activity and playmate preferences: Implications for the development of sexual orientation. *Developmental Psychology, 31,* 31–42.

Berg, S. J., & Wynne-Edwards, K. E. (2001). Changes in testosterone, cortisol, and estradiol in men becoming fathers. *Mayo Clinic Proceedings, 76,* 582–592.

Berger, K. S. (2007). Update on bullying at school: Science forgotten? *Developmental Review, 27,* 90–126.

Berglund, A., & Rosenqvist, G. (2001). Male pipefish prefer dominant over attractive females. *Behavioral Ecology, 12,* 402–406.

Berglund, A., Rosenqvist, G., & Bernet, P. (1997). Ornamentation predicts reproductive success in female pipefish. *Behavioral Ecology and Sociobiology, 40,* 145–150.

Bergman, T. J., Beehner, J. C., Cheney, D. L., & Seyfarth, R. M. (2003, November 14). Hierarchical classification by rank and kinship in baboons. *Science, 302,* 1234–1236.

Berlin, B., Boster, J. S., & O'Neill, J. P. (1981). The perceptual bases of ethnobiological classification: Evidence from Aguaruna Jívaro ornithology. *Journal of Ethnobiology, 1,* 95–108.

Berlin, B., Breedlove, D. E., & Raven, P. H. (1966, October 14). Folk taxonomies and biological classification. *Science, 154,* 273–275.

Berlin, B., Breedlove, D. E., & Raven, P. H. (1973). General principles of classification and nomenclature in folk biology. *American Anthropologist, 75,* 214–242.

Berman, P. W. (1980). Are women more responsive than men to the young? A review of developmental and situational variables. *Psychological Bulletin, 88,* 668–695.

Berman, P. W., Monda, L. C., & Myerscough, R. P. (1977). Sex differences in young children's responses to an infant: An observation within a day-care setting. *Child Development, 48,* 711–715.

Bernasconi, G., Ashman, T.-L., Birkhead, T. R., Bishop, J. D. D., Grossniklaus, U., Kubli, E., et al. (2004, February 13). Evolutionary ecology of the prezygotic stage. *Science, 303,* 971–975.

Bernhardt, P. C., Dabbs, J. M., Fielden, J. A., & Lutter, C. D. (1998). Testosterone changes during vicarious experiences of winning and losing among fans at sporting events. *Physiology & Behavior, 65*, 59–62.

Best, D. L., & Williams, J. E. (1983). A cross-cultural viewpoint. In A. E. Beall & R. J. Sternberg (Eds.), *The psychology of gender* (pp. 215–248). New York: Guilford Press.

Betzig, L. L. (1986). *Despotism and differential reproduction: A Darwinian view of history.* New York: Aldine Publishing.

Betzig, L. L. (1989). Causes of conjugal dissolution: A cross-cultural study. *Current Anthropology, 30*, 654–676.

Betzig, L. L. (1993). Sex, succession, and stratification in the first six civilizations: How, powerful men reproduced, passed power on to their sons, and used power to defend their wealth, women, and children. In L. Ellis (Ed.), *Social stratification and socioeconomic inequality: Vol. 1. A comparative biosocial analysis* (pp. 37–74). Westport, CT: Praeger.

Betzig, L. L., & Turke, P. (1992). Fatherhood by rank on Ifaluk. In B. S. Hewlett (Ed.), *Father–child relations: Cultural and biosocial contexts* (pp. 111–129). New York: Aldine de Gruyter.

Birkhead, T. R., & Møller, A. P. (1996). Monogamy and sperm competition in birds. In J. M. Black (Ed.), *Partnerships in birds: The study of monogamy* (pp. 323–343). New York: Oxford University Press.

Birkhead, T. R., & Møller, A. P. (1998). *Sperm competition and sexual selection.* New York: Academic Press.

Bishop, K. M., & Wahlsten, D. (1997). Sex differences in the human corpus callosum: Myth or reality? *Neuroscience and Biobehavioral Reviews, 21*, 581–601.

Bjork, A., & Pitnick, S. (2006, June 8). Intensity of sexual selection along the anisogamy–isogamy continuum. *Nature, 441*, 742–745.

Björklund, A., Ginther, D. K., & Sundström, M. (2007). Family structure and child outcomes in the USA and Sweden. *Journal of Population Economics, 20*, 183–201.

Bjorklund, D. F., & Harnishfeger, K. K. (1995). The evolution of inhibition mechanisms and their role in human cognition and behavior. In F. N. Dempster & C. J. Brainerd (Eds.), *New perspectives on interference and inhibition in cognition* (pp. 141–173). New York: Academic Press.

Bjorklund, D. F., & Kipp, K. (1996). Parental investment theory and gender differences in the evolution of inhibition mechanisms. *Psychological Bulletin, 120*, 163–188.

Bjorklund, D. F., & Pellegrini, A. D. (2002). *The origins of human nature: Evolutionary developmental psychology.* Washington, DC: American Psychological Association.

Björkqvist, K., Osterman, K., & Lagerspetz, K. M. J. (1994). Sex differences in covert aggression among adults. *Aggressive Behavior, 20*, 27–34.

Black, F. L., & Hedrick, P. W. (1997). Strong balancing selection at HLA loci: Evidence from segregation in South Amerindian families. *Proceedings of the National Academy of Sciences USA, 94*, 12452–12456.

Black, J. M. (Ed.). (1996). *Partnerships in birds: The study of monogamy*. New York: Oxford University Press.

Black, J. M., Choudhury, S., & Owen, M. (1996). Do barnacle geese benefit from life-long monogamy? In J. M. Black (Ed.), *Partnerships in birds: The study of monogamy* (pp. 91–117). New York: Oxford University Press.

Blinkhorn, S. (2005, November 3). A gender bender. *Nature, 438,* 31–32.

Block, J. H. (1976). Issues, problems, and pitfalls in assessing sex differences: A critical review of *The psychology of sex differences*. *Merrill-Palmer Quarterly, 22,* 283–308.

Block, R. A., Arnott, D. P., Quigley, B., & Lynch, W. C. (1989). Unilateral nostril breathing influences lateralized cognitive performance. *Brain and Cognition, 9,* 181–190.

Bloom, P. (1996). Intention, history, and artifact concepts. *Cognition, 60,* 1–29.

Blum, D. (1997). *Sex on the brain: The biological differences between men and women.* New York: Viking.

Blurton Jones, N. G., Hawkes, K., & O'Connell, J. F. (1997). Why do Hadza children forage? In N. L. Segal, G. E. Weisfeld, & C. C. Weisfeld (Eds.), *Uniting psychology and biology: Integrative perspectives on human development* (pp. 279–313). Washington, DC: American Psychological Association.

Blurton Jones, N. G., Marlowe, F. W., Hawkes, K., & O'Connell, J. F. (2000). Paternal investment and hunter-gatherer divorce rates. In L. Cronk, N. Chagnon, & W. Irons (Eds.), *Adaptation and human behavior: An anthropological perspective* (pp. 69–90). New York: Aldine De Gruyter.

Blythe, P. W., Todd, P. M., & Miller, G. F. (1999). How motion reveals intention: Categorizing social interactions. In G. Gigerenzer, P. M. Todd, & the ABC Research Group (Eds.), *Simple heuristics that make us smart* (pp. 257–285). New York: Oxford University Press.

Boag, P. T. (1983). The heritability of external morphology in Darwin's ground finches (*Geospiza*) on Isla Daphne Major, Galápagos. *Evolution, 37,* 877–894.

Boag, P. T., & Grant, P. R. (1978, August 24). Heritability of external morphology in Darwin's finches. *Nature, 274,* 793–794.

Boehm, C. (1993). Egalitarian behavior and reverse dominance hierarchy. *Current Anthropology, 34,* 227–254.

Böer, M., & Sommer, V. (1992). Evidence for sexually selected infanticide in captive *Cercopithecus mitis*, *Cercocebus torquatus*, and *Mandrillus leucophaeus*. *Primates, 33,* 557–563.

Boesch, C., Crockford, C., Herbinger, I., Wittig, R., Moebius, Y., & Normand, E. (2008). Intergroup conflicts among chimpanzees in Taï National Park: Lethal violence and the female perspective. *American Journal of Primatology, 70,* 519–532.

Boesch, C., Kohou, G., Néné, H., & Vigilant, L. (2006). Male competition and paternity in wild chimpanzees of the Taï forest. *American Journal of Physical Anthropology, 130,* 103–115.

Bogaert, A. F. (2005). Age at puberty and father absence in a national probability sample. *Journal of Adolescence, 28,* 541–546.

Bogin, B. (1999). *Patterns of human growth* (2nd ed.). Cambridge, England: Cambridge University Press.

Bond, L., Carlin, J. B., Thomas, L., Rubin, K., & Patton, G. (2001, September 1). Does bullying cause emotional problems? A prospective study of young teenagers. *BMJ, 323,* 480–484.

Bonduriansky, R. (2001). The evolution of male mate choice in insects: A synthesis of ideas and evidence. *Biological Reviews, 76,* 305–399.

Bonnerup, J. A., Gramkow, A., Sorensen, P., Melbye, M., Adami, H.-O., Glimelius, B., & Frisch, M. (2000). Correlates of heterosexual behavior among 23–87 year olds in Denmark and Sweden, 1992–1998. *Archives of Sexual Behavior, 29,* 91–106.

Boone, J. L. (1986). Parental investment and elite family structure in preindustrial states: A case study of late medieval–early modern Portuguese genealogies. *American Anthropologist, 88,* 859–878.

Boone, J. L., & Kessler, K. L. (1999). More status or more children? Social status, fertility reduction, and long-term fitness. *Evolution and Human Behavior, 20,* 257–277.

Booth, A., Johnson, D. R., & Granger, D. A. (1999). Testosterone and men's health. *Journal of Behavioral Medicine, 22,* 1–19.

Borgerhoff Mulder, M. (1990). Kipsigis women's preferences for wealthy men: Evidence for female choice in mammals? *Behavioral Ecology and Sociobiology, 27,* 255–264.

Borgerhoff Mulder, M. (2000). Optimizing offspring: The quantity–quality tradeoff in agropastoral Kipsigis. *Evolution and Human Behavior, 21,* 391–410.

Borgia, G. (1985a). Bower destruction and sexual competition in the satin bower bird (*Ptilonorhynchus violaceus*). *Behavioral Ecology and Sociobiology, 18,* 91–100.

Borgia, G. (1985b). Bower quality, number of decorations and mating success of male satin bower birds (*Ptilonorhynchus violaceus*): An experimental analysis. *Animal Behaviour, 33,* 266–271.

Borgia, G. (1986). Satin bowerbird parasites: A test of the bright male hypothesis. *Behavioral Ecology and Sociobiology, 19,* 355–358.

Borgia, G. (1995a). Complex male display and female choice in the spotted bowerbird: Specialized functions for different bower decorations. *Animal Behaviour, 49,* 1291–1301.

Borgia, G. (1995b). Threat reduction as a cause of differences in bower architecture, bower decoration and male display in two closely related bowerbirds *Chlamydera nuchalis* and *C. maculata. Emu, 95,* 1–12.

Borgia, G. (2006). Preexisting male traits are important in the evolution of elaborated male sexual display. *Advances in the Study of Behavior, 36,* 249–302.

Borgia, G., & Coleman, S. W. (2000). Co-option of male courtship signals from aggressive display in bowerbirds. *Proceedings of the Royal Society of London B, 267,* 1735–1740.

Borgia, G., & Wingfield, J. C. (1991). Hormonal correlates of bower decoration and sexual display in the satin bowerbird (*Ptilonorhynchus violaceus*). *Condor, 93*, 935–942.

Borries, C., Launhardt, K., Epplen, C., Epplen, J. T., & Winkler, P. (1999). DNA analyses support the hypothesis that infanticide is adaptive in langur monkeys. *Proceedings of the Royal Society of London B, 266*, 901–904.

Bosacki, S. L. (2000). Theory of mind and self-concept in preadolescents: Links with gender and language. *Journal of Educational Psychology, 92*, 709–717.

Bosacki, S. L., & Astington, J. W. (1999). Theory of mind in preadolescents: Relations between social understanding and social competence. *Social Development, 8*, 237–254.

Boster, J. S. (1985). "Requiem for the omniscient informant": There's life in the old girl yet. In J. W. D. Dougherty (Ed.), *Directions in cognitive anthropology* (pp. 177–197). Urbana: University of Illinois Press.

Botvinick, M. M., Braver, T. S., Barch, D. M., Carter, C. S., & Cohen, J. D. (2001). Conflict monitoring and cognitive control. *Psychological Review, 108*, 624–652.

Bradley, B. J., Doran-Sheehy, D. M., Lukas, D., Boesch, C., & Vigilant, L. (2004). Dispersed male networks in Western gorillas. *Current Biology, 14*, 510–513.

Brändström, A. (1997). Life histories of lone parents and illegitimate children in nineteenth-century Sweden. In C. A. Corsini & P. P. Viazzo (Eds.), *The decline of infant and child mortality* (pp. 173–191). The Hague, Netherlands: Martinus Nijhoff.

Bravery, B. D., Nicholls, J. A., & Goldizen, A. W. (2006). Patterns of painting in satin bowerbirds *Ptilonorhynchus violaceus* and males' responses to changes in their paint. *Journal of Avian Biology, 37*, 77–83.

Breedlove, S. M. (2000, March 30). Finger-length ratios and sexual orientation: Measuring people's finger patterns may reveal some surprising information. *Nature, 404*, 455–456.

Bressan, P., & Stranieri, D. (2008). The best men are (not always) already taken. *Psychological Science, 19*, 145–151.

Brewer, D. D., Potterat, J. J., Garrett, S. B., Muth, S. Q., Roberts, J. M., Kasprzyk, D., et al. (2000). Prostitution and the sex discrepancy in reported number of sexual partners. *Proceedings of the National Academy of Sciences USA, 97*, 12385–12388.

Brodmann, K. (1909). *Vergleichende Lokalisationslehre der Grosshirnrinde in ihren Prinzipien dargestellt auf Grund des Zellenbaues* [Comparative localization of the cerebral cortex based on cell composition]. Leipzig, Germany: Barth.

Bronfenbrenner, U. (1986). Ecology of the family as a context for human development: Research perspectives. *Developmental Psychology, 22*, 723–742.

Bronte-Tinkew, J., Moore, K. A., & Carrano, J. (2006). The father–child relationship, parenting styles, and adolescent risk behaviors in intact families. *Journal of Family Issues, 27*, 850–881.

Brooks, R. (1999). Mate choice copying in guppies: Females avoid the place where they saw courtship. *Behaviour, 136*, 411–421.

Brothers, L. (1990). The social brain: A project for integrating primate behavior and neurophysiology in a new domain. *Concepts in Neuroscience, 1*, 27–51.

Brothers, L., & Ring, B. (1992). A neuroethological framework for the representation of minds. *Journal of Cognitive Neuroscience, 4*, 107–118.

Brothwood, M., Wolke, D., Gamsu, H., Benson, J., & Cooper, D. (1986). Prognosis of the very low birthweight baby in relation to gender. *Archives of Disease in Childhood, 61*, 559–564.

Brown, D. E. (1991). *Human universals*. Philadelphia: Temple University Press.

Brown, W. J., Mishra, G., Kenardy, J., & Dobson, A. (2000). Relationships between body mass index and well-being in young Australian women. *International Journal of Obesity, 24*, 1360–1368.

Browne, K. R. (2002). *Biology at work: Rethinking sexual equality*. New Brunswick, NJ: Rutgers University Press.

Buchan, J. C., Alberts, S. C., Silk, J. B., & Altmann, J. (2003, September 11). True paternal care in a multi-male primate society. *Nature, 425*, 179–181.

Buchanan, C. M., Maccoby, E. E., & Dornbusch, S. M. (1992). Adolescents and their families after divorce: Three residential arrangements compared. *Journal of Research on Adolescence, 2*, 261–291.

Buchanan, K. L. (2000). Stress and the evolution of condition-dependent signals. *Trends in Ecology and Evolution, 15*, 156–160.

Buck, R., Miller, R. E., & Caul, W. F. (1974). Sex, personality, and physiological variables in the communication of affect via facial expression. *Journal of Personality and Social Psychology, 30*, 587–596.

Buck, R. W., Savin, V. J., Miller, R. E., & Caul, W. F. (1972). Communication of affect through facial expression in humans. *Journal of Personality and Social Psychology, 23*, 362–371.

Buckle, L., Gallup, G. G., Jr., & Rodd, Z. A. (1996). Marriage as a reproductive contract: Patterns of marriage, divorce, and remarriage. *Ethology and Sociobiology, 17*, 363–377.

Bugental, D. B. (2000). Acquisition of the algorithms of social life: A domain-based approach. *Psychological Bulletin, 126*, 187–219.

Bugental, D. B., & Beaulieu, D. A. (2009). Sex differences in response to cautional threat. *Evolution and Human Behavior, 30*, 238–243.

Bukowski, W. M., Sippola, L. K., & Newcomb, A. F. (2000). Variations in patterns of attraction to same- and other-sex peers during early adolescence. *Developmental Psychology, 36*, 147–154.

Bulmer, M. (1994). *Theoretical evolutionary ecology*. Sunderland, MA: Sinauer Associates Publishers.

Burch, R. L., & Gallup, G. G., Jr. (2000). Perceptions of paternal resemblance predict family violence. *Evolution and Human Behavior, 21*, 429–435.

Burghardt, G. M. (2005). *The genesis of animal play: Testing the limits.* Cambridge, MA: MIT Press/Bradford Books.

Burkitt, J., Widman, D., & Saucier, D. M. (2007). Evidence for the influence of testosterone in the performance of spatial navigation in a virtual water maze in women but not in men. *Hormones and Behavior, 51,* 649–654.

Burley, N. (1986). Sexual selection for aesthetic traits in species with biparental care. *American Naturalist, 127,* 415–445.

Buss, A. H., & Portnoy, N. W. (1967). Pain tolerance and group identification. *Journal of Personality and Social Psychology, 6,* 106–108.

Buss, D. M. (1988). From vigilance to violence: Tactics of mate retention in American undergraduates. *Ethology and Sociobiology, 9,* 291–317.

Buss, D. M. (1989a). Conflict between the sexes: Strategic interference and the evocation of anger and upset. *Journal of Personality and Social Psychology, 56,* 735–747.

Buss, D. M. (1989b). Sex differences in human mate preferences: Evolutionary hypothesis tested in 37 cultures. *Behavioral and Brain Sciences, 12,* 1–49.

Buss, D. M. (2003). *The evolution of desire: Strategies of human mating* (2nd ed.). New York: Basic Books.

Buss, D. M., Larsen, R. J., Westen, D., & Semmelroth, J. (1992). Sex differences in jealousy: Evolution, physiology, and psychology. *Psychological Science, 3,* 251–255.

Buss, D. M., & Schmitt, D. P. (1993). Sexual strategies theory: An evolutionary perspective on human mating. *Psychological Review, 100,* 204–232.

Buss, D. M., & Shackelford, T. K. (1997). From vigilance to violence: Mate retention tactics in married couples. *Journal of Personality and Social Psychology, 72,* 346–361.

Buss, D. M., Shackelford, T. K., Choe, J. C., Buunk, B., & Dijkstra, P. (2000). Distress about mating rivals. *Personal Relationships, 7,* 235–243.

Buss, K. A., Brooker, R. J., & Leuty, M. (2008). Girls most of the time, boys some of the time: Gender differences in toddlers' use of maternal proximity and comfort seeking. *Infancy, 13,* 1–29.

Bussey, K., & Bandura, A. (1999). Social cognitive theory of gender development and differentiation. *Psychological Review, 106,* 676–713.

Butler, M. A., Sawyer, S. A., & Losos, J. B. (2007, May 10). Sexual dimorphism and adaptive radiation in *Anolis* lizards. *Nature, 447,* 202–205.

Butler, R., & Shalit-Naggar, R. (2008). Gender and patterns of concerned responsiveness in representations of mother–daughter and mother–son relationship. *Child Development, 79,* 836–851.

Butler, T., Imperato-McGinley, J., Pan, H., Voyer, D., Cordero, J., Zhu, Y.-S., et al. (2006). Sex differences in mental rotation: Top–down versus bottom–up processing. *NeuroImage, 32,* 445–456.

Buunk, B. P., Angleitner, A., Oubaid, V., & Buss, D. M. (1996). Sex differences in jealousy in evolutionary and cultural perspective: Tests from the Netherlands, Germany, and the United States. *Psychological Science, 7,* 359–363.

Buunk, B. P., Dijkstra, P., Fetchenhauer, D., & Kenrick, D. T. (2002). Age and gender differences in mate selection criteria for various involvement levels. *Personal Relationships, 9,* 271–278.

Byers, J. A., & Walker, C. (1995). Refining the motor training hypothesis for the evolution of play. *American Naturalist, 146,* 25–40.

Byrd-Craven, J., Geary, D. C., Rose, A. J., & Ponzi, D. (2008). Co-rumination increases stress hormone levels in women. *Hormones and Behavior, 53,* 489–492.

Byrd-Craven, J., Geary, D. C., Vigil, J. M., & Hoard, M. K. (2007). One mate or two? Life history traits and reproductive variation in low-income women. *Acta Psychological Sinica, 39,* 469–480.

Byrne, P., Becker, S., & Burgess, N. (2007). Remembering the past and imagining the future: A neural model of spatial memory and imagery. *Psychological Review, 114,* 340–375.

Byrne, R. (1995). *The thinking ape: Evolutionary origins of intelligence.* New York: Oxford University Press.

Byrnes, J. P., Miller, D. C., & Schafer, W. D. (1999). Gender differences in risk taking: A meta-analysis. *Psychological Bulletin, 125,* 367–383.

Cabeza, R., & Nyberg, L. (1997). Imaging cognition: An empirical review of PET studies with normal subjects. *Journal of Cognitive Neuroscience, 9,* 1–26.

Cahill, L. (2006). Why sex matters for neuroscience. *Nature Neuroscience Reviews, 7,* 477–484.

Cahill, S., & Mussap, A. J. (2007). Emotional reactions following exposure to idealized bodies predict unhealthy body change attitudes and behaviors in women and men. *Journal of Psychosomatic Research, 62,* 631–639.

Caillaud, D., Levréro, F., Gatti, S., Ménard, N., & Raymond, M. (2008). Influence of male morphology on male mating status and behavior during interunit encounters in Western lowland gorillas. *American Journal of Physical Anthropology, 135,* 379–388.

Cairns, R. B., Cairns, B. D., Neckerman, H. J., Fergusson, L. L., & Gariépy, J.-L. (1989). Growth and aggression: 1. Childhood to early adolescence. *Developmental Psychology, 25,* 320–330.

Campbell, A. (1995). A few good men: Evolutionary psychology and female adolescent aggression. *Ethology and Sociobiology, 16,* 99–123.

Campbell, A. (1999). Staying alive: Evolution, culture, and women's intrasexual aggression. *Behavioral and Brain Science, 22,* 203–252.

Campbell, A. (2002). *A mind of her own: The evolutionary psychology of women.* New York: Oxford University Press.

Campbell, A. (2004). Female competition: Causes, constraints, content, and contexts. *Journal of Sex Research, 41,* 16–26.

Campbell, A. (2008). The morning after the night before: Affective reactions to one-night stands among mated and unmated women and men. *Human Nature, 19,* 157–173.

Campbell, A., & Muncer, S. (2008). Intent to harm or injure? Gender and the expression of anger. *Aggressive Behavior, 34*, 282–293.

Campbell, B. C., Prossinger, H., & Mbzivo, M. (2005). Timing of pubertal maturation and the onset of sexual behavior among Zimbabwe school boys. *Archives of Sexual Behavior, 34*, 505–516.

Campbell, L., & Ellis, B. J. (2005). Commitment, love, and mate retention. In D. M. Buss (Ed.), *The evolutionary psychology handbook* (pp. 419–442). Hoboken, NJ: Wiley.

Campos, J. J., Campos, R. G., & Barrett, K. C. (1989). Emergent themes in the study of emotional development and emotion regulation. *Developmental Psychology, 25*, 394–402.

Capelli, C., Redhead, N., Abernethy, J. K., Gratrix, F., Wilson, J. F., Moen, T., et al. (2003). A Y chromosome census of the British isles. *Current Biology, 13*, 979–984.

Capitani, E., Laiacona, M., Mahon, B., & Caramazza, A. (2003). What are the facts of semantic category-specific deficits? A critical review of the clinical evidence. *Cognitive Neuropsychology, 20*, 213–261.

Caporael, L. R. (1997). The evolution of truly social cognition: The core configurations model. *Personality & Social Psychology Review, 1*, 276–298.

Caramazza, A., & Shelton, J. R. (1998). Domain-specific knowledge systems in the brain: The animate–inanimate distinction. *Journal of Cognitive Neuroscience, 10*, 1–34.

Card, N. A., Stucky, B. D., Sawalani, G. M., & Little, T. D. (2008). Direct and indirect aggression during childhood and adolescence: A meta-analytic review of gender differences, intercorrelations, and relations to maladjustment. *Child Development, 79*, 1185–1229.

Cárdenas, R. A., & Harris, L. J. (2007). Do women's preferences for symmetry change across the menstrual cycle? *Evolution and Human Behavior, 28*, 96–105.

Caro, T. M. (1980). Effects of the mother, object play, and adult experience on predation in cats. *Behavioral and Neural Biology, 29*, 29–51.

Carranza, J. (1996). Sexual selection for male body mass and the evolution of litter size in mammals. *American Naturalist, 148*, 81–100.

Carré, J. M., & McCormick, C. M. (2008). Aggressive behavior and change in salivary testosterone concentrations predict willingness to engage in a competitive task. *Hormones and Behavior, 54*, 403–409.

Carroll, L. (1871). *Through the looking-glass and what Alice found there.* London: Macmillan.

Carron, A. V., & Bailey, D. A. (1974). Strength development in boys from 10 through 16 years. *Monographs of the Society for Research in Child Development, 39*(4, Serial No. 157).

Carson, J., Burks, V., & Parke, R. D. (1993). Parent–child physical play: Determinants and consequences. In K. MacDonald (Ed.), *Parent–child play: Descriptions & implications* (pp. 197–220). Albany: State University of New York Press.

Carter, C. S., & Getz, L. L. (1993, June). Monogamy and the prairie vole. *Scientific American, 268,* 100–106.

Carvajal-Carmona, L. G., Soto, I. D., Pineda, N., Ortíz-Barrientos, D., Duque, C., Ospina-Duque, J., et al. (2000). Strong Amerind/White sex bias and a possible Sephardic contribution among the founders of a population in northwest Columbia. *American Journal of Human Genetics, 67,* 1287–1295.

Casey, M. B., & Brabeck, M. M. (1989). Exceptions to the male advantage on a spatial task: Family handedness and college major as factors identifying women who excel. *Neuropsychologia, 27,* 689–696.

Cashdan, E. (1993). Attracting mates: Effects of paternal investment on mate attraction strategies. *Ethology and Sociobiology, 14,* 1–24.

Cashdan, E. (1995). Hormones, sex, and status in women. *Hormones and Behavior, 29,* 354–366.

Cashdan, E. (2003). Hormones and competitive aggression in women. *Aggressive Behavior, 29,* 107–115.

Cavanna, A. E., & Trimble, M. R. (2006). The precuneus: A review of its functional anatomy and behavioral correlates. *Brain, 126,* 564–583.

Cavigelli, S. A., & Pereira, M. E. (2000). Mating season aggression and fecal testosterone levels in male ring-tailed lemurs (*Lemur catta*). *Hormones and Behavior, 37,* 246–255.

Ceci, S. J., & Williams, W. M. (Eds.). (2007). *Why aren't more women in science? Top researchers debate the evidence.* Washington, DC: American Psychological Association.

Ceci, S. J., & Williams, W. M., & Barnett, S. M. (2009). Women's underrepresentation in science: Sociocultural and biological considerations. *Psychological Bulletin, 135,* 218–261.

Cerda-Flores, R. M., Barton, S. A., Marty-Gonzalez, L. F., Rivas, F., & Chakraborty, R. (1999). Estimation of nonpaternity in the Mexican population of Nuevo Leon: A validation study with blood group markers. *American Journal of Physical Anthropology, 109,* 281–293.

Chagnon, N. A. (1977). *Yanomamö, the fierce people.* New York: Holt.

Chagnon, N. A. (1988, February 26). Life histories, blood revenge, and warfare in a tribal population. *Science, 239,* 985–992.

Chagnon, N. A. (1997). *Yanomamö* (5th ed.). Fort Worth, TX: Harcourt.

Charlesworth, B. (1993). The evolution of sex and recombination in a varying environment. *Journal of Heredity, 84,* 345–350.

Charlesworth, W. R., & Dzur, C. (1987). Gender comparisons of preschoolers' behavior and resource utilization in group problem-solving. *Child Development, 58,* 191–200.

Charlesworth, W. R., & LaFrenier, P. (1983). Dominance, friendship utilization and resource utilization in preschool children's groups. *Ethology and Sociobiology, 4,* 175–186.

Charman, T., & Clements, W. (2002). Is there a gender difference in false belief development? *Social Development, 11*, 1–10.

Charnov, E. L. (1993). *Life history invariants: Some explorations of symmetry in evolutionary ecology.* New York: Oxford University Press.

Charpentier, M., Peignot, P., Hossaert-McKey, M., Gimenez, O., Setchell, J. M., & Wickings, E. J. (2005). Constraints on control: Factors influencing reproductive success in male mandrills (*Mandrillus sphinx*). *Behavioral Ecology, 16*, 614–623.

Chavanne, T. J., & Gallup, G. G., Jr. (1998). Variation in risk taking behavior among female college students as a function of the menstrual cycle. *Evolution and Human Behavior, 19*, 27–32.

Chen, F.-C., & Li, W.-H. (2001). Genomic divergences between humans and other hominoids and the effective population size of the common ancestor of humans and chimpanzees. *American Journal of Human Genetics, 68*, 444–456.

Chen, Z., & Siegler, R. S. (2000). Across the great divide: Bridging the gap between understanding toddlers' and older children's thinking. *Monographs of the Society for Research in Child Development, 65*(2, Serial No. 261).

Cherlin, A. J., Furstenberg, F. F., Jr., Chase-Lansdale, P. L., Kiernan, K. E., Robins, P. K., Morrison, D. R., & Teitler, J. O. (1991, June 7). Longitudinal studies of effects of divorce on children in Great Britain and the United States. *Science, 252*, 1386–1389.

Chisholm, J. S. (1993). Death, hope, and sex: Life-history theory and the development of reproductive strategies. *Current Anthropology, 34*, 1–24.

Choi, J., & Silverman, I. (2003). Processing underlying sex differences in route-learning strategies in children and adolescents. *Personality and Individual Differences, 34*, 1153–1166.

Choi, J.-K., & Bowles, S. (2007, October 26). The coevolution of parochial altruism and war. *Science, 318*, 636–640.

Christenfeld, N. J. S., & Hill, E. A. (1995, December 14). Whose baby are you? *Nature, 378*, 669.

Christensen, A., & Heavey, C. L. (1990). Gender and social structure in the demand/withdraw pattern of marital conflict. *Journal of Personality and Social Psychology, 59*, 73–81.

Christie, J. F., & Johnsen, E. P. (1987). Reconceptualizing constructive play: A review of the empirical literature. *Merrill-Palmer Quarterly, 33*, 439–452.

Clark, D. A., Mitra, P. P., & Wang, S. S.-H. (2001, May 10). Scalable architecture in mammalian brains. *Nature, 411*, 189–193.

Clark, R. D., III, & Hatfield, E. (1989). Gender differences in receptivity to sexual offers. *Journal of Psychology & Human Sexuality, 2*, 39–55.

Clinton, W. L., & Le Boeuf, B. J. (1993). Sexual selection's effects on male life history and the pattern of male mortality. *Ecology, 74*, 1884–1892.

Cloutier, J., Heatherton, T. F., Whalen, P. J., & Kelley, W. M. (2008). Are attractive people rewarding? Sex differences in the neural substrates of facial attractiveness. *Journal of Cognitive Neuroscience, 20*, 941–951.

Clutton-Brock, T. H. (1988). Reproductive success. In T. H. Clutton-Brock (Ed.), *Reproductive success: Studies of individual variation in contrasting breeding systems* (pp. 472–485). Chicago, IL: The University of Chicago Press.

Clutton-Brock, T. H. (1989). Mammalian mating systems. *Proceedings of the Royal Society of London B, 236*, 339–372.

Clutton-Brock, T. H. (1991). *The evolution of parental care*. Princeton, NJ: Princeton University Press.

Clutton-Brock, T. H. (2007, December 21). Sexual selection in males and females. *Science, 318*, 1882–1885.

Clutton-Brock, T. H., Albon, S. D., & Guinness, F. E. (1985, January 10). Parental investment and sex differences in juvenile mortality in birds and mammals. *Nature, 313*, 131–133.

Clutton-Brock, T. H., Albon, S. D., & Guinness, F. E. (1988). Reproductive success in male and female red deer. In T. H. Clutton-Brock (Ed.), *Reproductive success: Studies of individual variation in contrasting breeding systems* (pp. 325-343). Chicago, IL: University of Chicago Press.

Clutton-Brock, T. H., Harvey, P. H., & Rudder, B. (1977, October 27). Sexual dimorphism, socionomic sex ratio and body weight in primates. *Nature, 269*, 797–800.

Clutton-Brock, T. H., Hodge, S. J., Spong, G., Russell, A. F., Jordan, N. R., & Bennett, L. L., et al. (2006, December 28). Intrasexual competition and sexual selection in cooperative mammals. *Nature, 444*, 1065–1068.

Clutton-Brock, T. H., & McComb, K. (1993). Experimental tests of copying and mate choice in fallow deer (*Dama dama*). *Behavioral Ecology, 4*, 191–193.

Clutton-Brock, T. H., & Vincent, A. C. J. (1991, May 2). Sexual selection and the potential reproductive rates of males and females. *Nature, 351*, 58–60.

Coates, J. M., & Herbert, J. (2008). Endogenous steroids and financial risk taking on a London trading floor. *Proceedings of the National Academy of Sciences USA, 104*, 6167–6172.

Cohen, D., Nisbett, R. E., Bowdle, B. F., & Schwarz, N. (1996). Insult, aggression, and the southern culture of honor: An "experimental ethnography." *Journal of Personality and Social Psychology, 70*, 945–960.

Cohen, L. B., & Gelber, E. R. (1975). Infant visual memory. In L. B. Cohen & P. Salapatek (Eds.), *Infant perception: From sensation to cognition* (pp. 347–403). New York: Academic Press.

Cohen-Bendahan, C. C. C., Buitelaar, J. K., van Goozen, S. H. M., & Cohen-Kettenis, P. T. (2004). Prenatal exposure to testosterone and functional cerebral lateralization: A study in same-sex and opposite-sex twins. *Psychoneuroendocrinology, 29*, 911–916.

Cohen-Bendahan, C. C. C., van de Beek, C., & Berenbaum, S. A. (2005). Prenatal sex hormone effects on child and adult sex-typed behavior: Methods and findings. *Neuroscience and Biobehavioral Reviews, 29,* 353–384.

Colegrave, N. (2002, December 12). Sex releases the speed limit on evolution. *Nature, 420,* 664–666.

Coleman, S. W., Patricelli, G. L., & Borgia, G. (2004, April 15). Variable female preferences drive complex male displays. *Nature, 428,* 742–745.

Collaer, M. L., & Hines, M. (1995). Human behavioral sex differences: A role for gonadal hormones during early development? *Psychological Bulletin, 118,* 55–107.

Collaer, M. L., Reimers, S., & Manning, J. T. (2007). Visuospatial performance on an Internet line judgment task and potential hormonal markers: Sex, sexual orientation, and 2D:4D. *Archives of Sexual Behavior, 36,* 177–192.

Collis, K., & Borgia, G. (1992). Age-related effects of testosterone, plumage, and experience on aggression and social dominance in juvenile male satin bowerbirds (*Ptilonorhynchus violaceus*). *Auk, 109,* 422–434.

Collis, K., & Borgia, G. (1993). Delayed plumage maturation, facilitated learning, and the cost of display and delayed plumage maturation in the satin bowerbird (*Ptilonorhynchus violaceus*). *Ethology, 94,* 59–71.

Colmenares, F. (1992). Clans and harems in a colony of hamadryas and hybrid baboons: Male kinship, familiarity and the formation of brother-teams. *Behaviour, 121,* 61–94.

Coluccia, E., Iosue, G., & Brandimonte, M. A. (2007). The relationship between map drawing and spatial orientation abilities: A study of gender differences. *Journal of Environmental Psychology, 27,* 135–144.

Coluccia, E., & Louse, G. (2004). Gender differences in spatial orientation: A review. *Journal of Environmental Psychology, 24,* 329–340.

Connellan, J., Baron-Cohen, S., Wheelwright, S., Batki, A., & Ahluwalia, J. (2001). Sex differences in human neonatal social perception. *Infant Behavior and Development, 23,* 113–118.

Conner, J. K. (2001). How strong is natural selection? *Trends in Ecology & Evolution, 16,* 215–217.

Constable, J. L., Ashley, M. V., Goodall, J., & Pusey, A. E. (2001). Noninvasive paternity assignment in Gombe chimpanzees. *Molecular Ecology, 10,* 1279–1300.

Cooke, L. P. (2004). The gendered division of labor and family outcomes in Germany. *Journal of Marriage and Family, 66,* 1246–1259.

Cooke, L. P. (2007). Persistent policy effects on the division of domestic tasks in reunified Germany. *Journal of Marriage and Family, 69,* 930–950.

Cooper, T. F., Lenski, R. E., & Elena, S. F. (2005). Parasites and mutational load: An experimental test of a pluralistic theory for the evolution of sex. *Proceedings of the Royal Society of London B, 272,* 311–317.

Cornelissen, P. L., Hancock, P. J. B., Kiviniemi, V., George, H. R., & Tovée, M. J. (in press). Patterns of eye movements when male and female observers judge female attractiveness, body fat, and hip-to-waist ratio. *Evolution and Human Behavior*.

Cornwallis, C. K., & Birkhead, T. R. (2007). Changes in sperm quality and numbers in response to experimental manipulation of male social status and female attractiveness. *American Naturalist, 170,* 758–770.

Cornwell, R. E., Smith, M. J. L., Boothroyd, L. G., Moore, F. R., Davis, H. P., Stirrat, M., et al. (2006). Reproductive strategy, sexual development and attraction to facial characteristics. *Philosophical Transactions of the Royal Society of London, B, 361,* 2143–2154.

Corter, C. M., & Fleming, A. S. (1995). Psychobiology of maternal behavior in human beings. In M. H. Bornstein (Ed.), *Handbook of parenting: Vol. 2. Biology and ecology of parenting* (pp. 87–116). Mahwah, NJ: Erlbaum.

Coss, R. G., & Goldthwaite, R. O. (1995). The persistence of old designs for perception. In N. S. Thompson (Ed.), *Perspectives in ethology: Behavioral design* (Vol. 11, pp. 83–147). New York: Plenum Press.

Costa, P. T., Jr., Terracciano, A., & McCrae, R. R. (2001). Gender differences in personality traits across cultures: Robust and surprising findings. *Journal of Personality and Social Psychology, 81,* 322–331.

Cowan, N. (1995). *Attention and memory: An integrated framework.* New York: Oxford University Press.

Cox, C. R., & Le Boeuf, B. J. (1977). Female incitation of male competition: A mechanism of sexual selection. *American Naturalist, 111,* 317–335.

Cox, M. J., Owen, M. T., Lewis, J. M., & Henderson, V. K. (1989). Marriage, adult adjustment, and early parenting. *Child Development, 60,* 1015–1024.

Crano, W. D., & Aronoff, J. (1978). A cross-cultural study of expressive and instrumental role complementarity in the family. *American Sociological Review, 43,* 463–471.

Crick, N. R., Casas, J. F., & Mosher, M. (1997). Relational and overt aggression in preschool. *Developmental Psychology, 33,* 579–588.

Cronin, H. (1991). *The ant and the peacock.* New York: Cambridge University Press.

Crow, J. F. (1997). The high spontaneous mutation rate: Is it a health risk? *Proceedings of the National Academy of Sciences, USA, 94,* 8380–8386.

Cruz García, G. S. (2006). The mother–child nexus. Knowledge and valuation of wild food plants in Wayanad, Western Ghats, India. *Journal of Ethnobiology and Ethnomedicine, 2,* 39. Retrieved October 12, 2008, from http://www.ethnobiomed.com/content/2/1/39

Cunningham, M. R. (1986). Measuring the physical in physical attractiveness: Quasi-experiments on the sociobiology of female beauty. *Journal of Personality and Social Psychology, 50,* 925–935.

Cunningham, M. R., Barbee, A. P., & Pike, C. L. (1990). What do women want? Facialmetric assessment of multiple motives in the perception of male facial physical attractiveness. *Journal of Personality and Social Psychology, 59,* 61–72.

Cusumano, D. L., & Thompson, J. K. (2000). Media influence and body image in 8–11-year-old boys and girls: A preliminary report on the multidimensional media influence scale. *International Journal of Eating Disorders, 29*, 37–44.

Dale, J. (2006). Intraspecific variation in coloration. In G. E. Hill & K. J. McGraw (Eds.), *Bird coloration: Vol. 2. Function and evolution* (pp. 36–86). Cambridge, MA: Harvard University Press.

Daly, M., & Wilson, M. (1982). Whom are newborn babies said to resemble? *Ethology and Sociobiology, 3*, 69–78.

Daly, M., & Wilson, M. (1983). *Sex, evolution and behavior* (2nd ed.). Boston: Willard Grant.

Daly, M., & Wilson, M. (1988a, October 28). Evolutionary social psychology and family homicide. *Science, 242*, 519–524.

Daly, M., & Wilson, M. (1988b). *Homicide.* New York: Aldine de Gruyter.

Daly, M., Wilson, M., & Weghorst, S. J. (1982). Male sexual jealousy. *Ethology and Sociobiology, 3*, 11–27.

Damasio, A. (2003). *Looking for Spinoza: Joy, sorrow, and the feeling brain.* Orlando, FL: Harcourt.

Darwin, C. R. (1845). *Journal of researches into the natural history and geology of the countries visited during the voyage of H.M.S. Beagle round the world, under the command of Capt. Fitz Roy, R.N.* (2nd ed.). London: John Murray.

Darwin, C. R. (1859). *On the origin of species by means of natural selection.* London: John Murray.

Darwin, C. R. (1871). *The descent of man, and selection in relation to sex* (Vols. 1 & 2). London: John Murray.

Darwin, C. R., & Wallace, A. (1858). On the tendency of species to form varieties, and on the perpetuation of varieties and species by natural means of selection. *Journal of the Linnean Society of London, Zoology, 3*, 45–62.

Darwin, F. (Ed.). (2000). *The autobiography of Charles Darwin.* Amherst, NY: Prometheus Books. (Original work published 1887)

Davies, P. T., & Cummings, E. M. (1994). Marital conflict and child adjustment: An emotional security hypothesis. *Psychological Bulletin, 116*, 387–411.

Davis, J., & Werre, D. (2008). A longitudinal study of the effects of uncertainty on reproductive behaviors. *Human Nature, 19*, 426–452.

Davis, J. N., & Daly, M. (1997). Evolutionary theory and the human family. *Quarterly Review of Biology, 72*, 407–435.

Davis, L. E., Cheng, L. C., & Strube, M. J. (1996). Differential effects of racial composition on male and female groups: Implications for group work practice. *Social Work Research, 20*, 157–166.

Dawkins, R. (1989). *The selfish gene* (2nd ed.). New York: Oxford University Press.

Dawkins, R., & Krebs, J. R. (1979). Arms races between and within species. *Proceedings of the Royal Society of London B, 205*, 489–511.

Day, M. H. (1994). The origin and evolution of man. In E. E. Bitter & N. Bittar (Eds.), *Evolutionary biology* (pp. 321–351). Greenwich, CT: JAI Press.

Day, L. B., Westcott, D. A., & Olster, D. H. (2005). Evolution of bower complexity and cerebellum size in bowerbirds. *Brain, Behavior and Evolution, 66*, 62–72.

Dean, C., Leakey, M. G., Reid, D., Schrenk, F., Schwartz, G. T., Stringer, C., & Walker, A. (2001, December 6). Growth processes in teeth distinguish modern humans from *Homo erectus* and earlier hominins. *Nature, 414*, 628–631.

Deaner, R. O. (2006). More males run relatively fast in U.S. road races: Further evidence of a sex difference in competitiveness. *Evolutionary Psychology, 4*, 303–314. Retrieved June 28, 2008, from http://www.epjournal.net/filestore/ep043033142.pdf

Deary, I. J., Irwing, P., Der, G., & Bates, T. C. (2007). Brother–sister differences in the *g* factor in intelligence: Analysis of full, opposite-sex siblings from the NLSY1979. *Intelligence, 35*, 451–456.

Deary, I. J., Thorpe, G., Wilson, V., Starr, J. M., & Whalley, L. J. (2003). Population sex differences in IQ at age 11: The Scottish mental survey 1932. *Intelligence, 31*, 533–542.

de Bruin, J. P., Bovenhuis, H., van Noord, P. A. H., Pearson, P. L., van Arendonk, J. A. M., te Velde, E. R., et al. (2001). The role of genetic factors in age at natural menopause. *Human Reproduction, 16*, 2014–2018.

DeBruine, L. M., Jones, B. C., Little, A. C., Boothroyd, L. G., Perrett, D. I., Penton-Voak, I. S., et al. (2006). Correlated preferences for facial masculinity and ideal or actual partner's masculinity. *Proceedings of the Royal Society of London B, 273*, 1355–1360.

Decaestecker, E., Gaba, S., Raeymaekers, J. A. M., Stoks, R., Van Kerckhoven, L., Ebert, D., & De Meester, L. (2007, December 6). Host–parasite 'Red Queen' dynamics archived in pond sediment. *Nature, 450*, 870–873.

de Gaudemar, B. (1998). Sexual selection and breeding patterns: Insights from salmonids (*Salmonidae*). *Acta Biotheoretica, 46*, 235–251.

de Lacoste-Utamsing, C., & Holloway, R. L. (1982, June 25). Sexual dimorphism in the human corpus callosum. *Science, 216*, 1431–1432.

Delahunty, K. M., McKay, D. W., Noseworthy, D. E., & Storey, A. E. (2007). Prolactin responses to infant cues in men and women: Effects of parental experience and recent infant contact. *Hormones and Behavior, 51*, 213–220.

Del Giudice, M. (2008). Sex-biased ratio of avoidant/ambivalent attachment in middle childhood. *British Journal of Developmental Psychology 26*, 369–379.

Del Giudice, M. (2009a). On the real magnitude of psychological sex difference. *Evolutionary Psychology, 7*, 264–279. Retrieved June 9, 2009, from http://www.epjournal.net/ep07264279

Del Giudice, M. (2009b). Sex, attachment, and the development of reproductive strategies. *Behavioral and Brain Sciences, 32*, 1–67.

Del Giudice, M., & Belsky, J. (in press). The development of sex differences in attachment: An evolutionary perspective. *Perspectives in Child Development*.

Delhey, K., Peters, A., & Kempenaers, B. (2007). Cosmetic coloration in birds: Occurrence, function, and evolution. *American Naturalist, 169,* S145–S158.

Demas, G. E., Albers, H. E., Cooper, M., & Soma, K. K. (2007). Novel mechanisms underlying neuroendocrine regulation of aggression: A synthesis of bird, rodent and primate studies. In J. D. Blaustein (Ed.), *Behavioral neurochemistry, neuroendocrinology and molecular neurobiology* (337–372). Berlin, Germany: Springer-Verlag.

Deregowski, J. B., Shepard, J. W., & Slaven, G. A. (1997). Sex differences on Bartel's task: An investigation into perception of real and depicted distances. *British Journal of Psychology, 88,* 637–651.

Derntl, B., Kryspin-Exner, I., Fernbach, E., Moser, E., & Habel, U. (2008). Emotion recognition accuracy in healthy young females is associated with cycle phase. *Hormones and Behavior, 53,* 90–95.

de Ruiter, J. R., & Inoue, M. (1993). Paternity, male social rank, and sexual behavior. *Primates, 34,* 553–555.

de Ruiter, J. R., & van Hooff, J. A. R. A. M. (1993). Male dominance rank and reproductive success in primate groups. *Primates, 34,* 513–523.

DeSoto, M. C., Bumgardner, J., Close, A., & Geary, D. C. (2007). Investigating the role of hormones in theory of mind. *North American Journal of Psychology, 9,* 535–544.

DeSteno, D. A., & Salovey, P. (1996). Evolutionary origins of sex differences in jealousy? Questioning the fitness of the model. *Psychological Science, 7,* 367–372.

Deviche, P., & Cortez, L. (2005). Androgen control of immunocompetence in the male house finch, *Carpodacus mexicanus* Müller. *Journal of Experimental Biology, 208,* 1287–1295.

de Visser, J. A. G. M., & Elena, S. F. (2007). The evolution of sex: Empirical insights into the roles of epistasis and drift. *Nature Reviews: Genetics, 8,* 139–149.

de Vlaming, V. L. (1979). Actions of prolactin among the vertebrates. In E. J. W. Barrington (Ed.), *Hormones and evolution* (pp. 561–642). New York: Academic Press.

DeVoogd, T. J. (1991). Endocrine modulation of the development and adult function of the avian song system. *Psychoneuroendocrinology, 16,* 41–66.

de Waal, F. B. M. (1982). *Chimpanzee politics: Power and sex among apes.* New York: Harper & Row.

de Waal, F. B. M. (1993). Sex differences in chimpanzee (and human) behavior: A matter of social values? In M. Hechter, L. Nadel, & R. E. Michod (Eds.), *The origin of values* (pp. 285–303). New York: Aldine de Gruyter.

de Waal, F. B. M. (2000, July 28). Primates—A natural heritage of conflict resolution. *Science, 289,* 586–590.

de Waal, F. B. M., & Lanting, F. (1997). *Bonobo: The forgotten ape.* Berkeley: University of California Press.

Diamond, J. M. (1966, March 4). Zoological classification system of a primitive people. *Science, 151,* 1102–1104.

Diamond, J. M. (1986). Biology of birds of paradise and bowerbirds. *Annual Review of Ecology and Systematics, 17,* 17–37.

Dickemann, M. (1981). Paternal confidence and dowry competition: A biocultural analysis of purdah. In R. D. Alexander & D. W. Tinkle (Eds.), *Natural selection and social behavior* (pp. 417–438). New York: Chiron Press.

Diener, E., & Seligman, E. P. (2002). Very happy people. *Psychological Science, 13,* 81–84.

Dimberg, U., & Öhman, A. (1996). Behold the wrath—Psychophysiological responses to facial stimuli. *Motivation & Emotion, 20,* 149–182.

DiPietro, J. A. (1981). Rough and tumble play: A function of gender. *Developmental Psychology, 17,* 50–58.

Dixon, A., Ross, D., O'Malley, S. L. C., & Burke, T. (1994, October 20). Paternal investment inversely related to degree of extra-pair paternity in the reed bunting. *Nature, 371,* 698–700.

Dixson, A. F. (1983). Observation on the evolution and behavioral significance of "sexual skin" in female primates. *Advances in the Study of Behavior, 13,* 63–106.

Dixson, A. F., Bossi, T., & Wickings, E. J. (1993). Male dominance and genetically determined reproductive success in the mandrill (*Mandrillus sphinx*). *Primates, 34,* 525–532.

Dloniak, S. M., French, J. A., & Holekamp, K. E. (2006, April 27). Rank-related maternal effects of androgens on behaviour in wild spotted hyaenas. *Nature, 440,* 1190–1193.

Dolan, B. M., Birtchnell, S. A., & Lacey, J. H. (1987). Body image distortion in non-eating disordered women and men. *Journal of Psychosomatic Research, 31,* 513–520.

Donaldson, R. S., & Kohl, S. G. (1965). Perinatal mortality in twins by sex. *American Journal of Public Health, 55,* 1411–1418.

Douadi, M. I., Gatti, S., Levrero, F., Duhamel, G., Bermejo, M., Vallet, D., et al. (2007). Sex-biased dispersal in western lowland gorillas (*Gorilla gorilla gorilla*). *Molecular Ecology, 16,* 2247–2259.

Draper, P. (1989). African marriage systems: Perspectives from evolutionary ecology. *Ethology and Sociobiology, 10,* 145–169.

Draper, P., & Harpending. H. (1982). Father absence and reproductive strategy. *Journal of Anthropological Research, 38,* 255–272.

Draper, P., & Harpending, H. (1988). A sociobiological perspective on the development of human reproductive strategies. In K. B. MacDonald (Ed.), *Sociobiological perspectives on human development* (pp. 340–372). New York: Springer-Verlag.

Dreher, J.-C., Schmidt, P. J., Kohn, P., Furman, D., Rubinow, D., & Berman, K. F. (2007). Menstrual cycle phase modulates reward-related neural function in women. *Proceedings of the National Academy of Sciences USA, 104,* 2465–2470.

Drigotas, S. M. (2002). The Michelangelo phenomenon and personal well-being. *Journal of Personality, 70,* 59–77.

Driscoll, I., Hamilton, D. A., Yeo, R. A., Brooks, W. M., & Sutherland, R. J. (2005). Virtual navigation in humans: The impact of age, sex, and hormones on place learning. *Hormones and Behavior, 47,* 326–335.

Dubb, A., Gur, R., Avants, B., & Gee, J. (2003). Characterization of sexual dimorphism in the human corpus callosum. *NeuroImage, 20,* 512–519.

Dufty, A. M., Jr., Clobert, J., & Møller, A. P. (2002). Hormones, developmental plasticity and adaptation. *Trends in Ecology & Evolution, 17,* 190–196.

Dugatkin, L. A. (1996). Interface between culturally based preferences and genetic preferences: Female mate choice in *Poecilia reticulata. Proceedings of the National Academy of Sciences USA 93,* 2770–2773.

Dugatkin, L. A., & Godin, J.-G. J. (1993). Female mate copying in the guppy (*Poecilia reticulata*): Age-dependent effects. *Behavioral Ecology, 4,* 289–292.

Dunbar, R. I. M. (1984). *Reproductive decisions: An economic analysis of gelada baboon social strategies.* Princeton, NJ: Princeton University Press.

Dunbar, R. I. M. (1993). Coevolution of neocortical size, group size and language in humans. *Behavioral and Brain Sciences, 16,* 681–735.

Dunbar, R. I. M. (1995). The mating system of callitrichid primates: I. Conditions for the coevolution of pair bonding and twinning. *Animal Behaviour, 50,* 1057–1070.

Dunbar, R. I. M., & Bever, J. (1998). Neocortex size predicts group size in carnivores and some insectivores. *Ethology, 104,* 695–708.

Dunn, J., Cutting, A. L., & Demetriou, H. (2000). Moral sensibility, understanding others, and children's friendship interactions in the preschool period. *British Journal of Developmental Psychology, 18,* 159–177.

Dupanloup, I., Pereira, L., Bertorelle, G., Calafell, F., Prata, M. J., Amorim, A., & Barbujani, G. (2003). A recent shift from polygyny to monogamy is suggested by the analysis of worldwide Y-chromosome diversity. *Journal of Molecular Evolution, 57,* 85–97.

Durante, K. M., Li, N. P., & Haselton, M. G. (2008). Changes in women's choice of dress across the ovulatory cycle: Naturalistic and laboratory task-based evidence. *Personality and Social Psychology Bulletin, 34,* 1451–1460.

Dyer, F. C. (1998). Cognitive ecology of navigation. In R. Dukas (Ed.), *Cognitive ecology: The evolutionary ecology of information processing and decision making* (pp. 201–260). Chicago: The University of Chicago Press.

Dykiert, D., Gale, C. R., & Deary, I. J. (2009). Are apparent sex differences in mean IQ scores created in part by sample restriction and increased male variance? *Intelligence, 37,* 42–47.

Eagly, A. H. (1987). *Sex differences in social behavior: A social-role interpretation.* Hillsdale, NJ: Erlbaum.

Eagly, A. H., & Karau, S. J. (2002). Role congruity theory of prejudice toward female leaders. *Psychological Review, 109,* 573–598.

Eagly, A. H., & Wood, W. (1999). The origins of sex differences in human behavior: Evolved dispositions versus social roles. *American Psychologist, 54,* 408–423.

Eals, M., & Silverman, I. (1994). The hunter-gatherer theory of spatial sex differences: Proximate factors mediating the female advantage in recall of object arrays. *Ethology and Sociobiology, 15,* 95–105.

East, M. L., Burke, T., Wilhelm, K., Greig, C., & Hofer, H. (2003). Sexual conflicts in spotted hyenas: Male and female mating tactics and their reproductive outcome with respect to age, social status and tenure. *Proceedings of the Royal Society of London B, 270*, 1247–1254.

Eaton, W. O., & Enns, L. R. (1986). Sex differences in human motor activity level. *Psychological Bulletin, 100*, 19–28.

Ecuyer-Dab, I., & Robert, M. (2004a). Have sex differences in spatial ability evolved from male competition for mating and female concern for survival? *Cognition, 91*, 221–257.

Ecuyer-Dab., I., & Robert, M. (2004b). Spatial ability and home-range size: Examining the relationship in Western men and women (*Homo sapiens*). *Journal of Comparative Psychology, 118*, 217–231.

Ecuyer-Dab., I., & Robert, M. (2007). The female advantage in object location memory according to the foraging hypothesis: A critical analysis. *Human Nature, 18*, 365–385.

Eder, D., & Hallinan, M. T. (1978). Sex differences in children's friendships. *American Sociological Review, 43*, 237–250.

Eens, M., & Pinxten, R. (2000). Sex-role reversal in vertebrates: Behavioural and endocrinological accounts. *Behavioural Processes, 51*, 135–147.

Eibl-Eibesfeldt, I. (1989). *Human ethology.* New York: Aldine de Gruyter.

Eichstedt, J. A., Serbin, L. A., Poulin-DuBois, D., & Sen, M. G. (2002). Of bears and men: Infants' knowledge of conventional and metaphorical gender stereotypes. *Infant Behavior & Development, 25*, 296–310.

Eisenberg, N., & Lennon, R. (1983). Sex differences in empathy and related capacities. *Psychological Bulletin, 94*, 100–131.

Eisenberg, N., Murray, E., & Hite, T. (1982). Children's reasoning regarding sex-typed toy choices. *Child Development, 53*, 81–86.

Ekman, P. (1992). Facial expressions of emotion: New findings, new questions. *Psychological Science, 3*, 34–38.

Ekstrom, A. D., Kahana, M. J., Caplan, J. B., Fields, T. A., Isham, E. A., Newman, E. L., & Fried, I. (2003, September 11). Cellular networks underlying human spatial navigation. *Nature, 425*, 184–187.

Ellis, B. J. (2004). Timing of pubertal maturation in girls: An integrated life history approach. *Psychological Bulletin, 130*, 920–958.

Ellis, B. J., & Essex, M. J. (2007). Family environments, adrenarche, and sexual maturation: A longitudinal test of a life history model. *Child Development, 78*, 1799–1817.

Ellis, B. J., McFadyen-Ketchum, S., Dodge, K. A., Pettit, G. S., & Bates, J. E. (1999). Quality of early family relationships and individual differences in the timing of pubertal maturation in girls: A longitudinal test of an evolutionary model. *Journal of Personality and Social Psychology, 77*, 387–401.

Ellis, B. J., & Symons, D. (1990). Sex differences in sexual fantasy: An evolutionary psychological approach. *Journal of Sex Research, 27*, 527–555.

Ellis, L. (1995). Dominance and reproductive success among nonhuman animals: A cross-species comparison. *Ethology and Sociobiology, 16,* 257–333.

Ellis, L., Hershberger, S., Field, E., Wersinger, S., Sergio, P., Geary, D., et al. (2008). *Sex differences: Summarizing more than a century of scientific research.* New York: Psychology Press.

Else-Quest, N. M., Hyde, J. S., Goldsmith, H. H., & Van Hulle, C. A. (2006). Gender differences in temperament: A meta-analysis. *Psychological Bulletin, 132,* 33–72.

Ember, C. R. (1978). Myths about hunter-gatherers. *Ethnology, 17,* 439–448.

Ember, C. R., & Ember, M. (1994). War, socialization, and interpersonal violence. *Journal of Conflict Resolution, 38,* 620–646.

Emlen, S. T., & Oring, L. W. (1977, July 15). Ecology, sexual selection, and the evolution of mating systems. *Science, 197,* 215–223.

Endicott, K. (1992). Fathering in an egalitarian society. In B. S. Hewlett (Ed.), *Father–child relations: Cultural and biosocial contexts* (pp. 281–295). New York: Aldine de Gruyter.

Endler, J. A., & Basolo, A. L. (1998). Sensory ecology, receiver bias and sexual selection. *Trends in Ecology and Evolution, 13,* 415–420.

Engelhardt, A., Heistermann, M., Hodges, J. K., Nürnberg, P., & Niemitz, C. (2006). Determinants of male reproductive success in wild long-tailed macaques (*Macaca fascicularis*)—Male monopolization, female mate choice, or post-copulatory mechanisms? *Behavioral Ecology and Sociobiology, 59,* 740–752.

Engh, A. L., Beehner, J. C., Bergman, T. J., Whitten, P. L., Hoffmeier, R. R., Seyfarth, R. M., & Cheney, D. L. (2006). Female hierarchy instability, male immigration and infanticide increase glucocorticoid levels in female chacma baboons. *Animal Behaviour, 71,* 1227–1237.

Engh, A. L., Funk, S. M., Van Horn, R. C., Scribner, K. T., Bruford, M. W., & Libants, S., et al. (2002). Reproductive skew among males in a female-dominated mammalian society. *Behavioral Ecology, 13,* 193–200.

Epstein, R. A., & Higgins, J. S. (2007). Differential parahippocampal and retrosplenial involvement in three types of visual scene recognition. *Cerebral Cortex, 17,* 1680–1693.

Ergon, T., Lambin, X., & Stenseth, N. C. (2001, June 28). Life-history traits of voles in a fluctuating population respond to the immediate environment. *Nature, 411,* 1043–1045.

Eriksson, J., Siedel, H., Lukas, D., Kayser, M., Erler, A., Hashimoto, C., et al. (2006). Y-chromosome analysis confirms highly sex-biased dispersal and suggests a low male effective population size in bonobos (*Pan paniscus*). *Molecular Ecology, 15,* 939–949.

Ermer, E., Cosmides, L., & Tooby, J. (2008). Relative status regulates risky decision making about resources in men: Evidence for the co-evolution of motivation and cognition. *Evolution and Human Behavior, 29,* 106–118.

Ernst, M., Maheu, F. S., Schroth, E., Hardin, J., Golan, L. G., Cameron, J., et al. (2007). Amygdala function in adolescents with congenital adrenal hyperplasia: A model for the study of early steroid abnormalities. *Neuropsychologia, 45*, 2104–2113.

Essock-Vitale, S. M., & McGuire, M. T. (1988). What 70 million years hath wrought: Sexual histories and reproductive success of a random sample of American women. In L. Betzig, M. Borgerhoff Mulder, & P. Turke (Eds.), *Human reproductive behaviour: A Darwinian perspective* (pp. 221–235). Cambridge, England: Cambridge University Press.

Estes, S., & Arnold, S. J. (2007). Resolving the paradox of stasis: Models with stabilizing selection explain evolutionary divergence on all timescales. *American Naturalist, 169*, 227–244.

Evans, J. P., Zane, L., Francescato, S., & Pilastro, A. (2003, January 23). Directional postcopulatory sexual selection revealed by artificial insemination. *Nature, 421*, 360–363.

Evans, J. St. B. T. (2002). Logic and human reasoning: An assessment of the deduction paradigm. *Psychological Bulletin, 128*, 978–996.

Evans, L. (2006). Innate sex differences supported by untypical traffic fatalities. *Chance, 19*, 10–15.

Ewen, J. G., & Armstrong, D. P. (2000). Male provisioning is negatively correlated with attempted extrapair copulation in the stitchbird (or hihi). *Animal Behaviour, 60*, 429–433.

Fabricius, W. V., & Luecken, L. J. (2007). Postdivorce living arrangements, parent conflict, and long-term physical health correlates for children of divorce. *Journal of Family Psychology, 21*, 195–205.

Fagan, J., & Palkovitz, R. (2007). Unmarried, nonresident fathers' involvement with their infants: A risk and resilience perspective. *Journal of Family Psychology, 21*, 479–489.

Fagan, J. F., III. (1972). Infants' recognition memory for faces. *Journal of Experimental Child Psychology, 14*, 453–476

Fagen, R. M. (1981). *Animal play behavior*. New York: Oxford University Press.

Fairbanks, L. A., & McGuire, M. T. (1995). Maternal condition and the quality of maternal care in vervet monkeys. *Behaviour, 132*, 733–754.

Faivre, B., Grégoire, A., Préault, M., Cézilly, F., & Sorci, G. (2003, April 4). Immune activation rapidly mirrored in a secondary sexual trait. *Science, 300*, 103.

Falk, D. (2001). The evolution of sex differences in primate brains. In D. Falk & K. R. Gibson (Eds.), *Evolutionary anatomy of the primate cerebral cortex* (98–112). Cambridge, England: Cambridge University Press.

Falk, D., Froese, N., Sade, D. S., & Dudek, B. C. (1999). Sex differences in brain/body relationships of rhesus monkeys and humans. *Journal of Human Evolution, 36*, 233–238.

Falk, D., Redmond, J. C., Jr., Guyer, J., Conroy, G. C., Recheis, W., Weber, G. W., & Seidler, H. (2000). Early hominid brain evolution: A new look at old endocasts. *Journal of Human Evolution, 38*, 695–717.

Fan, J., Dai, W., Liu, F., & Wu, J. (2005). Visual perception of male body attractiveness. *Proceedings of the Royal Society of London B, 272,* 219–226.

Fan, J., Liu, F., Wu, J., & Dai, W. (2004). Visual perception of female body attractiveness. *Proceedings of the Royal Society of London B, 271,* 347–352.

Farah, M. J., Meyer, M. M., & McMullen, P. A. (1996). The living/nonliving dissociation is not an artifact: Giving an a priori implausible hypothesis a strong test. *Cognitive Neuropsychology, 13,* 137–154.

Farris, C., Treat, T. A., Viken, R. J., & McFall, R. M. (2008). Perceptual mechanisms that characterize gender differences in decoding women's sexual intent. *Psychological Science, 19,* 348–354.

Faulkner, J., & Schaller, M. (2007). Nepotistic nosiness: Inclusive fitness and vigilance of kin members' romantic relationships. *Evolution and Human Behavior, 28,* 430–438.

Feinberg, M., Neiderhiser, J., Howe, G., & Hetherington, E. M. (2001). Adolescent, parent, and observer perceptions of parenting: Genetic and environmental influences on shared and distinct perceptions. *Child Development, 72,* 1266–1284.

Feingold, A. (1990). Gender differences in effects of physical attractiveness on romantic attraction: A comparison across five research paradigms. *Journal of Personality and Social Psychology, 59,* 981–993.

Feingold, A. (1992a). Gender differences in mate selection preferences: A test of the parental investment model. *Psychological Bulletin, 112,* 125–139.

Feingold, A. (1992b). Sex differences in variability in intellectual abilities: A new look at an old controversy. *Review of Educational Research, 62,* 61–84.

Feingold, A. (1994). Gender differences in personality: A meta-analysis. *Psychological Bulletin, 116,* 429–456.

Fejfar, M. C., & Hoyle, R. H. (2000). Effect of private self-awareness on negative affect and self-referent attribution: A quantitative review. *Personality and Social Psychology Review, 4,* 132–142.

Feldman, S. S., Nash, S. C., & Aschenbrenner, B. G. (1983). Antecedents of fathering. *Child Development, 54,* 1628–1636.

Feng, J., Spence, I., & Pratt, J. (2007). Playing an action video game reduces gender differences in spatial cognition. *Psychological Science, 18,* 850–855.

Ferguson, R. B. (1995). *Yanomami warfare: A political history.* Santa Fe, NM: School of American Research Press.

Ferrie, J. E., Head, J., Shipley, M. J., Vahtera, J., Marmot, M. G., & Kivimäki, M. (2007). BMI, obesity, and sickness absence in the Whitehall II study. *Obesity, 15,* 1554–1564.

Ferriman, K., Lubinski, D., & Benbow, C. P. (2009). Work preferences, life values, and personal views of top math/science graduate students and the profoundly gifted: Developmental changes and sex differences during emerging adulthood and parenthood. *Journal of Personality and Social Psychology, 97,* 517–532.

Feshbach, N. D. (1969). Sex differences in children's modes of aggressive responses toward outsiders. *Merrill-Palmer Quarterly, 15*, 249–258.

Festinger, L. (1954). A theory of social comparison processes. *Human Relations, 7*, 117–140.

Fieder, M., & Huber, S. (2007). The effect of sex and childlessness on the association between status and reproductive output in modern society. *Evolution and Human Behavior, 28*, 392–398.

Fieder, M., & Huber, S., Bookstein, F. L., Iber, K., Schafer, K., Winckler, G., & Wallner, B. (2005). Status and reproduction in humans: New evidence for the validity of evolutionary explanations on basis of a university sample. *Ethology, 111*, 940–950.

Figueiredo, G. M., Leitão-Filho, H. F., & Begossi, A. (1993). Ethnobotany of Atlantic forest coastal communities: Diversity of plant used in Gamboa. *Human Ecology, 21*, 419–430.

Figueiredo, G. M., Leitão-Filho, H. F., & Begossi, A. (1997). Ethnobotany of Atlantic forest coastal communities: II. Diversity of plant uses at Sepetiba Bay (SE Brazil). *Human Ecology, 25*, 353–360.

Figueredo, A. J., Vásquez, G., Brumbach, B. H., Schneider, S. M. R., Sefcek, J. A., Tal, I. R., et al. (2006). Consilience and life history theory: From genes to brain to reproductive strategy. *Developmental Review, 26*, 243–275.

Fink, B., & Penton-Voak, I. (2002). Evolutionary psychology of facial attractiveness. *Current Directions in Psychological Sciences, 11*, 154–158.

Fischer, H., Sandblom, J., Nyberg, L., Herlitz, A., & Bäckman, L. (2007). Brain activation while forming memories of fearful and neutral faces in women and men. *Emotion, 7*, 767–773.

Fisher, H. E. (1982). *The sex contract: The evolution of human behavior*. New York: Morrow.

Fisher, R. A. (1930). *The genetical theory of natural selection*. Oxford, England: Clarendon Press.

Fiske, S. T. (2002). What we know now about bias and intergroup conflict, the problem of the century. *Current Directions in Psychological Science, 11*, 123–128.

Fiske, S. T., & Taylor, S. E. (1991). *Social cognition* (2nd ed.). New York: McGraw-Hill.

Fitch, R. H., & Denenberg, V. H. (1998). A role for ovarian hormones in sexual differentiation of the brain. *Behavioral and Brain Sciences, 21*, 311–352.

Fivizzani, A. J., & Oring, L. W. (1986). Plasma steroid hormones in relation to behavioral sex role reversal in the spotted sandpiper, *Actitis macularia*. *Biology of Reproduction, 35*, 1195–1201.

Fleming, A. S., Corter, C., Stallings, J., & Steiner, M. (2002). Testosterone and prolactin are associated with emotional responses to infant cries in new fathers. *Hormones and Behavior, 42*, 399–413.

Fleming, A. S., O'Day, D. H., & Kraemer, G. W. (1999). Neurobiology of mother–infant interactions: Experience and central nervous system plasticity across development and generations. *Neuroscience and Biobehavioral Reviews, 23,* 673–685.

Fleming, I. A., & Gross, M. R. (1994). Breeding competition in a Pacific salmon (Coho: *Oncorhynchus kisutch*): Measures of natural and sexual selection. *Evolution, 48,* 637–657.

Flinn, M. V. (1988a). Mate guarding in a Caribbean village. *Ethology and Sociobiology, 9,* 1–28.

Flinn, M. V. (1988b). Parent–offspring interactions in a Caribbean village: Daughter guarding. In L. Betzig, M. Borgerhoff Mulder, & P. Turke (Eds.), *Human reproductive behaviour: A Darwinian perspective* (pp. 189–200). Cambridge, England: Cambridge University Press.

Flinn, M. V. (1992). Paternal care in a Caribbean village. In B. S. Hewlett (Ed.), *Father–child relations: Cultural and biosocial contexts* (pp. 57–84). New York: Aldine de Gruyter.

Flinn, M. V. (2006). Evolution and ontogeny of stress response to social challenges in the human child. *Developmental Review, 26,* 138–174.

Flinn, M. V., & England, B. G. (1997). Social economics of childhood glucocorticoid stress response and health. *American Journal of Physical Anthropology, 102,* 33–53.

Flinn, M. V., Geary, D. C., & Ward, C. V. (2005). Ecological dominance, social competition, and coalitionary arms races: Why humans evolved extraordinary intelligence. *Evolution and Human Behavior, 26,* 10–46.

Flinn, M. V., & Leone, D. V. (2006). Early family trauma and the ontogeny of glucocorticoid stress response in the human child: Grandmother as a secure base. *Journal of Developmental Processes, 1,* 31–68.

Flinn, M. V., & Low, B. S. (1986). Resource distribution, social competition, and mating patterns in human societies. In D. I. Rubenstein & R. W. Wrangham (Eds.), *Ecological aspects of social evolution: Birds and mammals* (pp. 217–243). Princeton, NJ: Princeton University Press.

Flinn, M. V., Quinlan, R. J., Decker, S. A., Turner, M. T., & England, B. G. (1996). Male–female differences in effects of parental absence on glucocorticoid stress response. *Human Nature, 7,* 125–162.

Foerster, K., Coulson, T., Sheldon, B. C., Pemberton, J. M., Clutton-Brock, T. H., & Kruuk, L. E. B. (2007, June 28). Sexually antagonistic genetic variation for fitness in red deer. *Nature, 447,* 1107–1110.

Foley, R. A. (1987). Hominid species and stone-tool assemblages: How are they related? *Antiquity, 61,* 380–392.

Foley, R. A. (1999). Hominid behavioral evolution: Missing links in comparative primate socioecology. In P. C. Lee (Ed.), *Comparative primate socioecology* (pp. 363–386). Cambridge, England: Cambridge University Press.

Foley, R. A., & Lahr, M. M. (1997). Mode 3 technologies and the evolution of modern humans. *Cambridge Archaeology Journal, 7,* 3–36.

Foley, R. A., & Lee, P. C. (1989, February 17). Finite social space, evolutionary pathways, and reconstructing hominid behavior. *Science, 243,* 901–906.

Folstad, I., & Karter, A. J. (1992). Parasites, bright males, and the immunocompetence handicap. *American Naturalist, 139,* 603–622.

Formisano, E., De Martino, F., Bonte, M., & Goebel, R. (2008, November 7). "Who" is saying "what?" Brain-based decoding of human voice and speech. *Science, 322,* 970–973.

Forsberg, A. J. L., & Tullberg, B. S. (1995). The relationship between cumulative number of cohabiting partners and number of children for men and women in modern Sweden. *Ethology and Sociobiology, 16,* 221–232.

Forsgren, E., Amundsen, T., Borg, A. A., & Bjelvenmark, J. (2004, June 3). Unusually dynamic sex roles in a fish. *Nature, 429,* 551–554.

Försterling, F., Preikschas, S., & Agthe, M. (2007). Ability, luck, and looks: An evolutionary look at achievement ascriptions and the sexual attribution bias. *Journal of Personality and Social Psychology, 92,* 775–788.

Fossey, D. (1984). *Gorillas in the mist.* Boston: Houghton Mifflin.

Fox, G. L. (1995). Noncustodial fathers following divorce. *Marriage & Family Review, 20,* 257–282.

Frank, L. G. (1986). Social organization of the spotted hyaena (*Crocuta crocuta*). I. Demography. *Animal Behaviour, 34,* 1500–1509.

Frayer, D. W., & Wolpoff, M. H. (1985). Sexual dimorphism. *Annual Review of Anthropology, 14,* 429–473.

Fredrickson, B. L., Roberts, T.-A., Noll, S. M., Quinn, D. M., & Twenge, J. M. (1998). That swimsuit becomes you: Sex differences in self-objectification, restrained eating, and math performance. *Journal of Personality and Social Psychology, 75,* 269–284.

Freedman, D. G. (1974). *Human infancy: An evolutionary perspective.* New York: Wiley.

Fukushima, H., & Hiraki, K. (2006). Perceiving an opponent's loss: Gender-related differences in the medial-frontal negativity. *SCAN, 1,* 149–157.

Furlow, F. B., Armijo-Prewitt, T., Gangestad, S. W., & Thornhill, R. (1997). Fluctuating asymmetry and psychometric intelligence. *Proceedings of the Royal Society of London B, 264,* 823–829.

Furstenberg, F. F., Jr., Morgan, S. P., & Allison, P. D. (1987). Paternal participation and children's well-being after marital dissolution. *American Sociological Review, 52,* 695–701.

Furstenberg, F. F., Jr., & Nord, C. W. (1985). Parenting apart: Patterns of child-rearing after marital disruption. *Journal of Marriage and the Family, 47,* 893–904.

Furstenberg, F. F., Jr., Peterson, J. L., Nord, C. W., & Zill, N. (1983). The life course of children of divorce: Marital disruption and parental contact. *American Sociological Review, 48,* 656–668.

Fusani, L., & Gahr, M. (2006). Hormonal influence on song structure and organization: The role of estrogen. *Neuroscience, 138*, 939–946.

Gabriel, S., & Gardner, W. L. (1999). Are there "his" and "hers" types of interdependence? The implications of gender differences in collective versus relational interdependence for affect, behavior, and cognition. *Journal of Personality and Social Psychology, 77*, 642–655.

Gabunia, L., Vekua, A., Lordkipanidze, D., Swisher, C. C., III, Ferring, R., Justus, A., et al. (2000, May 12). Earliest Pleistocene hominid cranial remains from Dmanisi, Republic of Georgia: Taxonomy, geological setting, and age. *Science, 288*, 1019–1025.

Gaertner, L., & Insko, C. A. (2000). Intergroup discrimination in the minimal group paradigm: Categorization, reciprocation, or fear? *Journal of Personality and Social Psychology, 79*, 77–94.

Gahr, M. (2003). Male Japanese quails with female brains do not show male sexual behaviors. *Proceedings of the National Academy of Sciences USA, 100*, 7959–7964.

Galea, L. A. M. (2008). Gonadal hormone modulation of neurogenesis in the dentate gyrus of adult male and female rodents. *Brain Research Reviews, 57*, 332–341.

Galea, L. A. M., & Kimura, D. (1993). Sex differences in route-learning. *Personality and Individual Differences, 14*, 53–65.

Galea, L. A. M., Lee, T. T.-Y., Kostaras, X., Sidhu, J. A., & Barr, A. M. (2002). High levels of estradiol impair spatial performance in the Morris water maze and increase 'depressive-like' behaviors in the female meadow vole. *Physiology & Behavior, 77*, 217–225.

Galea, L. A. M., Perrot-Sinal, T. S., Kavaliers, M., & Ossenkopp, K.-P. (1999). Relations of hippocampal volume and dentate gyrus width to gonadal hormone levels in male and female meadow voles. *Brain Research, 821*, 383–391.

Galef, B. G., Jr., & Laland, K. N. (2005). Social learning in animals: Empirical studies and theoretical models. *BioScience, 55*, 489–499.

Gallagher, H. L., & Frith, C. D. (2003). Functional imaging of 'theory of mind'. *Trends in Cognitive Sciences, 7*, 77–83.

Gallistel, C. R. (1990). *The organization of learning.* Cambridge, MA: MIT Press/ Bradford Books.

Gallup, G. G., & Burch, R. L. (2004). Semen displacement as a sperm competition strategy in humans. *Evolutionary Psychology, 2*, 12–23. Retrieved April 26, 2008, from http://www.epjournal.net/filestore/ep021223.pdf

Gangestad, S. W., Bennett, K. L., & Thornhill, R. (2001). A latent variable model of developmental instability in relation to men's sexual behavior. *Proceedings of the Royal Society of London B, 268*, 1677–1684.

Gangestad, S. W., & Buss, D. M. (1993). Pathogen prevalence and human mate preferences. *Ethology and Sociobiology, 14*, 89–96.

Gangestad, S. W., Garver-Apgar, C. E., Simpson, J. A., & Cousins, A. J. (2007). Changes in women's mate preferences across the ovulatory cycle. *Journal of Personality and Social Psychology, 92,* 151–163.

Gangestad, S. W., & Simpson, J. A. (2000). The evolution of human mating: Trade-offs and strategic pluralism. *Behavioral and Brain Sciences, 23,* 573–644.

Gangestad, S. W., & Thornhill, R. (1998). Menstrual cycle variation in women's preferences for the scent of symmetrical men. *Proceedings of the Royal Society of London B, 265,* 927–933.

Gangestad, S. W., & Thornhill, R. (2008). Human oestrus. *Proceedings of the Royal Society of London B, 272,* 2023–2027.

Gangestad, S. W., Thornhill, R., & Garver, C. E. (2002). Changes in women's sexual interests and their partner's mate retention tactics across the menstrual cycle: Evidence for shifting conflicts of interest. *Proceedings of the Royal Society of London B, 269,* 975–982.

Gangestad, S. W., Thornhill, R., & Garver-Apgar, C. (2005a). Adaptations to ovulation. In D. M. Buss (Ed.), *The evolutionary psychology handbook* (pp. 344-371). Hoboken, NJ: Wiley.

Gangestad, S. W., Thornhill, R., & Garver-Apgar, C. (2005b). Women's sexual interests across the ovulatory cycle depend on primary partner developmental instability. *Proceedings of the Royal Society of London B, 272,* 2023–2027.

Gangestad, S. W., Thornhill, R., & Yeo, R. A. (1994). Facial attractiveness, developmental stability, and fluctuating asymmetry. *Ethology and Sociobiology, 15,* 73–85.

Garai, J. E., & Scheinfeld, A. (1968). Sex differences in mental and behavioral traits. *Genetic Psychology Monographs, 77,* 169–299.

Garamszegi, L. Z., Heylen, D., Møller, A. P., Eens, M., & de Lope, F. (2005). Age-dependent health status and song characteristics in the barn swallow. *Behavioral Ecology, 16,* 580–591.

Gard, M. G., & Kring, A. M. (2007). Sex differences in the time course of emotion. *Emotion, 7,* 429–437.

Garver-Apgar, C. E., Gangestad, S. W., & Simpson, J. A. (2007). Women's perceptions of men's sexual coerciveness change across the menstrual cycle. *Acta Psychologica Sinica, 39,* 536–540.

Garver-Apgar, C. E., Gangestad, S. W., Thornhill, R., Miller, R. D., & Olp, J. J. (2006). Major histocompatibility complex alleles, sexual responsivity, and unfaithfulness in romantic couples. *Psychological Science, 17,* 830–835.

Gaulin, S. J. C. (1992). Evolution of sex differences in spatial ability. *Yearbook of Physical Anthropology, 35,* 125–151.

Gaulin, S. J. C., & Boster, J. S. (1990). Dowry as female competition. *American Anthropologist, 92,* 994–1005.

Gaulin, S. J. C., & Fitzgerald, R. W. (1986). Sex differences in spatial ability: An evolutionary hypothesis and test. *American Naturalist, 127,* 74–88.

Gaulin, S. J. C., & Fitzgerald, R. W. (1989). Sexual selection for spatial-learning ability. *Animal Behaviour, 37,* 322–331.

Gavrilets, S. (2000, February 24). Rapid evolution of reproductive barriers driven by sexual conflict. *Nature, 403,* 886–889.

Geary, D. C. (1995a). Reflections of evolution and culture in children's cognition: Implications for mathematical development and instruction. *American Psychologist, 50,* 24–37.

Geary, D. C. (1995b). Sexual selection and sex differences in spatial cognition. *Learning and Individual Differences, 7,* 289–301.

Geary, D. C. (1996). Sexual selection and sex differences in mathematical abilities. *Behavioral and Brain Sciences, 19,* 229–284.

Geary, D. C. (1998a). Functional organization of the human mind: Implications for behavioral genetic research. *Human Biology, 70,* 185–198.

Geary, D. C. (1998b). *Male, female: The evolution of human sex differences.* Washington, DC: American Psychological Association.

Geary, D. C. (2000). Evolution and proximate expression of human paternal investment. *Psychological Bulletin, 126,* 55–77.

Geary, D. C. (2002a). Sexual selection and human life history. In R. Kail (Ed.), *Advances in child development and behavior* (Vol. 30, pp. 41–101). San Diego, CA: Academic Press.

Geary, D. C. (2002b). Sexual selection and sex differences in social cognition. In A. V. McGillicuddy-De Lisi & R. De Lisi (Eds.), *Biology, society, and behavior: The development of sex differences in cognition* (pp. 23–53). Greenwich, CT: Ablex Publishing, with Greenwood Press.

Geary, D. C. (2005a). Evolution of paternal investment. In D. M. Buss (Ed.), *The evolutionary psychology handbook* (pp. 483–505). Hoboken, NJ: Wiley.

Geary, D. C. (2005b). *The origin of mind: Evolution of brain, cognition, and general intelligence.* Washington, DC: American Psychological Association.

Geary, D. C. (2007). Educating the evolved mind: Conceptual foundations for an evolutionary educational psychology. In J. S. Carlson & J. R. Levin (Eds.), *Educating the evolved mind: Vol. 2. Psychological perspectives on contemporary educational issues* (pp. 1–99). Greenwich, CT: Information Age.

Geary, D. C. (2008). An evolutionarily informed education science. *Educational Psychologist, 43,* 179–195.

Geary, D. C., & Bjorklund, D. F. (2000). Evolutionary developmental psychology. *Child Development, 71,* 57–65.

Geary, D. C., Byrd-Craven, J., Hoard, M. K., Vigil, J., & Numtee, C. (2003). Evolution and development of boys' social behavior. *Developmental Review, 23,* 444–470.

Geary, D. C., DeSoto, M. C., Hoard, M. K., Sheldon, M. S., & Cooper, L. (2001). Estrogens and relationship jealousy. *Human Nature, 12,* 299–320.

Geary, D. C., & Flinn, M. V. (2001). Evolution of human parental behavior and the human family. *Parenting: Science and Practice, 1*, 5–61.

Geary, D. C., & Flinn, M. V. (2002). Sex differences in behavioral and hormonal response to social threat: Commentary on Taylor et al. (2000). *Psychological Review, 109*, 745–750.

Geary, D. C., Rumsey, M., Bow-Thomas, C. C., & Hoard, M. K. (1995). Sexual jealousy as a facultative trait: Evidence from the pattern of sex differences in adults from China and the United States. *Ethology and Sociobiology, 16*, 355–383.

Geary, D. C., Vigil, J., & Byrd-Craven, J. (2004). Evolution of human mate choice. *Journal of Sex Research, 41*, 27–42.

Gelman, R. (1990). First principles organize attention to and learning about relevant data: Number and animate–inanimate distinction as examples. *Cognitive Science, 14*, 79–106.

Gelman, S. A. (2003). *The essential child: Origins of essentialism in everyday thought.* New York: Oxford University Press.

Gelman, S. A., Taylor, M. G., & Nguyen, S. P. (2004). Mother–child conversations about gender: Understanding the acquisition of essentialist beliefs. *Monographs of the Society for Research in Child Development, 69*(1, Serial No. 275).

Gerhardt, H. C., Humfeld, S. C., & Marshall, V. T. (2007). Temporal order and the evolution of complex acoustic signals. *Proceedings of the Royal Society of London B, 274*, 1789–1794.

Gerhardt, H. C., Tanner, S. D., Corrigan, C. M., & Walton, H. C. (2000). Female preference functions based on call duration in the gray tree frog (*Hyla versicolor*). *Behavioral Ecology, 11*, 663–669.

Geschwind, N., & Galaburda, A. M. (1987). *Cerebral lateralization: Biological mechanisms, associations, and pathology.* Cambridge, MA: MIT Press/Bradford Books.

Geschwind, N., & Levitsky, W. (1968, July 12). Human brain: Left–right asymmetries in temporal speech region. *Science, 161*, 186–187.

Ghiglieri, M. P. (1987). Sociobiology of the great apes and the hominid ancestor. *Journal of Human Evolution, 16*, 319–357.

Ghiselin, M. T. (1974). *The economy of nature and the evolution of sex.* Berkeley: University of California Press.

Giedd, J. N., Blumenthal, J., Jeffries, N. O., Castellanos, F. X., Liu, H., Zijdenbos, A., et al. (1999). Brain development during childhood and adolescence: A longitudinal MRI study. *Nature Neuroscience, 2*, 861–863.

Gigerenzer, G., Todd, P. M., & ABC Research Group (Eds.). (1999). *Simple heuristics that make us smart.* New York: Oxford University Press.

Gil, D., Graves, J., Hazon, N., & Wells, A. (1999, October 1). Male attractiveness and differential testosterone investment in zebra finch eggs. *Science, 286*, 126–128.

Gil-Burmann, C., Peláez, F., & Sánchez, S. (2002). Mate choice differences according to sex and age: An analysis of personal advertisements in Spanish newspapers. *Human Nature, 13*, 493–508.

Gilliard, E. T. (1969). *Birds of paradise and bowerbirds*. London: Weidenfeld & Nicolson.

Gilligan, C. (1982). *In a difference voice: Psychological theory and women's development*. Cambridge, MA: Harvard University Press.

Gilmore, J. H., Lin, W., Prastawa, M. W., Looney, C. B., Vetsa, Y. S., Knickmeyer, R. C., et al. (2007). Regional gray matter growth, sexual dimorphism, and cerebral asymmetry in the neonatal brain. *Journal of Neuroscience, 27*, 1255–1260.

Gindhart, P. S. (1973). Growth standards for the tibia and radius in children aged one month through eighteen years. *American Journal of Physical Anthropology, 39*, 41–48.

Gingerich, P. D. (2001). Rates of evolution on the time scale of the evolutionary process. *Genetica, 112/113*, 127–144.

Ginsburg, H. J., & Miller, S. M. (1982). Sex differences in children's risk-taking behavior. *Child Development, 53*, 426–428.

Goldberg, S., Blumberg, S. L., & Kriger, A. (1982). Menarche and interest in infants: Biological and social influences. *Child Development, 53*, 1544–1550.

Goldizen, A. W. (2003). Social monogamy and its variation in callitrichids: Do these relate to the cost of infant care? In U. H. Reichard & C. Boesch (Eds.), *Monogamy: Mating strategies and partnerships in birds, humans and other mammals* (pp. 232–247). Cambridge, England: Cambridge University Press.

Goldschmidt, T., Bakker, T. C. M., & Feuth-De Bruijn, E. (1993). Selective copying of mate choice of female sticklebacks. *Animal Behaviour, 45*, 541–547.

Goldstein, J. M., Jerram, M., Poldrack, R., Ahern, T., Kennedy, D. N., Seidman, L. J., & Makris, N. (2005). Hormonal cycle modulates arousal circuitry in women using functional magnetic resonance imaging. *Journal of Neuroscience, 25*, 9309–9316.

Goldstein, J. M., Seidman, L. J., Horton, N. J., Makris, M., Kennedy, D. N., Caviness, V. S., Jr., et al. (2001). Normal sexual dimorphism of the adult human brain assessed by in vivo magnetic resonance imaging. *Cerebral Cortex, 11*, 490–497.

Gonzalez-Bono, E., Salvador, A., Serrano, M. A., & Ricarte, J. (1999). Testosterone, cortisol, and mood in a sports team competition. *Hormones and Behavior, 35*, 55–62.

Good, C. D., Johnsrude, I., Ashburner, J., Henson, R. N. A., Friston, K. J., & Frackowiak, R. S. J. (2001). Cerebral asymmetry and the effects of sex and handedness on brain structure: A voxel-based morphometric analysis of 465 normal adult brains. *NeuroImage, 14*, 685–700.

Goodall, J. (1986). *The chimpanzees of Gombe: Patterns of behavior*. Cambridge, MA: Belknap Press.

Goodsori, J. L., Saldanha, C. J., Hahn, T. P., & Soma, K. K. (2005). Recent advances in behavioral neuroendocrinology: Insights from studies on birds. *Hormones and Behavior, 48*, 461–473.

Gottfredson, L. S. (1997). Why *g* matters: The complexity of everyday life. *Intelligence, 24*, 79–132.

Gottman, J. M. (1998). Psychology and the study of marital processes. *Annual Review of Psychology, 49*, 169–197.

Gouchie, C., & Kimura, D. (1991). The relationship between testosterone levels and cognitive ability patterns. *Psychoneuroendocrinology, 16,* 323–334.

Gould, E., Woolley, C. S., & McEwen, B. S. (1991). The hippocampal formation: Morphological changes induced by thyroid, gonadal and adrenal hormones. *Psychoneuroendocrinology, 16,* 67–84.

Gould, S. J., Hildreth, J. E. K., & Booth, A. M. (2004). The evolution of allo-immunity and the genesis of adaptive immunity. *Quarterly Review of Biology, 79,* 359–382.

Gowlett, J. A. J. (1992). Tools—The Paleolithic record. In S. Jones, R. Martin, & D. Pilbeam (Eds.), *The Cambridge encyclopedia of human evolution* (pp. 350–360). New York: Cambridge University Press.

Grabe, S., Ward, L. M., & Hyde, J. S. (2008). The role of the media in body image concerns among women: A meta-analysis of experimental and correlational studies. *Psychological Bulletin, 134,* 460–476.

Grachev, I. D., & Apkarian, A. V. (2000). Chemical heterogeneity of the living human brain: A proton MR spectroscopy study on the effects of sex, age, and brain region. *NeuroImage, 11,* 554–563.

Graham, J., Haidt, J., & Nosek, B. A. (2009). Liberals and conservatives rely on different sets of moral foundations. *Journal of Personality and Social Psychology, 96,* 1029–1046.

Grainger, S. (2004). Family background and female sexual behavior: A test of the father-absence theory in Merseyside. *Human Nature, 15,* 133–145.

Grammer, K., Renninger, L., Fischer, B. (2004). Disco clothing, female sexual motivation, and relationship status: Is she dressed to impress? *Journal of Sex Research, 41,* 66–74.

Grammer, K., & Thornhill, R. (1994). Human (*Homo sapiens*) facial attractiveness and sexual selection: The role of symmetry and averageness. *Journal of Comparative Psychology, 108,* 233–242.

Grant, B. R., & Grant, P. R. (1993). Evolution of Darwin's finches caused by a rare climatic event. *Proceedings of the Royal Society of London B, 251,* 111–117.

Grant, J. W. A., & Foam, P. E. (2002). Effect of operational sex ratio on female–female versus male–male competitive aggression. *Canadian Journal of Zoology, 80,* 2242–2246.

Grant, P. R. (1999). *Ecology and evolution of Darwin's finches.* Princeton, NJ: Princeton University Press.

Grant, P. R., & Grant, B. R. (2002, April 26). Unpredictable evolution in a 30-year study of Darwin's finches. *Science, 296,* 707–711.

Gray, J. A. (1987). Perspectives on anxiety and impulsivity: A commentary. *Journal of Research in Personality, 21,* 493–509.

Gray, J. P. (1985). *Primate sociobiology.* New Haven, CT: Hraf Press.

Gray, P. B. (2003). Marriage, parenting, and testosterone variation among Kenyan Swahili men. *American Journal of Physical Anthropology, 122,* 279–286.

Gray, P. B., Ellison, P. T., & Campbell, B. C. (2007). Testosterone and marriage among Ariaal men of northern Kenya. *Current Anthropology, 48,* 750–755.

Gray, P. B., Kahlenberg, S. M., Barrett, E. S., Lipson, S. F., & Ellison, P. T. (2002). Marriage and fatherhood are associated with lower testosterone in males. *Evolution and Human Behavior, 23,* 193–201.

Gray, P. B., Parkin, J. C., & Samms-Vaughan, M. E. (2007). Hormonal correlates of human paternal interactions: A hospital-based investigation in urban Jamaica. *Hormones and Behavior, 52,* 499–507.

Graziano, W. G., & Eisenberg, N. (1997). Agreeableness: A dimension of personality. In R. Hogan, J. Johnson, & S. Briggs (Eds.), *Handbook of personality psychology* (pp. 795–824). San Diego, CA: Academic Press.

Graziano, W. G., Jensen-Campbell, L. A., Shebilske, L. J., & Lundgren, S. R. (1993). Social influence, sex differences, and judgments of beauty: Putting the *interpersonal* back in interpersonal attraction. *Journal of Personality and Social Psychology, 65,* 522–531.

Gredlein, J. M., & Bjorklund, D. F. (2005). Sex differences in young children's use of tools in a problem-solving task. *Human Nature, 16,* 211–232.

Greenlees, I. A., & McGrew, W. C. (1994). Sex and age differences in preferences and tactics of mate attraction: Analysis of published advertisements. *Ethology and Sociobiology, 15,* 59–72.

Greenough, W. T., Black, J. E., & Wallace, C. S. (1987). Experience and brain development. *Child Development, 58,* 539–559.

Greenspan, J. D., Craft, R. M., LeResche, L., Arendt-Nielsen, L., Berkley, K. J., Fillingim, R. B., et al. (2007). Studying sex and gender differences in pain and analgesia: A consensus report. *Pain, 132,* S26–S45.

Greenwood, P. J. (1980). Mating systems, philopatry and dispersal in birds and mammals. *Animal Behaviour, 28,* 1140–1162.

Griffith, S. C., & Pryke, S. R. (2006). Benefits to females of assessing color displays. In G. E. Hill & K. J. McGraw (Eds.), *Bird coloration: Vol. 2. Function and evolution* (pp. 233–279). Cambridge, MA: Harvard University Press.

Griskevicius, V., Cialdini, R. B., & Kenrick, D. T. (2006). Peacocks, Picasso, and parental investment: The effects of romantic motives on creativity. *Journal of Personality and Social Psychology, 91,* 63–76.

Grön, G., Wunderlich, A. P., Spitzer, M., Tomczak, T., & Riepe, M. W. (2000). Brain activation during human navigation: Gender-different neural networks as substrate of performance. *Nature Neuroscience, 3,* 404–408.

Groos, K. (1898). *The play of animals.* New York: Appleton.

Gross, J. J., & John, O. P. (1998). Mapping the domain of expressivity: Multimethod evidence for a hierarchical model. *Journal of Personality and Social Psychology, 74,* 170–191.

Gross, M. R. (1985, January 3). Disruptive selection for alternative life histories in salmon. *Nature, 313*, 47–48.

Gross, M. R. (1996). Alternative reproductive strategies and tactics: Diversity within sexes. *Trends in Ecology and Evolution, 11*, 92–98.

Grossman, C. J. (1985, January 18). Interactions between the gonadal steroids and the immune system. *Science, 227*, 257–261.

Grossman, M., & Wood, W. (1993). Sex differences in intensity of emotional experience: A social role interpretation. *Journal of Personality and Social Psychology, 65*, 1010–1022.

Grossmann, T., & Johnson, M. H. (2007). The development of the social brain in infancy. *European Journal of Neuroscience, 25*, 909–919.

Grotpeter, J. K., & Crick, N. R. (1996). Relational aggression, overt aggression and friendship. *Child Development, 67*, 2328–2338.

Guéguen, N. (2007). Bust size and hitchhiking: A field study. *Perceptual and Motor Skills, 105*, 1294–1298.

Guégan, N. (in press). Menstrual cycle phases and female receptivity to a courtship solicitation: An evaluation in a nightclub. *Evolution and Human Behavior*.

Gunnar, M. R., & Donahue, M. (1980). Sex differences in social responsiveness between six and twelve months. *Child Development, 51*, 262–265.

Gur, R. C., Gunning-Dixon, F., Bilker, W. B., & Gur, R. E. (2002). Sex differences in temporo-limbic and frontal brain volumes of healthy adults. *Cerebral Cortex, 12*, 998–1003.

Gur, R.C., Turetsky, B. I., Matsui, M., Yan, M., Bilker, W., Hughett, P., & Gur, R. E. (1999). Sex differences in brain gray and white matter in healthy young adults: Correlations with cognitive performance. *Journal of Neuroscience, 19*, 4065–4072.

Gurven, M., Kaplan, H., & Gutierrez, M. (2006). How long does it take to become a proficient hunter? Implications for the evolution of extended development and long life span. *Journal of Human Evolution, 51*, 454–470.

Gustafsson, L. (1986). Lifetime reproductive success and heritability: Empirical support for Fisher's fundamental theorem. *American Naturalist, 128*, 761–764.

Gustafsson, L., & Qvarnström, A. (2006). A test of the "sexy son" hypothesis: Sons of polygynous collard flycatchers do not inherit their fathers mating status. *American Naturalist, 167*, 297–302.

Gustafsson, L., & Sutherland, W. J. (1988, October 27). The costs of reproduction in the collard flycatcher *Ficedula albicollis*. *Nature, 335*, 813–815.

Gutierres, S. E., Kenrick, D. T., & Partch, J. J. (1999). Beauty, dominance, and the mating game: Contrasts effects in self-assessment reflect gender differences in mate selection. *Personality and Social Psychology Bulletin, 25*, 1126–1134.

Guttentag, M., & Secord, P. (1983). *Too many women?* Beverly Hills, CA: Sage.

Hadfield, J. D., Burgess, M. D., Lord, A., Phillimore, A. B., Clegg, S. M., & Owens, I. P. F. (2006). Direct versus indirect sexual selection: Genetic basis of colour, size and recruitment in a wild bird. *Proceedings of the Royal Society of London B, 273,* 1347–1353.

Haidt, J. (2007, May 18). The new synthesis in moral psychology. *Science, 316,* 998–1002.

Haig, D. (1993). Genetic conflicts in human pregnancy. *Quarterly Review of Biology, 68,* 495–532.

Halari, R., Sharma, T., Hines, M., Andrew, C., Simmons, A., & Kumari, V. (2006). Comparable fMRI activity with differential behavioural performance on mental rotation and overt verbal fluency tasks in healthy men and women. *Experimental Brian Research, 169,* 1–14.

Haley, M. P., Deutsch, C. J., & Le Boeuf, B. J. (1994). Size, dominance and copulatory success in male northern elephant seals, *Mirounga angustirostris. Animal Behaviour, 48,* 1249–1260.

Hall, G. C. H., & Barongan, C. (1997). Prevention of sexual aggression: Sociocultural risk and protective factors. *American Psychologist, 52,* 5–14.

Hall, J. A. (1978). Gender effects in decoding nonverbal cues. *Psychological Bulletin, 85,* 845–857.

Hall, J. A. (1984). *Nonverbal sex differences: Communication accuracy and expressive style.* Baltimore: The Johns Hopkins University Press.

Hall, J. A., & Matsumoto, D. (2004). Gender differences in judgments of multiple emotions from facial expressions. *Emotion, 4,* 201–206.

Hall, J. A. Y., & Kimura, D. (1995). Sexual orientation and performance on sexually dimorphic motor tasks. *Archives of Sexual Behavior, 24,* 395–407.

Halpern, C. T., Udry, J. R., Campbell, B., & Suchindran, C. (1993). Relationships between aggression and pubertal increases in testosterone: A panel analysis of adolescent males. *Social Biology, 40,* 8–24.

Halpern, D. F. (2000). *Sex differences in cognitive abilities* (3rd ed.). Mahwah, NJ: Erlbaum.

Halpern, D. F., Benbow, C., Geary, D. C., Gur, R., Hyde, J., & Gernsbacher, M. A. (2007). The science of sex differences in science and mathematics. *Psychological Science in the Public Interest, 8,* 1–52.

Hamann, S., Herman, R. A., Nolan, C. L., & Wallen, K. (2004). Men and women differ in amygdala response to visual sexual stimuli. *Nature Neuroscience, 7,* 411–416.

Hames, R. (1992). Variation in paternal care among the Yanomamö. In B. S. Hewlett (Ed.), *Father–child relations: Cultural and biosocial contexts* (pp. 85–110). New York: Aldine de Gruyter.

Hames, R. (1996). Costs and benefits of monogamy and polygyny for Yanomamö women. *Ethology and Sociobiology, 17,* 181–199.

Hamilton, G., Stoneking, M., & Excoffier, L. (2005). Molecular analysis reveals tighter social regulation in immigration in patrilocal populations than in matrilocal populations. *Proceedings of the National Academy of Sciences USA, 102,* 7476–7480.

Hamilton, W. D. (1964). The genetical evolution of social behaviour. II. *Journal of Theoretical Biology, 7,* 17–52.

Hamilton, W. D. (1980). Sex versus non-sex versus parasite. *Oikos, 35,* 282–290.

Hamilton, W. D. (1990). Mate choice near or far. *American Zoologist, 30,* 341–352.

Hamilton, W. D., Axelrod, R., & Tanese, R. (1990). Sexual reproduction as an adaptation to resist parasites (A review). *Proceedings of the National Academy of Sciences USA, 87,* 3566–3573.

Hamilton, W. D., & Zuk, M. (1982, October 22). Heritable true fitness and bright birds: A role for parasites? *Science, 218,* 384–387.

Hampson, E. (1990a). Estrogen-related variations in human spatial and articulatory-motor skills. *Psychoneuroendocrinology, 15,* 97–111.

Hampson, E. (1990b). Variation in sex-related cognitive abilities across the menstrual cycle. *Brain and Cognition, 14,* 26–43.

Hampson, E., & Kimura, D. (1988). Reciprocal effects of hormonal fluctuations on human motor and perceptual-spatial skills. *Behavioral Neuroscience, 102,* 456–459.

Hampson, E., van Anders, S. M., & Mullin, L. I. (2006). A female advantage in the recognition of emotional facial expressions: Test of an evolutionary hypothesis. *Evolution and Human Behavior, 27,* 401–416.

Harasty, J., Double, K. L., Halliday, G. M., Kril, J. J., & McRitchie, D. A. (1997). Language-associated cortical regions are proportionally larger in the female brain. *Archives of Neurology, 54,* 171–176.

Harcourt, A. H., Harvey, P. H., Larson, S. G., & Short, R. V. (1981, September 3). Testis weight, body weight and breeding system in primates. *Nature, 293,* 55–57.

Harcourt, A. H., & Stewart, K. J. (2007). *Gorilla society: Conflict, compromise, and cooperation between the sexes.* Chicago: The University of Chicago Press.

Harris, C. R. (2000). Psychophysiological responses to imagined infidelity: The specific innate modular view of jealousy reconsidered. *Journal of Personality and Social Psychology, 78,* 1082–1091.

Harris, C. R. (2003). A review of sex differences in sexual jealousy, including self-report data, psychophysiological responses, interpersonal violence, and morbid jealousy. *Personality and Social Psychology Review, 7,* 102–128.

Harris, C. R., & Christenfeld, N. (1996). Gender, jealousy, and reason. *Psychological Science, 7,* 364–366.

Harris, C. R., Jenkins, M., & Glaser, D. (2003). Gender differences in risk assessment: Why do women take fewer risks than men? *Judgment and Decision Making, 1,* 48–63.

Harris, J. R. (1995). Where is the child's environment? A group socialization theory of development. *Psychological Review, 102,* 458–489.

Harris, L. T., & Fiske, S. T. (2006). Dehumanizing the lowest of the low. *Psychological Science, 17,* 847–853.

Hart, J., Jr., & Gordon, B. (1992, September 3). Neural subsystem for object knowledge. *Nature, 359,* 60–64.

Hartung, J. (1982). Polygyny and inheritance of wealth. *Current Anthropology, 23,* 1–12.

Hartung, J. (1995). Love thy neighbor: The evolution of in-group morality. *Skeptic, 3,* 86–99.

Harvey, P. H., & Clutton-Brock, T. H. (1985). Life history variation in primates. *Evolution, 39,* 559–581.

Harvey, P. H., Kavanagh, M., & Clutton-Brock, T. H. (1978). Canine tooth size in female primates. *Nature, 276,* 817–818.

Harvey, P. H., Martin, R. D., & Clutton-Brock, T. H. (1987). Life histories in comparative perspective. In B. B. Smuts, D. L. Cheney, R. M. Seyfarth, R. W. Wrangham, & T. T. Struhsaker (Eds.), *Primate societies* (pp. 181–196). Chicago: The University of Chicago Press.

Haselton, M. G., & Buss, D. M. (2000). Error management theory: A new perspective on biases in cross-sex mind reading. *Journal of Personality and Social Psychology, 78,* 81–91.

Haselton, M. G., & Gangestad, S. W. (2006). Conditional expression of women's desires and men's mate guarding across the ovulatory cycle. *Hormones and Behavior, 49,* 509–518.

Haselton, M. G., & Miller, G. F. (2006). Women's fertility across the cycle increases the short-term attractiveness of creative intelligence. *Human Nature, 17,* 50–73.

Haselton, M. G., Mortezaie, M., Pillsworth, E. G., Bleske-Rechek, A., & Frederick, D. A. (2007). Ovulatory shifts in human female ornamentation: Near ovulation, women dress to impress. *Hormones and Behavior, 51,* 40–45.

Hassan, B., & Rahman, Q. (2007). Selective sexual orientation-related differences in object location memory. *Behavioral Neuroscience, 121,* 625–633.

Hassett, J. M., Siebert, E. R., & Wallen, K. (2008). Sex differences in rhesus monkey toy preferences parallel those of children. *Hormones and Behavior, 54,* 355–358.

Hassrick, R. B. (1964). *The Sioux: Life and customs of a warrior society.* Norman: University of Oklahoma Press.

Hatfield, E., & Sprecher, S. (1995). Men's and women's preferences in marital partners in the United States, Russia, and Japan. *Journal of Cross-Cultural Psychology, 26,* 728–750.

Hauser, M. D. (1996). *The evolution of communication.* Cambridge, MA: MIT Press/ Bradford Books.

Hausmann, M., & Güntürkün, O. (2000). Steroid fluctuations modify functional cerebral asymmetries: The hypothesis of progesterone-mediated interhemispheric decoupling. *Neuropsychologia, 38,* 1362–1374.

Hausmann, M., Slabbekoorn, D., van Goozen, S. H. M., Cohen-Kettenis, P. T., & Güntürkün, O. (2000). Sex hormones affect spatial abilities during the menstrual cycle. *Behavioral Neuroscience, 114,* 1245–1250.

Haviland, J. J., & Malatesta, C. Z. (1981). The development of sex differences in nonverbal signals: Fallacies, facts, and fantasies. In C. Mayo & N. M. Henley (Eds.), *Gender and nonverbal behavior* (pp. 183–208). New York: Springer-Verlag.

Havliček, J., Dvořáková, R., Bartoš, L., & Flegr, J. (2006). Non-advertised does not mean concealed: Body odour changes across the human menstrual cycle. *Ethology, 112,* 81–90.

Hawkes, K., O'Connell, J. F., & Blurton Jones, N. G. (2001). Hunting and nuclear families. *Current Anthropology, 42*, 681–709.

Hawley, P. H. (1999). The ontogenesis of social dominance: A strategy-based evolutionary perspective. *Developmental Review, 19*, 97–132.

Hawley, P. H. (2003). Prosocial and coercive configurations of resource control in early adolescence: A case for the well-adapted Machiavellian. *Merrill-Palmer Quarterly, 49*, 279–309.

Hawley, P. H., Little, T. D., & Card, N. A. (2008). The myth of the alpha male: A new look at dominance-related beliefs and behaviors among adolescent males and females. *International Journal of Behavioral Development, 32*, 76–88.

Hayward, C. (Ed.). (2003). *Gender differences at puberty*. Cambridge, England: Cambridge University Press.

Heckhausen, J., & Schulz, R. (1995). A life-span theory of control. *Psychological Review, 102*, 284–304.

Hed, H. M. E. (1987). Trends in opportunity for natural selection in the Swedish population during the period 1650–1980. *Human Biology, 59*, 785–797.

Hedges, L. V., & Nowell, A. (1995, July 7). Sex differences in mental scores, variability, and numbers of high-scoring individuals. *Science, 269*, 41–45.

Hedrick, P. W., & Black, F. L. (1997a). HLA and mate selection: No evidence in South Amerindians. *American Journal of Human Genetics, 61*, 505–511.

Hedrick, P. W., & Black, F. L. (1997b). Random mating and selection in families against homozygotes for HLA in South Amerindians. *Hereditas, 127*, 51–58.

Heister, G., Landis, T., Regard, M., & Schroeder-Heister, P. (1989). Shift of functional cerebral asymmetry during the menstrual cycle. *Neuropsychologia, 27*, 871–880.

Heistermann, M., Ziegler, T., van Schaik, C., Launhardt, K., Winkler, P., & Hodges, J. K. (2001). Loss of oestrus, concealed ovulation and paternity confusion in free-ranging *Hanuman langurs. Proceedings of the Royal Society of London B, 268*, 2445–2451.

Herlihy, D. (1965). Population, plague and social change in rural Pistoia, 1201–1430. *The Economic History Review, 18*, 225–244.

Herlitz, A., Nilsson, L.-G., & Bäckman, L. (1997). Gender differences in episodic memory. *Memory & Cognition, 25*, 801–811.

Herlitz, A., & Rehnman, J. (2008). Sex differences in episodic memory. *Current Directions in Psychological Science, 17*, 52–56.

Herman, J. F., & Siegel, A. W. (1978). The development of cognitive mapping of the large-scale environment. *Journal of Experimental Child Psychology, 26*, 389–406.

Herman, R. A., Measday, M. A., & Wallen, K. (2003). Sex differences in infants in juvenile rhesus monkeys: Relation to prenatal androgen. *Hormones and Behavior, 43*, 573–583.

Hermans, E. J., Putman, P., Baas, J. M., Koppeschaar, H. P., & van Honk, J. (2006). A single administration of testosterone reduces fear-potentiated startle in humans. *Biological Psychiatry, 59*, 872–874.

Herndon, J. C., Tigges, J., Anderson, D. C., Klumpp, S. A., & McClure, H. M. (1999). Brain weight throughout the life span of the chimpanzee. *Journal of Comparative Neurology, 409,* 567–572.

Hewlett, B. S. (1988). Sexual selection and paternal investment among Aka pygmies. In L. Betzig, M. Borgerhoff Mulder, & P. Turke (Eds.), *Human reproductive behaviour: A Darwinian perspective* (pp. 263–276). Cambridge, England: Cambridge University Press.

Hewlett, B. S. (1992). Husband–wife reciprocity and the father–infant relationship among Aka pygmies. In B. S. Hewlett (Ed.), *Father–child relations: Cultural and biosocial contexts* (pp. 153–176). New York: Aldine de Gruyter.

Hewstone, M., Rubin, M., & Willis, H. (2002). Intergroup bias. *Annual Review of Psychology, 53,* 575–604.

Hill, A. V. S., Allsopp, C. E. M., Kwiatkowski, D., Anstey, N. M., Twumasi, P., Rowe, P. A., et al. (1991, August 15). Common West African HLA antigens are associated with protection from severe malaria. *Nature, 352,* 595–560.

Hill, G. E. (1991, March 28). Plumage coloration is a sexually selected indicator of male quality. *Nature, 350,* 337–339.

Hill, K. (1982). Hunting and human evolution. *Journal of Human Evolution, 11,* 521–544.

Hill, K., & Hurtado, A. M. (1996). *Ache life history: The ecology and demography of a foraging people.* New York: Aldine de Gruyter.

Hill, K., & Kaplan, H. (1988). Tradeoffs in male and female reproductive strategies among the Ache: Part 1. In L. Betzig, M. Borgerhoff Mulder, & P. Turke (Eds.), *Human reproductive behaviour: A Darwinian perspective* (pp. 277–289). Cambridge, England: Cambridge University Press.

Hill, R. (1945). Campus values in mate selection. *Journal of Home Economics, 37,* 554–558.

Hines, M., Brook, C., & Conway, G. S. (2004). Androgen and psychosexual development: Core gender identity, sexual orientation, and recalled childhood gender role behavior in women and men with congenital adrenal hyperplasia (CAH). *Journal of Sex Research, 41,* 75–81.

Hines, M., Fane, B. A., Pasterski, V. L., Mathews, G. A., Conway, G. S., & Brook, C. (2003). Spatial abilities following prenatal androgen abnormality: Targeting and mental rotations performance in individuals with congenital adrenal hyperplasia. *Psychoneuroendocrinology, 28,* 1010–1026.

Hines, M., Golombok, S., Rust, J., Johnston, K. J., & Golding, J. (2002). Testosterone during pregnancy and gender role behavior of preschool children: A longitudinal, population study. *Child Development, 73,* 1678–1687.

Hines, M., & Kaufman, F. R. (1994). Androgens and the development of human sex-typical behavior: Rough-and-tumble play and sex of preferred playmates in children with congenital adrenal hyperplasia (CAH). *Child Development, 65,* 1042–1053.

Hines, M., & Shipley, C. (1984). Prenatal exposure to diethylstilbestrol (DES) and the development of sexually dimorphic cognitive abilities and cerebral lateralization. *Developmental Psychology, 20*, 81–94.

Hirschenhauser, K., Frigerio, D., Grammer, K., & Magnusson, M. S. (2002). Monthly patterns of testosterone and behavior in prospective fathers. *Hormones and Behavior, 42*, 172–181.

Hirschenhauser, K., & Oliveira, R. F. (2006). Social modulation of androgens in male vertebrates: Meta-analyses of the challenge hypothesis. *Animal Behaviour, 71*, 265–277.

Ho, H.-Z., Gilger, J. W., & Brink, T. M. (1986). Effects of menstrual cycle on spatial information-processes. *Perceptual and Motor Skills, 63*, 743–751.

Hobolth, A., Christensen, O. F., Mailund, T., & Schierup, M. H. (2007). Genomic relationships and speciation times of human, chimpanzee, and gorilla inferred from a coalescent hidden Markov model. *PLoS Genetics, 3*, 294–304. Retrieved December 17, 2007, from http://www.plosgenetics.org/article/info:doi%2F10.1371%2Fjournal.pgen.0030007

Hoelzel, A. R., Le Boeuf, B. J., Reiter, J., & Campagna, C. (1999). Alpha-male paternity in elephant seals. *Behavioral Ecology and Sociobiology, 46*, 298–306.

Hoffman, J. I., Forcada, J., Trathan, P. N., & Amos, W. (2007, February 22). Female fur seals show active choice for males that are heterozygous and unrelated. *Nature, 445*, 912–914.

Hoffman, M. L. (1977). Sex differences in empathy and related behaviors. *Psychological Bulletin, 84*, 712–722.

Höglund, J., & Alatalo, R. V. (1995). *Leks*. Princeton, NJ: Princeton University Press.

Holder, C. F. (1892). *Along the Florida reef*. New York: Appleton.

Holding, C. S., & Holding, D. H. (1989). Acquisition of route network knowledge by males and females. *Journal of Genetic Psychology, 116*, 29–41.

Holloway, C. C., & Clayton, D. F. (2001). Estrogen synthesis in the male brain triggers development of the avian song control pathway in vitro. *Nature Neuroscience, 4*, 170–175.

Holloway, R. L. (1973). Endocranial volumes of early African hominids, and the role of the brain in human mosaic evolution. *Journal of Human Evolution, 2*, 449–459.

Holloway, R. L., Broadfield, D. C., & Yuan, M. S. (2004). *The human fossil record: Vol. 3. Brain endocasts—The paleoneurological record*. Hoboken, NJ: Wiley.

Hönekopp, J., Rudolph, U., Beier, L., Liebert, A., & Müller, C. (2007). Physical attractiveness of face and body as indicators of physical fitness in men. *Evolution and Human Behavior, 28*, 106–111.

Hopcroft, R. L. (2006). Sex, status, and reproductive success in the contemporary United States. *Evolution and Human Behavior, 27*, 104–120.

Horai, S., Hayasaka, K., Kondo, R., Tsugane, K., & Takahata, N. (1995). Recent African origin of modern humans revealed by complete sequences of hominoid mitochondrial DNAs. *Proceedings of the National Academy of Sciences USA, 92,* 532–536.

Horowitz, D. L. (2001). *The deadly ethnic riot.* Berkeley: University of California Press.

Houle, D. (1992). Comparing evolvability and variability in quantitative traits. *Genetics, 130,* 195–204.

Hrdy, S. B. (1979). Infanticide among animals: A review, classification, and examination of the implications for the reproductive strategies of females. *Ethology and Sociobiology, 1,* 13–40.

Hrdy, S. B. (2005). Comes the child before the man: How cooperative breeding and prolonged postweaning dependence shaped human potential. In B. S. Hewlett & M. E. Lamb (Eds.), *Hunter-gatherer childhoods: Evolutionary, developmental & cultural perspectives* (pp. 65–91). New Brunswick, NJ: Transaction Publishers.

Huffman, K. J., Nelson, J., Clarey, J., & Krubitzer, L. (1999). Organization of somatosensory cortex in three species of marsupials, *Dasyurus hallucatus, Dactylopsila trivirgata,* and *Monodelphis domestica:* Neural correlates of morphological specializations. *Journal of Comparative Neurology, 403,* 5–32.

Hume, D. K., & Montgomerie, R. (2001). Facial attractiveness signals different aspects of "quality" in women and men. *Evolution and Human Behavior, 22,* 93–112.

Humphrey, N. K. (1976). The social function of intellect. In P. P. G. Bateson & R. A. Hinde (Eds.), *Growing points in ethology* (pp. 303–317). New York: Cambridge University Press.

Humphreys, L. G., Lubinski, D., & Yao, G. (1993). Utility of predicting group membership and the role of spatial visualization in becoming an engineer, physical scientist, or artist. *Journal of Applied Psychology, 78,* 250–261.

Hurtado, A. M., & Hill, K. R. (1992). Paternal effect on offspring survivorship among Ache and Hiwi hunter-gatherers: Implications for modeling pair-bond stability. In B. S. Hewlett (Ed.), *Father–child relations: Cultural and biosocial contexts* (pp. 31–55). New York: Aldine de Gruyter.

Hutt, C. (1972). Sex differences in human development. *Human Development, 15,* 153–170.

Hyde, J. S. (2007). New directions in the study of gender similarities and differences. *Current Directions in Psychological Science, 16,* 259–263.

Hyde, J. S., & Linn, M. C. (1988). Gender differences in verbal ability: A meta-analysis. *Psychological Bulletin, 104,* 53–69.

Irons, W. (1979). Cultural and biological success. In N. A. Chagnon & W. Irons (Eds.), *Natural selection and social behavior* (pp. 257–272). North Scituate, MA: Duxbury Press.

Irons, W. (1993). Monogamy, contraception and the cultural and reproductive success hypothesis. *Behavioral and Brain Sciences, 16,* 295–296.

Irwing, P., & Lynn, R. (2005). Sex differences in means and variability on the progressive matrices in university students: A meta-analysis. *British Journal of Psychology, 96,* 505–524.

Isaac, J. L. (2005). Potential causes and life-history consequences of sexual size dimorphism in mammals. *Mammal Review, 35,* 101–115.

Izard, C. E. (1993). Organizational and motivational functions of discrete emotions. In M. Lewis & J. M. Haviland (Eds.), *Handbook of emotions* (pp. 631–641). New York: Guilford Press.

Jackson, D. N., & Rushton, J. P. (2006). Males have greater *g*: Sex differences in general mental ability from 100,000 17- to 18-year-olds on the Scholastic Assessment Test. *Intelligence, 34,* 479–486.

Jacob, S., McClintock, M. K., Zelano, B., & Ober, C. (2002). Paternally inherited HLA alleles are associated with women's choice of male odor. *Nature Genetics, 30,* 175–179.

Jacobs, L. F., Gaulin, S. J. C., Sherry, D. F., & Hoffman, G. E. (1990). Evolution of spatial cognition: Sex-specific patterns of spatial behavior predict hippocampal size. *Proceedings of the National Academy of Sciences USA, 87,* 6349–6352.

Jacobs, L. F., & Schenk, F. (2003). Unpacking the cognitive map: The parallel map theory of hippocampal function. *Psychological Review, 110,* 285–315.

Jacobziner, H., Rich, H., Bleiberg, N., & Merchant, R. (1963). How well are well children? *American Journal of Public Health, 53,* 1937–1952.

Jaeger, J. J., Lockwood, A. H., Van Valin, R. D., Jr., Kemmerer, D. L., Murphy, B. W., & Wack, D. S. (1998). Sex differences in brain regions activated by grammatical and reading tasks. *NeuroReport, 9,* 2803–2807.

Jaenike, J. (1978). An hypothesis to account for the maintenance of sex within populations. *Evolutionary Theory, 3,* 191–194.

Jaffe, K., Urribarri, D., Chacon, G. C., Diaz, G., Torres, A., & Herzog, G. (1993). Sex-linked strategies of human reproductive behavior. *Social Biology, 40,* 61–73.

Jakobsson, M., Scholz, S. W., Scheet, P., Gibbs, J. R., VanLiere, J. M., Fung, H.-C., et al. (2008, February 21). Genotype, haplotype and copy-number variation in worldwide human populations. *Nature, 451,* 998–1003.

James, T. W., & Kimura, D. (1997). Sex differences in remembering the locations of objects in an array: Location-shifts versus local exchanges. *Evolution and Human Behavior, 18,* 155–163.

James, W. H. (1993). The incidence of superfecundation and of double paternity in the general population. *Acta Geneticae Medicae et Gemellologiae, 42,* 257–262.

Jameson, K. A., Highnote, S. M., & Wasserman, L. M. (2001). Richer color experience in observers with multiple photopigment opsin genes. *Psychonomic Bulletin & Review, 8,* 244–261.

Jamieson, I. (1995). Do female fish prefer to spawn in nests with eggs for reasons of mate choice copying or egg survival? *American Naturalist, 145,* 824–832.

Jardine, R., & Martin, N. G. (1983). Spatial ability and throwing accuracy. *Behavior Genetics, 13,* 331–340.

Jarvinen, D. W., & Nicholls, J. G. (1996). Adolescent's social goals, beliefs about the causes of social success, and satisfaction in peer relations. *Developmental Psychology, 32,* 435–441.

Jasieńska, G., Ziomkiewicz, A., Ellison, P. T., Lipson, S. F., & Thune, I. (2004). Large breasts and narrow waits indicate high reproductive potential in women. *Proceedings of the Royal Society of London B, 271,* 1213–1217.

Jennings, K. D. (1975). People versus object orientation, social behavior, and intellectual abilities in preschool children. *Developmental Psychology, 11,* 511–519.

Jennions, M. D., Møller, A. P., & Petrie, M. (2001). Sexually selected traits and adult survival: A meta-analysis. *Quarterly Review of Biology, 76,* 3–36.

Jerison, H. J. (1973). *Evolution of the brain and intelligence.* New York: Academic Press.

Joffe, T. H. (1997). Social pressures have selected for an extended juvenile period in primates. *Journal of Human Evolution, 32,* 593–605.

Johanna, A., Forsberg, L., & Tullberg, B. S. (1995). The relationship between cumulative number of cohabiting partners and number of children for men and women in modern Sweden. *Ethology and Sociobiology, 16,* 221–232.

Johnson, A. M., Mercer, C. H., Erens, B., Copas, A. J., McManus, S., Wellings, K., et al. (2001, December 1). Sexual behaviour in Britain: Partnerships, practices, and HIV risk behaviors. *The Lancet, 358,* 1835–1842.

Johnson, E. S. (1984). Sex differences in problem solving. *Journal of Educational Psychology, 76,* 1359–1371.

Johnson, L. S., Kermott, L. H., & Lein, M. R. (1994). Territorial polygyny in house wrens: Are females sufficiently compensated for the cost of mate sharing? *Behavioral Ecology, 5,* 98–104.

Johnson, R. T., Burk, J. A., & Kirkpatrick, L. A. (2007). Dominance and prestige as differential predictors of aggression and testosterone in men. *Evolution and Human Behavior, 28,* 345–351.

Johnson, W., & Bouchard, T. J., Jr. (2007). Sex differences in mental abilities: *g* masks the dimensions on which they lie. *Intelligence, 35,* 23–39.

Johnson-Frey, S. H. (2003). What's so special about human tool use? *Neuron, 39,* 201–204.

Johnson-Laird, P. N. (1983). *Mental models.* Cambridge, England: Cambridge University Press.

Jonason, P. K. (2007). An evolutionary psychology perspective on sex differences in exercise behaviors and motivations. *Journal of Social Psychology, 147,* 5–14.

Jones, B. C., DeBruine, L. M., Little, A. C., Conway, C. A., Welling, L. L. M., & Smith, F. (2007). Sensation seeking and men's face preferences. *Evolution and Human Behavior, 28,* 439–446.

Jones, C. B. (2003). *Sexual selection and reproductive competition in primates: New perspectives and directions.* Norman, OK: American Society of Primatologists.

Jones, D. (1995). Sexual selection, physical attractiveness, and facial neoteny. *Current Anthropology, 36*, 723–748.

Jordan, K., Wüstenberg, T., Heinze, H.-J., Peters, M., & Jäncke, L. (2002). Women and men exhibit different cortical activation patterns during mental rotation tasks. *Neuropsychologia, 40*, 2397–2408.

Joseph, J. E., & Willingham, D. B. (2000). Effect of sex and joystick experience on pursuit tracking in adults. *Journal of Motor Behavior, 32*, 45–56.

Josephson, S. C. (2002). Does polygyny reduce fertility? *American Journal of Human Biology, 14*, 222–232.

Juby, H., Billette, J.-M., Laplante, B., & Le Bourdais, C. (2007). Nonresident fathers and children: Parents' new unions and frequency of contact. *Journal of Family Issues, 28*, 1220–1245.

Just, M. A., & Carpenter, P. A. (1985). Cognitive coordinate systems: Accounts of mental rotation and individual differences in spatial ability. *Psychological Review, 92*, 137–172.

Käär, P., Jokela, J., Merilä, J., Helle, T., & Kojola, I. (1998). Sexual conflict and remarriage in preindustrial human populations: Causes and fitness consequences. *Evolution and Human Behavior, 19*, 139–151.

Kahneman, D., & Tversky, A. (1982). The simulation heuristic. In D. Kahneman, P. Slovic, & A. Tversky (Eds.), *Judgment uncertainty: Heuristics and biases* (pp. 201–208). Cambridge, England: Cambridge University Press.

Kaiser, S. Walther, S., Nennig, E., Kronmüller, K., Mundt, C., Weisbrod, M., et al. (2008). Gender-specific strategy use and neural correlates in a spatial perspective taking task. *Neuropsychologia, 46*, 2524–2531.

Kalick, S. M., Zebrowitz, L. A., Langlois, J. H., & Johnson, R. M. (1998). Does human facial attractiveness honestly advertise health? Longitudinal data on an evolutionary question. *Psychological Science, 9*, 8–13.

Kamei, N. (2005). Play among Baka children in Cameroon. In B. S. Hewlett & M. E. Lamb (Eds.), *Hunter-gatherer childhoods: Evolutionary, developmental & cultural perspectives* (pp. 343–359). New Brunswick, NJ: Transaction Publishers.

Kanazawa, S. (2001). Why father absence might precipitate early menarche: The role of polygyny. *Evolution and Human Behavior, 22*, 329–334.

Kane, M. J., & Engle, R. W. (2002). The role of prefrontal cortex in working-memory capacity, executive attention, and general fluid intelligence: An individual-differences perspective. *Psychonomic Bulletin & Review, 9*, 637–671.

Kano, T. (1980). Social behavior of wild pygmy chimpanzees (*Pan paniscus*) of Wamba: A preliminary report. *Journal of Human Evolution, 9*, 243–260.

Kano, T. (1992). *The last ape: Pygmy chimpanzee behavior and ecology.* Palo Alto, CA: Stanford University Press.

Kansaku, K., & Kitazawa, S. (2001). Imaging studies on sex differences in the lateralization of language. *Neuroscience Research, 41*, 333–337.

Kansaku, K., Yamaura, A., & Kitazawa, S. (2000). Sex differences in lateralization revealed in the posterior language areas. *Cerebral Cortex, 10,* 866–872.

Kaplan, H. S., Hill, K., Lancaster, J., & Hurtado, A. M. (2000). A theory of human life history evolution: Diet, intelligence, and longevity. *Evolutionary Anthropology, 9,* 156–185.

Kaplan, H. S., & Lancaster, J. B. (2000). The evolutionary economics and psychology of the demographic transition to low fertility. In L. Cronk, N. Chagnon, & W. Irons (Eds.), *Adaptation and human behavior: An anthropological perspective* (pp. 283–322). New York: Aldine De Gruyter.

Kaplan, H. S., Lancaster, J. B., & Anderson, K. G. (1998). Human parental investment and fertility: The life histories of men in Albuquerque. In A. Booth & A. C. Crouter (Eds.), *Men in families: When do they get involved? What difference does it make?* (pp. 55–109). Mahwah, NJ: Erlbaum.

Kaplan, H. S., Lancaster, J. B., Bock, J. A., & Johnson, S. E. (1995). Does observed fertility maximize fitness among New Mexican men? A test of an optimality model and a new theory of parental investment in the embodied capital of offspring. *Human Nature, 6,* 325–360.

Karmiloff-Smith, A. (1992). *Beyond modularity: A developmental perspective on cognitive science.* Cambridge, MA: MIT Press/Bradford Books.

Kayser, M., Brauer, S., Weiss, G., Schiefenhövel, W., Underhill, P., Shen, P., et al. (2003). Reduced Y-chromosome, but not mitochondrial DNA, diversity in human populations from West New Guinea. *American Journal of Human Genetics, 72,* 281–302.

Keeley, L. H. (1996). *War before civilization: The myth of the peaceful savage.* New York: Oxford University Press.

Keightley, P. D., & Eyre-Walker, A. (2000, October 13). Deleterious mutations and the evolution of sex. *Science, 290,* 331–333.

Keil, F. C. (1992). The origins of an autonomous biology. In M. R. Gunnar & M. Maratsos (Eds.), *The Minnesota symposium on child psychology: Vol. 25. Modularity and constraints in language and cognition* (pp. 103–137). Hillsdale, NJ: Erlbaum.

Keil, F. C., Levin, D. T., Richman, B. A., & Gutheil, G. (1999). Mechanism and explanation in the development of biological thought: The case of disease. In D. L. Medin & S. Atran (Eds.), *Folkbiology* (pp. 285–319). Cambridge, MA: MIT Press/Bradford Books.

Kelley, J. (2004). Life history and cognitive evolution in the apes. In A. E. Russon & D. R. Begun (Eds.), *The evolution of thought: Evolutionary origins of great ape intelligence* (pp. 280–297). Cambridge, England: Cambridge University Press.

Kelly, S., & Dunbar, R. I. M. (2001). Who dares, wins: Heroism versus altruism in women's mate choices. *Human Nature, 12,* 89–105.

Kelso, W. M., Nicholls, M. E. R., Warne, G. L., & Zacharin, M. (2000). Cerebral lateralization and cognitive functioning in patients with congenital adrenal hyperplasia. *Neuropsychology, 14,* 370–378.

Kemp, D. J. (2006). Ageing, reproductive value, and the evolution of lifetime fighting behavior. *Biological Journal of the Linnean Society*, 88, 565–578.

Kempenaers, B., Lanctot, R. B., & Robertson, R. J. (1998). Certainty of paternity and paternal investment in eastern bluebirds and tree swallows. *Animal Behaviour*, 55, 845–860.

Kendler, K. S. (1996). Parenting: A genetic-epidemiologic perspective. *American Journal of Psychiatry*, 153, 11–20.

Kendler, K. S., Myers, J., & Prescott, C. A. (2005). Sex differences in the relationship between social support and risk for major depression: A longitudinal study of opposite-sex twin pairs. *American Journal of Psychiatry*, 162, 250–256.

Kendrick, K. M., & Keverne, E. B. (1991). Importance of progesterone and estrogen priming for the induction of maternal behavior by vaginocervical stimulation in sheep: Effects of maternal experience. *Physiology & Behavior*, 49, 745–750.

Kenrick, D. T., & Keefe, R. C. (1992). Age preferences in mates reflect sex differences in human reproductive strategies. *Behavioral and Brain Sciences*, 15, 75–133.

Kenrick, D. T., Keefe, R. C., Gabrielidis, C., & Cornelius, J. S. (1996). Adolescents' age preferences for dating partners: Support for an evolutionary model of life-history strategies. *Child Development*, 67, 1499–1511.

Kenrick, D. T., Li, N. P., & Butner, J. (2003). Dynamical evolutionary psychology: Individual decision rules and emergent social norms. *Psychological Review*, 110, 3–28.

Kenrick, D. T., Sadalla, E. K., Groth, G., & Trost, M. R. (1990). Evolution, traits, and the stages of human courtship: Qualifying the parental investment model. *Journal of Personality*, 58, 97–116.

Kenrick, D. T., Sundie, J. M., Nicastle, L. D., & Stone, G. O. (2001). Can one ever be too wealthy or too chaste? Searching for nonlinearities in mate judgment. *Journal of Personality and Social Psychology*, 80, 462–471.

Kensinger, E. A. (2007). Negative emotion enhances memory accuracy: Behavioral and neuroimaging evidence. *Current Directions in Psychological Science*, 16, 213–218.

Kerig, P. K., Cowan, P. A., & Cowan, C. P. (1993). Marital quality and gender differences in parent–child interaction. *Developmental Psychology*, 29, 931–939.

Kessler, R. C., Berglund, P., Demler, O., Jin, R., Merikangas, K. R., & Walters, E. E. (2005). Lifetime prevalence and age-of-onset distributions of DSM–IV disorders in the national comorbidity survey replication. *Archives of General Psychiatry*, 62, 593–602.

Ketterson, E. D., & Nolan, V., Jr. (1992). Hormones and life histories: An integrative approach. *American Naturalist*, 140, S33–S62.

Ketterson, E. D., & Nolan, V., Jr. (1999). Adaptation, exaptation, and constraint: A hormonal perspective. *American Naturalist*, 154, S4–S25.

Kiel, E. J., & Buss, K. A. (2006). Maternal accuracy in predicting toddlers' behaviors and associations with toddlers' fearful temperament. *Child Development*, 77, 355–370.

Kilpatrick, L. A., Zald, D. H., Pardo, J. V., & Cahill, L. F. (2006). Sex-related differences in amygdala functional connectivity during resting conditions. *Neuro-Image, 30,* 452–461.

Kim, J., Shen, W., Gallagher, D., Jones, A., Jr., Wang, Z., Wang, J., et al. (2006). Total-body skeletal muscle mass: Estimation by dual-energy X-ray absorptiometry in children and adolescents. *American Journal of Clinical Nutrition, 84,* 1014–1020.

Kimball, R. T. (2006). Hormonal control of coloration. In G. E. Hill & K. J. McGraw (Eds.), *Bird coloration: Vol. 1. Mechanisms and measurements* (pp. 431–468). Cambridge, MA: Harvard University Press.

Kimchi, T., Xu, J., & Dulac, C. (2007, August 30). A functional circuit underlying male sexual behavior in the female mouse brain. *Nature, 448,* 1009–1014.

Kimura, D. (1987). Are men's and women's brains really different? *Canadian Psychology, 28,* 133–147.

Kimura, D. (1999). *Sex and cognition.* Cambridge, MA: MIT Press/Bradford Books.

Kimura, D. (2002). Sex hormones influence human cognitive pattern. *Neuro-endocrinology Letters, 23,* S67–S77.

Kingsolver, J. G., Hoekstra, H. E., Hoekstra, J. M., Berrigan, D., Vignieri, S. N., Hill, C. E., et al. (2001). The strength of phenotypic selection in natural populations. *American Naturalist, 157,* 245–261.

Kinnison, M. T., & Hendry, A. P. (2001). The pace of modern life II: From rates of contemporary microevolution to pattern and process. *Genetica, 112/113,* 145–164.

Kirchengast, S., & Gartner, M. (2002). Changes in fat distribution (WHR) and body weight during the menstrual cycle. *Collegium Anthropologicum, 26,* S47–S57.

Kirk, K. M., Blomberg, S. P., Duffy, D. L., Heath, A. C., Owens, I. P., & Martin, N. G. (2001). Natural selection and quantitative genetics of life history-traits in Western women: A twin study. *Evolution, 55,* 423–435.

Kirkpatrick, M., & Ryan, M. J. (1991, March 7). The evolution of mating preferences and the paradox of the lek. *Nature, 350,* 33–38.

Kiros, G.-E., & Hogan, D. P. (2001). War, famine and excess child mortality in Africa: The role of parental education. *International Journal of Epidemiology, 30,* 447–455.

Kitange, H. M., Machibya, H., Black, J., Mtasiwa, D. M., Masuki, G., Whiting, D., et al. (1996, January 27). Outlook for survivors of childhood in sub-Saharan Africa: Adult mortality in Tanzania. *BMJ, 312,* 216–220.

Kivlighan, K. T., Granger, D. A., & Booth, A. (2005). Gender differences in testosterone and cortisol response to competition. *Psychoneuroendocrinology, 30,* 58–71.

Klein, R. P., & Durfee, J. T. (1978). Effects of sex and birth order on infant social behavior. *Infant Behavior and Development, 1,* 106–117.

Klindworth, H., & Voland, E. (1995). How did the Krummhörn elite males achieve above-average reproductive success? *Human Nature, 6,* 221–240.

Knauft, B. M. (1987). Reconsidering violence in simple human societies: Homicide among the Gebusi of New Guinea. *Current Anthropology, 28,* 457–500.

Knickmeyer, R. C., Baron-Cohen, S., Raggatt, P., & Taylor, K. (2005). Foetal testosterone, social relationships and restricted interests in children. *Journal of Child Psychology and Psychiatry, 46,* 198–210.

Knickmeyer, R. C., Baron-Cohen, S., Raggatt, P., Taylor, K., & Hackett, G. (2006). Fetal testosterone and empathy. *Hormones and Behavior, 49,* 282–292.

Knickmeyer, R. C., Wheelwright, S., Taylor, K., Raggatt, P., Hackett, G., & Baron-Cohen, S. (2005). Gender-typed play and amniotic testosterone. *Developmental Psychology, 41,* 517–528.

Knight, G. P., & Chao, C.-C. (1989). Gender differences in the cooperative, competitive, and individualistic social values of children. *Motivation and Emotion, 13,* 125–141.

Knight, G. P., Guthrie, I. K., Page, M. C., & Fabes, R. A. (2002). Emotional arousal and gender differences in aggression: A meta-analysis. *Aggressive Behavior, 28,* 366–393.

Kok, J., van Poppel, F., & Kruse, E. (1997). Mortality among illegitimate children in mid-nineteenth-century The Hague. In C. A. Corsini & P. P. Viazzo (Eds.), *The decline of infant and child mortality* (pp. 193–211). The Hague, Netherlands: Martinus Nijhoff.

Kokko, H. (1997). Evolutionarily stable strategies of age-dependent sexual advertisement. *Behavioral Ecology and Sociobiology, 41,* 99–107.

Kokko, H., Brooks, R., McNamara, J. M., & Houston, A. I. (2002). The sexual selection continuum. *Proceedings of the Royal Society of London B, 269,* 1331–1340.

Kolakowski, D., & Malina, R. M. (1974, October 4). Spatial ability, throwing accuracy and man's hunting heritage. *Nature, 251,* 410–412.

Kondrashov, A. S. (1988, December 1). Deleterious mutations and the evolution of sexual reproduction. *Nature, 336,* 435–440.

Kondrashov, A. S., & Crow, J. F. (1991, May 23). Haploidy or diploidy: Which is better? *Nature, 351,* 314–315.

Konner, M. (2005). Hunter-gatherer infancy and childhood: The !Kung and others. In B. S. Hewlett & M. E. Lamb (Eds.), *Hunter-gatherer childhoods: Evolutionary, developmental & cultural perspectives* (pp. 19–64). New Brunswick, NJ: Transaction Publishers.

Korchmaros, J. D., & Kenny, D. A. (2001). Emotional closeness as a mediator of the effect of genetic relatedness on altruism. *Psychological Science, 12,* 262–265.

Korpelainen, H. (2000). Fitness, reproduction and longevity among European aristocratic and rural Finnish families in the 1700s and 1800s. *Proceedings of the Royal Society of London B, 267,* 1765–1770.

Krebs, J. R., & Davies, N. B. (1993). *An introduction to behavioural ecology* (3rd ed.). Oxford, England: Blackwell Science.

Kring, A. M., & Gordon, A. H. (1998). Sex differences in emotion: Expression, experience, and physiology. *Journal of Personality and Social Psychology, 74,* 686–703.

Kruger, D. J. (2003). Evolution and altruism: Combining psychological mediators with naturally selected tendencies. *Evolution and Human Behavior, 24,* 118–125.

Kuba, M. J., Byrne, R. A., Mather, J. A., & Meisel, D. V. (2006). When do octopuses play? Effects of repeated testing, object type, age, and food deprivation in object play in *Octopus vulgaris. Journal of Comparative Psychology, 120,* 184–190.

Kuhl, P. K. (1994). Learning and representation in speech and language. *Current Opinion in Neurobiology, 4,* 812–822.

Kuhl, P. K., Andruski, J. E., Chistovich, I. A., Chistovich, L. A., Kozhevnikova, E. V., Ryskina, V., et al. (1997, August 1). Cross-language analysis of phonetic units in language addressed to infants. *Science, 277,* 684–686.

Kujawski, J. H., & Bower, T. G. R. (1993). Same-sex preferential looking during infancy as a function of abstract representation. *British Journal of Developmental Psychology, 11,* 201–209.

Kuhlmeier, V. A., & Boysen, S. T. (2002). Chimpanzees (*Pan troglodytes*) recognize spatial and object correspondences between a scale model and its referent. *Psychological Science, 13,* 60–63.

Kurland, J. A., & Gaulin, S. J. C. (2005). Cooperation and conflict among kin. In D. M. Buss (Ed.), *The evolutionary psychology handbook* (pp. 447–482). Hoboken, NJ: Wiley.

Kurosaki, M., Shirao, N., Yamashita, H., Okamoto, Y., & Yamawaki, S. (2006). Distorted images of one's own body activates the prefrontal cortex and limbic/paralimbic system in young women: A functional magnetic resonance imaging study. *Biological Psychiatry, 59,* 380–386.

Kurzban, R., & Weeden, J. (2005). Hurry date: Mate preferences in action. *Evolution and Human Behavior, 26,* 227–244.

Kvarnemo, C. (2006). Evolution and maintenance of male care: Is increased paternity a neglected benefit of care? *Behavioral Ecology, 17,* 144–148.

Kvarnemo, C., & Ahnesjö, I. (1996). The dynamics of operational sex ratios and competition for mates. *Trends in Ecology & Evolution, 11,* 404–408.

LaFontana, K. M., & Cillessen, A. H. N. (2002). Children's perceptions of popular and unpopular peers: A multimethod assessment. *Developmental Psychology, 38,* 635–647.

Laiacona, M., Barbarotto, R., & Capitani, E. (2006). Human evolution and the brain representation of semantic knowledge: Is there a role for sex differences? *Evolution and Human Behavior, 27,* 158–168.

Lamb, M. E., & Elster, A. B. (1985). Adolescent mother–infant–father relationships. *Developmental Psychology, 21,* 768–773.

Lamb, M. E., Frodi, A. M., Hwang, C.-P., & Frodi, M. (1982). Varying degrees of paternal involvement in infant care: Attitudinal and behavioral correlates. In M. E. Lamb (Ed.), *Nontraditional families: Parenting and child development* (pp. 117–137). Hillsdale, NJ: Erlbaum.

Lamb, M. E., Pleck, J. H., & Levine, J. A. (1986). Effects of paternal involvement on fathers and mothers. *Marriage & Family Review, 9,* 67–83.

Lampert, A., & Friedman, A. (1992). Sex differences in vulnerability and maladjustment as a function of parental investment: An evolutionary approach. *Social Biology, 39,* 65–81.

Lancaster, J. B. (1989). Evolutionary and cross-cultural perspectives on single-parenthood. In R. W. Bell & N. J. Bell (Eds.), *Interfaces in psychology: Sociobiology and the social sciences* (pp. 63–72). Lubbock: Texas Tech University Press.

Lancaster, J. B., & Lancaster, C. S. (1987). The watershed: Change in parental-investment and family-formation strategies in the course of human evolution. In J. B. Lancaster, J. Altmann, A. S. Rossi, & L. R. Sherrod (Eds.), *Parenting across the life span: Biosocial dimensions* (pp. 187–205). New York: Aldine de Gruyter.

Langergraber, K. E., Mitani, J. C., & Vigilant, L. (2007). The limited impact of kinship on cooperation in wild chimpanzees. *Proceedings of the National Academy of Sciences USA, 104,* 7786–7790.

Langlois, J. H., Kalakanis, L., Rubenstein, A. J., Larson, A., Hallam, M., & Smoot, M. (2000). Maxims or myths of beauty? A meta-analytic and theoretical review. *Psychological Bulletin, 126,* 390–423.

Langmore, N. E., Cockrem, J. F., & Candy, E. J. (2002). Competition for male reproductive investment elevates testosterone levels in female dunnocks, *Prunella modularis. Proceedings of the Royal Society London B, 269,* 2473–2478.

Lassek, W. D., & Gaulin, S. J. C. (2008). Waist-to-hip ratio and cognitive ability: Is gluteofemoral fat a privileged store of neurodevelopmental resources? *Evolution and Human Behavior, 29,* 26–34.

Lavelli, M., & Fogel, A. (2002). Developmental changes in mother–infant face-to-face communication: Birth to 3 months. *Developmental Psychology, 38,* 288–305.

Law, D. J., Pellegrino, J. W., & Hunt, E. B. (1993). Comparing the tortoise and the hare: Gender differences and experience in dynamic spatial reasoning tasks. *Psychological Science, 4,* 35–40.

Law, D. J., Pellegrino, J. W., Mitchell, S. R., Fischer, S. C., McDonald, T. P. & Hunt, E. B. (1993). Perceptual and cognitive factors governing performance in comparative arrival-time judgments. *Journal of Experimental Psychology: Human Perception and Performance, 19,* 1183–1199.

Law Smith, M. J., Perrett, D. I., Jones, B. C., Cornwell, R. E., Moore, F. R., Feinberg, D. R., et al. (2006). Facial appearance is a cue to oestrogen levels in women. *Proceedings of the Royal Society of London B, 273,* 135–140.

Laws, K. R., & Neve, C. (1999). A 'normal' category-specific advantage for naming living things. *Neuropsychologia, 37,* 1263–1269.

Lawson Handley, L. J., & Perrin, N. (2007). Advances in our understanding of mammalian sex-biased dispersal. *Molecular Ecology, 16,* 1559–1578.

Lazarus, R. S. (1991). *Emotion and adaptation.* New York: Oxford University Press.

Leadbeater, B. J., Blatt, S. J., & Quinlan, D. M. (1995). Gender-linked vulnerabilities to depressive symptoms, stress, and problem behaviors in adolescents. *Journal of Research on Adolescence, 5*, 1–29.

Leakey, M. G., Feibel, C. S., McDougall, I., Ward, C., & Walker, A. (1998, May 7). New specimens and confirmation of an early age for *Australopithecus anamensis*. *Nature, 393*, 62–66.

Leaper, C., Anderson, K. J., & Sanders, P. (1998). Moderators of gender effects on parents' talk to their children: A meta-analysis. *Developmental Psychology, 34*, 3–27.

Leaper, C., & Smith, T. E. (2004). A meta-analytic review of gender variations in children's language use: Talkativeness, affiliative speech, and assertive speech. *Developmental Psychology, 40*, 993–1027.

LeBas, N. R., Hockham, L. R., & Ritchie, M. G. (2003). Nonlinear and correlational sexual selection on 'honest' female ornamentation. *Proceedings of the Royal Society London B, 270*, 2159–2165.

Le Boeuf, B. J. (1974). Male–male competition and reproductive success in elephant seals. *American Zoologist, 14*, 163–176.

Le Boeuf, B. J., & Peterson, R. S. (1969, January 3). Social status and mating activity in elephant seals. *Science, 163*, 91–93.

Le Boeuf, B. J., & Reiter, J. (1988). Lifetime reproductive success in northern elephant seals. In T. H. Clutton-Brock (Ed.), *Reproductive success: Studies of individual variation in contrasting breeding systems* (pp. 344–362). Chicago: The University of Chicago Press.

Leenaars, L. S., Dane, A. V., & Marini, Z. A. (2008). Evolutionary perspective on indirect victimization in adolescence: The role of attractiveness, dating and sexual behavior. *Aggressive Behavior, 34*, 404–415.

Leggio, M. G. Molinari, M., Neri, P., Graziano, A., Mandolesi, L., & Petrosini, L. (2000). Representation of action in rats: The role of cerebellum in learning spatial performance by observation. *Proceedings of the National Academy of Sciences USA, 97*, 2320–2325.

Leigh, S. R. (1996). Evolution of human growth spurts. *American Journal of Physical Anthropology, 101*, 455–474.

Leighton, D. R. (1987). Gibbons: Territoriality and monogamy. In B. B. Smuts, D. L. Cheney, R. M. Seyfarth, R. W. Wrangham, & T. T. Struhsaker (Eds.), *Primate societies* (pp. 135–145). Chicago: The University of Chicago Press.

Leonard, C. M., Towler, S., Welcome, S., Halderman, L. K., Otto, R., Eckert, M. A., & Chiarello, C. (2008). Size matters: Cerebral volume influences sex differences in neuroanatomy. *Cerebral Cortex, 18*, 2352–2357

Leonard, W. R., & Robertson, M. L. (1994). Evolutionary perspectives on human nutrition: The influence of brain and body size on diet and metabolism. *American Journal of Human Biology, 6*, 77–88.

Leslie, A. M. (1987). Pretense and representation: The origins of "theory of mind." *Psychological Review, 94*, 412–426.

Leslie, A. M., Friedman, O., & German, T. P. (2004). Core mechanisms in 'theory of mind.' *Trends in Cognitive Sciences, 8*, 528–533.

Lessells, C. M. (2008). Neuroendocrine control of life histories: What do we need to know to understand the evolution of phenotypic plasticity? *Philosophical Transactions of the Royal Society of London B, 363*, 1589–1598.

Lever, J. (1978). Sex differences in the complexity of children's play and games. *American Sociological Review, 43*, 471–483.

Levine, S. C., Huttenlocher, J., Tayler, A., & Langrock, A. (1999). Early sex differences in spatial skill. *Developmental Psychology, 35*, 940–949.

Levine, S. C., Vasilyeva, M., Lourenco, S. F., Newcombe, N., & Huttenlocher, J. (2005). Socioeconomic status modifies the sex differences in spatial skill. *Psychological Science, 16*, 841–845.

Lévy, F., Keller, M., & Poindron, P. (2004). Olfactory regulation of maternal behavior in mammals. *Hormones and Behavior, 46*, 284–302.

Lévy, F., Kendrick, K. M., Keverne, E. B., Piketty, V., & Poindron, P. (1992). Intracerebral oxytocin is important for the onset of maternal behavior in inexperienced ewes delivered under peridural anesthesia. *Behavioral Neuroscience, 106*, 427–432.

Lewis, K. P., & Barton, R. A. (2004). Playing for keeps: Evolutionary relationships between social play and the cerebellum in nonhuman primates. *Human Nature, 15*, 5–21.

Li, J. Z., Absher, D. M., Tang, H., Southwick, A. M., Castro, A. M., Ramachandran, S., et al. (2008, February 22). Worldwide human relationships inferred from genome-wide patterns of variation. *Science, 319*, 1100–1104.

Li, N. P. (2007). Mate preference necessities in long- and short-term mating: People prioritize in themselves what their mates prioritize in them. *Acta Psychologica Sinica, 39*, 528–535.

Li, N. P., Bailey, J. M., Kenrick, D. T., & Linsenmeier, J. A. W. (2002). The necessities and luxuries of mate preferences: Testing the tradeoffs. *Journal of Personality and Social Psychology, 82*, 947–955.

Li, N. P., & Kenrick, D. T. (2006). Sex similarities and differences in preferences for short-term mates: What, whether, and why. *Journal of Personality and Social Psychology, 90*, 468–489.

Liben, L. S., Susman, E. J., Finkelstein, J. W., Chinchilli, V. M., Kunselman, S., Schwab, J., et al. (2002). The effects of sex steroids on spatial performance: A review and an experimental clinical investigation. *Developmental Psychology, 38*, 236–253.

Lie, H. C., Simmons, L. W., & Rhodes, G. (2009). Does genetic diversity predict health in humans? *PLoS ONE, 4*, e6391. doi: 10.1371/journal.pone.006391

Lijima, M., Arisaka, O., Minamoto, F., & Arai, Y. (2001). Sex differences in children's free drawings: A study on girls with congenital adrenal hyperplasia. *Hormones and Behavior, 40*, 99–104.

Lindenfors, P., Nunn, C. L., & Barton, R. A. (2007). Primate brain architecture and selection in relation to sex. *BMC Biology, 5*, 20. Retrieved December 16, 2007, from http://www.biomedcentral.com/1741-7007/5/20

Lindenfors, P., Tullberg, B. S., & Biuw, M. (2002). Phylogenetic analyses of sexual selection and sexual size dimorphism in pinnipeds. *Behavioral Ecology and Sociobiology, 52*, 188–193.

Lindsay, E. W., Colwell, M. J., Frabutt, J. M., & MacKinnon-Lewis, C. (2006). Family conflict in divorced and non-divorced families: Potential consequences for boys' friendship status and friendship quality. *Journal of Social and Personal Relationships, 23*, 45–63.

Linn, M. C., & Petersen, A. C. (1985). Emergence and characterization of sex differences in spatial abilities: A meta-analysis. *Child Development, 56*, 1479–1498.

Lippa, R. A. (2007). The preferred traits of mates in a cross-national study of heterosexual and homosexual men and women: An examination of biological and cultural influences. *Archives of Sexual Behavior, 36*, 193–208.

Little, A. C., Burt, D. M., Penton-Voak, I. S., & Perrett, D. I. (2001). Self-perceived attractiveness influences human female preferences for sexual dimorphism and symmetry in male faces. *Proceedings of the Royal Society of London B, 268*, 39–44.

Lockman, J. J. (2000). A perception–action perspective on tool use development. *Child Development, 71*, 137–144.

López, H. H., Hay, A. C., & Conklin, P. H. (2009). Attractive men induce testosterone and cortisol release in women. *Hormones and Behavior, 56*, 84–92.

Lorch, P. D. (2002). Understanding reversals in the relative strength of sexual selection on males and females: A role for sperm competition? *American Naturalist, 159*, 645–657.

Lovejoy, C. O. (1981, January 23). The origin of man. *Science, 211*, 341–350.

Low, A., Bentin, S., Rockstroh, B., Silberman, Y., Gomolla, A., Cohen, R., & Elbert, T. (2003). Semantic categorization in the human brain: Spatiotemporal dynamics revealed by magnetoencephalography. *Psychological Science, 14*, 367–372.

Low, B. S. (1988). Pathogen stress and polygyny in humans. In L. Betzig, M. Borgerhoff Mulder, & P. Turke (Eds.), *Human reproductive behaviour: A Darwinian perspective* (pp. 115–127). Cambridge, England: Cambridge University Press.

Low, B. S. (1989). Cross-cultural patterns in the training of children: An evolutionary perspective. *Journal of Comparative Psychology, 103*, 311–319.

Low, B. S. (1990a). Marriage systems and pathogen stress in human societies. *American Zoologist, 30*, 325–339.

Low, B. S. (1990b). Occupational status, landownership, and reproductive behavior in 19th-century Sweden: Tuna Parish. *American Anthropologist, 92*, 457–468.

Low, B. S. (2000). *Why sex matters: A Darwinian look at human behavior*. Princeton, NJ: Princeton University Press.

Low, B. S., & Clarke, A. L. (1992). Resources and the life course: Patterns through the demographic shift. *Ethology and Sociobiology, 13*, 463–494.

Low, B. S., Simon, C. P., & Anderson, K. G. (2002). An evolutionary ecological perspective on demographic transitions: Modeling multiple currencies. *American Journal of Human Biology, 14*, 149–167.

Low, L.-F., & Anstey, K. J. (2006). Hormone replacement therapy and cognitive performance in postmenopausal women—A review by cognitive domain. *Neuroscience and Biobehavioral Reviews, 30*, 66–84.

Loy, J. W., & Hesketh, G. L. (1995). Competitive play on the plains: An analysis of games and warfare among Native American warrior societies, 1800–1850. In A. D. Pellegrini (Ed.), *The future of play theory: A multidisciplinary inquiry into the contributions of Brian Sutton-Smith* (pp. 73–105). Albany: State University of New York Press.

Lubinski, D., & Benbow, C. P. (1994). The study of mathematically precocious youth: The first three decades of a planned 50-year study of intellectual talent. In R. F. Subotnik & K. D. Arnold (Eds.), *Beyond Terman: Contemporary longitudinal studies of giftedness and talent* (pp. 255–281). Norwood, NJ: Ablex.

Lubinski, D., Benbow, C. P., & Sanders, C. E. (1993). Reconceptualizing gender differences in achievement among the gifted. In K. A. Heller, F. J. Monks, & A. H. Passow (Eds.), *International handbook of research and development of giftedness and talent* (pp. 693–707). London, England: Pergamon Press.

Lubinski, D., Benbow, C. P., Shea, D. L., Eftekhari-Sanjani, H., & Halvorson, M. B. J. (2001). Men and women at promise for scientific excellence: Similarity not dissimilarity. *Psychological Science, 12*, 309–317.

Lubinski, D., & Dawis, R. V. (1992). Aptitudes, skills, and proficiencies. In M. D. Dunnette & L. M. Hough (Eds.), *The handbook of industrial/organizational psychology* (2nd ed., pp. 1–59). Palo Alto, CA: Consulting Psychologists Press.

Lubinski, D., & Humphreys, L. G. (1990). A broadly based analysis of mathematical giftedness. *Intelligence, 14*, 327–355.

Lucariello, J. M., Durand, T. M., & Yarnell, L. (2007). Social versus intrapersonal ToM: Social ToM is a cognitive strength for low- and middle-SES children. *Journal of Applied Developmental Psychology, 28*, 285–297.

Lucas, A., Morley, R., & Cole, T. J. (1998, November 28). Randomised trial of early diet in preterm babies and later intelligence quotient. *BMJ, 317*, 1481–1487.

Lucas, A., Morley, R., & Cole, T. J., Gore, S. M., Davis, J. A., Bamford, M. F. M., & Dossetor, J. F. B. (1989). Early diet in preterm babies and developmental status in infancy. *Archives of Disease in Childhood, 64*, 1570–1578.

Lueptow, L. B., Garovich-Szabo, L., & Lueptow, M. B. (2001). Social change and thepersistence of sex typing: 1974–1997. *Social Forces, 80*, 1–35.

Luster, T., & Okagaki, L. (1993). Multiple influences on parenting: Ecological and life-course perspectives. In T. Luster & L. Okagaki (Eds.), *Parenting: An ecological perspective* (pp. 227–250). Hillsdale, NJ: Erlbaum.

Lutchmaya, S., & Baron-Cohen, S. (2002). Human sex differences in social and non-social looking preferences, at 12 months of age. *Infant Behavior & Development, 25*, 319–325.

Lutchmaya, S., Baron-Cohen, S., & Raggatt, P. (2002a). Foetal testosterone and eye contact in 12-month-old human infants. *Infant Behavior & Development, 25*, 327–335.

Lutchmaya, S., Baron-Cohen, S., & Raggatt, P. (2002b). Foetal testosterone and vocabulary size in 18- and 24-month old infants. *Infant Behavior & Development, 24*, 418–424.

Lytton, H., & Romney, D. M. (1991). Parents' differential socialization of boys and girls: A meta-analysis. *Psychological Bulletin, 109*, 267–296.

Mac Arthur, R. H., & Wilson, E. O. (1967). *The theory of island biogeography*. Princeton, NJ: Princeton University Press.

Maccoby, E. E. (1988). Gender as a social category. *Developmental Psychology, 24*, 755–765.

Maccoby, E. E. (1990). Gender and relationships: A developmental account. *American Psychologist, 45*, 513–520.

Maccoby, E. E. (1998). *The two sexes: Growing up apart, coming together*. Cambridge, MA: Belknap Press.

Maccoby, E. E., Buchanan, C. M., Mnookin, R. H., & Dornbusch, S. M. (1993). Post-divorce roles of mothers and fathers in the lives of their children. *Journal of Family Psychology, 7*, 24–38.

Maccoby, E. E., & Jacklin, C. N. (1974). *The psychology of sex differences*. Palo Alto, CA: Stanford University Press.

Maccoby, E. E., & Jacklin, C. N. (1987). Gender segregation in childhood. In E. H. Reese (Ed.), *Advanced in child development and behavior* (Vol. 20, pp. 239–287). New York: Academic Press.

MacDonald, D. H., & Hewlett, B. S. (1999). Reproductive interests and forager mobility. *Current Anthropology, 40*, 501–523.

MacDonald, K. (1988). *Social and personality development: An evolutionary synthesis*. New York: Plenum Press.

MacDonald, K. (1992). Warmth as a developmental construct: An evolutionary analysis. *Child Development, 63*, 753–773.

MacDonald, K. (1993). Parent–child play: An evolutionary perspective. In K. MacDonald (Ed.), *Parent–child play: Descriptions & implications* (pp. 113–143). Albany: State University of New York Press.

MacDonald, K. (1996). What do children want? A conceptualisation of evolutionary influences on children's motivation in the peer group. *International Journal of Behavioral Development, 19*, 53–73.

MacDonald, K. (1997). Life history theory and human reproductive behavior: Environmental/contextual influences and heritable variation. *Human Nature, 8*, 327–359.

Machel, G. (1996). *Impact of armed conflict on children*. New York: United Nations. Retrieved June 5, 2008, from http://www.un.org/children/conflict/english/themachelstudy.html.

Machin, S., & Pekkarinen, T. (2008, November 28). Global sex differences in test score variability. *Science, 322*, 1331–1332.

Macrae, C. N., Alnwick, K. A., Milne, A. B., & Schloerscheidt, A. M. (2002). Person perception across the menstrual cycle: Hormonal influences on social–cognitive functioning. *Psychological Science, 13*, 532–536.

Madden, J. (2001). Sex, bowers and brains. *Proceedings of the Royal Society London B, 268*, 833–838.

Maestripieri, D. (2005). Effects of early experience on female behavioural and reproductive development in rhesus macaques. *Proceedings of the Royal Society London B, 272*, 1243–1248.

Maestripieri, D., & Ross, S. R. (2004). Sex differences in play among western lowland gorilla (*Gorilla gorilla gorilla*) infants: Implications for adult behavior and social structure. *American Journal of Physical Anthropology, 123*, 52–61.

Magee, S. E., Neff, B. D., & Knapp, R. (2006). Plasma levels of androgens and cortisol in relation to breeding behavior in parental male bluegill sunfish, *Lepomis macrochirus*. *Hormones and Behavior, 49*, 598–609.

Maggioncalda, A. N., Sapolsky, R. M., & Czekala, N. M. (1999). Reproductive hormone profiles in captive male orangutans: Implications for understanding developmental arrest. *American Journal of Physical Anthropology, 109*, 19–32.

Maguire, E. A., Burgess, N., Donnett, J. G., Frackowiak, R. S. J., Frith, C. D., & O'Keefe, J. (1998, May 8). Knowing where and getting there: A human navigational network. *Science, 280*, 921–924.

Maguire, E. A., Frackowiak, R. S. J., & Frith, C. D. (1996). Learning to find your way: A role for the human hippocampal formation. *Proceedings of the Royal Society of London B, 263*, 1745–1750.

Maguire, E. A., Frackowiak, R. S. J., & Frith, C. D. (1997). Recalling routes around London: Activation of the right hippocampus in taxi drivers. *Journal of Neuroscience, 17*, 7103–7110.

Maguire, E. A., Woollett, K., & Spiers, H. J. (2006). London taxi drivers and bus drivers: A structural MRI and neuropsychological analysis. *Hippocampus, 16*, 1091–1101.

Mahawar, M. M., & Jaroli, D. P. (2008). Traditional zootherapeutic studies in India: A review. *Journal of Ethnobiology and Ethnomedicine, 4*, 17. Retrieved October 10, 2008, from http://www.ethnobiomed.com/content/4/1/17

Majeres, R. L. (2007). Sex differences in phonological coding: Alphabet transformation speed. *Intelligence, 35*, 335–346.

Malt, B. C. (1995). Category coherence in cross-cultural perspective. *Cognitive Psychology, 29*, 85–148.

Maner, J. K., Miller, S. L., Schmidt, N. B., & Eckel, L. A. (2008). Submitting to defeat: Social anxiety, dominance threat, and decrements in testosterone. *Psychological Science, 19*, 764–768.

Mann, D. R., & Fraser, H. M. (1996). The neonatal period: A critical interval in male primate development. *Journal of Endocrinology, 149*, 191–197.

Manning, J. T. (1989). Age-advertisement and the evolution of the peacock's train. *Journal of Evolutionary Biology, 2*, 379–384.

Manning, J. T., Koukourakis, K., & Brodie, D. A. (1997). Fluctuating asymmetry, metabolic rate and sexual selection in human males. *Evolution and Human Behavior, 18*, 15–21.

Manning, J. T., Scutt, D., Whitehouse, G. H., & Leinster, S. J. (1997). Breast asymmetry and phenotypic quality in women. *Evolution and Human Behavior, 18*, 223–236.

Manson, J. H., & Wrangham, R. W. (1991). Intergroup aggression in chimpanzees and humans. *Current Anthropology, 32*, 369–390.

Marcus, G. (2004). *The birth of the mind: How a tiny number of genes creates the complexities of human thought.* New York: Basic Books.

Markovits, H., Benenson, J., & Dolenszky, E. (2001). Evidence that children and adolescents have internal models of peers interactions that are gender differentiated. *Child Development, 72*, 879–886.

Markus, H. (1977). Self-schemata and processing information about the self. *Journal of Personality and Social Psychology, 35*, 63–78.

Marler, C. A., & Ryan, M. J. (1997). Origin and maintenance of a female mating preference. *Evolution, 51*, 1244–1248.

Marler, P. (1991). The instinct to learn. In S. Carey & R. Gelman (Eds.), *The epigenesis of mind: Essays on biology and cognition* (pp. 37–66). Hillsdale, NJ: Erlbaum.

Marlowe, F. W. (2003). A critical person for provisioning by Hadza men: Implications for pair bonding. *Evolution and Human Behavior, 24*, 217–229.

Marlowe, F. W. (2004a). Marital residence among foragers. *Current Anthropology, 45*, 277–284.

Marlowe, F. W. (2004b). Mate preferences among Hadza hunter-gatherers. *Human Nature, 15*, 365–376.

Marmot, M. (2004). *The status syndrome: How social standing affects our health and longevity.* New York: Holt.

Martin, C. L., & Fabes, R. A. (2001). The stability and consequences of young children's same-sex peer interactions. *Developmental Psychology, 37*, 431–446.

Martin, C. L., Ruble, D. N., & Szkrybalo, J. (2002). Cognitive theories of early gender development. *Psychological Bulletin, 128*, 903–933.

Martin, R. (1997). "Girls don't talk about garages!": Perceptions of conversation in same- and cross-sex friendships. *Personal Relationships, 4*, 115–130.

Martin, W. J. (1949, March 12). Infant mortality. *BMJ, 1*, 438–441.

Martorell, R., Rivera, J., Kaplowitz, H., & Pollitt, E. (1992). Long-term consequences of growth retardation during early childhood. In M. Hernández & J. Argente (Eds.), *Human growth: Basic and clinical aspects* (pp. 143–149). Amsterdam, Netherlands: Elsevier Science.

Matthews, M. H. (1987). Sex differences in spatial competence: The ability of young children to map 'primed' unfamiliar environments. *Educational Psychology, 7*, 77–90.

Matthews, M. H. (1992). *Making sense of place: Children's understanding of large-scale environments*. Savage, MD: Barnes & Noble Books.

Maynard Smith, J. (1977). Parental investment: A prospective analysis. *Animal Behaviour, 25*, 1–9.

Maynard Smith, J., & Price, G. R. (1973, November 2). The logic of animal conflict. *Nature, 246*, 15–18.

Mayr, E. (1974). Behavior programs and evolutionary strategies. *American Scientist, 62*, 650–659.

Mayr, E. (1982). *The growth of biological thought*. Cambridge, MA: Belknap Press.

Mazur, A., & Booth, A. (1998). Testosterone and dominance in men. *Behavioral and Brain Sciences, 21*, 353–397.

Mazur, A., & Michalek, J. (1998). Marriage, divorce, and male testosterone. *Social Forces, 77*, 315–330.

McBurney, D. H., Simon, J., Gaulin, S. J. C., & Geliebter, A. (2002). Matrilateral biases in the investment of aunts and uncles: Replication in a population presumed to have high paternity certainty. *Human Nature, 13*, 391–402.

McBurney, D. H., Zapp, D. J., & Streeter, S. A. (2005). Preferred number of sexual partners: Tails of distributions and tales of mating systems. *Evolution and Human Behavior, 26*, 271–278.

McClure, E. B. (2000). A meta-analytic review of sex differences in facial expression processing and their development in infants, children, and adolescents. *Psychological Bulletin, 126*, 424–453.

McClure, E. B., Monk, C. S., Nelson, E. E., Zarahn, E., Leibenluft, E., Bilder, R. M., et al. (2004). A developmental examination of gender differences in brain engagement during evaluation of threat. *Biological Psychiatry, 55*, 1047–1055.

McDade, T. W., Reyes-García, V., Blackinton, P., Tanner, S., Huanca, T., & Leonard, W. R. (2007). Ethnobiological knowledge is associated with indices of child health in the Bolivian Amazon. *Proceedings of the National Academy of Sciences USA, 104*, 6134–6139.

McEwen, B. S., Biron, C. A., Brunson, K. W., Bulloch, K., Chambers, W. H., Dhabhar, F. S., et al. (1997). The role of adrenocorticoids as modulators of immune function in health and disease: Neural, endocrine and immune interactions. *Brain Research Reviews, 23*, 79–133.

McFadden, D. (1998). Sex differences in the auditory system. *Developmental Neuropsychology, 14*, 261–298.

McGlone, J. (1980). Sex differences in human brain asymmetry: A critical survey. *Behavioral and Brain Sciences, 3*, 215–263.

McGrew, W. C. (1992). *Chimpanzee material culture: Implications for human evolution*. New York: Cambridge University Press.

McGuinness, D., & Pribram, K. H. (1979). The origins of sensory bias in the development of gender differences in perception and cognition. In M. Bortner (Ed.), *Cognitive growth and development: Essays in memory of Herbert G. Birch* (pp. 3–56). New York: Brunner/Mazel.

McHale, J. P., Kuersten-Hogan, R., Lauretti, A., & Rasmussen, J. L. (2000). Parental reports of coparenting and observed coparenting behavior during the toddler period. *Journal of Family Psychology, 14*, 220–236.

McHale, S. M., Kim, J.-Y., Dotterer, A. M., Crouter, A. C., & Booth, A. (2009). The development of gendered interests and personality qualities from middle childhood through adolescence: A biosocial analysis. *Child Development, 80*, 482–495.

McHale, S. M., Shanahan, L., Updegraff, K. A., Crouter, A. C., & Booth, A. (2004). Developmental and individual differences in girls' sex-typed activities in middle childhood and adolescence. *Child Development, 75*, 1575–1593.

McHenry, H. M. (1992). Body size and proportions in early hominids. *American Journal of Physical Anthropology, 87*, 407–431.

McHenry, H. M. (1994a). Behavioral ecological implications of early hominid body size. *Journal of Human Evolution, 27*, 77–87.

McHenry, H. M. (1994b). Tempo and mode in human evolution. *Proceedings of the National Academy of Sciences USA, 91*, 6780–6786.

McHenry, H. M., & Coffing, K. (2000). *Australopithecus* to *Homo:* Transformations in body and mind. *Annual Review of Anthropology, 29*, 125–146.

McIntyre, M., Gangestad, S. W., Gray, P. B., Chapman, J. F., Burnham, T. C., O'Rourke, M. T., & Thornhill, R. (2006). Romantic involvement often reduces men's testosterone levels—But not always: The moderating role of extrapair sexual interest. *Journal of Personality and Social Psychology, 91*, 642–651.

McKeever, W. F. (1995). Hormone and hemisphericity hypotheses regarding cognitive sex differences: Possible future explanatory power, but current empirical chaos. *Learning and Individual Differences, 7*, 323–340.

McKenna, P., & Parry, R. (1994). Category specificity in the naming of natural and man-made objects: Normative data from adults and children. *Neuropsychological Rehabilitation, 4*, 255–281.

McKinnon, J. S., Mori, S., Blackman, B. K., David, L., Kingsley, D. M., & Jamieson, L., et al. (2004, May 20). Evidence for ecology's role in speciation. *Nature, 429*, 294–298.

McLain, D. K., Setters, D., Moulton, M. P., & Pratt, A. E. (2000). Ascription of resemblance of newborns by parents and nonrelatives. *Evolution and Human Behavior, 21*, 11–23.

McNamara, J. M., & Houston, A. I. (1996, March 21). State-dependent life histories. *Nature, 380*, 215–221.

McRae, K., Reiman, E. M., Fort, C. L., Chen, K., & Lane, R. D. (2008). Association between trait emotional awareness and dorsal anterior cingulate activity during emotion is arousal-dependent. *NeuroImage, 41*, 648–655.

Mealey, L. (1985). The relationship between social status and biological success: A case study of the Mormon religious hierarchy. *Ethology and Sociobiology, 6,* 249–257.

Meaney, M. J., Dodge, A. M., & Beatty, W. W. (1981). Sex-dependent effects of amygdaloid lesions on the social play of prepubertal rats. *Physiology & Behavior, 26,* 467–472.

Medin, D. L., & Atran, S. (Eds.). (1999). *Folkbiology.* Cambridge, MA: MIT Press/ Bradford Books.

Medin, D. L., & Atran, S. (2004). The native mind: Biological categorization and reasoning in development and across cultures. *Psychological Review, 111,* 960–983.

Medin, D. L., Ross, N. O., Atran, S., Cox, D., Coley, J., Proffitt, J. B., & Blok, S. (2006). Folkbiology of freshwater fish. *Cognition, 99,* 237–273.

Mehl, M. R., Vazire, S., Ramírez-Esparza, N., Slatcher, R. B., & Pennebaker, J. W. (2007, July 6). Are women really more talkative than men? *Science, 317,* 82.

Menken, J., Trussell, J., & Larsen, U. (1986, September 26). Age and infertility. *Science, 233,* 1389–1394.

Mennill, D. J., Ratcliffe, L. M., & Boag, P. T. (2002, May 3). Female eavesdropping on male song contests in songbirds. *Science, 296,* 873.

Merriwether, D. A., Huston, S., Iyengar, S., Hamman, R., Norris, J. M., Shetterly, S. M., et al. (1997). Mitochondrial versus nuclear admixture estimates demonstrate a past history of directional mating. *American Journal of Physical Anthropology, 102,* 153–159.

Mesquida, C. G., & Wiener, N. I. (1996). Human collective aggression: A behavioral ecology perspective. *Ethology and Sociobiology, 17,* 247–262.

Meuwissen, I., & Over, R. (1992). Sexual arousal across the menstrual phases of the human menstrual cycle. *Archives of Sexual Behavior, 21,* 101–119.

Miles, C., Green, R., & Hines, M. (2006). Estrogen treatment effects on cognition, memory and mood in male-to-female transsexuals. *Hormones and Behavior, 50,* 708–717.

Miles, W. R. (1910). A comparison of elementary and high school grades. *Pedagogical Seminary, 17,* 429–450.

Milinski, M. (2006). The major histocompatibility complex, sexual selection, and mate choice. *Annual Review of Ecology, Evolution, and Systematics, 37,* 159–186.

Miller, D. C., & Byrnes, J. P. (1997). The role of contextual and personal factors in children's risk taking. *Developmental Psychology, 33,* 814–823.

Miller, G. (2000). *The mating mind: How sexual choice shaped the evolution of human nature.* New York: Doubleday.

Miller, G., Tybur, J. M., & Jordan, B. D. (2007). Ovulatory cycle effects on tip earnings by lap dancers: Economic evidence for human estrous? *Evolution and Human Behavior, 28,* 375–381.

Miller, G. T., & Pitnick, S. (2002, November 8). Sperm-female coevolution in *Drosophila. Science, 298,* 1230–1233.

Miller, L. C., & Fishkin, S. A. (1997). On the dynamics of human bonding and reproductive success: Seeking windows on the adapted-for-human-environmental interface. In J. A. Simpson & D. T. Kenrick (Eds.), *Evolutionary social psychology* (pp. 197–235). Mahwah, NJ: Erlbaum.

Milner, A. D., & Goodale, M. A. (1995). *The visual brain in action*. New York: Oxford University Press.

Mintz, L. B., & Betz, N. E. (1986). Sex differences in the nature, realism, and correlates of body image. *Sex Roles, 15,* 185–195.

Mitani, J. C., & Amsler, S. J. (2003). Social and spatial aspects of male subgrouping in a community of wild chimpanzees. *Behaviour, 140,* 869–884.

Mitani, J. C., Gros-Louis, J., & Richards, A. F. (1996). Sexual dimorphism, the operational sex ratio, and the intensity of male competition in polygynous primates. *American Naturalist, 147,* 966–980.

Mitani, J. C., & Watts, D. P. (2005). Correlates of territorial boundary patrol behavior in wild chimpanzees. *Animal Behaviour, 70,* 1079–1086.

Mock, D. W., & Fujioka, M. (1990). Monogamy and long-term pair bonding in vertebrates. *Trends in Ecology & Evolution, 5,* 39–43.

Moffat, S. D., & Hampson, E. (1996). A curvilinear relationship between testosterone and spatial cognition in humans: Possible influence of hand preference. *Psychoneuroendocrinology, 21,* 323–337.

Moffat, S. D., Hampson, E., & Hatzipantelis, M. (1998). Navigation in a "virtual" maze: Sex differences and correlation with psychometric measures of spatial ability in humans. *Evolution and Human Behavior, 19,* 73–87.

Molfese, D. L., Freeman, R. B., & Palermo, D. S. (1975). The ontogeny of brain lateralization for speech & nonspeech stimuli. *Brain and Language, 2,* 356–368.

Møller, A. P. (1988, April 14). Female choice selects for male sexual tail ornaments in the monogamous swallow. *Nature, 332,* 640–642.

Møller, A. P. (1990a). Effects of a haematophagous mite on the barn swallow (*HIRUNDO RUSTICA*): A test of the Hamilton and Zuk hypothesis. *Evolution, 44,* 771–784.

Møller, A. P. (1990b). Parasites and sexual selection: Current status of the Hamilton and Zuk hypothesis. *Journal of Evolutionary Biology, 3,* 319–328.

Møller, A. P. (1994a). *Sexual selection and the barn swallow*. New York: Oxford University Press.

Møller, A. P. (1994b). Symmetrical male sexual ornaments, paternal care, and offspring quality. *Behavioral Ecology, 5,* 188–194.

Møller, A. P. (2000). Male parental care, female reproductive success, and extrapair paternity. *Behavioral Ecology, 11,* 161–168.

Møller, A. P., & Alatalo, R. V. (1999). Good-genes effects in sexual selection. *Proceedings of the Royal Society of London B, 266,* 85–91.

Møller, A. P., & Cuervo, J. J. (2000). The evolution of paternity and paternal care. *Behavioral Ecology, 11,* 472–485.

Møller, A. P., Soler, M., & Thornhill, R. (1995). Breast asymmetry, sexual selection, and human reproductive success. *Ethology and Sociobiology, 16,* 207–219.

Møller, A. P., & Tegelström, H. (1997). Extra-pair paternity and tail ornamentation in the barn swallow *Hirundo rustica. Behavioral Ecology and Sociobiology, 41,* 353–360.

Monteiro, J. M., Albuquerque, U. P., Lins-Neto, E. M. F., Araújo, E. L., & Amorim, E. L. C. (2006). Use patterns and knowledge of medicinal species among two rural communities in Brazil's semi-arid northeastern region. *Journal of Ethnopharmacology, 105,* 173–186.

Monto, M. A., & McRee, N. (2005). A comparison of male customers of female street prostitutes with national samples of men. *International Journal of Offender Therapy and Comparative Criminology, 49,* 505–529.

Moore, D. S., & Johnson, S. P. (2008). Mental rotation in human infants: A sex difference. *Psychological Science, 19,* 1063–1066.

Moore, S. L., & Wilson, K. (2002, September 20). Parasites as a viability cost of sexual selection in natural populations of mammals. *Science, 297,* 2015–2018.

Mordecai, K. L., Rubin, L. H., & Maki, P. M. (2008). Effects of menstrual cycle phase and oral contraceptive use on verbal memory. *Hormones and Behavior, 54,* 286–293.

Morgan, A. D., Gandon, S., & Buckling, A. (2005, September 8). The effect of migration on local populations in a coevolving host-parasite system. *Nature, 437,* 253–256.

Morgan, M. J., Adam, A., & Mollon, J. D. (1992). Dichromats detect colour-camouflaged objects that are not detected by trichromats. *Proceedings of the Royal Society of London B, 248,* 291–295.

Mori, A., Watanabe, K., & Yamaguchi, N. (1989). Longitudinal changes of dominance rank among females of the Koshima group of Japanese monkeys. *Primates, 30,* 147–173.

Morris, J. A., Jordan, C. L., & Breedlove, S. M. (2004). Sexual differentiation of the vertebrate nervous system. *Nature Neuroscience, 7,* 1034–1039.

Morrison, A. S., Kirshner, J., & Molho, A. (1977). Life cycle events in 15th century Florence: Records of the *Monte Delle Doti. American Journal of Epidemiology, 106,* 487–492.

Morrongiello, B. A., & Dawber, T. (2004). Identifying factors that relate to children's risk-taking decisions. *Canadian Journal of Behavioral Science, 36,* 255–266.

Mougeot, F., Redpath, S. M., & Piertney, S. B. (2006). Elevated spring testosterone increases parasite intensity in male red grouse. *Behavioral Ecology, 17,* 117–125.

Mougeot, F., Redpath, S. M., Piertney, S. B., & Hudson, P. J. (2005). Separating behavioral and physiological mechanisms in testosterone-mediated trade-offs. *American Naturalist, 166,* 158–168.

Mountain, J. L., Lin, A. A., Bowcock, A. M., & Cavalli-Sforza, L. L. (1993). Evolution of modern humans: Evidence from nuclear DNA polymorphisms. In M. J. Aitken, C. B. Stringer, & P. A. Mellars (Eds.), *The origins of modern humans and the impact of chronometric dating* (pp. 69–83). Princeton, NJ: Princeton University Press.

Mousseau, T. A., & Fox, C. W. (Eds.). (1998). *Maternal effects as adaptations*. New York: Oxford University Press.

Mousseau, T. A., & Roff, D. A. (1987). Natural selection and the heritability of fitness components. *Heredity, 59,* 181–197.

Moyo, S., Hawkridge, T., Mahomed, H., Workman, L., Minnies, D., Geiter, L. J., et al. (2007). Determining causes of mortality in children enrolled in a vaccine field trial in a rural area in the Western Cape province of South Africa. *Journal of Pediatrics and Child Health, 43,* 178–183.

Muehlenbein, M. P. (2006). Intestinal parasite infections and fecal steroid levels in wild chimpanzees. *American Journal of Physical Anthropology, 130,* 546–550.

Muehlenbein, M. P., & Bribiescas, R. G. (2005). Testosterone-mediated immune functions and male life histories. *American Journal of Human Biology, 17,* 527–558.

Muehlenbein, M. P., Watts, D. P., & Whitten, P. L. (2004). Dominance rank and fecal testosterone levels in adult male chimpanzees (*Pan troglodytes schweinfurthii*) at Ngogo, Kibale national park, Uganda. *American Journal of Primatology, 64,* 71–82.

Mueller, S. C., Temple, V., Oh, E., VanRyzin, C., Williams, A., Cornwell, B., et al. (2008). Early androgen exposure modulates spatial cognition in congenital adrenal hyperplasia. *Psychoneuroendocrinology, 33,* 973–980.

Muller, H. J. (1964). The relation of recombination to mutational advance. *Mutation Research, 1,* 2–9.

Muller, M. N., Kahlenberg, S. M., Emery Thompson, M., & Wrangham, R. W. (2007). Male coercion and the costs of promiscuous mating for female chimpanzees. *Proceedings of the Royal Society of London B, 274,* 1009–1014.

Muller, M. N., Thompson, M. E., & Wrangham, R. W. (2006). Male chimpanzees prefer mating with old females. *Current Biology, 16,* 2234–2238.

Muller, M. N., & Wrangham, R. W. (2004). Dominance, aggression and testosterone in wild chimpanzees: A test of the 'challenge hypothesis.' *Animal Behaviour, 67,* 113–123.

Munroe, R. H., Munroe, R. L., & Brasher, A. (1985). Precursors of spatial ability: A longitudinal study among the Logoli of Kenya. *Journal of Social Psychology, 125,* 23–33.

Murdock, G. P. (1981). *Atlas of world cultures*. Pittsburgh, PA: University of Pittsburgh Press.

Murphy, F. C., Nimmo-Smith, I., & Lawrence, A. D. (2003). Functional neuroanatomy of emotions: A meta-analysis. *Cognitive, Affective, & Behavioral Neuroscience, 3,* 207–233.

Murray-Close, D., Ostrov, J. M., & Crick, N. R. (2007). A short-term longitudinal study of growth of relational aggression during middle childhood: Associations with gender, friendship intimacy, and internalizing problems. *Development and Psychopathology, 19,* 187–203.

Nascimento, J. M., Shi, L. Z., Meyers, S., Gagneux, P., Loskutoff, N. M., Botvinick, E. L., & Berns, M. W. (2008). The use of optical tweezers to study sperm competition and motility in primates. *Journal of the Royal Society Interface, 5,* 297–302.

Nathans, J., Piantanida, T. P., Eddy, R. L., Shows, T. B., & Hogness, D. S. (1986, April 11). Molecular genetics of inherited variation in human color vision. *Science, 232,* 203–210.

National Academy of Sciences. (2006). *Beyond bias and barriers: Fulfilling the potential of women in academic science and engineering.* Washington, DC: National Academies Press.

Neal, J. K., & Wade, J. (2007). Courtship and copulation in the adult male green anole: Effects of season, hormone and female contact on reproductive behavior and morphology. *Behavioural Brain Research, 177,* 177–185.

Neave, N., & Wolfson, S. (2003). Testosterone, territoriality, and the 'home advantage.' *Physiology & Behavior, 78,* 269–275.

Neff, B. D. (2003, April 17). Decisions about parental care in response to perceived paternity. *Nature, 422,* 716–719.

Neff, B. D., & Pitcher, T. E. (2005). Genetic quality and sexual selection: An integrated framework for good genes and compatible genes. *Molecular Ecology, 14,* 19–38.

Neff, B. D., & Sherman, P. W. (2002). Decision making and recognition mechanisms. *Proceedings of the Royal Society of London B, 269,* 1435–1441.

Nei, M., & Hughes, A. L. (1991). Polymorphism and evolution of the major histocompatibility complex loci in mammals. In R. K. Selander, A. G. Clark, & T. S. Whittam (Eds.), *Evolution at the molecular level* (pp. 222–247). Sunderland, MA: Sinauer Associates.

Neiderhiser, J. M., Reiss, D., Lichtenstein, P., Spotts, E. L., & Ganiban, J. (2007). Father–adolescent relationships and the role of genotype-environment correlation. *Journal of Family Psychology, 21,* 560–571.

Neitz, M., Kraft, T. W., & Neitz, J. (1998). Expression of L cone pigment gene subtypes in females. *Vision Research, 38,* 3221–3225.

Nettle, D. (2002). Height and reproductive success in a cohort of British men. *Human Nature, 13,* 473–491.

Nettle, D. (2008). Why do some dads get more involved than others? Evidence from a large British cohort. *Evolution and Human Behavior, 29,* 416–423.

Neu, H. C. (1992, August 21). The crisis of antibiotic resistance. *Science, 257,* 1064–1073.

Neufang, S., Specht, K., Hausmann, M., Güntürkün, O., Herpertz-Dahlmann, R., Fink, G. R., & Konrad, K. (2009). Sex differences in the impact of steroid hormones on the developing human brain. *Cerebral Cortex, 19,* 463–473.

Newcombe, N. S., & Huttenlocher, J. (2006). Development of spatial cognition. In W. Damon (Gen Ed.) & D. Kuhl & R. S. Siegler (Vol. Eds.), *Cognition, perception, and language: Vol. 2. Handbook of child psychology* (6th ed., pp. 734–776). New York: Wiley.

Newman, M. L., Sellers, J. G., & Josephs, R. A. (2005). Testosterone, cognition, and social status. *Hormones and Behavior, 47*, 205–211.

Nicolaidis, C., Curry, M. A., Ulrich, Y., Sharps, P., McFarlane, J., Campbell, D., et al. (2003). Could we have known? A qualitative analysis of data from women who survived an attempted homicide by an intimate partner. *Journal of General Internal Medicine, 18*, 788–794.

Nicolson, N. A. (1987). Infants, mothers, and other females. In B. B. Smuts, D. L. Cheney, R. M. Seyfarth, R. W. Wrangham, & T. T. Struhsaker (Eds.), *Primate societies* (pp. 330–342). Chicago: The University of Chicago Press.

Nishida, T. (1979). The social structure of chimpanzees of the Mahale mountains. In D. A. Hamburg & E. R. McCown (Eds.), *The great apes* (pp. 73–121). Menlo Park, CA: Benjamin Cummings.

Nolan, J. M., & Robbins, M. C. (1999). Cultural conservation of medicinal plant use in the Ozarks. *Human Organization, 58*, 67–72.

Nolan, P. M., Hill, G. E., & Stoehr, A. M. (1998). Sex, size, and plumage redness predict house finch survival in an epidemic. *Proceedings of the Royal Society of London B, 265*, 961–965.

Nolen-Hoeksema, S. (1987). Sex differences in unipolar depression: Evidence and theory. *Psychological Bulletin, 101*, 259–282.

Nordling, D., Andersson, M., Zohari, S., & Gustafsson, L. (1998). Reproductive effort reduces specific immune response and parasite resistance. *Proceedings of the Royal Society of London, B, 265*, 1291–1298.

Norenzayan, A., & Shariff, A. F. (2008, October 3). The origin and evolution of religious prosociality. *Science, 322*, 58–62.

Nottebohm, F. (1970, February 13). Ontogeny of bird song. *Science, 167*, 950–956.

Nottebohm, F. (1980). Testosterone triggers growth of brain vocal control nuclei in adult female canaries. *Brain Research, 189*, 429–436.

Nottebohm, F. (1981, December 18). A brain for all seasons: Cyclical anatomical changes in song-control nuclei of the canary brain. *Science, 214*, 1368–1370.

Nottebohm, F. (2005). The neural basis of birdsong. *PLoS Biology, 3*, 759–761. doi:10.1371/journal.pbio.0030164.

Nottebohm, F., & Arnold, A. P. (1976, October 8). Sexual dimorphism in vocal control areas of the songbird brain. *Science, 194*, 211–213.

Nsubuga, A. M., Robbins, M. M., Boesch, C., & Vigilant, L. (2008). Patterns of paternity and group fission in wild multimale mountain gorilla groups. *American Journal of Physical Anthropology, 135*, 263–274.

Nussey, D. H., Postma, E., Gienapp, P., & Visser, M. E. (2005, October 14). Selection on heritable phenotypic plasticity in a wild bird population. *Science, 310,* 304–306.

Ober, C., Elias, S., Kostyu, D. D., & Hauck, W. W. (1992). Decreased fecundability in Hutterite couples sharing HLA-DR. *American Journal of Human Genetics, 50,* 6–14.

Ober, C., Weitkamp, L. R., Cox, N., Dytch, H., Kostyu, D., & Elias, S. (1997). HLA and mate choice in humans. *American Journal of Human Genetics, 61,* 497–504.

O'Connell, J. F., Hawkes, K., & Blurton Jones, N. G. (1999). Grandmothering and the evolution of *Homo erectus. Journal of Human Evolution, 36,* 461–485.

O'Connor, D. B., Archer, J., Hair, W. M., & Wu, F. C. W. (2001). Activational effects of testosterone on cognitive function in men. *Neuropsychologia, 39,* 1385–1394.

O'Connor, D. B., Archer, J., & Wu, F. C. W. (2004). Effects of testosterone on mood, aggression, and sexual behavior in young men: A double-blind, placebo-controlled, cross-over study. *Journal of Clinical Endocrinology & Metabolism, 89,* 2837–2845.

Oda, R. (2001). Sexual dimorphic mate preference in Japan: An analysis of lonely hearts advertisements. *Human Nature, 12,* 191–206.

Öhman, A. (2002). Automaticity and the amygdala: Nonconscious responses to emotional faces. *Current Directions in Psychological Science, 11,* 62–66.

O'Keefe, J., & Nadel, L. (1978). *The hippocampus as a cognitive map.* New York: Oxford University Press.

Olendorf, R., Rodd, F. H., Punzalan, D., Houde, A. E., Hurt, C., Reznick, D. N., & Hughes, K. A. (2006, June 1). Frequency-dependent survival in natural guppy populations. *Nature, 441,* 633–636.

Oliveira, R. F., Ros, A. F. H., & Gonçalves, D. M. (2005). Intra-sexual variation in male reproduction in teleost fist: A comparative approach. *Hormones and Behavior, 48,* 430–439.

Oliver, M. B., & Hyde, J. S. (1993). Gender differences in sexuality: A meta-analysis. *Psychological Bulletin, 114,* 29–51.

Oring, L. W., Lank, D. B., & Maxson, S. J. (1983). Population studies of the polyandrous spotted sandpiper. *Auk, 100,* 272–285.

Ormerod, B. K., Lee, T. T.-Y., & Galea, L. A. M. (2004). Estradiol enhances neurogenesis in the dentate gyri of adult male meadow voles by increasing survival of young granule neurons. *Neuroscience, 128,* 645–654.

Osofsky, J. D., & O'Connell, E. J. (1977). Patterning of newborn behavior in an urban population. *Child Development, 48,* 532–36.

Otter, K., Ratcliffe, L., Michaud, D., & Boag, P. T. (1998). Do female black-capped chickadees prefer high-ranking males as extra-pair partners? *Behavioral Ecology and Sociobiology, 43,* 25–36.

Owens, I. P. F., Burke, T., & Thompson, D. B. A. (1994). Extraordinary sex roles in the Eurasian dotterel: Female mating arenas, female–female competition, and female mate choice. *American Naturalist, 144,* 76–100.

Oxford, J., Ponzi, D., & Geary, D. C. (in press). Hormonal responses differ when playing violent games against an ingroup and outgroup. *Evolution and Human Behavior*.

Oxley, D. R., Smith, K. B., Alford, J. R., Hibbing, M. V., Miller, J. L., Scalora, M., et al. (2008, September 19). Political attitudes vary with physiological traits. *Science, 321*, 1667–1670.

Pääbo, S. (1999). Human evolution. *Trends in Genetics, 15*, M13–M16.

Paglin, M., & Rufolo, A. M. (1990). Heterogeneous human capital, occupational choice, and male–female earnings differences. *Journal of Labor Economics, 8*, 123–144.

Pakkenberg, B., & Gundersen, J. G. (1997). Neocortical neuron number in humans: Effect of sex and age. *Journal of Comparative Neurology, 384*, 312–320.

Palmer, C. T., Ellsworth, R. &, Steadman, L. B. (2009). Talk and tradition: Why the least interesting components of religion may be the most evolutionarily important. In E. Voland & W. Schiefenhvel (Eds.), The biological evolution of religious mind and behavior (pp. 105–116). New York: Springer-Verlag.

Palombit, R. A., Cheney, D. L., & Seyfarth, R. M. (2001). Female–female competition for male 'friends' in wild chacma baboons, *Papio cynocephalus ursinus*. *Animal Behaviour, 61*, 1159–1171.

Panksepp, J., Siviy, S., & Normansell, L. (1984). The psychobiology of play: Theoretical and methodological perspectives. *Neuroscience & Biobehavioral Reviews, 8*, 465–492.

Parameswaran, G. (2003). Experimenter instructions as a mediator in the effects of culture on mapping one's neighborhood. *Journal of Environmental Psychology, 23*, 409–417.

Parish, A. R. (1996). Female relationships in bonobos (*Pan paniscus*): Evidence for bonding, cooperation, and female dominance in a male-philopatric species. *Human Nature, 7*, 61–96.

Parke, R. D. (1995). Fathers and families. In M. H. Bornstein (Ed.), *Handbook of parenting: Vol. 3. Status and social conditions of parenting* (pp. 27–63). Mahwah, NJ: Erlbaum.

Parke, R. D., & Buriel, R. (1998). Socialization in the family: Ethnic and ecological perspectives. In W. Damon & E. Eisenberg (Eds.), *Handbook of child psychology* (5th ed., Vol. 3, pp. 463–552). New York: Wiley.

Parker, G. A., & Simmons, L. W. (1996). Parental investment and the control of selection: Predicting the direction of sexual competition. *Proceedings of the Royal Society of London B, 263*, 315–321.

Parker, J. G., & Asher, S. R. (1993). Friendship and friendship quality in middle childhood: Links with peer group acceptance and feelings of loneliness and social dissatisfaction. *Developmental Psychology, 29*, 611–621.

Parker, J. G., & Seal, J. (1996). Forming, losing, renewing, and replacing friendships: Applying temporal parameters to the assessment of children's friendship experiences. *Child Development, 67*, 2248–2268.

Parker, S. T., & McKinney, M. L. (1999). *Origins of intelligence: The evolution of cognitive development in monkeys, apes, and humans*. Baltimore: Johns Hopkins University Press.

Pascalis, O., de Haan, M., & Nelson, C. A. (2002, May 17). Is face processing species-specific during the first year of life? *Science, 296*, 1321–1323.

Pasternak, B., Ember, C. R., & Ember, M. (1997). *Sex, gender, and kinship: A cross-cultural perspective*. Upper Saddle River, NJ: Prentice-Hall.

Pasterski, V., Hindmarch, P., Geffner, M., Brook, C., Brain, C., & Hines, M. (2007). Increased aggression and activity level in 3- to 11-year-old girls with congenital adrenal hyperplasia (CAH). *Hormones and Behavior, 52*, 368–374.

Paterson, S., & Pemberton, J. M. (1997). No evidence for major histocompatibility complex-dependent mating patterns in a free-living ruminant population. *Proceedings of the Royal Society of London B, 264*, 1813–1819.

Patterson, N., Richter, D. J., Gnerre, S., Lander, E. S., & Reich, D. (2006, June 29). Genetic evidence for complex speciation of humans and chimpanzees. *Nature, 441*, 1103–1108.

Paul, L., & Hirsch, L. R. (1996). Human male mating strategies: II. Moral codes of "quality" and "quantity" strategies. *Ethology and Sociobiology, 17*, 71–86.

Pavio, A., & Clark, J. M. (1991). Static versus dynamic imagery. In C. Cornoldi & M. A. McDaniel (Eds.), *Imagery and cognition* (pp. 221–245). New York: Springer-Verlag.

Pawlowski, B., Atwal, R., & Dunbar, R. I. M. (2008). Sex differences in everyday risk-taking behavior in humans. *Evolutionary Psychology, 6*, 29–42. Retrieved April 28, 2008, from http://www.epjournal.net/filestore/ep062942.pdf

Pawlowski, B., & Dunbar, R. I. M. (2005). Waist-to-hip ratio versus body mass index as predictors of fitness in women. *Human Nature, 16*, 164–177.

Pawlowski, B., Dunbar, R. I. M., & Lipowicz, A. (2000, January 13). Tall men have more reproductive success. *Nature, 403*, 156.

Pawlowski, B., & Jasienska, G. (2005). Women's preferences for sexual dimorphism in height depend on menstrual cycle phase and expected duration of relationship. *Biological Psychology, 70*, 38–43.

Pawlowski, B., & Jasienska, G. (2008). Women's body morphology and preferences for sexual partners' characteristics. *Evolution and Human Behavior, 29*, 19–25.

Pawlowski, B., Lowen, C. B., & Dunbar, R. I. M. (1998). Neocortex size, social skills and mating success in primates. *Behaviour, 135*, 357–368.

Pearson, R., & Lewis, M. B. (2005). Fear recognition across the menstrual cycle. *Hormones and Behavior, 47*, 267–271.

Pedersen, F. A. (1991). Secular trends in human sex ratios: Their influence on individual and family behavior. *Human Nature, 2*, 271–291.

Pedersen, J. M., Glickman, S. E., Frank, L. G., & Beach, F. A. (1990). Sex differences in the play behavior of immature spotted hyenas, *Crocuta crocuta*. *Hormones and Behavior, 24*, 403–420.

Pedersen, W. C., Miller, L. C., Putcha-Bhagavatula, A. D., & Yang, Y. (2002). Evolved sex differences in the number of partners desired? The long and short of it. *Psychological Science, 13*, 157–161.

Pellegrini, A. D., & Bartini, M. (2001). Dominance in early adolescent boys: Affiliative and aggressive dimensions and possible functions. *Merrill-Palmer Quarterly, 47*, 142–163.

Pellegrini, A. D., & Bjorklund, D. F. (2004). The ontogeny and phylogeny of children's object and fantasy play. *Human Nature, 15*, 23–43.

Pellegrini, A. D., Dupuis, D., & Smith, P. K. (2007). Play in evolution and development. *Developmental Review, 27*, 261–276.

Pellegrini, A. D., & Smith, P. K. (1998). Physical activity play: The nature and function of a neglected aspect of play. *Child Development, 69*, 577–598.

Pellegrini, A. D., & Smith, P. K. (Eds.). (2005). *The nature of play: Great apes and humans*. New York: Guilford Press.

Pellis, S. M. (2002). Sex differences in play fighting revisited: Traditional and non-traditional mechanisms of sexual differentiation in rats. *Archives of Sexual Behavior, 31*, 17–26.

Pellis, S. M., & Iwaniuk, A. N. (2000). Comparative analyses of the role of postnatal development on the expression of play fighting. *Developmental Psychobiology, 36*, 136–147.

Pellis, S. M., & Pellis, V. C. (2007). Rough-and-tumble play and the development of the social brain. *Current Directions in Psychological Science, 16*, 95–98.

Penn, D. J. (2002). The scent of genetic compatibility: Sexual selection and the major histocompatibility complex. *Ethology, 108*, 1–21.

Penn, D. J., & Potts, W. K. (1999). The evolution of mating preferences and major histocompatibility complex genes. *American Naturalist, 153*, 145–164.

Penner, A. M. (2003). International gender × item difficulty interactions in mathematics and science achievement tests. *Journal of Educational Psychology, 95*, 650–655.

Penton-Voak, I. S., Perrett, D. I., Castles, D. L., Kobayashi, T., Burt, D. M., Murray, L. K., & Minamisawa, R. (1999, June 24). Menstrual cycle alters face preference. *Nature, 399*, 741–742.

Pergams, O. R. W., Barnes, W. M., & Nyberg, D. (2003, May 22). Rapid change in mouse mitochondrial DNA: Wild mice around Chicago may have switched genotype to keep pace with modern living. *Nature, 423*, 397.

Perloe, S. I. (1992). Male mating competition, female choice and dominance in a free ranging group of Japanese macaques. *Primates, 33*, 289–304.

Perrenoud, A. (1991). The attenuation of mortality crises and the decline of mortality. In R. Schofield, D. Reher, & A. Bideau (Eds.), *The decline of mortality in Europe* (pp.18–37). Oxford, England: Oxford University Press.

Perrett, D. I., Penton-Voak, I. S., Little, A. C., Tiddeman, B. P., Burt, D. M., Schmidt, N., et al. (2002). Facial attractiveness judgments reflect learning of parental age characteristics. *Proceedings of the Royal Society of London B, 269*, 873–880.

Perrone, M., Jr., & Zaret, T. M. (1979). Parental care patterns of fishes. *American Naturalist, 113*, 351–361.

Pérusse, D. (1993). Cultural and reproductive success in industrialized societies: Testing the relationship at the proximate and ultimate levels. *Behavioral and Brain Sciences, 16*, 267–322.

Pérusse, D., Neale, M. C., Heath, A. C., & Eaves, L. J. (1994). Human parental behavior: Evidence for genetic influence and potential implication for gene-culture transmission. *Behavior Genetics, 24*, 327–335.

Peters, M. (1997). Gender differences in intercepting a moving target. *Journal of Motor Behavior, 29*, 290–296.

Petralia, S. M., & Gallup, G. G., Jr. (2002). Effects of a sexual assault scenario on hand-grip strength across the menstrual cycle. *Evolution and Human Behavior, 23*, 3–10.

Petren, K., Grant, B. R., & Grant, P. R. (1999). A phylogeny of Darwin's finches based on microsatellite DNA length variation. *Proceedings of the Royal Society of London B, 266*, 321–329.

Petrie, M. (1994, October 13). Improved growth and survival of offspring of peacocks with more elaborate trains. *Nature, 371*, 598–599.

Petrie, M., Halliday, T., & Sanders, C. (1991). Peahens prefer peacocks with elaborate trains. *Animal Behavior, 41*, 323–331.

Petrinovich, L., & Baptista, L. F. (1987). Song development in the white crowned sparrow: Modification of learned song. *Animal Behaviour, 35*, 961–974.

Pfaff, D. W., Phillips, M. I., & Rubin, R. T. (2004). *Principles of hormone/behavior relations*. New York. Academic Press.

Pheasant, S. T. (1983). Sex differences in strength—Some observations on their variability. *Applied Ergonomics, 14*, 205–211.

Phillips, K., & Silverman, I. (1997). Differences in the relationship of menstrual cycle phase to spatial performance on two- and three-dimensional tasks. *Hormones and Behavior, 32*, 167–175.

Phillips, K. A., Menard, W., & Fay, C. (2006). Gender similarities and differences in 200 individuals with body dysmorphic disorder. *Comprehensive Psychiatry, 47*, 77–87.

Phillips, S. D., & Imhoff, A. R. (1997). Women and career development: A decade of research. *Annual Review of Psychology, 48*, 31–59.

Phoenix, C. H., Goy, R. W., Gerall, A. A., & Young, W. C. (1959). Organizing action of prenatally administered testosterone propionate on the tissues mediating mating behavior in the female guinea pig. *Endocrinology, 65*, 369–382.

Pigliucci, M. (2006). Genetic variance–covariance matrices: A critique of the evolutionary quantitative genetics research program. *Biology and Philosophy, 21*, 1–23.

Pinker, S. (1994). *The language instinct*. New York: Morrow.

Pinker, S. (1997). *How the mind works*. New York: Norton.

Pinker, S. (1999). *Words and rules: The ingredients of language*. New York: Basic Books.

Pinker, S. (2008). *The sexual paradox: Men, women, and the real gender gap*. New York: Scribner.

Pinker, S., & Bloom, P. (1990). Natural language and natural selection. *Behavioral and Brain Sciences, 13*, 707–784.

Pipitone, R. N., & Gallup, G. G., Jr. (2008). Women's voice attractiveness varies across the menstrual cycle. *Evolution and Human Behavior, 29*, 268–274.

Pitcher, E. G., & Schultz, L. H. (1983). *Boys and girls at play: The development of sex roles*. South Hadley, MA: Bergin & Garvey.

Pizzari, T., Cornwallis, C. K., Løvlie, H., Jakobsson, S., & Birkhead, T. R. (2003, November 6). Sophisticated sperm allocation in male fowl. *Nature, 426*, 70–74.

Platek, S. M., Burch, R. L., Panyavin, I. S., Wasserman, B. H., & Gallup, G. G., Jr. (2002). Reactions to children's face resemblance affects males more than females. *Evolution and Human Behavior, 23*, 159–166.

Plavcan, J. M. (2000). Inferring social behavior from sexual dimorphism in the fossil record. *Journal of Human Evolution, 39*, 327–344.

Plavcan, J. M. (2001). Sexual dimorphism in primate evolution. *Yearbook of Physical Anthropology, 44*, 25–53.

Plavcan, J. M., & van Schaik, C. P. (1997). Intrasexual competition and body weight dimorphism in anthropoid primates. *American Journal of Physical Anthropology, 103*, 37–68.

Plavcan, J. M., van Schaik, C. P., & Kappeler, P. M. (1995). Competition, coalitions and canine size in primates. *Journal of Human Evolution, 28*, 245–276.

Pleck, J. H. (1997). Paternal involvement: Levels, sources, and consequences. In M. E. Lamb (Ed.), *The role of the father in child development* (3rd ed., pp. 66–103). New York: Wiley.

Plomin, R., Fulker, D. W., Corley, R., & DeFries, J. C. (1997). Nature, nurture, and cognitive development from 1 to 16 years: A parent–offspring adoption study. *Psychological Science, 8*, 442–447.

Poelwijk, F. J., Kiviet, D. J., Weinreich, D. M., & Tans, S. J. (2007, January 25). Empirical fitness landscapes reveal accessible evolutionary paths. *Nature, 445*, 383–386.

Pollet, T. V., & Nettle, D. (2008). Driving a hard bargain: Sex ratio and male marriage success in a historical US population. *Biology Letters, 4*, 31–33.

Pomiankowski, A., & Møller, A. P. (1995). A resolution of the lek paradox. *Proceedings of the Royal Society of London B, 260*, 21–29.

Poon, A., & Chao, L. (2004). Drift increases the advantage of sex in RNA bacteriophage Φ6. *Genetics, 166*, 19–24.

Posner, M. I. (1994). Attention: The mechanisms of consciousness. *Proceedings of the National Academy of Sciences USA, 91*, 7398–7403.

Potthoff, R. F., & Whittinghill, M. (1965). Maximum-likelihood estimation of the proportion of nonpaternity. *American Journal of Human Genetics, 17*, 480–494.

Potts, W. K., Manning, C. J., & Wakeland, E. K. (1991, August 15). Mating patterns in seminatural populations of mice influenced by MHC genotype. *Nature, 352,* 619–621.

Pound, N. (2002). Male interest in visual cues of sperm competition risk. *Evolution and Human Behavior, 23,* 443–466.

Povinelli, D. J. (2000). *Folk physics for apes: The chimpanzees theory of how the world works.* New York: Oxford University Press.

Power, T. G. (2000). *Play and exploration in children and animals.* Mahwah, NJ: Erlbaum.

Pratto, F. (1996). Sexual politics: The gender gap in the bedroom, the cupboard, and the cabinet. In D. M. Buss & N. M. Malamuth (Eds.), *Sex, power, conflict: Evolutionary and feminist perspectives* (pp. 179–230). New York: Oxford University Press.

Pratto, F., & Hegarty, P. (2000). The political psychology of reproductive strategies. *Psychological Science, 11,* 57–62.

Pratto, F., Sidanius, J., & Stallworth, L. M., & Malle, B. (1994). Social dominance orientation: A personality variable predicting social and political attitudes. *Journal of Personality and Social Psychology, 67,* 741–763.

Pratto, F., Stallworth, L. M., Sidanius, J., & Siers, B. (1997). The gender gap in occupational role attainment: A social dominance approach. *Journal of Personality and Social Psychology, 72,* 37–53.

Price, G. R. (1970, August 1). Selection and covariance. *Nature, 227,* 520–521.

Pruett-Jones, S., & Pruett-Jones, M. (1994). Sexual competition and courtship disruptions: Why do male bowerbirds destroy each other's bowers? *Animal Behaviour, 47,* 607–620.

Pryce, C. R. (1993). The regulation of maternal behaviour in marmosets and tamarins. *Behavioural Processes, 30,* 201–224.

Pryce, C. R. (1995). Determinants of motherhood in human and nonhuman primates: A biosocial model. In C. R. Pryce, R. D. Martin, & D. Skuse (Eds.), *Motherhood in human and nonhuman primates: Biosocial determinants* (pp. 1–15). Basel, Switzerland: Karger.

Pugh, K. R., Shaywitz, B. A., Shaywitz, S. E., Shankweiler, D. P., Katz, L., Fletcher, J. M., et al. (1997). Predicting reading performance from neuroimaging profiles: The cerebral basis of phonological effects in printed word identification. *Journal of Experimental Psychology: Human Perception and Performance, 23,* 299–318.

Pusey, A., Williams, J., & Goodall, J. (1997, August 8). The influence of dominance rank on the reproductive success of female chimpanzees. *Science, 277,* 828–831.

Puts, D. A. (2005). Mating context and menstrual phase affect women's preferences for male voice pitch. *Evolution and Human Behavior, 26,* 388–397.

Puts, D. A. (2006). Cycle variation in women's preferences for masculine traits. *Human Nature, 17,* 114–127.

Puts, D. A., McDaniel, M. A., Jordan, C. L., & Breedlove, S. M. (2008). Spatial ability and prenatal androgens: Meta-analyses of congenital adrenal hyperplasia and digit ratio (2D:4D) studies. *Archives of Sexual Behavior, 37,* 100–111.

Quinlan, R. J. (2003). Father absence, parental care, and female reproductive development. *Evolution and Human Behavior, 24,* 376–390.

Quinlan, R. J. (2007). Human parental effort and environmental risk. *Proceedings of the Royal Society of London B, 274,* 121–125.

Quinn, P. C., & Liben, L. S. (2008). A sex difference in mental rotation in young infants. *Psychological Science, 19,* 1067–1070.

Quintana-Murci, L., Chaix, R., Wells, R. S., Behar, D. M., Sayar, H., Scozzari, R., et al. (2004). Where west meets east: The complex mtDNA landscape of the southwest and central Asian corridor. *American Journal of Human Genetics, 74,* 827–845.

Qvarnström, A., Brommer, J. E., & Gustafsson, L. (2006, May 4). Testing the genetics underlying the co-evolution of mate choice and ornament in the wild. *Nature, 441,* 84–86.

Qvarnström, A., Pärt, T., & Sheldon, B. C. (2000, May 18). Adaptive plasticity in mate preference lined to differences in reproductive effort. *Nature, 405,* 344–347.

Qvarnström, A., & Price, T. D. (2001). Maternal effects, paternal effects and sexual selection. *Trends in Ecology & Evolution, 16,* 95–100.

Rahman, Q., Andersson, D., & Govier, E. (2005). A specific sexual orientation-related difference in navigation strategy. *Behavioral Neuroscience, 119,* 311–316.

Rahman, Q., & Koerting, J. (2008). Sexual orientation-related differences in allocentric spatial memory tasks. *Hippocampus, 18,* 55–63.

Rahman, Q., & Wilson, G. D. (2003). Large sexual-orientation-related differences in performance on mental rotation and judgment of line orientation tasks. *Neuropsychology, 17,* 25–31.

Ray, J. C., & Sapolsky, R. M. (1992). Styles of male social behavior and their endocrine correlates among high-ranking wild baboons. *American Journal of Primatology, 28,* 231–250.

Raymond, C. L., & Benbow, C. P. (1986). Gender differences in mathematics: A function of parental support and student sex typing? *Developmental Psychology, 22,* 808–819.

Read, D. W., & LeBlanc, S. A. (2003). Population growth, carrying capacity, and conflict. *Current Anthropology, 44,* 59–85.

Read, J. S., Troendle, J. F., & Klebanoff, M. A. (1997). Infectious disease mortality among infants in the United States, 1983 through 1987. *American Journal of Public Health, 87,* 192–198.

Reavis, R., & Overman, W. H. (2001). Adult sex differences on a decision-making task previously shown to depend on the orbital prefrontal cortex. *Behavioral Neuroscience, 115,* 196–206.

Redouté, J., Stoléru, S., Grégoire, M.-C., Costes, N., Cinotti, L., Lavenne, F., et al. (2000). Brain processing of visual sexual stimuli in human males. *Human Brain Mapping, 11,* 162–177.

Reed, W. L., Clark, M. E., Parker, P. G., Raouf, S. A., Arguedas, N., Monk, D. S., et al. (2006). Physiological effects on demography: A long-term experimental study of testosterone's effects on fitness. *American Naturalist, 167,* 667–683.

Regalski, J. M., & Gaulin, S. J. C. (1993). Whom are Mexican infants said to resemble? Monitoring and fostering paternal confidence in the Yucatan. *Ethology and Sociobiology, 14,* 97–113.

Regan, P.C., & Dreyer, C. S. (1999). Lust? Love? Status? Young adults' motives for engaging in casual sex. *Journal of Psychology and Human Sexuality, 11,* 1–24.

Rehnman, J., & Herlitz, A. (2006). Higher face recognition ability in girls: Magnified by own-sex and own-ethnicity bias. *Memory, 14,* 289–296.

Rehnman, J., & Herlitz, A. (2007). Women remember more faces than men do. *Acta Psychologica, 124,* 344–355.

Reid, A. (1997). Locality or class? Spatial and social differentials in infant and child mortality in England and Wales, 1895–1911. In C. A. Corsini & P. P. Viazzo (Eds.), *The decline of infant and child mortality* (pp. 129–154). The Hague, Netherlands: Martinus Nijhoff.

Reid, I. (1998). *Class in Britain.* Cambridge, England: Polity Press.

Reid, J. M., Arcese, P., Cassidy, A. L. E. V., Hiebert, S. M., Smith, J. N. M., Stoddard, P., et al. (2005). Fitness correlates of song repertoire in free-living song sparrows (*Melospiza melodia*). *American Naturalist, 165,* 299–310.

Reinius, B., Saetre, P., Leonard, J. A., Blekhman, R., Merion-Martinez, R., Gilad, Y., & Jazin, E. (2008). An evolutionarily conserved sexual signature in the primate brain. *PLoS Genetics, 4,* 1–13. Retrieved September 2, 2008, from http://www.plosgenetics.org/article/info:doi%2F10.1371%2Fjournal.pgen.1000100

Reiss, D. (1995). Genetic influences on family systems: Implications for development. *Journal of Marriage and the Family, 57,* 543–560.

Reynolds, J. D. (1987). Mating system and nesting biology of the Red-necked Phalarope *Phalaropus lobatus:* What constrains polyandry? *Isis, 129,* 225–242.

Reynolds, J. D., & Székely, T. (1997). The evolution of parental care in shorebirds: Life histories, ecology, and sexual selection. *Behavioral Ecology, 8,* 126–134.

Reynolds, S. M., Dryer, K., Bollback, J., Uy, J. A. C., Patricelli, G. L., Robson, T., et al. (2007). Behavioral paternity predicts genetic paternity in satin bowerbirds (*Ptilonorhynchus violaceus*), a species with a non-resource-based mating system. *Auk, 124,* 857–867.

Reznick, D. N., & Bryga, H. A. (1996). Life-history evolution in guppies (*Poecilia reticulata: Poeciliidae*). V. Genetic basis of parallelism in life histories. *American Naturalist, 147,* 339–359.

Reznick, D. N., & Endler, J. A. (1982). The impact of predation on life history evolution in Trinidadian guppies (*Poecilia reticulata*). *Evolution, 36,* 160–177.

Reznick, D. N., & Ricklefs, R. E. (2009, February 12). Darwin's bridge between microevolution and macroevolution. *Nature, 457,* 837–842.

Reznick, D. N., Shaw, F. H., Rodd, F. H., & Shaw, R. G. (1997, March 28). Evaluation of the rate of evolution in natural populations of guppies (*Poecilia reticulata*). *Science, 275*, 1934–1937.

Rhen, T., & Crews, D. (2002). Variation in reproductive behavior within a sex: Neural systems and endocrine activation. *Journal of Neuroendocrinology, 14*, 517–531.

Rice, W. R. (2002). Experimental tests of the adaptive significance of sexual recombination. *Nature Reviews: Genetics, 3*, 241–251.

Richmond, B. G., & Jungers, W. L. (1995). Size variation and sexual dimorphism in *Australopithecus afarensis* and living hominoids. *Journal of Human Evolution, 29*, 229–245.

Ridley, M. (1993). *The red queen: Sex and the evolution of human nature*. New York: Penguin Books.

Rilling, J. K., Kaufman, T. L., Smith, E. O., Patel, R., & Worthman, C. M. (2009). Abdominal depth and waist circumference as influential determinants of human female attractiveness. *Evolution and Human Behavior, 30*, 21–31.

Robbins, M. M. (1999). Male mating patterns in wild multimale mountain gorilla groups. *Animal Behaviour, 57*, 1013–1020.

Robbins, M. M., Bermejo, M., Cipolletta, C., Magliocca, P., Parnell, R. J., & Stokes, E. (2004). Social structure and life-history patterns in Western gorillas (*Gorilla gorilla gorilla*). *American Journal of Primatology, 64*, 145–159.

Robbins, M. M., Robbins, A. M., Gerald-Steklis, N., & Steklis, H. D. (2007). Socioecological influences on the reproductive success of female mountain gorillas (*Gorilla beringei beringei*). *Behavioral Ecology and Sociobiology, 61*, 919–931.

Robbins, M. M., & Sawyer, S. C. (2007). Intergroup encounters in mountain gorillas of Bwindi Impenetrable National Park, Uganda. *Behaviour, 144*, 1497–1519.

Roberts, M. L., Buchanan, K. L., & Evans, M. R. (2004). Testing the immunocompetence handicap hypothesis: A review of the evidence. *Animal Behaviour, 68*, 227–239.

Roberts, M. L., Buchanan, K. L., Hasselquist, D., & Evans, M. R. (2007). Effects of testosterone and corticosterone on immunocompetence in a zebra finch. *Hormones and Behavior, 51*, 126–134.

Roberts, S. C., Havlicek, J., Flegr, J., Hruskova, M., Little, A. C., Jones, B. C., et al. (2004). Female facial attractiveness increases during the fertile phase of the menstrual cycle. *Proceedings of the Royal Society of London B, 271*, S270–S272.

Roberts, S. C., Little, A. C., Gosling, L. M., Perrett, D. I., Carter, V., Jones B. C., et al. (2005). MHC-heterozygosity and human facial attractiveness. *Evolution and Human Behavior, 26*, 213–216.

Robinson, J. G. (1982). Intrasexual competition and mate choice in primates. *American Journal of Primatology Supplement, 1*, 131–144.

Rodd, F. H., Reznick, D. N., & Skolowski, M. B. (1997). Phenotypic plasticity in life history traits of guppies: Responses to social environment. *Ecology, 78*, 419–433.

Rodman, P. S., & Mitani, J. C. (1987). Orangutans: Sexual dimorphism in a solitary species. In B. B. Smuts, D. L. Cheney, R. M. Seyfarth, R. W. Wrangham, &

T. T. Struhsaker (Eds.), *Primate societies* (pp. 146–164). Chicago: The University of Chicago Press.

Rodseth, L., Wrangham, R. W., Harrigan, A. M., & Smuts, B. B. (1991). The human community as a primate society. *Current Anthropology, 32,* 221–254.

Roff, D. A. (1992). *The evolution of life histories: Theory and analysis.* New York: Chapman & Hall.

Rogers, A. R., & Mukherjee, A. (1992). Quantitative genetics of sexual dimorphism in human body size. *Evolution, 46,* 226–234.

Rogers, M., Hennigan, K., Bowman, C., & Miller, N. (1984). Intergroup acceptance in classroom and playground settings. In N. Miller & M. B. Brewer (Eds.), *Groups in contact: The psychology of desegregation* (pp. 213–227). Orlando, FL: Academic Press.

Rohwer, S., Herron, J. C., & Daly, M. (1999). Stepparental behavior as mating effort in birds and other animals. *Evolution and Human Behavior, 20,* 367–390.

Rollet, C. (1997). Childhood mortality in high-risk groups: Some methodological reflections based on French experience. In C. A. Corsini & P. P. Viazzo (Eds.), *The decline of infant and child mortality* (pp. 213–225). The Hague, Netherlands: Martinus Nijhoff.

Roney, J. R., Mahler, S. V., & Maestripieri, D. (2003). Behavioral and hormonal responses of men to brief interactions with women. *Evolution and Human Behavior, 24,* 365–375.

Roney, J. R., & Simmons, Z. L. (2008). Women's estradiol predicts preferences for facial cues of men's testosterone. *Hormones and Behavior, 53,* 14–19.

Rose, A. J., & Asher, S. R. (1999). Children's goals and strategies in response to conflicts within a friendship. *Developmental Psychology, 35,* 69–79.

Rose, A. J., Carlson, W., & Waller, E. M. (2007). Prospective associations of co-rumination with friendship and emotional adjustment: Considering the socioemotional trade-offs of co-rumination. *Developmental Psychology, 43,* 1019–1031.

Rose, A. J., & Rudolph, K. D. (2006). A review of sex differences in peer relationship processes: Potential trade-offs for the emotional and behavioral development of girls and boys. *Psychological Bulletin, 132,* 98–131.

Rosen, B. N., & Peterson, L. (1990). Gender differences in children's outdoor play injuries: A review and an integration. *Clinical Psychology Review, 10,* 187–205.

Rosen, W. D., Adamson, L. B., & Bakeman, R. (1992). An experimental investigation of infant social referencing: Mothers' messages and gender differences. *Developmental Psychology, 28,* 1172–1178.

Rosenthal, R., Hall, J. A., DiMatteo, M. R., Rogers, P. L., & Archer, D. (1979). *Sensitivity to nonverbal communication: The PONS test.* Baltimore: The Johns Hopkins University Press.

Rotter, N. G., & Rotter, G. S. (1988). Sex differences in the encoding and decoding of negative facial emotions. *Journal of Nonverbal Behavior, 12,* 139–148.

Roulin, A. (1999). Nonrandom pairing by male barn owls (*Tyto alba*) with respect to a female plumage trait. *Behavioral Ecology, 10*, 688–695.

Roulin, A., Ducrest, A.-L., Balloux, F., Dijkstra, C., & Riols, C. (2003). A female melanin ornament signals offspring fluctuating asymmetry in the barn owl. *Proceedings of the Royal Society London B, 270*, 167–171.

Roulin, A., Jungi, T. W., Pfister, H., & Dijkstra, C. (2000). Female bard owls (*Tyto alba*) advertise good genes. *Proceedings of the Royal Society London B, 267*, 937–941.

Roulin, A., Riols, C. Dijkstra, C., & Ducrest, A.-L., (2001). Female plumage spottiness signals parasite resistance in the barn owl (*Tyto alba*). *Behavioral Ecology, 12*, 103–110.

Round, J. M., Jones, D. A., Honour, J. W., & Nevill, A. M. (1999). Hormonal factors in the development of differences in strength between boys and girls during adolescence: A longitudinal study. *Annals of Human Biology, 26*, 49–62.

Rowe, D. C. (1994). *The limits of family influence: Genes, experience, and behavior*. New York: Guilford Press.

Rowe, D. C. (2002). What twin and adoption studies reveal about parenting. In J. G. Borkowski, S. L. Ramey, & M. Bristol-Power (Eds.), *Parenting and the child's world: Influences on academic, intellectual, and social-emotional development* (pp. 21–34). Mahwah, NJ: Erlbaum.

Royle, N. J., Hartley, I. R., & Parker, G. A. (2002, April 18). Sexual conflict reduces offspring fitness in zebra finches. *Nature, 416*, 733–736.

Rozin, P. (1976). The evolution of intelligence and access to the cognitive unconscious. In J. M. Sprague & A. N. Epstein (Eds.), *Progress in psychobiology and physiological psychology* (Vol. 6, pp. 245–280). New York: Academic Press.

Rozin, P., & Fallon, A. (1988). Body image, attitudes to weight, and misperceptions of figure preferences of the opposite sex: A comparison of men and women in two generations. *Journal of Abnormal Psychology, 97*, 342–345.

Rubenstein, D. R. (2007). Female extrapair mate choice in a cooperative breeder: Trading sex for help and increasing offspring heterozygosity. *Proceedings of the Royal Society of London B, 274*, 1895–1903.

Rubin, K. H., Fein, G. G., & Vandenberg, B. (1983). Play. In P. Mussen & E. M. Hetherington (Eds.), *Handbook of child psychology: Socialization, personality, and social development* (4th ed., Vol. 4, pp. 693–774). New York: Wiley.

Ruff, C. B., Trinkaus, E., & Holliday, T. W. (1997, May 8). Body mass and encephalization in Pleistocene *Homo*. *Nature, 387*, 173–176.

Rushton, J. P. (1996). Self-report delinquency and violence in adult twins. *Psychiatric Genetics, 6*, 87–89.

Rushton, J. P., & Ankney, C. D. (1996). Brain size and cognitive ability: Correlations with age, sex, social class, and race. *Psychonomic Bulletin & Review, 3*, 21–36.

Rushton, J. P., & Ankney, C. D. (2009). Whole brain size and general mental ability: A review. *International Journal of Neuroscience, 119*, 691–731.

Russell, T. A., Tchanturia, K., Rahman, Q., & Schmidt, U. (2007). Sex differences in theory of mind: A male advantage on Happé's "cartoon" task. *Cognition and Emotion, 21*, 1554–1564.

Russon, A. E., & Begun, D. R. (Eds.). (2004). *The evolution of thought: Evolutionary origins of great ape intelligence*. Cambridge, England: Cambridge University Press.

Ryan, M. J., & Keddy-Hector, A. (1992). Directional patterns of female mate choice and the role of sensory biases. *American Naturalist, 139*, S4–S35.

Rymarczyk, K., & Grabowska, A. (2007). Sex differences in brain control of prosody. *Neuropsychologia, 45*, 921–930.

Sabini, J., & Green, M. C (2004). Emotional responses to sexual and emotional infidelity: Constants and differences across genders, samples, and methods. *Personality and Social Psychology Bulletin, 30*, 1375–1388.

Sæther, S. A., Fiske, P., & Kålås, A. (2001). Male mate choice, sexual conflict and strategic allocation of copulations in a lekking bird. *Proceedings of the Royal Society London B, 268*, 2097–2102.

Sagarin, B. J., Becker, D. V., Guadagno, R. E., Nicastle, L. D., & Millevoi, A. (2003). Sex differences (and similarities) in jealousy: The moderating influence of infidelity experience and sexual orientation of the infidelity. *Evolution and Human Behavior, 24*, 17–23.

Saino, N., Bolzern, A. M., & Møller, A. P. (1997). Immunocompetence, ornamentation, and viability of male barn swallows (*Hirundo rustica*). *Proceedings of the National Academy of Sciences USA, 94*, 549–552.

Saino, N., Incagli, M., Martinelli, R., & Møller, A. P. (2002). Immune response of male barn swallows in relation to parental effort, corticosterone plasma levels, and sexual ornamentation. *Behavioral Ecology, 13*, 169–174.

Saino, N., & Møller, A. P. (1994). Secondary sexual characteristics, parasites and testosterone in the barn swallow, *Hirundo rustica*. *Animal Behaviour, 48*, 1325–1333.

Saino, N., Møller, A. P., & Bolzern, A. M. (1995). Testosterone effects on the immune system and parasite infestations in the barn swallow (*Hirundo rustica*): An experimental test of the immunocompetence hypothesis. *Behavioral Ecology, 6*, 397–404.

Saino, N., Primmer, C. R., Ellegren, H., & Møller, A. P. (1997). An experimental study of paternity and tail ornamentation in the barn swallow (*Hirundo rustica*). *Evolution, 51*, 562–570.

Salvador, A. (2005). Coping with competitive situations in humans. *Neuroscience and Biobehavioral Reviews, 29*, 195–205.

Salzano, F. M., Neel, J. V., & Maybury-Lewis, D. (1967). Further studies of the Xavante Indians: I. Demographic data on two additional villages: Genetic structure of the tribe. *American Journal of Human Genetics, 19*, 463–489.

Sandberg, D. E., & Meyer-Bahlburg, H. F. L. (1994). Variability in middle childhood play behavior: Effects of gender, age, and family background. *Archives of Sexual Behavior, 23*, 645–663.

Sapolsky, R. M. (1993). The physiology of dominance in stable versus unstable social hierarchies. In W. A. Mason & S. P. Mendoza (Eds.), *Primate social conflict* (pp. 171–204). Albany: State University of New York Press.

Sapolsky, R. M. (2005, April 29). The influence of social hierarchy on primate health. *Science, 308,* 648–652.

Sargent, R. C., Rush, V. N., Wisenden, B. D., & Yan, H. Y. (1998). Courtship and mate choice in fishes: Integrating behavioral and sensory ecology. *American Zoologist, 38,* 82–96.

Sarkadi, A., Kristiansson, R., Oberklaid, F., & Bremberg, S. (2008). Fathers' involvement and children's developmental outcomes: A systematic review of longitudinal studies. *Acta Pædiatrica, 97,* 153–158.

Sasse, G., Muller, H., Chakraborty, R., & Ott, J. (1994). Estimating the frequency of nonpaternity in Switzerland. *Human Heredity, 44,* 337–343.

Sato, A., O'Huigin, C., Figueroa, F., Grant, P. R., Grant, B. R., Tichy, H., & Klein, J. (1999). Phylogeny of Darwin's finches as revealed by mtDNA sequences. *Proceedings of the National Academy of Sciences USA, 96,* 5101–5106.

Saucier, D., Bowman, M., & Elias, L. (2003). Sex differences in the effect of articulatory or spatial dual-task interference during navigation. *Brain and Cognition, 53,* 346–350.

Savin-Williams, R. C. (1987). *Adolescence: An ethological perspective.* New York: Springer-Verlag.

Sawaguchi, T. (1997). Possible involvement of sexual selection in neocortical evolution of monkeys and apes. *Folia Primatologica, 68,* 95–99.

Saxe, R., & Kanwisher, N. (2003). People thinking about people: The role of the temporo-parietal junction in "theory of mind." *NeuroImage, 19,* 1835–1842.

Scarr, S. (1992). Developmental theories of the 1990s: Developmental and individual differences. *Child Development, 63,* 1–19.

Scarr, S., & McCarthy, K. (1983). How people make their own environments: A theory of genotype leading to environment effects. *Child Development, 54,* 424–435.

Scarr, S., Phillips, D., & McCartney, K. (1989). Working mothers and their families. *American Psychologist, 44,* 1402–1409.

Schall, J. J., & Staats, C. M. (1997). Parasites and the evolution of extravagant male characteristics: *Anolis* lizards on Caribbean islands as a test of the Hamilton-Zuk hypothesis. *Oecologia, 111,* 543–548.

Schattmann, L., & Sherwin, B. B. (2007). Effects of pharmacologic manipulation of testosterone on cognitive functioning in women with polycystic ovary syndrome: A randomized, placebo-controlled treatment study. *Hormones and Behavior, 51,* 579–586.

Scheib, J. E., Gangestad, S. W., & Thornhill, R. (1999). Facial attractiveness, symmetry and cues of good genes. *Proceedings of the Royal Society of London B, 266,* 1913–1917.

Schiff, W., & Oldak, R. (1990). Accuracy of judging time to arrival: Effects of modality, trajectory, and gender. *Journal of Experimental Psychology: Human Perception and Performance, 16,* 303–316.

Schirmer, A., Kotz, S. A., & Friederici, A. D. (2005). On the role of attention for the processing of emotions in speech: Sex differences revisited. *Cognitive Brain Research, 24,* 442–452.

Schlupp, I., Marler, C., & Ryan, M. J. (1994, January 21). Benefit to male sailfin mollies of mating with heterospecific females. *Science, 263,* 373–374.

Schluter, D. (2001). Ecology and the origin of species. *Trends in Ecology and Evolution, 16,* 372–380.

Schmitt, D. P., & Buss, D. M. (1996). Strategic self-promotion and competitor derogation: Sex and context effects on the perceived effectiveness of mate attraction tactics. *Journal of Personality and Social Psychology, 70,* 1185–1204.

Schmitt, D. P., & 118 members of the International Sexuality Description Project. (2003). Universal sex differences in the desire for sexual variety: Tests from 52 nations, 6 continents, and 13 islands. *Journal of Personality and Social Psychology, 85,* 85–104.

Schmitt, D. P., & 121 members of the International Sexuality Description Project. (2004). Patterns and universals of mate preferences across 53 nations: The effects of sex, culture, and personality and romantically attracting another person's partner. *Journal of Personality and Social Psychology, 86,* 560–584.

Schmitt, D. P., & Realo, A., Voracek, M., & Allik, J. (2008). Why can't a man be more like a woman? Sex differences in big five personality traits across 55 cultures. *Journal of Personality and Social Psychology, 94,* 168–192.

Schneider, D. J. (1973). Implicit personality theory: A review. *Psychological Bulletin, 79,* 294–309.

Schoech, S. J., Mumme, R. L., & Wingfield, J. C. (1996). Prolactin and helping behaviour in the cooperatively breeding Florida scrub-jay, *Aphelocoma c. coerulescens. Animal Behaviour, 52,* 445–456.

Schöning, S., Engelien, A., Kugel, H., Schäfer, S., Schiffbauer, H., Zwitserlood, P., et al. (2007). Functional anatomy of visuo-spatial working memory during mental rotation is influenced by sex, menstrual cycle, and sex steroid hormones. *Neuropsychologia, 45,* 3202–3214.

Schultheiss, O. C., Dargel, A., & Rohde, W. (2003). Implicit motives and gonadal steroid hormones: Effects of menstrual cycle phase, oral contraceptive use, and relationship status. *Hormones and Behavior, 43,* 293–301.

Schultheiss, O. C., & Rohde, W. (2002). Implicit power motivation predicts men's testosterone changes and implicit learning in a contest situation. *Hormones and Behavior, 41,* 195–202.

Schultheiss, O. C., Wirth, M. M., & Stanton, S. J. (2004). Effects of affiliation and power motivation arousal on salivary progesterone and testosterone. *Hormones and Behavior, 46,* 592–599.

Schultheiss, O. C., Wirth, M. M., Torges, C. M., Pang, J. C., Villacorta, M. A., & Welsh, K. M. (2005). Effects of implicit power motivation on men's and women's implicit learning and testosterone changes after social victory or defeat. *Journal of Personality and Social Psychology, 88,* 174–188.

Schultz, H. (1991). Social differences in mortality in the eighteenth century: An analysis of Berlin church registers. *International Review of Social History, 36,* 232–248.

Schutter, D. J. L. G., Peper, J. S., Koppeschaar, H. P. F., Kahn, R. S., & van Honk, J. (2005). Administration of testosterone increases functional connectivity in a cortico-cortical depression circuit. *Journal of Neuropsychiatry and Clinical Neuroscience, 17,* 372–377.

Schützwohl, A., & Koch, S. (2004). Sex differences in jealousy: The recall of cues to sexual and emotional infidelity in personally more and less threatening context conditions. *Evolution and Human Behavior, 25,* 249–257.

Schwarz, S., & Hassebrauck, M. (2008). Self-perceived and observed variations in women's attractiveness throughout the menstrual cycle—A diary study. *Evolution and Human Behavior, 29,* 282–288.

Schyns, P. G., Bonnar, L., & Gosselin, F. (2002). Show me the features! Understanding recognition from the use of visual information. *Psychological Science, 13,* 402–409.

Scott, S. H. (2004). Optimal feedback control and the neural basis of volitional motor control. *Nature Reviews: Neuroscience, 5,* 534–546.

Scutt, D., & Manning, J. T. (1996). Symmetry and ovulation in women. *Human Reproduction, 11,* 2477–2480.

Sear, R. (2006). Height and reproductive success: How a Gambian population compares with the West. *Human Nature, 17,* 405–418.

Sear, R., & Mace, R. (2008). Who keeps children alive? A review of the effects of kin on child survival. *Evolution and Human Behavior, 29,* 1–18.

Sear, R., Steele, F., McGregor, I. A., & Mace, R. (2002). The effects of kin on child mortality in rural Gambia. *Demography, 39,* 43–63.

Seddon, N., Merrill, R. M., & Tobias, J. A. (2008). Sexually selected traits predict patterns of species richness in a diverse clade of suboscine birds. *American Naturalist, 171,* 620–631.

Seehausen, O., Terai, Y., Magalhaes, I. S., Carleton, K. L., Mrosso, H. D. J., Miyagi, R., et al. (2008, October 2). Speciation through sensory drive in cichlid fish. *Nature, 455,* 620–626.

Seielstad, M. T., Minch, E., & Cavalli-Sforza, L. L. (1998). Genetic evidence for a higher female migration rate in humans. *Nature Genetics, 20,* 278–280.

Selander, R. K. (1965). On mating systems and sexual selection. *American Naturalist, 99,* 129–141.

Sellen, D. W., Borgerhoff Mulder, M., & Sieff, D. F. (2000). Fertility, offspring quality, and wealth in Datoga pastoralists: *Testing evolutionary models of intersexual selection.* In L. Cronk, N. Chagnon, & W. Irons (Eds.), *Adaptation and human behavior: An anthropological perspective* (pp. 91–114). New York: Aldine De Gruyter.

Semino, O., Passarino, G., Oefner, P. J., Lin, A. A., Arbuzova, S., Beckman, L. E., et al. (2000, November 10). The genetic legacy of Paleolithic *Homo sapiens* in extant Europeans: A Y chromosome perspective. *Science, 290,* 1155–1159.

Serbin, L. A., Powlishta, K. K., & Gulko, J. (1993). The development of sex typing in middle childhood. *Monographs of the Society for Research in Child Development, 58* (No. 2, Serial No. 232).

Setalaphruk, C., & Price, L. L. (2007). Children's traditional ecological knowledge of wild food resources: A case study in a rural village in Northeast Thailand. *Journal of Ethnobiology and Ethnomedicine, 3,* 33. Retrieved October 12, 2008, from http://www.ethnobiomed.com/content/3/1/33

Setchell, J. M. (2003). The evolution of alternative reproductive morphs in male primates. In C. B. Jones (Ed.), *Sexual selection and reproductive competition in primates: New perspectives and directions* (pp. 413–435). Norman, OK: American Society of Primatologists.

Setchell, J. M., Charpentier, M., & Wickings, E. J. (2005). Mate guarding and paternity in mandrills: Factors influencing alpha male monopoly. *Animal Behaviour, 70,* 1105–1120.

Setchell, J. M., & Dixson, A. F. (2001). Changes in the secondary sexual adornments of male mandrills (*Mandrillus sphinx*) are associated with gain and loss of alpha status. *Hormones and Behavior, 39,* 177–184.

Setchell, J. M., Lee, P. C., Wickings, E. J., & Dixson, A. F. (2001). Growth and ontogeny of sexual size dimorphism in the mandrill (*Mandrillus sphinx*). *American Journal of Physical Anthropology, 115,* 349–360.

Setchell, J. M., Smith, T., Wickings, E. J., & Knapp, L. A. (2008). Social correlates of testosterone and ornamentation in male mandrills. *Hormones and Behavior, 54,* 365–372.

Setchell, J. M., & Wickings, E. J. (2005). Dominance, status signals and coloration in male mandrills (*Mandrillus sphinx*). *Ethology, 111,* 25–50.

Setchell, J. M., Wickings, E. J., & Knapp, L. A. (2006). Life history in male mandrills (*Mandrillus sphinx*): Physical development, dominance rank, and group association. *American Journal of Physical Anthropology, 131,* 498–510.

Shackelford, T. K., Buss, D. M., & Weekes-Shackelford, V. A. (2003). Wife killings committed in the context of a lovers triangle. *Basic and Applied Social Psychology, 25,* 137–143.

Shackelford, T. K., & Goetz, A. T. (2006). Comparative evolutionary psychology of sperm competition. *Journal of Comparative Psychology, 120,* 139–146.

Shackelford, T. K., & Larsen, R. J. (1997). Facial asymmetry as an indicator of psychological, emotional, and physiological distress. *Journal of Personality and Social Psychology, 72,* 456–466.

Shackelford, T. K., Voracek, M., Schmitt, D. P., Buss, D. M., Weekes-Shackelford, V. A., & Michalski, R. L. (2004). Romantic jealousy in early adulthood and in later life. *Human Nature, 15,* 283–300.

Shapiro, D. H., Jr., Schwartz, C. E., & Astin, J. A. (1996). Controlling ourselves, controlling our world: Psychology's role in understanding positive and negative consequences of seeking and gaining control. *American Psychologist, 51,* 1213–1230.

Shaywitz, B. A., Shaywitz, S. E., Pugh, K. R., Constable, R. T., Skudlarski, P., Fulbright, R. K., et al. (1995, February 2). Sex differences in the functional organization of the brain for language. *Nature, 373,* 607–609.

Sheeber, L. B., Davis, B., Leve, C., Hops, H., & Tildesley, E. (2007). Adolescents' relationships with their mothers and fathers: Associations with depressive disorder and subdiagnostic symptomatology. *Journal of Abnormal Psychology, 116,* 144–154.

Sheeran, P., & Orbell, S. (2000). Self-schemas and the theory of planned behaviour. *European Journal of Social Psychology, 30,* 533–550.

Sheldon, B. C. (2000). Differential allocation: Tests, mechanisms and implications. *Trends in Ecology and Evolution, 15,* 397–402.

Sheldon, B. C., Merilä, J., Qvarnström, A., Gustafsson, L., & Ellegren, H. (1997). Paternal genetic contribution to offspring condition predicted by size of male secondary sexual character. *Proceedings of the Royal Society of London B, 264,* 297–302.

Sheldon, M. S., Cooper, L. Geary, D. C., Hoard, M. K., & DeSoto, M. C. (2006). Estrogen fluctuation and sexual motives. *Personality and Social Psychology Bulletin, 32,* 1659–1673.

Shepard, R. N. (1994). Perceptual-cognitive universals as reflections of the world. *Psychonomic Bulletin & Review, 1,* 2–28.

Sherry, D. F., Forbes, M. R. L., Khurgel, M., & Ivy, G. O. (1993). Females have a larger hippocampus than males in the brood-parasitic brown-headed cowbird. *Proceedings of the National Academy of Sciences USA, 90,* 7839–7843.

Sherry, D. F., & Hampson, E. (1997). Evolution and the hormonal control of sexually-dimorphic spatial abilities in humans. *Trends in Cognitive Sciences, 1,* 50–56.

Sherry, D. F., Vaccarino, A. L., Buckenham, K., & Herz, R. S. (1989). The hippocampal complex of food-storing birds. *Brain, Behavior & Evolution, 34,* 308–317.

Shin, Y. W., Kim, D. J., Hyon, T., Park, H. J., Moon, W. J., Chung, E. C., et al. (2005). Sex differences in the human corpus callosum: Diffusion tensor imaging study. *NeuroReport, 16,* 795–798.

Shine, R. (1978). Propagule size and parental care: The "safe harbor" hypothesis. *Journal of Theoretical Biology, 75,* 417–424.

Shirao, N., Okamoto, Y., Mantani, T., Okamoto, Y., & Yamawaki, S. (2005). Gender differences in brain activity generated by unpleasant word stimuli concerning body image: An fMRI study. *British Journal of Psychiatry, 186,* 48–53.

Shtulman, A. (2006). Qualitative differences between naïve and scientific theories of evolution. *Cognitive Psychology, 52,* 170–194.

Shuster, S. M., & Wade, M. J. (2003). *Mating systems and strategies.* Princeton, NJ: Princeton University Press.

Shyue, S.-K., Hewett-Emmett, D., Sperling, H. G., Hunt, D. M., Bowmaker, J. K., Mollon, J. D., & Li, W.-H. (1995, September 1). Adaptive evolution of color vision in higher primates. *Science, 269,* 1265–1267.

Sidanius, J., & Ekehammar, B. (1983). Sex, political party preference, and higher-order dimensions of sociopolitical ideology. *Journal of Psychology, 115,* 233–239.

Sidanius, J., Pratto, F., & Bobo, L. (1994). Social dominance orientation and the political psychology of gender: A case of invariance? *Journal of Personality and Social Psychology, 67,* 998–1011.

Sidanius, J., Pratto, F., & Mitchell, M. (2001). In-group identification, social dominance orientation, and differential intergroup social allocation. *Journal of Social Psychology, 134,* 151–167.

Siefferman, L., & Hill, G. E. (2005). Blue structural coloration predicts incubation provisioning in eastern bluebirds. *Journal of Avian Biology, 36,* 488–493.

Siegler, R. S. (1996). *Emerging minds: The process of change in children's thinking.* New York: Oxford University Press.

Sigg, H., Stolba, A., Abegglen, J.-J., & Dasser, V. (1982). Life history of hamadryas baboons: Physical development, infant mortality, reproductive parameters and family relationships. *Primates, 23,* 473–487.

Silk, J. B. (1987). Social behavior in evolutionary perspective. In B. B. Smuts, D. L. Cheney, R. M. Seyfarth, R. W. Wrangham, & T. T. Struhsaker (Eds.), *Primate societies* (pp. 318–329). Chicago: The University of Chicago Press.

Silk, J. B. (1993). The evolution of social conflict among female primates. In W. A. Mason & S. P. Mendoza (Eds.), *Primate social conflict* (pp. 49–83). Albany: State University of New York Press.

Silk, J. B. (2007, September 7). Social components of fitness in primate groups. *Science, 317,* 1347–1351.

Silk, J. B., Alberts, S. C., & Altmann, J. (2003, November 14). Social bonds of female baboons enhance infant survival. *Science, 302,* 1231–1234.

Silverman, I., Choi, J., Mackewn, A., Fisher, M., Moro, J., & Ohshansky, E. (2000). Evolved mechanisms underlying wayfinding: Further studies on the hunter-gatherer theory of spatial sex differences. *Evolution and Human Behavior, 21,* 201–213.

Silverman, I., & Eals, M. (1992). Sex differences in spatial abilities: Evolutionary theory and data. In J. H. Barkow, L. Cosmides, & J. Tooby (Eds.), *The adapted mind: Evolutionary psychology and the generation of culture* (pp. 533–549). New York: Oxford University Press.

Simmons, L. W., & Kotiaho, J. S. (2007). Quantitative genetic correlation between trait and preference supports a sexually selected sperm process. *Proceedings of the National Academy of Sciences USA, 104,* 16604–16608.

Simner, M. L. (1971). Newborn's response to the cry of another infant. *Developmental Psychology, 5,* 136–150.

Simon, H. A. (1956). Rational choice and the structure of the environment. *Psychological Review, 63,* 129–138.

Sinervo, B., Miles, D. B., Frankino, A., Klukowski, M., & DeNardo, D. F. (2000). Testosterone, endurance, and Darwinian fitness: Natural and sexual selection on the physiological bases of alternative male behaviors in side-blotched lizards. *Hormones and Behavior, 38,* 222–333.

Sinervo, B., & Svensson, E. (1998). Mechanistic and selective causes of life history trade-offs and plasticity. *Oikos, 83,* 432–442.

Singh, D. (1993a). Adaptive significance of female physical attractiveness: Role of waist-to-hip ratio. *Journal of Personality and Social Psychology, 65,* 293–307.

Singh, D. (1993b). Body shape and women's attractiveness: The critical role of waist-to-hip ratio. *Human Nature, 4,* 297–321.

Singh, D. (1995a). Female health, attractiveness, and desirability for relationships: Role of breast asymmetry and waist-to-hip ratio. *Ethology and Sociobiology, 16,* 465–481.

Singh, D. (1995b). Female judgment of male attractiveness and desirability for relationships: Role of waist-to-hip ratio and financial status. *Journal of Personality and Social Psychology, 69,* 1089–1101.

Singh, D., & Bronstad, P. M. (2001). Female body odour is a potential cue to ovulation. *Proceedings of the Royal Society of London B, 268,* 797–801.

Slabbekoorn, D., van Goozen, S. H. M., Megens, J., Gooren, L. J. G., & Cohen-Kettenis, P. T. (1999). Activating effects of cross-sex hormones on cognitive functioning: A study of short term and long-term hormone effects in transsexuals. *Psychoneuroendocrinology, 24,* 432–447.

Slaby, R. G., & Frey, K. S. (1975). Development of gender constancy and selective attention to same-sex models. *Child Development, 46,* 849–856.

Slob, A. K., Bax, C. M., Hop, W. C. J., Rowland, D. L., & van der Werff ten Bosch, J. J. (1996). Sexual arousability and the menstrual cycle. *Psychoneuroendocrinology, 21,* 545–558.

Smith, E. A. (1998). Is Tibetan polyandry adaptive? Methodological and metatheoretical analyses. *Human Nature, 9,* 225–261.

Smith, E. A. (2004). Why do good hunters have higher reproductive success? *Human Nature, 15,* 343–364.

Smith, K. L., Cornelissen, P. L., & Tovée, M. J. (2007). Color 3D bodies and judgments of human female attractiveness. *Evolution and Human Behavior, 28,* 48–54.

Smith, L. L., & Hines, M. (2000). Language lateralization and handedness in women prenatally exposed to diethylstilbestrol (DES). *Psychoneuroendocrinology, 25,* 497–512.

Smith, P. K. (1982). Does play matter? Functional and evolutionary aspects of animal and human play. *Behavioral and Brain Sciences, 5,* 139–184.

Smith, R. L. (1984). Human sperm competition. In R. L. Smith, *Sperm competition and the evolution of animal mating systems* (pp. 601–659.). New York: Academic Press.

Smith, R. L., Rose, A. J., & Schwartz-Mette, R. A. (2009). Relational and overt aggression in childhood and adolescence: Clarifying mean-level gender differences and associations with peer acceptance. *Social Development.* Retrieved

April 12, 2009, from http://www3.interscience.wiley.com/journal/122280508/abstract?CRETRY=1&SRETRY=0

Smolak, L., & Murnen, S. K. (2008). Drive for leanness: Assessment and relationship to gender, gender role and objectification. *Body Image, 5*, 251–260.

Smuts, B. B. (1985). *Sex and friendship in baboons*. New York: Aldine Publishing Company.

Smuts, B. B. (1987). Gender, aggression, and influence. In B. B. Smuts, D. L. Cheney, R. M. Seyfarth, R. W. Wrangham, & T. T. Struhsaker (Eds.), *Primate societies* (pp. 400–412). Chicago: The University of Chicago Press.

Smuts, B. B. (1995). The evolutionary origins of patriarchy. *Human Nature, 6*, 1–32.

Smuts, B. B., Cheney, D. L., Seyfarth, R. M., Wrangham, R. W., & Struhsaker, T. T. (Eds.) (1987). *Primate societies*. Chicago: The University of Chicago Press.

Smuts, B., & Gubernick, D. J. (1992). Male-infant relationships in nonhuman primates: Paternal investment or mating effort? In B. S. Hewlett (Ed.), *Father–child relations: Cultural and biosocial contexts* (pp. 1–30). New York: Aldine de Gruyter.

Smuts, B., & Nicolson, N. (1989). Reproduction in wild female olive baboons. *American Journal of Primatology, 19*, 229–246.

Soma, K. K. (2006). Testosterone and aggression: Berthold, birds and beyond. *Journal of Neuroendocrinology, 18*, 543–551.

Sommer, I. E. C., Aleman, A., Bouma, A., & Kahn, R. S. (2004). Do women really have more bilateral language representation than men? A meta-analysis of functional imaging studies. *Brain, 127*, 1845–1852.

Sorci, G., Morand, S., & Hugot, J.-P. (1997). Host-parasite coevolution: Comparative evidence for covariation of life history traits in primates and oxyurid parasites. *Proceedings of the Royal Society of London B, 264*, 285–289.

Sowell, E. R., Peterson, B. S., Kan, E., Woods, R. P., Yoshii, J., Bansal, R., et al. (2006). Sex differences in cortical thickness mapped in 176 healthy individuals between 7 and 87 years of age. *Cerebral Cortex, 17*, 1550–1560.

Spelke, E. S. (2005). Sex differences in intrinsic aptitude for mathematics and science?: A critical review. *American Psychologist, 60*, 950–958.

Spelke, E. S., Breinlinger, K., Macomber, J., & Jacobson, K. (1992). Origins of knowledge. *Psychological Review, 99*, 605–632.

Spiers, H. J., Burgess, N., Maguire, E. A., Baxendale, S. A., Hartley, T., Thompson, P. J., & O'Keefe, J. (2001). Unilateral temporal lobectomy patients show lateralized topographical and episodic deficits in a virtual town. *Brain, 124*, 2476–2489.

Spinath, F. M., & O'Connor, T. G. (2003). A behavioral genetic study of the overlap between personality and parenting. *Journal of Personality, 71*, 785–808.

Spotts, E. L., Lichtenstein, P., Pedersen, N., Neiderhiser, J. M., Hansson, K., Cederblad, M., & Reiss, D. (2005). Personality and marital satisfaction: A behavioural genetic analysis. *European Journal of Personality, 19*, 205–227.

Sprecher, S., Sullivan, Q., & Hatfield, E. (1994). Mate selection preferences: Gender differences examined in a national sample. *Journal of Personality and Social Psychology, 66*, 1074–1080.

Sprengelmeyer, R., Perrett, D. I., Fagan, E. C., Cornwell, R. E., Lobmaier, J. S., Sprengelmeyer, A., et al. (2009). The cutest little baby face: A hormonal link to sensitivity in cuteness in infant faces. *Psychological Science, 20*, 149–154.

Spritzer, M.D., & Galea, L.A.M. (2007). Testosterone and dihydrotestosterone, but not estradiol, enhance hippocampal neurogenesis in adult male rats. *Developmental Neurobiology, 67*, 1321–1333.

Spritzer, M. D., Meikle, D. B., & Solomon, N. G. (2004). The relationship between dominance rank and spatial ability among male meadow voles (*Microtus pennsylvanicus*). *Journal of Comparative Psychology, 118*, 332–339.

Spritzer, M. D., Meikle, D. B., & Solomon, N. G. (2005). Female choice based on male spatial ability and aggressiveness among meadow voles. *Animal Behaviour, 69*, 1121–1130.

Spritzer, M. D., Solomon, N. G., & Meikle, D. B. (2005). Influence of scramble competition for mates upon the spatial ability of male meadow voles. *Animal Behaviour, 69*, 375–386.

Spritzer, M. D., Solomon, N. G., & Meikle, D. B. (2006). Social dominance among male meadow voles is inversely related to reproductive success. *Ethology, 112*, 1027–1037.

Stamps, J. A. (1995). Using growth-based models to study behavioral factors affecting sexual size dimorphism. *Herpetological Monographs, 9*, 75–87.

Stanley, J. C. (1993). Boys and girls who reason well mathematically. In G. R. Bock & K. Ackrill (Eds.), *The origins and development of high ability* (pp. 119–138). New York: Wiley.

Stanley, J. C., Benbow, C. P., Brody, L. E., Dauber, S., & Lupkowski., A. E. (1992). Gender differences on eighty-six nationally standardized aptitude and achievement tests. In N. Colangelo, S. G. Assouline, & D. L. Ambroson (Eds.), *Talent development: Proceedings from the 1991 Henry B. and Jocelyn Wallace national research symposium on talent development* (pp. 42–65). Unionville, NY: Trillium Press.

Stanovich, K. E., & West, R. F. (2000). Individual differences in reasoning: Implications for the rationality debate? *Behavioral and Brain Sciences, 23*, 645–726.

Stanton, S. J., & Schultheiss, O. C. (2007). Basal and dynamic relationships between implicit power motivation and estradiol in women. *Hormones and Behavior, 52*, 571–580.

Stearns, S. C. (1992). *The evolution of life histories*. New York: Oxford University Press.

Stearns, S. C., & Koella, J. C. (1986). The evolution of phenotypic plasticity in life-history traits: Predictions of reaction norms for age and size at maturity. *Evolution, 40*, 893–913.

Sterck, E. H. M., Watts, D. P., & van Schaik, C. P. (1997). The evolution of female social relationships in nonhuman primates. *Behavioral Ecology and Sociobiology, 41*, 291–309.

Stinson, S. (1985). Sex differences in environmental sensitivity during growth and development. *Yearbook of Physical Anthropology, 28*, 123–147.

Storey, A. E., Walsh, C. J., Quinton, R. L., & Wynne-Edwards, K. E. (2000). Hormonal correlates of paternal responsiveness in new and expectant fathers. *Evolution and Human Behavior, 21*, 79–95.

Strand, S., Deary, I. J., & Smith, P. (2006). Sex differences in cognitive ability test scores: A UK national picture. *British Journal of Educational Psychology, 76*, 463–480.

Strassmann, B. I. (1997). Polygyny as a risk factor for child mortality among the Dogon. *Current Anthropology, 38*, 688–695.

Strassmann, B. I. (2000). Polygyny, family structure, and child mortality: A prospective study among the Dogon of Mali. In L. Cronk, N. Chagnon, & W. Irons (Eds.), *Adaptation and human behavior: An anthropological perspective* (pp. 49–67). New York: Aldine De Gruyter.

Strassmann, B. I., & Gillespie, B. (2002). Life-history theory, fertility and reproductive success in humans. *Proceedings of the Royal Society of London B, 269*, 553–562.

Strayer, F. F., & Santos, A. J. (1996). Affiliative structures in preschool peer groups. *Social Development, 5*, 117–130.

Stringer, C. B. (1992). Evolution of early humans. In S. Jones, R. Martin, & D. Pilbeam (Eds.), *The Cambridge encyclopedia of human evolution* (pp. 241–251). New York: Cambridge University Press.

Strough, J., Berg, C. A., & Sansone, C. (1996). Goals for solving everyday problems across the life span: Age and gender differences in the salience of interpersonal concerns. *Developmental Psychology, 32*, 1106–1115.

Stumpf, H., & Stanley, J. C. (1998). Stability and change in gender-related differences on the College Board advanced placement and achievement tests. *Current Directions in Psychological Science, 7*, 192–196.

Suddendorf, T., & Busby, J. (2003). Mental time travel in animals? *Trends in Cognitive Sciences, 7*, 391–396.

Suddendorf, T., & Corballis, M. C. (1997). Mental time travel and the evolution of the human mind. *Genetic, Social, and General Psychology Monographs, 123*, 133–167.

Sultan, S. E. (2000). Phenotypic plasticity for plant development, function and life history. *Trends in Plant Science, 5*, 537–542.

Surbey, M. K., & Brice, G. R. (2007). Enhancement of self-perceived mate value precedes a shift in men's preferred mating strategy. *Acta Psychologica Sinica, 39*, 513–522.

Sutton-Smith, B., Rosenberg, B. G., & Morgan, E. F., Jr. (1963). Development of sex differences in play choices during preadolescence. *Child Development, 34*, 119–126.

Swenson, L. P., & Rose, A. J. (2003). Friends as reporters of children's and adolescents' depressive symptoms. *Journal of Abnormal Child Psychology, 31,* 619–631.

Symons, D. (1979). *The evolution of human sexuality.* New York: Oxford University Press.

Szykman, M., Engh, A. L., Van Horn, R. C., Funk, S. M., Scribner, K. T., & Holekamp, K. E. (2001). Association patterns among male and female spotted hyenas (*crocuta crocuta*) reflect male mate choice. *Behavioral Ecology and Sociobiology, 50,* 231–238.

Tajfel, H., & Turner, J. C. (1979). An integrative theory of intergroup conflict. In W. G. Austin & S. Worchel (Eds.), *The social psychology of intergroup relations* (pp. 33–47). Monterey, CA: Brooks/Cole.

Takahashi, H. (2004). Do males have a better chance of mating when the number of estrous females is equal to or greater than the males' ordinal rank? Testing the hypothesis in Japanese macaques. *American Journal of Primatology, 63,* 95–102.

Takahashi, H., Matsuura, M., Yahata, N., Koeda, M., Suhara, T., & Okubo, Y. (2006). Men and women show distinct brain activations during imagery of sexual and emotional infidelity. *NeuroImage, 32,* 1299–1307.

Takahata, Y., Huffman, M. A., Suzuki, S., Koyama, N., & Yamagiwa, J. (1999). Why dominants do not consistently attain high mating and reproductive success: A review of longitudinal Japanese macaque studies. *Primates, 40,* 143–158.

Tal, I., & Lieberman, D. (2007). Kin detection and the development of sexual aversions: Toward an integration of theories on family sexual abuse. In C. Salmon & T. Shackelford (Eds.), *Family relationships: An evolutionary perspective* (pp. 205–229). New York: Oxford University Press.

Tallal, P. (1991). Hormonal influences in developmental learning disabilities. *Psychoneuroendocrinology, 16,* 203–211.

Tanner, J. M. (1990). *Foetus into man: Physical growth from conception to maturity.* Cambridge, MA: Harvard University Press.

Taylor, A. B. (1997). Relative growth, ontogeny, and sexual dimorphism in Gorilla (*Gorilla gorilla gorilla* and G. *g. beringei*): Evolutionary and ecological considerations. *American Journal of Primatology, 43,* 1–31.

Taylor, M. D., Hart, C. L., Smith, G. D., Whalley, L. J., Hole, D. J., Wilson, V., & Deary, I. J. (2005). Childhood IQ and marriage by mid-life: The Scottish mental survey 1932 and the midspan studies. *Personality and Individual Differences, 38,* 1621–1630.

Taylor, S. E. (1982). The availability bias in social perception and interaction. In D. Kahneman, P. Slovic, & A. Tversky (Eds.), *Judgment uncertainty: Heuristics and biases* (pp. 190–200). Cambridge, England: Cambridge University Press.

Taylor, S. E., Klein, L. C., Lewis, B. P., Gruenewald, T. L., Gurung, R. A. R., & Updegraff, J. A. (2000). Biobehavioral responses to stress in females: Tend-and-befriend, not fight-or-flight. *Psychological Review, 107,* 411–429.

Teaford, M. F., & Ungar, P. S. (2000). Diet and the evolution of the earliest human ancestors. *Proceedings of the National Academy of Sciences USA, 97,* 13506–13511.

Teklehaymanot, T., & Giday, M. (2007). Ethnobiological study of medicinal plants used by people in Zegie Peninsula, Northwestern Ethiopia. *Journal of Ethnobiology and Ethnomedicine*, *3*, 12. Retrieved October 12, 2008, from http://www.ethnobiomed.com/content/3/1/12

Thilers, P. P. MacDonald, S. W. S., & Herlitz, A. (2006). The association between endogenous free testosterone and cognitive performance: A population-based study in 35 to 90 year-old men and women. *Psychoneuroendocrinology*, *31*, 565–576.

Thomas, J. R., & French, K. E. (1985). Gender differences across age in motor performance: A meta-analysis. *Psychological Bulletin*, *98*, 260–282.

Thomson, R., Pritchard, J. K., Shen, P., Oefner, P. J., & Feldman, M. W. (2000). Recent common ancestry of human Y chromosomes: Evidence from DNA sequence data. *Proceedings of the National Academy of Sciences USA*, *97*, 7360–7365.

Thornhill, R. (1976). Sexual selection and paternal investment in insects. *American Naturalist*, *110*, 153–163.

Thornhill, R., & Gangestad, S. W. (1993). Human facial beauty: Averageness, symmetry, and parasite resistance. *Human Nature*, *4*, 237–269.

Thornhill, R., & Gangestad, S. W. (1999). The scent of symmetry: A human sex pheromone that signals fitness? *Evolution and Human Behavior*, *20*, 175–201.

Thornhill, R., & Gangestad, S. W. (2008). *The evolutionary biology of human female sexuality*. New York: Oxford University Press.

Thornhill, R., Gangestad, S. W., Miller, R., Scheyd, G., McCollough, J. K., & Franklin, M. (2003). Major histocompatibility complex genes, symmetry, and body scent attractiveness in men and women. *Behavioral Ecology*, *14*, 668–678.

Thornhill, R., & Palmer, C. T. (2000). *The natural history of rape: Biological basis of sexual coercion*. Cambridge, MA: MIT Press.

Tiger, L., & Shepher, J. (1975). *Women in the kibbutz*. New York: Harvest Book.

Timberlake, W. (1994). Behavior systems, associationism, and Pavlovian conditioning. *Psychonomic Bulletin & Review*, *1*, 405–420.

Tobias, P. V. (1987). The brain of *Homo habilis*: A new level of organization in cerebral evolution. *Journal of Human Evolution*, *16*, 741–761.

Tomasello, M., & Call, J. (1997). *Primate cognition*. New York: Oxford University Press.

Tooby, J., & Cosmides, L. (1990). On the universality of human nature and the uniqueness of the individual: Role of genetics and adaptation. *Journal of Personality*, *58*, 17–67.

Torchin, M. E., Lafferty, K. D., Dobson, A. P., McKenzie, V. J., & Kuris, A. M. (2003, February 6). Introduced species and their missing parasites. *Nature*, *421*, 628–630.

Townsend, J. M., Kline, J., & Wasserman, T. H. (1995). Low-investment copulation: Sex differences in motivations and emotional reactions. *Ethology and Sociobiology*, *16*, 25–51.

Towson, S. M. J., Lerner, M. J., & de Carufel, A. (1981). Justice rules or ingroup loyalties: The effects of competition on children's allocation behavior. *Personality and Social Psychology Bulletin*, *7*, 696–700.

Træen, B., Holmen, K., & Stigum, H. (2007). Extradyadic sexual relationships in Norway. *Archives of Sexual Behavior, 36,* 55–65.

Tranel, D., Damasio, H., Denburg, J. L., & Bechara, A. (2005). Does gender play a role in functional asymmetry of the ventromedial prefrontal cortex? *Brain, 128,* 2872–2881.

Trivers, R. L. (1971). The evolution of reciprocal altruism. *Quarterly Review of Biology, 46,* 35–57.

Trivers, R. L. (1972). Parental investment and sexual selection. In B. Campbell (Ed.), *Sexual selection and the descent of man 1871–1971* (pp. 136–179). Chicago: Aldine Publishing.

Trivers, R. L. (1974). Parent–offspring conflict. *American Zoologist, 14,* 249–264.

Troxel, W. M., & Matthews, K. A. (2004). What are the costs of marital conflict and dissolution to children's physical health? *Clinical Child and Family Psychology Review, 7,* 29–57.

Trudel, G. (2002). Sexuality and marital life: Results of a survey. *Journal of Sex & Marital Therapy, 28,* 229–249.

Tulving, E. (2002). Episodic memory: From mind to brain. *Annual Review of Psychology, 53,* 1–25.

Turner, B. N., Iverson, S. L., & Severson, K. L. (1983). Seasonal changes in openfield behavior in wild male meadow voles (*Microtus pennsylvanicus*). *Behavioral and Neural Biology, 39,* 60–77.

Turner, C. F., Ku, L., Rogers, S. M., Lindberg, L. D., Pleck, J. H., & Sonenstein, F. L. (1998, May 8). Adolescent sexual behavior, drug use, and violence: Increased reporting with computer survey technology. *Science, 280,* 867–873.

Turner, P. J., & Gervai, J. (1995). A multidimensional study of gender typing in preschool children and their parents: Personality, attitudes, preferences, behavior, and cultural differences. *Developmental Psychology, 31,* 759–772.

Tutin, C. E. G. (1979). Mating patterns and reproductive strategies in a community of wild chimpanzees (*Pan troglodytes schweinfurthii*). *Behavioral Ecology and Sociobiology, 6,* 29–38.

Udry, J. R., Billy, J. O. G., Morris, N. M., Groff, T. R., & Raj, M. H. (1985). Serum androgenic hormones motivate sexual behavior in adolescent human males. *Fertility and Sterility, 43,* 90–94.

Underhill, P. A., Jin, L., Zemans, R., Oefner, P. J., & Cavalli-Sforza, L. L. (1996). A pre-Columbian Y chromosome-specific transition and its implications for human evolutionary history. *Proceedings of the National Academy of Sciences, USA, 93,* 196–200.

Underhill, P. A., Shen, P., Lin, A. A., Jin, L., Passarino, G., Yang, W. H., et al. (2000). Y chromosome sequence variation and the history of human populations. *Nature Genetics, 26,* 358–361.

United Nations (1985). *Socio-economic differentials in child mortality in developing countries.* New York: Author.

United Nations Children's Fund. (2005). *Early marriage: A harmful traditional practice*. New York: Author. Retrieved April 18, 2008, from http://www.childinfo.org/areas/childmarriage/docs/Early_Marriage%20Final.pdf

U.S. Department of Agriculture. (1986). *Insects and mites: Techniques for collection and preservation*. Washington, DC: Author.

van Anders, S., Hamilton, L. D., & Watson, N. V. (2007). Multiple partners are associated with higher testosterone in North American men and women. *Hormones and Behavior, 51*, 454–459.

van Anders, S., & Hampson, E. (2005). Testing the prenatal androgen hypothesis: Measuring digit ratios, sexual orientation, and spatial abilities in adults. *Hormones and Behavior, 47*, 92–98.

Van Bavel, J. J., Packer, D. J., & Cunningham, W. A. (2008). The neural substrates of in-group bias: A functional magnetic resonance imaging investigation. *Psychological Science, 19*, 1131–1139.

van Beek, Y., & Dubas, J. S. (2008). Age and gender differences in decoding basic and non-basic facial expressions in late childhood and early adolescence. *Journal of Nonverbal Behavior, 32*, 37–52.

Vandenberg, S. G., & Kuse, A. R. (1978). Mental rotations, a group test of three-dimensional spatial visualization. *Perceptual and Motor Skills, 47*, 599–604.

Van den Bosh, W. J. H. M., Huygen, F. J. A., Van den Hoogen, H. J. M., & Van Weel, C. (1992). Morbidity in early childhood: Differences between girls and boys under 10 years old. *British Journal of General Practice, 42*, 366–369.

van der Meij, L., Buunk, A. P., van de Sande, J. P., & Salvador, A. (2008). The presence of a woman increases testosterone in aggressive dominant men. *Hormones and Behavior, 54*, 640–644.

van der Sluis, S., Derom, C., Thiery, E., Bartels, M., Polderman, T. J. C., Verhulst, F. C., et al. (2008). Sex differences in the WISC–R in Belgium and the Netherlands. *Intelligence, 36*, 48–67.

van der Sluis, S., Posthuma, D., Dolan, C. V., de Geus, E. J. C., Colom, R., & Boomsma, D. I. (2006). Sex differences on the Dutch WAIS–III. *Intelligence, 34*, 273–289.

van Goozen, S. H. M., Cohen-Kettenis, P. T., Gooren, L. J. G., Frijda, N. H., & Van de Poll, N. E. (1994). Activating effects of androgens on cognitive performance: Causal evidence in a group of female-to-male transsexuals. *Neuropsychologia, 32*, 1153–1157.

van Goozen, S. H. M., Cohen-Kettenis, P. T., Gooren, L. J. G., Frijda, N. H., & Van de Poll, N. E. (1995). Gender differences in behaviour: Activating effects of cross-sex hormones. *Psychoneuroendocrinology, 20*, 343–363.

van Goozen, S. H. M., Slabbekoorn, D., Gooren, L. J. G., Sanders, G., Cohen-Kettenis, P. T. (2002). Organizing and activating effects of sex hormones in homosexual transsexuals. *Behavioral Neuroscience, 116*, 982–988.

van Honk, J., Schutter, D. J. L. G., Hermans, E. J., Putman, P., Tuiten, A., & Koppeschaar, H. (2004). Testosterone shifts the balance between sensitivity for punishment and reward in healthy young women. *Psychoneuroendocrinology, 29,* 937–943.

van Honk, J., Tuiten, A., Verbaten, R., van den Hout, M., Koppeschaar, H., Thijssen, J., & de Haan, E. (1999). Correlations among salivary testosterone, mood, and selective attention to threat in humans. *Hormones and Behavior, 36,* 17–24.

Van Valen, L. (1973). A new evolutionary law. *Evolutionary Theory, 1,* 1–30.

Van Vugt, M., De Cremer, D., & Janssen, D. P. (2007). Gender differences in cooperation and competition: The male-warrior hypothesis. *Psychological Science, 18,* 19–23.

Van Vugt, M., & Spisak, B. R. (2008). Sex differences in the emergence of leadership during competitions within and between groups. *Psychological Sciences, 19,* 854–858.

Velle, W. (1987). Sex differences in sensory functions. *Perspectives in Biology and Medicine, 30,* 490–522.

Vellenga, R. E. (1980). Molts of the satin bowerbird *Ptilonorhynchus violaceus*. *Emu, 80,* 49–54.

Vermeersch, H., T'Sjoen, G., Kaufman, J.-M., & Vincke, J. (2008). The roles of testosterone in aggressive and non-aggressive risk-taking in adolescent boys. *Hormones and Behavior, 53,* 463–471.

Verona, E., & Curtin, J. J. (2006). Gender differences in negative affective priming of aggressive behavior. *Emotion, 6,* 115–124.

Vervaecke, H., Stevens, J., & Van Elsacker, L. (2003). Interfering with others: Female–female reproductive competition in *Pan paniscus*. In C. B. Jones (Ed.), *Sexual selection and reproductive competition in primates: New perspectives and directions* (pp. 231–253). Norman, OK: American Society of Primatologists.

Vigil, J. M. (in press). A socio-relational framework of sex differences in the expression of emotion. *Behavioral and Brain Sciences*.

Vigil, J. M., & Geary, D. C. (2006). Family and community background and variation in women's life history development. *Journal of Family Psychology, 20,* 597–604.

Vigil, J. M., Geary, D. C., & Byrd-Craven, J. (2005). A life history assessment of early childhood sexual abuse in women. *Developmental Psychology, 41,* 553–561.

Vigil, J. M., Geary, D. C., & Byrd-Craven, J. (2006). Trade-offs in low-income women's mate preferences: Within-sex differences in reproductive strategy. *Human Nature, 17,* 319–336.

Vigilant, L., Hofreiter, M., Siedel, H., & Boesch, C. (2001). Paternity and relatedness in wild chimpanzee communities. *Proceedings of the National Academy of Sciences USA, 98,* 12890–12895.

Vining, D. R., Jr. (1986). Social versus reproductive success: The central theoretical problem of human sociobiology. *Behavioral and Brain Sciences, 9,* 167–216.

Vogt, C., & Shecht, F. (1887). *The natural history of the mammalia* (Divs. 1–6). London: Blackie.

Voigt, C., & Goymann, W. (2007). Sex-role reversal is reflected in the brain of African black coucals (*Centropus grillii*). *Developmental Neurobiology, 67,* 1560–1573.

Volk, T., & Atkinson, J. (2008). Is child death the crucible of human evolution? *Journal of Social, Evolutionary, and Cultural Psychology, 2,* 247–260.

von Schantz, T., Bensch, S. B., Grahn, M., Hasselquist, D., & Wittzell, H. (1999). Good genes, oxidative stress and condition-dependent sexual signals. *Proceedings of the Royal Society of London B, 266,* 1–12.

von Schantz, T., Göransson, G., Andersson, G., Fröberg, I., Grahn, M., Helgée, A., & Wittzell, H. (1989, January 12). Female choice selects for a viability-based male trait in pheasants. *Nature, 337,* 166–169.

von Schantz, T., Wittzell, H., Göransson, G., Grahn, M., & Persson, K. (1996). MHC genotype and male ornamentation: Genetic evidence for the Hamilton-Zuk model. *Proceedings of the Royal Society of London B, 263,* 265–271.

Voyer, D., Postma, A., Brake, B., & Imperato-McGinley, J. (2007). Gender differences in object location memory: A meta-analysis. *Psychonomic Bulletin & Review, 14,* 23–38.

Voyer, D., Voyer, S., & Bryden, M.P. (1995). Magnitude of sex differences in spatial abilities: A meta-analysis and consideration and consideration of critical variables. *Psychological Bulletin, 117,* 250–270.

Wada, J., Clark, R., & Hamm, A. (1975). Cerebral hemisphere asymmetry in humans: Cortical speech zones in 100 adult and 100 infant brains. *Archives of Neurology, 32,* 239–246.

Wade, J. (2005). Current research on the behavioral endocrinology of reptiles. *Hormones and Behavior, 48,* 451–460.

Wade, T. J. (2000). Evolutionary theory and self-perception: Sex differences in body esteem predictors of self-perceived physical and sexual attractiveness and self-esteem. *International Journal of Psychology, 35,* 36–45.

Wager, T. D., Phan, K. L., Liberzon, I., & Taylor, S. F. (2003). Valence, gender, and lateralization of functional brain anatomy in emotion: A meta-analysis of findings from neuroimaging. *NeuroImage, 19,* 513–531.

Wagner, H. L., Buck, R., & Winterbotham, M. (1993). Communication of specific emotions: Gender differences in sending accuracy and communication measures. *Journal of Nonverbal Behavior, 17,* 29–53.

Walker, R., Gurven, M., Hill, K., Migliano, A., Chagnon, N., De Souza, R., et al. (2006). Growth rates and life history traits in twenty-two small-scale societies. *American Journal of Human Biology, 18,* 295–311.

Walker, S. (2005). Gender differences in the relationship between young children's peer-related social competence and individual differences in theory of mind. *Journal of Genetic Psychology, 166,* 297–312.

Walker, S. P., Chang, S. M., Powell, C. A., & Grantham-McGregor, S. M. (2005, November 19). Effects of early childhood psychosocial stimulation and nutritional supplementation on cognition and education in growth-stunted Jamaican children: Prospective cohort study. *The Lancet, 366,* 1804–1807.

Wallace, A. R. (1892). Note on sexual selection. *Natural Science, 1,* 749–750. Retrieved April 12, 2009, from http://www.wku.edu/~smithch/wallace/S459.htm

Wallen, K. (1996). Nature needs nurture: The interaction of hormonal and social influences on the development of behavioral sex differences in rhesus monkeys. *Hormones and Behavior, 30,* 364–378.

Walter, M., Bermpohl, F., Mouras, H., Schiltz, K., Tempelmann, C., Rotte, M., et al. (2008). Distinguishing specific sexual and general emotional effects in fMRI—Subcortical and cortical arousal during erotic picture viewing. *NeuroImage, 40,* 1482–1494.

Walters, J. R. (1987). Transition to adulthood. In B. B. Smuts, D. L. Cheney, R. M. Seyfarth, R. W. Wrangham, & T. T. Struhsaker (Eds.), *Primate societies* (pp. 358–369). Chicago: The University of Chicago Press.

Walters, J. R., & Seyfarth, R. M. (1987). Conflict and cooperation. In B. B. Smuts, D. L. Cheney, R. M. Seyfarth, R. W. Wrangham, & T. T. Struhsaker (Eds.), *Primate societies* (pp. 306–317). Chicago: The University of Chicago Press.

Walters, S., & Crawford, C. B. (1994). The importance of mate attraction for intrasexual competition in men and women. *Ethology and Sociobiology, 15,* 5–30.

Walum, H., Westberg, L., Henningsson, S., Neiderhiser, J. M., Reiss, D., Igi, W., et al. (2008). Genetic variation in the vasopressin receptor 1a gene (AVPR1A) associates with pair-bonding behavior in humans. *Proceedings of the National Academy of Sciences USA, 105,* 14153–14156.

Wang, M.-H., & vom Saal, F. S. (2000, September 28). Maternal age and traits in offspring. *Nature, 407,* 469–470.

Wang, Z. X., Liu, Y., Young, L. J., & Insel, T. R. (2000). Hypothalamic vasopressin gene expression increases in both males and females postpartum in a biparental rodent. *Journal of Neuroendocrinology, 12,* 111–120.

Watson, J. T., & Adkins-Regan, E. (1989). Testosterone implanted in the preoptic area of male Japanese quail must be aromatized to activate copulation. *Hormones and Behavior, 23,* 432–447.

Watson, N. V., & Kimura, D. (1991). Nontrivial sex differences in throwing and intercepting: Relation to psychometrically-defined spatial functions. *Personality and Individual Differences, 12,* 375–385.

Watts, D. P. (1998). Coalitionary mate guarding by male chimpanzees at Ngogo Kibale National Park, Uganda. *Behavioral Ecology and Sociobiology, 44,* 43–55.

Watts, D. P., & Mitani, J. C. (2001). Boundary patrols and intergroup encounters in wild chimpanzees. *Behaviour, 138,* 299–327.

Watts, D. P., Muller, M., Amsler, S. J., Mbabazi, G., & Mitani, J. C. (2006). Lethal intergroup aggression by chimpanzees in Kibale National Park, Uganda. *American Journal of Primatology, 68,* 161–180.

Waynforth, D., Hurtado, A. M., & Hill, K. (1998). Environmentally contingent reproductive strategies in Mayan and Ache males. *Evolution and Human Behavior, 19,* 369–385.

Wedekind, C., Seebeck, T., Bettens, F., & Paepke, A. J. (1995). MHC-dependent mate preferences in humans. *Proceedings of the Royal Society of London B, 260,* 245–249.

Weeden, J., Abrams, M. J., Green, M. C., & Sabini, J. (2006). Do high-status people really have fewer children? Education, income, and fertility in the contemporary U.S. *Human Nature, 17,* 377–392.

Weeden, J., & Sabini, J. (2005). Physical attractiveness and health in Western societies: A review. *Psychological Bulletin, 131,* 635–653.

Wegner, K. M., Reusch, T. B. H., & Kalbe, M. (2003). Multiple parasites are driving major histocompatibility complex polymorphism in the wild. *Journal of Evolutionary Biology, 16,* 224–232.

Weiner, J. (1995). *The beak of the finch.* New York: Vintage Books.

Weingrill, T., Lycett, J. E., & Henzi, S. P. (2000). Consortship and mating success in chacma baboons (*Papio cynocephalus ursinus*). *Ethology, 106,* 1033–1044.

Weisner, T. S., & Wilson-Mitchell, J. E. (1990). Nonconventional family lifestyles and sex typing in six-year-olds. *Child Development, 61,* 1915–1933.

Weiss, P. H., Marshall, J. C., Wunderlich, G., Tellmann, L., Halligan, P. W., Freund, H.-J., et al. (2000). Neural consequences of acting in near versus far space: A physiological basis for clinical dissociations. *Brain, 123,* 2531–2541.

Weiss, P. H., Marshall, J. C., Zilles, K., & Fink, G. R. (2003). Are action and perception in near and far space additive or interactive factors? *NeuroImage, 18,* 837–846.

Welch, A. M., Semlitsch, R. D., & Gerhardt, H. C. (1998, June 19). Call duration as an indicator of genetic quality in male gray tree frogs. *Science, 280,* 1928–1930.

Welling, L. L., Jones, B. C., DeBruine, L. M., Smith, F. G., Feinberg, D. R., Little, A. C., & Al-Dujaili, E. A. S. (2008). Men report stronger attraction to femininity in women's faces when their testosterone levels are high. *Hormones and Behavior, 54,* 703–708.

Wells, B. E., & Twenge, J. M. (2005). Changes in young people's sexual behavior and attitudes, 1943–1999: A cross-temporal meta-analysis. *Review of General Psychology, 9,* 249–261.

Wells, J. C. K. (2000). Natural selection and sex differences in morbidity and mortality in early life. *Journal of Theoretical Biology, 202,* 65–76.

Wells, R. S., Yuldasheva, N., Ruzibakiev, R., Underhill, P. A., Evseeva, I., Blue-Smith, J., et al. (2001). The Eurasian heartland: A continental perspective on Y-chromosome diversity. *Proceedings of the National Academy of Sciences USA, 98,* 10244–10249.

Wenk, R. E., Houtz, T., Brooks, M., & Chiafari, F. A. (1992). How frequent is heteropaternal superfecundation? *Acta Geneticae Medicae et Gemellologiae, 41,* 43–47.

West, G. B., Brown, J. H., & Enquist, B. J. (2001, October 11). A general model for ontogenetic growth. *Nature, 413,* 628–631.

West, M. J., & King, A. P. (1980). Enriching cowbird song by social deprivation. *Journal of Comparative and Physiological Psychology, 94,* 263–270.

West, M. M., & Konner, M. J. (1976). The role of father: An anthropological perspective. In M. E. Lamb (Ed.), *The role of the father in child development* (pp. 185–217). New York: Wiley.

West-Eberhard, M. J. (1983). Sexual selection, social competition, and speciation. *Quarterly Review of Biology, 58,* 155–183.

West-Eberhard, M. J. (2003). *Developmental plasticity and evolution.* New York: Oxford University Press.

Westendorp, R. G. J., & Kirkwood, T. B. L. (1998, December 31). Human longevity at the cost of reproductive success. *Nature, 396,* 743–746.

Westneat, D. F., & Sherman, P. W. (1993). Parentage and the evolution of parental behavior. *Behavioral Ecology, 4,* 66–77.

Westneat, D. F., & Stewart, I. R. K. (2003). Extra-pair paternity in birds: Causes, correlates, and conflict. *Annual Review of Ecology, Evolution, & Systematics, 34,* 365–396.

Whalen, R. E. (1974). Sexual differentiation: Models, methods, and mechanisms. In R. C. Friedman, R. M., Richart, & R. L. Vande Wiele (Eds.), *Sex differences in behavior* (pp. 467–481). New York: Wiley.

Wheeler, M. E., & Fiske, S. T. (2002). Controlling racial prejudice and stereotyping: Changing social cognitive goals affects human amygdala and stereotype activation. *Psychological Bulletin, 121,* 331–354.

Whisman, M. A., & Snyder, D. K. (2007). Sexual infidelity in a national survey of American women: Differences in prevalence and correlates as a function of method of assessment. *Journal of Family Psychology, 21,* 147–154.

Whissell, C. (1996). Mate selection in popular women's fiction. *Human Nature, 7,* 427–447.

White, D. R. (1988). Rethinking polygyny: Co-wives, codes, and cultural systems. *Current Anthropology, 29,* 529–572.

White, D. R., & Burton, M. L. (1988). Causes of polygyny: Ecology, economy, kinship, and warfare. *American Anthropologist, 90,* 871–887.

Whitesell, N. R., & Harter, S. (1996). The interpersonal context of emotion: Anger with close friends and classmates. *Child Development, 67,* 1345–1359.

Whiting, B. B., & Edwards, C. P. (1973). A cross-cultural analysis of sex differences in the behavior of children aged three through 11. *Journal of Social Psychology, 91,* 171–188.

Whiting, B. B., & Edwards, C. P. (1988). *Children of different worlds: The formation of social behavior.* Cambridge, MA: Harvard University Press.

Whiting, B. B., & Whiting, J. W. M. (1975). *Children of six cultures: A psycho-cultural analysis.* Cambridge, MA: Harvard University Press.

Whitley, B. E., Jr., & Kite, M. E. (1995). Sex differences in attitudes toward homosexuality: A comment on Oliver and Hyde (1993). *Psychological Bulletin, 117,* 146–154.

Whitten, P. L. (1987). Infants and adult males. In B. B. Smuts, D. L. Cheney, R. M. Seyfarth, R. W. Wrangham, & T. T. Struhsaker (Eds.), *Primate societies* (pp. 343–357). Chicago: The University of Chicago Press.

Whitten, P. L., & Turner, T. R. (2004). Male residence and the patterning of serum testosterone in vervet monkeys (*Cercopithecus aethiops*). *Behavioral Ecology and Sociobiology, 56,* 565–578.

Wickings, E. J., Bossi, T., & Dixson, A. F. (1993). Reproductive success in the mandrill, *Mandrillus sphinx:* Correlations of male dominance and mating success with paternity, as determined by DNA fingerprinting. *Journal of Zoology, 231,* 563–574.

Widdig, A., Bercovitch, F. B., Streich, W. J., Sauermann, U., Nürnberg, P., & Krawczak, M. (2004). A longitudinal analysis of reproductive skew in male rhesus macaques. *Proceedings of the Royal Society of London, B, 271,* 819–826.

Widemo, M. S. (2006). Male but not female pipefish copy mate choice. *Behavioral Ecology, 17,* 255–259.

Wiessner, P. (2002). Hunting, healing, and *hxaro* exchange: A long-term perspective on !Kung (Ju/'hoansi) large-game hunting. *Evolution and Human Behavior, 23,* 407–436.

Wilcox, A. J., Weinberg, C. R., & Baird, D. D. (1995). Timing of sexual intercourse in relation to ovulation: Effects on the probability of conception, survival of the pregnancy, and sex of the baby. *New England Journal of Medicine, 333,* 1517–1521.

Wilczynski, W., Lynch, K. S., & O'Bryant, E. L. (2005). Current research in amphibians: Studies integrating endocrinology, behavior, and neurobiology. *Hormones and Behavior, 48,* 440–450.

Wilder, J. A., Kingan, S. B., Mobasher, Z., Pilkington, M. M., & Hammer, M. F. (2004). Global patterns of human mitochondrial DNA and Y-chromosome structure are not influenced by higher migration rates of females versus males. *Nature Genetics, 36,* 1122–1125.

Wiley, R. H. (1974). Evolution of social organization and life-history patterns among grouse. *Quarterly Review of Biology, 49,* 201–227.

Wiley, R. H., & Poston, J. (1996). Indirect mate choice, competition for mates, and coevolution of the sexes. *Evolution, 50,* 1371–1381.

Williams, C. L., Barnett, A. M., & Meck, W. H. (1990). Organizational effects of early gonadal secretions on sexual differentiation in spatial ability. *Behavioral Neuroscience, 104,* 84–97.

Williams, C. L., & Meck, W. H. (1991). The organizational effects of gonadal steroids on sexually dimorphic spatial ability. *Psychoneuroendocrinology, 16,* 155–176.

Williams, G. C. (1957). Pleiotropy, natural selection and the evolution of senescence. *Evolution, 11,* 398–411.

Williams, G. C. (1966). *Adaptation and natural selection: A critique of some current evolutionary thought.* Princeton, NJ: Princeton University Press.

Williams, G. C. (1975). *Sex and evolution.* Princeton, NJ: Princeton University Press.

Williams, G. C., & Mitton, J. B. (1973). Why reproduce sexually? *Journal of Theoretical Biology, 39,* 545–554.

Williams, J. M., Oehlert, G. W., Carlis, J. V., & Pusey, A. E. (2004). Why do male chimpanzees defend a group range? *Animal Behaviour, 68,* 523–532.

Williams, M. A., & Mattingley, J. B. (2006). Do angry men get noticed? *Current Biology, 16*, R402–R404.

Willingham, W. W., & Cole, N. S. (1997). *Gender and fair assessment.* Mahwah, NJ: Erlbaum.

Wilson, A. B., Ahnesjö, I., Vincent, A. C. J., & Meyer, A. (2003). The dynamics of male brooding, mating patterns, and sex roles in pipefishes and seahorses (family *Syngnathidae*). *Evolution, 57*, 1374–1386.

Wilson, A. J., & Réale, D. (2006). Ontogeny of additive and maternal genetic effects: Lessons from domestic animals. *American Naturalist, 167*, E-23–E-38. Retrieved March 12, 2009, from http://www.journals.uchicago.edu/doi/abs/10.1086/498138

Wilson, G. D. (1997). Gender differences in sexual fantasy: An evolutionary analysis. *Personality and Individual Differences, 22*, 27–31.

Wilson, J. F., Weiss, D. A., Richards, M., Thomas, M. G., Bradman, N., & Goldstein, D. B. (2001). Genetic evidence for different male and female roles during cultural transitions in the British isles. *Proceedings of the National Academy of Sciences USA, 98*, 5078–5083.

Wilson, M., & Daly, M. (1985). Competitiveness, risk taking, and violence: The young male syndrome. *Ethology and Sociobiology, 6*, 59–73.

Wilson, M., & Daly, M. (1997, April 26). Life expectancy, economic inequality, homicide, and reproductive timing in Chicago neighbourhoods. *BMJ, 314*, 1271–1274.

Wilson, M. L., Hauser, M. D., & Wrangham, R. W. (2001). Does participation in intergroup conflict depend on numerical assessment, range location, or rank for wild chimpanzees? *Animal Behaviour, 61*, 1203–1216.

Wilson, M. L., & Wrangham, R. W. (2003). Intergroup relations in chimpanzees. *Annual Review of Anthropology, 32*, 363–392.

Wilson, M. S., & Liu, J. H. (2003). Social dominance orientation and gender: The moderating role of gender identity. *British Journal of Social Psychology, 42*, 187–198.

Wingfield, J. C., Hegner, R. E., Dufty, A. M., Jr., & Ball, G. F. (1990). The "challenge hypothesis": Theoretical implications for patterns of testosterone secretion, mating systems, and breeding strategies. *American Naturalist, 136*, 829–846.

Wingfield, J. C., Lynn, S. E., & Soma, K. K. (2001). Avoiding the 'costs' of testosterone: Ecological bases of hormone-behavior interactions. *Brain, Behavior and Evolution, 57*, 239–251.

Winslow, J. T., Hastings, N., Carter, C. S., Harbaugh, C. R., & Insel, T. R. (1993, October 7). A role for central vasopressin in pair bonding in monogamous prairie voles. *Nature, 365*, 545–548.

Winstead, B. A. (1986). Sex differences in same-sex friendships. In V. J. Derlaga & B. A. Winstead (Eds.), *Friendship and social interaction* (pp. 81–99). New York: Springer-Verlag.

Wirth, M. M., & Schultheiss, O. C. (2007). Basal testosterone moderates responses to anger faces in humans. *Physiology & Behavior, 90*, 496–505.

Wirth, M. M., Welsh, K. M., & Schultheiss, O. C. (2006). Salivary cortisol changes in humans after winning or losing a dominance contest depend on implicit power motivation. *Hormones and Behavior, 49*, 346–353.

Wiszewska, A., Pawlowski, B., & Boothroyd, L. G. (2007). Father–daughter relationship as a moderator of sexual imprinting: A facialmetric study. *Evolution and Human Behavior, 28,* 248–252.

Witelson, S. F. (1976, July 30). Sex and the single hemisphere: Specialization of the right hemisphere for spatial processing. *Science, 193,* 425–427.

Witelson, S. F. (1991). Neural sexual mosaicism: Sexual differentiation of the human temporo-parietal region for functional asymmetry. *Psychoneuroendocrinology, 16,* 131–153.

Witelson, S. F., Glezer, I. I., Kigar, D. L. (1995). Women have greater density of neurons in posterior temporal cortex. *Journal of Neuroscience, 15,* 3418–3428.

Wojcieszek, J. M., Nicholls, J. A., Marshall, N. J., & Goldizen, A. W. (2006). Theft of bower decorations among male satin bowerbirds (*Ptilonorhynchus violaceus*): Why are some decorations more popular than others? *Emu, 106,* 175–180.

Wolf, L., Ketterson, E. D., & Nolan, V., Jr. (1988). Paternal influence on growth and survival of dark-eyed junco young: Do parental males benefit? *Animal Behaviour, 36,* 1601–1618.

Wolpoff, M. H. (1976). Some aspects of the evolution of early hominid sexual dimorphism. *Current Anthropology, 17,* 579–606.

Wood, B., & Collard, M. (1999, April 2). The human genus. *Science, 284,* 65–71.

Wood, J. L., Heitmiller, D., Andreasen, N. C., & Nopoulos, P. (2008). Morphology of the ventral frontal cortex: Relationship to femininity and social cognition. *Cerebral Cortex, 18,* 534–540.

Wood, J. L., Murko, V., & Nopoulos, P. (2008). Ventral frontal cortex in children: Morphology, social cognition, and femininity/masculinity. *Social Cognitive and Affective Neuroscience, 3,* 168–176.

Wood, W., & Eagly, A. H. (2002). A cross-cultural analysis of the behavior of women and men: Implications for the origins of sex differences. *Psychological Bulletin, 128,* 699–727.

Wrangham, R. W. (1980). An ecological model of female-bonded primate groups. *Behaviour, 75,* 262–300.

Wrangham, R. W. (1999). Evolution of coalitionary killing. *Yearbook of Physical Anthropology, 42,* 1–30.

Wrangham, R. W., & Peterson, D. (1996). *Demonic males: Apes and the origin of human violence.* New York: Houghton Mifflin.

Wrangham, R. W., Wilson, M. L., & Muller, M. N. (2006). Comparative rates of violence in chimpanzees and humans. *Primates, 47,* 14–26.

Wyckoff, G., Wang, W., & Wu, C. (2000, January 20). Rapid evolution of male reproductive genes in the descent of man. *Nature, 403,* 304–309.

Wynne-Edwards, K. E. (2001). Hormonal changes in mammalian fathers. *Hormones and Behavior, 40,* 139–145.

Xue, Y., Zerjal, T., Bao, W., Zhu, S., Lim, S.-K., Shu, Q., et al. (2005). Recent spread of a Y-chromosome lineage in northern China and Mongolia. *American Journal of Human Genetics, 77*, 1112–1116.

Yonker, J. E., Eriksson, E., Nilsson, L.-G., & Herlitz, A. (2003). Sex differences in episodic memory: Minimal influence of estradiol. *Brain and Cognition, 52*, 231–238.

Youniss, J. (1986). Development in reciprocity through friendship. In C. Zahn-Waxler, E. Cummings, & R. Iannotti. (Eds.), *Altruism and aggression: Biological and social origins* (pp. 88–106). New York: Cambridge University Press.

Yusuf, S., Hawken, S., Ôunpuu, S., Bautista, L., Franzosi, M. G., Commerford, P., et al. (2005, November 5). Obesity and risk of myocardial infarction in 27000 participants from 52 countries: A case-control study. *The Lancet, 366*, 1640–1649.

Zaadstra, B. M., Seidell, J. C., Van Noord, P. A. H., Te Velde, E. R., Habbema, J. D. F., Vrieswijk, B., & Karbaat, J. (1993, February 20). Fat and female fecundity: Prospective study of effect of body fat distribution on conceptions rates. *BMJ, 306*, 484–487.

Zahavi, A. (1975). Mate selection—A selection for a handicap. *Journal of Theoretical Biology, 53*, 205–214.

Zahn-Waxler, C., Radke-Yarrow, M., Wagner, E., & Chapman, M. (1992). Development of concern for others. *Developmental Psychology, 28*, 126–136.

Zahn-Waxler, C., Shirtcliff, E. A., & Marceau, K. (2008). Disorders of childhood and adolescence: Gender and psychopathology. *Annual Review of Clinical Psychology, 4*, 275–303.

Zeh, J. A., & Zeh, D. W. (1997). The evolution of polyandry II: Post-copulatory defences against genetic incompatibility. *Proceedings of the Royal Society of London B, 264*, 69–75.

Zerjal, T., Xue, Y., Bertorelle, G., Wells, R. S., Bao, W., Zhu, S., et al. (2003). The genetic legacy of the Mongols. *American Journal of Human Genetics, 72*, 717–721.

Ziegler, A., Kentenich, H., & Uchanska-Ziegler, B. (2005). Female choice and the MHC. *Trends in Immunology, 26*, 496–502.

Zuckerman, M., & Kuhlman, D. M. (2000). Personality and risk-taking: Common biosocial factors. *Journal of Personality, 68*, 999–1029.

Zuk, M., & Johnsen, T. S. (1998). Seasonal changes in the relationship between ornamentation and immune response in red jungle fowl. *Proceedings of the Royal Society of London B, 265*, 1631–1635.

Zuk, M., Johnsen, T. S., & Maclarty, T. (1995). Endocrine-immune interactions, ornaments and mate choice in red jungle fowl. *Proceedings of the Royal Society of London B, 260*, 205–210.

Zuk, M., Thornhill, R., & Ligon, J. D. (1990). Parasites and mate choice in red jungle fowl. *American Zoologist, 30*, 235–244.

INDEX

Castration, 94
Casual sex
    and intimacy, 191
    and men's mate choices, 202–205
    and sexual objectification, 354
    women's aversion to, 156
Caterpillars, 77
Cerebellum
    and bower complexity, 61
    and locomotor play, 84
Cerebral palsy, 293
Chacma baboons, 127
Chagnon, N. A., 217
Chakraborty, R., 158
Chao, C.-C., 334
Chapman, M., 296
Charman, T., 371
Chavanne, T. J., 199
Chen, K., 353
Chen, Z., 316
Chicago, Illinois, 170
Childhood, 284–286
Child rearing, 142
Chimpanzees
    brain size of, 135
    coalitional competition of, 117–120,
        251
    development of, 284
    formation of mental representations
        by, 274
    hormones of, 115, 116
    and human evolution, 138
    human similarity to, 131
    providing of food by, 125
    sexual division of labor of, 142
    and sperm competition, 232–233
Chisholm, J. S., 169
Cillessen , A. H. N., 239
Clark, R. D., 203
Clements, W., 371
Closed genetic program, 278
Cloutier, J., 359
Clutton-Brock, T. H., 5, 54
Coalitional behavior, 25
Coalitional violence, 219
Coalition competition. *See also*
        Ingroups; Outgroups
    of female primates, 25, 81, 128
    of male primates, 117–120

among men, 179–181, 215–217, 219,
        220, 226–227, 250–252,
        265–266, 373–377
    and play, as preparation for, 296,
        302–308
    and social development, a prepara-
        tion for, 324–331, 335–336
    in social groups, 265
Coates, J. M., 231
Cockrem, J. F., 98
Coevolution, 29, 31
Coffing, K., 134, 135
Cognition. *See also* Academic compe-
        tencies; Attentional control;
        Conscious–psychological; Folk
        biology; Folk heuristics; Folk
        physics; Folk psychology; Group
        schema; Intelligence; Language;
        Memory; Mental rotation tasks;
        Motion detection; Navigation;
        Nonverbal communication;
        Object location memory; Perfect
        world representations; Profile of
        nonverbal sensitivity; Represen-
        tation; Self awareness; Self
        knowledge; Self schema; Spatial
        cognition; Spatial memory;
        Spatial skills; Theory of mind;
        Vocabulary; Working Memory
    and brain evolution, 135
    as related to vulnerability and
        variability, 291–293
    and sex hormones, 102–105
    and skill development, as related to
        play, 307, 311–313, 315, 317
Cognitive male–male competition,
        61–64
Cohen, L. B., 299
Cohen-Kettenis, P. T., 242–243, 367
Cole, N. S., 419
Coley, J. D., 271
Collaer, M. L., 305
Collard flycatchers, 46, 72
Color blindness, 390–391
Colwell, M. J., 154
Common field voles, 75, 76
Communication, nonverbal, 264
Competencies, 289–291
Competition. *See also* Intrasexual com-
        petition; Sperm competition

Ekstrom, A. D., 400
Elbow-room model, 28
Elephant seals
    body size of, 70
    maturation of, 287
    physical competition of, 79, 111
    sexual selection of, 41, 42, 56–59
Elias, L., 396
Elias, S., 195
Ellis, B. J., 152, 204, 256
Ellis, L., *xiv*, 409
Elster, A. B., 167
Emotional intimacy, 191–192
Emotions, 257–260, 324, 359, 370–371.
        See also Feelings
Empathy, 296–297
Employment, 149
Encephalization quotient (EQ),
        136–137. *See also* Brain size
Endicott, K., 340
Endler, R. E., 72
England, 149
Episodic memory, 360, 399
EQ (encephalization quotient), 136–137
Equality, 334
Eriksson, E., 360
Ermer, E., 230
Ernst, M., 351
Escherichia coli, 31
Essex, M. J., 152
Essock-Vitale, S. M., 157–158
Estradiol, 210, 243, 366, 394
Estrogen
    and brain functioning, 351
    effect of, on language, 367–369
    expression of, 103
    and facial expressions, 360–361
    increases in, during puberty, 309
    and ovulatory cycle, 196, 198
    prenatal exposure to, 96
    and representation, 401
    and sexual selection, 93, 95
    and spatial ability, 403
    and women's competitiveness, 242,
        243
Ethnic conflict, 255
Eurasian dotterel, 42
Europe, 186, 188
Evans, J. P., 52
Evans, L., 415

Evans, M. R., 100–101
Ewen, J. G., 90
Exploratory play, 310–313
Expressed emotions, 259–260
Extrapair copulation. *See also* Cuckoldry
    and fatherhood, 157–158, 198
    and sex hormones, 103
Eye contact, 295, 300
Eye-motor coordination, 290
Eyssell, K. M., 260

Facial attractiveness, 193–194
Facial expression, 356–361
Facultative parental investment, 88–89,
        157
Fagan, J., 168
Fallow deer, 54
Fantasy
    and casual sex, 203–204
    in conscious–psychological control
        system, 256
    during ovulatory cycle, 207
    and puberty, 288
Fantasy play, 317
Father-absent societies, 171–173
Fatherhood, 145–176. *See also* Paternal
        investment
    abandonment as conflict in, 162–163
    biological correlates with, 164–167
    costs of, to fathers, 156–159
    cultural correlates with, 171–175
    developmental correlates with,
        169–171
    direct care of children as conflict in,
        159–163
    ecological correlates with, 171–175
    and mortality of children, 147–150
    physical health of children as benefit
        of, 150–151
    physical well-being of children as
        benefit of, 146–147
    reproductive maturation as benefit
        of, 151–152
    social correlates with, 167–169
    social well-being of children as
        benefit of, 152–156
Father-present societies, 172–173
Fauna, 272–273, 386–387, 389
Fear, 298
Feelings, 257, 260–261, 370–371.
        See also Emotions

Folstad, I., 99
Food
    access to, 129
    availability of, 22–25
    and marriage systems, 179
Foraging, 142, 387
Forsberg, A. J. L., 173
Fort, C. L., 353
Frabutt, J. M., 154
Frackowiak, R. S. J., 273
France, 149
Fraternal polyandry, 180
Frequency-dependent selection, 19
Frey, K. S., 340
Friendships, 326–328, 337, 371. *See also*
        Peer relationships
Frijda, N. H., 243, 367
Frith, C. D., 273
Fukushima, H., 372
Furstenberg, F. F., Jr., 162
Fusiform gyrus, 399–400

Gahr, M., 102
Galápagos islands, 21, 24
Galea, L. A. M., 104, 396
Gallup, G. G., Jr., 199
Games, 267, 386
Gamsu, H., 292
Gangestad, S. W., 194, 207
García, Cruz, 385
Garfish, 83–84
Garver-Apgar, C. E., 195, 355
Gaulin, S. J. C., 210, 241
Gay men, 203–204, 375, 393, 402–403
Geary, D. C., 138, 324, 337
Gebusi society, 219
Gee, J., 349
Gelada baboons
    and harems, 115, 116, 124
    sexual preferences of, 127
Gelber, E. R., 299
Gender, Ideology of, 268–271
Gender roles, 268, 340
Gender schemas, 301, 323
General intelligence, 411–412. *See also*
        Intelligence
Genes. *See also* DNA fingerprinting;
        Major histocompatibility com-
        plex; Mitochondrial DNA; Popu-

lation genetics; X-chromosme
        genes; Y-chromosome genes
    expression of, and hormones,
        350–352
    as factor in female choice, 46–49
    and physical attractiveness, 192–194
    of women's mate choices, 194–198
Genetic inheritance, 16
Genetic research, 113–114
Genetics
    population, 233–235
    and social well-being of child, 155
Genghis Khan, 235
Geography, 396
Gerhardt, H. C., 51
Geschwind, N., 364
Gestation, internal, 5, 36
Gienapp, P., 77
Gil, D., 52
Gilligan, C., 334
Gilstrap, B., 161
Glaser, D., 230
Glezer, I. I., 349
Goldstein, J. M., 360
Goldwaithe, R. O., 290–291
Gonzalez-Bono, E., 227
Goodale, M. A., 272
Goodall, J., 118–119
Good genes model, 5, 43–49, 51, 92,
        181, 200. *See also* Female choice
    and physical attractiveness, 192–194
    and women's mate choices at
        ovulation, 197–198
Good taste model, 43–46. *See also*
        - Female choice
Gooren, L. J. G., 243, 367
Gordon, A. H., 260
Gorillas
    female choice in, 140–141
    human similarity to, 131
    male–male competition of, 138–139
    and male philopatry, 117
    paternity rates of, 158
    and sperm competition, 232–233
Gossiping, 156, 329
Goymann, W., 103–104
Graduate Record Examination, 419
Graham, J., 334
Grandmothers, 148
Grant, Peter, 21

ABOUT THE AUTHOR

David C. Geary, PhD, is a Curators' Professor and Thomas Jefferson Professor in the Department of Psychological Sciences at the University of Missouri. After completing his doctorate in 1986 at the University of California, Riverside, he held faculty positions at the University of Texas at El Paso and the University of Missouri, first at the Rolla campus and then in Columbia. Dr. Geary served as chair of his department from 2002 to 2005 and as the University of Missouri's Middlebush Professor of Psychological Sciences from 2000 to 2003. He has published more than 185 articles, commentaries, and chapters across a wide range of topics, including cognitive, developmental, and evolutionary psychology; education; and medicine. He has written three sole-authored books, *Children's Mathematical Development: Research and Practical Applications*; *Male, Female: The Evolution of Human Sex Differences*; and *The Origin of Mind: Evolution of Brain, Cognition, and General Intelligence*. He also coauthored *Sex Differences: Summarizing More Than a Century of Scientific Research*. Dr. Geary served as a member of the President's National Mathematics Advisory Panel and chaired the Learning Processes subcommittee, is a recipient of a MERIT Award from the National Institutes of Health, and was appointed by President G. W. Bush to the National Board of Directors for the Institute for Education Sciences.